Sources of the Grail

The Grail appears to the Knights of the Round Table at Camelot.
by Christine Loring, from Mystic Gleams of the Holy Grail

Sources of the Grail

An anthology

Selected and introduced
by John Matthews

Lindisfarne Press

First published in 1996 by Floris Books in Great Britain
and in 1997 by Lindisfarne Press in the United States

Lindisfarne Press, RR 4, Box 94A1, Hudson, NY 12534

ISBN 0-940262-87-8

Printed in Great Britain
by Biddles Ltd, Guildford

Contents

To the Companions of the Quest,
Who know who they are.

The Quest for Wholeness

At the beginning of the twelfth century the poet Chrétien de Troyes composed a poem which he called *Il Conte del Graal* (The Story of the Grail). It told the story of a search, undertaken by a simple youth, brought up away from the ways of men, for a mysterious object known as the "Graal." But Chrétien left the poem unfinished, dying before he could complete it, and in so doing he created a mystery that has stirred the imagination of countless seekers ever since.

Yet the mystery refuses to be codified, identified or pinned down to a specific time or place. The setting is most often the Middle Ages and the elements of the story follow their own pattern: the Grail itself, variously described as a cup, a dish, a stone or a jewel; the presence of its guardian, the Wounded King, who rules over a devastated Wasteland; the Company surrounding the King; and the questing knights who must pose the right question to heal both king and land. Yet despite the millions of words written every year about the Grail, it remains an object of mystery. It is hidden, secret, as the medieval knight and poet Wolfram von Eschenbach wrote in his telling of the myth, where the Grail is:

> The wondrous thing hidden in the flower-garden of the
> king where the elect of all nations are called. *(Parzifal)*

The Grail, indeed, can be many things — it can be almost anything to anyone — or it may be something that has no form, or more than one form — it may not even exist at all in this dimension. The important thing is that it provides an object for personal search, for growth and human development. In fact, it is more often not the object those who seek it are concerned with but the *actions* of the Grail — the way it causes changes to happen — in the heart, in the mind, in the soul.

In the traditions relating to Western teachings of alchemy, this is reflected in the mystery surrounding the transformational quality of the Great Work that lies at the centre of the alchemist's striving for earthly perfection. The transmutation of base metal into gold is a metaphor for the transformation of the human spirit — a transformation that takes place within the alembic of the Grail. Those who encounter the mystery are never the same again. They are caught up into an entirely new frame of existence, no longer bounded by time and space, they are transformed by the process of what they encounter.

We are dealing here with high things, with a Mystery that is almost too much for us. But we can learn, and grow, from studying it, by sharing the adventure of the Quest with those far-off people of the Arthurian world — who in truth are not so far off at all. Whatever else it may be, the Grail story is first and foremost pure myth. And like all myths it is filled with metaphors.

The earliest stories of the Grail came into being during a time of extraordinary flux, when much of the western world was undergoing a simultaneous cultural renaissance combined with a period of spiritual re-definition. It is my belief that one of the reasons why the Grail has become such an important symbol for our own time is because we are also going through a similar period of cultural upheaval and spiritual re-assessment. We are in the process of re-defining much of our awareness of culture, of its importance and of its relevance. The same is true of spirituality. Perhaps at no other time in our history have we been so hungry for transcendental knowledge — a fact perhaps not unconnected with the extreme richness of spiritual traditions available to us. The Grail tradition is only one such focus. It happens to have a good deal to offer because there is so much within it that is relevant to us now — and which will, I think, continue to be relevant well into the next millennium.

The story begins in a distant time, when the Celtic peoples held sway in these islands. We first hear of a search — the word quest is not quite current yet — for a mysterious object known as the Cauldron. Sometimes it is described as a Cauldron of Inspiration, sometimes a Cauldron of Life and Death, sometimes it is a cauldron which belongs to a specific person — like the Irish father god, the Dagda, or the Welsh god of the Underworld, Arawn. But the first time we hear of anyone going in search of it that seeker is called Arthur — no, not King Arthur, but Arthur the hero — and thus begins a story which is still being told — how Arthur and his followers — heroes still, not yet knights in shining armour — go in search of — in quest of — a mysterious container, the discovery of which offers the reward of inspiration, knowledge, wisdom, or life. The old Welsh poem that describes this, the *Preiddeu Annwn,* dates from the ninth century in its written form but probably looks back to a much earlier time (the text, in a new translation forms the first chapter of this collection). It is some three hundred years later, at the beginning of the twelfth century, when the stories of King Arthur and his knights began to proliferate — that we next hear of this search, and the story then looks both backward and forward.

We still have the search, the quest, for the mysterious object. And, just as in the old Welsh poem, those who seek it are still Arthur and his followers — now Knights of the Round Table — who encounter various dangers in the form of strange beings or mysterious tests that must be overcome before the would-be seeker can achieve the mystery of the Grail; for, such it is now called. No one knows for sure what the word Grail even means, but it is nearly always (with one notable exception) described as a cup or container of some kind — though now it is what is contained within the vessel that is important.

At some point between the writing of the ninth-century poem about a hunt for a magical Cauldron, and the twelfth-century romances of Arthur and his knights, the old magical vessel has become identified with the Holy Grail — variously described as the Cup with which Jesus celebrated the Last Supper, and the vessel in which Joseph of Arimathea (Christ's "Uncle" in the apocryphal tales) catches some of the blood that issues from Jesus' wounds when his body is washed in preparation for burial in Joseph's own tomb.

A complex story emerges from this identification. Joseph is entrusted with the Grail and instructed by Christ himself in its mysteries — specifically called "secrets," which are not to be conveyed to everyone. The Grail is then conveyed by a long

11

route and by various hands, from Palestine to Britain, where it comes to rest for a time at Glastonbury. There a sacred enclosure is made to contain it, from which it subsequently disappears, to be sought thereafter by many who regard it as a most holy and sacred object, to come into contact with which is to be somehow changed — enlightened as we might say today.

The story now tells us that through the ages a particular family are given the task of guarding the Grail. All are descendants of Joseph of Arimathea and some perform their duties better than others. One — the Fisher King — is said to fail in his task to the extent that he receives a terrible wound, one which will only heal when the Grail is achieved, until when he is kept in suspended animation, in great pain, yet still sustained by the Grail. Importantly, it is said that when this man — the Grail King as he has become in the medieval stories — receives his wound, the land over which he rules becomes wounded also — that is it becomes waste, infertile, almost dead — and that it will only be restored to health when the king, the guardian of the Grail, is restored to health.

The origins of this story go back into the mists of time. In many cultures the monarch is sacred, and the relationship of the monarch with the land is seen as far more than that of ordinary people. In Irish tradition, the kings literally "married" the land, often mating with the spirit of "Eriu" (Ireland) in the form of a woman. And, only a man perfect in body and spirit could be king. Thus in the Grail story when the king fails in his duty (the reasons do not matter here) he is punished — he receives a wound that will not heal — and through him the land is poisoned, it becomes sick as he is sick, infertile as he is infertile (it is not without significance, I believe, that the wound is always depicted as being in the generative organs), dead to the extent that he is dead.

The crux of the story is that only through the successful achievement of the Grail's mystery can the king — and through him the land — receive healing. Each individual seeker has to undergo a rigorous series of tests and trials before he can attempt the great mystery. In the story only four — three men and one woman — succeed, and two die in the attempt. One, Dindrane, the innocent sister of Perceval, gives up her life for the healing of another; the other, Galahad, the pure in spirit,

12

relinquishes his life so that he may enter the state of ecstatic being of oneness with Deity. The others: Perceval, who is called the Perfect Fool, and Bors, who is Everyman, perceive the mystery each in their own way and live to tell of it. Perceval becomes the next Guardian of the Grail — which, once it is achieved, becomes available for the next seeker — Bors returns home to tell of the wonders.

But there are other dimensions to the story. The Grail itself can only be activated by the asking of a Question — the word Quest itself derives from the same root. Though it is couched in several forms, the mysterious question is usually "Whom does the Grail serve?" Everyone who seeks it has to ask — and answer — this question sooner or later. It may seem an odd thing to ask when you have travelled however many hundreds of miles, undergone countless adventures and trials and arrived at last in the presence of the Wounded King and his entourage of Grail maidens and youths.

The Grail is borne through the hall in procession with the spear that drips blood, a large shallow dish and either a candelabra or a sword. The Wounded King is then fed with a wafer from the chalice. In some versions this is all, in others the entire company is fed with the food they most desire, which can be interpreted as actual *or* spiritual food; the point being that it is either the Grail King or the Company who are served, in the literal sense, by the Grail. Why, then, the question?

In part, of course, it is a ritual question, requiring a ritual response that in turn triggers a sequence of events: the healing of King and Kingdom, the restoration of the Wasteland. In the texts, various answers are given: Whom does the Grail serve? Why, the Grail King, the Company of the Grail, all who seek it. It is this last answer that concerns us most.

The Grail is here shown to be a gateway, a nexus-point between two states of being — those which we may call, for convenience, the human and the divine, the worldly and the otherworldly. All who seek the Grail are in some senses seeking one of these alternative states, and the state of well-being which derives from them. We can see this in the very shape most often assumed by the Grail, that of a Chalice. The upper portion is open to receive the down-pouring of blessings of the spiritual realm: the lower half, stem and base, form an upward pointing triangle that represents our own aspirations. In the centre the two meet and are fused: the Grail operates its wonderful life-giving properties — we are each served in the way that the Fisher King is served.

But this only happens in response to the need and urgency, the drive of the Quester. The answer is simple: the Grail serves us according to the way we serve it. Like the king who serves the land as the land serves him, we stand in similar relation to the Grail. Our service, our love or hope or desire is offered up, accepted and transformed into pure energy. And, if we have behaved in a right manner on our quest, we reap the rewards, the divine sustenance of the Grail. And, if we open this out still further, our service helps transform the land on which we live and walk and have our being. The Grail does not need to be in view — it is present all around us, in every act of service we do, whether it be, symbolically, for the king or the land.

While the king and the land are suffering the Grail cannot pass openly among us. It is as though a gap had opened between two worlds or states of being, leaving us shut out, lost in the twilight looking for the shining power of the Grail ... or as some texts suggest, inhabiting a land where there are no chalices, no means of expressing our own love or hope for the world we inhabit.

A passage from a modern Grail story, *War in Heaven* by Charles Williams, sums this up. In this story, after many adventures, the moment has come when a celebration of the Eucharist is to be made, using the Grail itself as the chalice. Standing before it, one of the modern questers reflects on its long, strange history:

> "Neither is this Thou" he breathed: and answered: "Yet this also is Thou." He considered, in this, chalices offered at every altar, and was aware again of a general movement of all things towards a narrow channel. Of all material things still discoverable in the world the Graal had been nearest the Divine and Universal Heart. Sky and sea and land were moving, not towards the vessel but to all it symbolized and had held ... and through that gate ... all creation moved.

14

Even here, where the Grail is still an object at the end of the search, it remains that what it symbolizes is important, not the Grail itself — "through that gate all creation moved." The object is as mysterious, as "hidden" as ever.

It seems that what we have to understand from all of this is that the Grail serves us in proportion to our service to the land and to the world about us. It is not some wonder-working artefact but an active principle touched off by the accumulated longing of mankind for what was once ours — for the perfect state of being that can still be ours. It is this which gives the aura of a lost golden age to Arthur's realm and acts.

As we follow the Quest Knights through the forests adventurous of the Arthurian legends we see many turnings that lead to different places in the map of the soul's journey — nearly all of the characters are in some way archetypal — as are their adventures, their sufferings and their realizations. It would be wrong to regard the stories too literally, of course — they are not and never were intended as parables — though it must be said, by way of balance, that the medieval writers were far more aware of what they were writing than they are sometimes given credit for. This is why we need to go back to the texts as often as possible — to their infinite variety, complexity and subtlety, where we may find ever new meanings.

There is another story that speaks to us in a powerful way. It is also a Grail story, though less familiar than most (an extract from the text that contains it — *The Elucidation* — forms Chapter 4 of this collection).

In that story it is said that long before the age of Arthur there existed a number of sacred wells that nourished the land and quenched the thirst of all who journeyed to them. These wells had guardians — the Maidens of the Wells — whose task it was to offer care and refreshment to all who came there. Now there was a king who lived at that time, whose name was Amangons, and he conceived of a great desire for one of the maidens. When she would not respond to his advances he raped her, and stole the golden cup with which she was used to offer water from the well to weary travellers. When Amangons' men saw what had happened they went out into the land and each took one of the Maidens for their own, despoiling her and her well. And it is said that, in that time, the land "lost the Voices of the Wells," for the Maidens had been wont to sing and prophesy from the spirit of the Wells. And that with this loss came a withering up of the earth and a Wasting of the Land, so that this is seen as a part of the tradition of the unhealing wound that must be set right. And the story says that many years later, in the time of Arthur, he and his knights came upon the descendants of the Maidens of the Wells and the followers of Amangons, wandering in the forest, and that they swore to avenge the wrong that had been done and to restore the voices of the Wells. The story does not tell us if they succeeded, but it is said that the Quest for the Grail becomes one of the tasks undertaken by Arthur's men — from which we may assume that when the Grail is found, and the King restored, the Wells are restored also, and the land given back not only life but the water of life — and the Voices of the Wells.

In this story too, I think, we can see many resonances for our own time and our personal paths. Who among us has not wandered in the Waste Lands, or felt the parching thirst of those deprived of water from the Wells? Who is there who has not been, or still is, wounded in some part of the body, or the mind, or the spirit who would seek healing if they could find it? We are very much a Silent Planet (as the writer C.S. Lewis called the earth), and if we are to survive and reach out beyond ourselves we need the Voices of the Wells — not to tell us what to do, but to tell us what we are already doing, to offer us comfort and support and to point us gently to a way forward.

These are the things that make the Grail a myth for all times, and one which is just as current today as it ever was. There are many more stories than we have space for in this collection, many more versions of the central story. Yet each, in its own way, bears out the patterning of the original.

From its beginning in Celtic myth through its first shaping in the eleventh century, and since then in numerous versions, the stories of the Grail have remained in the forefront of mystical literature and have provided inspiration and insight for many modern travellers on the road to self-awareness and self-realization. The quests of the Grail knights — both successful and unsuccessful — offer rich parallels with our own journeys and we could do worse than study them for the illumination they can offer. The Grail tradition is very much an initiatory path, as Robert Crutwell shows in his essay (see page 419). And as a path it can open doorways into other realms of the spirit. The stories and myths of the Grail form an ongoing commentary on our own personal search for absolutes, for wholeness in a time of great fragmentation.

The Wounded King — and the Waste Land — are healed by and through these Mysteries, and the Grail becomes available for the process to begin again. A process that is still happening today. The mystery is still present, still accessible, to everyone — to all of us who are seekers, if we wish to take up the Quest.

It is this which made the Grail relevant then, which makes it relevant today, and which will continue to make it relevant in the future. Because in this theme alone — apart from others not touched upon here — there is a chord that we can all respond to in some degree: because we are all wounded and because we have all wounded the land — the earth on which we live — to some degree; and we would all like to find healing, in whatever form it comes, and see the land healed as well.

When, a few years ago, I edited a collection of essays by various hands, each of which sought to trace an aspect of the Grail in contemporary terms, I called it *At the Table of the Grail* because that is how I see all of those who go on the quest — as sitting down together at a great invisible table to share their realizations. In this book I quoted a passage from the thirteenth century romance of *Perlesvaus,* which seems to me to say a great deal about the reasons for the quest, now as much as then.

The scene is set not long after the Arthurian era. The Grail Castle, where so many strange and wondrous things have taken place, is described as ruinous and empty, a place of ghosts with its once sacred and mysterious nature already beginning to be forgotten. To this place come two young knights in search of adventure, after the manner of the old heroes of the Table Round:

> They were fair knights indeed, very young and high-
> spirited and they swore they would go, and full of
> excitement they entered the castle. They stayed there a
> long while, and when they left they lived as hermits,
> wearing hair-shirts and wandering through the forests,
> eating only roots; it was a hard life, but it pleased them

greatly, and when people asked them why they were living thus, they would only reply: "Go where we went, and you will know why." (Translated by Nigel Bryant)

This is exactly the experience of the many people who have been "going there" ever since, seeking the mysterious object of which they have heard such marvellous report — more often than not failing, but sometimes discovering things about themselves and their own inner state.

The Grail is a symbol for now as much as for any time — a contemporary symbol of an utterly current aspiration. The King — call him Arthur or Christ or the World Soul — is wounded *by* as well as for us. These wounds impinge upon everyone, and when they are healed so shall we all be, it is the same story, an utterly simple one: the Grail serves us; we serve the Grail; it will heal us when we use it to heal the wounds of creation.

And, the wonderful thing is that each one of us is *already* engaged upon this quest. Each has a chance to redeem the time in which we live, to awaken the Sleeping King, to bring the Wasteland back into flower. We are indeed all "grails" to some degree, and the true object of the Quest lies in making ourselves vessels for the light that will bring about these things.

Only then can we ourselves be healed, the Fisher King within us regain his strength so that the land can flower. When that moment comes there will no longer be any need for a Grail, it will be everywhere about us no longer hidden but openly recognized — its presence felt in every particle of our being. As another contemporary writer, Vera Chapman, writes:

> Like a plant that dies down in winter, and guards its
> seeds to grow again, so you ... must raise the lineage
> from which all Arthur's true followers are to grow — not
> by a royal dynasty, but by spreading unknown and
> unnoticed ... Names and titles will be lost, but the story
> and the spirit of Arthur [and the Grail] shall not be lost.
> For Arthur is a spirit and Arthur is the land of Britain. So
> shall Arthur conquer, not by war, nor by one kingship
> that soon passes away, but by the carriers of the spirit
> that does not die. *(The Three Damosels)*

We are all carriers of that spirit, and by seeking the inner reality of the Grail *behind* the symbols and stories, we are taking part in an ongoing work without which all we hold most dear would long ago have perished. And if people look at us askance as we wander through the world with a strange look in our eyes, we have only to give the same answer of those knights who visited the ruined Grail Castle: "Go where we went, and you will know why."

*   *   *

This book is intended to be read chronologically — though of course the reader is at liberty to range at will — and for this reason I have generally followed the principle of placing the texts first with the commentaries following. This is to allow the reader to become familiar with the texts before going on to read the commentaries. The texts themselves are placed chronologically (where dates are known) to show the development of the Grail story throughout the Middle Ages. My own introductory matter, which will be found at the beginning of each of the three sections, aims to place the stories in context and, where necessary, make them more readily understood. In the case of the more obscure or complex texts I have also provided brief summaries to give the reader some idea of where, within the structure of the whole, the extract printed here comes. Some of these commentaries were written by Robert Jaffray and come from his excellent book *King Arthur and the Holy Grail,* from which a further chapter "Glastonbury and Fécamp" appears as Chapter 18 of this collection. The remainder are written by myself and are indicated by the initials J.M.; those by Jaffray by the initials R.J.

The essays and papers printed here date from a considerable time-span, during which the various texts often became known by different titles. I have indicated throughout where these differ from currently accepted forms. Thus, for example, the text known as *Perlesvaus* has also, at various times, been referred to as *Perceval le Gallois* and *The High History of the Holy Graal.* In a similar fashion some of the medieval authors have undergone shifts in orthography, so that Chrétien de Troyes is sometimes referred to as "Chrestien." I have retained these spellings throughout as their original authors intended as this does not interfere with the understanding of the texts.

Of course the reading of these fragments and summaries are no substitute for reading the original texts in their entirety. Most of these are now available in good modern translations, and I have included a generous selection in the section on "Further Reading" at the end of the book. I hope that those who enjoy, as well as feel the power of these stories, will be encouraged to look further and to begin for themselves a deeper exploration of the history of the Grail.

John Matthews
Oxford, June 1996

Percival at Corbenic

Rachel Anand Taylor

Is it lost, the lonely sea-road of pine and cypress and laurel
    That leads to the Sacred Castle over the spun sea-spray?
To the hushed white hall still strewn with its ivory roses and coral
    Does the Masque of the Lance and the Cup take its marvellous
        mournful way?

Who is the jasmine-pale Damsel that bears the Mazer
    Over her head with its pointed coif and floating veil?
Who is the Weeper behind her? Clothed in soft silver and azure,
    Who is the Adon-boy that carries the Spear of the Graal?

And what of the Fisher-King, carved on the bier of his trances,
    Waiting with smooth-combed curls in his Easter white and gold
Mid his vigil of paladins, poised as from ritual dances,
    That wear the Sign of the Dove, whose beauty shall not grow old?

Still stands the destined Knight, aloof in his passionate patience,
    His hand over his eyes? Is he doomed to fulfil or to fail?
Shall he dare the hells and the heavens of the strange illuminations,
    Initiate at last of the dread mysterious Graal?

Lo! Is he here and now, Love's own ethereal Lover,
    To speak the miraculous Word, unseal the Sterile Hour
With his muted violin voice, that the Wounded King recover
    And all the wild Waste Land sing into fruit and flower?

That all the sad Waste World, by its five rejoicing Rivers
    Be washed of its blood and tears, an Earthly Paradise,
The vines and wheat and roses reply to the Word that delivers
    And ships ride white in their havens, and stars come back to
        their skies?

But the Courtesy of the Graal is long long since passed over:
Even through the Spring and the jonquils, rides hither no Logos, no Lover.

PART ONE

The Celtic Dream

The Celtic Dream

The first part of this collection contains a number of texts and commentaries relating to the Celtic origins of the Grail. While it was once a matter of hot debate, there is no longer any real doubt that a number of the most important themes and characters in the story originated here, and in the four texts that follow — only one of which, *The Elucidation,* is not actually Celtic in provenance, but preserves a distinctly Celtic story-line — we shall see the first appearance of the Quest for the Cauldron, the Wounded King, the Mysterious Procession of the Hallows and the cause of the Waste Land. Each of these themes, which are central to the story of the Grail in its more familiar, medieval form, began in the more ancient reaches of Celtic myth, and the presence of these characteristics continues throughout its long history.

The earliest analogue for the Grail story still extant is a medieval Welsh poem know as the *Preiddeu Annwn* or Spoils of the In-World. It deals with the quest by a hero named Arthur for a sacred object known as the Cauldron, and there is a sense in which all subsequent stories for the Quest flow out from this point. The poem dates, in its current form, from the ninth century, though it is attributed to the sixth century bard Taliesin, an ascription which I see no need to question. It is thus nearly contemporary with Arthur, and shows him already cast in the light of a hero who seeks entry to the Otherworld — for which Annwn is one of the many names — to discover and bring back a mystical object that has the power to give life and inspiration to those who possess it.

This much is clear enough from the poem itself — though much of it remains obscure, or requires extensive knowledge of Celtic mythology to fully grasp its meaning. Essentially, Arthur, accompanied by "three shiploads" of his warriors, sets out in

Prydwen his magical ship, in search of the Cauldron of Annwn, which is "warmed by the breath" of nine "muses" or "maidens" (for which we may perhaps read "priestesses") and protected by the dark soldiers of the Otherworld. To reach their goal Arthur and his men must first pass through nine "Caers" or cities, each one reflecting a different aspect of the Otherworld. On each of these they must face some kind of test — though the exact nature of these remains unclear.

Several heroes are mentioned by name, notably Lludd and Lleminawg, the latter of which may possibly be an early analogue for the famous Sir Lancelot of medieval romance. A "sentinel" is also mentioned with whom "it was difficult to converse." We may assume that Taliesin himself was one of those present as he speaks of himself in the first person throughout and seems to be describing an event in which he personally took part. Beyond this there are references to Pwyll and Pryderi — famous heroes of the Welsh myth-books collectively known as *The Mabinogion* — though not generally associated with Arthur.

Other references are less clear, but the overall picture is that most of the heroes lost their lives — or at least remained behind in the Otherworld — only seven returning — with or without the Cauldron is again not stated.

A great deal has been made of this poem as a clear indication of the presence of a Celtic proto-Grail quest. Certainly other evidence from Celtic literature — including the text of "Peredur" from which an extract will be found in Chapter 3, and the Story of Branwen, Daughter of Llyr (Chapter 2), as well as numerous references to magical and wonder-working Cauldrons — suggests that this may well be the point at which the stories of the Quest first coalesced from the various aural versions that had probably been circulating for a far longer time.

It is appropriate therefore to begin with this text, in a new translation, in which I have attempted to restore some of the more arcane meaning to the poem. For a fuller commentary readers are referred to my book *Taliesin: Shamanism and the Bardic Mysteries in Britain and Ireland*.

The story of *Branwen, Daughter of Llyr* is one of the four "Branches" of the *Mabinogion*, one of the prime sources for Celtic myth. On the surface it is not Arthurian, nor does it have anything to do with the story of the Grail. Yet, within this text lie several of the themes that underlie all of the later medieval versions of the story. They include the wounding of the King, and the presence of a magical dwelling where an object of sacred importance is kept.

Despite its title, the text has really less to do with Branwen than with her brother Bran, who is one of the most important figures in Celtic tradition. As with many other semi-divine figures in Celtic literature, Bran is presented as seemingly human, though his great size and his title "Bendegeid" or Blessed makes it apparent that behind the figure of the king of Britain lies a far older and more god-like character. His possession of a magical cauldron with the power to grant life confirms this and the story of his wounding, and of the magical events that follow upon this, tells us that Bran is a being of supra-human stock.

The theme of the Wounded King appears in all of the extant Grail texts from Chrétien's *Conte del Graal* onwards, and this has long been recognized as deriving ultimately from the Celtic tradition that makes the relationship of king and land supremely important. For a king to rule in Celtic times he had to be not only perfect in body and mind but also to be recognized by the spirit of the land itself. This spirit also took the form of a hideous woman with whom the would-be king must mate. At the crucial moment the woman was transformed and revealed herself to the king as the spirit of the land, Sovereignty. This relationship sealed the bond between ruler and land and as long as he upheld it the country remained in harmony. If, however, the king became physically maimed he could no longer rule, and the land itself became troubled or waste.

This is the origin of the Wounded King and Waste Land themes in the story of the Grail, and it is present in the story of *Branwen* in the episode where Bran, having being wounded, instructs his followers to cut off his head and carry it with them to the mysterious island of Gwales. Here, the head continues to speak, uttering stories, songs and prophecies, and offering the endless feast known as the Entertainment of the Noble Head. At the time of his wounding Bran is suddenly referred to by the name "Morddwyd Tyllyon" This was not really understood until it was pointed out that a translation of the name is "the pierced thighs." As the Wounded King of the Grail romances is also specifically wounded in the thighs, it became clear that Bran was a prototype of the Grail king, with his magical Cauldron an early analogue of the Grail itself. Given that the name of the Wounded King is often given as Bron or Brons the connection now appears well established, and the importance of this text in the history of the Grail is made clear. (For a more detailed account of this story and its significance see *Mabon and the Mysteries of Britain* by Caitlín Matthews.)

There are those who would say that the story of *Peredur* does not belong here, but should rather come after Chrétien's *Conte del Graal*. The reason for this is a continuing scholarly debate as to "which came first?" The problem arises from the fact that "Peredur," which is generally accepted as part of the Welsh saga-book *The Mabinogion*, dates, in manuscript form, from the late twelfth century (some would say even later) and thus antedates Chrétien's work by almost a century. This has led many commentators to assume that it is a later work, based on the *Conte*. However, I have no hesitation in believing that, from internal evidence, the story of *Peredur* is actually older than Chrétien's, and in fact probably contains at least part of a far earlier version of the Grail story. The influence of Chrétien seems clear enough — in that it tells substantially the same story — but there are several shifts of emphasis, as well as differences of omission and contraction, that make the Welsh text a very different tale.

I have therefore placed it here, among the early, Celtic versions of the Grail myth, where I feel it belongs. Those who wish to compare the two versions may read the whole of Chrétien's text in any one of several versions currently available, while referring back to the version included in *The Mabinogion,* an extract of which follows here.

The differences between the two works are marked by a variation in the motivation of the hero. While the two stories both begin with the innocent and foolish hero, brought up in isolation in the forest, and while both follow the overall direction of the plot, in *Peredur* the motivation for the hero's quest is one of vengeance rather than the vaguer motive of Perceval in the *Conte,* who seems rather to wander, aimlessly, in search of the Grail and the Fisher King. Two other episodes (only the first of which are featured here) concern Peredur's fight with the Nine Witches of Caer Loyw (Gloucester), a battle with a Dragon, and the hero's reigning with the Empress of Constantinople. The episode included here tells of Peredur's first coming to the castle of the Lame King, his viewing of the mysterious procession of objects including the Bleeding Lance and the Head in the Platter, which significantly replaces the Graal, described by Chrétien as a shallow dish in which there is no such grisly object. Also in this version Peredur is tested by a magical sword, which breaks each time he uses it, and which he is able to restore twice but not thrice — a sign that he has come into a third part of his strength. Peredur also meets the woman whom he is ever after to love, and his witnessing of blood from a raven's kill in the snow reminds him, in a memorable image, of the black hair, white skin and red lips of his lady. The fight with the Nine Witches is again not to be found in Chrétien's narrative, and is obviously more primitive than the *Conte*.

Finally in this group of four primal texts comes *The Elucidation,* which is actually not Celtic at all, being written in medieval French and dating from *c.* 1315. However, it is placed here because it preserves a part of the story that is very much older than the writings of Chrétien, to whose poem it is supposed to be a kind of prelude. Indeed, despite its title, it does nothing to "elucidate" Chrétien's text, and only becomes understandable when considered in the light of the Celtic mythlore discussed above.

I have studied this text for a number of years, and I am now convinced that it contains some of the earliest strands of Grail lore to be found in written form. The story that it tells, as discussed above in the general introduction, concerns events that took place long before the time of Arthur, and is possessed of a far more primal and distinctly pagan atmosphere than that of the later texts. It provides a convincing alternative for the cause of the Waste Land, which may, in fact, be older even than the story told in *Branwen*.

In the figure of Amangons, I believe we have a prototype of the evil magician Klingsor, who in Wolfram von Eschenbach's poem of *Parzival,* acts as a powerful opponent to the heroes of the Grail. (For a discussion of this character see below in the introduction to Part Two). He may also be equated with the invisible knight Garlon, mentioned in the "Book of Balin" from

Thomas Malory's *Morte d'Arthur* (included as part of Chapter 15 in the present collection), suggesting a possible connection between the two distinct versions of cause of the Waste Land.

Only the first half of the poem is presented here, but I hope to produce a full new translation with extended commentary in a forthcoming book. Those wishing to read the full text are referred to the edition of A.W. Thompson (in Old French) and the translation by Sebastian Evans, from which the extract included here is taken.

In the chapters that follow three of the foremost scholars in the discipline of the Celtic Grail traditions explore the sources and influence of Celtic literature on the development of the Grail story. Sir John Rhys, who was one of the first Arthurian scholars to recognize the importance of sources such as those discussed above, looks not only at the *Preiddeu Annwn*, but also at the Welsh version of the great Vulgate *Quest of the Holy Grail* (see Chapter 14), *Y Seint Greal*, and at the magical *mwys* or basket of Gwyddno Garanhir, yet another of the many proto-Grail objects to be found within Celtic tradition. He finds hidden versions, not only of Gwyddno himself, but of other characters familiar to readers of the medieval Grail romances.

The distinguished Dutch scholar A.G. van Hamel follows, turning his attention more in the direction of early Irish sources, where he finds concomitants for both the Fisher King and the Grail itself in the lives of the early Irish saints and in the remarkable text *The Fosterage of the House of the Two Goblets*, which mingles together Pagan and Christian elements in a surprising way and may well have provided some of the major themes within the Grail story.*

Finally A.C.L. Brown, whose seminal book *The Origin of the Grail Legend* (1943) was one of the earliest to study the Celtic origins in any depth, contributes a chapter on "The Irish Element in King Arthur and the Grail." Here he discovers many Celtic elements to be found within the thirteenth century text of *Sir Percyvelle of Galles* (Chapter 19 of this collection), which has retained, despite its late date, many elements only found elsewhere in Celtic textual sources.

* A translation of this text, with commentary, can be found in *The Element Encyclopedia of Celtic Wisdom* compiled and edited by Caitlín and John Matthews.

CHAPTER 1

The Spoils of Annwn

ATTRIBUTED TO TALIESIN
TRANSLATED BY JOHN MATTHEWS

In Caer Siddi Gwair's prison was readied,
As Pwyll and Pryderi foretold,
None before went there save he,
Where the heavy chains bound him.
Before the spoils of Annwn he sang forever
This eternal invocation of poets:
Save only seven, none returned from Caer Siddi.

Since my song resounded in the turning Caer,
I am pre-eminent. My first song
Was of the Cauldron itself.
Nine maidens kindled it with their breath —
Of what nature was it?
Pearls were about its rim,
Nor would it boil a coward's portion.
Lleminawg thrust his flashing sword
Deep within it;
And before dark gates, a light was lifted.
When we went with Arthur — a mighty labour —
Save only seven, none returned from Caer Fedwydd.

Pre-eminent am I
Since my song resounded
In the four-square city,
The Island of the Strong Door.
The light was dim and mixed with darkness,

Though bright wine was set before us.
Three shiploads of Prydwen went with Arthur —
Save only seven, none returned from Caer Rigor.

Worth more am I than the clerks
Who have not seen Arthur's might
Beyond Caer Siddi.
Six thousand stood upon its walls —
It was hard to speak with their leader.
Three shiploads of Prydwen went with Arthur —
Save seven only, none returned from Caer Goludd.

I merit more than empty bards
Who know not the day, the hour or the moment
When the wondrous child was born;
Who have not journeyed
To the courts of heaven;
Who know nothing of the meaning
Of the starry-collared ox
With seven score links in his collar.
We went with Arthur — that sorrowful journey —
Save seven only, none returned from
    Manawyddan's Caer.

I know more forever than the weak-willed clerks
Who know not the day of the king's birth,
Nor the nature of the beast they guard for him.
When we went with Arthur — lamentable day —
Save only seven, none returned from Caer Achren.

CHAPTER 2

Branwen, daughter of Llyr

Translated by Charlotte Guest

Here is the second portion of the Mabinogi

Bendigeid Vran, the son of Llyr, was the crowned king of this island, and he was exalted from the crown of London. And one afternoon he was at Harlech in Ardudwy, at his Court, and he sat upon the rock of Harlech, looking over the sea. And with him were his brother Manawyddan the son of Llyr, and his brothers by the mother's side, Nissyen and Evnissyen, and many nobles likewise, as was fitting to see around a king. His two brothers by the mother's side were the sons of Eurosswydd, by his mother, Penardun, the daughter of Beli son of Manogan. And one of these youths was a good youth and of gentle nature, and would make peace between his kindred, and cause his family to be friends when their wrath was at the highest; and this one was Nissyen; but the other would cause strife between his two brothers when they were most at peace. And as they sat thus, they beheld thirteen ships coming from the south of Ireland, and making towards them, and they came with a swift motion, the wind being behind them, and they neared them rapidly. "I see ships afar," said the king, "coming swiftly towards the land. Command the men of the Court that they equip themselves, and go and learn their intent." So the men equipped themselves and went down towards them. And when they saw the ships near, certain were they that they had never seen ships better furnished. Beautiful flags of satin were upon them. And behold one of the ships outstripped the others, and they saw a shield lifted up above the side of the ship, and the point of the shield was upwards, in token of peace. And the men drew near that they might hold converse. Then they put out boats and came towards the land. And they saluted the king. Now the king could hear them from the place where he was, upon the rock above their heads. "Heaven prosper you," said he, "and be ye welcome. To whom do these ships belong, and who is the chief amongst you?" "Lord," said they, "Matholwch, king of Ireland, is here, and these ships belong to him." "Wherefore comes he?" asked the king, "and will he come to the land?" "He is a suitor unto thee, lord" said they, "and he will not land unless he have his boon." "And what may that be?" inquired the king. "He desires to ally himself with thee, lord," said they "and he comes to ask Branwen the daughter of Llyr, that, if it seem well to thee, the Island of the Mighty may be leagued with Ireland, and both become more powerful." "Verily," said he "let him come to land, and we will take counsel thereupon." And the answer was brought to Matholwch. "I will go willingly," said he. So he landed, and they received him joyfully; and great was the throng in the palace that night, between his hosts and those of the Court; and next day they took counsel, and they resolved to bestow Branwen upon Matholwch. Now she was one of the three chief ladies of this island, and she was the fairest damsel in the world.

And they fixed upon Aberffraw as the place where she should become his bride. And they went thence, and towards Aberffraw the hosts proceeded; Matholwch and his host in their ships; Bendigeid Vran and his host by land, until they came to Aberffraw. And at Aberffraw they began the feast and sat down. And thus sat they, the King of the Island of the Mighty and Manawyddan the son of Llyr on one side, and Matholwch on the other side, and Branwen the daughter of Llyr beside him. And they were not within a house, but under tents. No house could ever contain Bendigeid Vran. And they began the banquet and caroused and discoursed. And when it was more pleasing to them to sleep than to carouse, they went to rest, and that night Branwen became Matholwch's bride.

And next day they arose, and all they of the Court, and the officers began to equip and to range the horses and the attendants, and they ranged them in order as far as the sea.

And behold one day, Evnissyen, the quarrelsome man of

whom it is spoken above, came by chance into the place, where the horses of Matholwch were, and asked whose horses they might be. "They are the horses of Matholwch, King of Ireland, who is married to Branwen, thy sister; his horses are they." "And it is thus they have done with a maiden such as she, and moreover my sister, bestowing her without my consent? They could have offered no greater insult to me than this," said he. And thereupon he rushed under the horses and cut off their lips at the teeth, and their ears close to their heads, and their tails close to their backs, and wherever he could clutch their eyelids, he cut them to the very bone, and he disfigured the horses and rendered them useless.

And they came with these tidings unto Matholwch, saying that the horses were disfigured, and injured so that not one of them could ever be of any use again. "Verily, lord," said one, "it was an insult unto thee, and as such was it meant." "Of a truth, it is a marvel to me, that if they desire to insult me, they should have given me a maiden of such high rank and so much beloved of her kindred, as they have done." "Lord," said another, "thou seest that thus it is, and there is nothing for thee to do but to go to thy ships." And thereupon towards his ships he set out.

And tidings came to Bendigeid Vran that Matholwch was quitting the Court without asking leave, and messengers were sent to inquire of him wherefore he did so. And the messengers that went were Iddic the son of Anarawc, and Heveydd Hir. And these overtook him and asked of him what he designed to do, and wherefore he went forth. "Of a truth," said he, "if I had known I had not come hither. I have been altogether insulted, no one ever had worse treatment than I have had here. But one thing surprises me above all." "What is that?" asked they. "That Branwen, the daughter of Llyr, one of the three chief ladies of this island, and the daughter of the King of the Island of the Mighty, should have been given me as my bride, and that after that I should have been insulted; and I marvel that the insult was not done me before they had bestowed upon me a maiden so exalted as she." "Truly, lord, it was not the will of any that are of the Court," said they, "nor of any that are of the council, that thou shouldest have received this insult; and as thou hast been insulted, the dishonour is greater unto Bendigeid Vran than unto thee." "Verily," said he, "I think so. Nevertheless he

35

cannot recall the insult." These men returned with that answer to the place where Bendigeid Vran was, and they told him what reply Matholwch had given them. "Truly," said he, "there are no means by which we may prevent his going away at enmity with us, that we will not take." "Well, lord," said they, "send after him another embassy." "I will do so," said he. "Arise, Manawyddan son of Llyr, and Heveydd Hir, and Unic Glew Ysgwyd, and go after him, and tell him that he shall have a sound horse for everyone that has been injured. And besides that, as an atonement for the insult, he shall have a staff of silver, as large and as tall as himself, and a plate of gold of the breadth of his face. And show unto him who it was that did this, and that it was done against my will; but that he who did it is my brother, by my mother's side, and therefore it would be hard for me to put him to death. And let him come and meet me," said he, "and we will make peace in any way he may desire."

The embassy went after Matholwch, and told him all these sayings in a friendly manner, and he listened thereunto. "Men," said he, "I will take counsel." So to the council he went. And in the council they considered that if they should refuse this, they were likely to have more shame rather than to obtain so great an atonement. They resolved therefore to accept it, and they returned to the Court in peace.

Then the pavilions and the tents were set in order after the fashion of a hall; and they went to meat, and as they had sat at the beginning of the feast, so sat they there. And Matholwch and Bendigeid Vran began to discourse; and behold it seemed to Bendigeid Vran while they talked, that Matholwch was not so cheerful as he had been the night before. And he thought that the chieftain might be sad, because of the smallness of the atonement which he had, for the wrong that had been done him. "Oh, man," said Bendigeid Vran, "thou dost not discourse tonight so cheerfully as thou wast wont. And if it be because of the smallness of the atonement, thou shalt add thereunto whatsoever thou mayest choose, and tomorrow I will pay thee the horses." "Lord," said he, "Heaven reward thee." "And I will enhance the atonement," said Bendigeid Vran, "for I will give unto thee a cauldron, the property of which is, that if one of thy men be slain today, and be cast therein, tomorrow he will be as well as ever he was at best, except that he will not regain his speech." And thereupon he gave him great thanks, and very joyful was he for that cause.

And the next morning they paid Matholwch the horses as long as the trained horses lasted. And then they journeyed into another commot, where they paid him with colts until the whole had been paid, and from thenceforth that commot was called Talebolyon.

And a second night they sat together. "My lord," said Matholwch, "whence hadst thou the cauldron which thou hast given me?" "I had it of a man who had been in thy land," said he, "and I would not give it except to one from there." "Who was it?" asked he. "Llassar Llaesgyvnewid; he came here from Ireland with Kymideu Kymeinvoll, his wife, who escaped from the Iron House in Ireland, when it was made red hot around them, and fled hither. And it is a marvel to me that thou shouldst know nothing concerning the matter." "Something I do know," said he, "and as much as I know I will tell thee. One day I was hunting in Ireland, and I came to the mound at the head of the lake, which is called the Lake of the Cauldron. And I beheld a huge yellow-haired man coming from the lake with a cauldron on his back. And he was a man of vast size, and of horrid aspect, and a woman followed after him. And if the man was tall, twice as large as he was the woman, and they came towards me and greeted me. "Verily," asked I, "wherefore are you journeying?" "Behold, this," said he to me, "is the cause that we journey. At the end of a month and a fortnight this woman will have a son; and the child that will be born at the end of the month and the fortnight will be a warrior fully armed." So I took them with me and maintained them. And they were with me for a year. And that year I had them with me not grudgingly. But thenceforth was there murmuring, because that they were with me. For, from the beginning of the fourth month they had begun to make themselves hated and to be disorderly in the land; committing outrages, and molesting and harassing the nobles and ladies; and thenceforward my people rose up and besought me to part with them and they bade me to choose between them and my dominions. And I applied to the council of my country to know what should be done concerning them; for of their own free will they will not go, neither could they be compelled against their will, through fighting. And [the people of the country] being in this strait, they caused a chamber to be made all of iron. Now when the chamber was ready, there came there every smith that was in Ireland, and every one who owned tongs and hammer. And they caused coals to be piled up as high as the top of the chamber. And they had the man, and the woman, and the children, served with plenty of meat and drink; but when it was known that they were drunk, they began to put fire to the coals about the chamber, and they blew it with bellows until the house was red hot all around them. Then was there a council held in the centre of the floor chamber. And the man tarried until the plates of iron were all of a white heat; and then, by reason of the great heat, the man dashed against the plates with his shoulder and struck them out, and his wife followed him; but except him and his wife none escaped thence. And then I suppose, lord," said Matholwch unto Bendigeid Vran, "that he came over unto thee." "Doubtless he came here," said he, "and gave unto me the cauldron." "In what manner didst though receive them?" "I dispersed them through every part of my dominions, and they have become numerous and are prospering everywhere, and they fortify the places where they are with men and arms, of the best that were ever seen."

That night they continued to discourse as much as they would, and had minstrelsy and carousing, and when it was more pleasant to sleep than to sit longer, they went to rest. And thus was the banquet carried on with joyousness; and when it was finished, Matholwch journeyed towards Ireland, and Branwen with him, and they went from Aber Menei with thirteen ships, and came to Ireland. And in Ireland was there great joy because of their coming. And not one great man or noble lady visited Branwen unto whom she gave not either a clasp, or a ring, or a royal jewel to keep, such as it was honourable to be seen departing with. And in these things she spent that year in much renown, and she passed her time pleasantly, enjoying honour and friendship. And in the meanwhile it chanced that she became pregnant, and in due time a son was born unto her, and the name that they gave him was Gwern the son of Matholwch, and they put the boy out to be foster-nursed, in a place where were the best men of Ireland.

And behold in the second year a tumult arose in Ireland, on account of the insult which Matholwch had received in Cambria, and the payment made him for his horses. And his foster-brothers, and such as were nearest unto him, blamed him openly for that matter. And he might have no peace by reason of the tumult until they should revenge upon him this disgrace. And the vengeance which they took was to drive away Branwen from the same chamber with him, and to make her cook for the Court; and they caused the butcher after he had cut up the meat to come to her and give her every day a blow on the ear, and such they made her punishment.

"Verily, lord," said his men to Matholwch, "forbid now the ships and the ferry boats and the coracles, that they go not into Cambria, and such as come over from Cambria hither, imprison them that they go not back for this thing to be known there." And he did so; and it was thus for not less than three years.

And Branwen reared a starling in the cover of the kneading trough, and she taught it to speak, and she taught the bird what manner of man her brother was. And she wrote a letter of her woes, and the despite with which she was treated, and she bound the letter to the root of the bird's wing, and sent it towards Britain. And the bird came to this island, and one day it found Bendigeid Vran at Caer Seiont in Arvon, conferring there, and it alighted upon his shoulder and ruffled its feathers, so that the letter was seen, and they knew that the bird had been reared in a domestic manner.

Then Bendigeid Vran took the letter and looked upon it. And when he read the letter he grieved exceedingly at the tidings of Branwen's woes. And immediately he began sending messengers to summon the island together. And he caused sevenscore and four countries to come unto him, and he complained to them himself of the grief that his sister endured. So they took counsel. And in the council they resolved to go to Ireland, and to leave seven men as princes here, and Caradawc, the son of Bran, as the chief of them, and their seven knights. In Edeyrnion were these men left. And for this reason were the seven knights placed in the town. Now the names of these seven men were, Caradawc the son of Bran, and Heveydd Hir, and Unic Glew Ysgwyd, and Iddic the son of Anarawc Gwalltgrwn, and Fodor the son of Ervyll, and Gwlch Minascwrn, and Llassar the son of

Llaesar Llaesgygwyd, and Pendaran Dyved as a young page with them. And these abode as seven ministers to take charge of this island; and Caradawc the son of Bran was the chief amongst them.

Bendigeid Vran, with the host of which we spoke, sailed towards Ireland, and it was not far across the sea, and he came to shoal water. It was caused by two rivers; the Lli and the Archan were they called; and the nations covered the sea. Then he proceeded with what provisions he had on his own back, and approached the shore of Ireland.

Now the swineherds of Matholwch were upon the seashore, and they came to Matholwch. "Lord," said they, "greeting be unto thee." "Heaven protect you," said he, "have you any news?" "Lord," said they, "we have marvellous news, a wood have we seen upon the sea, in a place where we never yet saw a single tree." "This is indeed a marvel," said he; "saw you aught else?" "We saw, lord," said they, "a vast mountain beside the wood, which moved, and there was a lofty ridge on the top of the mountain, and a lake on each side of the ridge. And the wood, and the mountain, and all these things moved." "Verily," said he "there is none who can know aught concerning this, unless it be Branwen."

Messengers then went unto Branwen. "Lady," said they, "what thinkest thou that this is?" "The men of the Island of the Mighty, who have come hither on hearing of my ill-treatment and my woes." "What is the forest that is seen upon the sea?" asked they. "The yards and the masts of ships," she answered. "Alas," said they, "what is the mountain that is seen by the side of the ships?" "Bendigeid Vran, my brother," she replied, "coming to shoal water; there is no ship that can contain him in it." "What is the lofty ridge with the lake on each side thereof?" "On looking towards this island he is wroth, and his two eyes, one on each side of his nose, are the two lakes beside the ridge."

The warriors and the chief men of Ireland were brought together in haste, and they took counsel. "Lord," said the nobles unto Matholwch, "there is no other counsel than to retreat over the Linon (a river which is in Ireland), and to keep the river between thee and him, and to break down the bridge that is across the river, for there is a loadstone at the bottom of the river that neither ship nor vessel can pass over." So they re-treated across the river, and broke down the bridge.

Bendigeid Vran came to land, and the fleet with him by the bank of the river. "Lord," said his chieftains, "knowest thou the nature of this river, that nothing can go across it, and there is no bridge over it?" "What," said they, "is thy counsel concerning a bridge?" "There is none," said he, "except that he who will be chief, let him be a bridge. I will be so," said he. And then was that saying first uttered, and it is still used as a proverb. And when he had lain down across the river, hurdles were placed upon him, and the host passed over thereby.

And as he rose up, behold the messengers of Matholwch came to him, and saluted him, and gave him greeting in the name of Matholwch, his kinsman, and showed how that of his goodwill he had merited of him nothing but good. "For Matholwch has given the kingdom of Ireland to Gwern the son of Matholwch, thy nephew and thy sister's son. And this he places before thee, as a compensation for the wrong and despite that has been done unto Branwen. And Matholwch shall be maintained wheresoever thou wilt, either here or in the Island of the Mighty." Said Bendigeid Vran, "Shall not I myself have the kingdom? Then peradventure I may take counsel concerning your message. From this time until then no other answer will you get from me." "Verily," said they, "the best message that we receive for thee, we will convey it unto thee, and do thou await our message unto him." "I will wait," answered he, "and do you return quickly."

The messengers set forth and came to Matholwch. "Lord," said they, "prepare a better message for Bendigeid Vran. He would not listen at all to the message we bore him." "My friends," said Matholwch, "what may be your counsel?" "Lord," said they, "there is no other counsel than this alone. He was never known to be within a house, make therefore a house that will contain him and the men of the Island of the Mighty on the one side, and thyself and thy host on the other; and give over thy kingdom to his will, and do him homage. So by reason of the honour thou doest him in making him a house, whereas he never before had a house to contain him, he will make peace with thee." So the messengers went back to Bendigeid Vran, bearing him this message.

41

And he took counsel, and in the council it was resolved that he should accept this, and this was all done by the advice of Branwen, and lest the country should be destroyed. And this peace was made, and the house was built both vast and strong. But the Irish planned a crafty device, and the craft was that they should put brackets on each side of the hundred pillars that were in the house, and should place a leather bag on each bracket, and an armed man in every one of them. Then Evnissyen came in before the host of the Island of the Mighty, and scanned the house with fierce and savage looks, and described the leather bags which were around the pillars. "What is in this bag?" asked he of one of the Irish. "Meal, good soul," said he. And Evnissyen felt about it until he came to the man's head, and he squeezed the head until he felt his fingers meet together in the brain through the bone. And he left that one and put his hand upon another, and asked what was therein. "Meal," said the Irishman. So he did the like unto every one of them, until he had not left alive, of all the two hundred men, save one only; and when he came to him, he asked what was there. "Meal, good soul," said the Irishman. And he felt about until he felt the head, and he squeezed that head as he had done the others. And, albeit he found that the head of this one was armed, he left him not until he had killed him. And then he sang an Englyn:

"There is in this bag a different sort of meal,
  The ready combatant, when the assault is made
  By his fellow-warriors, prepared for battle."

Thereupon came the hosts unto the house. The men of the Island of Ireland entered the house on the one side, and the men of the Island of the Mighty on the other. And as soon as they had sat down there was concord between them; and the sovereignty was conferred upon the boy. When the peace was concluded, Bendigeid Vran called the boy unto him, and from Bendigeid Vran the boy went unto Manawyddan, and he was beloved by all that beheld him. And from Manawyddan the boy was called by Nissyen the son of Eurosswydd, and the boy went unto him lovingly. "Wherefore," said Evnissyen, "comes not my nephew the son of my sister unto me? Though he were not king

42

of Ireland, yet willingly would I fondle the boy." "Cheerfully let him go to thee," said Bendigeid Vran, and the boy went unto him cheerfully. "By my confession to Heaven," said Evnissyen in his heart, "unthought of by the household is the slaughter that I will this instant commit."

Then he arose and took up the boy by the feet, and before any one in the house could seize hold of him, he thrust the boy headlong into the blazing fire. And when Branwen saw her son burning in the fire, she strove to leap into the fire also, from the place where she sat between her two brothers. But Bendigeid Vran grasped her with one hand, and his shield with the other. They all hurried about the house, and never was there made so great a tumult by any host in one house as was made by them, as each man armed himself. Then said Morddwyd tyllyon, "The gadflies of Morddwyd tyllyon's cow!" And while they all sought their arms, Bendigeid Vran supported Branwen between his shield and his shoulder.

Then the Irish kindled a fire under the cauldron of renovation, and they cast the dead bodies into the cauldron until it was full, and the next day they came forth fighting-men as good as before, except that they were not able to speak. Then when Evnissyen saw the dead bodies of the men of the Island of the Mighty nowhere resuscitated, he said in his heart, "Alas! woe is me, that I should have been the cause of bringing the men of the Island of the Mighty into so great a strait. Evil betide me if I find not a deliverance therefrom." And he cast himself among the dead bodies of the Irish, and two unshod Irishmen came to him, and, taking him to be one of the Irish, flung him into the cauldron. And he stretched himself out in the cauldron, so that he rent the cauldron into four pieces, and burst his own heart also.

In consequence of that the men of the Island of the Mighty obtained such success as they had; but they were not victorious, for only seven men of them all escaped, and Bendigeid Vran himself was wounded in the foot with a poisoned dart. Now the seven men that escaped were Pryderi, Manawyddan, Gluneu Eil Taran, Taliesin, Ynawc, Grudyen the son of Muryel, and Heilyn the son of Gwynn Hen.

And Bendigeid Vran commanded them that they should cut off his head. "And take you my head," said he, "and bear it even unto the White Mount, in London, and bury it there, with the face towards France. And a long time will you be upon the road. In Harlech you will be feasting seven years, the birds of Rhiannon singing unto you the while. And all that time the head will be to you as pleasant company as it ever was when on my body. And at Gwales in Penvro you will be fourscore years, and you may remain there, and the head with you uncorrupted, until you open the door that looks towards Aber Henvelen, and towards Cornwall. And after you have opened the door, there you may no longer tarry, set forth then to London to bury the head, and go straight forward."

So they cut off his head, and these seven went forward therewith. And Branwen was the eighth with them, and they came to land at Aber Alaw, in Talebolyon, and they sat down to rest. And Branwen looked towards Ireland and towards the Island of the Mighty, to see if she could descry them. "Alas," said she, "woe is me that I was ever born; two islands have been destroyed because of me!" Then she uttered a loud groan, and there broke her heart. And they made her a foursided grave, and buried her upon the banks of the Alaw.

Then the seven men journeyed forward towards Harlech, bearing the head with them; and as they went, behold there met them a multitude of men and of women. "Have you any tidings?" asked Manawyddan. "We have none," said they, "save that Caswallawn the son of Beli has conquered the Island of the Mighty, and is crowned king of London." "What has become," said they, "of Caradawc the son of Bran, and the seven men who were left with him on this island?" "Caswallawn came upon them, and slew six of the men, and Caradawc's heart broke for grief thereof; for he could see the sword that slew the men, but knew not who it was that wielded it. Caswallawn had flung upon him the Veil of Illusion, so that no one could see him slay the men, but the sword only could they see. And it liked him not to slay Caradawc, because he was his nephew, the son of his cousin. And now he was the third whose heart had broke through grief. Pendaran Dyved, who had remained as a young page with these men, escaped into the wood," said they.

Then they went on to Harlech, and there stopped to rest, and they provided meat and liquor, and sat down to eat and drink. And there came three birds, and began singing unto them a certain song, and all the songs they had ever heard were unpleasant compared thereto; and the birds seemed to them to be at a great distance from them over the sea, yet they appeared as distinct as if they were close by, and at this repast they continued seven years.

And at the close of the seventh year they went forth to Gwales in Penvro. And there they found a fair and regal spot overlooking the ocean; and a spacious hall was therein. And they went into the hall, and two of its doors were open, but the third door was closed, that which looked towards Cornwall. "See, yonder," said Manawyddan, "is the door that we may not open." And that night they regaled themselves and were joyful. And of all they had seen of food laid before them, and of all they had heard of, they remembered nothing; neither of that, nor of any sorrow whatsoever. And there they remained fourscore years, unconscious of having ever spent a time more joyous and mirthful. And they were not more weary than when first they came, neither did they, any of them, know the time they had been there. And it was not more irksome to them having the head with them, than if Bendigeid Vran had been with them himself. And because of these fourscore years, it was called "the Entertaining of the noble Head." The entertaining of Branwen and Matholwch was in the time that they went to Ireland.

One day said Heilyn the son of Gwynn, "Evil betide me, if I do not open the door to know if that is true which is said concerning it." So he opened the door and looked towards Cornwall and Aber Henvelen. And when they had looked, they were as conscious of all the evils they had ever sustained, and of all the friends and companions they had lost, and of all the misery that had befallen them, as if all had happened in that very spot; and especially of the fate of their lord. And because of their perturbation they could not rest, but journeyed forth with the head towards London. And they buried the head in the White Mount, and when it was buried, this was the third goodly concealment; and it was the third ill-fated disclosure when it was disinterred, inasmuch as no invasion from across the sea came to the island while the head was in that concealment.

And thus is the story related of those who journeyed over from Ireland.

In Ireland none were left alive, except five pregnant women in a cave in the Irish wilderness; and to these five women in the same night were born five sons, whom they nursed until they became grown-up youths. And they thought about wives, and they at the same time desired to possess them, and each took a wife of the mothers of their companions, and they governed the country and peopled it.

And these five divided it amongst them, and because of this partition are the five divisions of Ireland still so termed. And they examined the land where the battles had taken place, and they found gold and silver until they became wealthy.

And thus ends this portion of the Mabinogi, concerning the blow given to Branwen, which was the third unhappy blow of the island; and concerning the entertainment of Bran, when the hosts of sevenscore countries and ten went over to Ireland to revenge the blow given to Branwen; and concerning the seven years' banquet in Harlech, and the singing of the birds in Rhiannon, and the sojourning of the head for the space of fourscore years.

CHAPTER 3

Peredur the Son of Evrawc

TRANSLATED BY CHARLOTTE GUEST

Peredur was one of seven sons of the Earl Evrawc. The father and the other six sons fell in combats, and Peredur was brought up by his mother in the wilderness, where the boy was kept ignorant of wars and knights. Peredur met three knights, one of whom was Gwalchmai (Gawain). His mother told him they were angels, but Peredur found out that they were knights, and he decided to become one himself. The incident of the lady in the tent is told, and also the arrival at Arthur's court.

Peredur came to a lake, and saw an old man sitting on the shore, while his attendants were fishing. The old man went to a castle nearby, and Peredur followed him and accepted his invitation to sit down to meat. The old man explained that he was the brother of Peredur's mother and urged Peredur to remain at the castle and receive instructions as a knight. He also told Peredur that if he saw wonderful things he must not ask about them if no one should offer an explanation to him.

The next day Peredur came to another castle and found a stately old man sitting in the large hall; and he was welcomed to the repast that was served to the old man and his retinue. Accepting a test that was proposed, Peredur broke his sword thrice by cutting an iron ring with it. Twice the pieces of the broken ring and sword reunited themselves, but the third time they did not do so. The old man told him he had arrived at only two-thirds of his strength, but when he arrived at his full powers none would be able to withstand him. The old man further stated that he was another brother of Peredur's mother. Two youths entered the hall bearing a great spear with three streams of blood flowing from the point; and all the attendants wailed in grief, but the

*old man did not refer to it, and so Peredur asked no explanation. Then
entered two maidens bearing a salver on which was a man's head,
lying in blood, and again the company lamented. Afterwards they all
retired for the night. The meeting with a woman the next day is
related, and the receipt from her of sundry explanations; and also the
search by Arthur for Peredur. Then comes the visit of Peredur to a
castle where a lovely maiden was in distress through the attacks of her
enemies, whom Peredur vanquished. Being much attracted to the
maiden of the castle, he remained three weeks. After that he visited the
castle of the Nine Sorceresses of Gloucester and remained there also for
three weeks. Then is related how Peredur saw a raven that had alighted
on a dead bird, and how he compared the black raven and the white
snow, and the red blood, to the hair and the skin and the blushes of his
lady-love. Then comes the defeat of Kai, and the meeting with Gwalchmai, and the union with Arthur's company at Caerlleon, where
Peredur fell in love with Angharad Llaw Eurawc. Then follow a
number of adventures of minor importance.*

*The narrative then relates that when Peredur was at Arthur's court
a hideous maiden appeared riding a yellow mule. She reproached
Peredur for not asking about the wonders at the court of the lame
King, and said that if he had done so, the King would have been
restored to health and his lands would have had peace; and Peredur set
forth to learn about the mysteries that the maiden has mentioned.*

*Peredur met a priest and was rebuked for wearing armour on that
day, which was Good Friday; and after a short sojourn with the priest
he set forth to find the Castle of Wonders, which he finally reached.
Here he was joined by King Arthur and his men, and they slew the
sorceresses of Gloucester, who were there, and thus took vengeance,
since Peredur had learned that the bloody head he had seen at the
castle was that of his cousin who had been killed by the sorceresses,
and that they had also wounded his uncle. (R.J.)*

From *Peredur the Son of Evrawc*

And Peredur rode forward. And he came to a vast and desert
wood, on the confines of which was a lake. And on the other
side was a fair castle. And on the border of the lake he saw a
venerable, hoary-headed man, sitting upon a velvet cushion, and

having a garment of velvet upon him. And his attendants were fishing in the lake. When the hoary-headed man beheld Peredur approaching, he arose and went towards the castle. And the old man was lame. Peredur rode to the palace, and the door was open, and he entered the hall. And there was the hoary-headed man sitting on a cushion, and a large blazing fire burning before him. And the household and the company arose to meet Peredur, and disarrayed him. And the man asked the youth to sit on the cushion; and they sat down, and conversed together. When it was time, the tables were laid, and they went to meat. And when they had finished their meal, the man inquired of Peredur if he knew well how to fight with the sword. "I know not," said Peredur, "but were I to be taught, doubtless I should." "Whoever can play well with the cudgel and shield, will also be able to fight with a sword." And the man had two sons; the one had yellow hair, and the other auburn. "Arise, youths," said he, "and play with the cudgel and the shield." And so did they. "Tell me, my soul," said the man, "which of the youths thinkest thou plays best." "I think," said Peredur, "that the yellow-haired youth could draw blood from the other, if he chose." "Arise thou, my life, and take the cudgel and the shield from the hand of the youth with the auburn hair, and draw blood from the yellow-haired youth if thou canst." So Peredur arose, and went to play with the yellow-haired youth; and he lifted up his arm, and struck him such a mighty blow, that his brow fell over his eye, and the blood flowed forth. "Ah, my life," said the man, "come now, and sit down, for thou wilt become the best fighter with the sword of any in this island; and I am thy uncle, thy mother's brother. And with me shalt thou remain a space, in order to learn the manners and customs of different countries, and courtesy, and gentleness, and noble bearing. Leave, then, the habits and the discourse of thy mother, and I will be thy teacher; and I will raise thee to the rank of knight from this time forward. And thus do thou. If thou seest aught to cause thee wonder, ask not the meaning of it; if no one has the courtesy to inform thee, the reproach will not fall upon thee, but upon me that am thy teacher." And they had abundance of honour and service. And when it was time they went to sleep. At the break of day, Peredur arose, and took his horse, and with his uncle's permission he rode forth. And he came to a vast desert wood, and at the further end of the wood was a meadow, and on the other side of the meadow he saw a large castle. And thitherward Peredur bent his way, and he found the gate open, and he proceeded to the hall. And he beheld a stately hoary-headed man sitting on one side of the hall, and many pages around him, who arose to receive and to honour Peredur. And they placed him by the side of the owner of the palace. Then they discoursed together; and when it was time to eat, they caused Peredur to sit beside the nobleman during the repast. And when they had eaten and drunk as much as they desired, the nobleman asked Peredur whether he could fight with a sword? "Were I to receive instruction," said Peredur, "I think I could." Now, there was on the floor of the hall a huge staple, as large as a warrior could grasp. "Take yonder sword," said the man to Peredur, "and strike the iron staple." So Peredur arose and struck the staple, so that he cut it in two; and the sword broke into two parts also. "Place the two parts together, and reunite them," and Peredur placed them together, and they became entire as they were before. And a second time he struck upon the staple, so that both it and the sword broke in two, and as before they reunited. And the third time he gave a like blow, and placed the broken parts together, and neither the staple nor the sword would unite as before. "Youth," said the nobleman, "come now, and sit down, and my blessing be upon thee. Thou fightest best with the sword of any man in the kingdom. Thou hast arrived at two-thirds of thy strength, and the other third thou hast not yet obtained; and when thou attainest to thy full power, none will be able to contend with thee. I am thy uncle, thy mother's brother, and I am brother to the man in whose house thou wast last night." Then Peredur and his uncle discoursed together, and he beheld two youths enter the hall, and proceed up to the chamber, bearing a spear of mighty size, with three streams of blood flowing from the point to the ground. And when all the company saw this, they began wailing and lamenting. But for all that, the man did not break off his discourse with Peredur. And as he did not tell Peredur the meaning of what he saw, he forbore to ask him concerning it. And when the clamour had a little subsided, behold two maidens entered, with a large salver between them, in which was a man's head, surrounded by a profusion of blood. And thereupon the company of the court made so great an outcry, that it was irksome to be in the same hall with them. But at length they were silent. And when time was that they should sleep, Peredur was brought into a fair chamber.

And the next day, with his uncle's permission, he rode forth. And he came to a wood, and far within the wood he heard a loud cry, and he saw a beautiful woman with auburn hair, and a horse with a saddle upon it, standing near her, and a corpse by her side. And as she strove to place the corpse upon the horse, it fell to the ground, and thereupon she made a great lamentation. "Tell me, sister," said Peredur, "wherefore art thou bewailing?" "O! accursed Peredur, little pity has my ill-fortune ever met with from thee." "Wherefore," said Peredur, "am I accursed?" "Because thou wast the cause of thy mother's death; for when thou didst ride forth against her will, anguish seized upon her heart, so that she died; and therefore art thou accursed. And the dwarf and the dwarfess that thou sawest at Arthur's Court were the dwarfs of thy father and mother; and I am thy foster-sister, and this was my wedded husband, and he was slain by the knight that is in the glade in the wood; and do not thou go near him, lest thou shouldest be slain by him likewise." "My sister, thou dost reproach me wrongfully; through my having so long remained amongst you, I shall scarcely vanquish him; and had I continued longer, it would, indeed, be difficult for me to succeed. Cease, therefore, thy lamenting, for it is of no avail, and I will bury the body, and then I will go in quest of the knight, and see if I can do vengeance upon him." And when he had buried the body, they went to the place where the knight was, and found him riding proudly along the glade; and he inquired of Peredur whence he came. "I come from Arthur's Court." "And art thou one of Arthur's men?" "Yes, by my faith." "A profitable alliance, truly, is that of Arthur." And without further parlance, they encountered one another, and immediately Peredur overthrew the knight, and he besought mercy of Peredur. "Mercy shalt thou have," said he, "upon these terms, that thou take this woman in marriage, and do her all the honour and reverence in thy power, seeing thou hast, without cause, slain her wedded husband; and that thou go to Arthur's Court, and shew him that it was I that overthrew thee, to do him honour and service; and that thou tell him that

I will never come to his Court again until I have met with the tall man that is there, to take vengeance upon him for his insult to the dwarf and dwarfess." And he took the knight's assurance, that he would perform all this. Then the knight provided the lady with a horse and garments that were suitable for her, and took her with him to Arthur's Court. And he told Arthur all that had occurred, and gave the defiance to Kai. And Arthur and all his household reproved Kai, for having driven such a youth as Peredur from his Court.

Said Owain the son of Urien, "This youth will never come into the Court until Kai has gone forth from it." "By my faith," said Arthur, "I will search all the deserts in the Island of Britain, until I find Peredur, and then let him and his adversary do their utmost to each other."

Then Peredur rode forward. And he came to a desert wood, where he saw not the track either of men or animals, and where there was nothing but bushes and weeds. And at the upper end of the wood he saw a vast castle, wherein were many strong towers; and when he came near the gate, he found the weeds taller than he had seen them elsewhere. And he struck the gate with the shaft of his lance, and thereupon behold a lean, auburn-haired youth came to an opening in the battlements. "Choose thou, chieftain," said he, "whether shall I open the gate unto thee, or shall I announce unto those that are chief, that thou art at the gateway?" "Say that I am here," said Peredur, "and if it is desired that I should enter, I will go in." And the youth came back, and opened the gate for Peredur. And when he went into the hall, he beheld eighteen youths, lean and redheaded, of the same height, and of the same aspect, and of the same dress, and of the same age as the one who had opened the gate for him. And they were well skilled in courtesy and in service. And they disarrayed him. Then they sat down to discourse. Thereupon, behold five maidens came from the chamber into the hall. And Peredur was certain that he had never seen another of so fair an aspect as the chief of the maidens. And she had an old garment of satin upon her, which had once been handsome, but was then so tattered, that her skin could be seen through it. And whiter was her skin than the bloom of crystal, and her hair and her two eyebrows were blacker than jet, and on her cheeks were two red spots, redder than whatever is reddest. And the maiden welcomed Peredur, and put her arms about his neck, and made him sit down beside her. Not long after this he saw two nuns enter, and a flask full of wine was borne by one, and six loaves of white bread by the other. "Lady," said they, "Heaven is witness, that there is not so much of food and liquor as this left in yonder convent this night." Then they went to meat, and Peredur observed that the maiden wished to give more of the food and of the liquor to him than to any of the others. "My sister," said Peredur, "I will share out the food and the liquor." "Not so, my soul," said she. "By my faith but I will." So Peredur took the bread, and he gave an equal portion of it to each alike, as well as a cup full of the liquor. And when it was time for them to sleep, a chamber was prepared for Peredur, and he went to rest.

"Behold, sister," said the youths to the fairest and most exalted of the maidens, "we have counsel for thee." "What may it be?" she inquired. "Go to the youth that is in the upper chamber, and offer to become his wife, or the lady of his love, if it seem well to him." "That were indeed unfitting," said she. "Hitherto I have not been the lady-love of any knight, and to make him such an offer before I am wooed by him, that, truly, can I not do." "By our confession to Heaven, unless thou actest thus, we will leave thee here to thy enemies, to do as they will with thee." And through fear of this, the maiden went forth; and shedding tears, she proceeded to the chamber. And with the noise of the door opening, Peredur awoke; and the maiden was weeping and lamenting. "Tell me, my sister," said Peredur, "wherefore dost thou weep?" "I will tell thee, lord," said she. "My father possessed these dominions as their chief, and this palace was his, and with it he held the best earldom in the kingdom; then the son of another earl sought me of my father, and I was not willing to be given unto him, and my father would not give me against my will, either to him or any earl in the world. And my father had no child except myself. And after my father's death, these dominions came into my own hands, and then was I less willing to accept him than before. So he made war upon me, and conquered all my possessions, except this one house. And through the valour of the men whom thou hast seen, who are my foster-brothers, and the strength of the house, it can never be taken while food and drink remain. And now our provisions are exhausted; but, as thou hast seen, we have been fed by the nuns, to whom the country is free. And at length they also are without supply of food or liquor. And at no later date than tomorrow, the earl will come against this place with all his forces; and if I fall into his power, my fate will be no better than to be given over to the grooms of his horses. Therefore, lord, I am come to offer to place myself in thy hands, that thou mayest succour me, either by taking me hence, or by defending me here, whichever may seem best unto thee." "Go, my sister," said he, "and sleep; nor will I depart from thee until I do that which thou requirest, or prove whether I can assist thee or not." The maiden went again to rest; and the next morning she came to Peredur, and saluted him. "Heaven prosper thee, my soul, and what tidings dost thou bring?" "None other, than that the earl and all his forces have alighted at the gate, and I never beheld any place so covered with tents, and thronged with knights challenging others to the combat." "Truly," said Peredur, "let my horse be made ready." So his horse was accoutred, and he arose and sallied forth to the meadow. And there was a knight riding proudly along the meadow, having raised the signal for battle. And they encountered, and Peredur threw the knight over his horse's crupper to the ground. And at the close of the day, one of the chief knights came to fight with him, and he overthrew him also, so that he besought his mercy. "Who art thou?" said Peredur. "Verily," said he, "I am Master of the Household to the earl." "And how much of the countess's possessions is there in thy power?" "The third part, verily," answered he. "Then," said Peredur, "restore to her the third of her possessions in full, and all the profit thou hast made by them, and bring meat and drink for a hundred men, with their horses and arms, to her court this night. And thou shalt remain her captive, unless she wish to take thy life." And this he did forthwith. And that night the maiden was right joyful, and they fared plenteously.

And the next day Peredur rode forth to the meadow; and that day he vanquished a multitude of the host. And at the close of the day, there came a proud and stately knight, and Peredur overthrew him, and he besought his mercy. "Who art thou?" said Peredur. "I am Steward of the Palace," said he. "And how much of the maiden's possessions are under thy control?" "One-third part," answered he. "Verily," said Peredur, "thou shalt fully restore to the maiden her possessions, and, moreover, thou shalt give her meat and drink for two hundred men, and their horses and their arms. And for thyself, thou shalt be her captive." And immediately it was so done.

And the third day Peredur rode forth to the meadow; and he vanquished more that day than on either of the preceding. And at the close of the day, an earl came to encounter him, and he overthrew him, and he besought his mercy. "Who art thou?" said Peredur. "I am the earl," said he. "I will not conceal it from thee." "Verily," said Peredur, "thou shalt restore the whole of the maiden's earldom, and shalt give her thine own earldom in addition thereto, and meat and drink for three hundred men, and their horses and arms, and thou thyself shalt remain in her power." And thus it was fulfilled. And Peredur tarried three weeks in the country, causing tribute and obedience to be paid to the maiden, and the government to be placed in her hands. "With thy leave," said Peredur, "I will go hence." "Verily, my brother, desirest thou this?" "Yes, by my faith; and had it not been for love of thee, I should not have been here thus long." "My soul," said she, "who art thou?" "I am Peredur the son of Evrawc from the North; and if ever thou art in trouble or in danger, acquaint me therewith, and if I can, I will protect thee."

So Peredur rode forth. And far thence there met him a lady, mounted on a horse that was lean, and covered with sweat; and she saluted the youth. "Whence comest thou, my sister?" Then she told him the cause of her journey. Now she was the wife of the Lord of the Glade. "Behold," said he, "I am the knight through whom thou art in trouble, and he shall repent it, who has treated thee thus." Thereupon, behold a knight rode up, and he inquired of Peredur, if he had seen a knight such as he was seeking. "Hold thy peace," said Peredur, "I am he whom thou seekest; and by my faith, thou deservest ill of thy household for thy treatment of the maiden, for she is innocent concerning me." So they encountered, and they were not long in combat ere Peredur overthrew the knight, and he besought his mercy. "Mercy thou shalt have," said Peredur, "so thou wilt return by the way thou camest, and declare that thou holdest the maiden innocent, and so that thou wilt acknowledge unto her the reverse thou hast sustained at my hands." And the knight plighted him his faith thereto.

Then Peredur rode forward. And above him he beheld a castle, and thitherward he went. And he struck upon the gate with his lance, and then, behold, a comely auburn-haired youth opened the gate, and he had the stature of a warrior, and the years of a boy. And when Peredur came into the hall, there was a tall and stately lady sitting in a chair, and many handmaidens around her; and the lady rejoiced at his coming. And when it was time, they went to meat. And after their repast was finished, "It were well for thee, chieftain," said she, "to go elsewhere to sleep." "Wherefore can I not sleep here?" said Peredur. "Nine sorceresses are here, my soul, of the sorceresses of Gloucester, and their father and their mother are with them; and unless we can make our escape before daybreak, we shall be slain; and already they have conquered and laid waste all the country, except this one dwelling." "Behold," said Peredur, "I will remain here tonight, and if you are in trouble, I will do you what service I can; but harm shall you not receive from me." So they went to rest. And with the break of day, Peredur heard a dreadful outcry. And he hastily arose, and went forth in his vest and his doublet, with his sword about his neck, and he saw a sorceress overtake one of the watch, who cried out violently. Peredur attacked the sorceress, and struck her upon the head with his sword, so that he flattened her helmet and her headpiece like a dish upon her head. "Thy mercy, goodly Peredur, son of Evrawc, and the mercy of Heaven." "How knowest thou, hag, that I am Peredur?" "By destiny, and the foreknowledge that I should suffer harm from thee. And thou shalt take a horse and armour of me; and with me thou shalt go to learn chivalry and the use of thy arms." Said Peredur, "Thou shalt have mercy, if thou pledge thy faith thou wilt never more injure the dominions of the Countess." And Peredur took surety of this, and with permission of the Countess, he set forth with the sorceress to the palace of the sorceresses. And there he remained for three weeks, and then he made choice of a horse and arms, and went his way.

And in the evening he entered a valley, and at the head of the valley he came to a hermit's cell, and the hermit welcomed him gladly, and there he spent the night. And in the morning he arose, and when he went forth, behold a shower of snow had fallen the night before, and a hawk had killed a wild fowl in front of the cell. And the noise of the horse scared the hawk away, and a raven alighted upon the bird. And Peredur stood, and compared the blackness of the raven and the whiteness of the snow, and the redness of the blood, to the hair of the lady that best he loved, which was blacker than jet, and to her skin which was whiter than the snow, and to the two red spots upon her cheeks, which were redder than the blood upon the snow appeared to be.

Now Arthur and his household were in search of Peredur. "Know ye," said Arthur, "who is the knight with the long spear that stands by the brook up yonder?" "Lord," said one of them, "I will go and learn who he is." So the youth came to the place where Peredur was, and asked him what he did thus, and who he was. And from the intensity with which he thought upon the lady whom best he loved, he gave him no answer. Then the youth thrust at Peredur with his lance, and Peredur turned upon him, and struck him over his horse's crupper to the ground. And after this, four-and-twenty youths came to him, and he did not answer one more than another, but gave the same reception to all, bringing them with one single thrust to the ground. And then came Kai, and spoke to Peredur rudely and angrily; and Peredur took him with his lance under the jaw, and cast him from him with a thrust, so that he broke his arm and his shoulder-blade, and he rode over him one-and-twenty times. And while he lay thus, stunned with the violence of the pain that he had suffered, his horse returned back at a wild and prancing pace. And when the household saw the horse come back without his rider, they rode forth in haste to the place where the encounter had been. And when they first came there, they thought that Kai was slain; but they found that if he had a skilful physician, he yet might live. And Peredur moved not from his meditation, on seeing the concourse that was around Kai. And Kai was brought to Arthur's tent, and Arthur caused skilful physicians to come to him. And Arthur was grieved that Kai had met with this reverse, for he loved him greatly.

"Then," said Gwalchmai, "it is not fitting that any should disturb an honourable knight from his thought unadvisedly; for either he is pondering some damage that he has sustained, or he is thinking of the lady whom best he loves. And through such ill-advised proceeding, perchance this misadventure has befallen him who last met with him. And if it seem well to thee, lord, I will go and see if this knight hath changed from his thought; and if he has, I will ask him courteously to come and visit thee." Then Kai was wroth, and he spoke angry and spiteful words. "Gwalchmai," said he, "I know that thou wilt bring him because he is fatigued. Little praise and honour, nevertheless, wilt thou have from vanquishing a weary knight, who is tired with fighting. Yet thus hast thou gained the advantage over many. And while thy speech and thy soft words last, a coat of thin linen were armour sufficient for thee, and thou wilt not need to break either lance or sword in fighting with the knight in the state he is in." Then said Gwalchmai to Kai, "Thou mightest use more pleasant words, wert thou so minded: and it behoves thee not upon me to wreak thy wrath and thy displeasure. Methinks I shall bring the knight hither with me without breaking either my arm or my shoulder." Then said Arthur to Gwalchmai, "Thou speakest like a wise and prudent man; go, and take enough of armour about thee, and choose thy horse." And Gwalchmai accoutred himself, and rode forward hastily to the place where Peredur was.

And Peredur was resting on the shaft of his spear, pondering the same thought, and Gwalchmai came to him without any signs of hostility, and said to him, "If I thought that it would be as agreeable to thee as it would be to me, I would converse with thee. I have also a message from Arthur unto thee, to pray thee to come and visit him. And two men have been before on this errand." "That is true," said Peredur, "and uncourteously they came. They attacked me, and I was annoyed thereat, for it was not pleasing to me to be drawn from the thought that I was in, for I was thinking of the lady whom best I love, and thus was she brought to my mind: I was looking upon the snow, and upon the raven, and upon the drops of the blood of the bird that the hawk had killed upon the snow. And I bethought me that her whiteness was like that of the snow, and that the blackness of her hair and her eyebrows like that of the raven, and that the two red spots upon her cheeks were like the two drops of blood." Said Gwalchmai, "This was not an ungentle thought, and I should marvel if it were pleasant to thee to be drawn from it." "Tell me," said Peredur, "is Kai in Arthur's Court?" "He is," said he, "and behold he is the knight that fought with thee last; and it would have been better for him had he not come, for his arm and his shoulder-blade were broken with the fall which he had from thy spear." "Verily," said Peredur, "I am not sorry to have thus begun to avenge the insult to the dwarf and dwarfess." Then Gwalchmai marvelled to hear him speak of the dwarf and the dwarfess; and he approached him, and threw his arms around his neck, and asked him what was his name. "Peredur the son of Evrawc am I called," said he; "and thou, Who art thou?" "I am called Gwalchmai," he replied. "I am right glad to meet with thee," said Peredur, "for in every country where I have been I have heard of thy fame for prowess and uprightness, and I solicit thy fellowship." "Thou shalt have it, by my faith, and grant me thine," said he, "Gladly will I do so," answered Peredur.

So they rode forth together joyfully towards the place where Arthur was, and when Kai saw them coming, he said, "I knew that Gwalchmai needed not to fight the knight. And it is no wonder that he should gain fame; more can he do by his fair words than I by the strength of my arm." And Peredur went with Gwalchmai to his tent, and they took off their armour. And Peredur put on garments like those that Gwalchmai wore, and they went together unto Arthur, and saluted him. "Behold, lord," said Gwalchmai, "him whom thou hast sought so long." "Welcome unto thee, chieftain," said Arthur. "With me thou shalt remain; and had I known thy valour had been such, thou shouldst not have left me as thou didst; nevertheless, this was predicted of thee by the dwarf and the dwarfess, whom Kai ill-treated and whom thou hast avenged." And hereupon, behold there came the Queen and her handmaidens, and Peredur saluted them. And they were rejoiced to see him, and bade him welcome. And Arthur did him great honour and respect, and they returned towards Caerlleon.

And the first night Peredur came to Caerlleon to Arthur's Court, and as he walked in the city after his repast, behold, there met him Angharad Llaw Eurawc. "By my faith, sister," said Peredur, "thou art a beauteous and lovely maiden; and, were it pleasing to thee, I could love thee above all women." "I pledge my faith," said she, "that I do not love thee, nor will I ever do so." "I also pledge my faith," said Peredur, "that I will never speak a word to any Christian again, until thou come to love me above all men."

The next day Peredur went forth by the high road, along a mountain-ridge, and he saw a valley of a circular form, the confines of which were rocky and wooded. And the flat part of the valley was in meadows, and there were fields betwixt the meadows and the wood. And in the bosom of the wood he saw large black houses of uncouth workmanship. And he dismounted, and led his horse towards the wood. And a little way within the wood he saw a rocky ledge, along which the road lay. And upon the ledge was a lion bound by a chain, and sleeping. And beneath the lion he saw a deep pit of immense size, full of the bones of men and animals. And Peredur drew his sword and struck the lion, so that he fell into the mouth of the pit and hung there by the chain; and with a second blow he struck the chain and broke it, and the lion fell into the pit; and Peredur led his horse over the rocky ledge, until he came into the valley. And in the centre of the valley he saw a fair castle, and he went towards it. And in the meadow by the castle he beheld a huge grey man sitting, who was larger than any man he had ever before seen. And two young pages were shooting the hilts of their daggers, of the bone of the sea-horse. And one of the pages had red hair, and the other auburn. And they went before him to the place where the grey man was, and Peredur saluted him. And the grey man said, "Disgrace to the beard of my porter." Then Peredur understood that the porter was the lion.

And the grey man and the pages went together into the castle, and Peredur accompanied them; and he found it a fair and noble place. And they proceeded to the hall, and the tables were already laid, and upon them was abundance of food and liquor. And thereupon he saw an aged woman and a young woman come from the chamber; and they were the most stately women he had ever seen. Then they washed and went to meat, and the grey man sat in the upper seat at the head of the table, and the aged woman next to him. And Peredur and the maiden were placed together, and the two young pages served them. And the maiden gazed sorrowfully upon Peredur, and Peredur asked the maiden wherefore she was sad. "For thee, my soul; for, from when I first beheld thee, I have loved thee above all men. And

60

it pains me to know that so gentle a youth as thou should have such a doom as awaits thee tomorrow. Sawest thou the numerous black houses in the bosom of the wood? All these belong to the vassals of the grey man yonder, who is my father. And they are all giants. And tomorrow they will rise up against thee, and will slay thee. And the Round Valley is this valley called." "Listen, fair maiden, wilt thou contrive that my horse and arms be in the same lodging with me tonight?" "Gladly will I cause it so to be, by Heaven, if I can."

And when it was time for them to sleep rather than to carouse, they went to rest. And the maiden caused Peredur's horse and arms to be in the same lodging with him. And the next morning Peredur heard a great tumult of men and horses around the castle. And Peredur arose, and armed himself and his horse, and went to the meadow. Then the aged woman and the maiden came to the grey man: "Lord," said they, "take the word of the youth, that he will never disclose what he has seen in this place, and we will be his sureties that he keep it." "I will not do so, by my faith," said the grey man. So Peredur fought with the host, and towards evening he had slain the one-third of them without receiving any hurt himself. Then said the aged woman, "Behold, many of thy host have been slain by the youth; do thou, therefore, grant him mercy." "I will not grant it, by my faith," said he. And the aged woman and the fair maiden were upon the battlements of the castle, looking forth. And at that juncture, Peredur encountered the yellow-haired youth and slew him. "Lord," said the maiden, "grant the young man mercy." "That will I not do, by Heaven," he replied; and thereupon Peredur attacked the auburn-haired youth, and slew him likewise. "It were better that thou hadst accorded mercy to the youth before he had slain thy two sons; for now scarcely wilt thou thyself escape from him." "Go, maiden, and beseech the youth to grant mercy unto us, for we yield ourselves into his hands." So the maiden came to the place where Peredur was, and besought mercy for her father, and for all such of his vassals as had escaped alive. "Thou shalt have it, on condition that thy father and all that are under him go and render homage to Arthur, and tell him that it was his vassal Peredur that did him this service." "This will we do willingly, by Heaven." "And you shall also receive baptism; and I will send to Arthur, and beseech him to bestow this valley upon thee and upon thy heirs after thee for ever." Then they went in, and the grey man and the tall woman saluted Peredur. And the grey man said unto him, "Since I have possessed this valley I have not seen any Christian depart with his life, save thyself. And we will go to do homage to Arthur, and to embrace the faith and be baptized." Then said Peredur, "To Heaven I render thanks that I have not broken my vow to the lady that best I love, which was, that I would not speak one word unto any Christian."

That night they tarried there. And the next day, in the morning, the grey man, with his company, set forth to Arthur's Court; and they did homage unto Arthur, and he caused them to be baptized. And the grey man told Arthur that it was Peredur that had vanquished them. And Arthur gave the valley to the grey man and his company, to hold it of him as Peredur had besought. And with Arthur's permission, the grey man went back to the Round Valley.

Peredur rode forward next day, and he traversed a vast tract of desert, in which no dwellings were. And at length he came to a habitation, mean and small. And there he heard that there was a serpent that lay upon a gold ring, and suffered none to inhabit the country for seven miles around. And Peredur came to the place where he heard the serpent was. And angrily, furiously, and desperately fought he with the serpent; and at last he killed it, and took away the ring. And thus he was for a long time without speaking a word to any Christian. And therefrom he lost his colour and his aspect, through extreme longing after the Court of Arthur, and the society of the lady whom best he loved, and of his companions. Then he proceeded forward to Arthur's Court, and on the road there met him Arthur's household going on a particular errand, with Kai at their head. And Peredur knew them all, but none of the household recognized him. "Whence comest thou, chieftain?" said Kai. And this he asked him twice and three times, and he answered him not. And Kai thrust him through the thigh with his lance. And lest he should be compelled to speak, and to break his vow, he went on without stopping. "Then," said Gwalchmai, "I declare to Heaven, Kai, that thou hast acted ill in committing such an outrage on a youth like this, who cannot speak." And Gwalchmai returned back to Arthur's Court. "Lady," said he to

Gwenhwyvar, "seest thou how wicked an outrage Kai has committed upon this youth who cannot speak; for Heaven's sake, and for mine, cause him to have medical care before I come back, and I will repay thee the charge."

And before the men returned from their errand, a knight came to the meadow beside Arthur's Palace, to dare some one to the encounter. And his challenge was accepted; and Peredur fought with him, and overthrew him. And for a week he overthrew one knight every day.

And one day, Arthur and his household were going to Church, and they beheld a knight who had raised the signal for combat. "Verily," said Arthur, "by the valour of men, I will not go hence until I have my horse and my arms to overthrow yonder boor." Then went the attendants to fetch Arthur's horse and arms. And Peredur met the attendants as they were going back, and he took the horse and arms from them, and proceeded to the meadow; and all those who saw him arise and go to do battle with the knight, went upon the tops of the houses, and the mounds, and the high places, to behold the combat. And Peredur beckoned with his hand to the knight to commence the fight. And the knight thrust at him, but he was not thereby moved from where he stood. And Peredur spurred his horse, and ran at him wrathfully, furiously, fiercely, desperately, and with mighty rage, and he gave him a thrust, deadly-wounding, severe, furious, adroit, and strong, under his jaw, and raised him out of his saddle, and cast him a long way from him. And Peredur went back, and left the horse and the arms with the attendant as before, and he went on foot to the Palace.

Then Peredur went by the name of the Dumb Youth. And behold, Angharad Llaw Eurawc met him. "I declare to Heaven, chieftain," said she, "woful is it that thou canst not speak; for couldst thou speak, I would love thee best of all men; and by my faith, although thou canst not, I do love thee above all." "Heaven reward thee, my sister," said Peredur, "by my faith I also do love thee." Thereupon it was known that he was Peredur. And then he held fellowship with Gwalchmai, and Owain the son of Urien, and all the household, and he remained in Arthur's Court.

CHAPTER 4

The Elucidation

TRANSLATED BY SEBASTIAN EVANS

The story of the Grail falls into seven parts, in which Master Bleheris relates how the rich land of Logres came to be destroyed. Attendant upon the wells and springs of the land were damsels whose task it was to entertain all wayfarers and see them fed with rich fare, but King Amangons and his men raped the Maidens of the Wells and carried off their golden cups so that thereafter their wells dried up and the land became waste. No longer could the court of the Fisher King be found. Many years later the Round Table Knights, hearing of this evil deed, set out in search of the damsels and found many wandering in the woods, each protected by a knight. These they overthrew and sent to Arthur. One, Blihos Bleheris, knew the whole story and told Arthur that the maidens now wandering the woods were the offspring of the original Well Guardians and that they would wander so until they found again the court of the Rich Fisher.

Arthur's knights determined to go in search of the court, and of its master who knew much of the arts of magic and could change his semblance at will. Gawain was to find the court and have much joy there, but before that Perceval found it — that same Perceval who asked about whom the Grail served and also about the Cross of silver, but not why the Spear dripped with blood. And the story will tell how the Grail served all with rich food, but this is Perceval's story and should await its turn, for when the Good Knight shall come that has found the court of Rich Fisher three times, then shall the full story of the Grail be told. Indeed the court was found seven times in all, and of each discovery there is a tale (the text lists these stories but none appear to have a direct connection with the Grail and are anyway lost). After this the land was restored, the streams ran again and the forests were thicker than ever. And in the land the descendants of the Well Maidens built the Castle of the Maidens, the Perilous Bridge and the Orgellus Castle.

There follows an account of Perceval's parents, but this reads as though attached to the preceding matter, which will be seen to have little or nothing to do with Chrétien. It seems, rather, to be a much earlier story which the author (who also makes himself one of the characters) had heard and decided to add to the literature of the Grail. It does, however, offer several clues to the later material. The whole episode of the well maidens — obviously otherworld characters — their rape and the subsequent drying up of the land, offers a convincing explanation of the Waste Land; while the character of the Fisher King here plays a more important role — seeming more like a positive version of the enchanters Garlon or Klingsor, whose acquaintance we shall make in later texts but who oppose the Grail rather than becoming its guardians. There is, too, the suggestion of a cult of sacred wells, of an otherworld being who rules over them, and of the intermingling of human and fairy blood. As always in Arthurian matters the Kingdom of Logres is an inner realm of Britain within Britain, a shadowy place whose borders overlap those of Arthur. (J.M.)

From *The Elucidation*

By way of a noble commencement thereof, here worshipfully beginneth a Romance of the most delightsome story that may be, to wit, the story of the Graal, the secret whereof may no man tell in prose nor rhyme, for such a thing might the story turn out to be before it were all told that every man might be grieved thereof albeit he had in nowise misdone. Wherefore it is that the wise man leaveth it aside and doth simply pass on beyond, for, and Master Blihos lie not, the secret should no man tell.

Now listen to me, all ye my friends, and ye shall hear me set forth the story that shall be right sweet to hearken unto, for therein shall be the seven Wardens that hold governance throughout the whole world, and all the good stories that any hath told according as the writing shall set them forth; what manner folk the seven Wardens should be, and how they took unto them a chief, and whom they took, for never aforetime have ye heard tell the story truly set forth, and how great noise was there and great outcry, and how and for what cause was destroyed the rich country of Logres whereof was much talk in days of yore.

The kingdom turned to loss, the land was dead and desert in suchwise as that it was scarce worth a couple of hazel-nuts. For they lost the voices of the wells and the damsels that were therein. For no less thing was the service they rendered than this, that scarce any wandered by the way, whether it were at eventide or morning, but that as for drink and victual he would go so far out of his way as to find one of the wells, and then nought could he ask for of fair victual such as pleased him but incontinent he should have it all so long as he had asked in reason. For straightway, I wis, forth of the well issued a damsel — none fairer need he ask — bearing in her hand a cup of gold with larded meats, pasties, and bread, while another damsel bore a white napkin and a dish of gold or silver wherein was the mess which he that had come for the mess had asked for. Right fair welcome found he at the well, and if so it were that his mess did not please him, divers other they brought him all made to his wish with great cheer and great plenty. The damsels with one accord served fair and joyously all wayfarers by the roads that came to the wells for victual.

King Amangons, that was evil and craven-hearted, was the first to break the custom, for thereafter did many others the same according to the ensample they took of the King whose duty it was to protect the damsels and to maintain and guard them within his peace. One of the damsels did he enforce, and to her sore sorrow did away her maidenhead, and carried off from her the cup of gold that he took along with him, and afterward did make him every day be served thereof. Well deserved he to come to mishap thereby. For thenceforth never did the damsel serve any more nor issue forth of that well for no man that might come thither to ask for victual. And all the other damsels only served in such sort as that none should see them.

The other vassals that held of the King's honour, when they beheld this of their Lord that he enforced the damsels whereso-ever he found them comeliest, did all in like manner enforce them and carried off the cups of gold in suchwise that thereafter did no damsel issue forth of the wells nor none did service. This wot ye well, my Lords, that on this wise did the land turn to its downfall, and an evil end withal did the King make and all the others after him that had wrought the damsels sore annoy. In such sort was the kingdom laid waste that thenceforth was no tree leafy. The meadows and the flowers were dried up and the waters were shrunken, nor as then might no man find the Court of the Rich Fisherman that wont to make in the land a glittering glory of gold and silver, of ermines and minever, of rich palls of sendal, of meats and of stuffs, of falcons gentle and merlins and tercels and sparrow-hawks and falcons peregrine.

Then, when the Court was found, throughout the country was so great plenty of all manner riches such as I have named that I warrant you all men marvelled thereat both rich and poor. Thenceforward, as before it had lost every whit, so now in the kingdom of Logres was all the richesse in the world.

The Peers of the Table Round came in the time of King Arthur. So good as they were none ever seen. Knights were they so good, so worshipful, so strong, so proud, so puissant, and so hardy, that when they had heard the story of the adventures, they were fain incontinent to recover the wells. All with one accord sware an oath to protect the damsels that had been put out of them and the cups that had been carried away, and to destroy root and branch the kindred of them that had wrought them harm. For these dwelt so nigh the wells that the damsels came not forth; and if it were that they could catch any of them, her made they be slain by the sword or hanged. Alms made they and prayer to God that He would recover back the wells in such stablishment as they were aforetime, and that for His honour He would do them the service they asked of Him. Before they bethought them of asking so much, they could find nought. Never a voice could they hear from the wells, nor would no damsel issue therefrom.

But thereafter such adventure found they that they did very mightily marvel thereat. For in the forest found they damsels — fairer none would you ask — with whom were knights right well armed upon their destriers that protected the damsels. Together fought they against them that would fain have carried them off. Many a knight did they make die, for the damsels, I wis, had many a battle in the land. King Arthur thereby lost many a good knight without recovery, and many a good one did he gain thereby, as the story will tell you.

The Knight first conquered had to name Blihos Bliheris, and him did Messire Gauwains overcome through the great prowess whereof he is fulfilled. Him sent he to yield himself up to King Arthur; whereupon he mounted his horse as he that hath no mind to tarry; and when he came to the Court did yield himself up, albeit never was he there known of the King, nor none did he know. But right good stories he knew, such as that none could ever be aweary of hearkening to his words. They of the Court asked him of the damsels that rode by the forest albeit it were not yet summer, and good right had they so to ask and demand answer. And he knew how to tell them as much so that right willingly gave they ear to him, and many a night together were the damsels and the knights fain to hearken to him and seek him out.

He saith to them: "Much marvel have ye of the damsels that ye see go among these great forests, and never make ye an end of asking in what country we are born. I will tell ye the truth hereof. All we are born of the damsels, and never in the world were fairer, whom King Amangons did enforce. Never on any day of the world shall those wrongs be amended. The Peers of the Table Round of their courtesy and honour, of their prowess and valiance, are fain by force to recover the wells whereof these be the squires and knights and nobles. I will tell you the sum of the matter. These all shall journey in common, and the damsels in likewise that wander at large through this country by forest and field behoveth it thus to fare until such time as God shall give them to find the Court from whence shall come the joy whereby the land shall again be made bright. To them that shall seek the Court, shall befall adventures such as were never found nor told of in this land afore." Much to their liking was this that he said and sung unto them, and right well were they pleased ...

CHAPTER 5

The Origin of the Holy Grail

SIR JOHN RHYS

The romances are not very clear in whose keeping the Grail was, for some of them place it in that of Peles (Pelles), and some in that of Peleur (Pellean); so we should probably not greatly err in supposing it associated with both, a view which is easy to admit on Welsh ground, where Pwyll and Pryderi are always treated as standing in the relation of father and son to one another. But had Pwyll and Pryderi anything that might be set over against the Grail? Most assuredly they had, as witness the Taliessin poem which describes Arthur harrying Hades. The principal treasure, which he and his men carried away thence, was the Cauldron of the Head of Hades, that is to say, of Pwyll. In that poem (xxx), Pwyll and Pryderi are associated together, and the cauldron is found at a place called Caer Pedryvan, the Four-horned or Four-cornered Castle, in Ynys Pybyrðor or the Isle of the Active Door, the dwellers of which are represented quaffing sparkling wine in a clime that blends the grey twilight of the evening with the jet-black darkness of night; so lamps burn in the front of the gates of Uffern or Hell. Besides the names Caer Pedryvan and Uffern, it has these others: Caer Veðwit, meaning probably the Castle of Revelry, in reference to the wine-drinking there; Caer Golud, or the Castle of Riches; Caer Ochren, Caer Rigor, and Caer Vanðwy, all three of unknown interpretation; and, lastly, Caer Sidi, which is interesting as occurring in another Taliessin poem of similarly mythological import. The bard in this latter poem (xiv), represents himself singing before princes over their mead-cups, and the verses in point run thus:

69

Ys kyweir vyg kadeir ygkaer sidi.
Nys plawd heint a heneint a uo yndi.
Ys gwyr manawyt[an] a phryderi.
Teir oryan y am tan agan recdi.
Ac am y banneu ffrydyeu gweilgi.
Ar ffynnhawn ffrwythlawn yssyd oduchti.
Ys whegach nor gwin gwyn yllyn yndi.

Perfect is my chair[1] in Caer Sidi:
Plague and age hurt him not who's in it —
They know, Manawyðtan and Pryderi.
Three organs round a fire sing before it,
And about its points are ocean's streams
And the abundant well above it —
Sweeter than white wine the drink in it.

We do not pretend to understand this description, though the words used present no serious difficulty; but it is to be noticed that the name Sidi refers to the castle as a revolving one: compare the Welsh word *sidyll*, "a spinning wheel." This leads one to compare the words in the Taliessin poem with the account in the Welsh *Seint Greal* of a revolving castle, which Peredur entered. The passage runs thus: "And they rode through the wild forests, and from one forest to another until they arrived on clear ground outside the forest. And then they beheld a castle coming within their view on level ground in the middle of a meadow; and around the castle flowed a large river, and inside the castle they beheld large spacious halls with windows large and fair. They drew nearer towards the castle, and they perceived the castle turning with greater speed than the fastest wind they had ever known. And above on the castle they saw archers shooting so vigorously, that no armour would protect against one of the discharges they made. Besides this, there were men there blowing in horns so vigorously, that one might think one felt the ground tremble. At the gates were lions, in iron chains, roaring and howling so violently that one might fancy the forest and the castle uprooted by them." We are not told that either the warriors or the trumpeters were figures in metal, but we have here the music, which, in the poem, is produced by the three organs. We find nothing, however, to throw any light on the sweet fountain of Caer Sidi.

One would probably not greatly err in regarding the Turning Castle as a form of the abode of the king of the dead, and the swiftness of its revolution would explain such a name as that of the Isle of the Active or strenuous Door. The large river flowing round it reminds one of the castle of Peleur, entered by Gwalchmei; and the sequel of the story of the Turning Castle, showing, among other things, how the lions and the warriors offered no obstruction to Peredur when he galloped up to the gate, also recalls the behaviour of the lion and the metal men in the case of Gwalchmei's entry to the other castle. It remains to mention a remarkable circumstance in connection with Peredur's entrance into the Turning Castle, namely, that he was led by a lady, who took from him his spear and his shield to carry them before him. In other words, the warrior is protected by a woman, as when, in a well-known Irish story, Liban, leading Loeg, Cuchulinn's charioteer, to the other world, and arriving at a perilous point in the journey, took him by the shoulder. Loeg objected, reminding her that this was not what he had been most used to do, namely, to accept protection from a woman; thereupon she assured him, that, if he was to return alive, it must be so.[2] It has already been pointed out, that we have a blurred version of the same sort of thing in Rhiannon carrying the visitors to Pwyll's court on her back from the horseblock to the hall; and a line hitherto unexplained, in the beginning of the same Taliessin poem (xxx), seems to refer to this goddess with free access to both worlds. The bard, before describing Arthur's expedition to Caer Sidi or Caer Pedryvan, observes that before him nobody had been there, that is, nobody who returned, excepting one whom he calls Gweir. He would seem to have entered with the aid of Rhiannon, strangely called in this story the "apostle" or messenger of Pwyll and Pryderi; and he only returned after a terrible imprisonment there, an initiation which made him for ever a bard. In the other poem mentioned we have, instead of Pwyll and Pryderi as here, Manawyðan and Pryderi as in the Mabinogi bearing the former's name.

The same poem, in the lines already cited, speaks likewise of the sea surrounding the points or corners of Caer Sidi. The word used is *banneu* the plural of *ban*, the Welsh equivalent of the

Goidelic *benn,* "a horn, peak or gable," so well known as the word used in naming mountains in Scotland; *ban,* and especially *banneu* is so used also in Wales, as in the case of *Banneu Brycheiniog,* "the Beacons of Brecknock" where the word refers to the tops of those mountains; but it may mean more indefinitely the ends of anything, as in the phrase, *pedwar ban y byd,* "the four ends or corners of the world." We have it also in the name *Caer Pedryvan,* or the castle of the fourfold *ban.* What this may have exactly meant is not clear, as it might mean simply square, in reference to its having four corners or angles. Most probably it meant more, and it is worth while mentioning that the Irish story of Maildun's Boat speaks of an "Isle of the Four Precious Walls." These latter met in its centre and consisted respectively of gold, silver, copper, and crystal, the four parts into which they divided the island being allotted severally to kings and queens, youths and maidens. The adjective from *ban* was *bannawc,*[3] in modern Welsh *bannog,* "having points, peaks, or horns;" and the Kulhwch story refers to a mountain in the north called Bannawc. Bannawc was also probably the name which became the Benwyk of Malory's *Morte d'Arthur,* the Benoic of the Huth *Merlin,* as the name of the country of King Ban. The same adjective qualifying *caer* would in old Welsh yield Caer Bannauc, written later Caer Vannawc or Vannawg, and it is the former we probably have in the name given by the romancers as Carbonek. Malory calls the place both Carbonek and Corbyn, while in Manessier's continuation of Chrétien's *Conte du Graal* it even becomes Corbiere; but the *Queste du Saint Graal,* edited by Dr Furnivall for the Roxburghe Club, retains a form Corbenic, which is less estropié; and this is also the name given in the *Grand St Graal,* where it is stated that Corbenic was situated in the Terre Foraine. Now Carbonek was the name of the castle where Pelles lived and kept the Holy Grail, and Carbonek seems practically the same as Taliessin's Caer Pedryvan or the *Banneu* of Caer Sidi, with which we have found Pwyll Head of Hades associated, as well as his famous Cauldron.

With regard to that vessel, Taliessin, in poem xxx, mentions the following things respecting it. The Cauldron of the Head of Hades had a rim set with pearls adorning it; the fire beneath it was kindled by the breath of nine maidens; utterances might be heard issuing from it; and it would not boil food for a coward.

The other poem does not mention the cauldron as being at Caer Sidi, but says that he who has his seat there has nought to fear from plague or old age. Compare with this what is said of the Grail in the romances, where Pelles and his brother figure. The Grail, when it comes, feeds those at the table with whatever kind of food each one desires. But those who are not worthy are not allowed by it to remain or to approach too near with impunity. Similarly those who worship at the Grail Chapel at King Peleur's remain young nor mark the lapse of time. Add to this that the Grail heals the sick and wounded. By means of accounts other than those in which the Grail belongs to Pelles or Peleur, the correspondence between it and the Cauldron of Pwyll Head of Hades, might, perhaps, be more strikingly shown; but the foregoing is sufficiently near for our purpose. Now, as the original identity of Pelles and Peleur with Pwyll and Pryderi has been shown to be probable, as has also the identity of Carbonek, where the Holy Grail was kept, with Caer Pedryvan, where Pwyll's Cauldron was found by Arthur and his men, the conclusion is all but inevitable, that the famous Cauldron served as a prototype of the far more famous Grail.

In the romances to which we have had to refer in connection with Pelles and Peleur or Pellean, the owner of the Grail is called the Lame or Maimed King; but there are others which style him the Fisher King or the Rich Fisher. These latter appellations appear to be derived from a different Welsh original, and they subdivide themselves into two groups — those in which the counterparts of Pelles and Pellean are called Gonemans or Goon and the Fisher respectively; and those in which they are represented as being a father and son, called Bron and Alain. Let us begin with the latter, and first with Bron, in whose name we have one of the romancers' versions of the Welsh name Brân.

The banquet of seven years' duration around Brân's Head at Harlech, and the festivities of eighty years on the lonely isle of Gwales, are left undefined as to the means or manner of providing for them: the presence of the Venerable Head appears to have sufficed without even a reference to a magic cauldron or any other vessel of mysterious virtues. A remarkable cauldron, however, does figure earlier in the story of Brân more than once, but it answers quite another purpose there, namely, to bring Brân's fallen foes back to life, which will be found matched, in

Gerbert's Perceval, by the potion already mentioned as used by a hag working by the order of the King of the Waste City. This incident of the quickening of the dead occurs elsewhere, especially in Irish literature, as for example in the story of a war between the Cruithni or Picts and the mythic Men of Fidga: under the direction and spells of a druid called Drostan, the resuscitation is brought about by means of a bath of new milk at a place called Ard Lemnachta, or Sweetmilk Hill, in Leinster. It occurs also in the story of the battle of Moytura between the Fomori and the Tuatha Dé Danann, under the leadership of their king Nuadu and Lug the Longhanded: in this instance the quickening of the dead warriors is brought about by dipping them at night in a well of marvellous virtues; and it is resorted to until those on the other side find out what is going on, whereupon they pile a cairn of stones over the well.

This, however, does not help us very much in the matter: so let us try the vessels which are made by Welsh story the objects of quests in the romancers' sense of the word. One of them has just been discussed, the Cauldron of the Head of Hades, and allusion has been made in the previous chapter to another which is treated so in the story of Kulhwch and Olwen, namely the Cauldron of Diwrnach the Goidel. For this Arthur and his men had to undertake a dangerous expedition to Erinn, as already mentioned. The Kulhwch story, however, mentions the perilous quests of other vessels of various virtues, though it closes without showing how they were all achieved. Among others may be cited the *cîb* or bushel of Llwyr son of Llwyryon, which alone would be found capable of holding the mead to be brewed for Kulhwch and Olwen's wedding; the horn of Gwlgawt Gogodin, to supply the guests with drink at the feast; the *botheu* or bottles of Rhinnon Rhin Barnawt,[4] in which no drink was ever known to turn sour; and the bottles of Gwidolwyn the Dwarf, which would keep the drink put in them in the east without losing its warmth till it arrived in the west. This mysterious reference calls to mind the story of Joseph of Arimathea collecting the blood of Christ in the Holy Grail and bringing it himself to the west, or else giving it to another to bring.

The latter was none other than Bron, in whom, as already hinted, we have the Brân of Welsh literature; and, according to some of the romances, Bron, with all his people, is ordered to go to the West; and punning references are not wanting to Glaston-bury under the name of *Avalon,* as the land of sunset, *ou li soleil avaloit.* Their passage over the sea to these parts was rather pec-uliar: a certain number of the company is said to have floated across on a shirt stripped from the back of Joseph son of Joseph of Arimathea, and the bearers of the Grail, with Bron at their head, were conducted on their way by the mystic virtues of that holy vessel. This voyage at once recalls that of Brân the Blessed to Erinn, when his troops went over in ships, whilst the king himself waded across, carrying the musicians of his court on his shoulders. Further, Brân, as the centre of a perpetual banquet, has already been placed in juxtaposition with the Grail as means of feeding the faithful; and here we have the rarer attribute of conducting a following in the sea superadded to the other cha-racteristics of both alike, and serving to establish the soundness of the comparison. We have in reality to go further: it is not a case of similarity so much as of identity. The voyage of Bron is but a Christian version of the voyage of Brân, and one cannot be surprised to find one of the romances of the Quest of the Holy Grail stating that the vessel was in the keeping of Bron, repre-sented as dwelling "in these isles of Ireland."[5] This description, which may be regarded without any violence as including not only Erinn, but also Gwales and the other isles from Lundy and the Scillies to Bardsey and Man; not to mention the mythic meadows to which allusion has been made as moored in the same seas.

The story of Brân, however, as we have it, shows no vessel to set over against the Grail of Bron and his son Alain: what sort of vessel it should have been may be gathered from the pro-perties of Bron's Grail. Take the following instances: on one occasion ten or a dozen loaves, placed on the table on which stood the Grail, were found to suffice for more than five hundred hungry people. Another time, when the multitude clamoured that they and their children were dying of hunger, Bron was to go into the water and catch a fish, and the first he caught was to be set on the table; then the Grail also was to be set on the table and covered with a towel while the fish was placed opposite to it. This was duly done, and the people were bidden to seat themselves; and those of them who were not defiled with sin were filled with sweetness and the desire of their heart. Here putting the fish near the Grail would seem to indicate, that what was originally conceived as done was putting the fish simply in the vessel to cook; but such a commonplace treatment would not do, once the vessel had come to be reckoned holy. That the Grail would not feed those "polluted with sin" looks like a spiritualized version of such a property as that of which the Cauldron of the Head of Hades gave proofs in declining to cook for the craven or coward. In the version extant of the Brân story no such vessel is mentioned, and we are left to suppose that the food and drink came before the banqueters around the Venerable Head without the intervention of any visible service, after the manner of feasts in Welsh fairy tales and, for that matter, in Irish ones too, where the usual order is continuous feasting without attendance.[6]

The case is not represented as otherwise with the Grail, for when that vessel goes round feeding those deemed worthy, "none may see who carries it." Just as we hear nothing about attendance in the Brân story, so neither do we hear of vessels. Another version may very possibly have alluded to one or more; for how were Brân's friends supposed to carry his head about with them? Certainly not on a pole, as that of a foe. Most likely it was on a dish; nay, it is not improbable that Brân's head on a dish, and the poisoned spear with which he had been wounded, formed the originals which suggested the Head brought in on a dish and the Bleeding Spear at the court of Peredur's second uncle, as mentioned in a previous chapter. The former, in fact, holds in that story the place occupied by the Grail in most of the versions of Perceval's visit to that court. Enough in any case has been said to show that the origin of Bron's Grail is to be sought in a Welsh story about Brân the Blessed, though no such is extant in the precise form which that of the Grail would seem to postulate.

There remains to be mentioned more particularly another quest in the Kulhwch story, and this brings us at length to Gonemans and Goon: Yspyðaden, chief of giants, lays it down as one of the conditions on which Kulhwch is to wed his daughter Olwen, that his would-be son-in-law should procure for him the *Mwys* of Gwyðno Garan-hir, for the truculent father-in-law would not consent to eat out of any other vessel on the night of his daughter's wedding. So Kulhwch undertakes to procure it in due course, though the story makes no allusion later to the achievement of this quest. It does, however, what is more important for our purpose; it describes the *mwys* thus: it was such a vessel that though all the world should approach it, thrice nine men at a time, they would find in it the food each liked best. A later account of the *mwys* is to the effect, that one man's food put into it would be found to be no less than enough for a hundred, when the *mwys* came to be opened. It was thought to have finally disappeared with Merlin when he entered the Glass House in Bardsey, as were also the other treasures of Britain: the entire number was usually held to be thirteen.

This account of Gwyðno's *Mwys* is the most exact which Welsh literature probably contains of the pagan prototype of the Grail of Christian romance. In the first place, its supposed disappearance into the isle of Bardsey, off the westernmost point of North Wales, recalls "those isles of Erinn" where Bron was supposed to reside in charge of the Grail. In the next place, it will be noticed that the *mwys* was not a vessel for cooking food but for holding it, just as the Grail was. The later Welsh account speaks of it as a vessel to be opened, so that it might be regarded as some kind of a basket, box, or cask; and this harmonizes with the modern use of the word, which is explained by Dr Pughe to mean "a kind of covered basket, pannier, or hamper, also the quantity contained in such vessel: *mwys o ysgadain* [sic], a mease or five-score of herrings." Similarly Dr Davies explains it as a "vas quoddam, quoddam mensurae genus," adding that *mwys o ysgadan* is five hundred herrings, in which he was more correct than Dr Pughe: he also gives *mwys bara* as meaning *panarium,* that is to say a bread *mwys* or bread-basket. In old Cornish the word was *muis* or *moys* and meant a table. In Old Irish it was *mias,* and it had the meanings of table and of dish. So in modern Irish the charger on which the Baptist's head is placed, in Matt. xiv. 8, is called a *mias,* as also in the Scotch Gaelic version, but not in Manx Gaelic, where, however, the word occurs as *meays,* meaning a mease or five hundred fishes.

This meeting of the meanings of table, dish, basket, and hamper, would seem to receive its explanation in the etymology of the words *mwys* and *mias,* both of which are probably the Latin mensa, "table," borrowed.[7] As the ancient Brythons, like the Irish and presumably the Norsemen, had no tables in the Roman sense of the word, the borrowed word not only served to denote the borrowed idea of table, but it was also partly applied to that of the native substitute for a table, namely a dish or platter; and this would undoubtedly appear to have been the meaning of the word *mwys* in Yspyðaden's demand that Kulhwch should obtain the Mwys of Gwyðno, for him to eat out of it at the wedding feast. In other words, *Mwys Gwyðno* in the Kulhwch story meant neither more nor less than Gwydno's vessel. The only property recorded of it was its power of multiplying a hundredfold, or even more, any food placed in it; and this is in entire agreement with what is said of the Fisher King's Grail in the *Conte du S. Graal:* Chrétien speaks of it feeding the Fisher King's father and sustaining his life, while two of the other authors of that poem represent the Grail serving the guests abundantly with bread, and even with wine and all sorts of food. One of the two, Gautier, goes further, and characterizes the Grail in a way which recalls the spiritual properties of Bron's Grail, for he states that the devil might not lead any man astray on the same day he had seen the Grail. The passage has, however, been suspected of not being homogeneous with Gautier's other verses; but in any case it can throw no serious difficulty in the way of our identifying, in point of origin, the anonymous Fisher King's Grail with Gwyðno Garanhir's *Mwys*.

The question of the mutual influence of the various versions of the Grail legend is a difficult and complicate one; but we have an instance probably of the influence of the French romances on the Welsh story of Peredur, where it represents the first of his two uncles as lame and also associates him with fishing, for the two things seem to have belonged to different versions of the story. It is owing also possibly to a similar mixture of different versions, that both Gonemans or Gwyn and Bron bear the same title of fisher. At any rate, Welsh literature enables one to see a reason for it only in the case of the former; but let us first see how it has hitherto been treated. Some have supposed that the fishing incident in which Bron plays the part already described is to be taken as a sufficient explanation of the name. The title of Rich Fisher is given in one of the romances both to Bron and to his successors. We allude to the *Grand St Graal* representing Bron's youngest son, who had been made keeper of the Grail, ordered to take the net which was on the Grail table and to fish with it. Alain, for that was his name, did so, and caught one big fish; but the people murmured that it would not be enough. When, however, Alain had divided the fish into three parts and prayed that it might suffice, all the people were fed, including the sinners that time. So not only Bron, but also Alain acquired the title of Rich Fisher, and it was inherited by the Grail-keepers after him; but it is added, that they were more blessed than Alain, as they were all crowned kings, whereas he never wore a crown.

Such are the explanations hitherto attempted, and it is significant, that in the opinion of one of the most recent students of the Grail legend, they are not satisfactory; for Mr Nutt thinks it simpler to believe that in the original Celtic tradition the surname of Rich Fisher had a significance now lost. This appeal to Celtic tradition we gladly accept, believing as we do, that its significance is even now not altogether lost. Let us premise, that while the Fisher King's name is not given, that of a person treated sometimes as his brother is mentioned: Chrétien, in his *Conte du Graal,* calls him Gonemans of Gelbort; Gerbert, in his portion of the same poem, calls him Gornumant, and Manessier, in his portion of it, calls him Goon Desert, that is in other words, Goon of the Terre Gastee or the Waste Land. These names stand unmistakably for the Welsh Gwynwas and Gwyn, which, as explained in another chapter, meant one and the same personage; namely, that most usually known to Welsh literature as Gwyn son of Nûð, king of the fairies and the demons of the Other World.

Gwyn and Gwyðno are not represented in Welsh as brothers, as are Goon and the Fisher King by Manessier; but one of the most remarkable poems in the *Black Book of Carmarthen* consists of a dialogue between them, in the course of which they become great friends. So far, then, we have not made much progress towards the identification of Gwyðno with the anonymous Fisher; but let us come to the fishing. In the first place it may be worth mentioning, that Gwyðno has the standing epithet or surname of Garan-hir, which seems to have meant Long-crane or Tall-heron.[8] This, to say the least of it, is the reverse of incompatible with the idea of fishing. In the next place Gwyðno was famous as the owner, not only of the *Mwys,* but also of a weir in which fish to the value of a hundred pounds used to be caught on the Eve of the First of May every year; and connected with this is the well-known story of finding the baby-bard Taliessin there. For in those days, we are told, Gwyðno had an only son Elphin, who was the wildest and neediest of the young men of his time. So his father, anxious about him and fearing that he had been born in an evil hour, permitted him to draw the weir one First of May, in order to see whether no luck would fall to his share. Elphin with his men went at the proper time to examine the weir, and the latter were about to leave in sad disappointment, persuaded that Elphin had interrupted the luck of his father's weir, when Elphin observed a leathern bag on one of the poles of the weir. It is needless to relate, how he found the bag to contain the baby Taliessin, who at once began to address Elphin in elaborate verse, and to inform him that he would be of greater value to him than the fish caught in the weir had ever been to Gwyðno.

Here then in this story, some of the essentials of which occur in a Taliessin poem, we have an adequate explanation of the fact, that the Grail owner was called the Fisher King or the Rich Fisher. It will, however, have been noticed that the two fishers in the Welsh story are Gwyðno and his son Elphin, while the Grail legend only associates with the anonymous Fisher his brother Goon, but no son. So here again one has probably to fall back on the mutual influence of the Grail romances, for in the version previously discussed, we had not two brothers, but a father and son, named Bron and Alain, to wit that Alain who was less blessed than the other heads of his family, inasmuch as he never wore a crown, as they are represented doing. In this Alain or Alein, surnamed *le Gros,* Malory's Hellyas le Grose, we seem to have the representative of Gwyðno's son Elphin, who is described as less fortunate than the rest of his family, and as a sort of a luckless youth. Alain, however, is sometimes treated as the father of Perceval (Peredur), and the name is probably a distorted form, not of *Elphin* but of *Eliver:* perhaps one would not be far wrong in regarding Eliver and Elphin as confounded here with one another.[9] But we are not aware that Welsh literature mentions a son of Brân, called either Eliver or Elphin, any more than it gives Brân the surname of Fisher: so we are on the whole inclined to ascribe both to the influence of the romance in the form in which it reached Chrétien, Gerbert and

80

Manessier, on that other form in which it was known to Robert de Borron and the author of the *Grand St Graal*. This agrees with the fact of the probable priority of that of Chrétien and his continuators while on the other side one has to admit that the latter make no allusion to Alain; but this is no decisive proof that he did not figure in some of the versions which they worked into the poem of the *Conte du Graal*.

In this chapter the various versions of the Holy Grail have been treated as falling readily into three groups, namely, those in which the Grail belongs respectively to Pelles, to Bron, and to the anonymous Fisher. The Welsh origin of the Grail of the first and the third groups has been pointed out, while in the second group the Grail has been traced to the quarter in which alone its origin is to be sought. So this chapter might end at this point, were it not that we may here conveniently append a few more identifications of Grail names, which could not have been advantageously introduced at an earlier stage. They may have a bearing on the difficult question of the influence on one another of the Grail stories of the three groups just mentioned. In any case the reader may rest assured, that it only requires more patience, and more acquaintance with the French versions than the author possesses, to identify most of the Grail proper names in them.

Let us begin where we left off with Goon of the Desert or Gonemans of Gelbort, in whom we seem to have Gwyn ab Nûð. The following short and savage episode in the story of Kulhwch and Olwen makes Gwyn king of the North, and subject to Arthur as his suzerain: "A little previously Creiðylad daughter of Llûð the Silver-handed had gone with Gwythur son of Greidiawl, but before he had slept with her, Gwyn son of Nûð came and carried her away by force. Gwythur collected an army and fought with Gwyn; but Gwyn prevailed, and captured Greid, son of Eri, Glinneu eil Taran, Gwrgwst Ledlwm, and Dyvnarth his son. He captured also ... son of Nethawc, Nwython, and Kyledr the Wild his son. He killed Nwython, took out his heart, and forced Kyledr to eat his father's heart, and it is therefore Kyledr became wild. Arthur heard of this, and came to the North and summoned son of Nûð before him: he released his men from his prison and made peace between Gwyn son of Nûð and Gwythur son of Greidiawl. This was the

81

peace that was made, that the damsel be left at her father's house, untouched by either side; that the two suitors fight every First of May for ever thenceforth till the Day of Doom; and he who then proves victorious let him take the damsel."

Leaving this mythological joke for a while, we turn to a passage relative to Lancelot and his lineage in the *Queste du Saint Graal*, which will serve among other things as a specimen of the taste of some of the romancers who undertook to Christianize pagan stories: Lancelot, after having a vision in which he saw a man surrounded with stars, and accompanied by seven kings and two knights, "comes to a hermitage, confesses, tells his vision, and learns that it has a great meaning in respect of his lineage, which must be expounded at much length: forty-two years after the Passion of Christ, Joseph of Arimathea left Jerusalem, came to Sarras, helped Evelac, who received baptism at the hands of Josephes, together with his brother-in-law, Seraphe (who took the name Nasciens), and who became a pillar of the holy faith, so that the great secrets of the Holy Grail were opened to him, which none but Joseph had beheld before, and no knight after save in dream. Now Evelac dreamed that out of his nephew, son of Nasciens, came forth a great lake, whence issued nine streams, eight of the same size, and the last greater than all the rest put together; our Lord came and washed in the lake which King Mordrains [this is another name for Evelac] thus saw flowing from Celidoine's belly. This Celidoine was the man surrounded by stars in Lancelot's vision, and this because he knew the course of the stars and the manner of the planets, and he was first King of Scotland, and the nine streams were his nine descendants, of whom seven [were] Kings and two knights: first, Warpus; second, Chrestiens [another version gives the preferable reading *Nasciens*]; third, Alain li Gros; fourth, Helyas; fifth, Jonaans, who went to Wales and there took to wife King Moroneus' daughter; sixth, Lancelot, who had the King of Ireland's daughter to wife; seventh, Bans. These were the seven Kings who appeared to Lancelot. The eighth stream was Lancelot himself, the elder of the knights of the vision. The ninth stream was Galahad, begot by Lancelot upon the Fisher King's daughter, lion-like in power, deepest of all the streams."

In the *Grand St Graal* the names of Nascien's descendants, as given by Mr Nutt, are Celidoine, Marpus, Nasciens, Alains li

Gros, Ysaies, Jonans, Lancelot, Bans, Lancelot and Galahad. Now Warpus or Marpus, as the name is here given, can hardly be regarded as anything else than a faulty reproduction of the name given as Gwrgwst in the Welsh story: it was the name also of the father of a powerful king of Fortrenn in the eighth century, Ungust, son of Wrgust or Uurgust, or as he is usually called Aengus son of Fergus, according to the Anglo-Gaelic forms of the names. In the next place *Nascien* appears, as given by Manessier, in the form *Natiien,* which is evidently the same name as Baeda's Naiton; for so he calls the Pictish king driven from his throne by Aengus son of Fergus in the year 729. The same name is probably to be found in the Nwython of the Welsh story of Gwyn and Gwythur; further, the Celidoine of the *Grand St Graal,* wrongly explained to mean Heaven-given, is to be set over against Kyledr, as a faulty reproduction of a Welsh name. Thus Natiien and his son Celidoine are Nwython and his son Kyledr, and this is favoured by a sort of correspondence between their story and that of their Welsh counterparts. For the *Grand St Graal* mentions Nascien and his son Celidoine thrown into prison by a hater of Christians, who was called Kalafier. Nascien, however, is not killed like Nwython by his foe, for he is miraculously rescued by a hand which appears out of a cloud and strikes of his fetters, while Celidoine is also released and borne through the air by nine hands to the land of a King Label, whose daughter he marries later in this confused narrative,[10] whereas Kalafier dies killed by fire from heaven.

It is probable, with regard to Celidoine as the first king of Scotland, that we have to regard the original as Kelyðon who appears at the opening of the story of Kulhwch as Kelyðon Wledig or Prince Kelyðon. This latter is doubtless to be treated as the eponymus hero of Caledonia; and the conclusion one is forced to draw is, that the Grail name Celidoine covers the two Welsh ones of Kelyðon and Kyledr;[11] if indeed they be two, and the latter, which is obscure, be not rather an error to be corrected into Kelyðon. Thus it will be seen that all of them about which anything can be predicated point to the North. But the *Grand St Graal* connects Bron in a sort of way with them, while the Welsh Brân is not usually associated with the North. This would seem to indicate that here Bron has been substituted for the anonymous Fisher, whom we have identified with Gwyðno.

The name, however, of Gwyðno has already passed before us, but heavily disguised: the romancers give it at least two forms differing considerably from one another. The first to be mentioned, as the easier to recognize, is that of Nentre (nominative *Nentres)* king of Garlot. The kingdom of Gwyðno is in Welsh called the Hundred of the Bottom, for which the modern Welsh is Gwaelod, in older Welsh spelling Gwaelawt, which is the key to Malory's Garlot, Garlott, and Garloth. The oldest recorded spelling of Gwyðno's name occurs in the *Black Book of Carmarthen,* 49[b], as *Guitnev,* which according to the usual spellings and misreadings might result in Nentres and Neutres.[12]

The other disguise of Gwyðno's name is to be detected in the form of Mordrain, mentioned in a passage just quoted from the *Queste,* for it was a name of great importance in the Grail stories purporting to give the early history of the vessel. It is also Mordrain in the *Grand St Graal,* but Manessier makes it Noodran,[13] which comes considerably nearer the Welsh prototype. Now Mordrain or Noodran is represented as the designation adopted by Evalach or Evalac when he was baptized. But this is the Welsh Avałłach or Avałłon, which would imply the identification of Gwyðno with Avałłach. Nor is this all, for the Huth *Merlin* makes Neutre king of Sorhaut[14] the only time it mentions him, and it represents Garlot as the kingdom ruled over by Urien and his wife Morgue or Morgain la Fee. Add to this that the Huth *Merlin* had in the first instance made of Morgue or Morgain and Morgan two sisters, and given the one to Neutre to wife, and the other to Urien. This attribution of the same kingdom of Garlot, and virtually of the same wife, Morgen, to Neutre and Urien, suggests the identity of Neutre with Urien, and recalls the allusion to Elphin as the name of a son of Urien, as well as one of Gwyðno's.

Pwyll is found as Pelles in the Venedotian district of Gwyðno, but whether this is to be ascribed to the mutual influence of the Grail stories, it is difficult to decide, and all that we can say is that it is not the district with which Welsh literature is wont to associate Pwyll: that, as we have seen, was Dyved in South Wales, far enough from Arllechweð and Gwyðno's land, where one finds Peleur's Castle, together with a group of localities associated with it. In the *Seint Greal* the chief of these latter are called the Turning Castle, the Dead Castle, the Maidens' Castle, and Glannog's Isle. Now the king of the Dead Castle used to make war on his brother Peleur, after whose death he took possession of his castle, and held it until it was stormed by Peredur; the same wicked tyrant used to war also on the Queen of the Maidens of the Castle of Maidens; and among other places visited weekly by him was Glannog's Isle, overlooking which from the mainland was situated the Queen's Castle, which should accordingly have been situated near Penmon and the eastern point of Anglesey. For Glannog's Isle, in Welsh Ynys Lannog,[15] is known to have been a name of the island otherwise called Ynys Seirioel, or St Seiriol's Isle, in English Priestholm, more commonly known as Puffin Island, which is separated from Anglesey by a channel less than a mile wide. In the Welsh chronicle, published under the name of *Annales Canbriae* we are told that Cadwallon was blockaded in Glannog's Isle in the year 629 by the fleet of Edwin of Northumbria, but unsuccessfully, as the Welsh king made his escape to Ireland: *Obsessio Catguollaun regis in insula Glannauc.* Of this Glannauc or Glannog nothing is known except that he is called the father of Helig of Tyno Helig, or Helig's Hollow, the name of a country supposed in Welsh legend to have been overrun by the sea on the coast of North Wales. Helig is styled in full Helig Voel or H. the Bald, which reminds one of the name of Tegid the Bald, whose land was likewise regarded as submerged, namely, beneath the lake bearing his name near Bala, as mentioned in a previous chapter. On the other hand, we seem to have the other selves of Gwyðno and his son Elphin in Glannog and his son Helig. Lastly, the association of the Turning Castle with the flourishing country of which Glannog's Isle is the most conspicuous remnant, is worthy of note; for it has been essayed to identify the Turning Castle with Caer Sidi, where Taliessin, according to one of his boasts, had a firm seat: this is probably the key to the tradition, that the bard had land given him in Arłłechweð by Gwyðno.

The reader may perhaps, on perusing this chapter, think it strange that Celtic literature, at one time, busied itself so much about vessels, and especially cauldrons. But it can be shown that such vessels may have had a spiritual or intellectual significance, as for instance in connection with the notion of poetry. Thus allusion is made in the *Book of Taliessin* to three muses rising out of the cauldron of Ogyrven the Giant, whose name is associated with bardism and the origin of writing. Outside the Celtic domain one may point to the Dwarf's Cup as one of the old Norse terms symbolic of thought, wisdom, and especially the inspiration of poetry; and one might bring into the comparison the soma of Hindu religion. All these cases connecting the sacred vessel or its contents with poetry and inspiration, point possibly back to some primitive drink brewed by the early Aryan, and taken by the medicine-man in order to produce a state of ecstasy or intoxication. Lastly, the religion of ancient Greece may be said to offer, in its holy tripods, a curious parallel to the cauldrons of Taliessin. It is true that nothing quite so intractable as a cauldron is associated with the oracle, for example, of Apollo at Delphi; but what was a tripod but a contrivance for holding a vessel over a fire? In the case of Delphi the tripod was placed over a chasm in the ground, the exhalations from which may be regarded as a substitute for the blaze of fire fed, according to Taliessin, by the breath of nine maidens. In Hellas the tripod, instead of bearing the weight of a cauldron from which utterances issued or three muses ascended,[16] had seated on it the medium in person, and she was supposed to give her responses according as the invisible influence of the divinity prompted her. The Celtic treatment being more primitive, the cauldron remained, and one may presume that it required the services of a druid as its interpreter.

Notes

1 There is, so far as we know, no warrant for treating cadeir, "a chair," as a seat in the sense of an abode or mansion.

2 *Hib. Lec.* p.641; see also Windisch's *Irische Texte*, pp.210, 219.

3 This, mutated, becomes *vannawc* (written also *fannawc*) as does *mannawc*, with which it is not to be confounded. The latter is derived from *man*, as in *man geni*, "a birth-mark," Latin *menda*, "a fault or blemish."

4 Can this be an estropié form of *Rhiannon Rhian Varnawt*, or Rh. the sentenced Lady? See *R.B. Mab.* p.19, Guest, iii. 62 but note that the Kulhwch story (*R.B. Mab.* p.123) makes Rhinnon a male.

5 See Nutt, p.28, where he gives an abstract of the *Petit Saint Graal*, also termed by him the Didot-Perceval. The *Seint Greal* has made of Bron and Brân the curious conglomerate *Brwns Brandalis* who has a brother, *Brendalis* of Wales (pp.173, 548), both uncles to Peredur on his father's side. Now Brwns is nothing but the French nominative *Brons*, from *Bron*, and *Brandalis* of Wales

suggests that the more correct form was Bran Galis, or Brân of Wales, if indeed one should not rather say Bran of Gwales in reference to the Isle of the Banquet. Brandalis appears in Malory's narrative as Brandyles, but he gives him no very distinctive attributes.

6 The Irish phrase for "without attendance" was *cen rithgnom:* see *Tochmarc Becfola,* ed. by O'Looney in the *Irish MSS Series* of the Royal Irish Academy, i. 180; also the story of Condla Ruad in Windisch's *Irische Grammatik,* p.119, where he prints *can rithgnom.* Compare Rhys' Welsh Fairy Tales in the *Cymmrodo*r, v. 8a, vi. 195.

7 If this prove incorrect, then one has to regard the Irish *mias,* "table," and *mias,* "dish," as distinct words, and to treat them somewhat as indicated by Ducange, who gives a *mēsa,* "table," from Spain chiefly, and another *mēsa* or *meisa halecum,* which he explains to have meant a *doliolum,* or cask: this latter was in Old French *meise (maise)* and *moise.* Note that the "thrice nine men" at the *Mwys* may be taken as if meant to be a multiple of the Roman triclinium, the "thrice" being introduced to render the exaggeration required.

8 À propos of this crane, one is inclined to ask what may be the origin of the Crane in the *Seint Greal,* pp.231, 587, that used to give the alarm to a whole country. See also *Hib. Lec.* p.334, where the three baleful *birdez* of Thornton's *Morte Arthure* should be corrected into *bridez* or damsels.

9 The *Grand St Graal* tries to distinguish two Alains: see Nutt, p.62. The principal stages through which *Eliver* passed into *Alain* or *Alein* were probably Eliuer, Eluien, Elaien, Elain or Elein.

10 Here we apparently have Gwyn appearing under the name of Kalafier, which is obscure, while King Label and his daughter may perhaps be Llûð and his daughter Creiðylad; for Llûð's surname in its Welsh form of *Llaßereint* may be regarded as in part reflected by that of Label: the form to be expected was Laberēz, or Laberenz, the earlier portion of which is fairly represented by Label. The daughter's name does not appear, as the French romancer probably found it untractable, though in other hands it has yielded the well-known name of Cordelia.

11 Kyledyr looks like a sort of compromise between *Kelydon* and *Kynedyr* or *Kyuedyr:* see *R.B.Mab.* pp.112, 124.

12 For Nentres see Malory, i. 2, 8, 12, 18, and xix. 11: it is Neutres in the Huth *Merlin,* i. 120. The Welsh pronunciation of Gwyðneu would, in the orthography of the Venedotian version of the Welsh Laws be represented by Guetneu. which, misread Gnetnen, might result in a nominative Netnēs or Nētnes, Nentnes; and by the phonetic change of *tn* into *tr* we should have Nentres. Compare Castrar for Casnar or Castnar. Gwyðneu should, according to analogy, drop its final *u,* but it is not certain that this would occur early enough; but in case it did, the change to Nentres would be somewhat simpler. The same system of Welsh spelling would make Gwaelawt into Guaylaut, which a romancer might reduce to Gailot or Goilot, whence by the easy misreading of *i* into *r,* one would get Garlot.

13 See Nutt, p.20. The Welsh spelling here implied would probably be that of Gwydneu or Guydneu; and Noodran is probably for Noodrain = Noodren, *ßy* being misread into *oo,* as is easily done, in the *Red Book* for example, and as was actually done in making *Gßyn* into Goon. As to *ai* and *a* or *e* compare

Morgain and Morgan in the Huth M*erlin* (i. 120, ii. 225, &c.), for Welsh Morgen. With Mordrain compare Marpus (and Warpus), for Gwrgwst or Guorgust, but the former perhaps started from the mutated forms *Wydneu* and *Wrgust*. Lastly, with the *rdr* for *dr* compare the *rdr* of Mordred for Modred (Welsh Medrod), also the *ntr* of Nentres.

14 Urien and his wife are made king and queen of *Gore* (Gower) by Malory, whereas here we have not a peninsula, but islands; for *Sorhaut* doubtless stands for some such a form — as *Sorlianc* — of the name of the Scillies, called *Sorlingues* in modern French. The accusative singular, according to the best reading of the MSS of Sulpicius Severus was *Sylinancim*: see his *Chronica* (ii. 51), ed. by Halm.

15 See the *Seint Greal*, p.276, where the words are *ynys yrhonn aelwir lanoc,* and so in the version in Lord Mostyn's Library (MS 284); but had the scribe recognized the name he ought to have given it in his sentence the unmutated form of *Glannoc,* which seems to have been equally unknown to the editor of the *Seint Greal:* witness p.616, where he translates the above words, "an island that is called Lanoc." Neither seems to have bethought him that *Ynys* and *Glannoc* must, when joined together, become *Ynys Lannoc,* according to the rules of *sandhi* usual in Welsh.

16 This may have suggested the scenes of mystery commonly described in connection with the Holy Grail, as for instance by Malory, xvii. 20, where one reads, "thenne loked they and sawe a man come oute of the holy vessel that had alle the sygnes of the passion of Ihesu Cryste bledynge alle openly."

CHAPTER 6

The Celtic Grail

A.G. van Hamel

The problem of the origin of the Holy Grail in Arthurian literature has raised vehement passions among students of medieval romance. Is the miraculous Feeding Vessel rooted in the materials of Celtic romantic or folkloristic literature? Celticists will generally be inclined to answer this question in the affirmative. To them the atmosphere of the Grail legend is so closely akin to that well-known from the Irish tales that even without the existence of direct parallels they will not hesitate to declare it necessarily Celtic. On the other hand, scholars not having first-hand knowledge of the Celtic tongues, are usually reluctant to admit the Celtic roots of the luxuriant growth of legends centring about the Grail Castle. That King Arthur was a national hero of the Britons cannot be denied; but nowhere in Celtic legend or history is his story connected with any object recalling Crestien's grail. Then, why should this connection not have been brought about by the French poet himself, who simply desired to Christianize the matter he was working upon by introducing a scene recalling certain rites of the church? Because there is no sufficient reason to detach this one trait from the rest of the story, Celticists will reply; Welsh and particularly Irish literature abound with indirect evidence that justifies the assumption of a Celtic origin also for the Grail *motif* itself.

In the present study, which is intended as a further support for the Celtic theory, it cannot be the writer's object to give an exhaustive survey of the opinions expressed by scholars on the Grail controversy. Besides, they have been discussed at length by the late Professor Bruce in his well-known work on the *Evolution of Arthurian Romance*. Even those who, like the present writer, can in no way accept Professor Bruce's conclusions will readily admit their profound admiration for the impartiality with which he rendered his opponents' views. However, it seems necessary to sum up briefly the arguments of the most prominent champions on both sides, in order that it may be seen from the outset, which aspects of the problem require more light at the present stage of the discussion.

Among the advocates of the Celtic theory Professor A.C.L. Brown ranks foremost.[1] He was the first to identify the Lance and Grail in Arthurian romance with the treasures of the Tuatha Dé Danann, known from Irish mythology, and the Grail quest with the search for a cup-of-plenty that has to be won or recovered, as is related in such Irish tales as the Lad of the Ferule or the Second Battle of Mag Tuired. These parallels may be said to be striking, but Professor Brown contents himself with the equation of individual traits.

Professor W.A. Nitze, who also sides with the celticists, adopts a different method.[2] He sees the direct source of the Grail story in Celtic literature, as appears clearly, for instance, from his identification of Brons, the Fisher King, with Bran fab Llyr, the hero of the second branch of the Mabinogi *(Branwen ferch Llyr)*; he justly points our that Bran, too, was in the possession of a "cauldron of regeneration." However, in this direction a certain amount of work had been done before him by Alfred Nutt.[3] What is new in Nitze's theory is that he asks for the primitive meaning of the Grail and the other symbols belonging to it. He arrives at the conclusion that their origin lies in a prehistorical agrarian cult and its ritual, which must have existed among the Celts as among other people.

The theory of Celtic origin was altogether rejected by Professor J.D. Bruce.[4] His view that the antiquity of the Tuatha Dé Danann treasures could not be proved from Irish tradition, was dismissed once and for all by the sweeping criticism of Dr Vernam Hull,[5] so no more need be said about this. On the positive side, however, his opinion deserves our attention. He believes in a Christian origin of the Grail *motif*, which was combined by the French poets with the Great Fool *motif* and the doubtless Celtic Arthurian setting of the whole.

90

A similar view-point is taken by Professor W. Golther.[6] According to him the source of the Enchanted Castle, where the Grail appears, is a Breton tale, but the Lance and Grail were added by Crestien on purpose. With the French poet the Grail is only a sacramental chalice, as he knew it himself from the rites of the church. The reason for the connection of these two heterogeneous elements remains obscure.

It is manifest that against both theories objections may be raised. The Celtic theory allows no room for the Christian element which is so conspicuous in the Grail legend. If the combination of Celtic folklore and Christian spiritualism had been effected by Crestien or one of his immediate predecessors, there would necessarily remain traces of unsmoothness in their work. Besides, the parallels adduced from Celtic literature furnish an illustration of one or two traits in the continental romances, such as the Grail as a miraculous Feeding Vessel, or the quest that can only be accomplished by the chosen hero, but never yet was a Celtic story unearthed showing the principal elements of the Grail legend in due connection with one another. In fact, the evidence collected in the Celtic field is too fragmentary ever to convince strangers in Celtic literature. If celticists generally do believe in the Celtic origin of the Grail legend, they are rather prompted to this attitude by intuition than on account of the evidence laid before them.

On the other hand, the Christian theory will hardly satisfy the modern critic. If it is assumed with Golther that the whole of medieval Arthurian romance has its roots in Crestien de Troyes' *Contes del graal,* then it seems impossible to accept for the Lance and Grail, which form part and parcel of the Grail scene, an origin and a source different from those of the Enchanted Castle and its other attributes: why should these particular *motifs* be separated from the rest with which they are so closely interwoven? Of course, it would be an altogether different thing if the biblical frame of Robert de Boron's *Joseph* could be proved to be built upon materials independent from Crestien, for then the Christian allusions in the *Contes del graal* would reflect a strong and well-developed tradition which, for some reason or other, Crestien withheld from us in its fullness, leaving it to Robert to reveal it to later generations of poets and students. This hypothesis, however, suffers from a strong inner improbability, as no earlier Christian legend on Joseph of Arimathea and the Holy Grail is known to exist.

Along with the Celtic and the Christian theories there is yet a third doctrine, which has found some very eloquent advocates, the so-called ritual theory. However, this should not be placed on a level with the two older theories, for, although in direct opposition to a Christian origin of the Grail, it is in no way incompatible with a Celtic source for the Feeding Vessel of romantic poetry. This appears clearly from the opinion expressed by Nitze, which has been referred to already. If in the Grail ritual a reminiscence should be preserved of prehistoric agrarian mysteries, even then the direct source of the literary Grail legend may be seen in the Irish and Welsh tales as the reflections of those ancient cults. In this case the mythological problem does not affect in any degree the philological question of the literary sources of the Grail legend. But it becomes altogether different when the demands of strict philology are passed by in silence, and mystery cults from Greece or the East are directly compared to certain scenes from the Arthurian romances. Then the literary link is missing, and we may even be requested to believe that some of those ancient rites survived until the Middle Ages and found their direct reflection in the literature of the time. We know, in fact, of agrarian or fertility rites that were observed by the country people in the Middle Ages, and are so even at the present day. But when their pagan character was still very prominent, the church used to object to them in a very severe manner. This does not render this theory particularly attractive to modern criticism; moreover, it is but seldom applied with that methodical exactness which is so desirable in literary research.

The ritual theory was exposed in an admirable way by Miss Jessie L. Weston.[7] She derives the mysteries of the Grail from the eastern Adonis cult, whereas Nitze compares the Eleusinian mysteries. More important, however, is another point where she differs from Nitze. She leaves the philological side of the question out of account and explains the Grail legend directly from the ritual itself. Thus it becomes impossible to make her views harmonize with the Celtic theory which can be easily done in the case of Professor Nitze. But Celtic literature is there after all, and its many affinities to the Grail legend present themselves to the eye. They demand an explanation which the ritual theory does not afford.

Professor R.S. Loomis[8] goes even farther than Miss Weston in his identifications of elements of the Grail legend with Greek and Eastern myths and rites, but of these he also sees the reflection in our Irish and Welsh tales. In fact, his comparisons are more than anything else concerned with the remains of ancient Celtic literature. Still he considers the Grail legend in its many aspects as independent from the latter; he contents himself with stating an imposing number of similarities, and explains these from the common stock of prehistorical mythology. But he gives no answer to the question, where the literary source of the Grail legend is to be sought. We are indebted to Professor Loomis for throwing more light on the many affinities between the Celtic stories and medieval romance. Even if he did not intend to do so, his work has made the Celtic origin of the Grail legend more probable than it was before. But the direct source is still obscure. The objection raised against the Celtic theory that by searching for parallels it could illustrate individual elements and *motifs,* but never succeeded in presenting a Celtic story which, as a whole, corresponded to the Grail legend, still holds good. In this respect it matters little whether we accept the Eastern origin of much in both Celtic literature and medieval romance or not. Besides, the ritual theory leaves the Christian element in the Grail legend out of account. Yet, as has been said already, this is no less characteristic for the story of the Holy Grail than the numerous folkloristic traits connected with it. The results of the investigations of the ritual school do not disengage Celtic scholars from the duty of pointing out the direct Celtic source of the Grail legend, or at least the nearest approach to it.

What we should like to find is a well-connected Celtic story, containing as many Grail elements as possible, and that in a Christian setting. For, if the Grail legend sprang from a Celtic source, then folklore (or perhaps mythology) and Christianity must have been blended together there as much as in later medieval romance. These two elements, so contrary in appearance, met and united long before Crestien, for with him not one trace of their original contradiction remains. Hence among the components required for the prototype of the Grail story the

Christian frame is absolutely necessary. Of course, it cannot be expected that any surviving Celtic tale should contain the various folkloristic and Christian elements of the Grail legend in exactly the same order and the same connection. For this the methods of Celtic storytellers are too well-known. They liked to play with their *motifs* and to vary the setting. All we may look for is a number of Grail elements collected into one frame which bears some likeness to that of the romances. Could such a story be discovered, then the lesson taught by it would, no doubt, bring the Grail problem nearer to its solution.

A very remarkable story, entitled *Altromh Tighi dá Medar* (the Fosterage of the House of the two Goblets), was published not long ago by Miss M.E. Dobbs from the Book of Fermoy.[9] No other version is known, but from the text it can be proved that what the Book of Fermoy provides is only a copy from some earlier manuscript. Thus the modern character of the language cannot be used as a proof for a recent origin of the tale. The text suffers from corruptness and the interpretation is not always easy. The general trend of the story, however, is clear and may be summarized as follows.

Since the invasion of the Sons of Míl the Tuatha Dé Danann inhabit the hills and mounds of Ireland. Their chiefs are Manannan and Bodb Derg. Elcmar, who is settled in Brug na Bóinne and has Aengus 'Og, son of the Dagda, staying with him, prepares a feast, where he also invites Manannan. During the feast Aengus 'Og, stirred by Manannan's evil counsel, summons Elcmar to quit the Brug and thus becomes lord of the fairy palace. Then the Wedding-feast of the Brug is instituted, and when the time comes, Manannan's wife gives birth to a daughter, whose name is Curcóg. At the same time Eithne is born; she is the daughter of Dichu, the steward, and his wife, who are not of the Tuatha Dé Danann themselves. Eithne becomes one of Curcóg's handmaids and excels her mistress in beauty and chastity, her fame spreads all over Ireland. One day Aengus 'Og receives the visit of his brother Finnbarr Meada. Upon seeing the maidens he insults Eithne by using unbecoming language against her. Being deeply troubled, she shuns the intercourse of her comrades and refuses every sort of food. Henceforth she lives on the milk of Aengus' Dun Cow, which she drinks from a gold goblet; she milks the cow herself. This cow was brought home by Aengus, together with the Speckled Cow of Manannan, from an expedition the two fairy lords made to India, the righteous land; two silken spancels and two golden goblets came into their possession at the same time. These treasures were found in a house called the House of the two Goblets, so that the name of the story is *Oileamain tighi dá medar;* it is a story of great power and renown.

Manannan, who had heard about Eithne's strange behaviour, invites the maidens to his mansion in Emain Ablach. Here also Eithne tastes no food except the milk of the Speckled Cow from the Gold Goblet. Now Manannan understands the reason for Eithne's preference for the milk of the miraculous cows. She does not belong to the race of the Tuatha Dé Danann, and when Finnbarr insulted her, the demon left her heart and an angel came in its place, so that it is the Trinity she adores now. After a time Curcóg desires to return to the Brug and Eithne follows her. From that day till the time of Lóegaire mac Néill the maidens sojourn alternately with Aengus and with Manannan; Eithne never partakes of any other food but the milk of the Dun and the Speckled Cows.

One day, after Christianity has spread in Ireland, Curcóg and her maidens go to swim in the Boyne. When they leave the river in their magic mist, Eithne does not notice the departure of her comrades and remains alone. She puts on her garments and, while searching the banks of the river, she sees one of St Patrick's clerics standing in the door of a church and reading his New Testament. She entreats the cleric to give her a lesson in reading, and from the outset she is able to read the book as if she had possessed this art all her life. The cleric is highly astonished at this, and his amazement still grows when, after having caught a salmon for himself, and letting down the rod once more, in order to provide food for the maiden, he catches a salmon of miraculous size, whose like was never seen. Thus Eithne remains in the cleric's house for a long time. In the meantime Aengus and his followers are searching Ireland for her. At length they also come to the oratory on the Boyne, and the maiden, perceiving them, imparts her fear to the cleric that she will be taken away from him. She prays the Lord for comfort and succor, and suddenly St Patrick appears from the other side of the house. A conversation between Aengus and St

95

Patrick ensues, which ends in the holy man desiring the fairy prince to shun vain gods henceforth and adore the Trinity. Then Aengus and his household depart, uttering a heart-rending wailing cry. The cry causes Eithne's heart to leap in her bosom and after a fortnight she dies, having commended her soul to God and Patrick.

After Eithne the oratory is called Ceall Eithne. The cleric Ceasán, the king of Scotland's son, leaves his house and settles down in Fid Gaible, where Cluain Ceasáin is named after him. St Patrick imparts great power to the story and orders that no one shall talk or sleep when it is recited.

One of the outstanding characteristics of the above tale is the mixing together of Christianity and heathen mythology. It was customary with the Irish storytellers to introduce Christianity into the national literature, or at least to make the latter harmonize as much as possible with the former. In the Ulster Cycle, for instance, we learn that the indignation at the crucifixion of Christ was the indirect cause of king Conchobar's death; this happened after the king had declared to believe in Christ, so that the blood he lost at the moment of his death was a baptism to him, and he was the first pagan in Ireland who went to Heaven.[10] For the Finn Cycle the connections with Christianity are even stronger. This will appear clearly from a perusal of *Accallamh na Senórach*. Here the fundamental conception itself, the colloquy of Patrick with a surviving hero of the Fiann, rests on the desire to establish a relation between Christian and national tradition. But there is much in details also that points to the same tendency. Thus Patrick receives from two angels the order to note down the stories of the Fiann. Finn and his heroes believed in the Lord of Heaven and earth because He destroyed in one night the two hundred youths of Cormac mac Airt. Not only did Finn believe in God, but he knew that Patrick and Ciarán would come to Ireland. Cáilte requests Patrick to redeem his sister Rairiu from the torments of hell, and the saint does accordingly, implying also Cáilte's father and mother and Finn mac Cumhaill in his prayer to God. Here everything has been done in order to make the inevitable paganism of the Fenian heroes as inoffensive as it could possibly be.

Even in the Cycle of the Tuatha Dé Danann, the pagan deities of ancient Ireland, there are manifest traces of Christian influence. In one of the recensions of Lebor Gabála it is said of the Tuatha Dé Danann: *rofogloindset eólus 7 filidecht ar cach díamair dána 7 in cach léri legus, 7 cech amainsi eladan docuisin is do Thuathaib Dé Danann atberar atá bunad, ar cia lánic crelim, ni rodíchuirthe na dána sin ar at maithe, 7 ní derna deman maith etir. Is follus dano asa febaib 7 asa n-ai-dedaib mach do demnaib ná sídaigib do Thuathaib Dé Danann.* Perhaps the Irish belief in the inviolability of the arts was never better expressed. It is but natural that Christian allusions should also intrude into the traditions about these pagan deities. One of the prominent characters in *Accallamh na Senórach* is Cascorach mac Cáincinde from Síd Buidb Deirg; he is an art student *(damna olloman)* of the Tuatha Dé Danann. He visits Cáilte in order to learn the Fenian stories from him; but when he meets Patrick, who invites him to sing for him, he asks Heaven for his reward. Yet his *ceól sídhe* is by no means deprived of its original magic qualities, and sleep befalls the listening clerics. From that moment Cascorach determines that his aim is to win Heaven. A little later, when Patrick is sojourning at the court of king Eochaid Leithderg of Leinster, he is approached by another prince of the Tuatha Dé Danann, Donn son of Midir, who lays down his head in the bosom of the saint and gives him power over all the Tuatha Dé Danann. The scribe of the manuscript, edited by Windisch and Stokes, was so profoundly touched by this scene that he could not refrain from observing in a marginal note: *conid ann do chreidset Tuath dé Danann do Patraicc.*

No more instances of Christian variations on national Irish themes will be required. It is but natural that in *Altromh Tighi dá Medar* a similar combination should occur. In this respect the author of the story did not deviate from the practice of his fellow-craftsmen. But at the same time his work recalls the Grail romances, for which the interpenetration of Christianity and pre-Christian folklore is characteristic too. However, before following up this idea, it will be necessary to analyze our story so that we may get a clear insight into its structure and the antiquity and meaning of its elements. A distinction must be made between the Christian and the native matter, and then each must be criticized in itself. Let us begin with the non-Christian elements, that is, with the traditions concerned with the Tuatha Dé Danann.

In the opening paragraph, which is partly illegible in the manuscript, the text of the original has been abridged. As we have it, it contains a succinct survey of the events that led to the confinement of the Tuatha Dé Danann to the hills and mounds of Ireland. It seems to be drawn up from different sources, perhaps partly from a failing memory. The three Tuatha Dé Danann kings, Mac Cecht, Mac Cuill and Mac Gréine, sons of Cermad Midbél, are said to be defeated by Erimon in a number of battles. Among these are named the battle of Tailltiu, which is know from all authorities dealing with the subject, and battles at Druim Lighean and Loch Febail. Perhaps these two names refer to one and the same battle, and the composer of the story was mistaken in that he represented it as a fight between Erimon and the sons of Cermad Midbél. For the only mention made of Druim Lighean in connection with a meeting of the Tuatha Dé Danann and the Góedels is in a tradition transmitted by Keating but marked by him as unreliable, that Ith son of Míl, who had preceded his brothers on the way to Ireland in order to explore the country, was slain by the sons of Cermad Midbél not on Mag Itha, as is the common view, but at Druim Lighean. Owing to a mistake this battle could take the place of the battle of Sliab Mis, which is recorded by Lebor Gabála as the first victory of the sons of Míl over the Tuatha Dé Danann preceding the battle of Tailltiu.

After the defeats inflicted upon the sons of Cermad Midbél and their people, Erimon son of Míl shared the kingship of Ireland with his brother Emer, until the latter, stirred by the evil cousin of his wife, revolted against his elder brother, thus being the cause of the fierce battle of Geisill, where Emer was slain. This conflict between the two brothers is also recorded in Lebor Gabála (portion of the text not yet printed), where it is located at Bri Dam in Offaly, the name Geisill not being mentioned. The Four Masters, however, who also record a battle at Bri Dam, add: *as frisidhe asberar cath Geisille*. The source of this addition seems to be a short poem on this event, preserved by Keating (*Fuair*, sc. Eibhear, *i dtuath Ghéisille a ghoin*).[11] Thus the same poem would be the source of this passage in our story, which conclusion is confirmed by the fact that it is the only other authority to state the cause of Emer's refractoriness, namely the evil counsel of his own wife:

do ráidh bean Eibhir na geath
mun budh lé Druim caoin Clasach
Druim Beitheach, Druim Finghen finn,
nach beith aon-oidhche i nEirinn.

Thus the opening paragraph shows that our author draws rather from poetical than from historical or pseudo-historical sources, and, it would seem, sometimes from a defective memory, too.

Of an introductory character is also the second paragraph. After being defeated by the Sons of Míl, the Tuatha Dé Danann take the advice of Manannan, who tells them to scatter over the hills and plains of Ireland and to settle there in their magic dwellings. They do accordingly and make Bodb Derg and Manannan their rulers. A list of the principal fairy princes and their mansions ensues, along with a few further particulars on the establishment of the Tuatha Dé Danann. It need hardly be remarked that this conception is not that of official Irish history. Lebor Gabála states that after the decisive battle of Tailltiu the Tuatha Dé Danann are routed to the sea, and according to the Four Masters those that were not slain in the battle, are killed afterwards wherever they are seized. Keating and O'Flaherty in *Ogygia* hold similar views. In romantic literature, on the other hand, they are supposed to live on until the present day and to dwell in their old fairy mounds. It suffices to refer to *Accallamh na Senórach,* where a great number of stories about the Tuatha Dé Danann is related and where they have intercourse with the heroes of the Fiann. In such romantic tales as *Tochmarc Etáine, Cath Finntrága,* etc., contact of the fairies with mortals of the heroic age is regarded as a most natural thing.

The contradiction between these two conceptions is not difficult to explain. The Tuatha Dé Danann are the spirits of the land, so that no possession of the soil could be acquired by the Góedels until they were completely extinguished.[12] But at the same time they could still be represented as inhabiting the desert regions of the country, which were as yet no man's property. In historical literature, where the evolutions of the earliest events is depicted as a sequence of conquests, the former notion is followed up to its utmost consequences, whereas the romances must necessarily adopt the latter. Of a third notion, which locates the Tuatha Dé Danann as divine beings in the Elysian

Fields, Mag Meld or Tír Tairngire, manifest traces are also retained; there, in fact, is the residence of the powerful chief Manannan.

In our story Manannan is one of two supreme rulers of the Tuatha Dé Danann after the battle of Tailltiu. He takes a prominent position in Irish mythological literature. His residence is located outside Ireland, in Tír Tairngire or in Mag Meld; his palace is called Emain or Emna. In *Altromh Tighi dá Medar* he is also said to reside at Emain Ablach in Tír Tairngire. But no other authority makes him rule over the Tuatha Dé Danann together with Bodb Derg, and this is only natural, since his dwelling place is beyond the waves; in *Oided Cloinne Lir* it is expressly stated that there is but one ruler, Bodb Derg. The author of our tale obviously placed Manannan in the same position as Bodb Derg on account of the prominent part he plays in the story.

Thus the lord of the fairies in the strict sense of the word is Bodb Derg. He is known as king of the fairies of Munster, where local legends about him were current, he is especially famous for being one of the principal characters in one of the *remscéula* of the Táin. *Do chophur in da muccado*. His palace is called Síd Boidb or Síd ar Femun,[13] and he is said to have received the kingship of the Tuatha Dé Danann. In *Cath Finntrága* he also acts as the monarch who summons the fairy host in case of danger.

After the names of the two overlords there follows a list of the principal Tuatha Dé Danann chiefs and their dwelling places. A similar list occurs in the story how Aengus got Brug na Bóinne from his father, the Dagda, but the two lists are not identical or even related; this is the more striking as the contents of the two stories seem to be variants of the same theme.[14] Most, though not all, of the fairy princes mentioned in *Altromh Tighi dá Medar* are known from other sources. Midir in Síd Truim is an outstanding character in *Tochmarc Etáine*; according to Lebor Gabála he is the son of Inndúi. Sighmall and his mansion at Síd Nennta are all known from the Dindsenchas and from the story called *Sluagad Nathi maic Fiachra,* of which we have at present no manuscript version but a summary in O'Curry's *Manuscript Materials.* His father's name is given in § 3 as Cairpre Crom, what is confirmed by Lebor Gabála, his grandfather is Midir. Tadg Mór son of Nuadu occurs in *Acc. na Sen.* as one of the Tuatha Dé Danann, and there his residence is located in Síd

100

Almaine; when our story mentions Síd Droma Dean as his dwelling-place, this appears to be another name for the same locality, Síd Droma Dean being Fornocht near the Hill of Allen in Co. Kildare. According to the story of *Cath Cnucha* and the Dindsenchas, Tagd Mór does not belong to the Tuatha Dé Danann, but is a druid; so here *Altromh Tighi dá Medar* sides with *Accallamh na Senórach*. Finnbarr Meada Siuil (Knock Maa, Co. Galway), who plays an important part in our story, is also named in *Cath Finntrága* and in *Accallamh na Senórach*, but not in the Dindsenchasor Lebor Gabála; no other story about him is known to exist. Abartach son of Illathach of Síd Buide is one of the heroes in Cath Finntrága, where he overcomes the Cat-Heads; Abartach, father of Smirgat, may and may not be a different person. Fogartach of Síd Finnabrach is unknown, unless he is identical with Faghartach "rí na hInnia." Ilbreac at Síd Aeda of Ess Ruaid is the hero of the story in *Accallamh na Senórach*, where he and his brother Aed are involved in a war against Lir of Síd Findachaid; he also occurs in the prose Dindsenchas and in *Cath Finntrága*, where he is called the son of Manannan. Lir of Síd Finnachaid is known from other tales besides, such as *Oided Cloinne Lir* and *Cath Finntrága*, where he assails the Dog-Heads.[15] Derg Diansgothach of Síd Cleitidh, who figures last in the list, was Oisín's grandfather according to *Accallamh na Senórach*, and one of the leaders in the war against Lir; he is not known from other sources.

So far the Tuatha Dé Danann in *Altromh Tighi dá Medar*. This portion was minutely scrutinized as it proves beyond all doubt that the author was reproducing genuine romantic traditions, partly obscured in our days, but evidently closely related to those preserved in *Accallamh na Senórach* and other texts. This applies *also* to the ensuing passage on the articles that make it possible for the Tuatha Dé Danann to subsist in Ireland after the occupation by the Sons of Míl, namely the Feth Fiada (a magic veil which renders them invisible), the feast of Goibniu, by means of which their lords escape age and decay, and Manannan's swine, whose flesh revives their killed warriors. As to the Feth Fiada, the name varies in our written sources, and as a magic object it would require a separate study; let it suffice to say here that it is of frequent occurrence in the Irish romances. In *Accallamh na Senórach* it is mentioned as a magic covering, and the Tuatha Dé Danann are said to have the *fia fiad* at their disposal in order to make themselves invisible. It recalls the covering garment Cuchulinn received at the hands of Manannan, and the cloak that is laid aside by the Tuatha Dé Danann when they want to show themselves to mortals.[16] In our story it re-occurs in §§ 10 and 11, where the power of making invisible appears to be inherent to the *feth fiar*: Eithne cannot find back her friends, after they have departed in the magic veil, whereas she herself is no longer able to escape the indiscretion of the mortal eye. In a Christian sense the name *(Faeth fiada)* is used for St Patrick's hymn, which transformed the saint and his followers into deer in the eyes of their enemies.

Of the two remaining treasures the feast of Goibniu *(Aed Goibnenn)* is preserved by Bé Bind, daughter of Elcmar, wife of Aed of Ess Ruad, who dispenses it to the Tuatha Dé Danann: *"'cach áen robói ac ól fleide Goibnind acaind'* [sc. Tuatha Dé Danann], *ar in ingen, 'ní thic saeth na galur riu'."* The swine of Manannan are not mentioned in *Accallamh na Senórach*, but we hear about them in *Echtra Cormaic;* they are the food of the people of Tír Tairngire, and when they are being roasted, every fourth part of them will be read at the telling of a true story; in the whole there are seven of them.

The Tuatha Dé Danann are rich in miraculous objects. The four treasures they brought from their original homes were referred to already. Then there is Manannan's cloak, which keeps Cuchulinn and Fand separated for ever, and the cows of Manannan in Tír Tairngire, and many others. It is difficult to make out why *Altromh Tighi dá Medar* alludes to the three objects mentioned above only, except perhaps for the Feth Fiada, which plays a part in the story itself. At any rate the introduction is entirely built on well-known traditions of romantic literature. All its statements, though not derived from one single authority, are rooted in the ancient stock of Irish lore. It was doubtless composed for the sake of the ensuing tale of Eithne, but it is by no means fantastical. It strengthens our confidence in the genuineness of that story, even for such features as receive no support from any preserved text.

The three opening paragraphs of the Eithne story proper relate how Aengus 'Og, son of the Dagda, under the influence of Manannan's magic power, compels his fosterfather Elcmar to quit the fairy palace of Brug na Bóinne and to leave it to himself. A feast is prepared by Elcmar, which Manannan honours by his presence, and there Aengus is taught the spell that is to make him master of the Brug. A mistake in the editor's translation must needs render this passage obscure to those who do not consult the Irish text. When Manannan has been invited, Elcmar sends his steward Dichu with other servants in order to provide fish, fowl and venison for the banquet. In the meantime the guests arrive and feast on other provisions, as long as the steward does not return. After three days and three nights the feast is interrupted: *i cinn an ceathrumadh la d'fulair Manannan an teach d'folmughadh gunar fagad mac mna iar blais beatha isin bruidhin sin acht Manannan 7 Aengus.* The translation "on the fourth day Manannan *was obliged to clear the house*" spoils the meaning of the passage; in fact, it does not yield any good sense. What really happens is this: "at the end of the fourth day Manannan *ordered the house to be cleared* so that no mother's son with a living soul was left in this mansion except Manannan and Aengus." Manannan is the acting character in the whole scene. He turns out the other guests in order to remain in the Brug with no one else with him but Aengus, whom he is going to stir against Elcmar. He knows that the supreme powers of the world will have Aengus lord of the Brug and from the outset he is preparing Elcmar's expulsion. He is acting according to a fixed plan, and it may even be asked whether the sending away of Dichu the steward forms a part of it. It is necessary that Dichu shall be absent from the Brug at the moment when Aengus pronounces the charm against Elcmar, for one day Dichu will be the father of Eithne, God's chosen maiden. Though it is not expressly stated that Manannan has a share in Dichu's being sent on errand, it seems only natural that this should be the case. For he is both the exponent and the agent of Providence.[17]

Manannan's character in our story requires a closer study. Of course, more than anything else he is the Fairy Lord who resides in his wonderful palace at Emain Ablach in Tír Tairngire. When he feels himself neglected by Elcmar, who has been slow in the preparation of the feast, he resolves to banish him for ever from the Brug and to give his place to Aengus. In order to achieve this, Manannan avails himself of magic. He teaches Aengus a powerful charm *(sén 7 soladh)*, which Elcmar cannot possibly resist. The *sén 7 soladh* is a pagan element, which is well-known from *Accallamh na Senórach*. See, for instance, line 6218 sqq.: Ireland is being harassed by three demons and Cormac mac Airt summons the three sons of the king of Iruaith in order to drive them off by pronouncing a *sén 7 soladh* against them *(Eirgid a nert in tshéin seo 7 in tsholaid, a tri náimhde tuathchaecha ... do tshil Buadnaite ingine Irhuaith .i. ingen ind fhir ro gabustar 7 ro thidnaic in fír-Dia forórda 7 tigerna na n-uile dáine il-lámaib na nIubal n-amirsech.*[18] The charm as a means to rid oneself of foes or to subdue enemies is pagan in its origin and often applied by druids, magicians and poets. Tadg mac Nuadat, who according to our story is one of the Tuatha Dé Danann, used it against king Conn in order to recover his daughter when she was abducted by Cumall. From paganism, however, it found its way into Christianity, as the saints were obliged to attack the druids with their own weapons. This double character of the charm is very conspicuous in our story. Manannan does not conceal that what he is exercising against Elcmar is sheer *draoidheacht*. At the same time his actions are dictated by the will of God: He alone has power over the Tuatha Dé Danann, He can condemn them if He likes, He banished the angels from Heaven, made the Fir Bolg yield to the Tuatha Dé Danann, and these to the Sons of Míl. If Elcmar is to be expelled from the Brug, God has willed it, it is His *sén*.

In fact this whole portion of *Altromh Tighi dá Medar* consists of two series of *motifs* blended. At the bottom there is a typical Irish pagan story, belonging to the type called ´*Oegidecht*: Manannan, supreme ruler of the Tuatha Dé Danann, is entitled to receive a feast from Elcmar of the Brug; Elcmar, however, is slow in preparing it and is therefore banished from the Brug by means of a charm which Manannan induces Aengus to pronounce. The reason of Elcmar's expulsion, namely Manannan's discontent on account of the insufficient provisions for the feast, can only be understood at this stage. But a Christian super-structure has been added: Elcmar must leave the Brug because it is God's will that Aengus henceforth shall be lord of the radiant palace, and Manannan is only the agent of the divine power; as to Elcmar, no one but God himself knows where he goes after the fall, his fate recalls that of Lucifer.[19] Thus this portion of our story is characterized by a striking incongruity in the motivation. The theme is pagan but the interpretation is Christian.

It is in no way surprising that a series of Christian *motifs* was introduced into a tale which centers about Manannan. The Christian elements are characteristic of the whole Manannan cycle, and at the bottom of it all there is the *rapprochement,* if not the identification, of Tír Tairngire (Terra Repromissionis) and Paradise. In this respect the poem recited by Manannan in *Imram Brain* is very instructive. There is no more eloquent picture of Manannan's land and every trait of it recalls Paradise: it is sinless and without decay or death. These traits are doubtless original, they were not borrowed from Christianity. Manannan, who displays numerous characteristics of a fertility deity, is the god of many love-affairs,[20] in him love is deified and thus eternal youth belongs to him and his household by nature. Manannan's land is the pagan Elyseum. Since the notions of Tír Tairngire and Paradise intermingled, it is but natural that Manannan should also be endowed with divine qualities in the Christian sense. In the poem quoted from *Imram Brain* he possesses knowledge of the divine scheme in the world: in §§ 45–47 the fall of Adam is recorded, and in § 48 the coming of Christ is prophesied. Similarly in *Altromh Tighi dá Medar* he knows everything about the fall of the angels, and he understands that Eithne will not partake of the Tuatha Dé Danann's food because she adores the Trinity. Even the *sén 7 soladh* he uses against Elcmar is equated with God's curse of Lucifer. The only typically pagan feature of Manannan that was not Christianized is his presiding at the Wedding-feast of the Brug, the love-feast of the gods, which results in the birth of Manannan's daughter Curcóg and the number of maidens who are to serve her. Here he is the fertility god whose cult consists in a general courtship. The libertine character, which the scene doubtless had in a more primitive form, was mitigated by our author; the atmosphere from which it arose was evidently the same as that of the "forked story" about Manannan: with mutual consent he gives over his wife to a young Tuatha Dé Danann chief, Aillén son of Eogabal, while himself he enjoys the love of ´Aine, Aillén's sister.

One question concerning the role of Manannan remains: is the part he plays in the expulsion of Elcmar original, or was it only assigned to him when the Christian element was introduced and no one among the Tuatha Dé Danann seemed better qualified to act as God's agent than he? The latter view must be the correct one. That Elcmar is lord of the Brug, is a common tradition, he is usually called "Elcmar in Brogha.' That he is deceived by Aengus, who takes the Brug from him, is also told in other sources, though the circumstances are not the same. According to the introduction of *Tochmarc Etáine* Aengus obtains the Brug from Elcmar by exacting it from him for a day and a night: there has never been a day without a night since the creation, so that Aengus becomes master of the Brug for ever. The same *motif* occurs in one of the *remscéla* of the Táin, but here the Dagda, not Elcmar, is the deceived lord. Thus the version of *Tochmarc Etáine* agrees partially with that of this *remscél* of the Táin, partially with that of *Altromh Tighi dá Medar*. As there is no trace of dependence of one version upon the other the elements occurring in two of them must be considered as original, namely the rule of Elcmar over the Brug and Aengus' trick. Of these the former was eliminated in the *remscél*, the latter in *Altromh Tighi dá Medar*. Here, Aengus does not win the Brug by means of a witty play upon words, but by Manannan's *sén 7 soladh*. It would seem that this change was brought about by the desire to assign to Manannan a place in the story, and we are confirmed in this view by the observation that in both the *remscél* of the Táin and *Tochmarc Etáine* Midir figures as Aengus' counselor. Evidently *Altromh Tighi dá Medar* replaced Midir by Manannan on purpose, and Aengus' behaviour towards Elcmar had to be altered accordingly.

From the banishment of Elcmar onwards our story follows its own ways. When Elcmar has left the Brug, the steward returns with his wife and his son Roc;[21] he learns what has happened during his absence and, having escaped Manannan's charm, he remains at the Brug, where his wife gives birth to a daughter, Eithne. At the same time the maidens that were conceived during the general Wedding-feast, are born, and amongst them Curcóg, Manannan's daughter, ranks foremost. She is given over, like the other maidens, to Aengus, who becomes their fosterfather, and Eithne is appointed Curcóg's handmaid. When the maidens have grown up, Finnbarr of Meada comes to see them and his visit is the immediate cause of Eithne growing conscious of herself.

The maidens are brought before Finnbarr, he looks keenly at them, and upon perceiving Eithne, he pronounces a quatrain of a highly injurious character. The text of the quatrain is corrupt, and the editor's translation is not quite satisfactory. The following attempt at a restitution of the text cannot be much amiss:

> Ingen ríg-rechtaire in Broga,
> in géis co mine malach,
> is bean do chloinn etig duine
> doní in suide salach.[22]

(The daughter of the head-steward of the Brug, the swan with delicacy of eyebrows, is a woman of the disgusting race of man, who makes the dirty sitting.)

The offence is in the words *in suide salach*. For a moment they menace to destroy the brotherly love that prevails between Aengus and Finnbarr, but the latter makes amends and the feast is allowed to continue. Curcóg is seated between two princes, and Eithne at the other side of Aengus. However, the saintly maiden remains distressed and refuses for seven days and nights every sort of food and drink. Later on the cause of her behavior is revealed by Manannan: the insult has caused the guardian demon (*a deman comuidachta*) to leave the maiden's heart, and an angel came in his place.

Finnbarr's quatrain was intended as a poet's satire. The power of the poets to bring evil on those who were subject to their wrath, is too well-known to require further illustrations. Plummer states that by their libels they could even raise actual blotches or blisters on the face of the person satirized. It is but natural that shame befalls Eithne and that she declines food and drink. But the Christian application of the satire *motif* is remarkable and, as far as I know, unique: the lampoon of Finnbarr, who represents the evil powers of heathendom, is, of course, destructive in its effects, but to the evil powers themselves. Thus it becomes a help to the power of God, for which it has paved the way towards the maiden's heart. Finnbarr's outrageous words liberate Eithne from the shackles of paganism.

No less interesting are the words themselves used by Finnbarr to insult the maiden. When it is said of her that she "makes the dirty sitting," this can only mean that she has been sitting at a place where she does not belong, that her presence has reviled the seat she occupies among the inhabitants of the Brug. The sight of a human being sitting among the fairy lords is loathsome to Finnbarr, she must be the sooner the better removed through a poetical satire. This explains why it is expressly stated that after Finnbarr's apology the maiden is led towards the seat at Aengus' side: she has been sitting there before, but was thought unworthy of it by Finnbarr. It cannot be denied that this scene, though differently connected, resembles more closely that of the Siege Perilous, known among other authorities from the Didot Perceval,[23] than any other parallel adduced until now. Professor Loomis[24] has collected a number of allusions to more or less miraculous seats from Celtic literature, such as the sage's seat at Nuadu's court, occupied by Lug according to the *Second Battle of Mag Tuired,* or the Lía Fáil which used to shriek under the king of Ireland. These, in fact, have nothing in common with the Siege Perilous except a few irrelevant features. What imports in the scene of the Siege Perilous, is that it is said by Arthur to be reserved for the best knight in the world, and that Perceval, at his first visit to Arthur's court, attempts in vain to sit in it, but is allowed to occupy it when he becomes a guardian of the Grail. In the Joseph d'Arimathie it is destined for the son of Hebron. In the scene of Finnbarr and Eithne there is the same Christian setting: the seat at Aengus' side is destined for the heroïne, who is a Christian saint. But before she sits down in it, Finnbarr has attempted to keep her from it by means of satirical words, and she does not come to her right until the demon has left her heart. In the same way Arthur dissuades Perceval from sitting in the Siege Perilous, and when he disregards the king's warnings, this proves fatal for him. However, as soon as he has redeemed the Fisher King and the Grail from their enchantment — that means, as soon as he realized his Christian mission to the full — the Siege Perilous is his. The parallelism is striking, even the name *an suide salach* recalls the Siege Perilous. Of course, in the Didot Perceval there is a long interval from the hero's first attempt to his final triumph, while in the story of Eithne the two stages constitute but one scene, and besides, Arthur is guided by friendly intentions towards the hero, whereas Finnbarr is only prompted to the action he takes by malice. But the fundamental idea of the seat that can only be occupied by a Christian hero after he has grown fully conscious himself, connects the two stories closely together and points to the same atmosphere that engendered them.

The three paragraphs following the scene of Finnbarr's insult contain the story of Eithne's miraculous feeding. Aengus offers her the milk of his Dun Cow from a golden goblet. She milks the cow herself and lives on its milk until the time when she is sent to Manannan, who is to make out the cause of the sudden change in her. In Manannan's palace she refuses all sorts of food except the milk of his Speckled Cow; here, too, she does the milking herself, and drinks the milk from a gold goblet. Then Manannan, who never yet saw an illness he was not able to diagnose, reveals her secret: the demon has left her, and henceforth she harbors an angel in her heart. After a month and a fortnight Curcóg desires to leave Emain Ablach and to return to the Brug, and Eithne has to follow her. From that time till the days of king Lóegaire mac Néill the maidens sojourn alternately with Aengus and with Manannan, and Eithne never tastes any other food but the milk of the two cows. What strikes most in this passage is that Curcóg suddenly takes an active part in the development of events. Until now she has only been a figurant, Eithne's mistress, but outshone by her in virtue and saintliness. Here it is she who desires to return to the Brug and thus becomes the cause of the alternate dwelling of the maidens in Tír Tairngire and in Ireland. This must be an ancient and genuine trait. The natural tendency of the author would doubtless have been to make Eithne no less prominent at this point of his story than elsewhere. Besides, Manannan puts his exhortation to his daughter not to leave him yet, in verse; it is contained in six *debide* couplets which picture the delights of Tír Tairngire, its music, its rolling waves, its flocks of birds. Curcóg's unexpected initiative cannot be due to mere accident or to carelessness of the author. It is a rest of the original pagan frame, which is mostly obscured by the Christian superstructure, and obviously preserves the Irish version of the Proserpina myth. Curcóg is the god's daughter whose dwelling-place is alternately on earth and in the Other World, like Kore in Greek and Skadi in Scandinavian mythology.[25] The author was very felicitous in molding together this pagan myth and the Christian *motif* of Eithne's miraculous feeding. The former accounts for the number of two cows and two goblets, which in itself is in no way required for the development of the story of Eithne. The latter claims our attention presently.

Aengus reveals the story of the two cows and the two goblets, the *Altromh Tighi dá Medar* proper. When, long ago, Manannan and Aengus went on an expedition to the eastern world, they came to the Golden Pillars and thence proceeded to India. There they found the two horn-twisted cows that are always in milk, the two many-shaped golden goblets and the two spancels of rare silk. They took these precious treasures with them to Ireland and shared them, so that Aengus became the possessor of the Dun Cow, and Manannan of the Speckled Cow. The cows are never without milk, and it tastes of honey and intoxicating wine. In fact, there is nothing extraordinary in this story. It is only one of the numerous instances of miraculous feeding animals belonging to the Tuatha Dé Danann. Let it suffice to point Manannan's swine and his wife's seven cows whose milk is sufficient for the whole population of Tír Tairngire. The three cows of Echde gave enough milk to fill every day a cauldron of sixty sextarii.[26] Balor Balcbéimnech had a cow whose milk would fill twenty barrels if they were put under her.[27] Trostan, a Pictish druid, provided the Leinstermen with seven score hornless white cows, whose milk annihilated the effect of poisoned weapons. Irish hagiography also abounds with instances of miraculous food. Nearest to Aengus' Dun Cow is the Odhar Ciaráin, the Dun Cow of St Ciarán. When St Kevin was a child, a white cow came to nourish him, and nobody knew whence it came nor where it went. Feeding vessels are no less common than feeding animals. The Tuatha Dé Danann have the Dagda's cauldron as one of their four treasures and, besides, a drinking-horn which turns water into mead, as well as a vat where spittle becomes wine. In Tír-na-mban there are dishes where the food never vanishes.[28] St Brendan of Clonfert arrives at a column where he finds a mass chalice, and neither he nor his companions experience the want of food or drink owing to the delight they find in the column. The only difference between *Altromh Tighe dá Medar* and the parallels just quoted is the occurring of the miraculous cow and the salutary vessel combined. This, in fact, is not necessary for the logic of the tale and compilation of *motifs* would seem to be responsible for it. Besides, a parallel may be seen in Iuchna's cows and his cauldron which is their calf: thirty cows was the portion of the cauldron, and the full of it was milked from them as often as the birds were signing to them.

However, these parallels from Irish literature can never satisfy us entirely. They only prove that both feeding animals and feeding vessels were of common occurrence in mythological tales and in hagiography. The adversaries of a Celtic origin of the Grail were fully justified in objecting to the identification of the Grail with similar feeding vessels; for the essential quality of the Grail, its Christian character, is lacking from all these Irish parallels.[29] It is here that the importance of *Altromh Tighe dá Medar* lies. If it may be inferred from the title of our tale that originally the goblets were even more significant than the cows themselves, and that the introduction of the two miraculous cows is perhaps due to a comparatively recent compilation of *motifs*, then the feeding vessels of the House of the two Goblets provide the intermediate stage between the purely pagan vessels and the Holy Grail. Besides, this also holds good if the cows have been there from the beginning. The goblets of Manannan and Aengus are typical miraculous feeding vessels of the Tuatha Dé Danann, but at the same time the application of the *motif* is purely Christian: they furnish the only food Eithne can partake of from the moment the angel has come into her heart, and she lives on it until the day she meets the fishing cleric. Nowhere does the Irish story take us so near to the Holy Grail as here.

It is interesting to note that this Christian interpretation of a pagan *motif* has its roots in the religious, especially the ethic notions of paganism itself. In § 8, Manannan, explaining the cause of the influence exercised by the Speckled Cow's milk on Eithne, remarks that the cow was brought home by him from a righteous land, that is from India *(a tír firén tugadh hí .i. a hIndia)*. This trait, which fully accounts for the connection between the cow's milk and Eithne's growing Christian self-consciousness,[30] is at the same time representative for the ethical atmosphere of the Tuatha Dé Danann. It constitutes, in fact, the link between paganism and Christianity in our story. It enabled the author to mold the two contrasting elements into a unity without offending his sense of probability. Among the ethical norms of Irish paganism, truth and righteousness seem to have ranked foremost. Righteousness prevails in the land of the Tuatha Dé Danann. This is stated by the fairy champion who hands the silver branch with golden apples to Cormac. The pig of Manannan will not be roasted until a true story is told for every fourth part of it. His golden cup breaks into pieces when a lie is said in its presence. It is but natural that paganism itself should attribute the powers of a miraculous feeding vessel to its origin from a righteous land. Through this it supplied the foundation for a Christian interpretation. Irish paganism and Christianity were not opposed to one another in every respect; in their ethical principles, especially in their reverence for truth and justice, they concurred. This is the bridge that connected the two sections of the road leading from a Celtic feeding vessel to the Holy Grail. Let it be remembered that the Grail Castle, too, is a place of truth and righteousness. No man, says Crestien, who is a coward, a traitor or a liar can remain alive in it for one hour.[31] Here is a striking proof of the close affinity of atmosphere that unites our simple story and the Grail romances.

The Christian conclusion of the tale also contains a few remarkable and interesting features. A common *märchen-motif* is used as an introduction: One day, when the maidens are swimming in the Boyne, Eithne is left by her companions, who depart covered by the Féth Fiada. This happens in the days of king Lóegaire mac Néill. Being now visible herself, she is received by a cleric in his cell; he is Ceasán, son of the king of Scotland. She abjures the Tuatha Dé Danann and becomes a Christian. The divine power is revealed in her; she is able to read without ever having learned it, and an exceptionally large fish is supplied for her food. Then the story ends with a contention between St Patrick and Aengus who both desire to keep the saintly maiden for themselves, and when Aengus, who is compelled to give her up, utters a heart-rending cry, this is the cause of her death. Her name survives in that of Cell Eithne, and Ceasán moves to Fid Gaible.

Ceasán and his cell at Feeguile in Leinster are also known from *Accallamh na Senórach*,[32] the text which in so many other cases, too, appears to be the source of important details in *Altromh Tighi dá Medar*. When Cáilte tells the story of the yellow

112

nuts and the golden apples from Fid Gaible, St Patrick remarks; *is annsin atá fer gráda dom muinnter se .i. Cessán mac ríg Alban, 7 sacart méisi damsa he.* Probably he must be identified with *cruimther Cassán,* who is mentioned in the *Vita Tripartita* as one of the priests accompanying St Patrick; however, this Cassán is neither the son of the king of Scotland nor is his dwelling-place at Fid Gaible, so that once more our story appears to draw largely from the traditions of romantic literature. The most salient features in Eithne's intercourse with Ceasán are her ability to read without learning and the miraculous feeding fish. For both parallels can be adduced from Irish hagiography. Reading the psalms, of course, is a necessity in becoming a Christian, and of nearly all the Irish saints it is related how they receive in their youth the instruction required for the acquisition of this accomplishment. Eithne's teacher is Ceasán. It can scarcely be due to a mere accident that in the *Vita Tripartita* the boy named Lonán mac Senaig, when his mother asks Patrick's blessing for him, is handed over by the saint to the same Ceasán in order to instruct him: during twelve days he is reading the psalms. The suggestion does not seem too hazardous that Ceasán was chosen as the maiden's mentor on account of this passage in the *Vita Tripartita.* Of the boy Lonán mac Senaig, however, it is not expressly said that no teaching was needed to make him read. Perhaps this is a miraculous gift which in Irish hagiography was regarded as more natural for the female saints. St Ite at least was able to preach the divine precepts from the inspiration of the Holy Ghost only. Of the male saints, on the other hand, the names of their teachers are usually carefully recorded in their lives.

Miraculous fishing is one of the commonest features in Irish hagiography, and no particular written authority was needed to introduce it into the tale of Eithne and Ceasán. St Kevin used to receive his salmon every day from a friendly otter, which only stopped its charity when one of the monks, Cellach, started coveting its hide. When St Ciarán of Saiger is sitting with the bishop Germán by the side of a river, the saint learns that the next day he will receive the visit of the king of Cashel's son. "Take the fish that is passing by thee," he says to Germán, and the bishop does accordingly. The miracle of St Cainnech is even more striking. The saint orders his servants to beg fish from the fishermen. These, however, refuse to give anything to the saint of God. Then St Cainnech tells his men to dip his staff into the weir, and by this process they catch two salmon of marvellous size. The author of *Altromh Tighe dá Medar* had not to look far in order to collect this typical illustration of the divine power in his heroïne. The salmon Ceasán caught for Eithne was so heavy that it cost him an effort to carry it from the river to the church. This trait connects our story manifestly with the whole body of Irish hagiography.

At the same time it constitutes another link of the tale of Eithne with the Grail romances. According to Crestien, Perceval, before reaching the Grail Castle, finds the king and one of his followers angling in a boat; hence his name the Fisher-King. Later on the Grail-King's fishing plays no part whatever in the narrative. The explanation that the king, who is maimed and wounded, can neither ride nor walk and has therefore taken up fishing as a pastime, is too childish to be original and obviously occupies the place of something older and more genuine. Robert de Boron, who retains a few doubtless ancient traits that were neglected even by Crestien, such as the Siege Perilous, gives a precious hint as to the direction where we have to look for the meaning of the fishing. In his *Joseph* he makes king Bron catch a fish at the direction of a heavenly voice and place it on the table opposite the Grail. Here the fish is meant as miraculous food, no less than the Grail, and it comes to Bron as a divine gift. Obviously Bron is nourished with the fish he catches through the grace of God; thence his name the Rich Fisher. This explanation is not only a most natural and plausible one, but it is also supported by the numerous scenes of fishing saints in Irish hagiography. The king in Crestien's *Contes del Graal,* too, is doubtless occupied in fishing because, with the help of the divine power, he thus provides the food required for the inhabitants of the castle. Only the miraculous feeding on the fish has been somewhat obscured by that on the Holy Grail, so that the fishing lost much of its original significance, and was perhaps not even understood by the poet himself. With Robert de Boron the trait has preserved more of its primitive meaning, though here, too, the combination with the Grail renders it less transparent. The conditions under which both the Fisher-King and Ceasán are fishing are identical, and the meaning of the fishing scene as a miraculous way of providing food, is the same in both cases. In the Irish tale the feeding on a miraculous fish and on a golden goblet with milk from divine cattle are kept separate, whereas in the Grail romances the fish and the Grail occur combined. Still in the former as in the latter the same hero or heroïne has the benefit from both. It was a felicitous idea of the Irish storyteller to use the double *motif* for establishing a climax. With him the milk and the goblet are symbolical for the preparation of Eithne's mission, the fish for its realization.

Of the conclusion of our story little need be said. Aengus appears to claim his fosterdaughter, St Patrick opposes him. Eithne's soul belongs to Jesus and, though her heart is filled with sorrow for the lost splendor of the Brug, she declines to follow Aengus thither. The sadness that masters Eithne at this moment, engenders the elegiac tone characteristic of many Irish romances. The fairies have to stoop to the rising sun of Christianity. Aengus' woeful cry breaks the maiden's heart.[33] Patrick's dispute with Aengus recalls his numerous contentions with the druids;[34] according to *Accallamh na Senórach*, he was sent to Ireland *do sílad chreitmhe 7 crábaid 7 do dhíchur deman 7 druadh a hEirinn ... 7 do thairnrmh idhul 7 arracht 7 ealadhan ndráidhechta.* However, Aengus never becomes the hateful druid, he remains the beautiful prince from fairy land who can do no wrong but for his refusal to adore the true God. The scene has a close affinity to that where MoChóemóg saves the Children of Lir from king Lairgnén of Connacht and, by touching their magic cloak, redeems them from enchantment; here, as in our story, the objects of the conflict belong to the Tuatha Dé Danann but have already found their souls' satisfaction in Christianity. Thus even in the purely Christian portion, where no direct influence of any other known text can be traced, the Tale of the House of the two Goblets is nearer akin to romantic than hagiographic literature. The Children of Lir turn old and withered men when the magic of their race is taken from them; thus Eithne has to die upon hearing the parting lament of her former comrades. In the romances the voice of the heathen past was allowed to ring through.

The tale is concluded by an elegy for Eithne; it was pronounced by Patrick, who imparts supernatural power to the story and enumerates the cases where it will avail to recite it. It secures a safe passage on ships, a faithful wife and good children; it is a safeguard against rows in ale-houses and revolutions in palaces; it redeems from bondage and imprisonment and is a promise of victory. There can be little doubt that this idea of having a special power attached to the story by St Patrick, was borrowed from the *Vita Tripartita* where the *Faed Fiada*, an incantation of the same saint, is exalted in a similar manner: *et in summo abinde inter Hibernos habetur pretio, quia creditur, et multa experientia probatur, pie recitantes ab imminentibus animae et corporis praeservare periculis.*

The object of the tale *Altromh Tighi dá Medar* is the glorification of Cell Eithne on the Boyne, a place that remains as yet unidentified. The tenor of the story must have been Christian from the outset. But the ancient Irish did not shrink from using their pagan national traditions in extolling the Christian faith and its saints, especially if the domicile of the latter had direct connections with the ancient beliefs. In shaping a legend about Eithne's cell on the Boyne it was but natural to establish a relation with Aengus and the Brug. The author was not only a devout believer in the power of the saintly maiden, but also thoroughly trained in the romantic literature of his country. He collected the elements for his story from various existing tales. Thence *Altromh Tighi dá Medar* cannot be one of the earliest representatives of its type. At the same time, however, it never departs from what is rooted in the traditions and beliefs of primitive and Christian Ireland. It is typical for the way paganism and Christianity could get mixed up in those times. What makes the story particularly interesting is that it borrows its non-Christian elements from the so-called mythological cycle, not from Fenian themes. Of this there are not many instances; the best known of them is *Oided Cloinne Lir* where, however, there is not such a deep interpretation of the two elements. This points to a later origin of *Altromh Tighi dá Medar*.

How was our story composed? Eithne, the heroïne in her cell on the Boyne, not far from the Brug of Aengus, could be easily linked together with Curcóg, Manannan's daughter and the Irish Proserpina, who was said to sojourn in the Brug in summertime. Thus the myth of Curcóg becomes the base of the whole structure. According to that myth Curcóg was conceived by Manannan during the Wedding-feast of the Brug, but was handed over to Aengus to foster her. From the time she was a grown-up maiden, she stayed alternately with her father in Tír Tairngire and with Aengus of the Brug, thus symbolizing the regular change of the seasons. It cannot be made out, whether at this stage the miraculous feeding cows and goblets formed part of the story; the circumstance that at a later stage these are reserved for Eithne only, points in a different direction. At any rate the connection with both Manannan and Aengus was there from the very outset. This rendered the introduction of the Christian element the more easy as there was a strong tendency to identify Manannan's Land of Promise with the Christian Paradise. The ethical notions connected with both and the reverence as regards truth and righteousness in both Irish paganism and Christianity contributed to the *rapprochement* of the two religious systems.

The idea of Curcóg's conception during the general Wedding-feast of the Brug, implies that a great number of maidens were born along with her; these are her playmates and companions. Eithne, the future saintly maiden of the cell, became one of their number. She is Curcóg's Christian counterpart. The story of the maidens' birth and their fostering at the Brug developed under the influence of the tale of Roc mac Dichon, the steward, and his son; Eithne was likewise represented as the daughter of a steward, namely Dichu, father of Roc. This Dichu is not of the Tuatha Dé Danann race, what accounts for Eithne's innate inclination towards Christianity.

The history of Eithne from the moment she is left by her companions is influenced by *Oided Cloinne Lir*. When she sees Ceasán, the cleric, standing in the door of his oratory she embraces Christianity. This scene is elaborated through a series of *motifs* borrowed from Irish hagiography, especially the *Vita Tripartita*. The most outstanding among these are Eithne's ability to read the psalms without learning, the miraculously provided fish, the dispute of Patrick and Aengus, the supernatural power imparted to the story. But romantic features are not excluded, for such are the cry of Aengus and Ceasán's migration to Fid Gaible.

Of greater importance is the portion that precedes Eithne's parting with Curcóg and her damsels. Its structure can be best understood as a series of new motivations. If it should be asked how Eithne could be so readily accepted into God's special grace, the answer must be: because she had passed through a period of preparation. The notion of her being born on the same day as Curcóg and her subsisting until the time of St Patrick, implied a miraculous feeding during the long centuries of her life. For by partaking of the magic food of the Tuatha Dé Danann, she could not be prepared for her Christian mission. Thus the *motif* of the miraculous cows and the golden goblets was introduced; there must be two of either, as Eithne had to migrate with Curcóg from the Brug to Tír Tairngire and vice versa. Her sojourn with Manannan was employed to make the latter reveal the secret of Eithne's miraculous feeding. The double character of the food, its serving a Christian purpose and yet its being supplied by the Tuatha Dé Danann, was explained from its hailing from India, the righteous land. It remains doubtful whether in this portion the goblets are more primitive than the cows, as might be inferred from the title of the story; compilation of *motifs* from the beginning is also possible. Both feeding animals and feeding vessels are common in romantic literature. Even their Christian application is not new, as is testified to by many scenes in the saints' lives.

The next question would be: what made Eithne deviate from the practice of the Tuatha Dé Danann and require a special food for herself? Finnbarr's insult, is the answer. He accused her of "making the dirty sitting," for he recognized in her the being of different descent, the offspring of the race of man. Her only connection with the inhabitants of the Brug lies in her being the daughter of Dichu the steward.

An introduction as to how Aengus became master of the Brug was prefixed in order to illustrate the prominent position taken in our tale by Aengus and Manannan. The common version of this tradition was even altered, so that Manannan was represented as the principal actor in the whole scene. If any one should wonder that Dichu, the steward, should be present in the Brug after the expulsion of Elcmar, his lord, this objection is met by the intimation that Dichu had been sent off on errand at the moment when Manannan caused Aengus to pronounce the powerful *sén 7 soladh* against Elcmar. This implied a preceding feast, offered by Elcmar to Manannan, and the latter's dissatisfaction at the insufficient preparation of the feast. This is the cause of Manannan's proceeding severely against Elcmar, although at the same time his attitude is dictated by a vague vision of the things to come.

As in *Oided Cloinne Lir* a few notes are premised on the history of the Tuatha Dé Danann since the battle of Tailltiu. They are largely taken from romantic sources, such as *Accallamh na Senórach* and other Fenian tales. But everything has been done to make the character of Manannan as conspicuous as possible. No other story connects Manannan so closely with the other Tuatha Dé Danann. This observation illustrates his importance as the link between paganism and Christianity in our tale.

From the above the composition of *Altromh Tighi dá Medar* will be sufficiently clear. There is a mythical base with an elaborated Christian superstructure and romantic adornments. The borrowings are taken mostly from romantic literature and, to a much smaller extent, from hagiography. What strikes us most, however, are the numerous features our story has in common with the Grail romances. It will be necessary to view these separately at present.

First there is the fundamental conception. The Grail hero is a simple youth who, through an arduous life, rises to the highest degree of Christian chivalry. Thus Eithne, the steward's daughter, despised as she is by Finnbarr of Meada, ends as a saint of God. In both there is the manifestation of God's power; from the beginning both are chosen heroes, whose career is the gradual realization of the divine intention. The Grail hero reaches a preliminary stage that opens to him the road to higher perfection, at his first visit of the Grail Castle, when he is allowed to see the Grail and its knights. Eithne's first step on the way to sanctity is the moment when, surrounded by Tuatha Dé Danann, she drinks the milk of the Dun Cow from the golden goblet. When afterwards she finds Ceasán in his cell and stays with him, the divine gift in her becomes apparent. Similarly Perceval grows fully conscious of himself during his second visit at the Grail Castle. In the Grail romances the two visits are directed towards the same place, as is required by the logic of the story, especially the *motif* of the Neglected Question; this makes it necessary for the hero to return to the castle where he had failed to act at a previous occasion. The Irish story, on the other hand, localizes the two stages of the heroïne's self-realization in different places, the Brug and Ceasán's cell. At the Brug she manifests herself partially, and Manannan is needed to explain the cause of her extraordinary behavior; that her Christian vocation does not reveal itself at once in full splendor is due to the pagan character of the population of the Brug and of Ireland generally at that time. Later, in Ceasán's cell, the grace of God in her breaks forth in its full glory. Perceval, on the other hand, receives the first token of his mission in the Grail castle, though he fails to understand it; later on it is in the same Grail castle that he awakes to complete self-consciousness. Hence in the romances the Grail castle displays some of the characteristics combined that in the story of Eithne belong either to the Brug of Aengus or to Ceasán's cell. The Grail castle is absolutely Christian and the knights of the Holy Grail are a Christian brotherhood: in this regard it corresponds with the cell of Ceasán. But at the same time it is a magnificent palace and serves as a residence for the most glorious knighthood of the world. Here it recalls the Brug and its radiant fairy princes. The combination of Christian and pagan traits is responsible for the double character of the Grail Castle.

Nowhere does this double character appear more clearly than in the miraculous feeding of the Grail Castle. The king finds himself in possession of a feeding vessel, not unlike the goblets of Aengus and Manannan,[35] but at the same time he is the Fisher-King and thus recalls Ceasán, the fishing cleric. The two *motifs*, both based on the notion of the chosen hero being fed miraculously, are obviously combined in the Grail romances, owing to the localization of the two successive stages of the hero's self-realization at the same place. This combination does not render the primitive identity of the two *motifs* in the two legends less obvious. It only makes the fish in the feeding scene appear superfluous. Another difference between the Irish tale and the Grail romances is that the Grail supplies spiritual food to all the knights of the Castle, whereas the goblet and the milk of the miraculous cows are reserved for Eithne alone. This is a direct consequence of the Christian nature of the Grail Castle and the pagan character of the palace of Aengus.

The two traditions have another feature in common, namely the Siege Perilous or *an suide salach*. After what has been observed on this already, nothing more need be said. The Siege

Perilous is distinctive of the Grail Castle, the "dirty sitting" of Eithne occurs in the Brug. Once more the Grail Castle shows one of the characteristics of a Celtic fairy palace.

Of course, in the strict philological sense of the word, the idea of any genetical relation existing between the Grail romances and *Altromh Tighi dá Medar* is precluded. All the evidence available points to a comparatively recent origin of the Irish tale, which is composed out of elements gathered from all sides. Moreover, notwithstanding the striking similarities, the differences are too important to be explained through a diverging evolution from a common origin. The fundamental notion, that of the hero who attains complete self-consciousness in two successive stages, is identical. This can also be said of some accessory elements, such as the fairy character of the Grail Castle and the Brug, the feeding vessel, the miraculous fish, the Siege Perilous. But here is the end of it. The trend of the narrative is entirely different in one case from the other, and the features where the two traditions agree do not constitute the frame of an organic story.

The impossibility to establish a genetical connection between the two legends renders the problem of their undeniable affinity even more fascinating. The common germ can only be seen in the identity of atmosphere. The story of Eithne centres about Cell Eithne and is based on the combination of Irish heathendom and Christianity. Owing to this, typical pagan elements, originating from early Celtic mythology, could be applied in a Christian sense. Thus an atmosphere was created where mythology, Christianity and romance intermingle. When we attempted to picture the development of this atmosphere in the tale of Eithne, we tried more than anything else to realize how strange this evolution must appear to those not conversant with the inner problems of Celtic literature. To celticists it is of course quite natural.

It remains very doubtful whether the direct sources of the Grail romances will ever be known. However, since the story of Eithne was found, the Celtic origin of the Grail legend can hardly be denied any longer. Now at last we have an Irish tale that coïncides in a number of its most prominent elements with the Grail legend. The similarities are too strong to be accidental: the chosen hero, the Grail with its Quest, the Rich Fisher, the

Siege Perilous. Yet no tie unites Eithne with the Grail. The legend of Perceval simply arose from the same atmosphere as that of Eithne. It probably also has early connections with a place of both Christian devotion and pagan reminiscences, let us say Glastonbury. There a similar growth of ideas was possible as on the banks of the Boyne. For there, too, nothing was more natural than that a miraculous feeding vessel of the fairy host should acquire a Christian meaning and help the hero in the accomplishment of his task. The host itself could easily assume Christian characteristics, not unlike Manannan from Tír Tairngire, so that in the course of time it became the Knighthood of the Holy Grail. Christian associations furnished the Fisher-King, pagan beliefs the Siege Perilous. It is a strange coïncidence that exactly the same *motifs* should be linked together in the two legends under consideration. Obviously the circumstances were much alike. The primitive Celtic Grail story must have looked very much like that of the House of the two Goblets. Originally the identity of the constitutive elements doubtless appeared more clearly at the surface than under the cover of so many later accretions. Now that the Grail traditions in their primitive form are lost beyond repair, it is wise to learn the lesson taught by what remains in Ireland. Very often the comparison with Irish tales has induced scholars to proclaim the identity of *motifs* or traditions, where in reality only a superficial likeness could be established. This is altogether different in the case of *Altromh Tighi dá Medar* and the Grail legend. Here is a close agreement in a considerable number of marked features. It demands an explanation, also from those who still will reject the Celtic origin of the legend of the Holy Grail.

Notes

1   See, for instance, *The bleeding lance,* PMLA, 25, 1 sqq.; and *King Arthur and the Grail,* Medieval Studies in memory of Gertrude Schoepperle Loomis, 95 sqq. (Paris, 1927).

2   Of his writings may be mentioned *The Fisher King and the Grail Romances,* PMLA, 24, 365 sqq., and *The identity of Brons,* Medieval Studies etc, 135 sqq.

3   *Studies in the Legend of the Holy Grail, London,* 1888.

4   *The evolution of Arthurian romance,* p.269 sqq., Göttingen, 1923.

5   Zeitschr. für celt. Phil., 18, 73 sqq.

6 *Parzival in der deutschen Literatur,* p.12 sqq., Berlin, 1929.

7 *The legend of sir Perceval,* 2 vols., London 1906–9; *The Quest of the Holy Grail,* London, 1913; *From Ritual to Romance,* Cambridge, 1920.

8 *Celtic myth and Arthurian romance,* New York, 1927. See my criticism of this book in English Studies (Amsterdam) 9, 155 sqq.

9 Zeitschr. für celt. Philologie, 18, 189 sqq. [Now translated in Matthews and Matthews, *Encyclopedia of Celtic Wisdom,* 1996.]

10 *The death tales of the Ulster heroes,* Dublin, 1906, p.4 sqq. Of Cuchulinn it is also said: *et alii dicunt co ro chret Cuchulainn o sin,* Cormac's Glossary, p.31. Oisín is also said to have been baptized in blood, compare Béaloideas, 2, 259.

11 Geoffrey Keating, *The History of Ireland,* ed. P.S. Dineen, London 1908, II, 104.

12 Compare *Acc na Sen.,* i. 377, where Ruide son of Lugaid and his brothers see no other way of acquiring land for themselves but by fasting against the Tuatha Dé Danann.

13 See, for instance, *Lebor Gabála,* p.170, and E. Gwynn, *The metrical Dindsenchas,* vol. 3 (Dublin, 1913), p. 324.

14 An altogether different list of Tuatha Dé Danann chiefs occurs in *Cath Finntrága* (p. 14 sq.) and in *Tóruigheacht Diarmuda 7 Gráinne* (ed. O'Duffy, Dublin, 1903), 1, p.50 sq.

15 Manannan is called the son of Lir in Lebor Gabála p.169; usually he is the son of Elloth. O'Curry, *Ms. Mat.,* p.584 note, mentions a lost tale *Tre Cuairt Tigi Lir.* See also Bergin, *Béaloideas,* 2, 249.

16 *Rennes Dindsenchas,* Revue celtique, 16, 274. Compare also the cloak in which Grainne is carried off by Aengus, *Tóruigheacht Diarmuda 7 Gráinne,* ed. O'Duffy, Dublin, 1903, I, p.20. The fundamental notion is that of a mist in which the Táin is revealed by Fergus, LI., p.245.

17 Compare the sending away of the servant and his son by Saint German at the burning of Bemli's hall, *Irish Nennius,* § 16.

18 The reference to Christianity is especially interesting. Compare also *Acc. na Sen.* 6320, 6323, 6338. Manannan's exhortation to Aengus to drive Elcmar from the Brug recalls his advice to Mongán to avenge his father in *Tucait Baile Mongáin (ní fes ca sen as an dubbartus sin,* see The Voyage of Bran, I, p.61).

19 Compare p.198, l.21 sqq.: Elcmar is compared to the rebellious angels, whose presence in Heaven could no longer be tolerated by God; therefore they were sent to the prisons of Hell. In the same way Elcmar was rebellious in keeping the Brug from Aengus.

20 Compare, for instance, *Serglige Conculaind, Compert Mongáin.* Aengus and Midir are also famous for their amorous adventures, see Poet. Dinds., 3, 42. 350. 386.

21 Roc (p.196, l.4) and his father Dichu did not spring from the phantasy of the author. They also occur in *Tóruigheacht Diarmuda 7 Gráinne* (II, p.40), where a story is told about Roc that recalls that of Eithne and seems to have influenced it. Cróchnuit, daughter of Currach Life, bears a son to Donn O'Donnchudha; this is Diarmaid. After a time she has another son from Roc son of Dichu. Roc is the steward of Aengus. The two boys are fostered by Aengus, who loves them dearly. Donn grows jealous of the favor bestowed

123

by all the inhabitants of the Brug upon the son of Roc, and kills the boy. Then Roc touches his dead son with a magic wand, thus transforming him into a boar. He prophesies that the boar will be the cause of Diarmaid's death. — There is more in this tale to interest us than the mere names of Roc and Dichu. As in *Altromh Tighi dá Medar* two children are born that win the love of all who see them, especially of Aengus himself. One of them is the steward's son. Aengus becomes their fosterfather. The son of the steward is even more beloved than the other boy; thus Eithne surpasses Curcóg in many respects. So far the two stories show a close resemblance that can hardly be accidental, although the further development is entirely different. Of course, priority belongs to the purely pagan story of the two boys, and the names of Roc and Dichu in *Altromh Tighi dá Medar* look like a reference to it. The author seems to have framed a Christian and feminine counterpart to the older pagan tale.

22 The ms. has *Ingin righa in rachtaire Mumain / in géis min mhalla, / is bean do cloinn etig duine / do rinne in suidhi sala.* The prosodical form is Dechnad Fota. In the first line *Mumain* gives no sense, Dichu is never connected with Munster, and on p.202, l.8, he is called *reachtaire an brogha;* thus in Broga must be substituted for Mumain. *Righa in reachtaire* yields four syllables instead of three; the designation *ri-reachtaire* being used for the steward on p.194, l.38, this seems to present the likeliest substitute. For the second and fourth lines a full rhyme is required. In the fourth line *sala* is a vox nihili, it is obviously a mistake for *salach.* Then *malach* as the concluding word of line 2 becomes very plausible, no other case of *mala* "an eyebrow" would suit the exigencies of the rhyme, nor would any form of the adjective *mánla*. The genitive plural *malach* requires a preceding substantive, so that *min* must be changed into *co mine*, which at the same time furnishes the exact number a syllables for the line. The third line needs no corrections, but the interpretation of *duine* ("to us") proposed by Miss Dobbs, cannot be retained; there is a rhyme of *duine* with *suide* in the fourth line, which *dúine-ne* "to us" does not afford. Of the seven syllables in the last line one must necessarily be expunged; this can only be done by changing *dorinne* into *doni,* which form is read by the editor in the prose paraphrase of the quatrain, p.204, l.24. The correction of *sala* into *salach* has been accounted for already. The translation of "the dirty mess" for *in suide salach* was probably chosen by the editor to suit the station, but *suide* means "a sitting" or "a seat" and nothing else.

23 Compare J.L. Weston, *The legend of Sir Perceval,* II, 20 sqq. In Robert de Boron's Joseph d'Arimathie Moys, who attempts to sit in it, is swallowed by the earth.

24 See *Celtic myth and Arthurian romance,* p.215 sqq.

25 See R.S. Loomis, *Celtic myth and Arthurian romance,* p.285 sqq., where however, not one instance from Celtic literature is adduced that shows a real affinity to the Greek myth. In *Altromh Tighi dá Medar,* p.214, l.23, it is even stated that Curcóg passes the summer in the Brug *(do bi Curcog gu na banntrocht ar faighthi Brogha na Boinne a n-aimsir hsamhraidh)!*

26 See R.S. Loomis, op cit., p.240 sq., where more instances are given. The origin of the belief in supernatural cattle lies in the more primitive form of cow-worship, such as that of the Norwegian king Ogvaldr, who worshipped a cow and thought it salutary to drink its milk (Olafs Saga Tryggv., c.64).

27 See Larminie, *West-Irish Folktales*, p.4. Compare A.H. Krappe, *Balor with the Evil Eye*, p.1 sqq.

28 *The voyage of Bran*, § 62.

29 Except, of course, in the case of St Brendan's chalice.

30 St Patrick is also called *firén*, Poet. Dinds, l.64. The fact that India is mentioned as the righteous country has no further significance. The inference that the frequent occurrence of the wonder-cows in Indian stories (as, for instance, that of Viçvamitra and Vasistha, Mahabharata, I, 175; IX, 40, and Rämäyana, I, 52–65) was known in medieval Ireland, would be unfounded at the present state of our knowledge.

31 Compare R.S. Loomis, op cit., p.171.

32 See line 474, 487. Thus it would seem that Fid Gaible is Ceasán's historical seat. Our story located him on its own account at Cell Eithne during the first part of his life in order to make him the teacher of the heroïne.

33 Compare the cry of Aengus at the death of Diarmuid O'Duibhne, *Tór Diram. 7 Gráinne*, II, p. 54.

34 See *Vita Tripartita*, pp.44, 54–60, 92, 130, 138. For conflicts of other saints with druids, see Plummer, *Vitae Sanct. Hib.* I, clvi sqq. and notes.

35 It should be noticed that to the two goblets of Aengus and Manannan a quest is attached; they were brought from India, the righteous land. This means another point of agreement. However, the connection is altogether different, the Grail Quest being accomplished by the hero himself.

CHAPTER 7

The Irish Element in King Arthur and the Grail

Arthur C.-L. Brown

It is no more a paradox to speak of the Irish element in King Arthur and the Grail than it would be to speak of the English element in Abraham Lincoln. Lincoln was not born until the United States had been for more than a quarter of a century independent of England. He never set foot on English soil, and yet it is obvious that nobody can understand the main traits of his character except by considering the traditions and the history of the English people. King Arthur was a Welshman. The story of King Arthur and the Grail came to the French and English from the Welsh, and, it is thought, from the Bretons of the northwest corner of France. The scene of Arthur's exploits was never in Ireland; and yet it is true that the spirit of the Arthurian romances is either of Irish origin, or is at least best preserved in Ireland, and that the original idea of the Grail can only be grasped by a knowledge of Irish romantic fiction.

Just how Irish story made its way to Wales is not very clear, but scholarly opinion now favors the idea that a great portion of Irish fable did reach the Welsh. The Welsh and the Bretons spoke a different language from the Irish, but the *Four Branches of the Mabinogi,* which are among the oldest Welsh prose tales, although, to be sure, they do not mention Arthur, have been proved to be full of Irish material. Probably Welsh bards were in the habit of serving apprenticeship under Irish teachers, and made it their business to imitate their Irish brethren; probably they adopted Irish romantic tales inserting Welsh characters and

Welsh place-names. Certain it is, to mention but an example or two, that Arthur's famous sword, Excalibur, derives both name and character from an Irish fairy sword, Caladbolg, and that the central incident of the English romance, *Sir Gawain and the Green Knight,* comes, even to the details of the dialogue, from a similar adventure of Cuchulinn which is known to us in the Irish saga called *Fled Bricrend.*

Welsh fairy-lore, of course, closely resembled Irish, so that it is usually difficult in the case of a particular story to tell whether we are dealing with parallel developments in Irish and Welsh, or whether the latter folk actually borrowed from the former. Since, however, we have very few Welsh and very many Irish medieval documents we are forced in practice to study the origin of medieval romance in Irish story. Some of the elements of the fairy background in the Arthurian romances may prove to be genuine Welsh and not Irish, but at least this mythological framework cannot be understood except by a study of the Irish material. Without pressing the point of ultimate origin we may, perhaps, speak of the source of medieval fairy machinery as to be found in Irish literature.

Fairy incidents and fairy personages, which form the chief Celtic contribution to Arthurian medieval romance, were able to engage the attention of men of the twelfth century because of a conception of the fairies which was peculiar to the Celts. The Irish fairies are of human shape and appearance, and except for being subject to the mysterious rules of fairyland, very much of human passion and behavior. When Connla, as a ninth century document tells us, was countered by one of the everliving ones, he knew that she was a fairy solely by her "wonderful garments." When John Connors today meets a fairy king near Killarney, he spends several hours in his company before he finds out that he is anything other than "a very well dressed gentleman."

In their human size and behavior the fairies of the Celts are unlike the humpbacked gnomes, the tiny elves, and gigantic trolls, that people the fancy of the rest of Europe. Because of their quite normal appearance Irish fairies easily entered Arthurian romances, the men becoming enchanters or magicians, and the women, ladies of all-compelling beauty who exacted from proud knights abject submission and service. This kind of lady

127

caught the fancy of the French *trouvères* of the twelfth century. It supplied them with the capricious, independent, and marvelously beautiful heroines whom they sought for their romances of chivalry. Small change was necessary to make these other-world ladies seem human; they were almost humanized from the beginning, and, already in ancient Irish story, were confused with the daughters of men in the sagas, and still more in the chronicles of Ireland, the fairies were tied up with historic people and events, and thus a step was taken toward transforming them into men and women. Probably this rationalizing went still further in Wales and suggested the almost complete rationalization of the French Arthurian romances.

It is not known whether the Welsh attached to the heroic figure of Arthur many fantastic tales which came from Ireland. They needed only to substitute for the names of unfamiliar Irish heroes those of Arthur and his warriors to give us actual Arthurian fiction such as appears in *Kulhwch and Olwen*. But *Kulhwch and Olwen* stands by itself, and, in the absence of any other genuine Welsh medieval Arthurian tales, it is possible to hold that the Welsh went but a little way towards building up a heroic legend about Arthur. Some scholars maintain a sceptical position, and believe that in Wales stories were told about various heroes, and that the authors of the French romances were the first to connect all these tales with Arthur, and thus to create the fabric of Arthurian romance. In any case, the plots, the patterns, so to speak, of Arthurian story were of Celtic origin.

Upon these Celtic patterns, French artists embroidered the rich texture of Arthurian romance. They changed warriors into knights, and fairy women into elegant ladies, and wove round them the fascination of courtly love; they bespangled the narratives with castles, tournaments, and brilliant armour; they introduced something of a deeper spirit of Christianity by picturing a new courtesy on the part of the great toward the oppressed and the poor. After the twelfth century ecclesiastical influences more and more altered many of the romances.

Thus the Arthurian legend consists of Irish and Welsh fairy and heroic tales transformed by French artists. Its most characteristic and striking feature is the fairy element, which has become dimmed or rationalized, and forms what I have called the background. This fairy background was not the invention of the logical and realistic French genius, but was an heritage that came to them from the fancy of the Celts. Medieval romance is nothing else than a combination of this fairy background with twelfth-century chivalry. The most characteristic element in French Arthurian romance is not of French origin at all. The glimpse that French romance gives us of an unearthly land; the hints that it affords of men and women of marvelous power and beauty (and without these, romance would not be what it is) had their home not in France but in Ireland.

The Irish conception of the Other World, the Plain of Delight, is easy to grasp. If we undertake to picture an imaginary world, an obvious thing to do is to suppose that we have got beneath a lake or sea, and there met with a people who are more delightful and splendid than we. These happy folk will of course have golden hair, and marvelous beauty. Their houses will be of snow-white marble, and their furniture of gold and silver. They will drink out of crystal cups, and spend their time in feasting, playing chess, and listening to music

From this imaginary world, all unpleasant things will be excluded. Because the acquisition and preparation of daily food is tiresome, these imaginary people will have dishes that supply food of themselves, and never-failing goblets of wine. Their chess-boards will be of glittering bronze, and their chessmen of pure gold. Their music will be of such sweetness as to throw a man into a sleep, or a swoon. Because ordinary warfare is perilous, and dreadful, these imaginary folk will have magic armour that protects them from wounds, talismanic spears, and swords that never fail to bring victory. When people are very happy, they do not note the passage of time; consequently in this imaginary world many years pass as one day. All of these characteristics are actually found in a number of Irish fairy stories which were written down at least a thousand years ago. For example, the details given above are in the *Adventures of Loegaire*, which is in a manuscript almost eight hundred years old.

The oldest Irish fairy stories consist essentially of a description of a land like this. In the *Adventures of Connla*, a supernatural damsel comes in a wonderful ship of glass, and carries the hero away forever to a superbly beautiful land where there is no death or decay. In the *Voyage of Bran*, the hero visits an island paradise where the inhabitants are beautiful damsels, and where everything in the way of food, music, and other delight is present. Everyone knows that the Arthurian romances likewise contain pictures of such a fairyland where all is happiness and joy. In the part of the Perceval attributed to Wauchier is an account of the Castle of the Maidens which under the guise of a medieval castle with towers and halls, tapestry and furniture, reproduces with but superficial transformation such a dream paradise.

Furthermore, in the so-called "Elucidation" attached to the Perceval, we read of a time when beautiful damsels dwelt by springs, or in hills, along the highroads, each with a golden goblet, and inexhaustible food, and drink, with which to regale the wayfarer. Britain, or Logres as it is called, was then indeed a land of fairy. The golden cup, which each fairy damsel possessed, was of course a cup of plenty, and as such a kind of prototype of the grail. In origin, perhaps, every fairy palace had its "grail," that is its vessel of abundance. That fairies possess never-failing cups is a commonplace of folk-lore. Many stories, not all of which are of Celtic origin, illustrating this folk-belief have been assembled by Hartland in his *Science of Fairy-Tales*. A good example is the story called "The Luck of Eden Hall," which relates how a butler once stole from a band of dancing fairies a magic cup that is still kept at Eden Hall in Northumberland. In calling these fairy cups "grails," I am well aware that the grail became more than a vessel of abundance. My point is simply that in the fairy cup-of-plenty lies the germ idea of the grail, and that, therefore, in a sense, every fairy castle had a grail.

Now the trouble with the kind of story we have been describing is obviously that in it nothing thrilling happens. A mortal man penetrates to fairyland, and tells us of its delight, but that is all. To make an interesting story, fairyland must be in trouble, and need to be delivered. It must be enchanted by wicked giants, and need to be freed from an evil spell.

Very early we find Irish stories in which fighting is necessary in the other world. In the *Serglige Conculaind* Cuchulinn is summoned to the other world in order to free it from three hostile giants who are troubling the land. As a reward for slaying the giants, Cuchulinn receives the hand of a fairy queen. A famous

130

example of this type of story in French romance is *Ivain,* by Chrétien de Troyes. Ivain, who was one of Arthur's knights, visits a marvelous land where, after slaying a huge antagonist called Esclados the Red, he marries a queen of supernatural beauty. In this type of story the hero is a well known warrior, and so cannot be left perpetually in fairyland, like Connla and Bran. Therefore, both Cuchulinn in the Irish *Serglige Conculaind,* and Ivain in the French romance, after a time, make their way back to earth. In this kind of story, the lady was at first a fairy who controlled the whole plot, and the warrior or warriors whom the mortal hero had to fight, were her creatures who fought only to test the hero's valor and strength. But already in both these stories, certainly in the French, the combat has become a real one, and the original fairy is regarded rather as a princess in the power of a giant, and needing to be delivered.

Out of this conception of a princess in the power of a giant, arises by a natural development the notion of a fairyland as enchanted, or in the power of one or more giants. A struggle is going on between two supernatural races. The kindly race of fairies needs the aid of a particular hero to effect its disenchantment and to gain a victory over its giant foes.

This situation is clearly depicted in *The Adventures of Loegaire,* a story which has already been referred to. Here a fairy king named Fiachna is in danger from a foe named Goll. Loegaire goes to fairyland, kills Goll, and as a reward receives Fiachna's daughter. In this story, however, the quest for a fairy bride has dropped into second place. The primary object of Loegaire's visit is to free fairyland from oppression or enchantment.

This type of plot, namely the delivery of a fairyland from enchantment by giants, manifestly affords plenty of dramatic action, and provokes more interest than the simple visit to fairyland with which we began. Fairy stories of this kind are well known in later Middle Irish, and modern Irish, literature. A good example is a story called "The Lad of the Ferule," which has been edited by Dr Douglas Hyde in the first volume of the *Irish Texts Society.* The hero, Murough, son of Brian Boru, was enticed down into fairyland in order to slay a giant who was oppressing the country. He slew the giant and returned, bringing with him a cauldron of plenty as a gift from fairyland.

This formula which is found in modern Irish story telling, is very old. A story plot of this kind evidently lies at the basis of a mythological tale in Irish which is called the *Battle of Moytura*. Although the account of the battle as we have it probably belongs to the twelfth century, numerous references to it in Irish historical books and other documents prove that it must be one of the oldest Irish stories. In fact the character of the story plainly takes it back to pagan times. The plot, to put it in a few words, is that the land of the Tuatha Dé Danaan (who are the same as the fairies) has been ruined by giants called Fomorians, and is saved by the coming of a supernatural hero, Lug. He is the destined deliverer and brings talismans which give him victory over the Fomorians, and enable him to deliver the fairies. In a story of this kind, the marvelous belongings of the fairies come into especial prominence. The notion is that a race of giants has brought enchantment upon the fairies by stealing their marvelous gear. These giants have carried off the fairy cup-of-plenty, the original object from which the "grail" developed, and have stolen or broken the resistless sword and spear. The destined hero recovers these talismans, one by one, and thus is able to slay the giants, and dispel the enchantment. The plot which has been just outlined is, I believe, a very old form of the grail plot.

It is noteworthy that a plot like this conjectural reconstruction of an older form of the grail story is preserved in the English *Sir Perceval*, which in the extant version is nearly two hundred years later than the oldest French grail romances. Unexpected chance has preserved with little alteration a primitive story in English, whereas in France the older stories, in consequence of having been displaced by the more elaborate narratives of Chrétien and his followers, were neglected and forgotten.

In the English *Sir Perceval* King Arthur has a cup of gold which when stolen leaves him powerless and in a kind of enchantment. The gold cup is not called a talisman, nor is it said that Arthur and his knights owe their courage and prosperity to it. Whoever wrote *Sir Perceval* did not grasp the thread of his plot and did not realize that the gold cup was a talisman. From the progress of the story, it may be inferred that the gold cup originally had talismanic powers. When it is gone, King Arthur says that he is "sick and sore," and that in all his land "there is no man worthy to be a knight." The sweeping statement proves that the cup was originally a talisman-of-prosperity, and as such a prototype of the grail. The cup is, however, a much simpler thing than the grail, and those scholars are not wrong who have called this English romance a Perceval story with no grail in it.

Nor is it surprising to find, as in *Sir Perceval*, that before the cup-of-plenty developed into a grail, Arthur was the lord of the cup. From *Kulhwch and Olwen* we know that the Welsh thought of Arthur as a fairy king, and gave him many talismanic weapons including the elfin sword Caletvwlch (Excalibur). From Layamon, we know that he had a wonderful round table. It was inevitable that stories would arise ascribing to such a monarch the possession of a fairy cup-of-plenty, and some such story, I conjecture, lies at the basis of the English *Sir Perceval*.

When the cup-of-plenty developed into the more mysterious thing called the grail, and became in French romances the central object in the story, Arthur could not remain the ruler of the cup, for that person must be depicted as enchanted and in need of rescue. In no grail romance is Arthur the grail king, although he is always related to him or interested in him. In the English *Sir Perceval*, it was possible for Arthur to be lord of the cup because his enchantment and consequent helplessness are so slurred over as to be almost unintelligible, and consequently do not clash with the current conception of him as a feudal king

In the English *Sir Perceval* then, we conclude that Arthur was in fact enchanted by a number of giant foes. The enchantment was the result of a battle in which Perceval's father had been slain. Victory depended upon the possession of three or four talismans: Perceval's spear, the Red Knight's armour, and King Arthur's golden cup. This cup is not specifically described, but after it has been stolen by the Red Knight we learn that Arthur and his land are left incapable of defence. The loss of the cup plunged him and his land into an enchantment. Like other enchanted people, like Dornröschen, like Tennyson's Sleeping Beauty, Arthur cannot help himself, but must wait until the destined hero with the talismanic spear comes and kills the giants. After Perceval has killed the Red Knight (who is no doubt the king of the giants) he puts on the red armour (which is evidently one of the talismans), and clad in this, fights and kills two more giants, Gollerotherame, and his brother. When the golden cup is carried back to Arthur by Gawain, Arthur recovers his courage and ability. He sets out at once to find Perceval, and since the giants are all dead, the exploits of Perceval have restored the land (no doubt originally fairyland) to a state of happiness

The English *Sir Perceval* is a story which has been confused by a series of narrators who did not understand the plot. An earlier form of the tale must have described a world of imaginary happiness and plenty which has been enchanted and oppressed by a race of hostile giants, and which was finally freed by a destined hero. This is a plot full of action and interest, Paradise must be lost in order that there may be a struggle to regain it. Perceval's battles to overthrow the giants give vigorous action to the story.

If King Arthur were represented as living in a palace of unimaginable splendor, fed with every food that he could desire from an unfailing grail, and able to repel all his foes by the aid of unconquerable talismans, there would be no real story. The dream would be purely descriptive. If, however, Arthur is pictured as in trouble; as having fallen into the power of hostile giants until such a time as a destined hero may free him; we get a struggle, a drama, something that can hold our interest. It is not said in the English *Sir Perceval* that King Arthur is enchanted, but it is said that Sir Perceval's mother was driven insane by one of the giants, and that she was cured only by a magic remedy which Perceval found in the giant's castle. This seems a hint that originally enchantment by the giants hung over the fairy people in the story, and was dispelled by Perceval. In the motive of enchantment, can be found an explanation for the wounded king, the weeping women, the waste land, and the general unhappy condition of the grail kingdom; features some or all of which occur in all the grail romances. The land is waste because it is enchanted, and the women are bewailing an evil spell that rests upon them and their country. Fairyland is in the power of giants, and only a destined hero can kill the giants, and recover the talismans upon which prosperity depends.

It is now possible to understand the importance which, in most of the stories, is attached to Perceval's failure to inquire about the grail. The people of the grail castle are enchanted. It is the essence of enchantment that those under it cannot help themselves. They must remain passive, like the sleeping beauty behind her thorny hedge, until after a hundred years, the destined prince arrives. The people in the grail castle, however eagerly they may desire to be freed from enchantment, must not suggest their wants to Perceval. This is why the grail people watch so eagerly to see whether Perceval will ask the question, and why they blame him so bitterly when he departs the first time, leaving the question unasked. If Perceval had asked why the lance bled, and whom the grail served, it would have broken the spell. They would have known that he intended to slay the giants and break the enchantment. Other ideas have no doubt entered the various forms of the grail story, but it seems to me that this is the original idea out of which the legend has grown up, and that it is best preserved in the English *Sir Perceval.**

In the "Elucidation," which has been already referred to, the idea of enchantment is also present. The happy time when fairy damsels served wandering knights out of golden cups came to an end. An evil folk wronged the fairies, and they and their cups-of-plenty were no longer found. The court of the Fisher King, that filled all the land with abundance, also vanished. This passage is of the utmost interest because here we find a French writer connecting the Fisher King (and the grail) with fairy cups-of-plenty. It is what we should expect if the grail has developed from a fairy cup-of-plenty. The "Elucidation" goes on to declare that by and by King Arthur's knights will come, to find once more the palace of the fisher king, and drive out the evil folk, so that all the maidens may dispense hospitality out of golden cups as before. The "Elucidation" agrees, therefore, with the English *Sir Perceval,* in referring to an enchantment, and in treating the grail as only one of a number of marvelous golden cups.

Wauchier's account is thought by many scholars to represent the oldest form of the grail story which exists in French. As we have it, however, it has been worked over after the time of Chrétien, and has been modified to suit Christian ideas. It tells, for example, that the bleeding lance is the lance of Longinus, with which Christ as he hung on the cross was smitten through the side. In this story, as in several others of the French grail

---

* See A.C.-L. Brown "The Grail and the English Sir Perceval," *Mod. Phil.* 16, 113; 17, 311; 18, 201; 12, 79.

stories, the hero, before arriving at the grail castle proper, meets with the "adventure of the demon-hand." He arrives at midnight at an empty chapel in the forest, where he takes refuge from a great storm. Suddenly a black and hideous hand comes through the window and extinguishes the light in the chapel. The hero flees from the chapel into the storm, and soon after comes to the grail castle.

The English *Sir Perceval* suggests an explanation for the demon-hand. It will be remembered that in this romance, King Arthur's golden cup was carried off by the Red Knight. A comparison of older stories shows that the Red Knight was a kind of snatching demon who haunts your palace and carries off your feast or a portion of your feast. In folk-tales it is not uncommon to have this snatching demon remain outside the house, so that those within see only his ugly hand coming through a window or the roof to seize and carry off the food. In the English *Sir Perceval,* as we have seen, this snatching demon was originally a hostile giant and his stealing a part of the king's feast was a symbol of the enchantment which he cast upon the king and his land.

The explanation which I offer for the story of the demon-hand (which in the French romance comes just before the visit to the grail castle) is that it is a snatching-demon-episode which has got separated from the description of the grail castle, and is told as an introduction. It is easy to see why the episode was separated. After the cup-of-plenty had developed into the more mysterious grail, it could not be represented as snatched away by a profane hand. Originally it was the grail itself that the demon-hand carried off, just as an uncanny foe snatched the golden cup in the English *Sir Perceval.* The description of the chapel of the demon-hand in Wauchier's version is very like that of the grail castle: "A great and fair chapel stood in the midst of the forest. The door was open, and within [the chapel] the altar stood, all bare with neither cloth nor covering thereon, but a great candle-stick wrought of gold that stood alone, and therein a tall taper that burned clearly and shed a great light around" — "Even as Gawain looked, lo! a hand black and hideous, nought so marvelous had he beheld before, came through the window, and took the taper, and extinguished the flame. Thereupon came a voice of lament so loud and so dire that it seemed as if the chapel itself rocked therefrom." Gawain's steed made a spring and carried his master away from the chapel. In a short time Gawain arrived at the grail castle where he heard a loud lamentation, (doubtless because of an enchantment from which the people suffered). Then he saw the grail, the bleeding lance, and the broken sword. The people of the castle gave the hero the sword, and asked him to mend it. When he could not do this, they knew that he was not the destined hero. Soon afterward he fell asleep, and he awoke the next morning, on a lofty cliff beside the sea, with no castle any longer in sight. He had been told that the sword had slain the lord of the castle who lay dead within, and that the kingdom of Logres was destroyed, and the country laid waste by a stroke of the sword. From the analogy of the English *Sir Perceval*, we may conclude that it was the giant of the demon-hand who had killed the knight and laid waste the land. The destined hero must repair the sword, slay therewith the giant, avenge the dead king, and thus make the land fruitful again.

Another French grail story is told by Manessier as a continuation to the *Perceval*. Like the story just outlined, it is preserved only in a form later than Chrétien, and has been altered by ecclesiastical interpolations, but it seems to give the original plot in tolerably consistent form. Here the grail king and his brother, Goon Desert, are at war with two foes, Espinogre and his nephew, Partinal. Goon Desert slew Espinogre. In revenge Partinal slew Goon Desert, but his sword broke. Goon Desert's body was brought to the grail castle, together with the broken sword. The grail king wounded himself accidentally with the pieces of the sword, and his wound might not be healed until Goon Desert's death was avenged. All this appears to be a rationalization of an enchantment which rests upon the land until the giant Partinal is slain. Savage tribes often believe that the prosperity of their land depends upon the health of their king; a belief that has been traced in ancient Ireland. Manessier relates a prophecy that a knight should come, repair the sword, and avenge the death of Goon Desert.

Manessier goes on to say that Perceval, when he sets out on the grail quest, comes first to the Chapel of the Black Hand which we are told has killed over four thousand knights. After many adventures he finds Partinal's castle, challenges him, cuts off his head, and carries it with him. At length he approaches the grail castle. As soon as the warders of the castle tell the king that a knight is approaching with a head hanging at his saddle-bow, the king springs to his feet and is cured of his wound. Partinal's head is stuck on a pike on the tower of the castle. After this there is no mention of enemies or danger. Without doubt the enchantment is ended, and the grail king is restored to his former splendor. Later Perceval himself becomes the grail king.

The grail story belongs to the oldest part of the Arthurian legend. It, and the main outlines of the Arthur story, have plots which can be pointed out in Ireland long before they are known anywhere else. We have, therefore, in the Arthur stories, material which is in part of Irish invention, although no doubt changed somewhat by the Welsh who transmitted it. Through the great stories of Arthur and the grail, the art of the Irish story-teller influenced all the literatures of western Europe.

The Medieval Quest

The Medieval Quest

With Part Two we move into the period when the stories of the Grail burst, literally, on the scene, and became, for the space of a hundred years, the most popular and often written about subject for the poets and romancers of the Middle Ages. Chrétien de Troyes, attached to the court of Marie de Champagne, already famous for his Arthurian stories of Lancelot, Erec and Cliges, chose for the subject of what was to be his final (unfinished) work, a story that he may well have heard on the lips of wandering Breton story-tellers, who had carried the stories of Arthur and his deeds from Celtic Britain into France and Gaul not long after his disappearance in the sixth century. The poem breaks off in the middle of a sentence, having told of Perceval's early adventures, as well as those of Sir Gawain, in pursuit of the Grail. Others took up his story within a year, expanding it to enormous lengths without bringing it to a satisfactory conclusion. The episode included here, in the translation of Roger Sherman and Laura Hibberd Loomis, describes Perceval's first visit to the Grail Castle, his failure to ask the all important Question, and the subsequent realization of the task that is to lead him on a series of adventures before he returns, once again, to the Castle.

Following on from this come two extracts from *The History of the Holy Grail* also sometimes known as the *Grand Saint Graal* or *Le Roman d'Estoire du Graal* by the thirteenth century Burgundian poet Robert de Borron. Drawing upon Christian apocryphal sources relating to Joseph of Arimathea and Pilate, de Borron places the origins of the Grail firmly within Christian tradition, identifying the sacred object specifically with the Cup of the Last Supper and the vessel in which some of Jesus' blood was later caught. Whether de Borron was the first to make this identification is unknown. He may have been copying from an earlier, now lost, source; but it is more than likely that he had come across the stories of the mysterious Grail, then circulating among the wandering *trouvères* and *conteurs* of the time, and that he chose to Christianize the story by adding in material from works such as *The Acts of Pilate* and the *Gospel of Nicodemus*. The two extracts given here are the rarely printed "Prologue" to the text, and an extensive extract from the opening of the poem, in which de Borron gives an account of the wonders that took place after the Crucifixion and the subsequent fate of the Grail and its guardians.

Next comes an extract from the Sixth Branch of *Perlesvaus* also known as *The High History of the Holy Grail*. Nothing is known of its author, though internal evidence suggests that it may have been written at Glastonbury, the Abbey famous for its Arthurian and Grail traditions. The text itself differs quite markedly from the others included here, including the fact that it brings Arthur himself more firmly into the picture as he witnesses a vision of the Grail that goes through five changes, none of which are described, as the mysteries of the Grail are such that ordinary men should not speak of them. There is indeed a dreamlike quality to this version of the story, with visits to Otherworldly islands and hints at a war between the Fisher King and the King of Castle Mortal — another aspect of the dark side of the Grail Family evidenced in characters such as Garlon, Amangons and Klingsor. The scene in which Perceval comes ashore from a mysterious ship, carrying a candelabra, and bringing the light of the Grail to the halls of Camelot reads like an Otherworldly visitation.

Branch Six deals with some of the adventures of Gawain, who in this romance plays a larger part than in many others. The entire section is a vivid parade of images, with Gawain wandering into first one astonishing scene then another. Here, as in several other texts, Gawain is associated with the Sword of John the Baptist, which may at one time have formed a separate, though related, story of Gawain's quest for this magical weapon. The episode of his battle with the giant, and his subsequent discovery of the king's dead son, who is then cooked and eaten by the inhabitants of the castle, reads like a distant memory of an ancient ritual, related here to the Christian Eucharist, but very different in kind. Gawain's own visit to the castle of the Fisher King follows, and here again the setting and the events that take place there are far more elaborate and symbolically strange than in any of the previous texts. *Perlesvaus* dates from the early part of the thirteenth century, but despite its obvious indebtedness to Chrétien's poem, it takes a very different direction, drawing much of its symbolism from the apocalyptic writings of the Abbot Joachim da Fiore, and the vision of the Book of Revelations. It is thus not only one of the most powerful of the Grail texts, but also the most purely mystical — as opposed to the theological dimension of works like the *Quest del Saint Graal* (see below) and the earlier writings of Robert de Borron.

Wolfram von Eschenbach's *Parzival*, which follows next in our sequence, is also full of highly charged symbolism, though derived mainly form Eastern sources. Despite its immense length — more than three times that of the original — Wolfram's poem actually follows the internal structure of Chrétien's earlier work closely. Wolfram differs in the immense amount of symbolic detail with which he elaborates on the theme of the earlier poem, extending it to more than three times its original length. In addition he includes lengthy accounts of the building of the Grail Temple, guarded by the "Templiessen," and in establishing a powerful opponent to the hero in the figure of Klingsor, an evil magician who castrates himself in imitation of the Wounded King, and who opposes the quest at every turn in the way, desiring to obtain the power of the Grail for himself. Wolfram also begins by telling the story of Parzival's parents, Gamuret and Hertzeloide, and in fact provides the hero with a half-brother, Feirefiz, the product of an earlier liaison between Gamuret and the Moorish Queen Belakane. Feirefiz is pied black and white, and at the end of the romance, having fallen in love with the Princess of the Grail, Repanse de Schoie, marries her and fathers a famous son — Prester John. Parzival has two sons by his wife Condwiramur, Kardeiss and Lohengrin, the Swan Knight, whose adventures are briefly related at the end of the poem. The extreme length and complexity of the work makes it difficult to summarize briefly, and as the work does follow the basic story line of the *Conte del Graal* I have not attempted to do so. The episode included here comes close to the middle of the story, where Parzival, worn out from his years of seeking, comes to the habitation of the hermit Trevrizent and pours out his heart to the wise old man. Much of his complaint is bitter, and directed towards an unfeeling deity. Trevrizent responds by explaining much of the true meaning of the Quest, and in setting the hero's feet upon the right path.

Another German Grail text, *Die Krone* (The Crown) follows. Its author, Heinrich von dem Türlin, knew Wolfram's work, but departed entirely from all previous Grail sources in making Gawain the central hero and Grail-winner. In this he may possibly have been drawing upon an even earlier source than that used by Chrétien — a source in which Gawain was indeed recognized as the rightful champion of the Grail. Certainly Gawain was a leading figure in Celtic tradition — and one of the earliest heroes mentioned in connection with Arthur. His subsequent demotion from hero to villain has been charted in my book *Gawain, Knight of the Goddess* in which I have shown that it was Gawain's association with more ancient, pagan beliefs that caused him to be replaced initially by Lancelot and later by Lancelot's son, Galahad, as the foremost of the Grail knights. The episode in which he reaches the Grail Chapel is one of the most powerful versions of these final mysteries. For many years this was the only part of this extraordinary work available in English; however it was recently translated and stands revealed as one of the more fascinating of the texts under discussion.

The *Vulgate Cycle* (nowadays known as the *Lancelot-Grail)* is the largest and most fully worked out version of the Arthurian myths to have survived. Dating from the middle of the thirteenth century, it covers the entire life and deeds of Arthur, relating all the events of the story to the central theme of the Quest. Beginning with the early history of the Grail, which follows the direction taken by Robert de Borron in its detailing of the events following the Crucifixion and the travels of the Grail, with its guardians, from the Holy Land to Britain, the cycle then treats of the early life of Arthur, his founding of the Round Table, the story of Merlin, and finally the begetting of Galahad and the events leading up to the Quest. The central story, from which the extract printed here is taken, concerns the search for the Grail itself, and its eventual discovery by the three successful knights: Galahad, Perceval and Bors. The tone of the romance is pious and it is larded with theological arguments and interpretations of every episode. This is not surprising as it was compiled, from already existing versions, by monks of the Cistercian Order, who saw in the popular romances of Arthur an opportunity to put forward many of the most powerful Christian teachings in a form that would reach the widest possible audience. The single master stroke of the cycle is the creation of Galahad. He is the son of Lancelot and the Grail princess, Elaine, and the engendering is brought about through a trick. Lancelot is made to believe he is summoned by Queen Guinevere, with whom he is in love; but it is Elaine he sleeps with, and upon whom he begets the child who will one day win the Grail. Thus out of the sinful love of Lancelot and Guinevere comes the birth of the Holy Knight — an extraordinary development of the story that was the work of a writer of genius. The episode included here deals with Lancelot's quest, an agonized search for a spiritual absolute that fails because, at bottom, he loves the Queen more than he loves God.

Sir Percyvelle of Galles, which follows here in its entirety, is a fourteenth century Middle English version of Chrétien's poem that preserves details from what may well have been the French poet's own source. As A.C.L. Brown points out in his essay on the Celtic sources of the Grail (Chapter 7), there are references that suggest links with the *Elucidation* (Chapter 4) and *Peredur* (Chapter 3), demonstrating the extraordinary tenacity of these ancient traditions to metamorphose through the ages, but still to retain some of their original shape and meaning. As early as line seven Percyvelle is said to have "drunk the water of the well," a possible reference to the magical wells in the *Elucidation.* As Brown also noted, the cup stolen from Arthur in this version of the story is the real focus of the quest. When it is gone Arthur is "sick and sore" and declares that no man is good enough to be made a knight. The suggestion is that Arthur is enchanted into a kind of stasis by the loss of the cup — a clear reference to the state of the Wounded King. There is little doubt, in fact, that Arthur himself once bore this title, and that the quest was not only to restore the Waste Land, but the whole of the Kingdom of Britain.

The final extract in this sequence of medieval texts comes from what is still the greatest single re-telling of the Arthurian cycle — Sir Thomas Malory's *Le Morte d'Arthur*. Printed in 1485 this work is a masterpiece of English prose and reads with all the verve and pace of a modern novel. Characterization and dialogue have a contemporary ring to them and whenever possible Malory allows the characters to speak for themselves. His source was the *Vulgate Cycle,* but he pared away all the theology, leaving the story to stand alone. He successfully shaped and adapted his sources to make something like a coherent whole out of widely divergent originals. Of Malory himself little or nothing is known for certain except for his own statement that he wrote the book while in prison. Several contenders for identification with this Malory have been put forward which, according to the argument one chooses to follow, make Malory either a political prisoner who fought on the losing side in the Wars of the Roses, or a criminal incarcerated for rape and theft. If the latter is the case then Malory must have written much of his book with extreme irony, as Arthur and his knights uphold very different standards. In effect the *Morte* is really a paean for the death of Chivalry, which its author (whoever he was) saw happening everywhere around him. The extracts printed here are from Books III and XVII respectively. The first deals with the cause of the Dolorous Blow, struck by the pagan knight Sir Balin who defends himself (unknowingly) with the sacred spear, which is one of the holy objects kept in the Chapel of the Grail. The second extract describes the final achieving of the Grail by Galahad, Perceval and Bors — a moving and powerful account of the experience of mystical rapture.

With this we reach the end of the selection of texts from this period when the Grail story was at its most popular and move on to three commentaries that look into the background of the works in question, and point towards some of the sources that influenced their authors. M. Gaster looks primarily to the East for inspiration, in particular the medieval romances of Alexander the Great, in which he sees a number of themes and descriptive passages that seem to have influenced the Grail story. He finds, in Alexander's journey to Paradise, several resonances not only for the descriptions of the Grail Temple, but also for the journey to the Holy City of Sarras, which, in the *Vulgate Cycle* and again in Malory's work, is the final destination of the Quest knights and the last resting place of the Grail.

This theme of oriental source material is taken up in the next article, by the distinguished orientalist Arthur Upham Pope, whose comparison of the thirteenth century poem *Der jungere Titurel,* attributed to Albrecht von Scharfenburg, with archeological and historical accounts of the Throne of Arches (Takht-i-Taqdis) a temple commissioned by the Persian-Sesanian king Chosroes II and built at Shiz, a sacred site deep in the mountains of Azerbaijan. The remarkable similarities between the actual sites and Albrecht's description of the Temple of the Grail certainly give pause for thought, and bring into focus some of the many questions relating to the actuality of many of the sites and events described in the medieval romances of the Grail.

The final chapter in this section is by Robert Jaffray and is concerned with two more sites associated with the mystical history of the Grail. These are Glastonbury in Somerset and Fécamp in Northern France. Both places have stories of the appearance of holy relics relating to the Crucifixion — the Cup of the Last Supper at Glastonbury, and some of the Holy Blood at Fécamp. Both places and their stories certainly influenced the writers and compilers of the Grail texts, and while the stories of Glastonbury are well known, those of Fécamp deserve to be better known, for the light they may well throw upon some of the more obscure corners of the Grail myth.

CHAPTER 8

Perceval: or
The Story of the Grail
by Chrétien de Troyes

TRANSLATED BY ROGER SHERMAN LOOMIS
AND LAURA HIBBARD LOOMIS

Perceval is brought up by his mother in the forest, where in ignorance of the ways of the world he happily hunts game with roughly made throwing spears. Then one day he meets three knights in the wood. Thinking them angels because of the brilliance of their armour, he questions them concerning their origin. Learning from them of Arthur's court and the institution of knighthood he vows to go there in search of adventure, and ignoring his mother's anguished request that he should remain with her he rides off on an ancient nag to find his way in the world of chivalry. Before he departs his mother gives him certain advice: always to give help to any women in distress, but take no more from them by way of reward than a kiss — though if one should also wish to give him a ring let him take that also. Also if he meets with anyone on the road he should not part from them without knowing their name, for those who conceal such things are of no good to anyone.

Armed with this advice, the first person Perceval encounters along the way is a beautiful woman in a scarlet pavilion, whose ring he takes and whom he kisses. He then proceeds to Arthur's court where he enters in time to witness the arrival of a red knight who spills wine in the queen's lap and carries off her golden cup. Still mindful of his mother's instructions Perceval pursues the knight, kills him and returns the cup to the queen — acquiring the red knight's armour

148

on the way by the simple expedient of cooking the body over a slow fire!

At the court he seeks training in knightly pursuits and then sets out on further adventures. The most important of these is when he arrives at the castle of the Fisher King, whom he finds presiding over a hall in which are four hundred men sitting round a fire while an old man lies upon a couch close by. The Fisher King presents Perceval with a Sword which he accepts unthinkingly. A procession passes through the hall, led by a squire carrying a spear from which blood drips upon the ground, followed by two squires each carrying a ten-branched candle-stick. After this comes a damsel carrying a "Grail" which blazes with a light so bright that it puts out the light of the candles and of the stars. Following her is another maiden carrying a Talleors (variously translated as meaning a dish, a bowl, a casket or a tabernacle). Perceval watches all this but fails to ask its meaning. He retires for the night and on waking finds the castle deserted. He sets out in search of the Fisher King and his people, but no sooner has he crossed the drawbridge than the whole castle vanishes. Perceval then encounters a damsel cradling the body of a knight in her arms and lamenting bitterly. She tells him that the Fisher King has long since received a wound in the thighs, which has never healed, though it might well have done so had Perceval asked about the procession of the Grail. She also informs him that the sword which he was given at the castle will break if he is not careful, but that in such a case he can restore it by dipping it in a lake near which its maker, the smith Trebuchet, dwells.

Returning to Arthur's court Perceval is upbraided by a hideous damsel who appears from nowhere to mock him for so foolishly failing to ask the Question which would have healed the king and made his country prosperous again. Determined to right this wrong, and to learn more of the mysterious Grail, Perceval sets forth again and after many adventures meets with a band of pilgrims who reproach him for bearing arms on Good Friday. Five years have passed since he left Arthur's court and in his eagerness to discover more about the Grail he has forgotten God. Perceval confesses his sins to a forest hermit and learns from him that his mother died of grief after he left her. He feels great remorse but has still not rediscovered the Castle of the Grail.

Here the story changes course to deal with the adventures of Gawain, whose quest is to free an imprisoned damsel. By way of reward she shows him an underground crypt where the Sword of Judas Maccabeus is kept. It is now called the Sword of the Strange Girdle

149

and we shall encounter it again in other of our texts. Continuing his adventures, which at this point have nothing to do with the Grail, Gawain is ferried over a rise to a magical Castle of Ladies where many damsels are held prisoner awaiting the one who will deliver or marry them, thus putting an end to the enchantments of the place. Gawain undergoes many trials and tests in this place, including the adventure of the Perilous Bed, which is so designed that anyone who sets foot upon it or attempts to lie down, is at once assailed by invisible opponents, who fling spears and fire arrows at him, and is then attacked by a lion. But Gawain overcomes them all and is proclaimed lord of the castle. (J.M.)

From *Perceval*

Then the monks, nuns, and all the others went their ways, and Perceval set forth, lance in rest, armed at all points as he had come there. All day he journeyed without meeting earthly creature or Christian man or woman to direct him. He did not cease to beseech the Lord, the sovereign Father, if it were His will, to grant that he might find his mother in life and health. He was still praying when he came at the bottom of a hill to a river. Gazing upon the deep and rapid water, he did not dare to descend into it but said: "Ah, Almighty God, if I could cross this stream, I believe I would find my mother, if she is still alive."

So he rode along the bank till he came to a cliff washed by the stream, so that he could not pass. Then he caught sight of a boat floating downstream and two men in it. He waited, expecting them to come up to him. But they stopped in the middle of the river and dropped anchor. The man in the bow had a line and was baiting his hook with a fish somewhat larger than a minnow. The knight, not knowing where to find passage, greeted them and asked: "Sirs, tell me if there is a ford or a bridge on this river?"

The fisherman answered: "No, brother, on my faith there is not for twenty leagues up or down a boat larger than this, which would not carry five men, and one cannot cross on horseback, for there is no ferry, bridge, or ford."

"Then tell me, in God's name, where I may find shelter."

The fisherman replied: "Indeed you will have need of that and more. I will myself give you lodging tonight. Ride up by the cleft in this rock, and when you have reached the top, you will see before you in a valley a house where I dwell, near the river and near the wood."

Without further pause the knight ascended, and at the top of the hill he gazed long ahead without seeing anything but sky and earth. He exclaimed: "What has brought me here? Stupidity and trickery. God bring shame on him today who sent me here! Truly he put me on the right path when he said that at the top I would spy a house! Fisherman, you foully deceived me if you spoke out of malice!"

At that instant he spied before him in a valley the top of a tower. One might seek as far as Beirut without finding one as noble or as well situated. It was square, built of dark stone, and flanked by two lesser towers. The hall stood in front of the tower, and before the hall an arcade. As the youth descended he confessed that the fisherman had given him good directions, and praised him and no longer called him a treacherous liar, since now he had found harborage. So he proceeded to the gate, before which there was a drawbridge lowered. As he crossed, four squires came to meet him; two removed his arms; a third let his horse away to give him fodder and oats; the fourth clad the youth in a scarlet mantle, fresh and new. Then they led him to the arcade, and be assured that none as splendid could be found as far as Limoges. There he waited till the lord of the castle sent two squires to fetch him, and he accompanied them to the square hall, which was as long as it was wide. In the middle he saw, sitting on a couch, a handsome nobleman with grizzled locks, on his head a sable cap, black as a mulberry, with a crimson lappet below and a robe of the same. He was reclining on his elbow, and in front of him a great fire of dry branches blazed between four columns. Four hundred men could seat themselves comfortably around it. The four strong columns which supported the hood of the fireplace were of massive bronze.

The squires brought the youth before his host and stood on either side of him. When the lord saw him approach, he promptly greeted him, saying: "Friend, do not take it amiss if I do not rise to meet you, but I cannot do so easily."

"In God's name, sire, do not speak of it, for, as God may give me joy and health, it does not offend me."

The nobleman raised himself with difficulty, as much as he could, and said: "Friend, draw nearer; do not be abashed but sit here at my side, for so l bid you."

As the youth sat beside him, the nobleman inquired: "Friend, from what place did you come today?"

"Sire, this morning I left the castle called Belrepeire."

"So help me God," exclaimed the nobleman, "you have had a long day's ride. You must have departed before the watchman blew his horn at dawn."

"No," the youth answered, "prime had already been rung, I assure you."

As they talked, a squire came in at the door, a sword suspended from his neck. He handed it to the rich host, who drew it halfway from the sheath and observed where it was forged, for it was written on the blade. He saw too that it was of such fine steel that it could not break save only in one peril which no one knew but him who had forged and tempered it. The squire who had brought it announced: "Sire, the fair-haired maiden, your beautiful niece, sends you this gift. You have never seen one lighter for its length and breadth. You may present it to whom you please, but my lady would be glad if you would bestow it where it would be well employed. He who forged it made only three, and he will die before he can make another."

At once the lord, taking the sword by the hangings, which were worth a great treasure, gave it to the newcomer. The pommel was of the best gold of Arabia or Greece, and the sheath was covered with Venetian gold embroidery. This richly mounted sword the lord gave to the youth, saying: "Good sir, this was destined for you, and I desire you to have it. Gird it on and then draw it."

The youth thanked him and fastened the girdle so that it was not too tight. Then he drew out the naked blade from the sheath and after holding it a little put it back. Rest assured that it became him well hanging at his side, and better still when gripped in his fist; and it surely seemed that it would do him knightly service in time of need. Looking about, he noted standing behind him around the brightly burning fire some squires, and he entrusted the sword to the keeping of the one who had charge of his arms. Then he returned to his seat beside the lord, who showed him great honour. The light of the candles was the brightest that one could find in any mansion.

While they were talking of this and that, a squire entered from a chamber, grasping by the middle a white lance, and passed between the fire and those seated on the couch. All present beheld the white lance and the white point, from which a drop of red blood ran down to the squire's hand. The youth who had arrived that night watched this marvel, but he refrained from asking what this meant, for he was mindful of the lesson which Gornemant gave him, warning him against too much speech, and he feared that if he asked, it would be considered rude. So he held his peace.

Then two other squires came in, right handsome, bearing in their hands candelabra of fine gold and niello work, and in each candelabrum were at least ten candles. A damsel came in with these squires, holding between her two hands a grail. She was beautiful, gracious, splendidly garbed, and as she entered with the grail in her hands, there was such a brilliant light that the candles lost their brightness, just as the stars do when the moon or the sun rises. After her came a damsel holding a carving platter of silver. The grail which preceded her was of refined gold; and it was set with precious stones of many kinds, the richest and the costliest that exist in the sea or in the earth. Without question those set in the grail surpassed all other jewels. Like the lance, these damsels passed before the couch and entered another chamber.

The youth watched them pass, but he did not dare to ask concerning the grail and whom one served with it, for he kept in his heart the words of the wise nobleman. I fear that harm will come of this, because I have heard say that one can be too silent as well as be too loquacious. But, for better or for worse, the youth put no question.

The lord then ordered the water to be brought and the cloths to be spread, and this was done by those whose duty and custom it was. The lord and his guest washed their hands with moderately warm water. Two squires brought a wide table top of ivory, which, according to the story was all of a piece, and they held it a moment before the lord and the youth, till two other squires came bringing trestles. The wood of which they were made possessed two virtues which made them last forever. Of what were they made? Of ebony. What is the property of that wood? It cannot rot and it cannot burn; these two dangers it does not heed. The table top was placed on the trestles, and the cloth was laid. What should I say of the cloth? No legate, cardinal, or even pope ever ate on one so white.

The first course was a haunch of venison, peppered and cooked in grease. There was no lack of clear wine or grape juice to drink from a cup of gold. Before them a squire carved the peppered venison which he had set on a silver carving platter, and then he placed the slices on large pieces of bread in front of them.

Meanwhile the grail passed again before them, and still the youth did not ask concerning the grail, whom one served with it. He restrained himself because the nobleman had so gently charged him not to speak too much, and he had treasured this in his heart and remembered it. But he was silent longer than was proper, for as each course was served, he saw the grail pass before him in plain view, and did not learn whom one served with it though he would have liked much to know. Instead he said to himself that he would really ask one of the squires of the court before he departed, but would wait till the morning when he took leave of the lord and his attendants. So he postponed the matter and put his mind on eating and drinking, in no stingy fashion were the delicious viands and wines brought to the table. The food was excellent; indeed, all the courses that king or count or emperor are wont to have were served to that noble and the youth that night.

After the repast the two passed the evening in talk, while the squire made up the beds for the night and prepared the rarest fruits: dates, figs, nutmegs, cloves, pomegranates, electuaries, gingerbread of Alexandria, aromatic jelly, and so forth. Afterwards they had many draughts of piment without honey or pepper, mulberry wine, and clear syrup. At all this the youth wondered, for he had never experienced the like. At last the nobleman said: "Friend, it is time to go to bed, and do not take it ill that I depart to my chamber to sleep. And when you please, you may lie here. Because of my infirmity I must be carried."

Four nimble and strong servants came out of a chamber, took hold by the four corners the coverlet of the couch on which the nobleman was lying, and carried him away. Other squires remained with the youth to serve him as was needed. When he wished, they removed his hose and other clothing and put him to bed in white linen sheets.

He slept till break of day, but the household had already risen. When he looked about, he saw no one, and was obliged to get up alone; though he was annoyed, he rose since he must, drew on hose without help, and took his arms, which he found at the head of the dais, where they had been brought. When he had armed himself well, he walked past the doors of chambers which he had seen open the night before. But all in vain, for he found them closed. He shouted and knocked. No one opened; there was no response. When he had called long enough, he went to the door of the hall, found it open, descended the steps, and found his horse saddled and his lance and shield leaning against the wall. He then mounted and searched about the courtyard, but saw neither servant nor squire. He rode to the gate and found the drawbridge lowered, for it had been so left that nothing should prevent him from passing it freely at any hour. Then he thought, since the bridge was down, that the squires must have gone into the forest to examine the nets and traps. So, having no reason to wait longer, he said to himself that he would follow after them and learn, if possible, from one of them why the lance bled and whither the grail was carried. He passed out through the gate, but before he had crossed the drawbridge, he felt that the feet of his horse were rising, and the animal made a great leap, and if he had not done so, both he and his rider would have come to grief. The youth turned his head to see what had happened and perceived that someone had raised the drawbridge. He called out, but no one answered.

"Speak," said he, "you who have raised the bridge! Speak to me! Where are you, for I do not see you? Show yourself, and I would ask you a question."

Thus he wasted his words, for no one would reply. So he rode toward the forest and entered on a path where there were fresh hoofprints of horses. "This is the way," said he to himself, "which the men I am seeking have taken."

Then he galloped through the forest as long as the track

155

lasted, until he spied by chance a maiden under an oak tree, crying and lamenting in her distress. "Alas, wretch that I am, in an evil hour was I born! Cursed be that hour and that in which I was begotten! Never before has anything happened to enrage me so. Would that God had not pleased to make me hold my dead lover in my arms! He would have done better to let me die and let my lover live. O Death, why did you take his soul rather than mine? When I see him whom I loved best dead, what is life worth? Without him I care nothing for my life and my body. Death, cast out my soul that it may, if his soul deigns to accept it, be its handmaid and companion."

Thus she was mourning over the headless body of a knight which she clasped. The youth did not stop when he saw her, but approached and greeted her. She returned his greeting with head lowered, but did not cease her lament. The youth asked: "Who killed this knight who lies in your lap?"

"Good sir," the maiden replied, "a knight killed him this very morning. But one thing I see which amazes me. For people say that one may ride twenty-five leagues in the direction from which you came without finding an honest and clean lodging place, and yet your horse's flanks are smooth and his hide is curried. Whoever it was who washed and combed him, fed him on oats and bedded him with hay, the beast could not have a fuller belly and a neater hide. And you yourself look as if you had enjoyed a night of comfortable repose."

"By my faith, fair lady," said he, "I had indeed as much comfort last night as was possible, and if it appears so, there is good reason. If anyone gave a loud shout here where we are, it would be heard clearly where I lay last night. You cannot know this country well, for without doubt I have had the best lodging I ever enjoyed."

"Ah, sir, did you lie then at the dwelling of the rich Fisher King?"

"Maiden, by the Saviour, I do not know if he is fisherman or king, but he is very rich and courteous. I can say no more than that late last evening I met two men floating slowly in a boat. One was rowing, the other was fishing with a hook, and he directed me to his house and there gave me lodging."

The maiden said: "Good sir, he is a king, I assure you, but he was wounded and maimed in a battle so that he cannot move himself, for a javelin wounded him through the two thighs. He is still in such pain that he cannot mount a horse, but when he wishes to divert himself, he has himself placed in a boat and goes fishing with a hook; therefore he is called the Fisher King. He can endure no other pastime, neither hunting nor hawking, but he has his fowlers, archers, and huntsmen to pursue game in his forests. Therefore he enjoys this place; in all the world no better dwelling could be found for his purposes, and he has built a mansion befitting a rich king."

"Damsel," said he, "by my faith, what you say is true, for last evening I was filled with wonder as soon as I came before him. I stood at a little distance, but he told me to come and sit beside him, and bade me not think that he did not rise out of pride, for he had not the strength."

"Surely he did you a great honour when he seated you beside him. Tell me, when you were sitting there, did you see the lance of which the point bleeds, though there is no flesh or vein there?"

"Did I see it? Yes, by my faith."

"Did you ask why it bled?"

"I said nothing about it."

"So help me God, learn, then, that you have done ill. Did you see the grail?"

"Yes, indeed."

"And who held it?"

"A maiden."

"And whence did she come?"

"From a chamber."

"Whither did she go?"

"Into another chamber."

"Did no one precede the grail?"

"Yes."

"Who?"

"Only two squires."

"What did they hold in their hands?"

"Candelabra full of candles."

"Who came after the grail?"

"Another maiden."

"What did she hold?"

"A little carving dish of silver."

"Did you not ask anyone where they were going?"

"No question came from my mouth."

"So help me God, that was worse. What is your name, friend?"

Then he who did not know his name divined it and said that his name was Perceval of Wales. He did not know whether he told the truth or not, but it was the truth though he did not know it. When the damsel heard it, she rose and faced him, saying angrily: "Your name is changed, good friend."

"What is it?"

"Perceval the wretched! Ah, unfortunate Perceval, how unlucky it was that you did not ask all those things! For you would have cured the maimed King, so that he would have recovered the use of his limbs and would have ruled his lands and great good would have come of it! But now you must know that much misery will come upon you and others. This has happened to you, understand, because of your sin against your mother; she has died of grief for you. I know you better than you know me, for you do not know who I am. I was reared with you in the house of your mother long ago. I am your first cousin and you are mine. I grieve no less because you have had the misfortune not to learn what is done with the grail and to whom it is carried than because of the death of your mother or because of this knight whom I loved dearly, seeing he called me his dear mistress and loved me as a brave and loyal knight."

"Ah, cousin," said Perceval, "if what you say is true, tell me how you know it."

"I know it," the damsel answered, "as truly as one who saw her laid in the earth."

"Now may God of his goodness have mercy on her soul!" cried Perceval. "It is a sorrowful tale you have told. Now that she is laid in earth, what is there left for me to seek? For I was journeying only to see her. I must now take another road. If you are willing to accompany me, I should be pleased. He who lies dead here can no longer serve you, I warrant. The dead to the dead, the living to the living. Let us go together, for it seems very foolish for you to watch here alone over this body. Let us pursue the slayer, and I promise and swear that, if I overtake him, either he will force me to surrender, or I will force him."

She, unable to suppress the great woe in her heart, said:

"Good friend, I cannot go with you or leave my lover until I have buried him. If you listen to me, follow this paved road, since it is by this way that the evil, insolent knight who killed my sweet lover departed. So help me God, I have not said this because I wish you to pursue him, though I wish him as much harm as if he had slain me. But where did you get the sword which hangs at your left side and which has never drawn blood and has never been unsheathed in the hour of need? I know well where it was forged and by whom. Do not trust it, for it will betray you in battle and fly in pieces."

"Fair cousin, one of the nieces of my good host sent it to him last evening, and he gave it to me, and I was well pleased. But you terrify me if what you have said is true. Tell me now, if you know: if the sword should break, will it ever be repaired?"

"Yes, but with much hardship. If one could find the way to the lake which is near the Firth of Forth, he could have it hammered, tempered, and made whole again. If chance should take you there, go to a smith called Trebuchet, because he made it and will reforge it; it can be done by no other man."

"Surely," said Perceval, "if it breaks, I shall be in grievous peril."

CHAPTER 9

The History of the Holy Grail

Robert de Borron

*The author begins by stating that the tale he is about to tell is taken
from a book which was given to him by Our Lord Himself, in Brittany,
717 years after His Passion. The narrative begins with Joseph of
Arimathea and corresponds in its main points with the commencement
of Borron's Joseph; but with a different treatment of details. It relates
that Joseph and a number of converts took the Holy Dish (i.e. the dish
of the Paschal Supper) in a wooden ark and travelled to Sarras "between Babiloine and Salemandre," whence the Saracens came, and
where Evalach reigned; and also how the latter was converted to
Christianity through the efforts of Josephes, the son of Joseph, who had
been consecrated there as a Bishop by Jesus Christ in a wonderful
ceremony which had revealed the presence of the relics of the Passion
in the ark which he had brought with him. A description is given of
Evalach's successful fight against Tholomers, King of Egypt, through
the Almighty's aid, and the conversion of Séraphe, the brother-in-law
of Evalach. After baptism, Evalach was called Mordrains, and Séraphe
Nasciens. It is then related that Mordrains undertook the forcible conversion of his subjects, and that Josephes, engaging in physical combat,
was wounded in the thigh by an angel carrying a lance, the head of
which remained in the wound. Josephes was told he should have confined himself to spiritual work.*

*The story then states that Josephes showed the ark and the Holy
Vessel to Mordrains and Nasciens, and that the latter referred to it as
the Grail, making use of a play upon words similar to that which is
contained in Borron's Joseph. An angel appeared, drew out the lance-
head, and foretold the wonderful adventures which would come to them
in the lands where God would lead them — all connected with the
lance and the Holy Grail. The marvels of the Grail would only be seen*

160

thereafter by one man who would be the last of Nascien's race; and the lance would later wound also a King descended from Josephes, who would be healed when the good knight, descended from Nasciens might learn to know the wonders of the Holy Grail. The angel's message connected the lance symbolically with the one which pierced the side of Our Lord on the Cross.

After this there is a long section covering some wonderful adventures which befell Mordrains and Nasciens, including a prophetical dream of Mordrains in relation to the descent of the Grail knight from Nasciens. Mordrains and Nasciens were each conveyed by supernatural power to separate distant islands. Nasciens discovered there a ship without captain or crew. He found therein among other wonderful things a mysterious sword with strange hangings lying on a bed, which could only be used by one who surpassed all other men in goodness and bravery. A long explanation follows to show that the sword was David's and that the ship had been built by Solomon.

Celidoine, the son of Nasciens, joined his father and they set sail in Solomon's ship, being afterwards joined by Mordrains; and a variety of adventures follow.

The story then relates that Joseph, Josephes, and their followers had gone to Great Britain with the Holy Grail. They had crossed from the Continent on the shirt of Josephes which miraculously sustained them on the water. Mention is made of the birth of a son to Joseph, who receives the name of Galahad. After sundry adventures Joseph went to preach in Norgales (North Wales), taking the Holy Grail with him. There he and his companion were imprisoned by King Crudel. King Mordrains, being warned by a dream of Joseph's troubles, took ship and went to his assistance. He finally arrived in Great Britain, and rescued Joseph and his friends. The next day while Josephes was officiating as a priest before the Grail, Mordrains was moved by curiosity to come too near and was stricken by blindness and paralysis. A voice told him that when the Good Knight should come he would be healed. He retired to a monastery to await this event, and after many years Perceval le Gallois and Galahad saw him there.

In the course of Josephes' travels he was one day sitting at the table with his companions; and the Grail was placed thereon. One seat was left vacant between Josephes and Brons to represent the seat occupied by the Saviour at the Last Supper. Moys attempted to occupy this seat but was carried away in flames by mysterious hands.

One of Brons' twelve sons, Alain le Gros, choosing to remain *unmarried, was allotted to the service of the Grail, and was to be Grail Keeper after Josephes' death. One day, at Josephes' orders, Alain caught a fish which miraculously sufficed to feed many; and he was called the Rich Fisher; and all Grail Keepers would hereafter bear this title. In the course of his travels Josephes was seized by some heathen, and wounded by a sword which broke, leaving its point in the wound; but Josephes withdrew the point, and said the sword should not be mended except by him who should gain the Perilous Seat in the time of King Arthur. Joseph's son Galahad became king of Cocelice (Hocelice), and reigned so well that the name of the kingdom was afterwards called Gales (Wales) after him.*

The deaths of Joseph and Josephes are related — both being buried in Scotland — the former in the Abbey of Glays — and Alain took charge of the Grail, for which a castle was built, called Corbenic.

After Alain's death his brother Josue became Grail Keeper. One of his successors was Pellehans, called the Maimed King because he was wounded in battle in the two thighs. He could not be healed until the good knight Galahad should come. Pellehans was followed by his son Pelles, from whose daughter Lancelot begat Galahad, born out of wedlock. (R.J.)

1. The History of the Holy Grail
(prologue and introduction)

TRANSLATED BY ADRIAN PATERSON*

He who cleaveth to and judgeth the least and the sinfullest of this world extendeth greeting at the beginning of this story to all those whose hearts and faith are in the Holy Trinity, which is the Father, which is the Son, which is the Holy Ghost — The

---

* From the twelfth century French of the Sire Robert de Borron. Originally published in: *Studies in Comparative Religion,* vol. 8. no.1, Winter, 1974. This medieval French text, together with a Middle English translation done in the reign of Henry VI, was published in London in 1861 by the Roxburgh Club and again in 1874 by the Early English Text society. But in both these editions the Prologue and the Introduction are given in the French only, for the sole surviving manuscript of the English version, now in the library of Corpus Christi College, Cambridge, is defective at the beginning.

Father by whom all things are established and receive the beginnings of life — the Son by whom all things are delivered from the torments of Hell and brought back to the joy which lasteth forever — the Holy Ghost by whom all things escape from the hands of the evil spirit and are filled with joy by the illumination of Him who is the True Enlightener and the True Comforter. The name of him who writeth this story is not named nor clarified from the beginning, but from the words which shall follow will a large number perceive what his name is, the country where he was born and a great part of his descent. But at the beginning he wisheth not to disclose himself, and for this he hath three reasons. The first is that if he named himself and said that God had discovered through him so high a story as that of the Holy Grail which is the highest story that there can be, the wicked and the envious would turn on him in their baseness. The other reason is that some could hear of his name who knew him and would think less of the story because so wretched a person had put it into writing. The other reason is that if he had put his name to the story and someone found something misrelated by fault of bad scribe who afterwards might transcribe it from one book into another, they would put all the blame on his name; for in all times there are more mouths that speak ill than good and more is one man blamed for one single ill than he is praised for a hundred goodnesses; and for that reason he does not wish that his name shall be too soon discovered. But whatever he may wish to happen in this, he will be sooner found out than he would like it. But he will tell openly very soon how he was bidden make the story of the Holy Grail manifest.

It happened on the 717th year after the passion of our Lord Jesus Christ, that I, most sinful of all sinners, was in the wildest place that I ever wish to get to know of and removed from all Christian peoples. But besides telling that the place was very wild I should also say that it was very pleasant and full of delights, for a man who wholly belongeth to God seeth all secular things by opposites. I was sitting thus in the place you have heard me mention on the Thursday in Holy Week and when Good Friday came I had said the service pleasing to our Lord which is called Tenebrae; then a great desire for sleep seized me and I began to slumber, but it did not last long before

163

a voice called me four times by my name. It said to me — "Wake thyself and understand in one thing three and from three things one and as much can the One as the Three." At once I woke up and saw so great a brightness that never before saw I so great a one. And then I saw before me the most beautiful man that there ever was and when I saw Him I was amazed and knew not what to say nor to do, and He said to me — "Understandest thou the words that I have spoken to thee?" and I answered Him fearfully, "Sire, I am not yet wholly certain of it;" and He saith to me, "It is the recognition of the Trinity that I have brought to thee; and it is because of this," He went on, "that thou hast been in doubt whether the Trinity has three Persons and they only one Godhead and one Power." "Never have I had doubts excepting only in this one point." And again He saith to me: "Canst thou understand and perceive who I am?" and I answered to Him that my eye was a mortal one and that it could not behold so great a brightness, nor am I yet capable of saying what all mortal languages had difficulty in expressing. And He bent Himself towards me and He breathed freely into my face and then was I aware that I had eyes a hundredfold more clear than I had before and I felt before my mouth a great miracle of tongues. And He said to me — "Canst thou still not understand nor know who I am?" and when I wished to speak to Him I saw a great flame of fire which leapt from the midst of my mouth. I was so much afraid that I could say never a word; and He said — "Be not afraid. I am the Fountain of Wisdom. I am that One to whom Nicodemus said 'Master, we know who you are.' I am He of whom the Scripture saith 'All Wisdom cometh from our Lord.' I am the perfect Master. I am come to thee because I wish that thou receive instruction in all things in which thou doubtest; and I will make thee certain and through thee will it be exposed to all those that shall hear it told." After these words He took me by the hand and gave me a book which was in no direction larger than the palm of a man's hand and when He had given it to me He said that He had given me in that book so great a wonder that no mortal heart could think nor know one greater. "Nor ever wilt thou be in doubt of any thing but thou be able to confirm it in this book and herein are my secrets which no man may behold if he is not first cleansed by true confession and in such a way

I tell it as by the language of the heart and as with a closed mouth and no words, for it cannot be named by mortal language without the four elements being disturbed by it, for the Heavens will weep at it, the air become troubled at it, the earth collapse through it and the water change its colour by it — all this is this manual and herein is more still, for if a man shall behold it in perfect faith it shall profit both the soul and the body, for never shall man be so in error if he look therein but he will not also be full of a greater joy than any man can devise nor ever, whatever sin he may have committed in this century, shall he die a sudden death; this is the Way of Life;" and when he had said this, a voice loud as thunder cried out and when it had cried out, there came a noise so great from above that in my opinion the firmament was crumbling and the Earth had collapsed and if the light before had been great, now it was a hundred times more bright for I thought I had lost my sight by it and there I lay on the earth as if in a swoon and when this emptiness of head was passed I opened my eyes and I saw about me nothing of what I had seen before and I was holding it all a dream until I found in my hand the small book just as the Great Master had put it there.

Then I rose up very happy and rejoicing greatly and I set myself to prayer and orison and I yearned very much for the day to come; and when it was day, I began to read and found the beginning of my lineage which I had very much wanted to see and when I had looked at it much I marvelled how in so small a book there could be so many words and thus I looked through a third of the book until I had found a great part of my lineage and I saw there the lives and the names of all that I scarcely dared say I knew not that I was descended from them and when I saw their good lives and the travail that they had suffered on earth for the Creator, I could not think how I could so amend my soul as to be worthy to be led back to them, nor was I aware of being a man in my relationship to them, but only the features of a man.

When I had thought this over for a long time, I looked before me and saw that there was written "Here beginneth the Holy Grail" and when I had read so much that midday was passed, I found "Here beginneth the Great Fear." I then read on so much that I saw many terrible things and God knoweth that I had great doubts in seeing them nor would I have dared to see them if this had not been commanded me by Him by Whom all things are commanded and governed; and when I had seen this, I began to think very hard and as I was thinking this I saw a ray as a burning fire and it descended from heaven and came before my eyes like lightning and it was very like a clap of thunder so the brightness was great and lasted long; and then it appeared before my eyes so that my whole eye glittered through it and then fell I in a swoon and when it pleased our Lord again, I knew He lifted me up and afterwards I saw such a great obscurity that one could see nothing more than one can see on the darkest night of winter and this darkness lasted the time to take a hundred steps. Then it pleased God that the darkness should pass away and it grew lighter little by little until the sun returned to his former brightness. Afterwards there came where I was such a sweet scent as if all the spices of the world had been strewn there and after this I heard the gentlest song which was ever sung; and those who sang were so close to me that I felt they were visible things and as if I could touch them with my hands, but I could see none of them but well I understood that they praised our Lord and they said towards the end of their song "Glory and honour be prepared to the Restorer of Life and the Destroyer of Death." This praise I heard quite well, but in all the rest I heard nothing of it and afterwards they sounded a clarion of bells and when they had ceased to sound it, they began their song again. Seven times did their voices sing in this way; at the eighth song it broke so that I was aware that they sank below and then was I aware that the wings of all the birds of the world were passing before me and when the voices had departed, then the great fragrance which I had smelt before and which had so pleased me returned. Then the singing began again and I began to think of this great marvel when I heard a voice which said to me — "Leave thy thoughts and render what thou owest to thy Creator." Then I rose and saw that the Nones of the day was past and I marvelled greatly, for I thought it was still morning because I had looked so long at the book which pleased me very much. Then I began the service of our Lord as it is laid down for that day on which He died for us and wherefore one communeth not for the figure must be reversed until Sunday and on Good Friday one does not hallow it since it would have no meaning on the same day on which He was sacrificed on the Cross: and when with the help of God I had finished this and wished to receive my Saviour, an angel took me by the two hands and told me — "These three persons are due to be received by you; therefore I shall make you understand what they mean and in this beyond certainty." At this word he raised me aloft and carried me to a place where if all mortal tongues spoke and all hearts and ears listened to them, they would not any of them understand such great joys without receiving from them an hundredfold as great ones again and if I said this was in the third heaven where St Paul was carried, l should not be intending to lie. But I do no dare to boast of it, though I can well say that there was shown to me the sceptre of which Paul saith no mortal tongue may reveal it and when I had seen such great marvels, then the angel carried me and said to me — "Hast thou seen great marvels?" and I said that I never thought such great ones could exist and he said to me that he would show me even greater ones. Then he took me and carried me again to another stage which was a hundred times more clear to behold. This was more coloured than any heart could devise, and there he showed me the power of the Trinity openly, and I saw them separately the Father, the Son and the Holy Ghost, and I saw that these three persons belonged to one deity and one person and yet I say that I saw there three persons, one separated from the other; wherefore I shall enrage the envious whose only work is to blame others and who will say that I go against the authority of St John, the high evangelist, who saith that never mortal man saw the Father nor ever shall be able to, with which I am in complete accord. But all those who have listened to this have not heard it well, for there he speaketh of mortal man, but once the soul is separated from the body it is therefore a thing spiritual and well can look upon the Father; and while I was beholding this great marvel, there came a thunderclap and after this thunderclap came half again as many celestial things as before and I lay again as in a swoon. There I saw so great a marvel that I cannot tell of it. In due course the angel took me and brought me back to that place where he had taken me from and he said to me before he returned my spirit to its body that I had seen many marvels; and I replied to him that there was no mortal who if he heard it told would not hold it for a lie, and he said to me "Art thou still not very certain of what thou hast been in doubt about?" and I said to him that there was no man in the world how disbelieving soever whom, if he could listen to me, I would not make understand clearly how all the points of the Trinity are, because I have seen it and learnt it. Then he put my spirit back into my body and told me that from that time onwards I was never again to be in doubt and I leaped as one who wakes up and I thought to see the angel but he was already gone and I looked about me and saw my saviour before me and in the same manner as before the angel had taken me away; it shone in good faith. Then I took the manual and placed it in the place where the sacrament was for it was a very beautiful place and a proper one; and when I had gone out from the Chapel, I saw that it was near night time and then I entered into my house and ate there such food as God had given to me.

And so passed that day and the night all until the day of the Resurrection of the Saviour and when it had pleased Him that I had done the service of that day which is as high as the day of our salvation, as He Himself who made the day holy, I make a pledge that I should hasten to the book for its good words rather than take any meat, for so sweet were the words that they made me forget my hunger and when I came to the chest where I had put the small book, it was nowhere to be found there and when I saw this I was much grieved and knew not what to do and I marvelled how it could have got taken away from that place, for I had found it shut as before and as I was in this manner a voice said to me — "What dost thou marvel at? In such a way did Jesus Christ rise from the tomb without opening it, but comfort thyself and go and take food for it behoves thee to suffer before thou canst have the book back;" and when I heard that I would have it again I held myself well paid. I went and ate and when I had eaten I prayed to our Lord that He would give me possession of what I desired. Then a voice said to me, "This the High Master biddeth thee. Tomorrow when thou hast sung the Mass, thou shalt go and eat and then thou shalt set out upon Jesus Christ's business, and when thou hast left this place, thou shalt go by the path which leadeth to the high-road; and this road will lead thee until thou comest to the 'Siegestone.' Then thou shalt abandon that road and go at once along a path which will lead thee to a crossroads of seven ways which is on the plain of the 'Bewildered Vale' and when thou comest to the 'Fountain of Grief' there where the Great Slaughter lately was, thou shalt find a beast whose like thou hast never seen before. Here see to it that thou follow wherever it shall lead thee; and when thou hast lost it in the Land of Negnes, there shalt thou finish thy wanderings and there shalt thou know why the Great Master has sent thee thither."

Then the voice stopped speaking; and I rose on the morrow and sang mass and then I breakfasted and made the sign of the Holy Cross upon myself and upon my habitation. Then I set out all alone just as the voice had told me and when I had passed the sward, I went on until I came to the valley of the Dead. That Valley I should know well because I had been there before and had seen there a battle between two of the best knights whom one knoweth of in any land. Then I continued until I came to the crossroads. There I looked about me and saw a cross at the edge of the fountain and under this cross there knelt that beast which the voice had told me of and when it saw me, it rose and looked at me for a long time and I at it. But the more I looked at it, the more I marvelled at it, for it was different from all other beasts, for it was white as new snow and had the head and neck of a sheep; it had the feet of a dog and the thighs of one which were black as coal; and it had the breast, the hindquarters and the body of a wolf and the tail of a lion. Thus diverse was the beast and when I had sufficiently looked at it, I signalled it to go before and it entered the first way which it found on the right and we continued until evening began to set in and then it turned through a thick dingle and I after it and so we wandered on until it was night and then we came out of the heath and entered into a forest high and deep and when we were at the bottom of a valley, there saw I a lodge. I was very glad thereat. For I saw in it a man who was dressed in religious vestures and when he saw me he took off his hood and knelt before me. And I raised him up and told him that I too was a sinner like himself and could not give him the blessing; and what more shall I say; he would not rise in my presence before I had given him the blessing. Whereat I was very heavy of heart for I was not worthy to give benediction, and when I had given it him, he lead me by the hand into his lodge and when we had eaten he asked me much about myself for the goodman thought there was more good in me than there was and I answered him from beginning to end. In the morning the goodman implored me to sing his mass and I did it. Afterwards I started on my way and he escorted me and when we were outside the gateway then saw I the beast which had led me and I had not seen it before I had first seen the goodman in the evening. Then I started on my way and my wanderings and the goodman escorted me far enough and on taking his leave implored me to pray for him. I agreed to pray for him if he would pray for me and he said that he would do it.

Then he returned and I went after the beast through the midst of the forest until we came to a very beautiful moor; and already midday was passed when I saw before me a very beautiful pine tree and under this pine tree there was one of the most beautiful fountains in the world. In this fountain there was some gravel as red as fire and burning and the water was as cold as ice and changed its colour three times a day, for it became green and was as bitter as the great sea. Under this pine the beast lay down and made as if to rest itself and I looked about me and saw coming a messenger on a horse very fast and when he came near me, he dismounted and knelt before me and drew forth a napkin from his breast and said to me — "Sire, my lady saluteth you, she who received the knights of the Golden Circle on the day when the great marvel was known by him whom you know and she sendeth you to eat of such meat as she has." And I took the cloth and undid it and I drew from it a cake very beautiful and very good and he prepared me a full pot of cervoise and a little cup. I ate and drank very gratefully as much as I wished for I was very hungry and when I had eaten I said to the valet that he was to salute the lady from me in the name of the True Creator and he said that he would do that very willingly and with much pleasure. Then he departed down the valley; and between us we wandered on until evening began to set in and until we came to a crossroads where there was a cross where the beast stopped and immediately I heard a horse whinney and come towards me and now I saw coming towards me a knight who led a number of others with him and when he saw I was a man of religion he jumped down from his horse as did all the others. Then he saluted me and asked me to make his house my inn for the night and then he called his squire and gave him his horse to lead to the hostel and bade him bid his mesne that they should deck out the house in good manner.

Then he led me to his house and gave me very good cheer; and all those of the house as well. But one thing happened which much displeased me for he began to implore of me a chain which I wore round me. He said that he had seen me elsewhere and named the place correctly to me; but then did not know how to ask me to make anything known to him. He was an excellent host to me that night and in the morning I rose and he put me on my way and when I came outside the doorway, I found the beast before me and was very pleased thereat. We wandered on until the third hour. Then I saw a way which led out of the forest. I continued until I came to a large mansion and a church very beautiful and when I came to the church I found there beautiful nuns who were chanting their hours and when they saw that I was a priest they asked me to sing them mass and I did it and afterwards they gave me dinner and begged me much to stay with them two days or three. But that was to no purpose, as I started on my way with thebeast and when we came to the big stone where there was a cross and on the cross words which said that here I should achieve my journey, when I looked about me I saw not the beast nor did I know what had become of it and I looked at the letters which told me all that I had to do.

Then I started on my way. I entered a path to the right in the middle of the most beautiful forest which was ever seen and I wandered on until the forest became clearer and then I looked about me and saw on a lawn a very beautiful chapel but I still had half a league to do, and now I heard a cry so hideous and terrible that never was so hideous a one heard. I was very astonished thereat. But nevertheless I did not leave off going on thus for our Saviour wished it and when I came to it I found it already open and I found a man lying on the threshold in a swoon and I looked at him and I saw that he had his eyes turned into his head. I immediately made the sign of the cross before his face and he rose up from that moment to a sitting posture and then I perceived that the devil was entered into his body. I told him to leave it but he said that he would not yet on no account and I knew well that it was time I entered into the chapel and looked towards the altar and there I saw a small book. I rendered thanks to Jesus Christ first and carried it in front of me and when I came near to the possessed one, the devil began to repent and then there came so many devils that I never thought there had been so many in the world and when they saw the small book they all fled and the one that was in the body could not go out through the mouth because of the book and the sign of the cross. He began to cry — "Remove the small book and I will go away;" and I told him to go out underneath it and he did so very soon, and when he was gone out he departed at such speed that I thought he would knock down the forest before him. Then I took the man in my arms and carried him to before the altar and remained there until it was day: and then I asked him if he would eat and he asked me who I was: and I told him not to be afraid for I was come there for his good and I asked him what meat he was used to eat: and he said that meat which he was accustomed to eat for he had passed twenty four years and a half as a hermit and he had spent nine years eating only herbs and fruit nor so long as he lived would he eat other food unless God sent it to him.

And there I left him very hungry as one who had not eaten since the devil had entered into his body. Then I said in order my hours and sang mass, then I came back to the place where I had left the goodman and I found him asleep; and I who had not slept that night slept a little and when I was asleep I was aware that I was near a fountain at the foot of a hill and I saw a man who offered me apples and pears. Then I awoke and went to the hill and there I found a man at the fountain and when he saw me he brought me some apples and put them in my lap and he told me that every day from then onwards I was to go and fetch our food at that fountain and at the Great Master's command. Then I carried them to the goodman and readily did he eat of them for he was very hungry as he had fasted much and was hardly able to support himself on his feet. I was in his company until he was wholly recovered; and when the 8th day after Easter came we went away, which weighed heavily upon him and after that he related to me how the illness had first come to him, and he said it came to him through a sin he had committed. He did not think in his whole life he had sinned excepting only this one which mortal flesh can guard itself against once it has received the cowl and when he had confessed himself he asked me to pray to our Lord that through His gentle pity He should keep him from the sin through which he had merited His wrath.

Then we embraced one another and left each other with much weeping and if one may judge a man by looking at him, I do not think that one can find a better than him. When he had conveyed me as far as his gateway, there I found the beast that had led me and when the goodman saw the beast he asked what it was; and I told him that I had no other guide on the way and he said to me that very well ought one to serve that Lord who so protected his servants; nor could I ever perceive that any except him saw the beast, but again I thought of the word spoken before, for our Lord judgeth so well that there is none who if he had done all the goodnesses and then undone one would not lose everything and he who hath committed all the sins of the world if he cry God mercy for them will not have a hundred times greater joy than the other. And thus must he have lost God's love through one misdeed, though he had been in His service for the greater part of his life. Then we parted and came to the Way where we were come before. We journeyed on until I was come on the Saturday to my dwelling and when I was come there I sang Vespers and Compline and then went and ate what God pleased and then went and lay down on my bed for I was very tired. And when I had lain down there appeared the High Master to me as He had also before appeared and He told me to take the book on the first working day and write what was in it in another book and take from the alm's room what it behoved to write with, as I should find it there. In the morning I rose up as He had bidden and found all that was necessary for writing, pen, ink, parchment and knife; and when Sunday was passed and I had sung mass on Monday I took the book; and the beginning of the writing was of the Crucifixion of Jesus Christ ...

2.*

The first part of the History of the Holy Grail *tells of the betrayal and crucifixion of Christ; how Joseph of Arimathea asked for his body from Pontius Pilate; how, after the resurrection, Joseph was cast in prison because the body had disappeared; how Vespasian, son of the Roman Emperor Titus [!] was smitten with leprosy and cured by Veronica's veil; how in gratitude for his recovery through this relic he came to Jerusalem to avenge Christ's death, and found Joseph alive in the prison where he had been left and forgotten many years before. During this time Christ had appeared to Joseph and given him the Grail, the vessel of the Last Supper, which had miraculously sustained him without food and drink. He now departs with his sister and his brother-in-law, Bron, and a band of followers.*

Thus did Vespasian avenge the death of Jesus, whom he greatly loved. When Joseph had done he asked leave of Vespasian to depart, and he went with his folk into distant lands, where they dwelt a long time. While they abode there Joseph gave them good instruction, as he was well enabled to: he bade them work, and they did so without demur; thus they fared well for a long time and they lacked nought. But afterwards things fared ill, and I shall tell you in what wise: whatever they wrought or labored at by day or night turned to evil hap, nor would they longer yield themselves to suffer it. This evil came because of one sole sin that began to be amidst them, wherewith they were greatly soiled: it was the sin of lechery, most vile and unclean. When they saw that they might not suffer or endure this evil, they came straightway to Hebron, who was very close to Joseph, and told him that good fortune was fleeing from them and all ills were pursuing them:

"Nor did ever folk as great as we have so much evil hap; we suffer too great mis-ease, more than others have: wherefore we wish thee for the love of God to tell Joseph of it, since all of us are dying of hunger, and well-nigh mad. We suffer too great

---

* Originally published in *Mediaeval Narrative: a Book of Translations* by Margaret Schlauch. Prentice-Hall: New York, 1928.

want, we and our wives and children." And when Hebron heard this he had great pity thereof and asked them if they had endured this a long time. "Yea, certainly, so long as we might. For the love of God we pray thee, go thou and make inquiry of Joseph why it hath come upon us that we have lost everything, and if it be by our sins or his that our goods are gone." Hebron told them that he would gladly go and ask it of him. Thus he went to Joseph and recounted to him the great shame and mis-ease that the folk about him were suffering, and the mischief that they had; and how they begged to be let know the truth of it. Then Joseph began to pray the Son of God with loyal heart to let him know the course of this affair. And Joseph began to fear that he might have mis-done aught in the sight of God, whereat God might be angered at him, and he was very sorrowful. Then he said,

"Hebron, I shall have knowledge of this; and if I know it I shall tell thee too."

Joseph went to his Vessel and knelt before it weeping, and he said, "O Lord Who didst put on flesh in the Virgin and wert born of her, Thou didst come of Thy pity and tenderness and didst desire to consort with us because of Thy love for us and to save Thy creatures, who wished to obey thee and follow Thy will. Sire, I saw Thee dead as truly as I saw Thee living, and after death I beheld Thee alive and speaking to me in the tower where I was immured: then Thou didst me great kindness; and there, Lord, Thou didst command me, when Thou didst bring me this Vessel, that any time I willed to have secrets of Thee, I should come before this precious Vessel wherein is Thy glorious blood. Therefore I do pray and ask of Thee to give me counsel in this matter that my people ask of me (they are in need of bread and meat): that they may work Thy pleasure and accomplish Thy will." Then the Voice that came of the Holy Spirit spoke to Joseph:

"Joseph, be not dismayed; thou hast no blame in this folly."

"Then, Sire, of Thy pity suffer that I remove from my company those that have sinned."

"That, Joseph, thou shalt not do; but I command thee one thing of great significance: thou shalt take the Vessel of My blood and openly make test of it regarding these sinners, with the Vessel quite unveiled. Remember that I was sold and betrayed, smitten and outraged: I knew it should be so but never did I wish to speak thereof before I was in the house of Simon with my friends, and I told them that he who was to betray Me was eating with Me. He who knew he had done this thing was ashamed and withdrew, nor was he ever My disciple thereafter, but there was another in his place. None shall take his place until thou art seated there. Thou knowest well that I was seated at Simon's table, where I ate and drank: there I foresaw clearly the torment that was to come upon Me. In the name of that table I cause now another to be decked, and thou shalt have it. Thou shalt summon Bron thy brother-in-law, who is a good man, and naught shall come of him but good. Cause him therefore to go down to the water to seek and catch a fish, and the first he takes he shall bring to thee. Knowest thou what thou shalt do with it? Thou shalt place it on that table, and the Vessel also, where it most pleases thee, if it be but in the center, and thou shalt cover it over with a napkin. When thou hast done this without fail, take thou again the fish that Hebron hath caught thee and place it down in the part opposite to the Vessel. And when thou hast done all this, call together all thy people and tell them they shall see wherefore they have been so afflicted, and who hath deserved, for his sins, that they had such a mis-chance. And when thou hast taken thy seat in that part where I did sit at the Last Supper, what time I ate with My disciples, seat thou Bron at thy right hand: then thou wilt see that Bron will hold him from that place. That empty place signifies the seat of Judas who left our company in his folly when he perceived that he had betrayed me. That place may not be filled until Enygeus shall have a child of Bron her husband, whom thou and thy sister do so love: and when the child is born, his place shall be assigned there.

"When thou hast done all this thou shalt call thy people and tell them, if they believe in God the Father of all the world, and in the Son and Holy Ghost (which is the blessed Trinity, holy and one), and in all the commandments and teachings I gave unto them when I spoke to them through thee of the three virtues that are one; if they have guarded all this well, nor transgressed upon it, let them come and be seated; thou shalt will it by the grace of Our Lord, Who does good and honour to His people."

Joseph fulfilled the commandment of our Lord, and summoned them even as God had instructed him. One part of the people seated themselves, but the others did not. The table was full, save for the place that might not be filled; and those who sat perceived a sweetness which was the completion of the desire of their hearts; and they who felt this grace forgot speedily enow the others, who had it not. One of those who were seated — his name was Peter — looked behind him and beheld those where standing; he prayed right humbly,

"Tell me truly, of your love, can ye feel or perceive aught of the good that we feel?"

They answered, "Not a whit."

Then said Peter to them, "Then let no man doubt that ye are assoiled of that foul sin which ye have caused Joseph to ask of, for which ye have lost grace."

Thereafter they issued from the house for very shame, and there was not one of them that wept not and made sorry cheer. When the service was done each man arose. They went among the others; but Joseph commanded them to return daily for this grace, without delay. Thus Joseph knew and discovered the sinners by the showing of almighty God, and thus was the Vessel first cherished and proved.

Long time they had this grace; and the others, who were deprived of it, questioned often those who were included, saying, "What is the nature of this grace, and what do ye feel therewith? Who is it that hath given you this gift and informed you with it?"

They answered, "No heart of man might suffice to imagine the great delight we have of it, nor the joy in which we abide and sojourn until the morning. Of whom might come this abundant grace that filleth the heart of man and woman and restores the soul entire?"

To them Joseph made answer, "This good cometh of Jesus the Blessed, who saved Joseph in the prison where he was put without cause."

"This Vessel that we have seen hath never been revealed to us; what it is we know not, howsoever we may surmise."

They said, "It is by this Vessel we are parted from you, for it belongeth to no sinner; to no fellowship or love."

"Ye can see it clearly: but tell us what desire or pleasure have ye when one sayeth to you 'Be seated now;' and can ye tell who it was that did that sin for which ye were cast forth from grace?"

They said, "We go hence like caitiffs and leave you; but if it please you, tell us (for we know that ye know) what we shall say when we are asked wherefore we have left you."

"Hearken what ye shall reply when ye are challenged, and it will be a true response; that we have remained in the grace of God our Father, and Jesus Christ, and the Holy Ghost, strengthened by Joseph's belief and his providing for us."

"And how shall that Vessel be spoken of, in which ye take such delight? Tell us how it is named when one speaks of it?"

Peter replied, "I seek not to conceal it; it shall rightly be called the Grail, for much gree doth he have of it that sees it: to all it is agreeable and fair, and those who may endure it take delight in seeing it and partaking of its fellowship: they have as much joy as a fish of the sea that, having been held in a man's hand, is allowed to escape and swim away in the water."

When they heard this they were well-pleased, nor would they grant it any other name than Grail, and well might they be agreed thereon. Thus all of those who departed thence, and eke all who remained, called the Vessel Grail for the reason I have said.

The folk that remained designated the third hour as the time when they went to the Grail, and that they called its service; and since this thing is true we call it the History of the Grail, and it will have the name of Grail from that time henceforward.

The false folk who departed left behind one of their number who was called Moses and who seemed wise to the people, ingenious in observation and artful in words. He made good commencement and ending, and of his knowledge made semblant that he was wise and piteous. He said that he would not quit this folk that God so filled with the grace of the Holy Ghost. Then he wept and made great moan, and sad and piteous cheer, very marvellous to see; and if anyone passed before him, he prayed him of his grace to intercede that Joseph might have mercy on him. This he begged fast and often, as it appeared with simple heart.

"For the sake of God, pray Joseph to grant me the grace of reconciliation." Many times he begged this, until it chanced one day that they were gathered together, and pity for Moses seized them; they said that they would speak of it to Joseph, and pray it of him. When they saw Joseph, they fell before his feet, all of them, and each man begged and pressed him to have pity on Moses. Joseph was greatly amazed at what they asked, and he said to them, "What would ye? Tell me what ye pray of me."

And they answered with all speed, "The greater part of our people are departed from us, and only one hath remained, who weeps right tenderly, and cries and makes great dole, saying that he will never leave this place so long as he lives. He prays us to pray thee by the grace we have in thy fellowship with great joy and lordship that he may be partaker in it, for we too desire it."

Joseph replied without retreat, "It is not for me to give it, for God our Lord gives that to whomsoever He wills. Those to whom He giveth it of a truth are those who of a right should have it: and this man, methinks, is not such from his bearing, God knows. We must know this, as I think, that he may not deceive us. If he be not good he will deceive himself, and he shall pay for it first."

[MS Lacuna]

"Thou didst desire to suffer earthly torment and endure death for us on earth. As truly as Thou didst save me and deliver me from the prison where Vespasian found me when he descended into the dungeon; and as Thou didst grant me, what time Thou gavest me the Vessel, that Thou wouldst come to me without delay when I required Thee in my need; even as truly as I believe in Thee, reveal to me what hath befallen Moses and whether he is utterly lost, that I may know it certainly and tell it to my folk, whom Thou hast given me as fellows, of Thy great courtesy."

The Voice came to Joseph and replied to him, "Joseph, the significance is now come to thee of what I said when thou didst found the table, that this place should be held in remembrance of the place of Judas, that he lost in his ignorance. I said that he would betray Me and that that place would not be filled before the day of Judgment, which all folk still await: and thou thyself mayest fill it when thou shalt bear hence the memory of thy death; but I tell thee for thy comfort that this place shall not be filled until the third man comes descended of thy lineage and

179

issued of thy kin: Hebron will beget and thy sister Enygeus bear, and the son of his son shall fill this place. Thou askest what hath befallen Moses who is lost: hearken and I shall tell thee.

"When his companions departed and left him here with thee, and he would not go with the others, but remained alone, he did that to deceive thee, and now he hath received his reward. He might not know nor believe that thy folk could have so much grace, and he remained merely to bring shame on the company. Know that he is cast down into the abyss and lost utterly: no one will speak more of him in fable or in song until he comes who is to fill the empty place: but there is no need to speak more of him. Those who constitute My fellowship and thine shall cry out upon Moses and accuse him greatly. Thus shalt thou tell and recount to thy disciples. Think now what thou hast achieved: with Me thou shalt find it even so."

Thus the Holy Ghost spoke to Joseph and revealed the evil work of Moses, telling him how it was; and Joseph did not conceal it from Bron or his fellows, but he told them openly what he had heard of Jesus Christ and how the matter stood, and what had been done with Moses. And all of them said, "Great is the might of God: a fool is he who chases folly for this dolorous life."

Long time did Bron and his wife abide together, until they had twelve sons, fair and gentle and well grown. They had the burden of them (as it well befit them) until Enygeus spoke to Bron her lord and said, "Sir, thou shouldst ask of Joseph my brother what we shall do with our children: they are now tall and well grown, and we ought do nothing with them unless we speak with him."

Bron said, "I too had thought to speak with thee of this: gladly will I go to him and ask it of him."

Bron went to Joseph and told him how it stood and what he willed, and that his sister had sent him thither in the matter.

"Sir, we have twelve great sons; we wish not to dispose of them nor do ought with them save through thee: tell me therefore what to do."

"Let them be in the fellowship of God; there they shall not suffer lack. I shall pray for it gladly when I find the time and place." Thereafter they let all that be until a day when Joseph was come to worship before the Vessel, and he remembered with gladness what Bron had asked of him, whereat he wept right tenderly and prayed to God:

"Our Father, almighty King, if it please Thee, let me know Thy will in this thing, what shall be done with my nephews and what labor shall be given them. Reveal and show me this thing, if it please Thee."

And God sent to Joseph an angel who said unto him, "God sendeth me to thee: knowest thou what He commandeth thee through me? So much will He do for thy nephews as thou dost pray and ask: He wisheth that they be brought and turned to the service of God, being His disciples with a master over them. If they wish to have wives they shall have them: and he who hath none, let him know the wedded men shall serve him: but do thou command their father and mother to bring before thee him who desireth no wife. Cause them to obey thee, and when they have come to thee, be not afeared, but before thou goest there thou shalt hear the voice of the Holy Ghost."

Joseph learned well what the angel said to him, and when the angel departed, Joseph abode in great joy for the good tidings, knowing that he would have all those youths. He went to Bron and told him the counsel he had received:

"Knowest thou," said he, "what I ask of thee? Teach thy children to observe and uphold the law of God: they may have wives in the manner of other folk, by espousal; but if there is one of them that desireth not to be wedded, but rather remain in my house, let him abide with me."

Bron said, "It shall be at thy commandment and pleasure." Bron went to his wife and told her what Joseph had said. When Enygeus had heard it she was delighted in heart and said to Bron, "Haste thee then, my lord, and do as thou art bound to do."

Bron called his children and asked them what was the life each chose to lead. They said, "We wish to accord with thy will and commandment." And thereat all were rejoiced, but Bron urged them until they had spouses and were wedded; and he commanded them to bear them loyally and fairly in the company of their dames: they were to be lords and their wives ladies. They took them according to the ancient law, without pride or arrogance, in the manner of Holy Church, and Joseph instructed them what they should take and what leave, and how maintain themselves. Thus the matter was concluded. Each one hath taken his spouse save only one, who had rather be cut and flayed than take a wife; there might be none for him, he said. When Bron heard this he marvelled greatly, and took him apart for privy rede. He said, "My son, why wilt thou take no wife, as thou shouldst, and as thy brothers have done?"

"Speak not thus to me, for so long as I live I shall never have espousal nor take a wife." Eleven of the sons were married, and Bron took the twelfth to his uncle Joseph, and told it him.

When Joseph heard this he smiled and said, "This one belongeth to me, for he shall be truly mine. If thou and my sister are agreed betwixt the two of you, ye shall give him to me."

They answered, "Gladly, lord: he shall be thine without regret or wrath." Joseph took him in his arms and embraced him, and he told the father and his sister that they might depart and leave the youth with him. Bron departed with his wife, and the young man abode with Joseph.

Then said Joseph, "Fair nephew, of a truth thou shouldst be greatly rejoiced, for our Lord of His pleasure hath chosen thee out to serve Him and exalt His sweet name, that may not be sufficiently praised. Fair sweet nephew, thou shalt be captain and governor over thy brethren. Stir not from beside me; remember what I shall tell thee. If our chosen Saviour Jesus Christ but wills it, of His power He shall appear to me, I well believe."

Joseph went unto his Vessel, and right humbly he prayed God to reveal how he should do well for his nephew. Joseph ended his prayer and anon he heard the Voice replying to him, "Thy nephew is sage and simple and well instructed, retentive and well-attempered: he will believe thee in all things, and will hold all thou shalt say to him. Hearken how thou shalt instruct him: tell him of My love for thee and for all folk who are well endoctrined; tell him how I was bought, sold, and delivered, and eke struck and reviled, being betrayed by one of My disciples, and spat upon and bound to the post, and how they did Me all the ill they might, for on the next day they hanged Me; and tell him thou didst take Me from the cross and wash My wounds, and didst receive My blood in this Vessel; and how thou wert taken by the Jews and put in the dungeon's depth, and how I comforted thee when I found thee there: for there I gave a gift to thee and all thy line, to all who may know and understand it. Tell him of the life and the love I gave to all thy company, and recall that I gave thee dominion over the heart of man in thy fellowship. Conceal nought of this from thy nephew; and all folk who know it and recount it perfectly shall have grace and pleasance, those who do dwell upon the earth. I shall guard their heritage for them and help them; they may not be wrongfully judged nor maimed for the sake of that whereof they do sacrament in remembrance of Me.

"When thou hast revealed him all of this, bear My Vessel to him and tell him what is within: some part of the blood that flowed from Me. If he believes this truly he shall have confirmation of his faith. Tell him how the Enemy ensnares and deceives My friends and those who follow Me; let him beware, I pray him. Forget not to tell him that he shall guard himself from anger, and be not quarrelsome; ill guided is he who sees not clear. Let him keep the matter close, for this will free him most speedily from ill thought or wrath or dole. He shall have need of these things, and they will protect him from the Enemy, who will then have no part in him. Let him beware of the delight of the flesh, and let him not be a dawdler, for all too quickly might the flesh entrap him and put him to sorrow and sin.

"When thou hast told him all this, pray of him to retell it to his fellows, without fail, to all that he shall know to be good men. He shall then speak of Me wherever he may be, far and near, for the more good he speaketh thereof, the more good he will find therein. Tell him that he shall have a son as heir, who shall guard the Vessel, wherefore thou shouldst make revelation to him of us and our fellowship. Forget not after all of this that he shall have the guard of his brothers and sisters. He shall depart towards the west, to the most distant places he can find; and wherever he cometh he shall exalt my name throughout the entire country, and pray to his Father to have His grace, and he shall have it. Tomorrow, when ye are gathered, ye shall see a great light descend in your midst, bearing a letter. This letter shall be given over to Peter to read, and thou shalt command him to depart to whatever place he wills, whither his heart most draweth him; and let him not be dismayed, for he shall not be forgotten of Me. When thou hast commanded this, ask him whither he desireth most to go: he will tell thee without doubt that he will go to the vale of Avaron and dwell in that country. That land is stretched out towards the west. There he will tarry and await the son of Alan; nor may he depart or leave this earth until he hath one who will read that letter for him, and tell him what this Vessel is, and what became of Moses, who was lost. When he has heard and seen and known these things he will die and come into joy without fail. And when thou hast said all this, send for thy nephews, and tell them all the words that I have spoken, and all this instruction, passing over nought."

Alan was converted and fulfilled of the grace of God. Joseph had heard and well remembered what the Voice had said: he called his nephew Alan and told him point by point all that he knew of Jesus Christ, and what the Voice had told him thereof. Messire Robert de Boron sayeth that if he willed to name all that might be put in this book, it would be doubled more than a hundred times. But he who may have this small part can surely know (if he will hearken well he may learn enough of good) the things that Joseph revealed and taught unto his nephew.

And when he had instructed him in all this, he said to him, "Fair nephew, thou shouldst be a good man, for thou hast gained much grace of God." Then Joseph led him apart, and told his father and his mother that he would watch over and govern his brothers and sisters, and they yielded them to be governed by him. If they had doubt of anything they were to seek counsel of him; if they did this it would be well, but if they did not, evil would befall them. He commanded Bron his father and he urged his wife, for he wished them to give him the seigneury over their sons and daughters, great and small alike: the more might they fear and trust and love him, and he would govern them well until each one trusted in him.

The next day when they were at the service, as the history telleth us, a great light appeared to them bearing a letter, and all of them arose at once. Joseph took it, and calling Peter he said to him, "Fair brother Peter, He Who redeemed us all from Hell, hath chosen thee as messenger, and thou shalt carry this letter into whatever place thou wilt."

When Peter heard Joseph speak he said he might not believe that God had made him a messenger, nor did it befit him to carry the letter. He however said, "He knoweth thee better than thyself: but one thing we pray thee of thy love for us, that thou tell us into what parts thou wilt go."

Peter said, "I know it well though none hath told me: no messenger thou hast seen knows better without announcement. I shall go into that western land that is very savage, into the vale of Avaron, to await God's mercy; and do thou too have mercy on me, and pray God that I go not contrary to His will by any strength, boldness, nor deceit, nor say aught contrary to His will. Pray thou also that the Enemy may not tempt nor destroy me, nor cut me off from the love of God." And all of them replied as one, "May God, Who hath the power, save thee!"

They departed into the house of Bron, and called his children, and to all of them Bron said, "My sons and daughters, never may ye have Paradise save by obedience; therefore I desire that all of you obey one man alone; and whatsoever I may give of grace and good for my son Alan I deliver over to him, and it shall not be in vain. I bid him and pray him to guard him well, and eke that ye obey him as ye should your lord. If ye have need of counsel, go to him without delay, and he will give it you in all loyalty. One thing I dare well advise you: undertake no thing contrary to his commandment; do his will devotedly."

So the youths departed from their father and it was their good will to trust in Alan their brother. He went into a distant land and took with him his brothers; in all places where he came he announced the death of Jesus Christ and preached His name even as Joseph taught him, and he found much grace among all men. So they departed; but now I shall leave telling of them and return. Peter now spoke to Joseph and the rest and said, "Now it behooveth me to go, methinks."

"According to God's commandment be it!"

Thereafter they held a gathering and begged Peter not to go; he replied anon that he had no desire to tarry, for he must needs go. "But I shall stay for you this day and then depart tomorrow, after we have been at service." Thus it stood as they devised.

Our Lord, who knew how the affair should proceed, sent an angel unto Joseph who comforted him greatly and told him not to be dismayed, for he was not forgot. "It behooveth thee to do My will, to record the love of thee and Me. Peter must depart from you: knowest thou wherefore? Thou didst venture to retain him this day, and he to remain: this God wished to reveal that he might speak truth, telling no falsehood when he seeth thy Vessel and the rare good things that I have told thee. Joseph, it befits those things that have a good commencement to end thereafter. Our Lord knows that Bron hath been a good man, and therefore of His will He had him fish in the water and catch that fish that is in thy service. God wishes and decrees that he shall have thy Vessel and guard it after thee. Teach him how he shall hold and maintain it, and of the love thou hast for Me, and I have ever had for thee; teach him the disposition and all the nature of God, all that thou hast heard of Him since thou wert born. Put him in belief of Me, and teach him well. Tell him how God came to thee in the prison holding thy Vessel, and how he delivered it unto thy hands: he spoke to thee holy words that are sweet and precious, gracious and full of pity, and rightly are they, called Secrets of the Grail. When thou hast done this fair and well, commend the Vessel to him to guard thereafter, and let him not in any wise misuse it, for all the fault will be on him, and dearly will he pay for it. And those who wish to call him rightly shall hereafter name him the Rich Fisher. Ever shall he wax in honour for the sake of the fish he caught at the commencement of that grace; and it is fitting that thou make him lord and master thereof. Even as the mount progresses and ever grows the smaller, so this folk must go into the west. So soon as ever he is seized of thy Vessel and holds it, he must needs depart straightway for the west into whatever place he wills to go; and when he pauses wheresoever he wishes to abide, he shall await the son of his son in all security; and when that son arrives, the Vessel shall be given over to him, and do thou tell him and command him to charge him with its keeping thereafter. Then hall be accomplished and revealed the significance of the blessed Trinity which we have devised in three parts, and of that third part, I tell thee truly, Jesus Christ, Who is Lord of all things, shall do His will, without any let. When thou givest over the Vessel and all things to Bron and art dis-seized thereof, all these things being accomplished, then Peter shall depart (I would not have him tarry), for he may say truly that he will have seen Hebron the Rich Fisher possessed of the Vessel and the honour. For this reason Peter abode until the morrow, and then departed. When thou hast done this he will

186

leave and pass over land and sea; and He Who watches over all things will guard him well; and when thou hast done this thou shalt depart from this world and enter into perfect joy which is My lot and the portion of all good men in life everlasting. Thou and the heirs of thy race, all that are born of thy sister, shall be saved; and they who learn to say this shall be most loved and cherished, most honoured and feared of good folk and the people."

And Joseph did all that the Voice commanded him. The next day all of them assembled and tarried for the service, and Joseph told again all that the Voice had said, saving only the word that Christ spoke to him in the dungeon. This word he taught to the Rich Fisher, and when he had said these things he also gave them to him written down. He revealed these secrets to him privily. When they had all listened and hearkened well to Joseph telling them that he would depart from their company and be with them no longer, they were greatly dismayed. And when they saw Joseph dis-seized of his office they had great pity, for they knew that he had delivered over his grace and his commandment, but they knew not how.

The Rich Fisher was now possessed of the Grail and all commandments. Joseph took leave when they arose, and greatly did they weep. They sighed and lamented right humbly, and many prayers they made, which God holds dear. Joseph remained three days in the company of the Rich Fisher to do him honour, nor did he refuse. On the third day he said to Joseph, "Hearken to me, Joseph, for a space: truly I tell thee that I desire to depart; if it please thee, I would go by thy will."

"It pleases me well," answered Joseph, "for these things come of God. I know what thou wilt bear away, and in what land thou wilt go. Depart thou: I remain, and I shall be at God's commandment."

So Joseph tarried. The Good Fisher departed — he it is of whom many wise words are told — into the land where he was born, and Joseph remained. Messire Robert de Boron says, if we would know it, that it is meet to tell where Alan went, the son of Hebron: into what land he fared, what befell him, what son he had, and who mothered it; what also befell Peter and where he went and in what place he will be recovered, albeit he may scarce be found; and also what befell Moses who was so long lost, for he must be found, so it is said, where the Rich Fisher fared and tarried: and he may have cunning to lead back him who had to depart.

These four things must all be assembled and recounted, each one alone as it was; but well I believe that no man might do it unless he had heard tell before the greater story of the Grail, which is all true. At this time as I recount it for my Lord Walter of Mont-Belyal, there was never before recounted the Great History of the Grail by any mortal man; but I let it be known by all those who would have this book, that if God gives me health and life, well-being and will to assemble all these parts, it shall be done if I may find them writ in books. And likewise if I leave out one part and fail to recount it, still it is needful to tell the fifth and forget the other four until I may return to my telling with more leisure, and to this work. Each part would be needful of itself; but if I leave them entire, I know of no man so wise who would not think them wholly lost, not knowing what had become of them, nor what division I might have made of them.

CHAPTER 10

Perlesvaus: or, The High History of the Holy Graal

TRANSLATED BY SEBASTIAN EVANS

The romance begins by alluding to the "Graal" as the vessel into which the Saviour's blood flowed. The author is given as "Josephus" but the Welsh version says that this was not Joseph of Arimathea. The prelude says the story is about the Good Knight, pure in body and bold in heart — called Perlesvax, Pellesvaus, Percevax, Perceval (Welsh version Poredur) who was of the lineage of "Joseph of Abarimacie." This Joseph was his mother's uncle, and he kept the Grail and the Lance.

It is further stated that the hero's mother was Ygloas (or Yglais) and her brothers were the Fisher King (Welsh, Peleur) the King of the Lower Folk, Pelles, and the King of the Chastel Mortel. His father was Alain li Gros (Welsh, Earl Evrawg) who was one of twelve brothers. Perceval had a sister Dindrane (Welsh, Danbrann, Landran).

The narrative begins with a reference to the demoralization of Arthur's court on account of his lack of interest in good things. The Knights of the Round Table had dwindled from 366 to about 25. Arthur went to a chapel and hermitage for counsel, and was informed that great sorrow was over the land because a young knight had visited the Fisher King and had seen the Grail and the Lance, but had not asked any questions about them. From a damsel he learned the story of the knight, who was called Perlesvax. While yet a boy he had seen two armed knights fighting; he had killed one of them with his javelin, and had gone with the other to Arthur's court, much to the grief of his father and mother.

King Arthur returned to Cardeil (Carduel; Welsh, Caerlleon) and arranged to hold court at Pannenoisance (Welsh, Penneissense) on the Welsh coast. There was a great assembly. Three damsels came with greetings from the Fisher King who was in a grievous condition because of the failure of a visitor to ask about the Holy Grail. On their way back to the Fisher King's castle they met Gauvains (Gawain; Welsh, Gwalchmai), the nephew of King Arthur. Gauvains' wanderings and adventures are detailed, until finally he arrived at the castle of the Fisher King. Here he was admitted and taken into the presence of the King who was ill, and lying on a bed. Gauvains presented to the King the sword with which John the Baptist was beheaded, which he had obtained in the course of his journeys. He was led into a hall where he sat down to a bounteous repast with twelve ancient looking knights. Two damsels entered, one bearing the Grail and the other the Bleeding Lance; and it seemed to Gauvains as if the blood from the Lance ran into a chalice that was in the Grail. The damsels went out; and, when they returned, there seemed to be three of them, and in the midst of the Grail the figure of a child. Again the damsels went out, and again they returned and now there was above the Grail a crowned King, on a cross, with a spear in his side. The knights were distressed that Gauvains said nothing, and they finally left the room; and Gauvains lay on a couch and slept all night. In the morning he found his horse awaiting him, and he left the castle after being informed that for his lack of speaking the previous evening he could not be permitted to hear mass in the chapel.

Journeying on, he met Lancelot and told of his visit to the Grail Castle. He expressed sorrow at his omission to say what he should have said, but he took comfort in the fact that the Best Knight had already been there and had failed in like manner.

Lancelot's adventures are now told; and allusion is made to the illness of Perceval "the widow's son," which had lasted since he was at the castle of the Fisher King, whence he had gone to the hermitage of his uncle King Pelles, for recovery. Perceval met Lancelot and fought him without recognizing him, but later learned that he was Lancelot, the son of his father's cousin, King Ban of Benoic.

Lancelot, in the course of his wanderings, came to a river whereon was a boat containing an oarsman, two knights, and a damsel holding in her lap the head of a knight. There was also another knight in the boat, who was fishing. They directed him to the nearest castle, where the Fisher King lived. He stopped at a chapel for confession, and told the hermit who was at the chapel about his love for Queen Guinevere, and was rebuked by the hermit, who told him that for this he could not see the Grail. He arrived at the castle and was taken before the Fisher King as the latter lay on his bed. They conversed about Perceval, who had been at the castle without being recognized. Lancelot was well entertained, but the Grail did not appear; and in time he made his way back to Arthur's court.

Various adventures are related of Gauvains, Lancelot, and Perceval. The latter finally came to the hermitage of King Pelles and learned that land of the Fisher King had been seized by the King of Castle Mortal, and that the sacred relics were no longer there, and the Fisher King himself was dead. Perceval pressed on and attacked the Grail Castle, and was in the act of capturing it when the King of Castle Mortal slew himself. Perceval took possession, and the household of the Fisher King returned; and the Grail and the Lance and the sword with which St John was beheaded were all brought back.

Arthur heard of Perceval's victory and started on a pilgrimage to the Grail Castle with Gauvains and Lancelot, but was obliged to send Lancelot back on account of a report that the kingdom had been pillaged by Briant of the Isles and the treacherous Kay, who had slain Lohot (Welsh, Loawt or Llacheu), Arthur's son. He also heard that Queen Guinevere was dead.

When Arthur arrived at the castle which formerly belonged to the Fisher King, he visited the chapel where the Grail was kept, and saw the Fisher King's tomb. The castle had three names: Eden (Welsh, Edom), Chateau de Joie and Chateau des Armes (Welsh, Castle of Souls). At the service in the chapel the Grail appeared in five different manners — the last being in the form of a chalice. Lancelot went to Cardeil, stopping en route at Avalon (Welsh, Avallach) where he found the Queen's body in a coffin at a chapel. Arthur and Gauvains followed in course of time. Later Arthur became suspicious of Lancelot's loyalty and cast him into prison, but afterwards released him.

The romance closes with the announcement which a mysterious voice made to Perceval, that the Grail would not long remain in its castle, but that he would soon be informed where it would be. Soon afterwards Perceval went away in a ship, and was seen no more. (R.J.)

Branch VI

I

Messire Gawain rode until he came to a forest, and seeth a land right fair and rich in a great enclosure of wall, and round the land and countryside within, the wall stretched right far away. Thitherward he cometh and seeth but one entrance thereinto, and he seeth the fairest land that ever he beheld and the best garnished and the fairest orchards. The country was not more than four leagues Welsh in length, and in the midst thereof was a tower on a high rock. And on the top was a crane that kept watch over it and cried when any strange man came into the country. Messire Gawain rode amidst the land and the crane cried out so loud that the King of Wales heard it, that was lord of the land. Thereupon, behold you, two knights that come after Messire Gawain and say to him: "Hold, Sir Knight, and come speak with the king of this country, for no strange knight passeth through his land but he seeth him." "Lords," saith Messire Gawain, "I knew not of the custom. Willingly will I go."

They led him thither to the hall where the King was, and Messire Gawain alighteth and setteth his shield and his spear leaning against a mounting-stage and goeth up into the hall. The King maketh great joy of him and asketh him whither he would go "Sir," saith Messire Gawain, "Into a country where I was never." "Well I know," saith the king, "where it is, for that you are passing through my land. You are going to the country of King Gurgalain to conquer the sword wherewith St John was beheaded."

II

"Sir," saith Messire Gawain, "You say true. God grant me that I may have it!" "That may not be so hastily," saith the King, "For you shall not go forth of my land before a year." "Ha, Sir," saith Messire Gawain, "For God's sake, mercy!" "None other mercy is here," saith the King. Straightway he maketh Messire Gawain be disarmed and afterward maketh bring a robe wherewith to apparel him, and showeth him much honour. But ill is he at ease, wherefore he saith to him: "Sir, wherefore are you fain to hold me here within so long?" "For this, that I know well you will have the sword and will not return by me." "Sir," saith Messire Gawain, "I pledge you my word that, so God give me to conquer it, I will return by you." "And I will allow you to depart from me at your will. For nought is there that I so much desire to see."

He lay the night therewithin, and on the morrow departed thence and issued forth of the land right glad and joyful. And he goeth toward the land of King Gurgalain. And he entereth into a noisome forest at the lower part and findeth at the right hour of noon a fountain that was enclosed of marble, and it was overshadowed of the forest like as it were with leaves down below, and it had rich pillars of marble all round about with fillets of gold and set with precious stones. Against the master-pillar hung a vessel of gold by a silver chain, and in the midst of the fountain was an image as deftly wrought as if it had been alive. When Messire appeared at the fountain, the image set itself in the water and was hidden therewith. Messire Gawain goeth down, and would fain have taken hold on the vessel of gold when a voice crieth out to him: "You are not the Good Knight unto whom is served thereof and who thereby is made whole."

Messire Gawain draweth him back and seeth a clerk come to the fountain that was young of age and clad in white garments, and he had a stole on his arm and held a little square vessel of gold, and cometh to the little vessel that was hanging on the marble pillar and looketh therein, and then rinseth out the other little golden vessel that he held, and then setteth the one that he held in the place of the other.

III

Therewith, behold, three damsels that come of right great beauty, and they had white garments and their heads were covered with white cloths, and they carried, one, bread in a little golden vessel, and the other wine in a little ivory vessel, and the third flesh in one of silver. And they come to the vessel of gold that hung against the pillar and set therein that which they have brought, and afterward they make the sign of the cross over the pillar and come back again. But on their going back, it seemed to Messire Gawain that only one was there. Messire Gawain much marvelled him of this miracle. He goeth after the clerk that carried the other vessel of gold, and saith to him: "Fair Sir, speak to me." "What is your pleasure?" saith the clerk. "Whither carry you this golden vessel and that which is therein?" "To the hermits," saith he, "that are in this forest, and to the Good Knight that lieth sick in the house of his uncle King Hermit." "Is it far from hence?" saith Messire Gawain. "Yea, Sir," saith the clerk, "to yourself. But I shall be there sooner than will you." "By God," saith Messire Gawain, "I would fain I were there now, so that I might see him and speak to him." "That believe I well," saith the clerk, "But now is the place not here."

Messire Gawain taketh leave and goeth his way and rideth until he findeth a hermitage and seeth the hermit therewithout. He was old and bald and of good life. "Sir," saith he to Messire Gawain, "Whither go you?" "To the land of King Gurgalain, Sir; is this the way?" "Yea," saith the hermit, "But many knights have passed hereby that hither have never returned." "Is it far?" saith he. "He and his land are hard by, but far away is the castle wherein is the sword." Messire Gawain lay the night therewithin. On the morrow when he had heard mass, he departed and rode until he cometh to the land of King Gurgalain, and heareth the folk of the land making dole right sore. And he meeteth a knight that cometh a great pace to a castle.

IV

"Sir," saith Messire Gawain, "Wherefore make the folk of this castle such dole, and they of all this land and all this country? For I hear them weep and beat their palms together on every side." "Sir," saith he, "I will tell you. King Gurgalain had one only son of whom he hath been bereft by a Giant that hath done him many mischiefs and wasted much of his land. Now hath the King let everywhere be cried that to him that shall bring back his son and slay the Giant he will give the fairest sword of the world, the which sword he hath, and of all his treasure so much as he may be fain to take. As at this time, he findeth no knight so hardy that he durst go; and much more blameth he his own law than the law of the Christians, and he saith that if any Christian should come into his land, he would receive him."

Right joyous is Messire Gawain of these tidings, and departeth from the castle and rideth on until he cometh to the castle of

King Gurgalain. The tidings come to the King that there is a Christian come into his castle. The King maketh great joy thereof, and maketh him come before him and asketh him of his name and of what land he is. "Sir," saith he, "My name is Gawain and I am of the land of King Arthur." "You are," saith he, "of the land of the Good Knight. But of mine own land may I find none that durst give counsel in a matter I have on hand. But if you be of such valour that you be willing to undertake to counsel me herein, right well will I reward you. A Giant hath carried off my son whom I loved greatly, and so you be willing to set your body in jeopardy for my son, I will give you the richest sword that was ever forged, whereby the head of St John was cut off. Every day at right noon is it bloody, for that at that hour the good man had his head cut off."

The King made fetch him the sword, and in the first place showeth him the scabbard that was loaded of precious stones and the mountings were of silk with buttons of gold, and the hilt in likewise, and the pommet of a most holy sacred stone that Enax, a high emperor of Rome, made be set thereon. Then the King draweth it forth of the scabbard, and the sword came forth thereof all bloody, for it was the hour of noon. And he made hold it before Messire Gawain until the hour was past, and thereafter the sword becometh as clear as an emerald and as green. And Messire Gawain looketh at it and coveteth it much more than ever he did before, and he seeth that it is as long as another sword, albeit, when it is sheathed in the scabbard, neither scabbard nor sword seemeth of two spans length.

V

"Sir Knight," saith the King, "This sword will I give you, and another thing will I do whereof you shall have joy." "Sir," saith Messire Gawain, "And I will do your need, if God please and His sweet Mother." Thereupon he teacheth him the way whereby the Giant went, and the place where he had his repair, and Messire Gawain goeth his way thitherward and commendeth himself to God. The country folk pray for him according to their believe that he may back repair with life and health, for that he goeth in great peril. He hath ridden until that he cometh to a great high mountain that has round about a land that the

Giant had all laid waste and the enclosure of the mountain went round about for a good three leagues Welsh, and therewithin was the Giant, so great and cruel and horrible that he feared no man in the world, and for a long time had he not been sought out by any knight, for none durst won in that quarter. And the pass of the mountain whereby he went to his hold was so strait that no horse might go through; wherefore behoveth Messire Gawain leave his horse and his shield and spear and to pass beyond the mountain by sheer force, for the way was like a cut between sharp rocks. He is come to level ground and looketh before him and seeth a hold that the Giant had on the top of a rock, and espieth the Giant and the lad where they were sitting on the level ground under a tree. Messire Gawain was armed and had his sword girt on, and goeth his way thitherward. And the Giant seeth him coming and leapeth up and taketh in hand a great axe that was at his side, and cometh toward Messire Gawain all girded for the fight and thinketh to smite him a two-handed stroke right amidst the head. But Messire Gawain swerveth aside and bestirreth him with his sword and dealeth him a blow such that he cut off his arm, axe and all. And the Giant returneth backward when he feeleth himself wounded, and taketh the King's son by the neck with his other hand and grippeth him so straitly that he strangleth and slayeth him. Then he cometh back to Messire Gawain and falleth upon him and grippeth him sore strait by the flanks, and lifteth him three foot high off the ground and thinketh to carry him to his hold that was within the rock. And as he goeth thither he falleth, Messire Gawain and all, and he lieth undermost. Howbeit he thinketh to rise, but cannot, for Messire Gawain sendeth him his sword right through his heart and beyond. Afterward, he cut off the head and cometh there where the King's child lay dead, whereof is he right sorrowful. And he beareth him on his neck, and taketh the Giant's head in his hand and returneth there where he had left his horse and shield and spear, and mounteth and cometh back and bringeth the King's son before the King and the head of the Giant hanging.

VI

The King and all they of the castle come to meet him with right great joy, but when they see the young man dead, their great joy is turned into right great dole thereby. And Messire Gawain alighteth before the castle and presenteth to the King his son and the head of the Giant. "Certes," saith he, "might I have presented him to you on live, much more joyful should I have been thereof." "This believe I well," saith the King, "Howbeit, of so much as you have done am I well pleased, and your guerdon shall you have." And he looketh at his son and lamenteth him right sweetly, and all they of the castle after him. Thereafter he maketh light a great show of torches in the midst of the city, and causeth a great fire to be made, and his son be set thereon in a brazen vessel all full of water, and maketh him be cooked and sodden over this fire, and maketh the Giant's head be hanged at the gate.

VII

When his son was well cooked, he maketh him be cut up as small as he may, and biddeth send for all the high men of his land and giveth thereof to each so long as there was any left. After that, he maketh bring the sword and giveth it to Messire Gawain, and Messire Gawain thanketh him much thereof. "More yet will I do for you," saith the King. He biddeth send for all the men of his land to come to his hall and castle. "Sir," saith he, "I am fain to baptize me." "God be praised thereof," saith Messire Gawain. The King biddeth send for a hermit of the forest, and maketh himself be baptized, and he had the name of Archis in right baptism; and of all them that were not willing to believe in God, he commanded Messire Gawain that he should cut off their heads.

VIII

In such wise was this King baptized that was the lord of Albanie, by the miracle of God and the knighthood of Messire Gawain, that departeth from the castle with right great joy and rideth until he is come into the land of the King of Wales and bethought him he would go fulfil his pledge. He alighted before the hall, and the King made right great cheer when he saw him come. And Messire Gawain hath told him: "I come to redeem my pledge. Behold, here is the sword." And the King taketh it in his hand and looketh thereon right fainly, and afterward maketh great joy thereof and setteth it in his treasury and saith:

"Now have I done my desire." "Sir," saith Messire Gawain, "Then have you betrayed me." "By my head," saith the King, "That have I not, for I am of the lineage of him that beheaded St John, wherefore have I a better right to it than you." "Sir," say the knights to the King, "Right loyal and courteous knight is Messire Gawain, wherefore yield him that which he hath conquered, for sore blame will you have of evil-treating him." "I will yield it," saith the King, "on such condition that the first damsel that maketh request of him, what thing soever she may require and whatsoever it be shall not be denied of him." And Messire Gawain agreeth thereto, and of this agreement thereafter did he suffer much shame and anguish and was blamed of many knights. And the King yielded him the sword. He lay the night therewithin, and on the morrow so soon as he might, he departed and rode until he came without the city where the burgess gave him the horse in exchange for his own. And he remembered him of his covenant, and abideth a long space and leaneth him on the hilt of his sword until the burgess cometh. Therewithal made they great joy the one of the other, and Messire showeth him the sword, and the burgess taketh it and smiteth his horse with his spurs and goeth a great gallop toward the city. And Messire Gawain goeth after a great pace and crieth out that he doth great treachery. "Come not after me into the city," saith the burgess, "for the folk have a commune." Howbeit, he followeth after into the city for that he might not overtake him before, and therein he meeteth a great procession of priests and clerks that bore crosses and censers. And Messire Gawain alighteth on account of the procession, and seeth the burgess that hath gone into the church and the procession after. "Lords," saith Messire Gawain, "Make yield me the sword whereof this burgess that hath entered your church hath plundered me." "Sir," say the priests, "Well know we that it is the sword wherewith St John was beheaded, wherefore the burgess hath brought it to us to set with our hallows in yonder, and saith that it was given him." "Ha, lords!" saith Messire Gawain, "Not so! I have but shown it to him to fulfil my pledge. And he hath carried it off by treachery."

Afterward he telleth them as it had befallen him, and the priests make the burgess give it up, and with great joy Messire Gawain departeth and remounteth his horse and issueth forth of the city. He hath scarce gone far before he meeteth a knight that came all armed, as fast as his horse could carry him, spear in rest. "Sir," saith he to Messire Gawain, "I have come to help you. We were told that you had been evil-entreated in the city, and I am of the castle that succoureth all strange knights that pass hereby whensoever they have need thereof." "Sir," saith Messire Gawain, "Blessed be the castle! I plain me not of the trespass for that right hath been done me. And how is the castle named?" "Sir, they call it the Castle of the Ball. Will you return back thither with me, since you are delivered, and lodge there the night with Messire, that is a right worshipful man and of good conditions?" Therewith they go together to the castle, that was right fair and well-seeming. They enter in, and when they were within, the Lord, that sate on a mounting-stage of marble, had two right fair daughters, and he made them play before him with a ball of gold, and looked at them right fainly. He seeth Messire Gawain alight and cometh to meet him and maketh him great cheer. Afterward, he biddeth his two daughters lead him into the hall.

IX

When he was disarmed, the one brought him a right rich robe, and after meat the two maidens sit beside him and make him right great cheer. Thereupon behold you, a dwarf that issueth forth of a chamber, and he holdeth a scourge. And he cometh to the damsels and smiteth them over their faces and their heads. "Rise up," saith he, "ye fools, ill-taught! Ye make cheer to him whom you ought to hate! For this is Messire Gawain, King Arthur's nephew, by whom was your uncle slain!" Thereupon they rise, all ashamed, and go into the chamber, and Messire Gawain remaineth there sore abashed. But their father comforteth him and saith: "Sir, be not troubled for aught that he saith, for the dwarf is our master; he chastiseth and teacheth my daughters, and he is wroth for that you have slain his brother, whom you slew the day that Marin slew his wife on your account, whereof we are right sorrowful in this castle." "So also am I," saith Messire Gawain, "But no blame of her death have I nor she, as God knoweth of very truth."

X

Messire Gawain lay the night at the castle, and departed on the morrow, and rode on his journeys until he cometh to the castle at the entrance to the land of the rich King Fisherman, where he seeth that the lion is not at the entrance nor were the serjeants of copper shooting. And he seeth in great procession the priests and them of the castle coming to meet him, and he alighteth, and a squire was apparelled ready, that took his armour and his horse, and he showeth the sword to them that were come to meet him. It was the hour of noon. He draweth the sword, and seeth it all bloody, and they bow down and worship it, and sing *Te Deum laudamus.* With such joy was Messire Gawain received at the castle, and he set the sword back in his scabbard, and kept it right anigh him, and made it not known in all the places where he lodged that it was such. The priests and knights of the castle make right great joy, and pray him right instantly that so God should lead him to the castle of King Fisherman, and the Graal should appear before him, he would not be so forgetful as the other knights. And he made answer that he would do that which God should teach him.

XI

"Messire Gawain," saith the master of the priests, that was right ancient: "Great need have you to take rest, for meseemeth you have had much travail." "Sir, many things have I seen whereof I am sore abashed, nor know I what castle this may be." "Sir," saith the priest, "This castle is the Castle of Inquest, for nought you shall ask whereof it shall not tell you the meaning, by the witness of Joseph, the good clerk and good hermit through whom we have it, and he knoweth it by annunciation of the Holy Ghost." "By my faith," saith Messire Gawain, "I am much abashed of the three damsels that were at the court of King Arthur. Two of them carried, the one the head of a king and the other of a queen, and they had in a car an hundred and fifty heads of knights whereof some were sealed in gold, other in silver, and the rest in lead." "True," saith the priest, "For as by the queen was the king betrayed and killed, and the knights whereof the heads were in the car, so saith she truth as Joseph witnesseth to us, for he saith of remembrance that by envy was

200

Adam betrayed, and all the people that were after him and the people that are yet to come shall have dole thereof for ever more. And for that Adam was the first man is he called King, for he was our earthly father, and his wife Queen. And the heads of the knights sealed in gold signify the new law, and the heads sealed in silver the old, and the heads sealed in lead the false law of the Sarrazins. Of these three manner of folk is the world stablished." "Sir," saith Messire Gawain, "I marvel of the castle of the Black Hermit, there where the heads were all taken from her, and the Damsel told me that the Good Knight should cast them all forth when he should come. And the other folk that are therewithin are longing for him." "Well know you," saith the priest, "that on account of the apple that Eve gave Adam to eat, all went to hell alike, the good as well as the evil, and to cast His people forth from hell did God become man, and cast these souls forth from hell of His bounty and of His puissance. And to this doth Joseph make us allusion by the castle of the Black Hermit, which signifieth hell, and the Good Knight that shall thence cast forth them that are within. And I tell you that the Black Hermit is Lucifer, that is Lord of hell in like manner as he fain would have been Lord of Paradise." "Sir," saith the priest, "By this significance is he fain to draw the good hermits on behalf of the new law wherein the most part are not well learned, wherefore he would fain make allusion by ensample." "By God," saith Messire Gawain, "I marvel much of the Damsel that was all bald, and said that never should she have her hair again until such time as the Good Knight should have achieved the Holy Graal." "Sir," saith the good man, "Each day full bald behoveth her to be, ever since bald she became when the good King fell into languishment on account of the knight whom he harboured that made not the demand. The bald damsel signifieth Joseu Josephus, that was bald before the crucifixion of Our Lord, nor never had his hair again until such time as He had redeemed His people by His blood and by His death. The car that she leadeth after her signifieth the wheel of fortune, for like as the car goeth on the wheels, doth she lay the burden of the world on the two damsels that follow her; and this you may see well, for the fairest followeth afoot and the other was on a sorry hackney, and they were poorly clad, whereas the third had costlier attire. The shield whereon was the red cross, that she left at the court of King Arthur, signifieth the most holy shield of the rood that never none durst lift save God alone." Messire Gawain heareth these and much pleaseth him thereof, and thinketh him that none durst set his hand to nor lift the shield that hung in the King's hall, as he had heard tell in many places; wherefore day by day were they waiting for the Good Knight that should come for the shield.

XII

"Sir," saith Messire Gawain, "By this that you tell me you do me to wit that whereof I was abashed, but I have been right sorrowful of a lady that a knight slew on my account though no blame had she therein, nor had I." "Sir," saith the priest, "Right great significance was there in her death, for Josephus witnesseth us that the old law was destroyed by the stroke of a sword without recover, and to destroy the old law did Our Lord suffer Himself to be smitten in the side of a spear. By this stroke was the old law destroyed, and by His crucifixion. The lady signifieth the old law. Would you ask more of me?" saith the priest. "Sir," saith Messire Gawain, "I met a knight in the forest that rode behind before and carried his arms upside down. And he said that he was the Knight Coward, and his habergeon carried he on his neck, and so soon as he saw me he set his arms to rights and rode like any other knight." "The law was turned to the worse," saith the priest, "before Our Lord's crucifixion, and so soon as He was crucified, was again restored to right." "Even yet have I not asked you of all," saith Messire Gawain, "For a knight came and jousted with me party of black and white, and challenged me of the death of the lady on behalf of her husband, and told me and I should vanquish him that he and his men would be my men. I did vanquish him and he did me homage." "It is right," saith the priest, "On account of the old law that was destroyed were all they that remained therein made subject, and shall be for ever more. Wish you to enquire of aught further?" saith the priest. "I marvel me right sore," saith Messire Gawain, "of a child that rode a lion in a hermitage, and none durst come nigh the lion save the child only, and he was not of more than six years, and the lion was right fell. The child was the son of the lady that was slain on my account." "Right well have you spoken," saith the priest, "in reminding me thereof. The child signifieth the Saviour of the world that was born under the old law and was circumcized, and the lion whereon he rode signifieth the world and the people that are therein, and beasts and birds that none may govern save by virtue of Him alone." "God!" saith Messire Gawain, "How great joy have I at heart of that you tell me! Sir, I found a fountain in a forest, the fairest that was ever seen, and an image had it within that hid itself when it saw me, and a clerk brought a golden vessel and took another golden vessel that hung at the column that was there, and set his own in place thereof. Afterward, came three damsels and filled the vessel with that they had brought thither, and straightway meseemed that but one was there." "Sir," saith the priest, "I will tell you no more thereof than you have heard, and therewithal ought you to hold yourself well apaid, for behoveth not discover the secrets of the Saviour, and them also to whom they are committed behoveth keep them covertly."

XIII

"Sir," saith Messire Gawain, "I would fain ask you of a King. When I had brought him his son back dead, he made him be cooked and thereafter made him be eaten of all the folk of his land." "Sir," saith the priest, "Already had he leant his heart upon Jesus Christ, and would fain make sacrifice of his flesh and blood to Our Lord, and for this did he make all those of his land eat thereof, and would fain that their thoughts should be even such as his own. And therefore was all evil belief uprooted from his land, so that none remained therein." "Blessed be the hour," saith Messire Gawain, "that I came herewithin!" "Mine be it!" saith the priest. Messire Gawain lay therewithin the night, and right well lodged was he. The morrow, when he had heard mass, he departed and went forth of the castle when he had taken leave. And he findeth the fairest land of the world and the fairest meadow-grounds that were ever seen, and the fairest rivers and forests garnished of wild deer and hermitages. And he rideth until he cometh one day as evening was about to draw on, to the house of a hermit, and the house was so low that his horse might not enter therein. And his chapel was scarce taller, and the good man had never issued therefrom of forty years past. The Hermit putteth his head out of the window when he seeth Messire Gawain and saith, "Sir, welcome may you be," saith he. "Sir, God give you joy, Will you give me lodging tonight?" saith Messire Gawain. "Sir, herewithin none harboureth save the Lord God alone, for earthly man hath never entered herewithin but me this forty year, but see, here in front is the castle wherein the good knights are lodged." "What is the castle?" "Sir, the good King Fisherman's, that is surrounded with great waters and plenteous in all things good, so the lord were in joy. But behoveth them harbour none there save good knights only." "God grant," saith Messire Gawain, "that I may come therein!"

XIV

When he knoweth that he is nigh the castle, he alighteth and confesseth him to the hermit, and avoweth all his sins and repenteth him thereof right truly. "Sir," saith the hermit, "Now forget not, so God be willing to allow you, to ask that which the other knight forgat, and be not afeard for aught you may see at the entrance of the castle, but ride on without misgiving and adore the holy chapel you will see appear in the castle, there where the flame of the Holy Spirit descendeth each day for the most Holy Graal and the point of the lance that is served there." "Sir," saith Messire Gawain, "God teach me to do His will!" He taketh leave, and goeth his way and rideth until the valley appeareth wherein the castle is seated garnished of all things good, and he seeth appear the most holy chapel. He alighteth, and then setteth him on his knees and boweth him down and adoreth right sweetly. Thereafter he remounteth and rideth until he findeth a sepulchre right rich, and it had a cover over, and it lay very nigh the castle, and it seemed to be within a little burial ground that was enclosed all round about, nor were any other tombs therein. A voice crieth to him as he passeth the burial-ground: "Touch not the sepulchre, for you are not the Good Knight through whom shall it be known who lieth therein." Messire Gawain passeth beyond when he had heard the voice and draweth nigh the entrance of the castle, and seeth that three bridges are there, right great and right horrible to pass. And three great waters run below, and him seemeth that the first bridge is a bowshot in length and in breadth not more than a foot. Strait seemeth the bridge and the water deep and swift and wide. He knoweth not what he may do, for it seemeth him that none may pass it, neither afoot nor on horse.

XV

Thereupon, lo you, a knight that issueth forth of the castle and cometh as far as the head of the bridge, that was called the Bridge of the Eel, and shouteth aloud: "Sir knight, pass quickly before it shall be already night, for they of the castle are awaiting us." "Ha," saith Messire Gawain, "Fair sir, but teach me how I may pass hereby." "Certes, Sir Knight, no passage know I to this entrance other than this, and if you desire to come to the castle, pass on without misgiving." Messire Gawain hath shame for that he hath stayed so long, and forthinketh him of this that the Hermit told him, that of no mortal thing need he be troubled at the entrance of the castle, and therewithal that he is truly confessed of his sins, wherefore behoveth him be the less adread of death. He crosseth and blesseth himself and commendeth himself to God as he that thinketh to die, and so smiteth his horse with his spurs and findeth the bridge wide and large as soon as he goeth forward, for by this passing were proven most of the knights that were fain to enter therein. Much marvelled he that he found the bridge so wide that had seemed him so narrow. And when he had passed beyond, the bridge, that was a drawbridge, lifted itself by engine behind him, for the water below ran too swiftly for other bridge to be made. The knight draweth himself back beyond the great bridge and Messire Gawain cometh nigh to pass it, and this seemed him as long as the other. And he seeth the water below, that was not less swift nor less deep, and, so far as he could judge, the bridge was of ice, feeble and thin, and of a great height above the water, and he looked at it with much marvelling, yet natheless not for that would he any the more hold back from passing on toward the entrance. He goeth forward and commendeth himself to God, and cometh in the midst thereof and seeth that the bridge was the fairest and richest and strongest he had ever beheld, and the abutments thereof were all full of images. When he was beyond the bridge, it lifted itself up behind him as the other had done, and he looketh before him and seeth not the knight, and is come to the third bridge and nought was he adread for anything he might see. And it was not less rich than the other, and had columns of marble all round about, and upon each a knop so rich that it seemed to be of gold. After that, he beholdeth the gate over against him, and seeth Our Lord there figured even as He was set upon the rood, and His Mother of the one side and St John of the other, whereof the images were all of gold, with rich precious stones that flashed like fire. And on the right hand he seeth an angel, passing fair, that pointed with his finger to the chapel where was the Holy Graal, and on his breast had he a precious stone, and letters written above his head that told how the lord of the castle was the like pure and clean of all evil-seeming as was this stone.

XVI

Thereafter at the entrance of the gate he seeth a lion right great and horrible, and he was upright upon his feet. So soon as he seeth Messire Gawain, he croucheth to the ground, and Messire Gawain passeth the entrance without gainsay and cometh to the castle, and alighteth afoot, and setteth his shield and his spear against the wall of the hall, and mounteth up a flight of marble steps and cometh into a hall right fair and rich, and here and there in divers places was it painted with golden images. In the midst thereof he findeth a couch right fair and rich and high, and at the foot of this couch was a chess-board right fair and rich, with an orle of gold all full of precious stones, and the pieces were of gold and silver and were not upon the board. Meanwhile, as Messire Gawain was looking at the beauty of the chess-board and the hall, behold you two knights that issue forth of a chamber and come to him. "Sir," say the knights, "Welcome may you be." "God give you joy and good adventure," saith Messire Gawain. They make him sit upon the couch and after that make him be disarmed. They bring him, in two basins of gold, water to wash his face and hands. After that, come two damsels that bring him a rich robe of silk and cloth of gold. Then they make him do on the same. Then say the two damsels to him, "Take in good part whatsoever may be done to you therewithin, for this is the hostel of good knights and loyal." "Damsels," saith Messire Gawain, "So will I do. Gramercy of your service." He seeth well that albeit the night were dark, within was so great brightness of light without candles that it was marvel. And it seemed him the sun shone there.

Wherefore marvelled he right sore whence so great light should come.

XVII

When Messire Gawain was clad in the rich robe, right comely was he to behold, and well seemed he to be a knight of great valour. "Sir," say the knights, "May it please you come see the Lord of this castle?" "Right gladly will I see him," saith he, "For I would fain present him with a rich sword." They lead him into the chamber where lay King Fisherman, and it seemed as it were all strown and sprinkled of balm, and it was all strown with green herbs and reeds. And King Fisherman lay on a bed hung on cords whereof the stays were of ivory; and therein was a mattress of straw whereon he lay, and above, a coverlid of sables whereof the cloth was right rich. And be had a cap of sables on his head covered with a red samite of silk, and a golden cross, and under his head was a pillow all smelling sweet of balm, and at the four corners of the pillow were four stones that gave out a right great brightness of light; and over against him was a pillar of copper whereon sate an eagle that held a cross of gold wherein was a piece of the true cross whereon God was set, as long as was the cross itself, the which the good man adored. And in four tall candlesticks of gold were four tall wax tapers set as often as was need. Messire Gawain cometh before the King and saluteth him. And the King maketh him right great cheer, and biddeth him be welcome. "Sir," saith Messire Gawain, "I present you with the sword whereof John was beheaded." "Gramercy," saith the King: "Certes, I knew well that you would bring it, for neither you nor other might have come in hither without the sword, and if you had not been of great valour you would not have conquered it." He taketh the sword and setteth it to his mouth and his face and so kisseth it right sweetly and maketh right great joy thereof. And a damsel cometh to sit at the head of the bed, to whom he giveth the sword in keeping. Two others sit at his feet that look at him right sweetly. "What is your name?" saith the King. "Sir, my name is Gawain." "Ha, Messire Gawain," saith he, "This brightness of light that shineth there within cometh to us of God for love of you. For every time that a knight cometh hither to harbour within this castle it appeareth as brightly as you see it now. And greater cheer would I make you than I do were I able to help myself, but I am fallen into languishment from the hour that the knight of whom you have heard tell harboured herewithin. On account of one single word he delayed to speak, did this languishment come upon me. Wherefore I pray you for God's sake that you remember to speak it, for right glad should you be and you may restore me my health. And see here is the daughter of my sister that hath been plundered of her land and disherited in such wise that never can she have it again save through her brother only whom she goeth to seek; and we have been told that he is the Best Knight of the world, but we can learn no true tidings of him." "Sir," saith the damsel to her uncle the King, "Thank Messire Gawain of the honour he did to my lady-mother when he came to her hostel. He stablished our land again in peace, and conquered the keeping of the castle for a year, and set my lady-mother's five knights there with us to keep it. The year hath now passed, wherefore will the war be now renewed against us and God succour us not, and I find not my brother whom we have lost so long." "Damsel," saith Messire Gawain, "I helped you so far as I might, and so would I again and I were there. And fainer am I to see your brother than all the knights of the world. But no true tidings may I hear of him, save so much, that I was at a hermitage where was a King hermit, and he bade me make no noise for that the Best Knight of the world lay sick therewithin, and he told me that his name was Par-lui-fet. I saw his horse being led by a squire before the chapel, and his arms and shield whereon was a sun figured." "Sir," saith the damsel, "My brother's name is not Par-lui-fet, but Perlesvax in right baptism, and it is said of them that have seen him that never comelier knight was known." "Certes," saith the King, "Never saw I comelier than he that came in hither nor better like to be good knight, and I know of a truth that such he is, for otherwise never might he have entered hereinto. But good reward of harbouring him had I not, for I may help neither myself nor other. For God's sake, Messire Gawain, hold me in remembrance this night, for great affiance have I in your valour." "Certes, Sir, please God, nought will I do within yonder, whereof I may be blamed of right."

208

XVIII

Thereupon Messire Gawain was led into the hall and findeth twelve ancient knights, all bald, albeit they seemed not to be so old as they were, for each was of an hundred year of age or more and yet none of them seemed as though he were forty. They have set Messire Gawain to eat at a right rich table of ivory and seat themselves all round about him. "Sir," saith the Master of the Knights, "Remember you of that the good King hath prayed of you and told you this night as you have heard." "Sir," saith Messire Gawain, "God remember it!" With that bring they larded meats of venison and wild-boar's flesh and other in great plenty, and on the table was rich array of vessels of silver and great cups of gold with their covers, and the rich candlesticks where the great candles were burning, albeit their brightness was hidden of the great light that appeared within.

XIX

Thereon, lo you, two damsels that issue forth of a chapel, whereof the one holdeth in her hands the most Holy Graal, and the other the Lance whereof the point bleedeth thereinto. And the one goeth beside the other in the midst of the hall where the knights and Messire Gawain sat at meat, and so sweet a smell and so holy came to them therefrom that they forgat to eat. Messire Gawain looketh at the Graal, and it seemed him that a chalice was therein, albeit none there was as at this time, and he seeth the point of the lance whence the red blood ran thereinto, and it seemeth him he seeth two angels that bear two candlesticks of gold filled with candles. And the damsels pass before Messire Gawain, and go into another chapel. And Messire Gawain is thoughtful, and so great a joy cometh to him that nought remembereth he in his thinking save of God only. The knights are all daunted and sorrowful in their hearts, and look at Messire Gawain. Thereupon behold you the damsels that issue forth of the chamber and come again before Messire Gawain, and him seemeth that he seeth three there where before he had seen but two, and seemeth him that in the midst of the Graal he seeth the figure of a child. The Master of the Knights beckoneth to Messire Gawain. Messire Gawain looketh before him and seeth three drops of blood fall upon the table. He was all abashed to look at them and spake no word.

XX

Therewith the damsels pass forth and the knights are all adread and look one at the other. Howbeit Messire Gawain may not withdraw his eyes from the three drops of blood, and when he would fain kiss them they vanish away, whereof he is right sorrowful, for he may not set his hand nor aught that of him is to touch thereof. Therewithal behold you the two damsels that come again before the table and seemeth to Messire Gawain that there are three, and he looketh up and it seemeth him to be the Graal all in flesh, and he seeth above, as him thinketh, a King crowned, nailed upon a rood, and the spear was still fast in his side. Messire Gawain seeth it and hath great pity thereof, and of nought doth he remember him save of the pain that this King suffereth. And the Master of the knights summoneth him again by word of mouth, and telleth him that if he delayeth longer, never more will he recover it. Messire Gawain is silent, as he that heareth not the knight speak, and looketh upward. But the damsels go back into the chapel and carry back the most Holy Graal and the Lance, and the knights make the tablecloths be taken away and rise from meat and go into another hall and leave Messire Gawain all alone. And he looketh all around and seeth the doors all shut and made fast, and looketh to the foot of the hall and seeth two candlesticks with many candles burning round about the chess-board, and he seeth that the pieces are set, whereof the one sort are silver and the other gold. Messire Gawain sitteth at the game, and they of gold played against him and mated him twice. At the third time, when he thought to revenge himself and saw that he had the worse, he swept the pieces off the board. And a damsel issued forth of a chamber and made a squire take the chess-board and the pieces and so carry them away. And Messire Gawain, that was way-worn of his wanderings to come thither where he now hath come, slept upon the couch until the morrow when it was day, and he heard a horn sound right shrill.

XXI

Thereupon he armeth him and would fain go to take leave of King Fisherman, but he findeth the doors bolted so that he may not get forth. And right fair service seeth he done in a chapel, and right sorrowful is he for that he may not hear the mass. A damsel cometh into the hall and saith to him: "Sir, now may you hear the service and the joy that is made on account of the sword you presented to the good King, and right glad at heart ought you to have been if you had been within the chapel. But you lost entering therein on account of a right little word. For the place of the chapel is so hallowed of the holy relics that are therein that man nor priest may never enter therein from the Saturday at noon until the Monday after mass." And he heard the sweetest voices and the fairest services that were ever done in chapel. Messire Gawain answereth her not a word so is he abashed. Howbeit the damsel saith to him "Sir, God be guardian of your body, for methinketh that it was not of your own default that you would not speak the word whereof this castle would have been in joy." With that the damsel departeth and Messire Gawain heareth the horn sound a second time and a voice warning him aloud: "He that is from without, let him go hence! for the bridges are lowered and the gate open, and the lion is in his den. And thereafter behoveth the bridge be lifted again on account of the King of the Castle Mortal, that warreth against this castle, and therefore of this thing shall he die."

XXII

Thereupon Messire Gawain issueth forth of the hall and findeth his horse all made ready at the mounting-stage, together with his arms. He goeth forth and findeth the bridges broad and long, and goeth his way a great pace beside a great river that runneth in the midst of the valley. And he seeth in a great forest a mighty rain and tempest, and so strong a thunder-storm ariseth in the forest that it seemeth like all the trees should be uprooted. So great is the rain and the tempest that it compelleth him set his shield over his horse's head lest he be drowned of the abundance of rain. In this mis-ease rideth he down beside the river that runneth in the forest until he seeth in a launde across the river a knight and a damsel right gaily appointed riding at pleasure, and the knight carrieth a bird on his fist, and the damsel hath a garland of flowers on her head. Two brachets follow the knight. The sun shineth right fair on the meadow and the air is right clear and fresh. Messire Gawain marvelleth much of this, that it raineth so heavily on his way, whereas, in the meadow where the knight and the damsel are riding, the sun shineth clear and the weather is bright and calm. And he seeth them ride joyously. He can ask them naught for they are too far away. Messire Gawain looketh about and seeth on the other side the river a squire nearer to him than is the knight. "Fair friend," saith Messire Gawain, "How is this that it raineth upon me on this side the river, but on the other raineth it not at all?" "Sir," saith the squire, "This have you deserved, for such is the custom of the forest." "Will this tempest that is over me last for ever?" saith Messire Gawain. "At the first bridge you come to will it be stayed upon you," saith the squire.

XXIII

Therewith the squire departeth, and the tempest rageth incontinent until he is come to the bridge; and he rideth beyond and cometh to the meadow, and the storm is stayed so that he setteth his shield to rights again upon his neck. And he seeth before him a castle where was a great company of folk that were making great cheer. He rideth until he cometh to the castle and seeth right great throng of folk, knights and dames and damsels. Messire Gawain alighteth, but findeth in the castle none that is willing to take his reins, so busied are they making merry. Messire Gawain presenteth himself on the one side and the other, but all of them avoid him, and he seeth that he maketh but an ill stay therewithin for himself, wherefore he departeth from the castle and meeteth a knight at the gate. "Sir," saith he, "What castle is this?" "And see you not," saith the knight, "that it is a castle of joy?" "By my faith," saith Messire Gawain, "They of the castle be not over-courteous, for all this time hath none come to take my reins." "Not for this lose they their courtesy," saith the knight, "For this is no more than you have deserved. They take you to be as slothful of deed as you are of word, and they saw that you were come through the Forest Perilous whereby pass all the discomfited, as well appeareth by your arms and your horse." Therewith the knight departeth, and

Messire Gawain hath ridden a great space sorrowful and sore abashed, until he cometh to a land parched and poor and barren of all comfort, and therein findeth he a poor castle, whereinto he cometh and seeth it much wasted, but that within was there a hall that seemed haunted of folk. And Messire Gawain cometh thitherward and alighteth, and a knight cometh down the steps of the hall right poorly clad. "Sir," saith the knight to Messire Gawain, "Welcome may you be!" After that, he taketh him by the hand and leadeth him upward to the hall, that was all waste. Therewithal issue two damsels from a chamber, right poorly clad, that were of passing great beauty, and make great cheer to Messire Gawain. So, when he was fain to disarm, behold you thereupon a knight that entereth into the hall, and he was smitten with the broken end of a lance through his body. He seeth Messire Gawain whom he knoweth. "Now haste!" saith he, "and disarm you not!" "Right joyful am I that I have found you! I come from this forest wherein have I left Lancelot fighting with four knights, whereof one is dead, and they think that it is you, and they are of kindred to the knight that you slew at the tent where you destroyed the evil custom. I was fain to help Lancelot, when one of the knights smote me as you may see." Messire Gawain goeth down from the hall and mounteth all armed upon his horse.

XXIV

"Sir," saith the knight of the hall, "I would go help you to my power, but I may not issue forth of the castle until such time as it be replenished of the folk that are wont to come therein and until my land be again given up to me through the valour of the Good Knight." Messire Gawain departeth from the castle as fast as horse may carry him, and entereth the forest and followeth the track of the blood along the way the knight had come, and rideth so far in the forest as that he heareth the noise of swords, and seeth in the midst of the launde Lancelot and the three knights, and the fourth dead on the ground. But one of the knights had drawn him aback, for he might abide the combat no longer, for the knight that brought the tidings to Messire Gawain had sore wounded him. The two knights beset Lancelot full sore, and right weary was he of the buffets that he had given and received. Messire Gawain cometh to one of the knights and smiteth him right through the body and maketh him and his horse roll over all of a heap.

XXV

When Lancelot perceiveth Messire Gawain, much joy maketh he thereof. In the meanwhile as the one held the other, the fourth knight fled full speed through the midst of the forest, and he that the knight had wounded fell dead. They take their horses, and Messire Gawain telleth Lancelot he hath the most poverty-stricken host that ever he hath seen, and the fairest damsels known, but that right poorly are they clad. "Shall we therefore take them of our booty?" "I agree," saith Lancelot, "But sore grieveth me of the knight that hath thus escaped us." "Take no heed!" saith Messire Gawain, "We shall do well enough herein." Thereupon they return back toward the poor knight's hostel and alight before the hall, and the Poor Knight cometh to meet them, and the two damsels, and they deliver to them the three horses of the three knights that were dead. The knight hath great joy thereof, and telleth them that now is he a rich man and that betimes will his sisters be better clad than are they now, as well as himself.

XXVI

Thereupon come they into the hall. The knight maketh one of his own squires stable the horses and the two damsels help disarm Lancelot and Messire Gawain. "Lords," saith the knight, "So God help me, nought have I to lend you wherewith to clothe you, for robe have I none save mine own jerkin." Lancelot hath great pity thereof and Messire Gawain, and the two damsels take off their kirtles that were made like surcoats of cloth that covered their poor shirts, and their jackets that were all to-torn and ragged and worn, and present them to the knights to clothe them. They were fain not to refuse, lest the damsels should think they held them not in honour, and did on the two kirtles right poor as they were. The damsels had great joy thereof that so good knights should deign wear garments so poor. "Lords," saith the Poor Knight, "The knight that brought the tidings hither, and was stricken through of a lance-shaft, is dead and lieth on a bier in a chapel within the castle, and he confessed himself right well to a hermit and bade salute you

214

both, and was right fain you should see him after that he were dead, and he prayed me instantly that I would ask you to be tomorrow at his burial, for better knights than be ye might not be thereat, so he told me." "Certes," saith Lancelot, "A good knight was he, and much mischief is it of his death; and sore grieveth me that I know not his name nor of what country he was." "Sir," saith Messire Gawain, "He said that you should yet know it well." The two good knights lay the night at the castle, and the Poor Knight lodged them as well as he might. When it cometh to morning, they go to the chapel to hear mass and to be at the burial of the body. After that they take leave of the Poor Knight and the two damsels and depart from the castle all armed. "Messire Gawain," saith Lancelot, "They know not at court what hath become of you, and they hold you for dead as they suppose." "By my faith," saith Messire Gawain, "thitherward will I go, for I have had sore travail, and there will I abide until some will shall come to me to go seek adventure." He recounteth to Lancelot how the Graal hath appeared to him at the court of King Fisherman: "And even as it was there before me, I forgat to ask how it served and of what." "Ha, Sir," saith Lancelot, "Have you then been there?" "Yea," saith he, "And thereof am I right sorry and glad: glad for the great holiness I have seen, sorry for that I asked not that whereof King Fisherman prayed me right sweetly." "Sir," saith Lancelot, "Right sorely ill have you wrought, nor is there nought whereof I have so great desire as I have to go to his castle." "By my faith," saith Messire Gawain, "Much shamed was I there, but this doth somewhat recomfort me, that the Best Knight was there before me that gat blame thereof in like manner as I." Lancelot departeth from Messire Gawain, and they take leave either of other. They issue forth of a forest, and each taketh his own way without saying a word.

CHAPTER 11

Parzival: a Knightly Epic by Wolfram von Eschenbach

TRANSLATED BY J.L. WESTON

Book IX: Trevrezent

"And, Sir Host, I yet more would tell thee, where cloister or church
   shall be
And men unto God give honour, there no eye hath looked on me,
And naught but strife have I sought me, tho' the time as thou sayst be
   long,
For I against God bear hatred, and my wrath ever waxeth strong.
For my sorrow and shame hath He cherished, and He watched them
   greater grow
Till too high they waxed, and my gladness, yet living, He buried low!
And I think were God fain to help me other anchor my joy had found
Than this, which so deep hath sunk it, and with sorrow hath closed it
   round.
A man's heart is mine, and sore wounded, it acheth, and acheth still,
Yet once was it glad and joyous, and free from all thought of ill!
Ere sorrow her crown of sorrow, thorn-woven, with stern hand pressed
On the honour my hand had won me o'er many a foeman's crest!
And l do well to lay it on Him, the burden of this my shame,
Who can help if He will, nor withholdeth the aid that men fain would
   claim.
But *me* alone, hath He helped not, whate'er men of Him may speak,
But ever He turneth from me, and His wrath on my head doth wreak!"

Then the hermit beheld him sighing, "Sir Knight, thou shalt put away
Such madness, and trust God better, for His help will He never stay.
And His aid to us here be given, yea, alike unto me and thee,

216

But 'twere best thou shouldst sit beside me, and tell here thy tale to me,
And make to me free confession — How first did this woe begin?
What foe shall have worked such folly that God should thine hatred
     win?
Yet first would I pray thee, courteous, to hearken the word I say,
For fain would I speak Him guiltless, ere yet thou thy plaint shall lay
'Gainst Him, Who denieth never unto sinful man His aid,
But ever hath answered truly, who truly to Him hath prayed."

"Tho' a layman I was yet ever in books might I read and learn
How men, for His help so faithful, should ne'er from His service turn.
Since aid He begrudged us never, lest our soul unto Hell should fall,
And as God Himself shall be faithful, be *thou* faithful whate'er befall;
For false ways He ever hateth — and thankful we aye should be
When we think of the deed, so gracious, once wrought of His love so
     free!
For *our* sake the Lord of Heaven in the likeness of man was made,
And Truth is His name, and His nature, nor from Truth shall He e'er
     have strayed.
And this shalt thou know most surely, God breaketh His faith with
     none.
Teach thy thoughts ne'er from Him to waver, since Himself and His
     ways are One!"

"Wouldst thou force thy God with thine anger? He who heareth that
     thou hast sworn
Hatred against thy Maker, he shall hold thee of wit forlorn!
Of Lucifer now bethink Thee, and of those who must share his fall,
Bethink thee, the angel nature was free from all taint of gall,
Say, whence sprang that root of evil which spurred them to endless
     strife,
And won its reward in Hell's torments, and the death of an outcast life?
Ashtaroth, Belcimon, and Belat, Rhadamant, yea, and many more!
Pride and anger the host of Heaven with Hell's colours have painted
     o'er!

"When Lucifer and his angels thus sped on their downward way,
To fill their place, a wonder God wrought from the earth and clay:
The son of His hands was Adam, and from flesh of Adam, Eve
He brought, and for Eve's transgression, I ween, all the world doth
     grieve.
For she hearkened not her Creator, and she robbed us of our bliss.
And two sons sprang forth from her body, and the elder he wrought
     amiss,

217

Since envy so worked upon him that from wrath there sprang disgrace,
And of maidenhood did he rob her who was mother of all his race!
Here many a one doth question, an the tale be to him unknown,
How might such a thing have chancèd? It came but by sin alone!"

Quoth Parzival, "Now, I think me that never such thing might be,
And 'twere better thou shouldst keep silence, than tell such a tale to
     me!
For who should have borne the father, whose son, as thou sayest, reft
Maidenhood from his father's mother? Such riddle were better left!"
But the hermit again made answer, "Now thy doubt will I put away,
O'er my falsehood thou canst bemoan thee if the thing be not truth I
     say,
For the *Earth* was Adam's mother, of the *Earth* was Adam fed,
And I ween, tho' a man she bare here, yet still was the Earth a maid.
And here will I read the riddle, he who robbed her of maidenhood
Was Cain the son of Adam, who in wrath shed his brother's blood:
For as on the Earth, so stainless, the blood of the guiltless fell,
Her maidenhood fled her ever! And true is the tale I tell.
For wrath of man and envy, thro' Cain did they wake to life,
And ever from that day forward thro' his sin there ariseth strife.

"Nor on earth shall aught be purer than a maiden undefiled,
Think how pure must be a maiden, since God was a Maiden's Child!
Two men have been born of maidens, and God hath the likeness ta'en
Of the son of the first Earth-Maiden, since to help us He aye was fain.
Thus grief alike and gladness from the seed of Adam spring,
Since He willed to be Son of Adam, Whose praises the angels sing.
And yet have we sin as our birthright, and sin's pain must we ever
     bear,
Nor its power may we flee! Yet pity He feeleth for our despair,
Whose Strength is aye linked with Mercy, and with Mercy goes hand
     in hand,
And for man, as a Man, He suffered, and did falsehood by truth
     withstand.

"No longer be wroth with thy Maker! If thou wouldst not thy soul were
     lost —
And here for thy sin do penance, nor longer thus rashly boast,
For he who, with words untamèd, is fain to avenge his wrong,
His own mouth shall, I ween, speak his judgment ere ever the time be
     long.
Learn faith from the men of old-time, whose rede ever waxeth new,
For Plato alike and the Sibyls in their day spake words so true,

218

And long years ere the time had ripened His coming they did foretell
Who made for our sin's Atonement, and drew us from depths of Hell.
God's Hand from those torments took us, and God's Love lifted us on
      high,
But they who His love disdainèd, they yet in Hell's clutches lie!

"From the lips of the whole world's Lover came a message of love and
      peace,
(For He is a Light all-lightening, and never His faith doth cease,)
And he to whom love He showeth, findeth aye in that Love his bliss,
Yet twofold I ween is the message, and His token some read amiss;
For the world may buy, as it pleaseth, God's Wrath or His Love so
      great.
Say, which of the twain wilt thou choose here, shall thy guerdon be
      Love or Hate?
For the sinner without repentance, he flieth God's faith and Face,
But he who his sin confesseth, doth find in His presence grace!

"From the shrine of his heart, who shall keep Him? Tho' hidden the
      thought within,
And secret, and thro' its darkness no sunbeam its way may win,
(For thought is a secret chamber, fast locked, tho' no lock it bear,)
Yet, tho' against man it be closèd, God's light ever shineth there.
He pierceth the wall of darkness, and silent and swift His spring,
As no sound betrayed His coming, as no footstep was heard to ring,
So silent His way He goeth — And swift as our thoughts have flown,
Ere God passed of our heart the threshold, our thoughts unto Him were
      known!
And the pure in heart He chooseth; he who doth an ill deed begin,
Since God knoweth the thoughts of all men, full sorely shall rue his sin.
And the man who by deeds God's favour doth forfeit, what shall he
      gain?
Tho' the world count him honour-worthy, his soul seeketh rest in vain.
And where wilt thou seek for shelter if *God* as thy foeman stand,
Who of wrath or of love giveth payment, as men serve Him, with equal
      hand?
Thou art lost if thy God be against thee — If thou wouldst His favour
      earn,
Then away from thy wrath and thy folly thy thoughts to His goodness
      turn!"

Quoth Parzival, "Here I thank thee, from my heart, that such faithful
      rede
Thou hast given of him who withholdeth from no man his rightful meed,

But evil, as good, requiteth — Yet my youth hath been full of care,
And my faith hath but brought me sorrow, and ill to this day I fare!"

Then the hermit he looked on the Waleis, "If a secret be not thy grief,
Right willing thy woe I'll hearken, I may bring thee perchance relief;
Of some counsel may I bethink me such as yet to thyself dost fail!"
Quoth Parzival, "Of my sorrows the chiefest is for the Grail,
And then for my wife — none fairer e'er hung on a mother's breast,
For the twain is my heart yet yearning, with desire that ne'er findeth
    rest."

Quoth his host, "Well, Sir Knight, thou speakest, such sorrow is good
    to bear;
If thus for the wife of thy bosom thy heart knoweth grief and care,
And Death find thee a faithful husband, tho' Hell vex thee with
    torments dire
Yet thy pains shall be swiftly ended, God will draw thee from out Hell-
    fire.
But if for the *Grail* thou grievest, then much must I mourn thy woe,
O! foolish man, since fruitless thy labours, for thou shalt know
That none win the Grail save those only whose names are in Heaven
    known,
They who to the Grail do service, they are chosen of God alone;
And mine eyes have surely seen this, and sooth is the word I say!"
Quoth Parzival, "Thou hast been there?" "Sir Knight," quoth the hermit,
    "Yea!"
But never a word spake our hero of the marvels himself had seen,
But he asked of his host the story, and what men by "The Grail" should
    mean?
Spake the hermit, "Full well do I know this, that many a knightly hand
Serveth the Grail at Monsalväsch, and from thence, throughout all the
    land,
On many a distant journey these gallant Templars fare,
Whether sorrow or joy befall them, for their sins they this penance bear!

"And this brotherhood so gallant, dost thou know what to them shall
    give
Their life, and their strength and their valour — then know, by a *stone*
    they live,
And that stone is both pure and precious — Its name hast thou never
    heard?
Men call it *Lapis Exilis* — by its magic the wondrous bird,
The Phoenix, becometh ashes, and yet doth such virtue flow
From the stone, that afresh it riseth renewed from the ashes glow,

220

And the plumes that erewhile it moulted spring forth yet more fair and
      bright —
And tho' faint be the man and feeble, yet the day that his failing sight
Beholdeth the stone, he dies not, nor can, till eight days be gone,
Nor his countenance wax less youthful — If one daily behold that
      stone,
(If a man it shall be, or a maiden 'tis the same,) for a hundred years,
If they look on its power, their hair groweth not grey, and their face
      appears
The same as when first they saw it, nor their flesh nor their bone shall
      fail
But young they abide for ever — And this stone all men call the Grail.

"And Its holiest power, and the highest shall I ween be renewed today,
For ever upon Good Friday a messenger takes her way.
From the height of the highest Heaven a Dove on her flight doth wing,
And a Host, so white and holy, she unto the stone doth bring.
And she layeth It down upon It; and white as the Host the Dove
That, her errand done, swift wingeth her way to the Heaven above.
Thus ever upon Good Friday doth it chance as I tell to thee:
And the stone from the Host receiveth all good that on earth may be
Of food or of drink, the earth beareth as the fulness of Paradise.
All wild things in wood or in water, and all that 'neath Heaven flies,
To that brotherhood are they given, a pledge of God's favour fair,
For His servants He ever feedeth and the Grail for their needs doth
      care!

"Now hearken, the Grail's elect ones, say who doth their service claim?
On the Grail, in a mystic writing, appeareth each chosen name,
If a man it shall be, or a maiden, whom God calls to this journey blest.
And the message no man effaceth, till all know the high behest,
But when all shall the name have read there, as it came, doth the
      writing go:
As children the Grail doth call them, 'neath its shadow they wax and
      grow.
And blessèd shall be the mother whose child doth the summons hear,
Rich and poor alike rejoiceth when the messenger draweth near,
And the Grail son or daughter claimeth! They are gathered from every
      land,
And ever from shame and sorrow are they sheltered, that holy band.
In Heaven is their rewarding, if so be that they needs must die,
Then bliss and desire's fulfilment are waiting them all on high!

"They who took no part in the conflict, when Lucifer would fight

With the Three-in-One those angels were cast forth from Heaven's
      height.
To the earth they came at God's bidding, and that wondrous stone did
      tend,
Nor was It less pure for their service, yet their task found at last an end.
I know not if God forgave them, or if they yet deeper fell,
This one thing I know of a surety, what God doeth, He doeth well!
But ever since then to this service nor maiden nor knight shall fail,
For God calleth them all as shall please Him! — and so standeth it with
      the Grail!"

Quoth Parzival, "So, since knighthood may conquer, with spear and
      shield,
Both the fame of *this* life, and the blessing which Paradise shall yield,
Since my soul ever longed for knighthood, and I fought where'er strife
      might be,
And my right hand hath neared full often the guerdon of victory,
If God be the God of battles, if He know how a man should fight,
Let Him name me as one of His servants, of the Grail let Him make me
      knight:
They shall own that I fear no danger, nor from strife would I turn
      aside!"
But the hermit made answer gently, "First must thou beware of pride,
For lightly may youth mislead thee; and the grace of humility
Mayst thou lose, and the proud God doth punish, as full surely is
      known to me!"
And tears filled his eyes to o'erflowing, and his sad thoughts awhile
      did turn
To a story of old, and our hero he bade from its lesson learn.

And he quoth, "Sir Knight, at Monsalväsch a king reigned in days of
      yore,
His name all men know as Anfortas, and I weep for him evermore.
Yea, and thou too shalt mourn his sorrow, for bitter the woe, I ween,
And the torment of heart and body that his guerdon from pride hath
      been.
For his youth and his worldly riches they led him an evil road,
And he sought for Frau Minne's favour in paths where no peace abode.

"But the Grail all such ways forbiddeth, and both knight alike and
      squire
Who serve the Grail must guard them from the lust of untamed desire.
By meekness their pride must be conquered, if they look for a heavenly
      prize,

222

And the brotherhood holdeth hidden the Grail from all stranger eyes:
By their warlike skill and prowess the folk from the lands around,
They keep afar, and none knoweth where the Grail and Its Burg are
    found
Save those whom the Grail shall summon within Monsalväsch' wall —
Yet *one,* uncalled, rode thither and evil did then befall,
For foolish he was, and witless, and sin-laden from thence did fare,
Since he asked not his host of his sorrow and the woe that he saw him
    bear.
No man would I blame, yet *this* man, I ween, for his sins must pay,
Since he asked not the longed-for question which all sorrow had put
    away.
(Sore laden his host with suffering, earth knoweth no greater pain.)
And before him King Lähelein came there, and rode to the Lake
    Brimbane.
Libbèals, the gallant hero, a joust there was fain to ride,
And Lähelein lifeless left him, on the grass by the water-side,
(Prienlascours, methinks, was his birthplace) and his slayer then led
    away
His charger, so men knew the evil thus wrought by his hand that day.

"And I think me, Sir knight, *thou* art Lähelein? For thou gavest unto my
    care
A steed that such token showeth as the steeds of the Grail Knights bear!
For the white dove I see on its housing, from Monsalväsch it surely
    came?
Such arms did Anfortas give them while joy yet was his and fame.
Their shields bare of old the token, Titurel gave it to his son
Frimutel, and such shield bare that hero when his death in a joust he
    won.
For his wife did he love so dearly no woman was loved so well
By man, yet in truth and honour, — and the same men of thee shall tell
If thou wakenest anew old customs, and thy wife from thine heart dost
    love —
Hold thou fast to such fair example lest thy steps from the right path
    rove!
And in sooth thou art wondrous like him who once o'er the Grail did
    reign,
Say, what is thy race? whence art thou? and tell me I pray thy name!"

Each gazed for a space on the other, and thus quoth Parzival,
"Son am I to a king and hero who through knightly courage fell,
In a joust was he slain — Now I pray thee, Sir Hermit, of this thy grace,
That thou, in thy prayers henceforward, wilt give to his name a place.

Know, Gamuret, did they call him, and he came from fair Anjou —
Sir Host I am not Lähelein; if ever such sin I knew
'Twas in my days of folly, yet in truth have I done the same,
Here I make of my guilt confession, and my sin unto thee I name,
For the prince who once fell a victim unto my sinful hand
Was he whom men called 'the Red Knight,' Prince Ither of Cumberland.
On the greensward I lifeless stretched him, and as at my feet he lay,
Harness, and horse, and weapons, as my booty I bare away!"

Spake the host as his words were ended, (the tale he ill pleased must
        hear,)
"Ah! world, wherefore deal thus with us? since sorrow and grief and
        fear
Far more than delight dost thou give us! Say, is this thy reward alone?
For ever the song that thou singest doth end in a mournful tone!"
And he spake, "O thou son of my sister, what rede may I give to thee?
Since the knight thou hast slain in thy folly, thy flesh and thy blood
        was he!
If thou, blood-guiltiness bearing, shalt dare before God to stand,
For one blood were ye twain, to God's justice thy life shall repay thine
        hand.
Say, for Ither of Gaheviess fallen, what payment dost think to give?
The crown he of knightly honour! God gave him, while he might live,
All that decketh man's life; for all evil his true heart did truly mourn,
True balsam was he of the faithful, to honour and glory born.
And shame fled before his coming, and truth in his heart did dwell,
And for love of his lovely body many women shall hate thee well!
For well did they love his coming, and to serve them he aye was fain,
But their eyes that shone fair for his fairness he ne'er shall rejoice again!
Now, may God show His mercy to thee whose hand hath such evil
        wrought,
Herzeleide the queen, thy mother, thou too to her death hast
        brought—"
"Nay! Nay! not so, holy father! What sayest thou?" quoth Parzival,
"Of what dost thou here accuse me? Were I king o'er the wondrous
        Grail
Not all Its countless riches would repay me if this be sooth,
These words that thy lips have spoken! And yet if I, in very truth,
Be son unto thy sister, then show that thou mean'st me well,
And say, without fear or falsehood, are these things true that thou dost
        tell?"

Then the hermit he spake in answer, "Ne'er learnt I to deceive,
Thy mother she died of sorrow in the day thou her side didst leave,

224

Such rewarding her love won for her! *Thou* wast the beast that hung
On her breast, the wingèd dragon that forth from her body sprung,
That spread its wings and left her: in a dream was it all foretold
Ere yet the sorrowing mother the babe to her breast did hold!

"And two other sisters had I, Schoisianè she was one;
She bare a child — Woe is me, her death thro' this birth she won!
Duke Kiot of Katelangen was her husband, and since that day
All worldly joy and honour he putteth from him away.
Siguné, their little daughter, was left to thy mother's care:
And sorrow for Schoisianè in my heart do I ever bear!
So true was her heart and faithful, an ark 'gainst the flood of sin.
A maiden, my other sister, her pure life doth honour win,
For the Grail she ever tendeth — Rèpanse de Schoie, her name,
Tho' none from Its place may move It whose heart showeth taint of
        shame,
In *her* hands is It light as a feather — And brother unto us twain
Is Anfortas, by right of heirship he king o'er the Grail doth reign;
And he knoweth not joy, but sorrow, yet one hope I ween is his,
That his pain shall at last be turnèd to delight and to endless bliss.
And wondrous the tale of his sorrow, as, nephew, I'll tell to thee,
And if true be thine heart and faithful his grief shall thy sorrow be!

"When he died, Frimutel, our father, they chose them his eldest son
As Lord of the Grail and Its knighthood, thus Anfortas his kingdom
        won,
And of riches and crown was he worthy, and we were but children
        still —
When he came to the years of manhood, when love joyeth to work her
        will
On the heart, and his lips were fringèd with the down of early youth,
Frau Minne laid stress upon him who for torment hath little ruth.
But if love the Grail King seeketh other than he find writ,
'Tis a sin, and in sorrow and sighing full sore shall he pay for it!

"And my lord and brother chose him a lady for service fair,
Noble and true he deemed her, I say not what name she bare;
Well he fought in that lady's honour, and cowardice from him fled,
And his hand many a shield-rim shattered, by love's fire was he
        venture led.
So high stood his fame that no hero in knightly lands afar
Could he brook to be thought his equal, so mighty his deeds of war,
And his battle-cry was 'Amor,' yet it seemeth unto me
Not all too well such cry suiteth with a life of humility.

"One day as the king rode lonely, in search of some venture high
(Sore trouble it brought upon us,) with love's payment for victory,
For love's burden lay heavy on him, in a joust was he wounded sore
With a poisoned spear, so that healing may be wrought on him
    nevermore.
For thine uncle, the King Anfortas, he was smitten thro' the thigh
By a heathen who with him battled, for he jousted right skilfully.
He came from the land of Ethnisé — where forth from fair Paradise
Flow the streams of the River Tigris, and he thought him, that heathen
    wise,
He should win the Grail, and should hold It — On his spear had he
    graven his name,
From afar sought he deeds of knighthood, over sea and land he came.
The fame of the Grail drew him thither, and evil for us his strife,
His hand joy hath driven from us and clouded with grief our life!

"But thine uncle had battled bravely and men praised his name that
    day —
With the spear-shaft yet fast in his body he wended his homeward way.
And weeping arose and wailing as he came once again to his own,
And dead on the field lay his foeman, nor did we for his death make
    moan!

"When the king came, all pale and bloodless, and feeble of strength and
    limb,
Then a leech stretched his hand to the spear-wound, and the iron he
    found fast within,
With the hilt, wrought of reed, and hollow, and the twain from the
    wound he drew.
Then I fell on my knees, and I vowed me to God, with a heart so true,
That henceforward the pride of knighthood, and its fame, would I
    know no more,
If but God would behold my brother and would succour his need so
    sore.
Then flesh, wine, and bread I forswore there, and all food that by blood
    might live,
That lust might no longer move me my life I to God would give,
And I tell thee, O son of my sister, that the wailing arose anew
When my weapons I put from off me and ungirded my sword so true,
And they spake, 'Who shall guard our mysteries? who shall watch o'er
    the wondrous Grail?'
And tears fell from the eyes of the maidens, but their weeping might
    naught avail!

226

"To the Grail, then, they bare Anfortas, if Its virtue might bring relief;
But, alas! when his eyes beheld It yet heavier waxed his grief
As the life sprang afresh within him, and he knew that he might not
    die;
And he liveth, while here I hide me in this life of humility,
And the power of the Grail, and Its glory, with their monarch have
    waxen weak.
For the venom, his wound that poisoned, tho' the leeches their books
    did seek
Yet found they nor help nor healing — Yea, all that their skill might
    learn
'Gainst the poison of Aspis, Elkontius, of Liseis, and Ecidemon,
All spells 'gainst the worm empoisoned, 'gainst Jecis or Meàtris;
Or all that a wise man knoweth of roots or of herbs; I wis
Naught was there in all might help him; nor rede I a longer tale
Since *God* willeth not his healing what man's skill may aught avail?

"Then we sent to the mystic waters, in a far-off land they rise,
Pison, Gihon, Tigris, Euphrates, the rivers of Paradise,
And so near they flow that the perfumes which breathe from its scented
    air
Shall yet to their streams be wafted — If their waters perchance might
    bear
Some plant from the wondrous garden that might succour us in our
    woe,
But vain thought, and fruitless labour, fresh sorrow our heart did know!

"Nor here did we end our labour, for again for the bough we sought
Which the Sibyl unto Aeneas as a shield 'gainst Hell's dangers brought.
'Gainst the smoke and the fire of Phlegethon, and the rivers that flow
    in Hell
Would it guard, and for long we sought it, for we thought, if such
    chance befell
That the spear in Hell-fire was welded, and the poison from Hell did
    spring
That thus of our joy had robbed us, then this bough might salvation
    bring!

"But Hell, it knew naught of the poison! There liveth a wondrous bird
Who loveth too well her fledglings — Of the Pelican's love we heard,
How she teareth her breast and feedeth her young with the quickening
    food
Of her own life-blood, and then dieth — So we took of that bird the
    blood,

227

Since we thought that her love might help us, and we laid it upon the
sore
As best we could — Yet, I wot well, no virtue for us it bore!

"A strange beast, the Unicorn, liveth, and it doth in such honour keep
The heart of a spotless maiden that it oft at her knee will sleep.
And the heart of that beast we took us, and we took us the red-fire
stone
That lies 'neath its horn, if the king's wound might its healing virtue
own.
And we laid on the wound the carbuncle, and we put it the wound
within,
Yet still was the sore empoisoned nor aid from the stone might win!

"And sore with the King we sorrowed — Then a magic herb we found,
(Men say, from the blood of a dragon it springeth from out the ground,)
With the stars, and the wind, and the heaven, close-bound, doth it win
its power,
Lest perchance, by the flight of the dragon, when the stars bring the
circling hour,
And the moon draweth near to her changing, (for sorer then grows the
pain,)
The herb might our grief have aided — Yet its magic we sought in vain!

"Then the knights of the Grail knelt lowly, and for help to the Grail
they prayed,
And, behold! the mystic writing, and a promise it brought of aid,
For a knight should come to the castle, and so soon as he asked the
king
Of the woe that so sorely pained him his question should healing bring.
But let them beware, man or maiden, or child, should they warn the
knight
Of his task, he no healing bringeth, greater waxeth the sorrow's might.
And the writing it ran, 'Ye shall mark this, forewarning shall bring but
ill,
And in the first night of his coming must the healer his task fulfil,
Or the question shall lose its virtue; but if at the chosen hour
He shall speak, *his* shall be the kingdom, and the evil hath lost its
power.
So the hand of the Highest sendeth to Anfortas the end of woe,
Yet *King* shall he be no longer tho' healing and bliss he know.'

"Thus we read in the Grail that our sorrow should come to an end that
day

228

That the knight should come who the meaning of the grief that he saw
      should pray —
Then salve of Nard we took us, and Teriak, and the wound we dressed,
And we burnt wood of Lignum Aloe for so might the king find rest.
Yet ever he suffereth sorely — Then fled I unto this place,
And my life little gladness knoweth till my brother hath gotten grace.
And the knight, he hath come, and hath left us, and ill for us all that
      day,
(But now did I speak of his coming,) sorrow-laden he rode away,
For he saw his host's woe and asked not, 'What aileth thee here, mine
      host?'
Since his folly such words forbade him great bliss shall he there have
      lost!"

Then awhile did they mourn together till the mid-day hour drew near,
And the host spake, "We must be seeking for food, and thine horse, I
      fear,
As yet shall be lacking fodder; nor know I how we shall feed
If not God in His goodness show us the herbs that shall serve our need,
My kitchen but seldom smoketh! Forgive thou the lack today,
And abide here, so long as shall please thee, if thy journey shall brook
      delay.
Of plants and of herbs would I teach thee much lore, if so be the grass
Were not hidden by snow — God grant us that this cold may be soon
      o'erpast —
Now break we yew-boughs for thy charger, far better its fare hath been
Erewhile 'neath the roof of Monsalväsch than shall here be its lot I ween!
Yet never a host shall ye meet with who rider alike and steed
Would as gladly bid share of his substance as I, had I all ye need!"

Then the twain they went forth on their errand — Parzival for his steed
      had care,
While the hermit for roots was seeking since no better might be their
      fare;
And the host his rule forgat not, he ate naught, whate'er he found,
Till the ninth hour, but ever hung them, as he drew them from out the
      ground,
On the nearest shrub, and there left them; many days he but ill might
      fare
For God's honour, since oft he lost them, the shrubs which his roots did
      bear.

Nor grudged they aught of their labour: then they knelt by the
      streamlet's flow,

And the roots and the herbs they washed there, and no laughter their
      lips might know.
Then their hands they washed, and the yew-boughs Parzival together
      bound
And bare them unto his charger ere the cavern again he found;
Then the twain by the fireside sat them, nor further might food be
      brought,
Nor on roast nor on boiled they fed them, nor found in their kitchen
      aught.
Yet so true was the love and the honour Parzival to the hermit bare
That he deemed he enough had eaten, and no better had been his fare
With Gurnemanz of Graharz, or e'en in Monsalväsch hall,
When the maidens passed fair before him and the Grail fed them each
      and all.

Then his kindly host quoth, "Nephew, despise not this food, for know
Lightly thou shalt not find one who shall favour and kindness show,
Of true heart, without fear of evil, as fain would I show to thee."
And Parzival quoth, "May God's favour henceforward ne'er light on
      me
If food ever better pleased me, or I ate with a better will
What a host ever set before me, such fare doth content me still."

Their hands they need not wash them for such food as before them lay,
'Twas no fish, that their eyes had harmèd as men oft are wont to say.
And were I or hawk or falcon I had lent me to the chase,
Nor stooped to the lure unwilling, nor fled from my master's face,
But an they no better fed me than at noontide they fed, these twain,
I had spread my wings right swiftly, nor come to their call again!

Why mock at this folk so faithful? 'Twas ever my way of old —
Yet ye know why, forsaking riches, they chose to them want and cold,
And the lack of all things joyful, such sorrow and grief of heart
They bare of true heart, God-fearing, nor had they in falsehood part;
And thus from the hand of the Highest they won payment for grief and
      woe,
And alike should the twain God's favour, as of old, so hereafter know.

Then up stood they again, and they gat them, Parzival and the holy
      man,
To the steed in its rocky stable, and full sadly the host began
As he spake to the noble charger, "Woe is me for thy scanty fare,
For the sake of the saddle upon thee and the token I see thee bear!"

When their care for the horse was ended, then sorrow sprang forth
    anew,
Quoth Parzival, "Host and uncle, my folly I needs must rue,
And fain would I tell the story if for shame I the word may speak;
Forgive me, I pray, of thy kindness, since in thee do l comfort seek,
For sorely, I ween, have I sinnèd; if thou canst no comfort find
No peace may be mine, but for ever the chains of remorse shall bind.
Of true heart shalt thou mourn my folly — He who to Monsalväsch
    rode,
He who saw Anfortas' sorrow, he who spake not the healing word,
'Twas I, child and heir of misfortune, 'twas I, Parzival, alone,
Ill have I wrought, and I know not how I may for such ill atone!"

Spake the hermit, "Alas! my nephew, thou speakest the words of woe,
Vanished our joy, and sorrow henceforth must we grasp and know,
Since folly of bliss betrayed thee: senses five did God give to thee,
And methinks, in the hour of thy testing, their counsel should better be.
Why guarded they not thine honour, and thy love as a man to men,
In the hour that thou satst by Anfortas? Of a truth hadst thou spoken
    then!

"Nor would I deny thee counsel; mourn not for thy fault too sore,
Thou shalt, in a fitting measure, bewail thee, and grief give o'er.
For strange are the ways, and fitful, of mankind, oft is youth too wise
And old age turneth back to folly, and darkened are wisdom's eyes,
And the fruit of a life lieth forfeit, while green youth doth wax old and
    fade —
Not in this wise true worth shall be rooted, and payment in praise be
    paid.
Thine youth would I see fresh blooming, and thine heart waxing strong
    and bold,
While thou winnest anew thine honour, nor dost homage from God
    withhold.
For thus might it chance unto thee to win for thyself such fame
As shall make amends for thy sorrow, and God thee, as His knight,
    shall claim!

"Thro' my mouth would God teach thee wisdom; now say, didst thou
    see the spear,
In that wondrous Burg of Monsalväsch? As ever the time draws near
When Saturn his journey endeth — (that time by the wound we know,
And yet by another token, by the fall of the summer snow)
Then sorely the frost doth pain him, thy king and uncle dear,
And deep in the wound empoisoned once more do they plunge the spear,

One woe shall help the other, the spear cure the frost's sharp pain,
And crimson it grows with his life-blood ere men draw it forth again!

"When the stars return in their orbit, then the wailing it waxeth sore,
When they stand in opposition, or each to the other draw.
And the moon, in its waxing and waning, it causeth him bitter pain —
In the time that I erst have told thee then the king little rest may gain;
His flesh thro' the frost it groweth colder than e'en the snow,
But men know that the spear sharp-pointed doth with fiery venom
        glow,
And upon the wound they lay it, and the frost from his flesh so cold
It draweth, and lo! as crystals of glass to the spear doth hold,
And as ice to the iron it clingeth, and none looseth it from the blade.
Then Trebuchet the smith bethought him, in his wisdom two knives he
        made,
Of silver fair he wrought them, and sharp was the edge and keen —
(A spell on the king's sword written had taught him such skill I ween,)
Tho' no flame on earth can kindle Asbestos, as men do tell,
And never a fire may harm it, if these crystals upon it fell
Then the flame would leap and kindle and burn with a fiery glow
Till th'Asbestos lay in ashes, such power doth this poison know!

"The king, he rideth never, nor yet may he walk, or lie,
And he sitteth not, but, reclining, in tears his sad days pass by.
And the moon's changes work him evil — To a lake they call Brimbane
They bear him full oft for fishing that the breezes may soothe his pain.
This he calleth his day for hunting, tho' what booty shall be his share,
And he vex himself to gain it, for his host 'twould be meagre fare!
And from this there sprang the story that he should but a Fisher be,
Tho' little he recked the fable, no merchant I ween was he
Of salmon or aye of lamprey, he had chosen far other game
Were he freed from the load of sorrow and the burden of bitter pain."

Quoth Parzival, "So I found him; the king's skiff at anchor lay,
And for pastime, e'en as a fisher, the even he wore away;
And many a mile had I ridden that day, since from Pelrapär
When the sun stood high in the heaven, at noontide I forth must fare;
And at even I much bethought me where my shelter that night might be,
Then my uncle did fair entreat me, and my host for a space was he."

"A perilous way didst thou ride there," spake the host, "one that well
        they guard
Those Templars, nor strength nor cunning brings a traveller thro' their
        ward,

232

For danger full oft besets him, and oft he his life shall lose,
Life against life is their penance, all quarter these knights refuse.

"Yet scatheless I passed that woodland in the day that I found the king
By the lake," quoth the knight, "and at even his palace with grief did
    ring,
And sure, as they mourned, I think me, no folk ever mourned before!
In the hall rose the voice of wailing as a squire sprang within the door,
And a spear in his hand he carried, and to each of the walls he stept,
Red with blood was the spear, as they saw it, the people they mourned
    and wept."

Then answered the host, "Far sorer than before was the monarch's pain,
In this wise did he learn the tidings that Saturn drew near again,
And the star with a sharp frost cometh, and it helpeth no whit to lay
The spear on the sore as aforetime, *in* the wound must it plunge alway!
When that star standeth high in heaven the wound shall its coming
    know
Afore, tho' the earth shall heed not, nor token of frost shall show.
But the cold it came, and the snow-flakes fell thick in the following
    night
Tho' the season was spring, and the winter was vanquished by
    summer's might.
As the frost to the king brought sorrow and pain, so his people true
Were of joy bereft, as the moment of his anguish thus nearer drew."

And Trevrezent quoth, "In sorrow that folk hath both lot and part,
When the spear thro' the king's wound pierceth, it pierceth each faithful
    heart.
And their love to their lord, and their sorrow, such tears from their
    eyelids drew
That, methinks, in those bitter waters had they been baptized anew."

Spake Parzival unto the hermit, "Five-and-twenty they were, the maids
I saw stand before the monarch, and courteous their part they played."
And the host spake, "By God's high counsel such maidens alone avail
For the care of this wondrous mystery, and do service before the Grail.
And the Grail, It chooseth strictly, and Its knights must be chaste and
    pure, —
When the star standeth high in the heaven then grief must that folk
    endure,
And the young they mourn as the aged, and God's wrath it lasts for
    aye,
And ne'er to their supplication doth He hearken and answer 'Yea.'

"And, nephew, this thing would I tell thee, and my word shalt thou
    well believe,
They who to the Grail do service, they take, and again they give.
For they take to them little children, noble of birth and race —
If a land be without a ruler, and its people shall seek God's Face
And crave of His Hand a monarch, then He hearkeneth to their prayer,
And a knight, from the Grail host chosen, as king to that land doth fare.
And well shall he rule that people, and happy shall be that land,
For the blessing of God goeth with him and God's wisdom doth guide
    his hand.

"God sendeth the *men* in secret, but the *maidens* in light of day
Are given unto their husbands; thus none spake to his wooing, Nay,
When King Kastis wooed Herzeleide, but joyful our sister gave,
Yet ne'er might her love rejoice him for Death dug at his feet a grave.
But in life had he given thy mother both Norgals and fair Waleis,
Those kingdoms twain and their cities, Kingrivals and Kanvoleis.
'Twas a fair gift, and known of all men — Then they rode on their
    homeward way,
But Death met them upon their journey, and he made of the king his
    prey,
And over both Waleis and Norgals Herzeleide, as queen, did reign,
Till Gamuret's right hand valiant won the maid, and her kingdoms
    twain.

"Thus the Grail Its maidens giveth, in the day, and the sight of men,
But It sendeth Its knights in the silence and their children It claims
    again, —
To the host of the Grail are they counted, Grail servants they all shall be,
So the will of God standeth written on the Grail for all men to see.

"He who would to the Grail do service, he shall women's love
    forswear:
A wife shall none have save the Grail king, and his wife a pure heart
    must bear,
And those others whom God's Hand sendeth, as king, to a kingless
    land —
But little I recked such counsel, to love's service I vowed my hand,
As the pride of my youth constrained me, and the beauty of woman's
    eyes,
And I rode full oft in her service, and I battled for knighthood's prize.
Fain was I for wild adventure, on jousting no more I thought,
So fair shone the love-light on me ever fiercer the strife I sought.
And thro' far-off lands and distant, in the service of love I fared,

234

And to win sweet love's rewarding right valiant the deeds I dared.
If heathen my foe or Christian, what mattered it unto me?
The fiercer the strife that beset me, the fairer my prize should be!

"And thus, for the love of woman, in three parts of the earth I fought,
In Europe, and far off Asia, and in Afric I honour sought.
If for gallant jousting I lusted I fought before Gaurivon;
By the mystic Mount of Fay-Morgan I many a joust have run.
And I fought by the Mount Agremontin, where are fiery men and
     fierce,
Yet the other side they burn not tho' their spears thro' the shield can
     pierce.
In Rohas I sought for ventures, and Slavs were my foemen then,
With lances they came against me and I trow they were gallant men!

"From Seville I took my journey, and I sailed o'er the tideless sea
Unto Sicily, since thro' Friant and Aquilea should my journey be.
Alas! alas! woe is me, for I met with thy father there,
I found him, and looked upon him, ere I from Seville must fare.
For e'en as I came to the city he there for a space abode,
And my heart shall be sore for his journey, since thence to Bagdad he
     rode,
And there, as thyself hast spoken, in a knightly joust he fell,
And forever my heart must mourn him, and my tongue of his praises
     tell!

"A rich man shall be my brother, nor silver nor gold would spare
When in secret I forth from Monsalväsch at his will and his word did
     fare;
For I took me his royal signet, and to Karkobra I came,
Where Plimizöl to the wide sea floweth, and the land, Barbigöl, they
     name.
And the Burg-grave he knew the token, ere I rode from the town again
Of horses and squires, as failed me, he raised me a gallant train,
And we rode thence to wild adventures, and to many a knightly deed,
For nothing had he begrudged me of aught that might serve my need.
Alone came I unto the city, and there at my journey's end
Did I leave those who had fared thence with me, and alone to
     Monsalväsch wend.

"Now hearken to me, my nephew, when thy father first saw my face
Of old in Seville's fair city, there did he such likeness trace
To his wife, fair Herzeleide, that he would me as brother claim,
Tho' never before had he seen me, and secret I held my name.

And in sooth was I fair to look on, as ever a man might be,
And my face by no beard was hidden; and sweetly he spake to me,
When he sought me within my dwelling — Yet many an oath I swore
And many a word of denial, yet ever he pressed me more
Till in secret at last I told him, his kinsman was I in truth,
And greatly did he rejoice him when he knew that his words were
      sooth!

"A jewel he gave unto me, and I gave to him at his will;
Thou sawest my shrine, green shall grass be, yet that shineth greener
      still,
'Twas wrought from the stone he gave me — a better gift he gave,
For his nephew as squire he left me, Prince Ither, the true and brave.
His heart such lore had taught him that falsehood his face did flee,
The King of Cumberland was he, who, thou sayest, was slain by thee.
Then no longer might we delay us, but we parted, alas! for aye.
He rode to the land of Baruch, unto Rohas I took my way.

"In Celli three weeks I battled, and I deemed 'twas enough for fame,
From Rohas I took my journey and unto Gandein I came,
('Twas that town from which first thy grandsire, his name of Gandein
      did take,)
And many a deed did Ither, and men of his prowess spake.
And the town lieth near the river, where Graien and Drave they meet,
And the waters I ween are golden, — there Ither found guerdon sweet,
For thine aunt, Lamire, she loved him, she was queen of that fair land,
Gandein of Anjou, her father, he gave it unto her hand.
And Lamire was her name, but her country shall be Styria to this
      day —
And many a land must he traverse who seeketh for knightly fray.

"It grieveth me sore for my red squire, men honoured me for his sake,
And Ither was thy near kinsman tho' of *that* thou small heed didst take!
Yet God *He* hath not forgotten, and thy deed shall He count for sin,
And I wot thou shalt first do penance ere thou to His peace shalt win.
And, weeping, this truth I tell thee, two mortal sins shall lie
On thine heart, thou hast slain thy kinsman, and thy mother, thro' thee,
      must die.
And in sooth shalt thou sore bewail her; in the day thou didst leave her
      side,
So great was her love, and faithful, that for grief at thy loss she died.
Now do thou as here I rede thee, repent thee and pay sin's cost,
That thy conflict on earth well ended thy soul be not ever lost."

Then the host he quoth full kindly, "Nephew, now say the word,
Whence hast thou yon gallant charger? Not yet I the tale have heard!"
"In a joust, Sir Host, did I win it, when I rode from Siguné's cell
In a gallop I smote the rider and he from the saddle fell,
And the steed was mine, I rode hence, — from Monsalväsch he came,
      the knight."
Quoth the host, "Is the man yet living who thus with thee did fight?"
"Yea, I saw him fly before me, and beside me stood his steed."
"Nay, if thou in such wise dost bear thee thou art scant of wit indeed!
The Grail-knights dost thou rob, and thinkest their friendship thereby
      to win?"
"Nay, my uncle, in strife I won it, and he who shall count it sin
Let him ask how the thing hath chanced thus, 'twas a fair fight we
      fought, we twain,
Nor was it for naught that I took it, for first had my steed been slain!"

Quoth Parzival, "Who was the maiden who the Grail in her hands did
      bear,
Her mantle, that eve, she lent me?" — Quoth the hermit, "That lady fair
Is thine aunt, if her robe she lent thee of the loan shalt thou not be vain,
For surely she deemed that hereafter thou shouldst there as monarch
      reign.
And the Grail, and herself, yea and I too, should honour thee as our lord:
And a gift didst thou take from thine uncle, for he gave thee, I ween, a
      sword,
And sin hast thou won in the wearing, since thy lips, which to speak
      are fain,
There spake not the mystic question which had loosened his sorrow's
      chain,
And that sin shalt thou count to the other, for 'tis time that we lay us
      down."
Nor couches nor cushions had they, but they laid them upon the ground,
And for bedding the rushes served them — too humble, I ween, such
      bed
For men of a race so noble, yet they deemed they were not ill-sped.

Then twice seven days he abode there, with the hermit his lot did share,
And the herb of the ground was his portion — yet he sought not for
      better fare,
Right gladly he bare such hardness that should bring to him food so
      sweet,
For as priest did his host absolve him, and as knight gave him counsel
      meet!

Quoth Parzival to the hermit, "Say who shall he be, who lay
Before the Grail? grey was he, yet his face it was as the day!"
Spake the host, "Titurel thou sawest, and he shall grandsire be
To thy mother, first king and ruler of the Grail and Its knights was he.
But a sickness hath fallen on him, and he lieth, nor findeth cure,
Yet his face on the Grail yet looketh, by Its power shall his life endure!
Nor his countenance changeth colour, and his counsel shall aye be
      wise —
In his youth he rode far and jousted, and won to him valour's prize.

"An thou wouldst that thy life be adornèd with true worth as thy
      crown of fame,
Then ne'er mayst thou hate a woman, but shall honour, as knight, her
      name,
For women and priests, thou knowest, unarmèd shall be their hand,
Yet the blessing of God watcheth o'er them, and as shield round the
      priest doth stand;
For the priest, he careth for thee, that thine end may be free from ill,
So treat thou no priest as a foeman, but serve him with right good will.
For naught on the earth thou seest that is like to his office high,
For he speaketh that word unto us which our peace and our life did buy;

And his hand hath been blest for the holding of the pledge on the altar
      laid,
To assure us of sin's forgiveness, and the price for our pardon paid.
And a priest who from sin doth guard him, and who to his Lord shall
      give
Pure heart and pure hand for His service, say, what man shall holier
      live?"

Now this day was their day of parting — Trevrezent to our hero spake,
"Leave thou here they sins behind thee, God shall me for thy surety
      take,
And do thou as I have shown thee, be steadfast and true of heart!"
Think ye with what grief and sorrow the twain did asunder part.

CHAPTER 12

Die Krone (The Crown) by Heinrich von dem Türlin

TRANSLATED BY J.L. WESTON

The early parts of the story have nothing to do with the Grail, though they do include some strange episodes. Suffice it to say that by verse nineteen thousand of the poem Gawain is in search of the Grail, accompanied by Lancelot, Kay and a knight called Colgrevance (interestingly, this same grouping of characters reappears later in Malory and in another of Chrétien's Arthurian poems unconnected with the Grail). They part at a crossroads and each undergoes a series of adventures. Gawain arrives at the Castle of Wonders, where he meets with the sister of the magician who owns it — here called Gansgutor but fulfilling a similar role to that of Klingsor. She warns him to take care not to fall asleep if he wishes to learn of the Grail. Eventually, after several further adventures, Gawain makes his rendezvous with Lancelot and Colgrevance (Kay has been imprisoned elsewhere) and the three enter the Grail Castle. Here they are led into a hall of surpassing splendour, where the floor is strewn with roses and an ancient man lies on a bed watching two youths playing chess. As evening approaches the hall fills with youths and maidens, and a single youth enters with a sword which he lays before the old man. Gawain is offered a drink, which he refuses. His comrades, however, accept and fall instantly asleep. Then two damsels enter carrying lights, followed by two knights with a Spear and two more women with a Toblier *(possibly* tailleor, *a dish or plate) on which are three drops of blood. They are followed by the most beautiful woman ever created, carrying a box and accompanied by a weeping maiden.*

The Spear is laid on the table and next to it the Toblier. *In the box*

239

carried by the beautiful woman is a piece of bread which she breaks into three, giving one piece to the old man. Gawain now recognizes her as the magician's sister and at once asks concerning the events he has witnessed. The people in the hall leap up with cries of joy. The old man tells Gawain that these are the mysteries of the Grail which none have seen save Parzival who failed to ask about them. Through his question Gawain has freed both the living and the dead, for though they seem real enough the old man and his companions are really ghosts — only the fair lady and the weeping maiden are living beings, who because of their purity are allowed to possess the Grail and feed him from it once a year. All Gawain's adventures have come from the Grail, and now that he has succeeded where all others have failed he must accept as a reward the Sword, which will help him in every danger he encounters from now onwards. After this no one will see the Grail again and he must ask no more concerning it. As daybreak falls the old man finishes his story and at once he and the court vanish away, leaving only the magician's sister and her attendant. (J.M.)

Sir Gawain at the Grail castle

Long and weary were the journeyings that good knight, Sir Gawain, made in search of the Grail; for he came even to a land wherein from the waxing to the waning of the moon there lacked not adventures stiff and stern. Yet his manhood stood him in good stead at need, otherwise had the toil and the strife weakened him overmuch. Howsoe'er it vexed him sorely. Yet the road led him at the last to a rich and goodly land, so well tilled that naught was lacking of the fruits of the earth, corn, and vines, and fair trees, all whereby man might live grew freely on either hand. That was right pleasing to Sir Gawain, who was worn with travel, for the land was like unto a garden, green, and in nowise bare, and of right sweet odour; it might well be held for an earthly Paradise, since 'twas full of all delights that heart of man might desire.

But ere ever he came within its borders a strange adventure befell him, for he saw a fiery sword, the breadth whereof he might not measure, which kept the entry to a fastness, within which stood a dwelling, cunningly builded, but the walls whereof were clear and transparent as glass; naught that passed there-

240

in might be held secret but 'twould have been seen without. I wot not how it chanced, but 'twas void and bare, and Sir Gawain deemed it strange and of ill omen; I think me well 'twas of ill, for 'twas a wild land, but therewith he left it behind him.

So the knight journeyed through that fair country, where he found all that heart desired, or that was needful to the body, so that his strength came again unto him, and he was wholly recovered of the pains which he had endured. And when he had ridden a twelve days' journey through the woodland he came again to an open country, and there he did meet with his comrades, Sir Lancelot and Sir Calogreant, whereat he was greatly rejoiced. The twain had wandered far astray, and save for their arms he might scarce have known them. He found them sleeping under a tree, whither his road led him, and for very joy he wakened them. Then they greeted each other gladly, and told each to the other the toils and the troubles that had befallen them as they rode singly or in company on their quest.

No longer might they abide there, for it drew towards nightfall; and as they went their way they beheld and saw how on the same track a squire spurred swiftly towards them, nor would he slacken his pace ere they met; right friendly was his mien as he bade Sir Gawain and his comrades be welcome to God, and to his lord, and to himself, in sooth he spoke truly and in no mockery, for good token he gave thereafter of his truth. He prayed them, in the name of his lord, that since they were come into his land they would do him so much honour as to turn aside unto his dwelling, for they were on the right road, and 'twas nigh at hand.

Sir Gawain made answer, "I thank ye right heartily, ye and your lord, know that we will gladly come unto your dwelling an' we be not forbidden by sword-thrust." The squire spake again, "This will I tell ye surely, follow ye this road straight unto the Burg, 'tis here full nigh at hand; I, having shown ye the road, will hasten thither, and ride ye as softly as ye will." With that he turned him again, and had swiftly outridden them.

Know ye that the knights were not over-long upon the road, for the twain, Sir Lancelot and Sir Calogreant, were sore a-hungered; sudden they saw before them a castle, fair to look upon, and they deemed they should find a goodly lodging therein. Without, on a meadow, was a great company of knights, who vied with each other in skilful horsemanship, as knights are wont to do. Without spear or shield, in courteous wise they rode hither and thither on the open field; but when the three had come so near that they took knowledge of them, that noble folk left their sport, and rode swift as flight over the meadow toward the road, and received the guests with gentle greeting, as is love's custom, bidding them welcome to their lord's land. With that they took them in safe-conduct, and led them even to the castle — I wot Sir Gawain there found gladsome gain!

The Burg was fairly builded, and therein dwelt a great folk, knights and ladies, who were right joyful as was fitting, that did Sir Gawain mark right well, and drew comfort therefrom. So well did they receive him that it grieved him naught that he was come unto their company; they beheld him right gladly, and all that was needful to him they gave him with full hand. So went he with the twain, Sir Lancelot and Sir Calogreant, unto the lord of the castle, even as they showed him the road.

'Twas the fairest palace ever builded, an the tale lie not no richer might tongue of man describe, or heart of man conceive. Never might the host be vexed through poverty, a courteous prince he was and good, and wise withal I ween. For the summer's heat his hall was all bestrewn with roses, whereof the perfume rejoiced him greatly. White was his vesture, cunningly wrought and sewn with diaper work of gold, 'twas a skilful hand that wrought it! Before him sat two youths of noble birth, whom he ever kept in his company; they jested lightly, the one with the other, the while they played at chess before his couch, and the lord leaned him over towards the board, for it gladdened him to behold the game, and to hearken to their jesting.

When Sir Gawain entered the hall the host received him and his two comrades well, and bade them be seated; Sir Gawain he made to sit beside him on the couch, on a cushion of rose-coloured silk did they sit together. In sooth there was pleasure enow of question and answer, and of knightly talk betwixt the host and Sir Gawain; and they who sat at the chess board jested and made merry. Thus they made pastime till nightfall, and then were the tables set that all might eat, nor was any man forgotten, there was space for all.

Then the knights arose, and Sir Gawain also, but the host spake to them all by name, for right well he knew them, and bade them sit by him, which they were nothing loth to do. With that there came a great company of knights and ladies, who saluted the host, as is the fashion of women, and sat them all down. Long was the hall and wide, yet 'twas full in every part, and all the tables filled. After them came full twenty chamberlains, young men of noble birth and courteous bearing, who bare napkins and basins, that did the knights mark well; behind them were a great company, bearing candles and candlesticks without number, with that was the hall so light 'twere hard to tell whether 'twere day or night. And there followed thirty minstrels, and others who sang full many a tuneful melody, all with one accord rejoiced and sang praises.

The two knights and Sir Gawain sat beside their host, yet not on a level, for Sir Gawain sat above, and they below, and the host 'twixt the three. The others sat all around the hall, and ate each twain together, a knight with his lady. And when all were seated, and were fain to eat, then there came into the hall a wondrous fair youth, of noble bearing, and in his hand he held a sword, fair and broad, and laid it down before the host. With that Sir Gawain 'gan to bethink him what this might betoken. After the youth came cupbearers, who passed through the hall, serving wine to all who were seated ere they might eat. Sir Gawain and his comrades did they serve first of all, the while the host sat beside them and did neither eat nor drink. Nor would Sir Gawain drink, but for his comrades twain they were so sore vexed by thirst, that even though he bade them refrain yet must they drink withal, and thereafter did they fall into a deep slumber, and when Sir Gawain beheld this it vexed him sorely.

Oft-times did the lord of the castle pray Sir Gawain to drink, as a courteous host doth his guest, but otherwise was he minded, and well on his guard, lest he too fall asleep.

At the last came in fair procession, as it were, four seneschals, and as the last passed the door was the palace filled — nor were it fitting that I say more. In the sight of all there paced into the hall two maidens fair and graceful, bearing two candlesticks; behind each maid there came a youth, and the twain held between them a sharp spear. After these came other two maidens, fair in form and richly clad, who bare a salver of gold and precious stones, upon a silken cloth; and behind them, treading soft and slow, paced the fairest being whom since the world began God had wrought in woman's wise, perfect was she in form and feature, and richly clad withal. Before her she held on a rich cloth of samite a jewel wrought of red gold, in form of a base, whereon there stood another of gold and gems, fashioned even as a reliquary that standeth upon an altar. This maiden bare upon her head a crown of gold, and behind her came another, wondrous fair, who wept and made lament, but the others spake never a word, only drew nigh unto the host and bowed them low before him.

Sir Gawain might scarce trust his senses, for of a truth he knew the crowned maiden well, and that 'twas she who aforetime had spoken to him of the Grail, and bade him an he ever saw her again, with five maidens in her company, to fail not to ask what they did there — and thereof had he great desire.

As he mused thereon the four who bare spear and salver, the youths with the maidens, drew nigh and laid the spear upon the table, and the salver beneath it. Then before Sir Gawain's eyes there befell a great marvel, for the spear shed three great drops of blood into the salver that was beneath, and the old man, the host, took them straightway. Therewith came the maiden of whom I spake, and took the place of the other twain, and set the fair reliquary upon the table — that did Sir Gawain mark right well — he saw therein a bread, wherof the old man brake the third part, and ate.

With that might Sir Gawain no longer contain himself, but spake, saying, "Mine host, I pray ye for the sake of God, and by His Majesty, that ye tell me what meaneth this great company, and these marvels I behold?" And even as he spake all the folk, knights and ladies alike, who sat there, sprang from their seats with a great cry, and the sound as of great rejoicing. Straightway the host bade them again be seated as before, and make no sound until he bade, and this they did forthwith.

At the sound of the great cry the twain, Sir Lancelot and Sir Calogreant, wakened, for through the wine they had drunk they slept soundly, but even as they beheld the maidens who stood around the board, and the marvels that had chanced, they sank back into slumber, and so it was that for five hours sleep kept fast hold of them, the while the old man spake thus:

"Sir Gawain, this marvel which is of God may not be known unto all, but shall be held secret, yet since ye have asked thereof, sweet kinsman and dear guest, I may not withhold the truth. 'Tis the Grail which ye now behold. Herein have ye won the world's praise, for manhood and courage alike have ye right well shown, in that ye have achieved this toilsome quest. Of the Grail may I say no more save that ye have seen it, and that great gladness hath come of this your question. For now are many set free from the sorrow they long had borne, and small hope had they of deliverance. Great confidence and trust had we all in Perceval, that he would learn the secret things of the Grail, yet hence did he depart even as a coward who ventured naught, and asked naught. Thus did his quest miscarry, and he learned not that which of a surety he should have learned. So had he freed many a mother's son from sore travail, who live, and yet are dead. Through the strife of kinsmen did this woe befall, when one brother smote the other for his land: and for that treason was the wrath of God shown on him and on all his kin, that all were alike lost.

"That was a woeful chance, for the living they were driven out, but the dead must abide in the semblance of life, and suffer bitter woe withal. That must ye know — yet had they hope and comfort in God and His grace, that they should come even to the goal of their grief, in such fashion as I shall tell ye.

"Should there be a man of their race who should end this their sorrow, in that he should demand the truth of these marvels, that were the goal of their desire; so would their penance be fulfilled, and they should again enter into joy: alike they who lay dead and they who live, and now give thanks to God and to ye, for by ye are they now released. This spear and this food they nourish me and none other, for in that I was guiltless of the deed God condemned me not. Dead I am, though I bear not the semblance of death, and this my folk is dead with me. However that may be, yet though all knowledge be not ours, yet have we riches in plenty, and know no lack. But these maidens they be not dead, nor have they other penance save that they be even where I am. And this is by the command of God, that by this His mystery, which ye have here beheld, they shall nourish me once, and once alone, in the year. And know of a truth that the adventures ye have seen came of the Grail, and now is the penance perfected, and for ever done away, and your quest hath found its ending."

Therewith he gave him the sword, and told him he were right well armed therewith, and however much he might bear it in strife never would it break, and he bade him wear it all his days. Thus did he end his tale, telling no more, save that he might now leave the quest he had undertaken, and that for the rest, on the morrow should his toil be ended. And in so far as concerned the maidens 'twas through their unstained purity, and through no misdoing, that God had thus laid on them the service of the Grail; but now was their task ended, and they were sad at heart, for they knew well that never more should the Grail be so openly beheld of men, since that Sir Gawain had learned its secrets, for 'twas of the grace of God alone that mortal eyes might behold it, and its mysteries henceforth no tongue might tell.

With this speaking the night had passed, and the day began to dawn, and as his tale was done, lo! from before Sir Gawain's eyes the old man vanished, and with him the Grail, and all that goodly company, so that in the hall there abode none save the three knights and the maidens.

And Sir Gawain was somewhat sorry, when he saw his host no more, yet was he glad when the maiden spake, saying that his labour was now at an end, and he had in sooth done all that pertained unto the Quest of the Grail, for never elsewhere in any land, save in that Burg alone, might the Grail have been beheld. Yet had that land been waste, but God had hearkened to their prayer, and by his coming had folk and land alike been delivered, and for that were they joyful.

That day Sir Gawain abode there with his comrades, who rejoiced greatly when they heard the tale, and yet were sorrowful in that they had slumbered when the Grail passed before them, and so beheld it not. Good hostelry they found in that Burg, and when the morning dawned and they must needs depart then was many a blessing called down upon Sir Gawain by those maidens, that he might live many years in bliss and honour, this they prayed of a true heart, since he had set them free, and one blessing surely seeketh another. So the good knight departed from among them. Thus doth the Quest of Sir Gawain find an ending.

CHAPTER 13

The Quest for the Holy Grail

TRANSLATED BY W.W. COMFORT

The Knights of the Round Table were assembled at Camelot on Whitsun Eve, in the year 454. A damsel arrived from King Pelles and took Lancelot out into the forest and led him to a nunnery where he met his cousins Boort (or Bors) and Lionel. The nuns showed a wonderful youth called Galahad, and some thought he was Lancelot's son. Lancelot knighted the boy.

On Lancelot's return to Arthur's court a block of red marble was seen floating in the water, and in it was fastened a sword on which was written that only the best knight in the world could withdraw it. Gawain, Perceval, and others made the attempt but failed. An armoured Knight then appeared, being announced as of the line of David and Joseph of Arimathea. He sat in the Perilous Seat at the Round Table without receiving damage, and explained that he was the nephew of King Pelles, and that the Rich Fisher was his grandfather. He was thus recognized as the son of Lancelot and of the daughter of the Fisher King. It was reported in the court that Galahad would end the wonders of Great Britain and that by him the maimed King would be healed. He succeeded easily in withdrawing the sword from the block of marble.

A young maiden then appeared, and grieved that Lancelot should no longer be the best knight, and said that a hermit called Nasciens desired them to know that he would send the Holy Grail on that day to feed the knights of the Round Table. A tournament was arranged and Galahad showed his great skill. After Vespers they sat down to meat, thunder was heard and a bright light was seen. The Grail came into the presence of the diners, covered with white samite, and borne by unseen hands; and the room was filled with delicious perfumes. As the Grail passed around, each person received abundant food.

The Grail having passed out of their presence, Gawain informed the Knights that no one had heretofore been served thus except at the court of the maimed King. They all vowed to seek the Grail for a year and a day, or longer if need be, as they had not yet seen the vessel itself. They set forth, following different routes.

Galahad took no shield with him, but after five days' journey he arrived at an abbey where he obtained a mysterious shield originally belonging to King Evalac of the City of Sarras, and endowed with supernatural power by Josephus (the son of Joseph of Arimathea) for Evalac (afterwards called Mordrains), who had brought the shield to Great Britain. Josephus had come to Great Britain with his father Joseph. They had been imprisoned there by King Crudel and rescued by Mordrains. The shield could not be used by anyone until Galahad should come, the last of the race of Mordrain's brother-in-law Nasciens.

In the course of his journeyings Galahad came to the Castle of Maidens and delivered the captives who were confined there, and who represented the good souls imprisoned in Hell before the advent of Jesus Christ.

The story then relates various adventures of Gawain and Galahad, which are not of special importance.

Lancelot's wanderings led him to a chapel; and he lay down to sleep at the foot of a cross which stood just outside. While he was half asleep a sick knight approached on a bier drawn by two horses. The knight lamented his illness, and the Holy Grail came from the chapel towards the knight and healed him; and then he left, swearing that he would not rest until he could learn why the Grail appeared in so many places in Logres (England), and who brought it there. Lancelot awoke, and was informed by a voice that on account of his love for Guinevere he was not fit to stay near the Holy Grail.

Perceval also had interesting adventures. He learned from his aunt, a recluse, formerly Queen of the Waste Land, that he and Galahad and Bors would succeed in their quest of the Grail, and he received an explanation of the three great tables; the first, at which our Lord ate with his Apostles; the second, the table used by Joseph of Arimathea, when he came to England with four thousand companions, at which was a seat which no one but Josephus could occupy; the third, the Round Table, made in the time of Merlin. At this last there was one seat called the Perilous Seat, which could only be occupied by one who would achieve the Grail. He also learned that the Lance as well as the

Grail was an object of inquiry so that its mysteries might be understood; and that the maimed King was at Castle Corbenic.

Perceval came to a monastery where he saw King Evalac (now called Mordrains) on a bed, suffering from wounds and totally blind because he had made an effort to see the Grail itself, after he and his brother-in-law Nasciens had rescued Joseph from the prison into which King Crudel had thrown him after his arrival in England with the Holy Grail. Evalac had been waiting four hundred years for the good knight to come when he would be healed.

Various adventures follow, relating to Perceval, Lancelot, Gawain, and Bors — the most important of which is a vision which came to Lancelot and revealed to him the future greatness of his son Galahad.

Galahad, in his wanderings, was conducted by a damsel (afterwards shown to be Perceval's sister) to a ship in which were Perceval and Bors; and after sailing for fourteen days they came to a desert isle and found another ship lying there. On this ship they found a sword with strange hangings, which, with the bed on which it lay, was made the subject of a long explanation by the damsel. The ship had been built by Solomon and the sword had belonged to David. Perceval's sister made new hangings from her own hair. Galahad took the sword, but it came afterwards into the possession of Perceval.

Lancelot's journeys at last led to a castle wherein was a room containing the Holy Grail. He saw a priest there celebrating Mass, and attempted to enter the room but was struck down by a wind, and rendered dumb for fourteen days, during which he took no food. It was the Castle Corbenic. In due season he dined with King Pelles; and the Grail in some mysterious way provided all with abundant food. After this, Lancelot returned to Arthur's court.

Galahad and Perceval journeyed together for five years; then they met Bors, and they all arrived together at Castle Corbenic. There they found King Pelles. The broken sword with which Joseph had been wounded was brought before them, and Galahad alone could join the pieces. It was then given to Bors. At vesper time four damsels carried into the room a bed on which was a crowned man, who greeted Galahad as his deliverer from suffering. A man in the garb of a bishop appeared in a chair borne by angels and sat before the table on which was the Holy Grail. On his forehead was written that he was Joseph (son of Joseph of Arimathea) the first Bishop of Christendom. From the altar came four angels — two with lights, one with a cloth of red samite, and one with a bleeding lance. The Bishop began to celebrate the Sacrament, and when he raised the wafer it took a man's form. Joseph then vanished. From the Grail came a man with blood flowing from wounds in hands and feet and body, who gave the Sacrament to Galahad and his companions, and told them that the Grail was the dish used in the Last Supper. The holy vessel would be taken to the City of Sarras; and Galahad, Perceval and Bors should follow it there after Galahad had healed the maimed King. Galahad and his companions set sail in Solomon's ship, in which they found the Holy Grail. On landing, they were imprisoned by King Escorant and fed during that period by the Holy Grail. Galahad was made King after Escorant's death. On the anniversary of Galahad's crowning, the Bishop appeared again and showed the Holy Grail to Galahad; and then Galahad died, and angels took his body. The Grail and the Lance were taken to heaven. Perceval died a year after this, and Bors then returned to Great Britain; and his tale was written down and kept in the Abbey of Salisbury. (R.J.)

Chapter V

Now the story tells that when Galahad had left the Maidens' Castle he rode until he came to the Forest Gaste. One day it happened that he met Lancelot and Perceval who were riding in company; but they did not recognize him, not having had an occasion to see his arms before. So Lancelot attacked him first and broke his lance against Galahad's breast. Then Galahad struck him so hard that he upset him and his horse in a pile, but he did him no other harm. Having broken his lance, he drew his sword and dealt Perceval such a blow that he split his helmet and cap of mail; and if the sword had not turned in his hand, he would surely have killed him. However, Perceval had not the strength to keep his saddle, but fell to the ground so weak and stunned from the terrific blow he had received that he did not know whether it was night or day. Now this conflict was waged in front of a hermitage where a recluse dwelt. When she saw Galahad going away, she called to him: "Farewell now, and may God lead you! Certainly, if they had known you as well as I know you, they would never have been so bold as to attack you." When Galahad heard these words, he was in great fear of being recognized. So he spurred his horse and rode away as fast as he could urge him. Now when the two knights saw that he was going away, they mounted their steeds as quickly as possible. But when they saw that they could not follow him, they turned back so abashed and so angry that they would fain have died at once; for their lives were hateful to them. So they struck into the Forest Gaste.

Lancelot was in the Forest Gaste, wretched and furious at having lost trace of the knight. And he said to Perceval: "What can we do?" and he replied he could think of no plan to pursue. For the knight went away so fast that they could not follow after him. "You see yourself," said he, "that night has surprised us in a place whence we cannot escape unless some chance should assist us. So it seems to me that we had better go back to the road. For if we begin to wander about here, I think we shall not get back to the right road for a long time. Now you may do what you please; but I see more advantage in our turning back than in pushing forward." Then Lancelot said that he would not agree to turn back, but would go after the knight with the white shield: for he would never be satisfied until he learned who he was. "You can at least wait," said Perceval, "until the morrow comes. Then you and I will pursue the knight." But Lancelot said he would do nothing of the kind. "God help you, then," said Perceval; "for today I go no farther, but I'll turn back to the recluse who said she knew well who he was."

Thus the companions separated, and Perceval returned to the recluse. Meanwhile Lancelot rode in pursuit of the knight hither and thither through the forest, following no trail or pathway, but going at random where chance took him. His regret was great that he could see neither in the distance nor near at hand any path to follow, for the night was very dark. Yet he pushed on until he came to a stone cross at the parting of two ways in a deserted place. And looking more closely at the cross as he drew near, he saw beside it a marble stone on which he thought he saw some writing. But the night was so dark that he could not make out what the writing said. And looking about the cross, he saw a very ancient chapel whither he turned in the hope of finding someone. When he was close to it he dismounted and, tying his horse to an oak-tree, he removed his shield from his neck and hung it on the tree. Then, coming to the chapel, he found it deserted and in ruins. And when he was about to enter, he found at the entrance some iron prongs so closely joined together that it would be no easy task for anyone to get in. Looking through the bars he saw inside an altar very richly adorned with silken cloths and other things, and before it stood a silver candelabra holding six burning tapers which cast a bright light around. At the sight of this, he yearned to enter to see who inhabited the place: for he could not imagine that there should be such beautiful things in such a remote place. So he examined the grill, and when he found he could not go farther, he was so distressed that he left the chapel and led his steed back by the bridle to the cross, where he took off the saddle and bridle and let him browse. Then he unlaced his helmet and set it down before him, and he removed his sword and lay down upon his shield in front of the cross and being weary fell into a light doze, though he could not entirely banish from his mind the Good Knight with the white shield.

When he had been there for some time, he saw coming in a litter borne by two palfreys, a sick knight who was lamenting bitterly. And when he drew near Lancelot, he stopped and gazed at him, but did not say a word, thinking he was asleep. Nor did Lancelot say a word, but lay as one in a doze between a sleep and wakefulness. And the knight in the litter who had stopped at the cross began to bewail his fate aloud, crying: "Ah! God, is there to be no end to my distress? Ah! God, when will the Holy Vessel come who will cause my agony to cease? Ah! God, did ever mortal man suffer so grievously as I suffer, and for so little guilt?" For a long time the knight thus complained and bewailed his woes and his pains to God. But Lancelot did not stir nor say a word, lying still as one in a trance, though he saw him and heard what he said.

And when the knight had waited for a long time in this way, Lancelot looked and saw approaching in the direction of the chapel the silver candelabra which he had seen in the chapel with the tapers. As he looked at the candelabra, he saw it moving toward the cross, but he could not see who was bearing it; and he was filled with wonder. Next he saw drawing near upon a silver table the Holy Vessel which he had seen once before at the Fisher King's, the very same which was called the Holy Grail. As soon as the sick knight saw it approaching, he fell his full length upon the ground, and with hands clasped

252

toward it, he exclaimed: "Fair sire God, who hast wrought so many miracles in this and other lands through this Holy Vessel which I see drawing near, Father, look upon me in pity, that this woe which I suffer may be speedily relieved, and that I too may enter upon the Quest even as other worthy men have done." Then he dragged himself along by his arms to the stone where the table rested with the Holy Vessel upon it. And he raised himself up by his two hands until he could kiss the silver table and touch it with his eyes. As soon as he had done this he felt, as it were, cured of his woes: so he uttered a great sigh and said: "Ah! God, I am healed." And at once he fell asleep. Now when the Vessel had stayed there a while, the candelabra moved away toward the chapel and the Vessel with it so that Lancelot did not know by whom it could be carried either when it approached or when it withdrew. However, it came about that either because he was wearied by his labours or because of sin which had overcome him, he did not stir when the Holy Grail passed by nor did he manifest any concern for it; wherefore later on the Quest many a word of shame was said to him and many a misfortune befell him.

When the Holy Grail had left the cross and returned to the chapel, the knight of the litter rose up restored and sound and kissed the cross. At once there appeared a squire bringing some fine rich arms, and going up to the knight he asked him how it was with him. "Well, in faith," said he, "thank God: I was healed at once as soon as the Holy Grail visited me. But I marvel at yon knight who is sound asleep and never woke up when it passed by." "In truth," said the squire, "he is some knight who is living in some great sin which he has never confessed, and of which he is perchance so guilty before Our Lord that He would not permit him to behold this fair adventure." "Surely," the knight replied, "he is unfortunate, whoever he be; for I believe he is one of the companions of the Round Table who have taken up the Quest of the Holy Grail." "Sire," said the squire, "I have brought here your arms, which you may take when you please." The knight replied that now he needed nothing else. So he armed himself and put on his iron greaves and his hauberk. Then taking Lancelot's sword and helmet, the squire gave them to him, and then he put the saddle and bridle on Lancelot's horse. When he had equipped the steed, he said to his lord: "Mount now, sire, for you are not lacking a good horse and a good sword. Truly, I have given you nothing which will not be better used by you than by that wretched knight lying yonder." The moon had now risen fair and clear, for it was already past midnight. And the knight inquired of the squire how he knew about the sword; and he replied that he knew it must be good by its beauty: for he had already drawn it from the scabbard and had thought it so beautiful that he had coveted it. And when the knight was fully armed and mounted upon Lancelot's steed, he raised his hand toward the chapel and swore that with the help of God and the saints he would never cease his wanderings until he found out how it was that the Holy Grail appeared in so many places in the kingdom of Logres, and by whom it was brought to England and for what purpose, unless someone else should anticipate him in discovering the truth. "So help me God," said the valet, "you have said enough. Now may God grant you to come out with honour from this Quest, and with salvation of your soul; for surely you cannot long maintain it without running danger of death." "If I die," the knight replied, "it will be rather to my honour than my shame. For no man of honour ought to refuse to undertake this Quest either for fear of death or love of life." Then he and his squire, taking the arms of Lancelot, left the cross and rode whither they were led by chance.

Now when he had gone perhaps half a league or more, it happened that Lancelot sat up like one who now for the first time was completely awake. And he wondered whether what he had seen had been a dream or a reality, for he did not know whether he had beheld the Holy Grail in fact or only in a dream. Then he stood up and saw the candelabra in front of the altar, but he saw no sign of what he would more like to see, that is the Holy Grail, about which he would fain learn the truth if possible.

When Lancelot had stood for a long time before the iron bars striving to catch a glimpse of what he most desired to see, a voice was heard saying to him: "Lancelot, harder than stone, more bitter than wood, more barren and stripped than the fig-tree, how wert thou so bold as to dare to enter the place where the Holy Grail reposed? Get thee hence, for the place is already polluted by thy presence." Hearing these words, he was so sorrowful that he knew not what to do. So he went away sighing deeply and weeping, and he cursed the hour he was born, for he knew well he had come to a place where he would have no more honour, since he had failed to learn the truth about the Holy Grail. But he did not forget the three expressions that had been addressed to him, nor will he forget them as long as he lives, nor will he be much relieved until he learns why he was addressed in this manner. And coming to the cross he found neither his helmet nor his sword nor his horse: then he perceived it had been the reality which he had beheld. Then he began a great marvellous lament, reproaching himself as a sorrowful wretch: "Ah! God, now my sins and my wicked life appear openly. Now I see that my own wickedness has been the cause of my confusion more than anything else. For when I ought to have reformed my conduct, the devil destroyed me by taking from me my sight so that I could not see anything that came from God. It is no wonder that I cannot see clearly, for since I was first made a knight there has been no time when I was not covered with the darkness of mortal sin, for more than any other man I have lived in the lust and degradation of this world."

Thus Lancelot violently reproached and blamed himself and uttered his lament all night. When the day dawned fair and clear and the birds began to sing in the woods and the sun began to shine among the trees, he saw the fine weather and heard the song of the birds which had many a time brought joy to his heart; then he saw himself stripped of his arms and his horse and everything, and he realized that in truth Our Lord was angry with him. And he thought he could never again find anything in the world to restore his joy to him. For he had been wanting at the very place where he expected to find his joy and every earthly honour, that is in the adventures of the Holy Grail. And this it was that made him disconsolate.

And when he had for a long time lamented and raved and regretted his misfortune, he left the cross and went through the forest on foot, without helmet, sword or shield. So he did not go back to the chapel where he had heard the three strange words addressed to him; but he turned off by a path which led him at the hour of prime to a hill where he found a hermitage and a hermit who was about to begin the mass and who had already donned the robes of Holy Church. Gloomy, pensive and im-measurably sad, he entered the chapel, and kneeling in the middle of the chancel he confessed his sins and cried aloud upon Our Lord for forgiveness for the evil deeds he had done in this world. Then he gave heed to the mass celebrated by the worthy man and his clerk. When the mass was over and the good man had laid aside the robes of Our Lord, Lancelot called him aside and begged him for God's sake to give him advice. And when the hermit asked him who he was, he replied that he belonged to King Arthur's household and was a companion of the Round Table. Then the good man asked him: "What do you want advice about? Is it a confession you wish to make?" "Yes, sire," he replied. "Then in Our Lord's name, let us proceed," the hermit said.

Then he led him in front of the altar and they sat down together. When the good man asked him his name, he said he was Lancelot of the Lake, son of King Ban of Benoyc. Then when the worthy man heard that he was Lancelot of the Lake, the man in the world of whom most good was spoken, he was amazed to see him display such grief, and he said to him:

"Sire, you owe a great debt to God for making you so fair and valiant that we know no one in the world who is your match for beauty and valour. He has given you the intelligence and the memory you possess, and you ought to deal so kindly with Him that His love may be safely bestowed in you and that the devil may derive no advantage from the great talent He has granted you. So serve Him with all your power and do His commandments. With the talent He has given you, serve not His mortal enemy, the devil. For if He has been generous to you above all others and He should lose after all, then you would be greatly to be blamed.

"So be not like the unprofitable servant of whom it speaks in the Gospel, whom one of the evangelists mentions when he tells that a certain rich man handed over to three of his servants a great part of his gold. For to one he gave one besant, and to another two, and to the other five. He to whom he gave five increased them so that when he came before his master to give him an account of his profits, he said: 'Lord, thou gavest me five besants: behold, here they are with five others which I have gained.' And when the lord heard it, he replied: 'Come, good and faithful servant: I admit thee into the company of my household.' Afterward came he who had received the two besants and told his master that he had gained two others. And his lord replied to him as he had done to the other servant. But it happened that he who had only received one had buried it in the earth and had fled from before his master's face, not daring to come forward. This was the wicked servant, the false simoniac, the hypocritical heart into which the flame of the Holy Spirit never entered. Therefore he cannot burn with the love of Our Lord nor kindle those to whom He announced the holy gospel. For as the holy scripture says: 'He who is not on fire himself will not burn another,' which is to say: 'If the flame of the Holy Spirit does not warm him who speaks the Gospel word, then the man who hears it will neither burn nor be warmed.'

"These words I have quoted because of the great gift which Our Lord has bestowed on you. For I see that He has created you fairer and better than other men, so far as can be judged from the outward semblance. And if you in spite of this gift which He has granted you are His enemy, then be sure that He will reduce you to nothingness in a short time, if you do not beseech Him for mercy in true confession and in hearty repentance and in amendment of your life. But I promise you that, if you beseech His mercy in this way, He is kind and loves the true repentance of the sinner more than He does the error, and He will raise you up stronger and more vigorous than you ever were before."

"Sire," said Lancelot, "this parable which you have shown me of the three servants who had received the besants, distresses me more than anything else. For I know well that Jesus Christ furnished me in childhood with all the good graces that any man could have; but because He was so generous to me with what I have so ill repaid Him, I know that I shall be judged as the wicked servant who hid his besant in the earth. For all my life I have served His enemy, and have warred against Him by my sin. Thus I have slain myself in the road which one finds at the beginning to be broad and seductive: that is the beginning of sin. The devil showed me the sweetness and the honey; but he did not show me the eternal punishment to be suffered by him who travels that road."

When the worthy man heard these words, he wept and said to Lancelot: "Sire, I know that no one continues in this path you mention who is not consigned to an endless death. But just as you may see how a man sometimes loses his road when he falls asleep and returns to it when he wakes up, so it is with the sinner who is lulled asleep in mortal sin and loses the right path, but later returns to his way, that is his Creator, and directs himself to the High Lord who cries continually: 'I am the way, the truth, and the life.'" At that moment he looked and beheld a cross on which the sign of the true Cross was portrayed; and pointing it out to Lancelot, he said: "Sire, do you see that cross?" "Yes," he replied. "Then know truly," said the hermit, "that that figure has stretched out its arms as if to draw all men unto it. In like manner Our Lord stretched out His arms to receive every sinner, you and all others who appeal to Him, and He cries continually: 'Come, come!' And since He is so kind as to receive all men and women who return to Him, know that He will not refuse you, if you offer yourself up to Him in the way I describe, with true confession of mouth and repentance of heart and amendment of life. So recount your state and your affairs to Him in my hearing, and I will do my best to help you to find succour, and I will counsel you as best I may."

Lancelot was still a while as one who never admitted his relations with the queen, and would never mention them as long as he lived, unless great pressure should be brought upon him. Then he heaved a sigh from the depths of his heart and was so moved that he could not utter a word. Though he would fain speak, he did not dare, being more cowardly than brave. Meanwhile the good man exhorted him to confess his sin and have it out; otherwise he would be ashamed for not doing as he was bid, and he further assured him of eternal life if he confessed his sin and of hell if he concealed it. He spoke to him so kindly and so appealingly that finally Lancelot began to speak:

"Sire, the fact is that I am dead in sin because of my lady whom I have loved all my life, and she is Queen Guinevere, the wife of King Arthur. It is she who has given me abundance of gold and silver and the valuable gifts which I have sometimes handed on to poor knights. It is she who has set me up in great luxury in the high places I occupy. It is for love of her that I have performed the great deeds of prowess of which the whole world talks. It is she who has raised me from poverty to riches and from misery to all the blessings earth affords. But I know well that because of my sin with her Our Lord is sorely displeased with me as He clearly revealed to me last night." Then he told him how he had beheld the Holy Grail without stirring in its presence either to do it honour or to prove his devotion to Our Lord.

Then when he had rehearsed his state and all his past life to the worthy man, he begged him for God's sake to counsel him. "Certainly, sire," he then replied, "there is no use in counselling you unless you promise God that you will never again fall into this sin. But if you were willing to renounce it altogether and cry for mercy and heartily repent, I think that Our Lord would still recall you to the number of His servants and would open for you the door of Heaven, where eternal life is prepared for those who enter in. But in your present state of mind there is no use in giving you advice. For it would be as in the case of the man who built a strong, high tower upon a poor foundation: and it turned out that when he had built for some time, it all fell in a heap. In like manner all my trouble would be wasted on you, if you did not receive my advice gladly and apply it. It would be like the seed sown upon the rock, which the birds carry off and scatter so that it never yields anything." "Sire," said he, "you cannot tell me anything that I will not do, if God grant me life." "Then I insist," said the worthy man, "that you promise me that you will never wrong your Creator by committing mortal sin with the queen or any other woman or in any other way which would anger Him." And this he promised like a loyal knight.

"Now tell me again," said the good man, "of your experience with the Holy Grail." Then he told him and repeated the three words which the voice had said to him in the chapel when he had been called a stone, wood, and a fig-tree. "Now in God's name," said he, "tell me the meaning of these three things. For I never heard anything which I so desired to understand. Therefore, I pray you to explain them to me: for I know that you know their meaning." Then the worthy man began to think a long while, and when he spoke, he said: "I am certainly not astonished, Lancelot," said he, "that these three words have been addressed to you. For you have always been the most marvellous man in the world, and so it is not strange that more marvellous words should be addressed to you than to others. And since you desire to know their meaning, I will gladly tell you. So listen.

"You say that you were told: 'Lancelot, harder than stone, more bitter than wood, more barren and stripped than the fig-tree, get thee hence.' When you were called harder than stone, a strange thing is to be understood. For every stone is hard by nature, the only difference being in degree. By the stone with its hardness is meant the sinner who has become so lulled and hardened in his sin that his heart cannot be softened by fire or water. It cannot be softened by fire; for the fire of the Holy Spirit cannot penetrate it or find access because of the filthy vessel and the mortal sins which have been increased and accumulated day by day. And it cannot be softened by water; for the word of the Holy Spirit, which is the sweet water and the gentle rain, cannot be received into such a heart as his. For Our Lord will never seek lodgment in a place where His enemy is, but insists that the place where He lodges be clean and purged of all vice and filth. Now the sinner is likened to a stone because of the exceeding hardness which He finds in him. But it remains to be seen why you are harder than stone, that is, why you are a greater sinner than all others." And, saying that, he began to think and then continued:

"I will tell you wherein you are worse than other sinners. You have heard of the three servants to whom the rich man gave the besants to increase and multiply. The two who had received most were good and faithful servants, wise and prudent. And the other, who had received less, was a stupid and disloyal servant. Now consider whether you could be one of His servants to whom Our Lord gave the five besants to multiply. It seems to me that to you He gave much more. For if one were to consider the knights of the world, methinks he could not find a man to whom Our Lord has granted so much grace as He has bestowed upon you. He gave you exceeding beauty; He gave you intelligence and discretion to distinguish the good from the evil; He gave you prowess and valour. And moreover He gave you happiness so generously that you have risen far above where you began. All these things Our Lord granted you in order that you might be His knight and servant. But He did not give you these things in order that they should be wasted on you, but that they should be increased and improved. But you have been such a wicked and disloyal servant that you have forsaken Him and served His enemy, for you have continually been at strife with Him. You have been like the wicked soldier who leaves his lord as soon as he has received his wages and goes to help his enemy. Thus you have acted toward Our Lord: for as soon as He had paid you richly and well, you left Him to go and serve him who is always at war with Him. This would not be done by any man, I think, whom He had paid as well as He has paid you. Thus you may see that you are harder than stone, and a greater sinner than any other. However, whoever wishes may interpret the word stone in another manner. For a multitude of people saw sweet water issue from the rock in the desert beyond the Red Sea where the people of Israel tarried so long a time. There it was clearly seen that when the people were athirst and quarrelled with each other, Moses came to a hard old rock and said, just as if it were ipossible: 'Can we not draw water from this rock?' And immediately there issued water from the rock in such plenty that all the people had enough to drink, and their murmuring was appeased and their thirst assuaged. Thus one can say that sometimes sweetness has issued even from a rock; but none ever issued from you, wherefore you can plainly see that you are harder than stone."

"Sire," said Lancelot, "now tell me why it was said that I was more bitter than wood." "I will tell you," the hermit made reply. "Now listen to me. I have shown you that in you there is nothing but hardness, and where hardness is there can be no sweetness, and we ought not to expect to find anything there but bitterness; and there is as much of bitterness in you as there ought to be of sweetness. So you are like the dead and rotten wood in which no sweetness is to be found, but only bitterness. Now I have shown you how you are harder than stone and more bitter than wood.

"Now the third thing to explain is how you are more barren and stripped than a fig-tree. The fig-tree here concerned is mentioned in the Gospel where it speaks of Palm Sunday when Our Lord entered the city of Jerusalem on an ass, the day when the children of the Hebrews sang to welcome Him the sweet

261

songs of which Holy Church reminds us each year on the day
we call the day of palms. That day the High Lord, the High
Master, the High Prophet preached in the city of Jerusalem
surrounded by those in whom all hardness was lodged. And
when He had toiled all day and had finished His sermon, He
found no one in the city who would lodge Him, wherefore He
went forth from the city. And when He was outside the city, He
saw by the road a fig-tree which was fine-looking and well
furnished with leaves and branches, but without fruit. And Our
Lord came to the tree, and when He saw it bare of fruit, He was
angered and cursed the tree which bore no fruit. So it was with
the fig-tree outside of Jerusalem. Now consider whether you
might be such an one, only more barren and stripped than it
was. When the High Lord came to the tree, He found on it
leaves which He might have picked, had He wished. But when
the Holy Grail passed where you were, it found you so stripped
as to be without any good thought or intention; rather it found
you mean and filthy and lying in luxury and stripped of leaves
and blossoms, that is to say, of all good works. Therefore, you
were told what you have reported to me: 'Lancelot, harder than
stone, more bitter than wood, more barren and stripped than a
fig-tree, get thee hence.'"

"Certainly, sire," said Lancelot, "you have spoken and shown
me clearly that I have good reason to be called a stone, wood,
and a fig-tree; for all those things you have mentioned are found
in me. But since you told me that I have not gone so far astray
that I may not yet return, if I am willing to keep from falling
again into mortal sin, I promise God first and you afterward that
I will never resume the life I have so long led, but will observe
chastity and keep my body as pure as I can. But I could not
cease from chivalry and feats of arms so long as I remain strong
and healthy as I am now." When the good man heard these
words, he was very happy and replied: "Without doubt, if you
willingly renounced your sin with the queen, I tell you truly that
Our Lord would love you again, and would succour you, and
would look upon you with pity, and would grant you power to
achieve many a thing which you cannot do now because of your
sin." "Sire," said Lancelot, "I renounce them all, and will never
more sin with her or anyone else."

When the worthy man heard that, he prescribed such penance

as he thought he could accomplish, then absolved him and blessed him and invited him to spend that day with him. And he replied that he must needs do so, as he had no horse to mount, nor shield nor lance nor sword. "I can help you about that," the hermit said, "before tomorrow evening. For close by there lives a brother of mine who is a knight and who will send me a horse and arms and everything else required as soon as I send word to him." Lancelot replied that in that case he would gladly stay, which made the good man happy and glad.

Thus Lancelot tarried with the hermit who exhorted him to do the right. And he gave him so much good advice that Lancelot repented of the life he had so long led. For he saw clearly that if he should die, his soul would be lost; and his body peradventure would suffer too, if it could be reached by punishment. So he repented that he had ever cherished this mad love for the queen, for he had ill spent his time. So he blamed himself and was ashamed, and promised in his heart that he would never again relapse. But now the story ceases to speak of him and returns to Perceval.

CHAPTER 14

Syr Percyvelle of Galles

TRANSLATED BY J.L. WESTON

Dear Lords, listen now to me,
Hearken words but two or three
Of a hero fair and free,
   Who was fierce in fight;
His right name was Percyvelle,
He was fostered on the fell,
Drank the water of the well
   Yet was valiant wight.
Of a nobleman the son,
Who, since that he first begun,
Goodly praise and worship won
   When he was made knight.
In the good King Arthur's hall
He was best beloved of all,
Percyvelle they did him call
   Whoso reads aright.

Who the tale aright can read
Knows him one of doughty deed,
A stiff knight upon a steed,
   Wielding weapons bold;
Therefore did the King Arthour
Do unto him great honour,
Gave his sister Acheflour
   For to have and hold
As his wife, to his life's end;
And with her broad lands to
     spend,
For right well the knight he kenned

Gave her to his hold.
And of goodly gifts full share
Gave he with his sister there,
(As it pleased the twain full fair,)
   With her, robes in fold.

There he gave him robes in fold,
And broad lands of wood and
     wold
With a store of goods untold
   That the maid he take;
To the kirk the knight did ride
There to wed that gentle bride
For rich gifts and lands so wide
   And for her own sake;
Sithen, without more debate,
Was the bridal held in state
For her sake who, as her mate,
   This good knight would take;
Afterward, withouten let,
A great jousting there was set,
And of all the knights he met
   None would he forsake.

None would he forsake that stead,
Not the Black Knight, nor the Red,
None who there against him sped
   With or shaft or shield;
There he did as noble knight,

Who well holdeth what he hight,
And full well he proved his might,
   All to him must yield;
There full sixty shafts I say
Brake Syr Percyvelle that day, —
On the wall his bride, she lay,
   Watched him weapons wield.
Tho' the Red Knight, he had sworn,
From his saddle is he borne,
And, well nigh of life forlorn,
   Lieth on the field.

As he lay there on the wold
Many a man must him behold
Who, thro' shield and armour's
   hold,
   'Stonied was that tide;
All men marvelled who were
   there,
Whether great or small they were,
That thus Percyvelle should dare
   Doleful dints abide;
There was no man, great or small,
No, not one amongst them all,
Who on grass dare risk a fall
   And would 'gainst him ride;
There Syr Percyvelle that day
Bare the tourney's prize away,
Homeward did he take his way,
   Blithe was she, his bride!

But tho' blithe the bride, and gay
That her lord had won the day
Yet the Red Knight sick he lay
   Wounded by his hand;
Therefore goodly gifts he plight
That, an he recover might,
And again by day or night,
   In the field might stand,
That he'ld quit him of the blow
Which he from his hand must
   know,
Nor his travail fruitless go,
   Nor be told in land

That Syr Percyvelle, in field,
Thus had shamed him under
   shield —
Payment full for that he'ld yield
   If in life he stand!

Now in life they be, the two,
But the Red knight naught may
   do
To bring scathe upon his foe
   Till the harm befell;
As it chanced, there fell no strife
Till that Percyvelle, in life,
Had a son by his young wife,
   After him to dwell;
And whenas that child was born
He bade call him on the morn
By the name his sire had worn,
   Even Percyvelle;
Then the knight was fain to make
Feast for this, his young son's
   sake,
Thus without delay they spake
   And of jousting tell.

Now of jousting do they tell,
And they say, Syr Percyvelle,
In the field he thinks to dwell
   As he aye has done;
There a jousting great they set
E'en of all the knights they met
For he would his son should get
   That same fame anon;
When thereof the Red Knight
   heard
Blithe was he of that same word,
Armed him swift with shield and
   sword,
   Thither hath he gone;
'Gainst Syr Percyvelle would ride
With broad shield and shaft that
   tide,
There his vow he would abide,
   Mastery maketh moan!

265

Mastery, it hath made moan —
Percyvelle right well hath done
For the love of his young son,
   On the opening day;
Ere the Red knight thither won
Percyvelle smote many a one,
Duke, earl, knight, and eke baron
   Vanquished in the play;
Honour had he won for dower, —
Came the Red Knight in that hour
But, "Woe worth false armour"
   Percyvelle may say!
There Syr Percyvelle was slain —
That the Red Knight was full fain
In his heart, I will maintain,
   When he went his way!

When he went upon his way,
Then no man durst aught to say
Were it earnest, were it play,
   For to bid him bide;
Since that he had slain right there
The best champion that was e'er,
With full many a wound so sare,
   'Stonied all that tide!
Then no better rede had they
Than the knight to lowly lay,
As men must the dead alway,
   And in earth must hide:
She who was but now his wife
Sorely might she rue her life,
Such a lord to lose in strife,
   She ailed not for pride.

Now is Percyvelle, the knight,
Slain in battle and in fight,
And her word that lady plight,
   Keep it if she may,
That ne'er, so her vow doth run,
She will dwell with her young son
Where such deeds of arms were
   done,
   Nor by night, nor day.
In the woodland shall he be,

Where, forsooth, he naught shall
   see
But the green and leafy tree,
   And the groves so gray;
Never shall his mind be bent
Nor on joust nor tournament,
But in the wild wood content,
   He with beasts shall play!

There with wild beasts should he
   play —
Thus her leave she took straight-
   way,
Both of king and lord that day,
   Gat her to the wood;
Left behind her bower and hall,
But one maid she took withal,
Who should answer to her call,
   When in need she stood;
Other goods would she have
   naught,
But a flock of goats she brought,
For their milk might serve, she
   thought,
   For their livelihood;
And of all her lord's fair gear
Naught she beareth with her here
Save a little Scottish spear,
   Serve her son it should.

And when her young son should
   go
In the woodland to and fro,'
That same spear, I'ld have ye know,
   She gave him one day;
"Mother sweet," then straight
   quoth he,
"Say, what may this strange thing
   be,
Which ye now have given me,
   What its name, I pray?"
Then she spake, that fair ladie,
"Son," she quoth, "now hearken
   me,

This a doughty dart shall be
  Found in woodland way."
Then the child was pleased at
    heart
That she gave to him this dart,
Therewith he made many smart
  In the woodland gay.

Thus amid the woodland glade
Dart in hand, the lad, he strayed,
Underneath the wild wood's
    shade,
  Throve there mightily,
And with this, his spear, would
    slay
Of wild beasts and other prey
All that he might bear away,
  Goodly lad was he;
Small birds too, he shot them
    there,
Many a hart and hind so fair
Homeward to his mother bare,
  Never lack had she.
So well did he learn to shoot,
There was no beast went afoot,
But in flight might find small
    boot,
  Run them down would he!

All the prey he marked, it fell —
Thus he grew and throve right
    well,
Was a strong lad, sooth to tell,
  Tho' his years were few;
Fifteen winters, yea, and more,
Dwelt he in those holts so hoar,
Naught of nurture nor of lore
  From his mother knew;
Till it fell upon a day,
That to him she thus did say:
"Sweet son, now I rede thee pray
  To God's Son so true,
By His aid to prosper thee,
So that, by His Majesty,

Thou a good man well may'st be
  And long life thy due!"

"Mother sweet," then answered
    he,
"Say, what kind of god is He
Whom thou now hast bidden me
  In this wise to pray?"
"Son, 't is the great God of
    Heaven,"
So she spake, "within days seven
Hath He made both Earth and
    Heaven,
  Ere closed the sixth day."
"By great God," his answer ran,
"An I may but meet that man,
Then, with all the craft I can,
  I to Him will pray!"
Thus then, did he live and wait,
E'en within his mother's gate,
For the great God lay in wait,
  Find Him if he may!

Then, as thro' holts hoar he fled,
So the chance befell that stead,
That three knights toward him
    sped,
  Of King Arthur's inn;
One, King Urien's son, Ywain,
And with him was good Gawain,
And Sir Kay rode with the twain,
  All were of his kin;
Thus in raiment rich they ride,
But the lad had naught that tide
Wherewith he his bones might
    hide,
  Saving a goat's skin;
Burly was he, broad to see,
On each side a skin had he,
Of the same his hood should be
  Even to his chin.

The hood came but to his chin,
And the flesh was turned within,

267

The lad's wit, it was full thin
　　When he should say aught;
And the knights were all in green,
Such as he had never seen,
Well he deemed that they had
　　　　been
　　The great God he sought;
And he spake: "Which of ye three
Shall in sooth the great God be,
Who, my mother told to me,
　　Hath　this　wide　world
　　wrought?"
Straight made answer Sir Gawain,
Fair and courteous spake again:
"Son, so Christ to me be fain,
　　Such shall we be naught."

Then he quoth, the foolish child,
Who had come from woodland
　　　　wild,
To Gawain the meek and mild,
　　Soft of speech and fair:
"I shall slay ye now all three
Save ye straightway tell to me
What things ye shall surely be,
　　Since no Gods ye were?"
Swift he answered him, Sir Kay,
"Yea, and then who should we
　　　　say
Were our slayer here today
　　In this woodland bare?"
At Kay's words he waxed full
　　wroth,
Save a great buck 'twixt them
　　both
Stood, I trow me, little loth,
　　Had he slain him there.

But Gawain, he quoth to Kay:
"Thy proud words shall us betray,
I would win this child with play,
　　Would'st thou hold thee still."
"Sweet son," in this wise spake
　　he,

"Knights, I trow we be, all three,
With King Arthur dwelling free
　　Who waits on the hill."
Quoth then Percyvelle, so light,
He who was in goatskin dight:
"Will　King　Arthur　make　me
　　knight,
　　An I seek him still?"
Then Sir Gawain answered there:
"That to say, I do not dare,
To the king I rede thee fare,
　　Ask of him his will."

Thus to know King Arthur's will,
Where he tarried stayed they still,
And the child he hastened, till
　　To his home be came.
As he sped him thro' the wood,
There he saw a full fair stud
Both of colts and mares so good,
　　But not one was tame;
And he said: "Now, by Saint John,
Such beasts as I now see yon,
Such the knights did ride upon,
　　Knew I but their name!
But as I may thrive, or thee,
E'en the biggest that I see
It shall shortly carry me
　　Home unto my dame!"

"When I come unto my dame
An I find her, at this same,
She will tell to me the name
　　Of this stranger thing."
Then, I trow, the biggest mare
Swiftly did he run down there,
Quoth: "I trow thou shalt me bear
　　With morn, to the King."
Saddle-gear the lad did lack,
Sprang upon the horse's back,
She bare him the homeward track,
　　Failed him for no thing.
Then his mother, woe-begone,
Wist not what to do anon,

When she saw her youthful son
  A steed with him bring.

Horse she saw him homeward
    bring;
And she wist well by that thing
What is in-born out will spring
  Spite of wiles she sought.
Swift she spake, the fair ladie:
"That this dole I needs must dree,
For the love of thy body
  That I dear have bought!"
"Dear son," so she spake him fair,
"Much unrest for thee I bear,
What wilt do with this same mare
  That thou home hast brought?"
But the boy was blithe and gay
When he heard his mother say
This, the brood-mare's name
    alway,
  Of naught else he thought.

Now he calleth her a mare,
E'en as did his mother ere,
Such he deemed all horses were,
  And were named, i' fay;
"Mother, on yon hill I've been,
There three knights I now have
    seen,
And with them have spoke, I ween,
  These words did I say:
I have promised them all three,
That I with their king will be,
Such an one shall he make me
  As they be today."
Thus he sware by God's great
    Might:
"I shall keep the words I plight,
Save the king shall make me
    knight
  Him with morn I'll slay."

Spake the mother full of woe,
For her son she grievéd so

That she thought she death
    should know,
  Knelt down on her knee:
"Son, hast ta'en to thee this rede,
Thou wilt turn to knightly deed,
Now where'er strange fate may
    lead,
  This I counsel thee;
Morn is furthermost Yule-day,
And thou say'st thou wilt away
To make thee knight, if so thou
    may,
  So hast told to me;
Dost of nurture little know,
Now in all things measure show
If in hall or bower thou go,
  And of hand be free."

Then she quoth, the lady bright:
"Where thou meetest with a
    knight
Doff thy hood to him forthright,
  Greet him courteously;"
"Mother sweet," he answered
    then,
"Saw I never any men,
If a knight I now should ken
  Tell the sign whereby?"
Then she showed him miniver,
For such robes she had by her,
"Son, where thou shalt see such
    fur
  On their hoods to lie."
"By Great God," then answered
    he,
"Where that I a knight may see
Mother, as thou biddest me,
  Even so do I."

All that night till it was day
He beside his mother lay,
With the morn he would away,
  May what will betide;
Bridle had he never none,

In its stead, he naught hath won,
But a withy took anon
   This, his steed, to guide;
Then his mother took a ring,
Bade the same again to bring:
"This shall be our tokening
   Here I'll thee abide."
Ring and spear he taketh there,
Springeth up astride the mare,
From the mother who him bare
   Forth the lad doth ride.

Fytte II
On his way, as he did ride,
Stood a hall, his way beside,
"Now for aught that may betide
   Here within will I."
Without let within he strode,
Found a broad board set with
     food,
A well plenished fire of wood
   Burning bright thereby.
And a manger too, he found,
Therein corn, it lay, unground,
To the same his mare he bound
   E'en with his withy.
Said: "My mother counselled me
That I should of measure be,
Half of all that here I see
   I shall let it lie."

Thus the corn, he parts it fair,
One half gives unto his mare,
To the board betakes him there
   Well assured that tide;
Found a loaf of bread so fine,
And a pitcher, full of wine,
And a mess, whereon to dine,
   With a knife beside.
All the meat he findeth there
With his hands, in even share
He doth part — "One half the fare
   Shall for other bide."
And the one half eateth he,

Could he more of measure be?
He of hand would fain be free,
   Tho' he had no pride!

Tho' the lad he had no pride,
Further did he go that tide
To a chamber there beside
   Wonders more to see;
Clothing rich he there found
   spread,
Slept a lady there, on bed, —
Quoth: "A token that we wed
   Shalt thou leave with me."
Then he kissed her, that sweet
   thing.
From her finger took a ring,
His own mother's tokening
   Left her there in fee.
Then he went forth to his mare,
The short spear he with him bare,
Leapt aloft as he was ere,
   On his way rides he.

Now upon his way rides he,
Marvels more full fain to see,
And a knight he needs must be
   With no more delay.
He came where the king should
   be,
Served of the first mess was he,
And to him, right hastily,
   Doth he make his way;
Hindrance brooked not, nor debate,
E'en at wicket, door, or gate,
Gat in swift, nor thought to wait,
   Masterful, that day;
E'en at his first entering,
This, his mare, no lie I sing,
Kissed the forehead of the king,
   Came so close alway.

Startled was the king, I trow,
And his hands, he raised them
   now,

Turned aside from off his brow
  Muzzle of the mare;
And he quoth: "Fair child, and
    free,
Stand thou still, aside of me,
Say from whence thou now shalt
    be,
  And thy will declare?"
Quoth the fool to Arthur mild:
"I be mine own mother's child
Come from out the woodland
    wild
  Unto Arthur fair;
Yesterday I saw knights three,
Such an one make thou of me
Here, on this my mare by thee,
  Ere thy meat thou share."

Out then spake Sir Gawain free,
Carver to the king was he,
Saith: "Forsooth, no lie this be,
  I was one, i' fay.
Child, now take thou my blessing
For thy fearless following,
Here in sooth hast found the king
  Who makes knights alway."
Then quoth Percyvelle the free:
"Now, if this King Arthur be,
Look a knight he make of me
  Even as I say:"
Tho' he were uncouthly dight,
He sware: "By God's mickle
    Might,
Save the king shall make me
    knight,
  Here I shall him slay."

All who heard him, young and
    old,
Marvelling, the king behold
That he suffer words so bold
  From so foul a wight;
Stayed his horse the king be-
    side —

Arthur looked on him that tide,
Then for sorrow sore he sighed
  As he saw that sight;
Tears fell from his eyes apace,
Following each the other's trace,
Quoth the king: "Alas, this place
  Knew me, day, or night —
That without him I should be
Living, who was like to thee,
Who so seemly art to see
  An thou wert well dight!"

Quoth the king: "Wert better
    dight,
Thou wert like unto a knight,
Whom I loved with all my might
  Whiles he was in life;
And so well he wrought my will,
In all ways of knightly skill,
That my sister, of goodwill,
  Gave I him for wife.
For him must I make my moan,
He, now fifteen years agone,
By a thief to death was done
  For a little strife;
Sithen am I that man's foe,
For to wreak upon him woe,
Death thro' me he may not know
  He in crafts is rife!"

Quoth: "His crafts they be so rife
There is no man now in life
Who, with sword, or spear, or
    knife,
  'Gainst him may avail,
Save but Percyvelle's young son;
An he knew what he had done,
The book saith, he might anon
  'Venge his father's bale," —
The lad deemed too long he
    stayed
Ere that he a knight was made,
That he e'er a father had,
  Knowledge did him fail;

271

Thus his meaning less should be
When unto the king said he:
"Sir, now let thy chattering be,
   I heed not such tale."

Quoth: "I think not here to stand,
Nor thy chatter understand,
Make me knight with this, thy
   hand,
   If it may be done."
Courteously, the king, he hight
That he now would dub him
   knight
If that he adown would light
   Eat with him at noon;
Saw the king his face so free,
Evermore he trowed that he,
This child, of a sooth should be
   Percyvelle's own son;
And it ran in the king's mood,
Acheflour, his sister good,
How she gat her to the wood
   With her boy alone.

This boy, he came from the wood,
Evil knew he not, nor good,
And the king, he understood,
   He was a wild wight;
So he spake him fair withal —
Then he lighted down in hall,
Bound his mare among them all,
   To the board was dight;
But, ere that he might begin,
Or unto the meat might win,
'Mid them all, the hall within,
   Came he, the Red Knight;
Pricking on a blood-red steed,
Blood-red too, was all his weed,
Fain to mock them all at need
   With crafts, as he might.

With his crafts began to call,
Loudly hailed them recreants all,—
King and knights within that wall

At the board they bide;
Roughly took the cup in hand
That before the king did stand,
None withstood him, all that band
   Deemed him mad that tide;
Portion full of wine it bare,
The Red Knight, he drank it there,
And the cup was very fair
   All of red gold tried.
In his band, as there it stood,
Took he up that cup so good,
Left them sitting at their food,
   And from thence did ride.

As from them he rode away,
He who made this tale doth say
The grief that on Arthur lay
   Never tongue might tell;
"Ah, dear God!" the king, he said,
"Thou Who all this wide world
   made,
Shall this man be ever stayed,
   Yon fiend forced to dwell?
Five years has he, in this way,
Borne my cup from me away,
And my good knight did he slay,
   E'en Syr Percyvelle.
Sithen, has he taken three,
And from hence he rideth free
Ere that I may harness me
   Him in field to fell!"

"Peter!" Percyvelle doth cry,
"Strike that knight adown will I,
And thy cup bring presently,
   Wilt thou make me knight."
"As I be true king," said he,
"I will make a knight of thee
If again thou bringest me
   This, my cup so bright."
Up he rose, I trow, the king,
To his chamber hastening,
Thence good armour would he
   bring

That the lad be dight;
Ere the armour down was cast,
Percyvelle from hall had passed,
On his track he followed fast
    Whom he thought to fight.

With his foe he goes to fight,
He none other wise was dight
But in goatskins three, to sight,
    As a fool he were;
Cried: "Man, on thy mare now
    hear,
Bring again now the king's gear,
Or I'll smite thee with my spear,
    And make thee less fair!"
After the Red Knight would ride
Boldly, would for nought abide,
Quoth: "A knight I'll be this tide,
    Of thine armour heir!"
And he sware by Christ's sore
    Pain:
"Save thou bring this cup again
With my dart thou shalt be slain,
    Cast down from thy mare!"
When the knight beheld him so,
Fool he deemed who was his foe
Since that he had called it so,
    This his steed, a mare.

Thus to see him well with sight
He his vizor raised forthright,
To behold how he was dight
    Whose words sense did lack;
Quoth: "An I reach thee, thou
    fool,
I will cast thee in the pool,
E'en for all the Feast of Yule,
    As thou wert a sack!"
Then quoth Percyvelle the free:
"Fool or no, whate'er I be,
This I trow, we soon shall see
    Whose brows shall be black!"
There his skill the lad would try,
At the knight a dart let fly,

Smote him full there in the eye,
    Came out at the back!

For the blow that he must bear,
From the saddle shaken there,
Who the sooth will hearken fair,
    The Red Knight was slain!
On the hill he fell down dead,
While his steed, at will it fled,
Percyvelle quoth in that stead:
    "Art a lazy swain!"
Quoth the child in that same tide:
"Would'st thou here my coming
    bide,
I to catch thy mare will ride,
    Bring her thee again;
Then I trow we twain with might,
Will as men together fight,
Each of us as he were knight
    Till the one be slain."

Now the Red Knight lieth slain,
Left for dead upon the plain,
And the boy doth ride amain,
    After his good steed;
But 't was swifter than the mare,
For naught else it had to bear
But the harness, fast and fair
    Fled, from rider freed;
Big with foal the mare that tide,
Of stout make was she beside,
Little power to run when tried,
    Nor pursue with speed;
The lad saw how it should be,
Swift adown to foot sprang he,
And the right way hastily
    Ran, as he had need.

Thus, fleet-foot, the lad he fled,
On his way he surely sped,
Caught, strong-hand, the steed
    that stead,
    Brought it to the knight;
"Now a fell foe shalt thou be,

Wilt not steal away from me,
Now I pray thou dealest free
  Blows, as fits a knight!
See, thy mare I bring thee here,
Mickle of thy other gear,
Mount, as when thou first anear
  Came, an thou wilt fight!"
Speechless still the knight he lay,
He was dead, what could he say?
The child knew no better way
  Than adown to light.

Percyvelle adown is light,
Of his arms would spoil the
  knight,
But he might not find aright,
  How was laced the weed;
Armed was he from head to heel
In iron harness, and in steel;
The lad knew not how to deal,
  Aid himself in need;
Quoth: "My mother counselled me
When my dart should broken be,
From the iron burn the tree,
  Fire is now my need."
Thus he seeks a flint straightway,
His fire-iron he takes that day,
And with never more delay
  He a spark hath freed.

Kindles there a flame, I trow,
Mid the bushes seeking now,
Swift he gathers branch and
  bough,
  That a fire would make;
There a great blaze doth he light,
Thinks therein to burn the knight,
Since he knew no better sleight
  This, his gear, to take.
Now Sir Gawain, he was dight,
Followed fast to see the fight
'Twixt the lad, and the Red
  knight,
  All for the boy's sake;

Found the Red Knight where he
  fell,
Slain was he by Percyvelle,
And a fire, that burnt right well,
  Birch and oak did make!

Of these twain the fire alway,
Great the brands and black, that
  day;
"With this fire what wilt thou,
  say?"
  Quoth he, soft and still.
"Peter!" quoth the boy also,
"An I thus the knight might know,
From his iron I'll burn him so,
  Right here, on the hill."
Answered him the good Gawain:
"Since the Red Knight thou hast
  slain,
To disarm him am I fain,
  Wilt thou hold thee still."
Then Sir Gawain down did light,
Took his harness from the knight,
On the child the same did dight,
  E'en at his own will.

In his armour doth he stand,
Takes the knight's neck in his
  hand,
Casts him on the burning brand
  There to feed the flame;
Then quoth Percyvelle in boast:
"Lie thou still therein and roast,
I keep nothing of thy cost,
  Naught that from thee came."
Burns the knight, and none doth
  heed
Clad the boy is in his weed,
And hath leapt upon his steed,
  Well-pleased, at that same;
He looked downward at his feet,
Saw his gear so fair and meet,
"Men may me as knight entreat,
  Call me by that name!"

274

Quoth Gawain the boy unto:
"From this hill I rede we go,
Hast done what thou willed to do,
    Near it draws to night."
Quoth the lad: "Dost trow this
        thing,
That unto thy lord and king,
I myself again will bring
    This, his gold so bright?
Nay, so I may thrive, or thee,
I'm as great a lord as he,
Ne'er today he maketh me,
    Any way a knight!
Take thou now the cup so fair,
And thyself the present bear,
Forth in land I'll further fare
    Ere from steed I light."

Neither would the lad alight,
Nor would wend with that good
        knight,
Forth he rideth all the night,
    So proud was he then;
Till at morn, on the fourth day,
With a witch met, so men say,
And his horse and fair array,
    She right well might ken;
And she deemed that it had been
The Red Knight, whom she had
        seen
In those arms afore, I ween,
    Such steed spurred he then;
Swiftly she to him would hie,
Quoth: "In sooth I tell no lie,
Men said, thou didst surely die,
    Slain by Arthur's men!

"Of my men one but now came
From yon hill, and at that same,
Where thou see'st the fierce fire
        flame,
    Said that thou wast there!"
Percyvelle he sat stone still,
Answer made he none, until

She had spoken all her will,
    Never word spake there:
"I on yonder hill have been,
Nothing else I there have seen,
But goat-skins, naught else, I
        ween,
    Than such worthless fare."
"My son, tho' thou there wast slain,
And thine armour from thee ta'en,
I could make thee whole again,
    Hale, as thou wert e'er."

Then by that wist Percyvelle
It had servéd him right well
That wild fire he made on fell,
    When the knight was slain;
And he deemed 'twere well that
        she
In that self-same place should be;
That old witch on spear bare he
    To the fire again;
There in mickle wrath and ire
Cast the witch into the fire:
"With the son thou didst desire
    Lie ye still, ye twain."
Thus the lad, he left them there,
And upon his way did fare,
Such-like deeds to do and dare,
    Was the child full fain.

Came he by a forest side,
There ten men, he saw them ride,
Quoth: "For aught that may
        betide
    With them would I be."
When the ten they saw him, they
Deemed him the Red Knight
        alway,
Who would seek them all to slay,
    Fast they turned to flee;
Since he so was clad that stead,
For their life from him they fled,
Aye the faster that they sped
    Faster followed he.

275

Till he knew one for a knight,
Of the miniver had sight,
Put his vizor up forthright:
    "Sir, God look on thee!'

Quoth the child: "God look on
    thee!"
Quoth the knight: "Well may'st
    thou be,
Ah! Lord God, now well is me
    That I live this day!"
By his face right well he thought
The Red Knight it should be
    naught,
Who as foeman had them sought,
    Boldly there did stay;
For it seemed him by the sight
That the lad had slain the knight
In whose armour he was dight,
    Rode his steed alway;
Soon the knight, he spoke again,
And to thank the child was fain;
"Thou the fiercest foe hast slain
    Who beset me aye!"

Quoth then Percyvelle the free,
Saith: "Now wherefore did ye flee
All of ye when ye saw me
    Riding here anigh?"
Then he spake, that agéd knight,
Who was past his day of might,
Nor with any man might fight,
    Answered, loud and high,
Saying: "These nine children here
They be all my sons so dear
Since to lose them I must fear
    For that cause fled I,
For we deemed that it had been
The Red Knight we now had seen,
He had slain us all, I ween,
    With great cruelty.

"Without mercy he were fain
One and all of us were slain,

To my sons he'd envy ta'en
    Most of any men:
Fifteen years agone, 't is true,
That same thief my brother slew
And hath set himself anew
    For to slay us then;
Fearing lest my sons should know
When they should to manhood
    grow,
And should slay him as their foe
    Where they might him ken.
Had I been in that same stead
When he smote my brother dead,
I had never eaten bread,
    Till I'd burned him then!"

"Burned," quoth Percyvelle, "he is,
I sped better than I wist," —
As the last word he must list
    Blither waxed the knight;
By his hall their road it fell,
Strait he prayed that Percyvelle
There awhile with them should
    dwell,
    And abide that night.
Well it should his guest befall —
So he brought him to the ball,
Spake him fair, that he withal
    From his steed should light;
Then, the steed in stable set,
To the hall the lad doth get,
And, with never further let,
    They for meat are dight.

Meat and drink for them were
    dight,
Men were there to serve aright,
And the lad found with the
    knight,
    Enow, to his hand.
As at meat they sat, and ate,
Came the porter from the gate,
Said, a man without did wait,
    From the Maiden-Land;

Saith: "Sir, he doth pray of thee
Meat and drink for charitie,
For a messenger is he,
   Nor for long may stand."
The knight bade him come within,
For he said: "It is no sin
That the man who meat may win
   Fill the traveller's hand."

Came the traveller at that stead,
By the porter thither led,
Hailed the knight who sat at
     bread
   On the daïs on high.
And the knight, he asked him
     there
Courteously, whose man he were?
And how far he thought to fare?
   "Tell me without lie."
"From the Lady Lufamour
Am I sent to King Arthour,
That he lend, for his honour
   To her grief an eye;
There hath come a Soudan bold,
Ta'en her lands, slain young and
     old,
And besieged her in her hold,
   Plagues her ceaselessly!

"Saith, at peace he'll leave her
     ne'er —
Since the maid is wondrous fair,
And hath mickle wealth for share,
   He doth work her woe.
Thus in grief she leads her life,
All her men he fells in strife,
Vows he'll have her for his wife,
   And she will not so;
By that Soudan's hand, I ween,
Slain have sire and uncle been,
Slain hath she her brothers seen,
   He is her worst foe!
He so closely her hath sought
To one castle is she brought,

From those walls he yieldeth
     naught,
   Ere he come her to.

"Saith, he will her favours know—
Liever she to death would go
Than that he, her bitterest foe,
   Wed her as his wife!
But he is so valiant wight,
All his foes he slays forthright,
And no man may with him fight,
   Tho' his fame were rife!"
Then quoth Percyvelle: "I pray
Thou wilt show to me the way,
Thither, as the road it lay,
   Without any strife!
Might I with that Soudan meet,
Who a maid doth so entreat,
He full soon his death should
     meet,   ·
   I remain in life!"

But the messenger, he sware,
He should bide there where he
     were:
"To King Arthur will I fare,
   There mine errand say.
Mickle sorrow me betide
If I longer here abide,
But from hence I now will ride
   Swiftly as I may."
When the lad in this wise spake
Prayer to him the knight doth
     make,
His nine sons with him to take,
   But he saith him "Nay."
Yet so fair his speech shall be
That he taketh of them three,
In his fellowship to be,
   Blither then were they.

Of their errand blithe they were,
Busked them, on their way to
     fare,

Mickle mirth then made they there,
　Little their amend!
He had ridden but a while,
Scarce the mountenance of a mile,
He bethought him of a guile
　They the worse did wend!
They with him to fare were fain —
Otherwise thought their chieftain,
Sendeth ever one again
　Back, at each mile's end,
Till they one and all were gone —
Then he rideth on alone
Spurring over stock and stone
　Where no man him kenned.

Known of no man would he be;
Ever further rideth he
'Midst a strange folk, verilie,
　Valiant deeds to do;
Now, I trow, hath Percyvelle
With two uncles spoken well,
Nor might one the other tell,
　Or his true name know;
Now upon the way he's set
That shall lead him, without let,
Till the Soudan he has met,
　Blacked his brows with blow.
Percyvelle no more I'll sing,
On his way God shall him bring —
Unto Arthur now, the king,
　Thither will we go.

On our way we'll go anon —
To Caerbedd the king has gone,
Mourning doth he make and moan,
　He doth sigh full sore;
Woe its will on him doth wreak,
And his heart is waxen weak
For he deems that he shall speak
　With Percyvelle no more.

As abed he lieth there
Came the messenger, who bare
Letters from the lady fair,
　Stood the king before;
Arthur might not stand that day,
Read the script as there he lay:
"This thy message," doth he say,
　"Answered is before."

Quoth: "Thine answer dost thou see,
He who sick and sore may be
Scarce may fare afar, that he
　In the field may fight!"
Cried the messenger withal,
Quoth: "Woe worth this wicked hall,
Why did I not turn at call,
　Go back with that knight?"
"What knight was that?" quoth the king;
"Whom thou meanest in this thing,
In my land is no lording
　Worthy name of knight!"
Quoth the messenger straightway:
"This his name he would not say,
Fain were I to know alway
　What the lad, he hight.

"This much had I from that knight,
He 'His mother's son' was hight,
In what manner he was dight
　Now I shall ye tell;
Worthy wight was he to see,
Burly, bold of body he,
Blood-stained arms should, verilie,
　Tale of battle tell;
He bestrode a blood-red steed,
Aketoun, and other weed,
All of that same hue indeed,
　They became him well!"

Then he gave command, the king,
Horse and armour forth to bring:
"May I trow thy chattering,
   That was Percyvelle!"

For the love of Percyvelle
They to horse and armour fell,
There would they no longer dwell,
   Forth to fare were fain:
Fast they ride upon their way,
They were sore afeard that day
Ere they come unto the fray
   That he should be slain;
Arthur with him taketh three
Knights, the fourth himself shall
      be,
Now so swiftly rideth he
   Follow may no swain.
Now the king is on his way,
Let him come whene'er he may
I will seek now in my play
   Percyvelle again.

Seek we Percyvelle again, —
He hath passed out on the plain,
Over moorland, and mountain
   Seeketh Maiden-Land;
Till toward the eventide
Warriors bold he saw abide,
With pavilions pitched in pride
   Round a city stand;
Hunting was the Soudan then,
He had left there many men,
Twenty score, an ye would ken,
   Should the gates command;
Ten score, while the day was
      light,
And eleven, through the night,
All of them were armed aright,
   Weapons in their hand.

There with weapons in their hand
They would fight e'en as they
      stand,

Sitting, lying, all that band,
   Eleven score of men;
Riding as one rides a race,
Ere he wist, in little space,
Thro' the thickest press, apace,
   Rode he 'mongst them then;
Started up a soldier bold,
Of his bridle layeth hold,
Said that he would fain be told
   Of his errand then;
Said he: "I be come here fain
For to see a proud Soudain,
He, i' faith, shall soon be slain
   If I might him ken!

"If to know that man I may,
Then at morn, when dawns the
      day,
Fast together shall we play
   With our weapons tried!"
When they heard that he, in fray,
Thought their Soudan for to slay
Each one fell on him that day,
   There to make him bide;
When he saw he thus was stayed,
Him, who hand on bridle laid;
Rode he down, and undismayed,
   There, the gate beside,
Thrust with spear about him
      there,
And his point through many bare,
There was no man who might
      dare
   Face the lad that tide.

Who in town the tidings tell
Say, beneath his feet they fell,
That bold body, Percyvelle
   Sped, his foes to still;
Thought, 'twas small speed with
      his spear,
Tho' it shore thro' many sheer,
Folk enow he found them here,
   Had of fight his fill;

From the hour of middle night,
Even till the morning light,
Were they ne'er so wild, or wight,
   He wrought at his will;
And he dealt thus with his brand,
There was none might 'gainst him
      stand,
Half a blow take from his hand
   Struck with such good-will.

Now he striketh them, I ween,
Till the Paynim's heads are seen
Hop as hailstones on the green,
   Round about the grass;
Thus he dealt them many a blow,
Till the dawn began to show
He had laid their lives full low,
   All who there would pass;
When his foes thus slain should be
Very weary then was he,
This I tell ye verilie,
   He but cared the less,
An he living were, or dead,
So he found him in such stead
He might peaceful lay his head,
   Surety find in stress.

There be found no surety
Save what 'neath the wall should
      be,
There a fair place chooseth he,
   And adown did light;
There he laid him down that tide,
And the steed stood him beside,
For the foal was fain to bide,
   Wearied with the fight.
On the morn, when it was day,
On the wall the watchman lay,
Saw signs of an ugly fray
   On the plain there dight;
Yet more marvel should there be,
Living man was none to see, —
Then they call that fair ladie
   To behold that sight.

Comes the lady to that sight;
Lufamour, that maiden bright,
Mounts the wall, that from the
      height,
   She may see the field;
Heads and helmets, many a one,
(Trow me, lie I tell ye none,)
There they lay the grass upon,
   With them many a shield;
'T was a marvel great they
      thought,
Who had such a wonder wrought
In such wise to death had brought
   All that folk on field,
And within the gate came ne'er
For to tell what men they were,
Tho' they knew the maid was
      there
   Fair reward to yield.

Their reward she fain would pay—
Forth in haste they go their way
If on field they find them aye
   Who had done this deed.
'Neath their band they looked
      around,
Saw a mickle steed that stound,
Blood-stained knight who lay on
      ground
   By a blood-red steed;
Then she quoth, that lady bright:
"Yonder doth there lie a knight,
Who has surely been in fight
   If I right may read;
Either hath that man been slain,
Or to slumber is he fain,
Or he is in battle ta'en,
   Blood-stained is his weed."

Quoth she: "Blood-stained is his
      weed,
Even so his goodly steed,
Such knight in this land, indeed,
   Did I never see;

What may he be, if he rise?
He is tall as there he lies,
And well made in every wise
   As a man may be."
Then she called her chamberlain,
Who by name hight fair Hatlayne,
The courtesy of good Gawain
   In hall practised he;
Then she bade him go his way —
"If yon knight he live alway,
Bid him come to me straightway,
   Pray him courteously."

Now to pray him as he can
'Neath the wall he swiftly ran,
Warily he waked the man,
   But the steed stood still;
As the tale was told to me
Down he kneeled on his knee,
Mildly hailed the knight so free,
   Spake him soft and still;
"This my lady, Lufamour,
She awaits thee in her bower,
Prayeth thee, for thine honour
   Come, if so thou will."
When he heard her message there
Up he rose with him to fare,
That man, who a stout heart bare,
   Would her prayer fulfil.

Now her prayer to fulfil
Followed he her servant's will,
Went his way with him, until
   To that maid came he;
Very blithe that maiden bright
When she saw that lad with sight,
For she trowed that he was wight,
   Asked him fair and free —
Of that lad she asks alway,
(Tho' he fain had said her nay,)
If he wist who did then slay
   Who her foes should be?
Quoth he: "None of them I sought,
I had with the Soudan fought

To a stand they had me brought,
   Slain they were by me."

Quoth he: "There they needs must
     stay!"
Lufamour, that lady gay,
By his words she knew straight-
     way
   That the lad was wight;
And the maid was blithe that
     stound
That she such an aid had found
'Gainst the Soudan, who was
     bound
   With them all to fight;
Straight she looked upon him
     there,
Thought him meet her land to
     share
If on field he won her fair
   With mastery and might;
Then they stabled there his steed,
And himself to hall they lead,
For delaying was no need,
   They to dine are dight.

Set the lad on daïs fair,
And with richest dainties there,
'T is no lie I now declare,
   Serve him speedily;
Sat him on a chair of gold
By the mildest maid on mold,
And the fairest to behold,
   As at meat sat she;
There she made him semblance
     good,
As they fell there to their food,
Skilfully she soothed his mood
   At meat, mirthfully;
That for this, her sake, I trow,
He doth undertake, and vow,
He will slay the Soudan now,
   And that speedily.

Quoth he: "Without any let
When I have the Soudan met,
A sad stroke on him I'll set
　　That his pride shall spill."
Quoth the lady fair and free:
"Who my foeman's bane shall be
He shall have my land and me,
　　Rule us as he will."
There his meal had been but small
When word came unto the hall
Saying, many men withal
　　Harnessed were on hill.
Woeful for their fellows slain
They the city nigh had ta'en,
Men within the hold amain
　　Tolled the bell with will.

Now they toll the common bell;
Word is come to Percyvelle
He no longer there would dwell,
　　Leapt from daïs that day.
Lust for fighting did he know,
Crying: "Kinsmen, now I go
All yon men I'll lay them low
　　Ere I cease to slay!"
Then she kissed him without let,
On his head the helm she set,
To the stable did he get
　　Where his steed did stay.
There were none with him to fare
For no man from thence he'ld
　　spare,
Forth he rides, and hastes him
　　there
　　To the thickest fray.

To the press he came apace
Riding as one rides a race,
All the folk before his face
　　They of strength had none;
Tho' to take him fain they were
Yet their blows, they harmed him
　　ne'er,
'T was as they had smitten there

On a right hard stone;
Were they weak, or were they
　　wight,
All on whom his brand did smite
Felled their bodies were forthright
　　Better fate had none;
And I wot so swift he sped
Ere the sun was high o'er head
He that folk had smitten dead
　　Left in life not one.

When they all were slain, then he
Looked around him, fain to see
If anigh him more should be
　　Who would with him fight;
As he, hardy, did behold,
Lo, he saw far off on wold,
Four knights under shield so bold
　　Thither ride aright;
The first should King Arthur be,
Then Ywain, flower of chivalry,
And Gawain, he made them three,
　　Kay, the fourth was hight;
Percyvelle, he spake full fair:
"Now to yonder four I'll fare,
If the Soudan shall be there
　　Do, as I am plight."

Now to hold the troth he plight
'Gainst the four he rideth right,
On the wall, the lady bright
　　Lay, and did behold,
How these many men he'd slain,
Sithen, turned his steed again
'Gainst four knights doth ride
　　amain
　　Further on the wold;
Then I trow she was full woe
When she saw him further go
And to seek four knights as foe
　　Shield and shaft uphold;
Mickle men and stern they ride,
And right well she deemed that
　　tide

That with bale they'd make him
    bide
  Who was her strong hold.

Tho' he was her surest hold
Yet that maid must needs behold
How he rideth forth on wold
    'Gainst the four amain;
Then King Arthur quoth forth-
    right:
"Hither comes a valiant knight
Who, because he seeketh fight,
  Forth to ride is fain;
If to fight he fares anon
And we four should strive 'gainst
    one,
Little fame we then had won
  If he soon were slain."
Fast the four, they forward ride,
And the lot they cast that tide,
Sought who first the joust should
    bide,
  That fell to Gawain.

When unto Gawain it fell
Thus to ride 'gainst Percyvelle,
Then the chance it pleased him
    well,
  From them did he fare;
Ever nearer as he drew,
Ever better then he knew
Of the arms and steed the hue
  That the lad he bare;
"Ah! dear God," quoth Gawain
    free,
"Now what may this venture be?
An I slay him, or he me,
  Sorry fate it were!
We be sisters' sons, we twain,
Were one by the other slain
He who lives might mourn amain
  That be born was e'er!"

Of his skill no proof he showed

Sir Gawain, as there he rode,
Drew his rein, and there abode
  To himself quoth low:
"Now an unwise man I be
Thus to vex me foolishly;
None shall aye so hardy be
  But his peer may know;
Percyvelle, he slew that knight,
Yet another, e'en as wight,
May in that same gear be dight,
  Taken all him fro
If my kinsman I should spare
And his gear another ware
Who should overcome me there
  That would work me woe!

"That would work me mickle
    woe —
Now, as I on earth may go
It shall ne'er befall me so
  If I right may read;
One shaft shall I send, to wit,
And will seek first blow to hit,
Then shall I know, by my wit,
  Who doth wear that weed."
No word more he saith that tide
But together swift they ride,
Men, who joust were bold to bide
  And stiff knights on steed;
Strong and stalwart steeds had
    they,
And their shields failed not that
    day,
But their spears brake in that fray,
  As behoved them need.

Spears, that erst were whole, they
    brake, —
With that, Percyvelle, he spake,
In this wise a tale would make
  That on his tongue lay;
Saith: "My way I wide have gone,
Yet, I trow me, such Soudan,
I' faith, saw I never none,

Ne'er by night or day:
I have slain, if I thee ken,
Twenty score of these, thy men,
Yet of all whom I slew then
    Deemed it but a play,
'Gainst the dint I took from thee
Ne'er such debt was owed by me,
Two for one, my pay shall be
    If so be I may!"

Then he answered, Sir Gawain,
(Sooth it is, be ye certain
Of that same was he full fain
    Where in field they fight;)
For, by these, his words so wild
Of a fool, the knight so mild
Wist full well it was the child
    Percyvelle, the wight —
Quoth: "No Soudan now I be,
But that same man, certainly,
Who thy body aided thee
    First in arms to dight;
Thy stout heart I praise alway
Tho' thy words were rough today,
And my name, the sooth to say
    Is Gawain, the knight!"

Quoth he: "Who will read aright
Knows me for Gawain the
    knight."
Then the twain, they ceased to
    fight,
    As good friends of old;
Quoth: "Bethink thee, when thy
    foe
Thou wast fain in fire to throw
To disarm thou didst not know
    This, his body cold;" —
Then was Percyvelle the free
Joyful, as he well might be,
For he wist well it was he
    By this token told;
Then as Gawain did him pray,
He his vizor raised straightway

With good cheer they kissed that
    day
    Those two barons bold.

Now they kiss, the barons twain,
Sithen talked, as they were fain,
Then, by them he draweth rein,
    Arthur, king, and knight;
Then, as they afore had done,
Gave he thanks to God anon.
Mickle mirth, I trow, they won,
    That they met aright;
Sithen, without more delay,
To the castle made their way
And with them he rides that day
    Percyvelle the wight;
Ready was the porter there,
Thro' the gate the knights they
    fare,
Blither heart no lady bare
    Than Lufamour, the bright!

"Succour great thou dost me send,
This my castle to defend
If the Soudan 'gainst me wend
    Who is my worst foe!"
Then they set their steeds in stall
And the king wends to the hall,
His knights follow him withal
    Since 't was fitting so;
Ready was their meal that day,
And thereto they take their way
With the king, the lady gay,
    And the knights also.

Welcome good she gave her guest,
Rich meats proffered of the best,
Dearest drinks at their behest
    Brought for them, I ween,
Ate and drank with mirth on
    mold,
Sithen talked, and tales they told
Of deeds that were wrought of old
    Both the king and queen;

And the first thing, did she pray
Of King Arthur, he would say
Of child Percyvelle alway
   What his life had been?
Lufamour, she wondered sore,
That he arms so bravely bore,
Yet knew naught of knightly lore
   As she well had seen.

She had seen, with this same child,
Naught but words and works so
    wild,
Marvelled much, that lady mild,
   Of his folly there;
Then hath Arthur shewn, that
    stead,
How that Percyvelle was bred
From the first, till he was led
   Forth, on field to fare;
How his father, slain was he,
And his mother fain would flee,
Dwell alone 'neath woodland tree,
   None her flight to share;
"There he dwelt for fifteen year,
Had for fellow the wild deer,
Little need ye wonder here
   That so wild he were!"

When he told this tale withal
To that lady fair in hall
Gracious words had he at call
   For them everyone;
Then quoth Percyvelle, the wight:
"If I be not yet a knight
Thou shalt keep thy promise plight
   Thou would'st make me one!"
Then the king he answered so:
"Other deeds thou needs must do,
'Gainst the Soudan shalt thou go,
   Thus thy spurs be won!"
Then quoth Percyvelle the free:
"Soon as I the Soudan see,
Even so, I swear to thee,
   Shall the deed be done!"

"As I sware," so doth he say,
"That I would the Soudan slay,
I will work as best I may
   That word to maintain."
That day did they no more deed,
Those knights, worthy under
    weed,
Busked them there, to bed to
    speed
   Great and small were fain;
Till ere morn hath waxen high
Comes the Soudan with a cry
All his folk, he found them lie,
   They'd been put to pain;
Soon he asked who was the knight
Who had slain his men with might
And in life had left the fight,
   Mastery to gain?

Now to win the mastery
To the castle doth he cry
If one were with heart so high
   Fain with him to fight?
Man for man to challenge fain:
"Tho' he all his folk hath slain,
He shall find Gollrotherame
   Meet him as is right;
But this forward I demand,
That thereto ye set your hand,
He who shall the better stand,
   Prove the most of might,
That he slay his foe this tide,
He the land, both broad and wide,
Holds, and taketh for his bride
   Lufamour, the bright!"

And that same, the King Arthour,
And the lady Lufamour,
All who were within that tower
   Granted readily;
They called Percyvelle the wight,
And the king there dubbed him
    knight
Tho' he little knew in sight

Stout of heart was he;
Bade him that he be to praise,
Gentle, and of courteous ways,
And Syr Percyvelle the Gallays,
　　Should his title be.
Thus the king, in Maiden-land,
Dubbed him knight with his own
　　hand,
Bade him firm 'gainst foe to stand,
　　Plague him ceaselessly.

Little peace he took that same,
'Gainst the Soudan swift he came,
Who hight Gollerotherame,
　　And was fell in fight;
In the field so broad and wide
No more carping made that tide
But together soon they ride
　　With their shafts aright;
Then the Soudan, strong in weed,
Percyvelle bare from his steed,
Two land's length, I trow, indeed,
　　With mastery and might;
On the earth the Soudan lay,
And his steed, it fled away,
Jesting, Percyvelle doth say:
　　"Hast the troth I plight!

"I thee plight a blow, I trow,
And methinks, thou hast it now,
Were it so, 't would please me, thou
　　Ne'er of this should mend!"
O'er the Soudan did he stay,
As upon the ground he lay,
Held him down to earth alway
　　E'en with his spear-end.
Fain he had his foeman slain,
E'en that miscreant Soudane,
But no way could find again,
　　Had small skill to wend;
Then he thinks, the lad so bold,
Of wild works he wrought of old,
"Had I now a fire on wold
　　Burning were thine end!"

Quoth: "I'ld burn thee here
　　forthright,
Then thou should'st have no more
　　might
'Gainst a woman aye to fight,
　　I would teach thee fair!"
Quoth the good Gawain that day:
"Thou could'st, didst thou know
　　the way,
And would'st light from steed
　　alway
Overcome him there."
Light of mood, the boy, and gay,
Thinks　　on　　other　　thing
　　straightway.
Quoth: "A *steed*, now didst thou
　　say?
　　I deemed this a *mare!*"
In the stead there, as he stood,
Little recked for ill or good,
Swiftly did he change his mood
　　Slacked his spear point there.

When he up his spear had ta'en,
With that, Gollerotherame,
This same miscreant Soudane,
　　Sprang upon his feet,
Forth his sword then draweth he,
Strikes at Percyvelle the free,
And the boy scarce skilled should
　　be
　　These, his wiles, to meet;
But the steed, at his own will,
Saw the sword, and stayed not
　　still,
Leapt aside upon a hill,
　　Five strides maketh fleet;
Even as he sprang there-by,
Then the Soudan raised a cry,
Waked the boy full suddenly
　　From his musings sweet.

He in musing deep did stay,
All his dreams then fled away,

Lighted down without delay
  'Gainst him for to go;
Quoth: "I trow, hast taught to me
How I best may deal with thee."
Swift, his sword then draweth he,
  Struck hard at his foe;
Thro' the neck-bone shore the
    blade,
Mouthpiece, gorget, useless laid,
And the Soudan's head he made
  Fly the body fro.'
Then he strode, the knight so
    good,
To his steed, as there it stood,
That fair maiden mild of mood,
  Much mirth might she know.

Very mirthful he, that tide,
To the castle did he ride,
Boldly there did he abide
  With that maiden bright;
Joyful were they everyone
That the Soudan was undone,
And he had the woman won
  By mastery and might.
Said of Percyvelle, that he
Worthy was a king to be,
Since he kept full faithfully
  That which he had hight.
There was nothing more to say
But, on the appointed day,
He wed Lufamour, the may,
  Percyvelle, the wight.

Now has Percyvelle the wight
Wedded Lufamour, the bright,
King hath he become of right
  Of that land so wide;
Then King Arthur, on a day,
Thought no longer there to stay,
Took leave of the lady gay
  And from thence would ride;
Percyvelle there leaveth he
King of all that land to be

Since with ring, the knight so free,
  Wed that maid as bride.
Sithen, on th'appointed day,
Rode the king upon his way,
As for certain sooth I say,
  Nor would more abide.

Now doth Percyvelle abide
There, within those boroughs wide,
For her sake who was his bride,
  Wedded there with ring;
Well he wielded rule in land,
All men bowed them to his hand,
At his will the folk, they stand,
  Know him for their king;
Thus within that burg, right well,
Till the twelvemonth's end, it fell,
With his true love did he dwell,
  Thought of ne'er a thing,
Thought not how his mother, she,
Dwelt beneath the greenwood tree,
How her drink should water be
  That from well doth spring.

Drinks spring-water from the well,
Eats of herbs, no lie I tell,
With none other thing doth dwell
  In the holts so sere;
Till it chanced upon a day
As within his bed he lay,
To himself he 'gan to say
  Soft, with sigh and tear:
"Last Yule day, methinks it were,
I on wild ways forth did fare,
Left my mother man-less there
  In the woodland drear —"
To himself then sayeth he:
"Blithe, I ween, I ne'er may be
Till I may my mother see,
  Or of her may hear."

Now to wot how she doth fare
That good knight doth armour
    bear,

287

Nor would longer linger there
  Spite of aught they say;
Up he rose within that hall,
Took his leave of one and all,
Both of great and eke of small,
  Forth would go his way,
Tho' she doth him straight en-
    treat,
Lufamour, his true love sweet,
While the days of Yule fast fleet
  He with her should stay,
He denied her of that thing,
But a priest he bade them bring,
Bade a Mass for him to sing,
  Rode forth that same day.

Now from thence the knight doth
    ride,
Never man he wist that tide
Whitherward he thought to ride
  His grief to amend;
Forth he rideth all alone,
Goeth from them everyone,
None might know where he is
    gone
  Or might with him wend;
Forward doth he take his way,
'T is the certain sooth I say,
Till a road he found alway
  By a forest end.
Then he heard, the road anigh,
As it were a woman's cry
Praying Mary mild, on high,
  She would succour send.

Praying Mary, mild of mood,
She would send her succour
    good —
As he came there thro' the wood
  He a marvel found;
For a lady, fair to see,
Stood fast bounden to a tree,
'T is the sooth I say to ye,
  Hand and foot were bound;

When her plight he thus did know
Fain was he to ask her who
He should be, who served her so,
  As he thus had found?
Saith she: "Sir, 't is the Black
    Knight,
He who is my lord by right,
Who in this wise hath me dight
  Brought me to this stound."

Quoth she: "Here he left me
    bound
For a fault that he hath found,
Yet I warrant thee this stound,
  Evil did I none!
For it chanced e'en as I say,
That upon my bed I lay
As it were the last Yule-Day,
  Now a twelvemonth gone,
Were he knight, or were he king,
One in jest hath done this thing,
He with me exchanged a ring,
  Richer had I none!
That man did I never see
Who made this exchange with me,
But I wot, whoe'er he be,
  He the better won! "

Quoth: "The better doth he own,
For such virtue in a stone,
In this world I ne'er have known,
  Set within a ring,
For the man who doth it wear,
Or upon his body bear,
Never blow may harm him there,
  Or to death him bring."
Percyvelle wist without fail,
When he heard that lady's tale,
He had brought her into bale
  When he changed her ring;
Straightway to her speaketh he,
To that lady fair and free:
"I shall loose thee from that tree
  By my faith as king!"

Percyvelle was king and knight,
Well he held what he had hight,
And he loosed that lady bright,
　Who stood bound to tree;
Down she sat, the lady fair,
Percyvelle beside her there,
Wayworn, since he far did fare,
　Fain to rest was he;
Deemed he well might rest that
　tide,
Yet short leisure might he bide,
As he lay, the dame beside,
　His head on her knee,
She waked Percyvelle the wight,
Bade him flee with all his might:
"Yonder cometh the Black Knight,
　Slain thou sure shalt be!"

Quoth she: "Sir, thou sure shalt
　die,
This I tell thee certainly,
Yonder, see, he draweth nigh
　Who shall slay us two."
But the knight he answered free:
"Thou but now didst say to me
That no dint my death should be,
　Nor should work me woe."
Then his helm on head he set,
But, ere he to horse might get,
The Black Knight with him hath
　met,
　Hailed him as his foe;
Quoth he: "How? What dost thou
　here?
Would'st thou then thy playmate
　cheer?
For this shalt thou pay full dear
　Ere I hence shall go!"

Quoth the knight: "Ere hence I go,
I shall surely slay ye two,
And the like of ye also,
　Fair reward to yield!"
Then quoth Percyvelle the free:

"Now, methinks, we soon shall
　see
Who of us shall worthy be
　To be slain in field!"
No word more they spake that
　tide,
But right soon together ride,
As men who would war abide
　Stiff, with shaft and shield.
And Syr Percyvelle, the wight,
He hath borne down the Black
　Knight,
Then, I trow, the lady bright
　Succoured him on field;

His best succour did she wield,
Save she there had been his shield,
He had sure been slain on field,
　Swift and certainly;
For as Percyvelle the keen
Fain the Black Knight's bane had
　been
Came the lady in between,
　And did "Mercy!" cry;
For her sake did he forbear,
And he made the Black Knight
　swear
To forgive that lady fair,
　Put his ill-will by;
And, himself, he sware that day
That he ne'er beside her lay,
Wronged her not in any way
　That were villainy!

"Villainy I did her ne'er,
When I saw her sleeping there,
Then I kissed that lady fair,
　That to own, I'm fain!
From her hand I took a ring,
And I left her slumbering,
And the truth of that same thing
　Will I here maintain!"
That naught else had chanced,
　that, he

Sware by Jesu, verilie,
For that same, right readily,
   Here would he be slain!
"Ready is the ring, I trow,
If mine own wilt give me now,
Of that same exchange, I vow,
   Shall I be full fain!"

Quoth: "Mine own I'll gladly
   take —"
In this wise the Black Knight
   spake:
"No denial will I make
   Thou too late shalt be!
Swift that ring did I demand
Drew it there from off her hand,
To the lord of this same land,
   Bare it speedily!
Mourning sore, that ring I bare,
To a good man took it there,
No more stalwart giant shall fare
   On this earth than he!
There is neither knight nor king
Who durst ask from him that ring,
But that same to death he'll bring,
   Hot his wrath shall be!"

"Be he hot, or be he cold —"
Thus spake Percyvelle the bold,
(For the tale that knight had told
   He waxed wroth that day;)
Quoth: "On gallows high may he
Hang, who gives this ring to thee
Ere mine own thou bringest me,
   Which thou gav'st away!
If none other way there be
Then right soon shalt tell to me
What like man, in sooth, is he
   Who is strong in fray?
I to speak no more be fain,
I must win it back again,
Lost thy share in these rings twain
   Tho' more precious they!"

Quoth: "Had they more precious
   been —"
Quoth the knight in wrath, I
   ween,
"That with small delay be seen,
   What like man is he,
If to keep thy word thou dare,
Percyvelle of Gallays, fare
To yon lofty palace, there
   Should he surely be;
Thy ring with that giant grim,
(Bright the stone, and nothing
   dim,)
There, forsooth, shalt find with
   him,
   Given it was by me.
In that hold, or eke without, —
Or, perchance, he rides about, —
But of thee he'll have small doubt
   As thou sure shalt see!"

Quoth the knight: "Thou sure
   shalt see,
That I tell thee certainlie," —
On his way then rideth he
   Wondrous swift that tide;
Stood the giant in his hold
Who was lord o'er wood and
   wold,
Saw Syr Percyvelle the bold
   O'er his land to ride;
On his porter calls, I ween,
Saith: "Now say, what may this
   mean?
For a bold man have I seen
   O'er my lands to ride.
Reach me down my plaything
   there,
And against him will I fare,
Better lot at Rome he'ld share
   As I thrive, this tide!"

An he thrive, or vanquished be,
Club of iron taketh he,

And 'gainst Percyvelle the free,
  Goes his way forthright,
Weighty blows that club should
    deal,
That a knight full well should feel,
For the head, well wrought of
    steel,
  Twelve stone weighed aright;
Bound the staff with iron band,
And with ten stones of the land,
One was set behind his hand,
  Was for holding dight;
Three and twenty, fully told,
Ill might any man on mold,
As the tale it now is told,
  'Gainst such weapon fight!

Thus, to smite each other down,
Met they on a moorland brown,
A full mile from any town,
  'Neath their shield so bold;
Then he quoth, the giant wight,
Soon as he beheld that knight:
"Mahoun, praiséd be thy might!"
  Did him well behold;
"Art thou he, now tell me true,
Who Gollerotherame slew,
Other brother ne'er I knew
  Than himself, of old?"
Then quoth Percyvelle the free:
"Thro' God's Grace, I'll so serve
    thee,
And such giants as ye be
  Slay them all on fold!"

Such a fight was seldom seen,
For the dale it rang, I ween
With the dints that passed bet-
    ween
  These two, when they met;
The giant, with his weapon fell,
Fain had smitten Percyvelle,
Bending low, he swerved full
    well,

  And a stroke swift set;
The giant's blow, it went astray,
Hard as flint the club alway,
Ere the staff he well might stay,
  Or his strength might let,
In the earth the club, it stood,
To the midmost of the wood,
Percyvelle, the hero good,
  Forth his sword would get.

Forth he drew his sword that day,
Smote the giant without delay,
Nigh unto his neck alway
  Even as he stood,
Strikes his hand off with a blow,
His left foot doth cleave also,
Dealt such dints upon his foe,
  Nighed him as he would;
Percyvelle he quoth: "I ween,
Had thy weapon smaller been
Better luck thy hand had seen,
  Thou hadst done some good;
Now, I trow, that ne'er again
Shall thy club from earth be ta'en,
Or thy way thou ridest fain,
  Ne'er, upon the Rood!"

Quoth he: "By the Holy Rood,
As in evil aye thou stood,
Of thy foot thou get'st no good,
  Save that hop thou may!"
Then his club aside he laid,
Smote the hero undismayed,
In the neck, with knife's sharp
    blade,
  Near enow were they.
Wrathful at the blow, I ween,
The giant's head he smote off
    clean,
As none had aforetime been,
  Both hands were away!
Then his head from off him
    drave —
He was a discourteous knave

Thus a giant's beard to shave,
  I forsooth, may say!

Then, as I the sooth may say,
Left the giant where he lay
And rode forth upon his way
  To the fortress-hold;
When he saw his lord was dead,
Then the porter swiftly sped,
From the knight, the keys, that
    stead,
  Would he not withhold;
Percyvelle, ere other thing,
Prayed the porter of the ring,
Thereof, could he tidings bring?
  And straightway he told,
Showed him straightway to the
    kist,
Where the treasure was, he wist,
Bade him take there, as he list,
  All he would of gold.

Percyvelle, from treasure hold
Speedy, turned out all the gold,
There, before him on the mold,
  Fell the ring he sought;
Stood the porter at his side,
Saw the ring from coffer glide,
And he quoth: "Woe worth the
    tide
  That same ring was wrought!"
Percyvelle, he answered free,
Asked him why, and wherefore,
    he
Banned that ring so bitterly,
  What was in his thought?
Then the porter answered fair,
By his loyalty he sware:
"I the truth will here declare
  And delay for naught."

Quoth: "The truth I tell to thee,
The knight whose this ring should
    be

As a present gave it free,
  And hath hither brought;
He, forsooth, my master there,
Took the gift with favour fair,
Lord of this land was he e'er,
  For his marvels wrought.
Dwelling nigh, there chanced to
    be
At that time, a fair ladie,
And my lord, right loyally,
  Loved her, as I thought;
So it chanced upon a day
As in sooth I now shall say,
That my lord went forth to play,
  And her love besought.

"Now the lady doth he pray
His true love to be alway,
Pleading straitly, that he may
  Of her favoured be;
As his first prayer he would
    bring,
He would proffer her the ring,
When she saw that tokening,
  Sore dismayed was she;
Wept, and wailed, and cried
    amain:
'Traitor, thou my son hast slain,
And the ring from him hast ta'en
  That was given by me!'
Then her clothes from off her tare,
Gat her to the woodland there,
Witless doth that lady fare
  This the cause shall be!

"Even for such cause as this
Is the lady mad, I wis,
Wild within the wood she is
  Ever since that tide;
Fain would I her succour be,
But whene'er she seeth me
From me swiftly doth she flee,
  Will for naught abide."
Quoth Syr Percyvelle that day:

"Now will I without delay
Strive to make that lady stay,
    But I will not ride;
But afoot I now will go,
An that lady shall me know
I may bring her out of woe
    For her son she'll bide!"

Quoth: "For this, her son, she'll
        bide,
But ahorse I will not ride
Till that lady I have spied,
    Speed as best I may;
With none armour that may be,"
Quoth the knight: "I'll cover me,
Till that I my mother see,
    Or by night or day;
But the self-same garb I ware
When from her I forth did fare,
That, I think again to bear
    After other play;
And I trow that never more
Come I from the holts so hore
Till her lot, who once me bore,
    I again may say."

"This for sooth I think to say." —
With that would he go his way,
With the morn, at dawn of day,
    Forth the knight did fare;
All his harness left within,
Did on him a coat of skin,
To the woodland forth did win
    'Mid the holts so bare;
Seven days long in vain he
        sought,
Of his mother found he naught,
Nor of meat or drink he thought,
    He was full of care;
On the ninth day it befell
That he came unto a well
Nigh where he was wont to
        dwell,
    And refresh him there.

He had drunk his fill that tide,
Further thought to wander wide,
When he saw, close to his side,
    That same lady free;
But, whenas she saw him there,
She with threats would 'gainst
        him fare.
And swift answer did she dare
    E'en that fair ladie;
She began to call and cry,
Saying: "Such a son had I!"
Then his heart for joy beat high,
    Blithe, I trow, was he;
As he came to her anear,
So that she his voice might hear,
Spake he: "Sweet my mother dear,
    Bide ye there for me!"

By that time so nigh was he
That she might in no wise flee,
This I tell ye certainly,
    She must needs abide;
Sprang on him in wrath so keen,
That of very truth, I ween,
Had her strength but greater been
    He were slain that tide;
But the stronger was he e'er,
Up he took his mother there,
On his back the lady bare,
    Pure, I trow, his pride.
To the castle gate that day
Hastens he, the nearest way,
And the porter without stay,
    Opens to him wide.

Bare his mother in that day, —
He who made the tale doth say
With what robes they had alway
    Wrapped her warmly there;
There the lord a drink had
        wrought,
And that same the porter brought,
For none other had he thought
    Save that lady fair.

293

Then for so the tale they tell,
With a spoon they fed her well,
And asleep she swiftly fell
    As I now declare;
And the lady sleeping lay
Three nights, and three days,
        alway
Doth the porter with her stay
    Wakes and watches there.

Thus the porter watched her there,
Loyal love to her he bare,
Till at last the lady fair
    Wakened, so I ween;
Then distraught was she no more,
But herself in such wise bore
As one hale, who ne'er of yore,
    Otherwise had been;
Then they kneeléd down, the
        three,
Gave God thanks on bended knee
That men thus His grace should
        see
    As on them was seen.

Sithen, go they on their way,
And a rich bath make straight-
        way,
For that lady, robed her gay,
    Both in gray and green.

Percyvelle without delay,
'T is the sooth to ye I say,
Took his mother, and his way
    Homeward rideth he;
Then great lords, and his sweet
        queen,
Welcomed him with joy, I ween,
When they him in life had seen
    Blithe they well may be.
Then he fared to Holy Land,
Cities won with his strong hand,
There was slain, I understand,
    This his end should be!
Jesu Christ, high Heaven's King,
Who is Lord of everything,
Grant to us His dear blessing,
    Amen, for charitie.

CHAPTER 15

Le Morte d'Arthur

Sir Thomas Malory

Book III

Chapter XII

How a sorrowful knight came before Arthur, and how Balin fetched him, and how that knight was slain by a knight invisible.

Within a day or two King Arthur was somewhat sick, and he let pitch his pavilion in a meadow, and there he laid him down on a pallet to sleep, but he might have no rest. Right so he heard a great noise of an horse, and therewith the king looked out at the porch of the pavilion, and saw a knight coming even by him, making great dole. Abide, fair sir, said Arthur, and tell me wherefore thou makest this sorrow. Ye may little amend me, said the knight, and so passed forth to the castle of Meliot. Anon after there came Balin, and when he saw King Arthur he alighted off his horse, and came to the king on foot, and saluted him. By my head, said Arthur, ye be welcome. Sir, right now came riding this way a knight making great mourn, for what cause I cannot tell; wherefore I would desire of you of your courtesy and of your gentleness to fetch again that knight either by force or else by his good will. I will do more for your lordship than that, said Balin; and so he rode more than a pace, and found the knight with a damosel in a forest, and said, Sir knight, ye must come with me unto King Arthur, for to tell him of your sorrow. That will I not, said the knight, for it will scathe

295

me greatly, and do you none avail. Sir, said Balin, I pray you make you ready, for ye must go with me, or else I must fight with you and bring you by force, and that were me loath to do. Will ye be my warrant, said the knight, an I go with you? Yea, said Balin, or else I will die therefore. And so he made him ready to go with Balin, and left the damosel still. And as they were even afore King Arthur's pavilion, there came one invisible, and smote this knight that went with Balin throughout the body with a spear. Alas, said the knight, I am slain under your conduct with a knight called Garlon; therefore take my horse that is better than yours, and ride to the damosel, and follow the quest that I was in as she will lead you, and revenge my death when ye may. That shall I do, said Balin, and that I make vow unto knighthood; and so he departed from this knight with great sorrow. So King Arthur let bury this knight richly, and made a mention on his tomb, how there was slain Herlews le Berbeus, and by whom the treachery was done, the knight Garlon. But ever the damosel bare the truncheon of the spear with her that Sir Herlews was slain withal.

Chapter XIII

How Balin and the damosel met with a knight which was in likewise slain, and how the damosel bled for the custom of a castle.

So Balin and the damosel rode into a forest, and there met with a knight that had been a-hunting, and that knight asked Balin for what cause he made so great sorrow. Me list not to tell you, said Balin. Now, said the knight, an I were armed as ye be I would fight with you. That should little need, said Balin, I am not afeard to tell you, and told him all the cause how it was. Ah, said the knight, is this all? here I ensure you by the faith of my body never to depart from you while my life lasteth. And so they went to the hostelry and armed them, and so rode forth with Balin. And as they came by an hermitage even by a churchyard, there came the knight Garlon invisible, and smote this knight, Perin de Mountbeliard, through the body with a spear. Alas, said the knight, I am slain by this traitor knight that rideth invisible. Alas, said Balin, it is not the first despite he hath done me; and there the hermit and Balin buried the knight under a rich stone and a tomb royal. And on the morn they found letters of gold written, how Sir Gawaine shall revenge his father's death, King Lot, on the King Pellinore. Anon after this Balin and the damosel rode till they came to a castle, and there Balin alighted, and he and the damosel went to go into the castle, and anon as Balin came within the castle's gate the portcullis fell down at his back, and there fell many men about the damosel, and would have slain her. When Balin saw that, he was sore aggrieved, for he might not help the damosel. Then he went up into the tower, and leapt over walls into the ditch, and hurt him not; and anon he pulled out his sword and would have foughten with them. And they all said nay, they would not fight with him, for they did nothing but the old custom of the castle; and told him how their lady was sick, and had lain many years, and she might not be whole but if she had a dish of silver full of blood of a clean maid and a king's daughter; and therefore the custom of this castle is, there shall no damosel pass this way but she shall bleed of her blood in a silver dish full. Well, said Balin, she shall bleed as much as she may bleed, but I will not lose the life of her whiles my life lasteth. And so Balin made her to bleed by her good will, but her blood helped not the lady. And so he and she rested there all night, and had there right good cheer, and on the morn they passed on their ways. And as it telleth after in the Sangreal, that Sir Percivale's sister helped that lady with her blood, whereof she was dead.

Chapter XIV

How Balin met with that knight named Garlon at a feast, and there he slew him, to have his blood to heal therewith the son of his host.

Then they rode three or four days and never met with adventure, and by hap they were lodged with a gentle man that was a rich man and well at ease. And as they sat at their supper Balin overheard one complain grievously by him in a chair. What is this noise? said Balin. Forsooth, said his host, I will tell you. I was but late at a jousting, and there I jousted with a knight that is brother unto King Pellam, and twice smote I him down, and then he promised to quit me on my best friend; and so he wounded my son, that cannot be whole till I have of that knight's blood, and he rideth alway invisible; but I know not his name. Ah! said Balin, I know that knight, his name is Garlon, he hath slain two knights of mine in the same manner, therefore I had liefer meet with that knight than all the gold in this realm, for the despite he hath done me. Well, said his host, I shall tell you, King Pellam of Listeneise hath made do cry in all this country a great feast that shall be within these twenty days, and no knight may come there but if he bring his wife with him, or his paramour; and that knight, your enemy and mine, ye shall see that day. Then I behote you, said Balin, part of his blood to heal your son withal. We will be forward to-morn, said his host. So on the morn they rode all three toward Pellam, and they had fifteen days' journey or they came thither; and that same day began the great feast. And so they alighted and stabled their horses, and went into the castle; but Balin's host might not be let in because he had no lady. Then Balin was well received and brought unto a chamber and unarmed him; and there were brought him robes to his pleasure, and would have had Balin leave his sword behind him. Nay, said Balin, that do I not, for it is the custom of my country a knight always to keep his weapon with him, and that custom will I keep, or else I will depart as I came. Then they gave him leave to wear his sword, and so he went unto the castle, and was set among knights of worship, and his lady afore him.

Soon Balin asked a knight, Is there not a knight in this court whose name is Garlon? Yonder he goeth, said a knight, he with the black face; he is the marvellest knight that is now living, for he destroyeth many good knights, for he goeth invisible. Ah well, said Balin, is that he? Then Balin advised him long: If I slay him here I shall not escape, and if I leave him now, peradventure I shall never meet with him again at such a steven, and much harm he will do an he live. Therewith this Garlon espied that this Balin beheld him, and then he came and smote Balin on the face with the back of his hand, and said, Knight, why beholdest me so? for shame therefore, eat thy meat and do that thou came for. Thou sayest sooth, said Balin, this is not the first despite that thou hast done me, and therefore I will do what I came for, and rose up fiercely and clave his head to the shoulders. Give me the truncheon, said Balin to his lady, wherewith he slew your knight. Anon she gave it him, for alway she bare the truncheon with her. And therewith Balin smote him through the body, and said openly, With that truncheon thou hast slain a good knight, and now it sticketh in thy body. And then Balin called unto him his host, saying, Now may ye fetch blood enough to heal your son withal.

Chapter XV

How Balin fought with King Pellam, and how his sword brake, and how he gat a spear wherewith he smote the dolorous stroke.

Anon all the knights arose from the table for to set on Balin, and King Pellam himself arose up fiercely, and said, Knight, hast thou slain my brother? thou shalt die therefore or thou depart. Well, said Balin, do it yourself. Yes, said King Pellam, there shall no man have ado with thee but myself, for the love of my brother. Then King Pellam caught in his hand a grim weapon and smote eagerly at Balin; but Balin put the sword betwixt his head and the stroke, and therewith his sword burst in sunder. And when Balin was weaponless he ran into a chamber for to seek some weapon, and so from chamber to chamber, and no weapon he could find, and always King Pellam after him. And at the last he entered into a chamber that was marvellously well dight and richly, and a bed arrayed with cloth of gold, the richest that might be thought, and one lying therein, and thereby stood a table of clean gold with four pillars of silver that bare up the table, and upon the table stood a marvellous spear strangely wrought. And when Balin saw that spear, he gat it in his hand and turned him to King Pellam, and smote him passingly sore with that spear, that King Pellam fell down in a swoon, and therewith the castle roof and walls brake and fell to the earth, and Balin fell down so that he might not stir foot nor hand. And so the most part of the castle, that was fallen down through that dolorous stroke, lay upon Pellam and Balin three days.

Book XVII

Chapter XVIII

How Galahad came to King Mordrains, and of other matters and adventures.

Now, saith the story, Galahad rode many journeys in vain. And at the last he came to the abbey where King Mordrains was, and when he heard that, he thought he would abide to see him. And upon the morn, when he had heard mass, Galahad came unto King Mordrains, and anon the king saw him, which had lain blind of long time. And then he dressed him against him, and said: Galahad, the servant of Jesu Christ, whose coming I have abiden so long, now embrace me and let me rest on thy breast, so that I may rest between thine arms, for thou art a clean virgin above all knights, as the flower of the lily in whom virginity is signified, and thou art the rose the which is the flower of all good virtues, and in colour of fire. For the fire of the Holy Ghost is taken so in thee that my flesh which was all dead of oldness is become young again. Then Galahad heard his words, then he embraced him and all his body. Then said he: Fair Lord Jesu Christ, now I have my will. Now I require thee, in this point that I am in, thou come and visit me. And anon Our Lord heard his prayer: therewith the soul departed from the body.

And then Galahad put him in the earth as a king ought to be, and so departed and so came into a perilous forest where he found the well the which boileth with great waves, as the tale telleth to-fore. And as soon as Galahad set his hand thereto it ceased, so that it brent no more, and the heat departed. For that it brent it was a sign of lechery, the which was that time much used. But that heat might not abide his pure virginity. And this was taken in the country for a miracle. And so ever after was it called Galahad's well.

Then by adventure he came into the country of Gore, and into the abbey where Launcelot had been to-forehand, and found the tomb of King Bagdemagus, but he was founder thereof, Joseph of Aramathie's son; and the tomb of Simeon where Launcelot had failed. Then he looked into a croft under the minster, and there he saw a tomb which brent full marvellously. Then asked he the brethren what it was. Sir, said they, a marvellous adventure that may not be brought unto none end but by him that passeth of bounty and of knighthood all them of the Round Table. I would, said Galahad, that ye would lead me thereto. Gladly, said they, and so led him till a cave. And he went down upon greses, and came nigh the tomb. And then the flaming failed, and the fire staunched, the which many a day had been great. Then came there a voice that said: Much are ye beholden to thank Our Lord, the which hath given you a good hour, that ye may draw out the souls of earthly pain, and to put them into the joys of paradise. I am of your kindred, the which hath dwelled in this heat this three hundred winter and four-and-fifty to be purged of the sin that I did against Joseph of Aramathie. Then Galahad took the body in his arms and bare it into the minster. And that night lay Galahad in the abbey; and on the morn he gave him service, and put him in the earth afore the high altar.

Chapter XIX

How Sir Percivale and Sir Bors met with Sir Galahad, and how they came to the Castle of Carbonek, and other matters.

So departed he from thence, and commended the brethren to God; and so he rode five days till that he came to the Maimed King. And ever followed Percivale the five days, asking where he had been; and so one told him how the adventures of Logris were enchieved. So on a day it befell that they came out of a great forest, and there they met at traverse with Sir Bors, the which rode alone. It is none need to tell if they were glad; and them he saluted, and they yielded him honour and good adventure, and everych told other. Then said Bors: It is mo than a year and an half that I ne lay ten times where men dwelled, but in wild forests and in mountains, but God was ever my comfort.

Then rode they a great while till that they came to the castle of Carbonek. And when they were entered within the castle King Pelles knew them; then there was great joy, for they wist well by their coming that they had fulfilled the quest of the Sangreal. Then Eliazar, King Pelles' son, brought to-fore them the broken sword wherewith Joseph was stricken through the thigh. Then Bors set his hand thereto, if that he might have soldered it again; but it would not be. Then he took it to Percivale, but he had no more power thereto than he. Now have ye it again, said Percivale to Galahad, for an it be ever enchieved by any bodily man ye must do it. And then he took the pieces and set them together, and they seemed that they had never been broken, and as well as it had been first forged. And when they within espied that the adventure of the sword was enchieved, then they gave the sword to Bors, for it might not be better set; for he was a good knight and a worthy man.

And a little afore even the sword arose great and marvellous, and was full of great heat that many men fell for dread. And anon alighted a voice among them, and said: They that ought not to sit at the table of Jesu Christ arise, for now shall very knights be fed. So they went thence, all save King Pelles and Eliazar, his son, the which were holy men, and a maid which was his niece; and so these three fellows and they three were there, no mo. Anon they saw knights all armed came in at the hall door, and did off their helms and their arms, and said unto Galahad: Sir, we have hied right much for to be with you at this table where the holy meat shall be departed. Then said he: Ye be welcome, but of whence be ye? So three of them said they were of Gaul, and other three said they were of Ireland, and the other three said they were of Denmark. So as they sat thus there came out a bed of tree, of a chamber, the which four gentlewomen brought; and in the bed lay a good man sick, and a crown of gold upon his head; and there in the midst of the place they set him down, and went again their way. Then he lift up his head, and said: Galahad, Knight, ye be welcome, for much have I desired your coming, for in such pain and in such anguish I have been long. But now I trust to God the term is come that my pain shall be allayed, that I shall pass out of this world so as it was promised me long ago. Therewith a voice said: There be two among you that be not in the quest of the Sangreal, and therefore depart ye.

Chapter XX

How Galahad and his fellows were fed of the Holy Sangreal, and how Our Lord appeared to them, and other things.

Then King Pelles and his son departed. And therewithal beseemed them that there came a man, and four angels from heaven, clothed in likeness of a bishop, and had a cross in his hand; and these four angels bare him up in a chair, and set him down before the table of silver whereupon the Sangreal was; and it seemed that he had in midst of his forehead letters the which said: See ye here Joseph, the first bishop of Christendom, the same which Our Lord succoured in the city of Sarras in the spiritual place. Then the knights marvelled, for that bishop was dead more than three hundred year to-fore. O knights, said he, marvel not, for I was sometime an earthly man. With that they heard the chamber door open, and there they saw angels; and two bare candles of wax, and the third a towel, and the fourth a spear which bled marvellously, that three drops fell within a box which he held with his other hand. And they set the candles upon the table, and the third the towel upon the vessel, and the fourth the holy spear even upright upon the vessel. And then the bishop made semblaunt as though he would have gone to the sacring of the mass. And then he took an ubblie which was made in likeness of bread. And at the lifting up there came a figure in likeness of a child, and the visage was as red and as bright as any fire, and smote himself into the bread, so that they all saw it that the bread was formed of a fleshly man; and then he put it into the Holy Vessel again, and then he did that longed to a priest to do to a mass. And then he went to Galahad and kissed him, and bade him go and kiss his fellows: and so he did anon. Now, said he, servants of Jesu Christ, ye shall be fed afore this table with sweet meats that never knights tasted. And when he had said, he vanished away. And they set them at the table in great dread, and made their prayers.

Then looked they and saw a man come out of the Holy Vessel, that had all the signs of the passion of Jesu Christ, bleeding all openly, and said: My knights, and my servants, and my true children, which be come out of deadly life into spiritual life, I will now no longer hide me from you, but ye shall see now a part of my secrets and of my hidden things: now hold and receive the high meat which ye have so much desired. Then took he himself the Holy Vessel and came to Galahad; and he kneeled down, and there he received his Saviour, and after him so received all his fellows; and they thought it so sweet that it was marvellous to tell. Then said he to Galahad: Son, wottest thou what I hold betwixt my hands? Nay, said he, but if ye will tell me. This is, said he, the holy dish wherein I ate the lamb on Sheer-Thursday. And now hast thou seen that thou most desired to see, but yet hast thou not seen it so openly as thou shalt see it in the city of Sarras in the spiritual place. Therefore thou must go hence and bear with thee this Holy Vessel; for this night it shall depart from the realm of Logris, that it shall never be seen more here. And wottest thou wherefore? For he is not served nor worshipped to his right by them of this land, for they be turned to evil living; therefore I shall disherit them of the honour which I have done them. And therefore go ye three tomorrow unto the sea, where ye shall find your ship ready, and with you take the sword with the strange girdles, and no more with you but Sir Percivale and Sir Bors. Also I will that ye take with you of the blood of this spear for to anoint the Maimed King, both his legs and all his body, and he shall have his health. Sir, said Galahad, why shall not these other fellows go with us? For this cause: for right as I departed my apostles one here and another there, so I will that ye depart; and two of you shall die in my service, but one of you shall come again and tell tidings. Then gave he them his blessing and vanished away.

Chapter XXI

How Galahad anointed with the blood of the spear the Maimed King, and of other adventures.

And Galahad went anon to the spear which lay upon the table, and touched the blood with his fingers, and came after to the Maimed King and anointed his legs. And therewith he clothed him anon, and start upon his feet out of his bed as an whole man, and thanked Our Lord that He had healed him. And that was not to the worldward, for anon he yielded him to a place of religion of white monks, and was a full holy man. That same night about midnight came a voice among them which said: My sons and not my chief sons, my friends and not my warriors, go ye hence where ye hope best to do and as I bade you. Ah, thanked be Thou, Lord, that Thou wilt vouchsafe to call us, Thy sinners. Now may we well prove that we have not lost our pains. And anon in all haste they took their harness and departed. But the three knights of Gaul, one of them hight Claudine, King Claudas' son, and the other two were great gentlemen. Then prayed Galahad to everych of them, that if they come to King Arthur's court that they should salute my lord, Sir Launcelot, my father, and all the fellowship of the Round Table; and prayed them if that they came on that part that they should not forget it.

Right so departed Galahad, Percivale and Bors with him; and so they rode three days, and then they came to a rivage, and found the ship whereof the tale speaketh of to-fore. And when they came to the board they found in the midst the table of silver which they had left with the Maimed King, and the Sangreal which was covered with red samite. Then were they glad to have such things in their fellowship; and so they entered and made great reverence thereto; and Galahad fell in his prayer long time to Our Lord, that at what time he asked, that he should pass out of this world. So much he prayed till a voice said to him: Galahad, thou shalt have thy request; and when thou askest the death of thy body thou shalt have it, and then shalt thou find the life of the soul. Percivale heard this, and prayed him, of fellowship that was between them, to tell him wherefore he asked such things. That shall I tell you, said Galahad; the other day when we saw a part of the adventures of the Sangreal I was in such a joy of heart, that I trow never man was that was earthly. And therefore I wot well, when my body is dead my soul shall be in great joy to see the blessed Trinity every day, and the majesty of Our Lord, Jesu Christ.

So long were they in the ship that they said to Galahad: Sir, in this bed ought ye to lie, for so saith the scripture. And so he laid him down and slept a great while; and when he awaked he looked afore him and saw the city of Sarras. And as they would have landed they saw the ship wherein Percivale had put his sister in. Truly, said Percivale, in the name of God, well hath my sister holden us covenant. Then took they out of the ship the table of silver, and he took it to Percivale and to Bors, to go to-fore, and Galahad came behind. And right so they went to the city, and at the gate of the city they saw an old man crooked. Then Galahad called him and bade him help to bear this heavy thing. Truly, said the old man, it is ten year ago that I might not go but with crutches. Care thou not, said Galahad, and arise up and shew thy good will. And so he assayed, and found himself as whole as ever he was. Than ran he to the table, and took one part against Galahad. And anon arose there great noise in the city, that a cripple was made whole by knights marvellous that entered into the city.

Then anon after, the three knights went to the water, and brought up into the palace Percivale's sister, and buried her as richly as a king's daughter ought to be. And when the king of the city, which was cleped Estorause, saw the fellowship, he asked them of whence they were, and what thing it was that they had brought upon the table of silver. And they told him the truth of the Sangreal, and the power which that God had sent there. Then the king was a tyrant, and was come of the line of paynims, and took them and put them in prison in a deep hole.

Chapter XXII

How they were fed with the Sangreal while they were in prison, and how Galahad was made king.

But as soon as they were there Our Lord sent them the Sangreal, through whose grace they were always fulfilled while that they were in prison. So at the year's end it befell that this King Estorause lay sick, and felt that he should die. Then he sent for the three knights, and they came afore him; and he cried them mercy of that he had done to them, and they forgave it him goodly; and he died anon. When the king was dead all the city was dismayed, and wist not who might be their king. Right so as they were in counsel there came a voice among them, and bade them choose the youngest knight of them three to be their king: For he shall well maintain you and all yours. So they made Galahad king by all the assent of the holy city, and else they would have slain him. And when he was come to behold the land, he let make above the table of silver a chest of gold and of precious stones, that filled the Holy Vessel. And every day early the three fellows would come afore it, and make their prayers.

Now at the year's end, and the self day after Galahad had borne the crown of gold, he arose up early and his fellows, and came to the palace, and saw to-fore them the Holy Vessel, and a man kneeling on his knees in likeness of a bishop, that had about him a great fellowship of angels, as it had been Jesu Christ himself; and then he arose and began a mass of Our Lady. And when he came to the sacrament of the mass, and had done, anon he called Galahad, and said to him: Come forth the servant of Jesu Christ, and thou shalt see that thou hast much desired to see. And then he began to tremble right hard when the deadly flesh began to behold the spiritual things. Then he held up his hands toward heaven and said: Lord, I thank thee, for now I see that that hath been my desire many a day. Now, blessed Lord, would I not longer live, if it might please thee, Lord. And therewith the good man took Our Lord's body betwixt his hands, and proffered it to Galahad, and he received it right gladly and meekly. Now wottest thou what I am? said the good man. Nay, said Galahad. I am Joseph of Aramathie, the which Our Lord hath sent here to thee to bear thee fellowship; and wottest thou wherefore that he hath sent me more than any other? For thou hast resembled me in two things; in that thou hast seen the marvels of the Sangreal, in that thou hast been a clean maiden, as I have been and am.

And when he had said these words Galahad went to Percivale and kissed him, and commended him to God; and so he went to Sir Bors and kissed him, and commended him to God, and said: Fair lord, salute me to my lord, Sir Launcelot, my father, and as soon as ye see him, bid him remember of this unstable world. And therewith he kneeled down to-fore the table and made his prayers, and then suddenly his soul departed to Jesu Christ, and a great multitude of angels bare his soul up to heaven, that the two fellows might well behold it. Also the two fellows saw come from heaven an hand, but they saw not the body. And then it came right to the Vessel, and took it and the spear, and so bare it up to heaven. Sithen was there never man so hardy to say that he had seen the Sangreal.

CHAPTER 16

The Legend of the Grail

M. Gaster

In the history of medieval romances there is none so complicated as that of the romance of the Holy Grail. Many a scholar
has tried to solve the problem of its origin, and yet a final
solution is still wanting.

No one who has ever trodden the enchanted land on which
the castle which contained the Holy Grail stood could entirely
escape the charm that overhangs it. Just as difficult as was the
ancient quest in romance, is the modern quest after the origin
and sources of this remarkable and weird tale.

This romance now exists in various forms, more or less akin
to one another. These have been subdivided into groups,
according to the affinity in which the incidents narrated therein
stand to one another, and also in how far one tale is developed
more than the other: a work which has been successfully carried
out by Mr Nutt, who, in his admirable Studies on the Grail, has
endeavoured to disentangle the skein of this complicated
problem, and to make some order in the mass of versions, texts,
and alterations in which this legend has been preserved. Mr
Nutt rightly distinguishes between an *Early history* of the Grail
and *the Quest;* the former containing the origin and source of the
Grail, and the Quest, on the other hand, consisting of the description of the adventures the expected hero had to undergo
until he finally reached his goal. Stripped of all the embellish-
ments which made out of these simple facts the most renowned
of medieval romances, the numerous versions of it are practically one. The differences begin with the detailed accounts given
in the Early history, and still more with the peculiarities of the

Grail, of the hero and his achievements. The framework is the same, but the contents vary almost in every version.

At the head of the whole literature stands Chrestien de Troyes, the famous minstrel, who, as far as our present knowledge goes, was the first to sing the praise of the Grail, and of the hero in search of it. Next in point of time, and, as I may at once add, first in importance, is the German follower of Chrestien, Wolfram von Eschenbach. In spite of the likeness, there is also a very great diversity in the treatment of the Grail by both these writers. Besides, Wolfram claims an independent source for his poetical composition, ridiculing Chrestien for not following the original closely.

Everything tends to make us believe that there must have existed a common primary source whence both Chrestien and Wolfram drew their tale. Of what kind was this primary source, and how much did it contain? Were both those parts which we find afterwards united, or was only one of them contained in the original? Did Chrestien and Wolfram know the Early history of the Grail or not? I entirely agree with Mr Nutt that they, or even the original they followed, did not know much of it, the origin and properties of the Grail being only vaguely indicated. It is chiefly *the Quest* which plays the most important part in their poems. Whence did they take it from? It is round this question that a literary battle has now been fought for over fifty years. I do not flatter myself that I shall be able to bring the battle to an end, but I intend attacking this question from a different point of view altogether.

It is a futile attempt to reduce every incident of these poems to one and the same source. Every work of art, every poetical production is, to some extent, a kind of mosaic, a kind of blending in one of a mass of different, sometimes widely divergent, elements. Composite as our modern knowledge is, so must also have been that of the ancient or medieval author who drew the elements of the romance, not from one source alone, but from many, sometimes quite different ones.

Two main sources of inspiration have been suggested by the various writers on this subject. To some, the legend in its *entirety* owes its origin to Christian lore; others have divided the matter, assigning the Early history to the Christian source, whilst the other — Quest — would be of *Celtic* (Welsh) origin. It is remarkable, however, that both sections have totally ignored another main source of medieval poetry and of modern civilization; I mean the old classical literature of Greece and Rome. But before proceeding further, I must first make clear my standpoint.

The Celtic origin does not rest upon documentary proof, upon older texts and MSS than Chrestien's poem, but on parallels to be found in Celtic folk-lore, and some later versions. I still hold to the theory that these versions are, in fact, only variations of Chrestien's poem of later origin, and that, through the instrumentality of such versions and adaptations, these romances entered into the possession of the people, and became its unwritten lore, the modern folk lore.

Far, therefore, from being the primitive source for Chrestien or his predecessor, modern tales are merely the reflex of that written literature, and are by no means anterior to it. Parallels adduced from modern tales do not therefore prove that these tales were the direct sources whence Chrestien drew the elements of his poem, but, as I contend, they are the outcome of that literature.

We must look for older parallels than the time of Chrestien, older than the second half of the twelfth century. We must study first the surroundings in which Chrestien grew up, what amount of knowledge was accessible to him, what great events stirred the nations of Europe, and what kind of literary currents swayed the people at that time. It is only by answering such questions that we can come to a more positive result, and then draw our inference also for Wolfram, and for the host of Chrestien's continuators. These also must have had access to some store of similar learning, to be able to tread in his footsteps, and to take up the thread where his dying hand let it fall. A few lays cannot, and could not, suffice for the explanation of the great mass of incidents embodied in these romances.

It must also first be proved how such Celtic tales, if they existed at all, could come to the knowledge of a French poet, living as he did in France, of whose sojourn in England not a trace has been found. One has only to compare the widely different parallels adduced from Celtic lore, to be convinced that Chrestien, or the author of the original which he adopted, must have had a herculean task to perform, to alter and change, to blend and to assimilate, an immense mass of tales, mythical and heroical and mould them together into one tale, which, after all, does not appear in a coherent form in any of its modern parallels. For it must be borne in mind that such a Celtic tale, containing most of the striking incidents, and older than the time of Chrestien, has not yet been discovered. What we have instead is a number of lays, or other tales, where either the one or the other incident is said to occur, the similarity not being absolutely identical, and in very many cases only the result of skilful interpretation.

If one should follow the same line of argumentation, one could easily adduce parallels to those Celtic lays and tales from various quarters of the globe, which would thus destroy the claim of the Celtic origin. The moment the same incident could be proved to exist elsewhere we might just as well consider it to have originated there also, and not be limited to Celtic lore alone. We would have then one source more for the supposed origin of the legend: the folk-lore of Europe.

The natural way, however, is to look for *one* central tale, containing a sufficient number of incidents complete in itself; and round that tale, other minor incidents drawn from various quarters, could have been added *afterwards* by the continuator and amplifier of the tale.

But that primary one must already contain the most important incidents, and at the same time this primitive tale must contain that of the *Grail* as one of its incidents, but only in a vague, indefinite form, so as to afford the possibility for the double interpretation of the Grail as presented on one side by Chrestien, and on the other by Wolfram.

The problem, therefore, is to find a tale containing some of the principal elements of the Quest, the Grail or something akin to it being an important one; this Grail, or whatever would be standing for it, must be conceived in a vague, indefinite form, so as to be able to be filled with any kind of interpretation — religious, material, metaphysical, according to the poetical bent and the intentions of the poets. It is, further, an absolute necessity that such a tale should be of an older date than the time of Chrestien, and also it will have to be shown that it was, or could have been, accessible to him.

Before I proceed further, let us first examine the state of things as they existed in Europe at the end of the twelfth century, the psychological condition, in the midst of which Chrestien lived, and moved, and wrote.

It is in the twelfth century that the great French epical poetry flourished. Through patient investigation it has been proved that the history of the old Merovingian period was changed by the *trouveur* in some of these epopees into the history of Charlemagne. A battle at Roncesvalles became the theme of one of the most celebrated old French romances, the chanson de Roland, and this was soon followed by a stately line of Chansons de Geste. Once started on the line of changing old history into modern, poets took a bolder course, and changed heroes of antiquity into national ones. Very well known is the tendency of the age to connect their own national history with that of the Greeks and Romans. The *Roman de Brut* of Wace, the old chronicles of Geoffrey and others, are examples of this tendency. Homer, i.e., Dictys and Dares, Virgil, and other writers of classical antiquity, furnished the materials for the writers of the middle ages, who drew upon them largely, only altering them, so that from Greek and Latin they became French and English.

The crusades had furnished further new themes for the fancy of the *trouveur* of the time. The whole world was stirred to its innermost depth by that general upheaving; the exploits of the first and second crusade had already begun to belong to the history of the past, when Chrestien began his poem. How many oriental legends were brought home and circulated by various pilgrims, especially such as were in Jerusalem, now once again in the hands of the infidels? The highest aim of the Christian world of that epoch was to regain possession of those sacred places; and the Order of the Templars represented the most ideal aspirations of the time — to live a chaste life, and to be found worthy to keep watch over the Lord's sanctuary.

Rumours of a great Christian kingdom in the far East, the kingdom of Prester John, reached Europe at the time and like lightning these tidings spread from country to country, reviving the hopes of the crusaders by announcing help from an unexpected quarter in the deadly fight against the Mahommedan power.

At the same time a great dogmatic change was taking place in the teachings of the Church. The theory of Paschasius Radbertus found many adversaries, but no less adherents, and the twelfth century is the time when that dispute reached its climax, and the dogma of *Transubstantiation* was finally settled. The mystery of the sacrament, and the more than symbolic meaning of the Eucharist, was the central point of this dogma which has profoundly altered the Catholic Church, and was in later times one of the principal elements of discord between the Reformed church and the Church of Rome.

In naming these factors, classical literature, so to say modernized in an epical form, the French Chansons de Geste, the Crusades and the legends of Palestine, and, finally, the question of transubstantiation and the pseudo-epigraphic literature of the mystery of the sacrament, I have pointed out the chief sources to which the romance of the Holy Grail owes its origin, without any further admixture of Celtic tales or lays, or Celtic mythology. The life that is described in the romances is that of the authors' time. Knightly deeds, adventures, miracles, and spells all belong to the machinery of the romantic literature of the time, and though important for determining the exact character of the surroundings, vary, as is natural, in every version, and if more MSS had been preserved the number of variations might have increased.

I shall now proceed to prove my case as far as possible in the order indicated.

Classical Influence. Working the romance backwards to its primitive form, we shall find that the main feature of the Quest may be summarized as follows:

A young man starts on an unheard of adventure, which no human being has ever achieved before him. It is by mere chance that he alights at the very spot where he had determined to go, although nothing definite is said as to the nature of that adventure. What he has to do, or to see, or to accomplish, is by no means clear. He himself does not know what to do, and fails thus in his first attempt.

According to Chrestien,[1] he comes to a river, upon which there is a boat, wherein are two men fishing. One of them, in reply to his questions, directs him for a night's shelter to his own castle hard by. Perceval starts for it, and at first, unable to find it, reproaches the fisher. Suddenly he perceives the castle before him, enters therein, is disarmed, clad in a scarlet mantle, and led into a great hall. Therein is a couch, upon which lies an old man; near him is a fire, around which some four hundred men are sitting. Perceval tells his host that he has come from Beau-Repaire. A squire enters, bearing a sword, and on it is written that it will never break, save in one peril, and that known only to the maker of it. 'Tis a present from the host's niece, to be bestowed where it will be well employed. The host gives it to Perceval, "to whom it was adjudged and destined." Hereupon enters another squire, bearing in his hand a lance, from the head of which a drop of blood runs down on the squire's hand. Perceval would have asked concerning this wonder, but he minds him of Goneman's counsel not to speak or inquire too much. Two more squires enter, holding each a ten-branched candlestick, and with them a damsel, a "Graal" in her hands. The Graal shines so that it puts out the light of the candles, as the sun does that of the stars. Thereafter follows a damsel holding a (silver) plate. All defile past between the fire and the couch, but Perceval does not venture to ask wherefore the Grail is used. Supper follows, and the Grail is again brought, and Perceval knowing not its use, had fain asked, but always refrains when he thinks of Gonemans, and finally puts off his questions till the morrow. After supper the guest is led to his chamber, and on the morrow, awakening, finds the castle deserted. Issuing forth, he finds his horse saddled, and the drawbridge down. Thinking to find the castle dwellers in the forest, he rides forth, but the drawbridge closes so suddenly behind him, that had not the horse leapt quickly forward, it had gone hard with steed and rider. In vain Perceval calls: none answer.

More elaborate is the version of Heinrich von dem Türlin.[2] "After monthlong wanderings, he meets with Lancelot and Calocreant, and all three come to the Grail castle. They are led into a hall, which passes in splendour aught earthly eye ever saw. The floor is strewn with roses; on a bed lies an old man in gold-embroidered garments, and watches two youths playing at chess. Towards night the hall fills with knights and dames; a youth enters, bearing a sword, which he lays before the old man ... Then enter two damsels, bearing lights, followed by two knights, with a spear, and two more damsels, with a toblier of gold and jewels. After them comes the fairest woman ever God created, and with her a maiden weeping. The spear is laid on the table, by it the 'toblier,' wherein are three drops of blood. In the box borne by the fair lady is a piece of bread, one-third part of which she breaks off and gives to the old man. Gawain, recognizing in her Gansguoter's sister, stays no longer, but asks what these wonders mean. Straightway knights and dames, all with mighty shout, leap from table, and great joy arises. The old man says what he has seen is the Grail; none saw it before save Parzival, and he asked not. By his question Gawain has delivered from long waiting and suffering both those which are dead and those which live. The old man himself and his companions are really dead, though they seem it not, but the lady and her damsels are living; for their unstained womanhood God has granted them to have the Grail, and therewith yearly to feed the old man."

So in all the versions it is a magnificent castle, wherein the one constantly-recurring figure is that of an old, sick or dead man, surrounded by jewels, plates or dishes of gold, and a mysterious thing, a cup with blood, or a box with bread, and a bloody lance. Only in Wolfram is it a mysterious rock or a jewel upon which a dove lays once a year a holy wafer. The hero asks, or omits to ask, and upon that action the whole tale turns. It is not, however, clear from the beginning what kind of task the hero has to achieve, nor is it more clear afterwards when he has achieved it. This portion seems not to be in the original, as not one version can clearly account for it. The original tale must have been also quite obscure on this point, thus affording free scope to the poet to interpret and to use it according to his own fancy. The less definite the task was the easier it was for the subsequent author to introduce into it what was nearest to him, and to give to it either a material or a spiritual meaning; the whole history of the legend points to such a kind of development as that which it really did undergo.

But whence comes that fundamental motive, an adventurous knight endowed with superior gifts, striving after an undertaking quite unique, never attempted before and never afterwards?

A glance over the literary activity in France at the time will give us the answer.

It was in the middle of the twelfth century that the Trojan war had been made the theme of an elaborate epos of thirty thousand verses by Benoît de St More, who, basing his work upon that of Dares Phrygius, Paulus Orosius, Ovid, etc., wrote his *Roman de Troie*. At about the same time the fabulous history of *Alexander the Great* was changed into a national epos by Alberic de Besançon, Alexander de Bernay (*c.* 1150), and very much amplified by Lambert li Tort (*c.* 1190–1200), the contemporary of Chrestien. One has only to see how they dealt with their originals, how they transferred the whole scenery from hoary antiquity to their own time, and to their own courts, to understand the liberty a poet of those times could take with his originals.

Seeing the manner in which the old kings and heroes were changed into knights and squires, the old gods into magicians and fairies, I do not think that I shall be considered very bold if I say that the legend of the Quest is nothing else but also a transformation of the most interesting episodes of that very legend of Alexander; the hero of the Grail romance is none else but Alexander, the Quest the counterpart of his attempt to force the Gates of Paradise, and the wonderful castle or temple, the one that Alexander saw in his marvellous expedition.

There is not one old version in which that journey — the *Iter ad Paradisum* — is not contained either in an amply developed form, or in an abridged one; but all contain the description of that marvellous castle. As we shall see presently, not only is it contained in the Greek text known under the name of Callisthenes (book iii, Ch. 28), but also in the Latin version of Julius Valerius, and in that of the Archipresbyter Leo. The oldest French versions and the German of Lamprecht, which is based upon these French poems, contain it also. Thus, there is no difficulty from a historical and literary point of view; this legend was earlier than Chrestien, this legend was then not only accessible, but surely *well known to Chrestien*.

Starting from the oldest version, I will give here an accurate translation of the "Pseudo-Callisthenes'" version:

"We sailed away from that river, and came to a large island, 150 furlongs distant from the mainland, and there we found the city of the sun. This city had twelve towers, built of gold and emerald. The walls, the circumference of which was about 150 furlongs, were made of Indian stones. In the middle of the town there was an altar built, like the towers, of gold and emerald. Seven steps led up to the altar, at the top there stood a chariot with horses and driver, made likewise of gold and emerald. But all these things were partly invisible on account of the fog. The priest of the sun, Aeteops, was clothed in real Cyssus. He spoke to us in a savage tongue and ordered us to leave that city. After we had left we wandered about for seven days. Everywhere was darkness; not even fire lit up those parts. So we turned back and came to the fields of Nysa, and there we saw a high mountain. We climbed to the top, and there beautiful houses, full of gold and silver, met our view; and these were enclosed by a wall of sapphire, with 150 steps cut into it, and upon the top stood a round temple, with seven pillars of sapphire and a hundred steps. Inside and outside were images of demi-gods, bacchantes, satyrs, and of others, initiated in the sacred mysteries, but old Maron sat on a beast of burden. A couch was placed in the middle of the temple; on this couch lay a man clothed in silk. I could not see his face, for it was veiled; but I saw strength and greatness. In the middle of the temple there was a golden chain weighing a hundred pounds, and suspended from it was a transparent wreath; a precious stone which illumined the whole temple, took the place of fire. From the ceiling hung also a gold cage, in which was a bird about the size of a dove. This bird called out to me in the voice resembling man's, the following, in Greek: 'Alexander, cease now to oppose (the) god; return to your home, and hasten not through thoughtlessness (reckless-ness) your transit to the celestial regions.' And as I was about to take down the bird and the lamp, which I intended to send to you, it seemed to me as if he who was resting on the couch moved. Then my friends said to me, 'Forbear, for it is holy.' And as I was going out into the grounds of the temple, I saw two amphoras of gold which were capable of holding sixty metretes; we measured them at table. I commanded the soldiers to en-camp there, and to enjoy themselves.

"A house also stood there, and it contained many beautiful and valuable goblets of precious stones. But just as we and the army were on the point of sitting down to the repast, there was heard suddenly a heavy thunder of flutes and cymbals, and pipes and trumpets, and kettledrums and zitters; and the whole mountain was covered with smoke, as if a heavy storm had broken down on us. Seized with fear, we hastened away, and wandered on until we came to the castle of Cyrus; and we came across many deserted towns, and one beautiful city, in which there was a house, in which the king himself received. I was told that there was a bird that spoke with human voice. I went into the house, and saw many wonderful sights, for the whole house was of gold. From the middle of the ceiling hung suspended a golden cage, like the one which I have mentioned before. In it was a bird like a dove, of gold colour; it was told to me that this bird prophesied to the king through its different tones, and that it was holy. I also saw an amphora capable of holding sixty metretes. The goldwork was marvellous, for all round it were figures, and above these a sea-battle, and in the middle was an inscription; everything was made and finished with gold. This amphora was said to be Egyptian, having been brought from the city of Memphis at the time when the Persians conquered Egypt. There was a house there, built in Greek style, in which the king had held his receptions, and in which there was a picture of the sea-fight of Xerxes. In this house there stood also a golden throne, inlaid with precious stones; and there was also a sweet-sounding zitter, whose strings moved of their own accord. Around it there stood a golden sideboard sixteen ells wide, and next to it another twenty ells wide; six steps led the way to it, and on the top of these stood an eagle with his wings spread out over the whole sideboard. There was also of gold a wild vine, with seven branches all worked in gold." So far Pseudo-Callisthenes. The text of Valerius has some variations, which I think essential, and I therefore mention them here. In fact, we have here two accounts, one of the temple of the sun, and the other of the palace of Cyrus and Xerxes. Being very much like one another, these two have been blended into one tale, some of the first description being left out by ignorant copyists, who took the former to be a mere narration of the latter (*Zacher,* pp. 170, 171).

The text of Valerius has now the following very remarkable detail in the description as he says of the palace, whilst, in fact, the *temple* is meant, as will be seen from the very wording, which runs as follows:

"In the temple hung from the ceiling a tropheum aureum (*Cod. Mediolan.:* stropaeum aureum), from that 'trophaeum' hung a ball in the form of 'vertiginis coelitis' (the heavenly). Upon that ball sat the image of a dove, which prophesied to the king.

And as I was about to take down that 'trophaeum' which I intended to send to you, those present counselled me not to do it, as it was a sacred place, and that I should not expose myself to the dangers awaiting the intruder."

It is obvious that this passage here belongs to the description of the temple, as it has nothing whatsoever to do with the palace of Xerxes; and so we find it also afterwards in the Latin and French versions of the Alexander legend.

Substituting Perceval for Alexander, we have in this chapter the central *motives* of the Grail legend: the marvellous castle or temple Alexander had been the only mortal who could reach after long and severe hardship; the mysterious old man on the couch, who appears in the romances as the maimed, sick king; the marvellous stone or cage, with the mysterious dove endowed with supernatural gifts — what could be more welcome for a poet than such a figure as that of the unknown powerful and yet half-concealed man lying on a couch? Fancy was quite free to picture in him either an ideal or a physical sufferer, tortured by a wound, inflicted either by a shaft, or by the dart of sin. Nothing could therefore adapt itself better to another cycle of tales and legends than the things seen in the temple; the jewel, or the dove, the huge amphoras and cauldrons, the numerous demi-gods and mystics, they could afterwards be substituted by Christian emblems or by other conceptions, drawn from different sources. The vagueness of the objects beheld in the temple, which can be seen already in the Latin versions of Valerius, whose words (almost unintelligible) I have retained, is the same which clings to the Grail, to the castle, its inmates, and the task of the hero.

It is, therefore, neither a feud-quest nor an unspelling-quest, to which two formulas Mr Nutt has reduced the legend (p. 181), but simply the journey to the earthly Paradise, and the marvellous castle or temple of the sun, which form the primitive nucleus of the romance.

Following up that clue we shall be able to explain many an incident in the romance through the legend of Alexander. There is in the romance the chief fisher standing by the river, who directs Perceval to the castle. In the legend it is not a fisher, but a *fish*, which is quickened to life by being dipped into the water of the river, which attracts the attention of Alexander and arouses his curiosity. He follows up the river, and is thus led to Paradise. Out of that fish there grew the fisher-king. I need not further insist upon the almost identical legend of the dove sitting on the ball (or jewel) and prophesying to the king in a human voice — i.e., to the man lying on the couch — and the dove which lays a holy wafer upon the stone in Wolfram's, and the bread by which the sick king is kept alive in Heinrich's poem. Perceval is led by lights to the magic castle, which are almost identical with the lights that go before Alexander in the version of Valerius.

We shall see presently how deeply these elements taken from the legend of Alexander, have been modified through the agency of Christian ideas and Christian conceptions. This episode with the lights, and especially that of the tree full of lights whereupon one child (two children) sits, will find its explanation later on.

There is, further, that peculiar country *Sarras,* mentioned as the land whence the *Saracens* came. The nomenclature in these romances, both that of persons and that of places, is one which deserves a careful investigation. If we could succeed in fixing some of the most important localities, much will be won for the date, age, and probable origin of the sources. I cannot linger over that important question here, nor even touch it more than I have done. It opens a wide prospect where fancy would display itself in etymological plays, riddles and solutions. The country of *Sarras* is one of these. As far as I have been able to investigate there is no trace of a country bearing such a name in the East. Looking to the legend of Alexander, I think the mystery will be solved. After leaving the Temple of the Sun, Alexander went to the country of Xerxes and delivered decisive battles (so in Valerius). In the French version (v. G. Paris, i, p.189f) of Thomas of Kent, we have there (Ch. ccxxx) substituted for Xerxes and his army: "de gens touz nuz sunt apellez *serres,*" and "del pople qu'est apellés *Serres* et de lur dreiture," "coment les *Serres* guierent Alix" (Chs. ccxxxii, ccxxxiii). The gymnosophists take the place of the Persians and are called the people of Xerxes. Out of this *Serres–Xerxes* grew the Sarras of the Grail cycle. These few examples suffice to establish a close connection also between minor details in the Alexandreid and in the Grail. The central portion has been taken over bodily and forms the central portion of the Grail, with all the peculiarities which tend to explain the further development this legend went through, until it reached that stage in which we find it.

By being connected with Alexander's journey to Paradise the legend of the Quest, which in its primitive form must also have been a search after it, is brought into close alliance with the numerous tales of saints journeying to Paradise: the legend of the three monks, that of St Macarius in the desert[3] (in itself only a modification of Alexander's), and St Brendan, not to mention ever so many more.

The description of the palace or castle is revived and amplified in the famous letter of Prester John, which became known at that time, and is directly quoted by Wolfram. Here the Christian element begins to creep in and leads the way to the other profound modifications which the legend underwent. We can see the transition from the heathen temple to a Christian palace (church) with a king (priest); coming thus nearer to certain forms of the Grail legend. In another place I intend studying the letter of Prester John, and of showing the sources whence it was derived. It will be shown there that it owes its origin, to some extent, to Jewish tales and Jewish descriptions of travels; and some light may be thrown on Flegetanis the Jew, to whom, according to Wolfram, Kyot owed the original of the Grail legend.

I must incidentally mention that a careful comparison of Chrestien's poem with the French "Chansons de Geste" will reveal the great dependence of the former upon the latter. Many an incident, many a description is undoubtedly taken over. I limit myself here to one, because Mr Nutt gives it such prominence; I mean the *Stag hunt*. Instead of having anything to do with the "lay of the fool," the connection with it being far from clear, or convincing, the true explanation is given in incident 70 of the *Queste* (Nutt, p. 49); there we read: "On the morrow they meet a white stag led by four lions; these come to a hermitage and hear mass, the stag becomes a man and sits on the altar; the lions become a man, an eagle, a lion, and an ox, all winged." There is not the slightest doubt as to who is represented here under the guise of a stag: it is Christ with the four Apostles, each in that form in which they have been represented by art.

This symbolism is not the author of the Queste's own

invention. We meet it more than once in the "Chansons de Geste" (V.P. Rajna. *Le origini dell'epopea francese*, Florence, 1884, p.252 and p.706ff). It can be traced even to a much older source, viz., the famous life of St Eustachius Placida, so closely resembling the framework of a romance, that it has indeed become a popular tale and it has been incorporated into the *Gesta Romanorum*, ed. Oesterley (Ch. 110), and *Legenda aurea* of Jacobus à Voragine. This hero-saint is drawn away from his companions by the appearance of a stag, whom he pursues, and which turns out afterwards to be Christ himself. The Stag has thus a symbolical meaning, and is of purely Christian origin.

The greatest modification in the tale, however, is that wrought in the character and attributes of the Holy Grail. I proceed, therefore, to investigate this second most important element of the legend.

There is, first, the question whence the name? What is the meaning of it? This question is the more necessary, as the oldest writers themselves do not know its exact meaning and have recourse to explanations which in the best case are mere plays upon the word. Paulin Paris, in his *"Romans de la Table Ronde,"* suggests that the name *Grail* is nothing else but a modification of the Latin *Graduale*, the name of a book used in the liturgy of the Church, wherein the tale was written down. The romances themselves afford examples enough to connect the tale with books preserved in the Church; the introduction to the Grand St Graal lets the book come down directly from heaven.

I can adduce another positive proof, viz., that a book used in the Church did bear the name of *Grael*. Philipp of Thaün, one of the oldest Norman poets (1100–1135), who wrote his *Computus* undoubtedly before the first half of the twelfth century, i.e., at least fifty years before Chrestien, gives a list of books which every good clergyman is expected to possess. He says:

> Iço fut
> li saltiers
> E li antefiniers
> Baptisteries, *Graels*
> Hymniers e li messels
> Tropiers e leçunier, etc.
> (M.F. Mann, *Physiologus*, I. Halle 1884, p. 6f)

This being the case, the Grail must have been either a book containing psalms chanted during the liturgy, or a description of some sort of theological legend or tale connected with the liturgy.

If the book was called Sanct Grael, and by popular etymology connected with *sang* (blood), we can easily understand one of the main developments of the legend, for nothing would be simpler than to explain it first as the blood of Christ, and then as the vessel destined to receive it. But this is undoubtedly the youngest of all the variations, and must be studied together with the sources and origin of the early history.

Chrestien and Gautier knew nothing of its previous history, and in the few passages in which the Grail occurs it is vaguely indicated as having food-giving properties without any other spiritual or theological gifts. Again, in Wolfram's version it has quite a different character altogether: it is a stone which yields all manner of food and drink, the power of which is sustained by a dove which every week lays a wafer upon it, is given, after the fall of the rebel angels, in charge to Titurel and his dynasty, is by them preserved in the Grail castle, Mont Salvatsch, and is guarded by a sacred order of knighthood whom it chooses itself (Nutt, p. 25).

If we follow up closely the different versions, we can easily observe the increase of the properties assigned to the Grail, and through the Grail to the Grail-keeper and Grail-seeker. We can see how the author of each new version tried to outdo his predecessor, and thus in time a complete history of the Grail appears, of which nothing was known before.

The connection, further, with Britain is one of the latest developments, and has nothing whatsoever to do with the primitive history of the Grail, with which it became later connected. I must leave that point untouched, as I wish to go straight to the question of the Grail itself. I have already stated, at the beginning, that the temple of the Grail in the poem is the temple of Jerusalem, and the Grail in its double character a certain sacred stone in the Holy place.

The change from the temple of the sun to a Christian church is only natural and quite in accordance with the spirit of the time. Besides, the legend of Prester John with his palace-church paved the way for the transition, and certainly none was better known or more renowned than that of Jerusalem, of which numerous legends were circulated by pilgrims from the Holy Land swarming through Europe, not to speak of the crusades and the numerous expeditions to Palestine. We can trace those legends which I shall mention later on more fully, through a great number of Christian writers, ranging from the twelfth century back to the third. From such legends is derived also the double character assigned to the Grail, that of a holy cup or vessel, with an eucharistical symbolism, and that of a sacred stone existing from the creation of the world, and carried about by the angels of heaven. Both are derived from a more primitive notion, viz., from the legends connected with a sacred stone which served as an altar in that very church. In this peculiar character we can trace it back to the first century, and, perhaps, to an earlier tradition preserved by Jewish writers.

It is well known that many ancient legends connected with the temple of Solomon have been adapted in later times to serve Christian notions. I mention, for instance the legend of Golgotha and the head of Adam, the legend of the beam in the temple which became afterwards the cross, that of the queen of Sheba, and the Sybilla, and so very many other legends and apocryphal tales, some of which are also to be found in the Grand St Graal, nay, form the greater part of its contents.

Now there was current at the time a peculiar legend connected with a certain stone that is still in existence; it is that stone which stands under a baldachin in the *Haram,* more precisely, in the *Kubbet-es-Sachra,* the *Temple of the Rock.* It is that famous building, erected by sultan El-Melik towards the end of the seventh century which so deeply impressed the Crusaders and the Templars, that they thought it was the real temple of Solomon. In order to watch this temple and keep it against the infidels, the knighthood of the Templars arose at the beginning of the eleventh century. They took the image of that dome as a crest. Many a church in Europe was built after this model; if I am not mistaken, the Temple church in London, where the quarters of the Knights Templar were, as well as similar buildings in Laon, Metz, etc.

The centre of that building is the rock, famous alike in Jewish, Mohamedan, and Christian legends; it is surrounded by a trellis of iron, with four lattice doors wrought by French artizans of the twelfth century, and is covered with red samite and gold fringes.

It would be almost impossible to give here all the legends that are told of this rock. I select only a few bearing on our subject. I begin with the oldest, that taken from the Jewish literature.

The first impulse to legendary development is the passage of the Bible: (Isaiah, xxviii, 16) "Therefore, thus saith the Lord God, Behold, I lay in Zion for a foundation a stone, a precious corner stone of sure foundation (Cf. I Pet. ii, v. 6.) Later fancy saw in that rock the stone of foundation, endowed it with supernatural origin and power, and gave it the name of *Eben shatya* — "the stone of foundation. This stone is the centre of the world, upon it stands the Temple, and that is the Stone upon which Jacob slept and saw the wonderful ladder with God standing on top of it." So runs one legend.

Another, more elaborate one, says: "When God created the world he took a stone (undoubtedly a precious one), engraved His holy and mysterious Name upon it, and sank it in the abyss to stem the underground waters; for when they behold the Holy Name they get overawed, and shrink back into their natural boundaries. Whenever a man utters an oath that stone comes up and receives that oath, and returns to its former place. If the oath is a true one, then the letters of the Holy Name get more deeply engraved, but if it is a false oath the letters are washed away by the waves, which surge and rise, and would overflow the world if God did not send an angel, *Jaazriel,* who possesses the seventy keys to the mysterious name of God, to engrave them anew, and thus to drive the flood back, for otherwise the world would be flooded."

As a continuation of this legend there exists another, according to which David, when he intended to lay the foundation of the Temple, brought that stone up from the depth, and if not for Divine intervention, would have brought about a second flood.

More ancient is the belief that upon that rock the holy ark, with the stone tables of the ten commandments, used to rest, and that they were hidden inside the rock at the moment of the destruction of the first temple.[4]

In the second book of the Maccabees the concealing of the holy vessels in a rock sealed with the ineffable name of God, is attributed to the Prophet Jeremiah — as is also the case in a certain apocryphal legend of Jeremiah, wherein also an incident occurs, which is absolutely identical with the legend of the Holy Grail. Both the keys of the temple and the Holy Grail are taken up to heaven by a mysterious hand reaching down from on high. But this I mention only incidentally. Let us proceed further with the *Eben Shatya*.

As the oldest tradition will have it, it was in the temple from the time of the first prophets, that is, it is recorded as having been from that time. It was therefore placed in the portion where the ark used to be before, in the Holy of Holies of the Temple; the High-priest entered there once a year to burn "sweet incense." This act was considered to be of symbolic importance, and the popular belief endows the rock with food-giving properties. "It is thence that Israel got abundance of food;" so runs the passage in the original. To complete the characteristics of this stone I have only to add another legend, which brings us directly in connection with Christianity. An old anti-Christian writing — perhaps that mentioned in the seventh century, but modified in later times[5] — has a peculiar tale about this stone.

It runs as follows:

"Now, at this time (i.e., in the time of Jesus) the unutterable name of God was engraved in the temple on the *Eben Shatya*. For when King David laid the foundations he found there a stone in the ground on which the name of God was engraved, and he took it and placed it in the Holy of Holies. But as the wise men feared lest some inquisitive youth should learn this Name, and be able thereby to destroy the world, they made by magic two brazen lions, which they sat before the entrance of the Holy of Holies, one on the right, the other on the left.

"Now if anyone were to go within and learn the Holy Name, then the lions would begin to roar as he came out so that out of alarm and bewilderment he would lose his presence of mind, and forget the Name.

"And Jesus left upper Galilee and came secretly to Jerusalem, and went into the temple, and learned there the holy writing, and after he had written the ineffable Name on parchment, he uttered it, with intent that he might feel no pain, and then he cut into his flesh, and hid the parchment with the inscription therein. Then he uttered the Name once more, and made so that his flesh healed up again.

"And when he went out of the door the lions roared and he forgot the Name. Therefore he hastened outside the town, cut into his flesh, took the writing out, and when he had sufficiently studied the signs he retained the Name in memory, 'and thus he wrought all the miracles through the agency of the ineffable name of God'."[6]

Taking all these elements together we have here clearly all the properties assigned to the Grail: the precious stone the centre of the temple, and further, the Keeper of the great secret, the mysterious words given to Joseph, and handed down by him to his descendants, the lions at the entrance against which Lancelot fought.

These are the primary elements for the later developments by Christians and Mohamedans; as that stone was equally holy to both, and the primitive legends were adapted to the altered circumstances, so, as we shall see, it became the altar upon which mass was celebrated, and the table of the Last Supper, the primitive form from which the later spiritual one was derived.

Well known is the interpretation of the text of Isaiah from which I started. In the first Epistle of Peter (ii, v.6), these very words are quoted, together with those from Psalm cxviii, 22, and Jesus is identified with the corner-stone, which in its turn was identified with the *Eben Shatya,* the stone of the world's foundation: He the stone, the altar, the sacrifice, thus the Eucharist.

At the place where the Temple stood a church was erected, or the Temple transformed into a church, called the Church of Mount Zion, first the abode of the Virgin Mary, then the Church of St James. One of the first pilgrims whose record is in existence, one from Bordeaux, *ca.* 333, shows the first phase of this transformation; he saw already there the "big corner-stone of which the Psalmist speaks."[7]

Antoninus, another, of the year 570, knows already more about it, for he says: "When you put your ear to it, you can hear the voices of many men." According to the Mohamedan legend one hears the noise of water. Both tales derived from the old legend mentioned above, that the stone shuts up the waters of the depth.

This church founded there is the mother church founded by the Apostles; and with this agrees the whole Christian antiquity.

In the same manner Evodius, Epiphanius, Hieronymus and many other ecclesiastical historians, unanimously assert that the scene of the Last Supper took place on Mount Zion. John of Wurzburg (1160–70; an older contemporary of Chrestien) says: "*The Coenaculum* is on Mount Sion, in the very spot where Solomon reared his splendid building, of which he speaks in his 'Song of Songs.'" The *table* of the Last Supper was also shown there as late as the twelfth and thirteenth centuries; and this table was identified with the altar upon which the Apostle John celebrated mass, which altar stands for that *corner-stone*.

There is a very interesting passage in Mandeville's description, a synchretistic account of what he saw on Mount Sion: "And 120 paces from that church (St James) is Mount Sion, where there is a fair church of Our Lady, where she dwelt and died, ... and there is the stone which the angel brought to Our Lady from Mount Sinai, which is of the same colour as that of St Catharine." And further on. "There is a part of the table on which Our Lord made His Supper, when he made his Maundy with his disciples and gave them his flesh and blood in form of bread and wine. And under that chapel, by a descent of thirty-two steps, is the place where Our Lord washed his disciples' feet, and the vessel which contained the water is still preserved ... And there is the altar where Our Lord heard the angels sing mass."

Almost identical with this description is that of Philip, of the twelfth or thirteenth century. The identification of stone and altar, and further altar and mass, is to be met with also elsewhere. It is in fact no more than a simple adaptation of the old notion, that the ark stood upon that stone and that the stone took the place of the altar. To identify the altar in the church and the sacrament with the fundamental events in the life and the teachings of Jesus is in perfect accord with the allegorical and mystical interpretations indulged in since ancient times. The mass in the oriental church has throughout only a symbolical meaning, and the Grail partakes thus of a double interpretation. To one it is merely a vessel or a cup, a portion for the whole, the natural change from the altar and mass to the most prominent *portion* of it; to another it is still a primitive rock made by hands of angels, and the food-giving wafer is brought by the dove which represents the Holy Spirit.

In one the change is more radical, and with the time becomes more mystical and symbolical; in the other the original form is better retained, and offers thus more elements for the re-construction of the oldest form of the legend. The *Munsalvasche,* where the castle stands, is nothing else than the "Mount of Salvation" — the Armenian church on Mount Sion is dedicated to the "Holy Saviour" the Salvator; and Wolfram was not alto-gether wrong when he accused Chrestien of having departed too much from the original conception.

In connection with the preceding, I will add now the interpre-tation of another name, *Corbenic,* not infrequent in the Grail romances, a name of some importance. According to *Queste,* In-cident 13 (Nutt, p. 73), Castle Corbenic is the place wherein the *maimed king dwells;* further, Incident 76; (p. 50) the same is again mentioned as the Castle of Peleur, or the Maimed King, i.e., the resting-place of the Grail. In the Grand St Graal, Incident 51 (p. 63) we read: "Here is the resting-place of the Holy Grail, a lordly castle is built for it hight *Corbenic,* which is *Chaldee,* and signifies 'holy vessel.'"

This interpretation is only half true, in so far as the word *Cor-benic* can be traced to a Hebrew or Chaldee word *Carbana,* the meaning of which is, *offering, sacrifice,* and not that which is as-signed to it by the author of the Grand St Graal, that of *holy vessel.*

This explanation agrees perfectly with the identification of the Grail with the *Altar*-stone, the place of sacrifices, mystical, sym-bolical or material.

Starting from the Slavonic, especially Russian legends, about the mysterious Altar-stone, which he brought in connection with the Grail, Prof. Wesselofsky has tried to prove its identity with that stone of the Christian Church of Zion mentioned by the pil-grims quoted above. The Jewish legends, however, which I have been able to add, have enabled me to trace that identity further, and to furnish those links which were missing, and to show the last sources to whom those Christian legends owed their origin. The name "Alatyr," which remained unexplained, is nothing else but the *Altar*-stone, as I have proved it to be.

The same causes, i.e., the same Palestinian legends, had the same result, viz., to produce an *ideal stone* both for the East and the West of Europe, but it remained to the genius of the different trouveurs, or Kaléki perchojie, to develop that idea according to the skill and perfection possible in those two regions. The one introduced it into the famous legend of Alexander, in order to substitute it for the meaningless stone mentioned there; the other connected it with other apocryphal tales and legends, and formed the famous Golubinaya Kniga of the Russian epos.

The legend of the Holy Grail had still to pass another stage of development, before it became what it is in some at least of the romances. It had to be entirely spiritualized. The Christian element so prominent in the Crusades pervaded the poem so thoroughly that to some it was nothing but the outcome of purely Christian canonical and non-canonical writings. By leaving the classical and local elements out of account, the Grail had still remained a puzzle to be solved.

I do not even attempt now to show all the parallels to the Christian apocryphal literature which we meet with in the different versions of the romance. The whole early history gives itself as such a tale; later on I may be permitted to show how inextricably interwoven with it are the apocryphal legends of Adam and Seth, the history of the Cross, a peculiar legend of Solomon and the Queen of Sheba, the legend of Sunday, and ever so many more allusions to such and similar apocryphal tales.

But there still remains the liturgical character which is given to the Grail in some of the versions of the romance. It serves to bring home to the reader or hearer a certain dogmatic teaching about the mystery of the Eucharist. The mystical procession, with the description of everything that occurred, points clearly to the fact of the transubstantiation of the sacrament, as a thing that did occur in the sight of the bystanders, as if it were a proof more to the truth and accuracy of this dogmatic teaching.

Has the author of the romance evolved it out of his own fancy, or does he follow here also some legend, which he adapts to his purposes?

There is no doubt that the question of the reality or non-reality of transubstantiation was at the time a burning one. The author or authors have shown themselves well versed in Christian and heathen lore, and on the other hand not much given to invent out of their own brains.

I do not know whether anybody has already pointed this out,

or has brought in connection with it the legend, which occurs to me as an almost direct source for that portion of the romances of the Grail.

It is besides localized in Jerusalem, and is directly connected with that very same church on Mount Sion of which the other *stone legend* speaks. I will deal now with this legend before concluding this, necessarily short, attempt to solve the question of the origin of the Grail. I have had to confine myself in many cases merely to indicating in a few words what required a special monograph, and I may return at another time to the study of those details at greater length.

Notes

1   Nutt, p. 11, Incid. 7.

2   Nutt, 27.

3   V. Graf, *Paradiso terrestro*, Torino, 1878.

4   *Joma*, f. 53b, f. 546; *Tanhuma*, ed. Buber, ii, p. 59, No. 59, 60, 61; *Levit. rab.* sect. 20; *Numb. rab.* sect. 12; *Cant. rab.* ad. Ch. iii, v. 18; *Pesikta. rab.* sect. 47; *Midrash Psalm*, Ps. 91, v. 12; *Yalkut Sim.* i. f. 35, § 120, f. 44d, § 145, etc.

5   Lipsius, *Pilatus Acten*, p. 29.

6   Baring-Gould, *Lost Gospels*, p. 77f.

7   A.N. Wesselofsky, *Razyskaniya vŭ oblasti russkago duhovnago stika*, iii, St Petersburg, 1881, p.4ff.

CHAPTER 17

Persia and the Holy Grail

ARTHUR UPHAM POPE

For nearly a thousand years the peoples of Europe were intensely absorbed and emotionally agitated by a series of strange legends about a sacred object of magical power called the Holy Grail. These legends were varied, confused and sometimes inconsistent, for in the course of their development they had been elaborated with details from folklores of several European and Oriental cultures. Yet from the eleventh to the nineteenth century a common and general faith was fervently accepted: there is a land far, far away, mysterious, inaccessible — an earthly paradise that lies at the true center of the world. There, crowning a great mountain, is a castle or temple of fabulous splendor containing the most precious of all objects, the Grail itself, charged with self-generating, self-renewing, overflowing abundance. An object of awe and reverence, the supreme goal of all desire, the ultimate secret of power and perfection, the divine symbol of life itself, its virtue will be imparted to whatever youth of noble birth can attain to it, even behold it.

This strange and deeply moving concept of the Grail permeated the entire consciousness of medieval Europe, everywhere kindling fervid enthusiasm, appearing constantly not only in folk lore, legend and romance, and in various decorative and ritual arts, but also in architecture which from time to time sought to reproduce the Temple of the Grail according to accepted descriptions, hoping thus to share in, and perpetuate, the magic virtues of the holy object.

The idea had a very long history, was probably ultimately derived from man's earliest fertility myths and rituals, vitalized and sustained by man's universal and persistent search for the elusive secret of life. Although never specifically sanctioned by ecclesiastical authority, it was finally, in later medieval times, assimilated to the Christian doctrine of the Redemption, the Grail being identified, alternatively, as the cup in which Joseph of Arimathea caught the blood of Christ or as the Chalice of the Last Supper, symbolizing man's ultimate salvation through divine Grace. "Through this fusion," writes J.M.E. Ross, "there was fashioned one of the richest influences which have ever inspired music, poetry and art." The Grail was "an abiding symbol for the moral and spiritual idealism of pilgrim humanity." Even in the late nineteenth century the legend was again given moving expression in Tennyson's very popular *Idylls of the King,* in Wagner's *Lohengrin* and *Parsifal,* which aroused pious fervor in several countries, and in Edwin Abbey's sumptuous murals in the Boston Public Library.

In short, the Grail legend entered into the language, the ideas and emotions of the Western world, kindling imagination and enhancing a central feature of Christian faith.

European scholars have for generations sought for the origins of this potent cult which evoked such ancient faith even though not inculcated by the Church. A substantial body of erudite research has been built up, but it has not yet provided a satisfactory explanation of how and where it all began. The consensus has been, until very recently, that the Grail stories were generated chiefly from French and Celtic sources, beginning in part as far back as the ninth century, with some earlier traces.

Some scholars, however, have suggested that the legend had been adapted from a pagan cult (notably, Jessie Weston, who focused chiefly on Adonis traditions); others, that it was a universal, ever-recurring theme born out of man's own deepest experience (a form of the "independent parallel invention hypothesis," proposed, for example, by Gaster). Still others (Wesselovsky, Staerk) saw Oriental derivations, not only in the rich romantic colouring, but also in some of the central ideas, notably certain marked resemblances to Babylonian fertility rituals and the magical renewal of abundance, which was also a primary function of the Grail. Finally, there were those (Nyberg, Herzfeld) who proposed a Persian location for the Castle of the Grail — Herzfeld, because he thought that the conventional description of the Grail castle resembled the ruined Palace of Ardashir dramatically crowning a cliff in Southern Persia, which might therefore have been the original model.

No one of these divergent theories has ever quite convinced a majority of serious scholars, each in turn being too general or lacking in specific confirming evidence. So until recently the origin of the Grail legends has remained speculative and controversial. But as one scholar (Ross) wrote nearly fifty years ago: "It must always be remembered that the discovery of some hitherto concealed manuscript might throw a flood of light on the whole subject and rearrange the knowledge now possessed."

That fortunate moment seems now to have arrived, and has been enriched with several apparently unrelated discoveries of critical importance which have been correlated and interpreted by a scholar of remarkable ability, Professor Lars Ivar Ringbom of Finland; and his conclusions point to Asian origins for the central concepts.[1]

The starting point was the publication by Dr Werner Wolf in 1942 of a recently discovered manuscript, with certain variants, of the poem *Der Jüngere Titurel*, by Albrecht (whose last name is unknown, though for a time he was called "von Scharffenberg"), written in 1270.[2] This professes to give a comprehensive account of the Grail, based on a compilation and completion of earlier writers like Wolfram von Eschenbach. Albrecht devotes 112 lines to a quite specific description of the Grail Temple (the first that we have) and its site, Mount Salvat, so specific, even to measurements, that it seems to be reporting fact rather than poetic fancy.

Many attempts have been made on the basis of this description theoretically to reconstruct the Grail Temple and to associate with it some known structures.[3] None, however, has been satisfactory, largely because the manuscripts of Albrecht's poem specify impossible dimensions, and cite 72 radial chapels — a number that defeats any feasible structural plan. Now Werner Wolf's publication, resting on the oldest and best manuscript, shows that the text should read 22, not 72 (for the purposes of the investigation a decisive number), and that the colossal dimensions are not affirmed in the original poem — corrections that result in a plan quite possible of construction.

Albrecht's description of the temple is somewhat confused by the inclusion of characteristic features of a Romanesque or perhaps Armenian church, which was not unknown, but at the core of his account are specific elements, quite foreign and exotic, clearly referring to some reality beyond the conventional and familiar — a domed structure surrounded by 22 radial chapels or arched recesses, with many distinctive decorative features, and set on a quite unusual and specifically described site.

As Albrecht tells it: In the Land of Salvation, in the Forest of Salvation, lies a solitary mountain called the Mountain of Salvation which King Titurel surrounded by a wall and on which he built a costly castle that he gave to serve as the Temple of The Grail, "because the Grail at that time had no fixed place, but floated, invisible, in the air." The Temple "was built of noble stone." The Mountain consisted of onyx and on the top grass, plants and a layer of earth were stripped off, uncovering the onyx which was levelled and polished until it shone like the moon. The resulting platform was one *klafter* (fathom: 6 feet) thick and from the edge of the steps to the temple walls it was 5 *klafter* (30 feet) wide.

The Temple itself was domed, round and high. It was roofed with gold and the interior of the dome was encrusted with sapphires, representing the blue vault of Heaven, and set with glistening carbuncles to mark the stars. The golden sun and silver moon moved through the Zodiac, and golden cymbals announced the seven canonical hours. "Neither inside or out is there a handsbreadth of the Temple that is not richly ornamented." Everywhere was gold, niello, enamel, enriched with jewels or set with coloured stones. Precious aloewood was used for the seats. Doors and railings were covered with gold. All want and poverty were banished far from the vicinity of the Temple.

Now, as Ringbom has pointed out, there was, in the distant land of Persia, at the sacred city of Shiz, another and very famous building, of fabulous opulence, domed, gilded and jewel-encrusted, also endowed with magical powers, also warding off want and poverty, life-protecting and life-sustaining, also set on a mountain. This building had been seen by many, had been described by geographers and historians as well as poets and mystics, and a drawing of it, approximately contemporary, exists. Indeed, there are so many similarities between these two buildings, their placement, structure and embellishment, their purposes and functions, that it seems as if they must be one and the same.

This other domed temple, perhaps the historical prototype of the Grail Temple, was the famous Takht-i-Taqdis, or Throne of Arches, commissioned by Chosroes II, the great Persian Sasanian King (590–628), and built at Shiz, the most sacred spot in the land, deep in the mountainous heart of Azerbaijan.[4] Shiz was, like Persepolis, the spiritual capital of the kingdom. Here were preserved the chronicles of the dynasty. Here Shapur, who designated himself "Brother of the Sun and Moon," deposited a copy of the *Avesta* with commentaries and a supplementary encyclopedia of all the knowledge of the time. Shiz was the closely guarded repository of the religious, intellectual and political authority of empire. Here was the sovereign Fire-temple, the Adhargushnasp, from whose sacred fire were replenished the fires of the other Temples. Here was the reputed birthplace of Zoroaster; and here were striking physical properties, particularly a miraculous lake, a bottomless, brimming reservoir which maintained a constant level without regard to seasons; self-generating, self-renewing, of overflowing abundance, conferring life and plenty on the surrounding land — proof of its supernatural, beneficent character.

Chosroes built his Takht as a thanksgiving for a victory which saved the régime, but it was not devised for ostentatious self-glorification. It was really a national effort, an expression of the national faith. It was not a throne in the ordinary sense, but a great pavillion, accommodating, round the King, a thousand of his nobles. Here the King, surrogate on earth of God, performed the crucial seasonal rites — the potent ceremonies which, by sympathetic magic, assisted the calendrical rotation, assuring the cooperation of the heavenly powers — the sun, moon, stars and rains — which were necessary for fertility, even, indeed, for the continued life of the people. It was thus, like Persepolis, a holy, cosmic structure, with the same supernatural function, and like Persepolis it had to be of utmost splendor, a supreme effort of king and nation. Indeed, for its construction Chosroes, with the consent of the nobles, lavished on it a sizeable, even imprudent proportion of the national treasure — and a formidable amount that was, thanks to the tribute which poured into the Iranian

State coffers from most of Western Asia, and even parts of India and China.

The Takht was built of precious woods; cedar and teak, overlaid with much gold. Only gold and silver nails were used. The risers of the steps were gold. The balustrades — like those of the Grail Temple — were gold; and again like the Grail Temple, the Takht was heavily encrusted with jewels. As in the Grail Temple, blue stones symbolized the sky — lapis lazuli and turquoise in the Takht, sapphires in the Grail Temple. In the Takht golden astronomical tables — which could be changed according to season — were set in the dome, and on these the stars were marked by rubies, recalling that the stars in the dome of the Grail Temple likewise were marked with red jewels — carbuncles, often rubies, though they might be other stones, provided they were red, for example, garnets. In both the sun and moon were displayed, rendered in precious metal. The astronomical adjustment of the Takht went even further: the whole building was set on rollers above a (hidden) pit in which horses worked a mechanism that turned the structure round through the Four Quarters, so that at every season it would be in correct correspondence with the heavens, thus making more potent the celebration of the appropriate rituals.

All the rest of the ornamentation and equipment of the Persian Temple were likewise of a magnificence and extravagance that only an unlimited imagination, unlimited funds and a great occasion could command. Its beauty and splendor would focus, so it was felt, the sympathetic attention and participation of the heavenly powers. The most sacred area, in the center, was enclosed in a vast curtain embroidered in gold, the patterns including the major astral symbols. Gold and silver braziers warmed the individual nobles while the upper arcades were enclosed in curtains of beaver or sable fur. To assure practical results, the major motivation, sympathetic magic was again employed — there were machines for creating the semblance of a storm: thunder, lightning, rain — all calculated to induce the outer heavens to send the real storm which would replenish the needy earth.

As the Throne of Chosroes faced a lake, so also, in several major reports, the Grail Temple is related to a body of water. In the earliest written account of Chrétien de Troyes (1180–90) the

Grail Castle stands beside a river. In Wolfram von Eschenbach's poem and in the Peredur story in the Welsh *White Book of Rhydderch* (1322)[5] it is beside a lake. The Grail Temple, in Albrecht's poem, is set in the midst of an artificial sea. These are European echoes of the Iranian insistence on water as an indispensable element in the fertility cult, and the ultimate purpose of fertility ceremonies. Other coincidences, though secondary, are still significant in the whole complex. In the Grail Temple, according to Albrecht, were used asbestos, associated with heat, and elitropia, associated with water and rain, suggestive of the main function of the Chosroes pavillion which was to control the heat of the sun and water from rain in order to promote life. Again, in the *White Book of Rhydderch*, Peredur makes a double visit to the Grail Castle, in the first emerging from a forest and finding a lake before the Castle, in the second approaching across a meadow. On another visit, later, he comes to the Castle by following a river through a valley. In this connection it is of some interest that the approach to the Takht from the south passes through a grove of trees, arriving at the lake where once stood the ceremonial pavillion; that from the north comes across a meadow, while the approach from the west (as well as the south) follows a stream up a valley. The Takht is approachable from only these three sides; the Grail Temple had doors only on these three sides.

One cultic parallel is particularly striking. The Grail Temple or Castle was the goal of a long and difficult journey which might be undertaken only by men of noble blood. And each Sasanian King was in honour bound to start, on the very day after his coronation at Ctesiphon, the long, arduous pilgrimage to the holy shrine of Shiz, entirely on foot, a tough journey of four hundred miles which might have taxed any of King Arthur's knights.

A hint of Iranian origins may also be contained in Albrecht's account where he tells of windmills forcing air through pipes down under the buildings (to make the fish and other monsters in the artificial sea move). Windmills were an invention of East Iran and the device by which air is forced down through pipes into the basement — the *Bad-gir* — is characteristic of Iran.

But the thesis that there is a certain relation between the throne of Chosroes and the Temple of the Grail does not rest on literary evidence alone. In 1937 an expedition of the Asia Institute (then the American Institute for Persian Art and Archeology) reached Takht-i-Suleiman, the present name for the ancient Shiz,[6] and found there substantial factual evidence of a correspondence of the site with Albrecht's description. Here was the mountain, a dome-like extinct volcano dramatically set apart from the surrounding terrain, with a plateau-like top, and it was ringed by a powerful, still-standing stone wall (40 feet high and 10 feet thick, built by the Parthians in the second century BC); here were remains of important buildings — Parthian, Sasanian and Islamic — testifying to the historic role of the site; here was a crystal lake in the center, and here also the flattened, smoothed-off area such as Albrecht described, and even more astonishing, a gleaming, crust-like deposit made by the mineral waters of the lake, which, particularly around the shores where it is more exposed, has taken on the appearance of onyx, with striations of white, buff, brown and other tints. These look sufficiently like onyx to justify Albrecht's assertions that the Grail Temple stood on a bed of onyx, which formed the substance of the mountain — a claim to some critics so fantastic as to deprive his other statements of credibility.

Moreover, Albrecht's remark that want was banished from the precincts of the Temple would be justified here at the Takht, for two unfailing streams pour out of the lake, miraculously conferring fertility, abundant and constant, on the green surrounding land.

Even more conclusive evidence of a dependent relation between Albrecht's Grail Temple and the Takht-i-Taqdis is furnished by an engraved bronze salver, in the Berlin Museum, which is either very late Sasanian or early post-Sasanian.[7] For this shows in elevation a domed palace which is elaborately decorated with symbols of fertility — trees, great blossoms, jars of the living water.

This building, depicted by the line engraving in the center of the salver, has been identified, by an intricate complex of internal evidence paralleling the literary records, as the Takht-i-Taqdis. A striking confirmation is that the rollers on which, according to Persian accounts, the building was set, are clearly shown in the drawing on the salver, a most unusual kind of foundation.

The building itself was interpreted by Strzygowski as an emblematic representation of the Holy Grail to which, when he reaffirmed it at the Second International Congress for Persian Art (London, 1931), Professor Sarre replied with great vigor that not one line of evidence had been produced — only affirmations. But Strzygowski's guess was apparently correct, for with Professor Wolf's publication of the more accurate Albrecht manuscript the two were virtually conclusively linked. For on the salver the central building is surrounded by twenty-two arched panels, each framing a decorative tree; and in the revised version of the Albrecht poem the rotunda of the Grail Temple is surrounded by twenty-two arcaded chapels, each decorated with an ornamental tree. The correspondence is the more impressive because the division of a circular area into twenty-two equal units is practically unprecedented in the decorative arts, and is difficult to achieve with ordinary craft methods.

On the salver the twenty-two arches represent, in a non-naturalistic, decoratively translated "perspective," an arcaded wall that evidently enclosed the Paradise Garden in which the Sasanian Temple would, in accordance with deeply rooted Iranian custom, have been set. Actually, the Temple could not have been encircled by merely twenty-two arches — they would have to have been of impossible heights and would have left conspicuous traces which the Institute's expedition would have seen. The number must be taken as "short hand" for 220 — just as the terminal zero is often dropped in writing Muslim dates, especially on works of art — it being obviously impossible to depict the full number on the salver. When 22 is thus understood as 220, the figure assumes a natural symbolic character quite lacking in 22, for 220 is divisible by four, important both in the practical design and symbolically because of the overshadowing concepts of the Four Quarters and the Four Seasons; and when divided by four it gives 55, also a "good" symbolic number, as five refers to the Four Quarters and the Center. Such a magnificent wall of arches round the Temple and its garden would justify the name: "The Throne of — Arches" — Takht-i-Taqdis.

Albrecht, or some lost predecessor's work from which he was borrowing, had with western literal-mindedness interpreted the decorative convention of flattening out a perspective as a ground plan, thus giving rise to the plan of radial chapels, and also the concept of the Grail Temple as circular.

Moreover, Albrecht, or his source, also interpreted the representation on the salver literally in respect of another important feature of the Grail Temple. For the engraving of the Takht-i-Taqdis in the center of the salver is miniature in scale in relation to the surrounding arcade; and Albrecht tells us that in the very center of the Grail Temple was a miniature replica of the temple itself, in which the Grail was deposited.

Again, the fact that it was presented on a *salver* would link the Takht with the Grail. For "grail," in Old French *"graal,"* meant originally "salver;" and a great salver, ceremoniously borne, was a major feature, usually the chief object, in the solemn procession within the Grail Castle which is the climax of the story. This salver bore a major object of the cult, either exposed but unexplained — like the severed head shown to Peredur; or concealed, and indicated as the Secret Object itself.

In Albrecht's account is another and almost more significant episode relevant to the fact that the Temple is illustrated on a salver; for according to him, the Grail was sent to India and as a result a replica of the Grail Temple was built there. This would be possible only if the Grail carried with it a representation of the Temple; and the big round bronze tray is a "graal" in the old literal sense of "salver" which does carry a detailed illustration of the Takht and its surrounding twenty-two arches which are echoed in Albrecht's Grail Temple.

It seems certain, then, that Albrecht, or his source, had seen an engraved salver like, or very similar to, the one in Berlin and knew that the building there represented was the Takht-i-Taqdis, so that he could supplement the illustration with other details that were known either from word-of-mouth tradition or in written reports — or the two combined.

But by what routes could this strange far-away building have become known to Europe and so deeply impressed Europeans? The problem is the more puzzling since the Takht-i-Taqdis was destroyed by Heraclius in 628, hardly twenty-five years after it was begun. The supreme and dramatic, particularly if it expresses the national genius and faith of a great people, travels far across many frontiers by virtue of its own momentum. In the case of the Throne of Chosroes, however, there were several ways in which it could reach the eager, wonder-loving mind of early medieval Europe. Some ten thousand returning officers and men of Heraclius' army must have been deeply impressed by the dazzling and quite unparalleled splendor of the Throne pavillion, which they helped to dismantle; an impression re-enforced by the strange storm-working machinery and the horrendous statue of Chosroes, arrogantly elevated high in the dome representing the vault of Heaven; by the magic of the constant lake, and, of course, as soldiers they must have been impressed by the site, its formidable wall, and the memory of the tragic defeat there of Marc Anthony. Returning, they would have had much to tell. Byzantine historians recognized the importance of Heraclius' triumph and reported it at some length in accounts now largely lost.[8]

There were, moreover, other and continuous avenues of communication. Persian Sasanian influences spread up through Christian Armenia, where there are many five-domed churches resembling the drawing on the salver, and round churches following the alternate interpretation; and Armenia was always in touch with the Christian West. In the eighth century there were Byzantine envoys at the Courts of the Caliphs of Baghdad where Sasanian memories were still very much alive, and Harun ar-Rashid was in touch with Charlemagne. Persia likewise had contacts with Egypt, and Egypt with Europe. The Irish missions to Egypt in the tenth century would have been a likely contact.

But far more important than these secondary contacts, and of poignant interest to the Christians of Europe, was the harrowing story which everybody knew of Chosroes' capture of Jerusalem in 614 and his seizure of the supreme Christian relic, the Cross itself, which the Sasanian monarch carried off to the sanctuary at Shiz. For the whole of devout Christianity this was a heart-breaking tragedy — never to be forgotten until it was retrieved, and again never to be forgotten when it was retrieved. And retrieved it was, when Heraclius took Shiz, destroyed the Takht and, in 629, carried the Cross back to Jerusalem in triumph and re-dedication. Medieval Europe, enveloping in its romantic devotion a great medley of traditions, most of them at least ultimately Oriental in origin, could hardly have failed to have absorbed the image and the feeling of the Takht-i-Taqdis, along with its legendary-repute.

342

Medieval Europe was, indeed, quite aware of the Asian world. Long before the Crusades, pilgrims sought the Holy land in such crowds that traffic out of Marseilles had to be officially regulated and each pilgrim, on boarding a vessel, was required to show his return ticket. Again, did not Abbott Suger say, "I love to talk with those who have been to the East and Jerusalem to see if their ways are not better than ours"? Everybody "knew" about a strange Christian king, Prester John, his fabulous palace and wide domains in Central Asia, or alternatively as King of Armenia and Egypt. Actually, Europe, partly because of the episode of the Cross, was well aware of the Palace of Chosroes, and it appears both in literature and the arts. German texts beginning as early as 1125 describe the Throne of Chosroes, with its jewelled dome, and the *Sächsischen Weltchronik* gives a miniature showing Chosroes seated on his throne high in the vault of Heaven. Other medieval accounts describe the mechanism for imitating rain; others ascribe to Chosroes fantastic powers — even to having covered his entire land with a heavenly vault. A Flemish tapestry, now in Saragossa Cathedral, made as late as about 1480, depicts Heraclius destroying the Throne of Chosroes.

The source or explanation for some of our formative and most persistent ideas cannot be found in our own history because they were engendered in the East before there was any Western culture, and they are far from obvious. Much research is needed; we must, of course, have far more facts about these remote sources.

But successful research into the cultural backgrounds of the Ancient Orient requires not merely more material and documentary "facts," but also, and quite urgently, a sympathetic understanding of presuppositions and attitudes fundamental in West Asian culture, wholly different from either the scientific or the common-sense assumptions of the Western world. We have persistently questioned the concepts and categories behind Asian cultures, but it has been in terms of those familiar to us. Consequently, the mentalities reflected in Asian cultural history often remain stubbornly opaque, they resist our insights and will continue to do so except when investigated in their own terms. More "facts" we certainly need, but uninterpreted "facts" are scarcely facts at all, and such "facts" seen against a Western, rather than an Eastern background are unreliable, if not down-right deceptive. The myths and postulates of ancient Oriental culture are involved in a remote and apparently foggy symbolism, often deeply connected with mystery cults and secret initiation rites, almost always involved deeply in complex religious systems and in many cases interwoven with astronomical concepts involving preconceptions and even images quite alien to both our experience and our information. Moreover, many centuries of cross-fertilization have often obscured the original strains, or crystallized them in formal simulacra or enmeshed them in references the original meanings of which have gone astray. Nonetheless, strange and irrational as ancient Asian cultural backgrounds may repeatedly seem, they have been evolved through profound and significant human experiences and this has given them initiating power as well as persistence.

If we try, however, to stretch these notions, images and the mythic complexes which are their matrix on the procrustean bed of Western rationalism, they will be deformed past recognition or evaluation, and quite devitalized, while under sympathetic exploration they can become very revealing and suggestive.

What is needed is still more and more open-minded and imaginatively sympathetic research into the genesis and development of the mythic web which is the backdrop of all Asian culture, further efforts to clarify and formulate the figures, types, their action-patterns and typical interrelations, a more critical — which also means a more open-minded — assessment of their role in cultural developments such as we have already had, to a considerable extent, in systematic surveys of ancient Egypt and in studies of early Mesopotamia.

The part that the Orient played in the Grail legends and cult, the influence of this whole complex on European art and architecture, and specifically in this case the part played by that extraordinary building, the Takht-i-Taqdis so ably studied by Ringbom, is but one of many instances of the stream of constructive influences that have issued from the Ancient East since before the dawn of Western civilization, a civilization which cannot be wholly or deeply understood without repeated references and new insights into Oriental sources.

Europe found her religious faiths — Greek, Roman or Northern — intellectually, morally and emotionally insufficient and

344

gradually replaced them with Christianity, an Oriental religion, after having earlier experimented with two other Eastern religions — Mithraism and Manichaeism. Rome, at the end, was pretty thoroughly orientalized. The incessant wars of Rome and Byzantium with Persia involved much cultural interchange. It was from the Orient that Europe learned many of the refinements of life: manners, costume, music. Troubadours and Minnesingers, their songs fashioned on Oriental models, introduced chivalry and heraldry, and profoundly influenced European literature. Europe depended largely on Arabic sources for knowledge of the Classics, and owed deep debts to the Near East in various sciences: medicine, astronomy, mathematics, navigation. Persia and Armenia made important contributions to the beginnings of Gothic architecture, and the eighty thuosand Persian coins of the tenth century alone found in Scandinavia witness the lively commerce between these regions. The flow of cultural contributions from the East was considerably augmented by the Crusades, and the extravagant enthusiasm of the eighteenth century for the Arabian Nights tales is a late example of Europe's continuing thirst for the release and stimulation that Oriental imagination and emotion provided.

Hence it should not be at all surprizing that the Takht-i-Taqdis, the fabulous temple that Chosroes II built on a strange mountain-top in northwest Persia, should have been the model for the Temple of the Grail, as the complex interlocking evidence from independent sources now shows. In fact, that various legends surrounding the Grail came into Europe from the Orient can now be substantiated by a mass of detailed evidence. Dr Phyllis Ackerman, who has contributed valuable ideas to this article, is bringing to conclusion several years of intensive research on certain Oriental sources of Grail mythology, the ways and reasons for the transformations of certain Oriental myths, more or less disguised, that reappear by traceable routes in the Grail cycle.

It is urgently to be hoped that there can be arranged a thoroughly equipped scientific expedition to the site of the Takht-i-Taqdis, to see if any traces whatever remain of the fabulous temple of Chosroes. Results of both investigations will be eagerly awaited by scholars of many countries.

Notes

1 *Graal Tempel und Paradies.* Stockholm, 1951.

2 Grundsätzliches zu einer Ausgaube des Jüngeren Titurel. *Ztschr. f. dtsch. Altertum,* Bd. 79, pp.49–113, 209–248.

3 Cf. Ringbom, *op. cit.,* Chaps. I, IV.

4 Cf. Arthur Christiansen, *L'Iran sous les Sassanids.* Copenhagen, 1936: references to "Takht-i-Taqdis." Shiz also reported at some length in Arabic and Persian sources: Asma (8th, 9th century); Ibn Khurdabih (9th c.); Tabari (9th, 10th c.); Masudi (10th c.); Ibn al Faqir (10th c.); Misar (10th c.); Yaqut (13th c.); Firdausi (10th c.); al Tha'alibi (10th c.); Mustawfi (14th c.).

5 A collection of Welsh bardic tales written down in 1322: cf. Peredur Son of Efrawg, G. and T. Jones, Trans., *The Mabinogion,* Everyman, London, 1957, pp.190f, 226.

6 Reported in *Bulletin of the American Institute for Persian Art and Archeology,* Vol IV, No. 2, Dec. 1937: articles by Pope, Crane, Wilber, Ackerman, pp.71–109; 28 illustrations.

7 Published by Strzygowski (1917, 1930), Sarre (1931), Pope (1932, 1938), Ackerman (1937, 1938), Reuther (1938), Ringbom (1951). For convenient illustrations see *Art Bulletin,* XV (1933), p. 10; *Bulletin American Institute Persian Art, op. cit.,* p.107; Survey of Persian Art, Vol 1, pp 555f; Vol III, p.2702; Vol IV, pl.1381.

8 Theophanos (8th c.); Nicephoros (8th c.); Georgios Monachos (9th c.); Ado of Vienne (9th c.); Gorgious Cedrenous (11th c.), using earlier material; Tzetes (12th c.)

CHAPTER 18

Glastonbury and Fécamp

ROBERT JAFFRAY

There are two localities which are of great interest in connection
with the story of the origin and development of these legends;
and we will do well to make them the subject of some investigation; viz., Glastonbury in Somerset, and Fécamp on the coast
of Normandy.

According to an ancient tradition, Glastonbury was the site of
the earliest Christian church in Great Britain, founded by Joseph
of Arimathea, who, according to the *Grand Saint Graal* romance,
brought the Holy Grail to Great Britain. William of Malmesbury,
writing in the first half of the twelfth century, refers in his *De
Antiquitate Glastoniensis Ecclesiae* to an ancient chronicle as authority for the statement that Joseph of Arimathea with twelve companions came to England as missionaries, and built a church at
a place called *Inisgutrin* (isle of glass) by the Britons; and that
the Angles, after their conquest of the land, rendered the name
in their language as Glastynbury. The ancient description of the
place as an island appears to have arisen from the fact that in
the olden time the site was surrounded by marshes. It has been
held that the text of *De Antiquitate* contains many interpolations
and that the genuineness of this and other passages is open to
grave doubts, especially as other early historians make no reference to the statement mentioned.[1] William's work also contains
other derivations of the name Glastynbury; this seems to
support the theory that his original text may have suffered
through interpolations. Whatever may be the truth about the
interpolations, the writing referred to above has been widely
accepted as authority for the Glastonbury tradition. The church

and abbey certainly existed at a very early date, and underwent many vicissitudes in the times of the Danes and the Normans. Local struggles for supremacy brought the monks of Glastonbury into disputes with neighboring ecclesiastical authorities, and it is held that the fabrication of documents relating to the history and importance of the Glastonbury foundation was resorted to on a large scale, in order to add to its prestige; so that full credence cannot always be given to the claims which were made in its behalf. Many relics were gathered there, including the body of Joseph of Arimathea; and the place became a great resort for pilgrims. At the time when William of Malmesbury wrote, there was an old wooden church with relics — St Mary's — and a larger stone church dedicated to Saint Peter and Saint Paul; also, on a neighboring hill called the Tor, a church dedicated to St Michael. After an extensive fire in 1184, a new church of St Mary was built as a large church, and dedicated in 1186.

Giraldus Cambrensis, who lived at the end of the twelfth century and the beginning of the thirteenth century, states that in his time the bodies of King Arthur and Queen Guinevere were exhumed at Glastonbury. This appears to have occurred in or about the year 1191.

Another tradition in regard to Glastonbury is found in the *Life* of *St Gildas*, dating from about the same period. Here it is related that Melwas, or Melvas, or Maelwas, King of Somerset, abducted Guinevere and carried her to his city of Glastonbury, i.e., the "City of Glass" (*Glastonia id est urbs vitrea*). This Melwas, although here represented as an earthly King, was originally a character in Celtic mythology; his kingdom was the Isle of Glass in the Otherworld — the Isle of Avalon of Celtic mythology. William of Malmesbury had already stated that the King and Queen had been buried at Glastonbury according to local tradition, and the identifying inscription is said to have referred to the place of burial as the "Isle of Avallonia."

Leaving aside a more detailed consideration of the different theories for the origin of the name of Glastonbury or the reason why it was referred to as the Isle of Avallonia, we can accept the fact that the place was at an early date brought into close connection with the story of Joseph of Arimathea, and, later, with the careers of King Arthur and Queen Guinevere, and that it was identified with the Avalon of Celtic mythology, i.e., the Otherworld.

From very early times there had existed among the Celts the belief in a Happy Otherworld — in one sense the abode of the dead, and yet also considered as a place to which mortals might go without dying, but from which they could not return alive to earth. The conception was not clearly fixed; there were many variations. One of them made it a Land of Women. It was always a place where heat and cold and illness and fatigue were unknown. The measures of time disappeared there. It was represented as an island lying in the distant sea, towards the West. It was sometimes called the Isle of Glass.

As far back as the seventh or eighth century this idea was shown in the ancient Irish tale *The Voyage of Bran Son of Febal* who was tempted by a strange woman to make a voyage over the seas to a distant island, the Land of Women, where there was no sickness, no unhappiness, no death. Bran stayed there for a period which seemed to be a year, but was really many years. In this case the visitor was enabled to return, but after he told of his adventures nothing more is known of him.[2]

A search for the antecedents of the idea of the Happy Otherworld would take us beyond the scope of our present subject; and the development of the idea in medieval times would of itself prove to be a subject of wide extent and great intricacy. For our present purpose it is sufficient to note the fact that there are many allusions to this Happy Otherworld in the Arthurian romances. Some of these show a more or less clear connection with Glastonbury. Chrétien's *Érec et Énide,* the earliest known of all the Arthurian romances, speaks of it as the *Isle de Voirre* (isle of glass) over which Maheloas reigned. It was a place where heat and cold, and tempest were unknown. The same author's Lancelot (called also *Le Conte de la Charette* or *Le Chevalier de la Charette)* tells of the rescue, at the hands of Lancelot, of Queen Guinevere, who had been abducted by Méléagant, son of King Bademagu of the land of Gorre whose chief city was Bade (Bath, in Somerset). Méléagant carried her to his country which is described as difficult of access, whence return was reported to be impossible. The similar incident in the *Life of St Gildas,* mentioned above, gives the abductor's name as Melwas, and the place of imprisonment as the City of Glass. All these rulers,

Maheloas, Méléagant, and Melwas, are held to indicate the same character, i.e., the King, or Prince, of the Dead.[3]

Other allusions in the romances deal with the mystery and enchantment of the Otherworld without connecting it with any particular locality.

Chrétien tells of Gawain's visit to an enchanted castle in a land whence people could not return, and where he was told that he must remain; but he broke the spell and was able to proceed. Wolfram related a similar incident at the Castle of Marvels built by the magician Klingsor, wherein were imprisoned numerous beautiful maidens. In the romance *Die Krone* Gawain visits Meideland, an isle of women. There are also instances in other stories, not mentioned in these pages, where Gawain is represented as visiting Fairyland. In the *Lanzelet* it is related that the infant Lancelot was carried away by a fairy queen to her kingdom of Meide-lant which was inhabited only by women; and there the boy was kept until he was fifteen years old. The *Prose Lancelot* includes practically the same incident, the fairy being named Viviane, The Lady of the Lake. The conception of the Otherworld was an unfailing source of material for the embellishment of these romances.

It is quite possible that the identification of Glastonbury with Avalon may have been due to the inventions of the monks, who, familiar with the Arthurian material, desired thus to glorify their place of residence. This result might have been reached by making interpolations in the work of William of Malmesbury (as mentioned above), or by inventing the story of the exhumation of the bodies of Arthur and Guinevere. A widely current belief existed that Arthur was not really dead. Geoffrey of Monmouth had stated that the great king had been taken mortally wounded to the island of Avalon to be healed. Wace, in his chronicle, repeated this statement, and also referred to the expectation that Arthur would return in course of time. Layamon stated that in Avalon he would be in the care of Argante[4] the Queen of Elves, and that he would be healed and would again come to his kingdom. Among the romances, as well as among the chronicles, we find some references of a similar character. The *Didot Perceval* leaves Arthur wounded at Avalon. The French *Mort Artu* relates that the king was carried away in a boat filled with women headed by Morgain la Fée, but does not mention Avalon. The

English *Morte Arthure* (of later date but deriving from an early French original) says he went to Avalon to be healed; and it states that he was buried at Glastonbury. Finally, the *Perlesvaus* alludes to Guinevere's tomb at Avalon; and the author states that the Latin original of his text was found in a holy house of religion in the island of Avalon. There is evidence to indicate that the monastery at Glastonbury was here referred to.[5]

But the special interest of Glastonbury is not alone in its identification with Avalon. The reputed visit of Joseph of Arimathea with his disciples, and the presence of his body there in company with other sacred relics, are important features in the record of that ancient abbey. Whatever may be our opinion of the historical accuracy of the claim for the personal presence of Joseph there, and the construction of the church, we can at least find some foundation for the belief that his body may have been brought there in the course of time. The *Chronicles of Senones* (Sens), dating from the early part of the thirteenth century, relate that Fortunat, patriarch of Grado, having made a pilgrimage to the East, was compelled to take refuge at the monastery of Moyenmoutier in the Vosges Mountains, and that he received a warm welcome there on account of the relics which he brought from the Holy Land, including the body of Joseph of Arimathea.

At a later time the body of Joseph was taken away by "strange monks." The visit of Fortunat was in the time of Charlemagne; and the writer of these *Chronicles* (Richer) states that the removal of Joseph's body appears to have taken place before the end of the tenth century. There does not seem to be any direct evidence that the relic was then taken to Glastonbury, but the reference to the "strange monks" and the persistence of the Glastonbury tradition, are considered to give some grounds for believing that this was the case.[6]

In connection with Joseph's visit to Great Britain it is related that his staff was planted and grew into the holy thorn bush on a hill near Glastonbury, and that he brought with him the blood which was taken from the Saviour's wounds. The latter one of these incidents necessitates reference to the Abbey at Fécamp, with which the legend of the Holy Blood is closely associated.[7] This legend may be briefly told as follows:

When the Saviour's body was removed from the Cross by

Joseph and Nicodemus, they scraped with a knife the blood which had dried on the wounds. At the death of Nicodemus he gave the blood to his nephew Isaac for safe-keeping. Isaac's wife was a Jewess; and, seeing her husband performing his devotions before his precious possession, she accused him of idolatry. Removing from Jerusalem to Sidon on this account, he learned there in a vision that Jerusalem would soon be destroyed; so he took two tubes of lead and placed therein the blood and the knife, and concealed them in the trunk of a fig-tree. The fissure in the tree closed up as by a miracle. Later, he was led by God to cut down the tree and cast it into the sea, and it was carried by God's care to the neighborhood of Fécamp on the northern coast of France. Here three saplings sprouted which were transplanted by a holy man living in the vicinity, but the trunk itself could not be moved. Later, an angel, disguised as a pilgrim, removed the trunk to another spot, where, at a time which appears to have been about the beginning of the sixth century, it manifested a miraculous power. A white stag, hunted by hounds, stood at bay by this tree-trunk, and neither the hounds nor the horses of the hunters would come near. The chief hunter, Duke Anségis, greatly astonished, prayed to God for an explanation of this wonder, and was led to erect a chapel on that spot. Years afterward, about 662, a new church and abbey were erected by St Wanninge (Waningus), to whom the story of the tree was revealed in a vision. The buildings were destroyed in one of the invasions of the Northmen, but they were rebuilt by William, son of Rollo, Duke of Normandy. William's son, Richard I, again rebuilt the church on a greater scale towards the end of the tenth century, and re-established the monastic discipline which had become demoralized. Having examined the archives of the abbey, he found there the tale of miracles which had been wrought by the Holy Blood. He discovered the trunk of the fig-tree, placed it in the wall of the church, and deposited the relic itself under a pillar near the altar. The chalice and paten in which the elements had been placed were taken to Fécamp. In the year 1171 Henry de Sully, fifth abbot of Fécamp, took all the holy relics from their hiding places and placed them on the altar.

It would be futile to attempt to draw the line between history and legend in the account of the many miracles which are recorded in connection with the relic; but there appears to be no doubt that the Holy Blood was a well-known relic at the abbey in the early part of the twelfth century, and that traditions about its early miraculous history were then in existence. The monastery flourished under Richard's successors, and was well-known throughout Europe.

In Wauchier's continuation of Chrétien's *Perceval*, where the visit of Perceval to Mont Dolorous is related, there is in several of the manuscripts a passage in which Wauchier refers for his authority to a tale which existed in writing at Fécamp. This may be only one of those mysterious references to unknown sources which are so common in these medieval writings, and which do not commend themselves to critical judgement in respect to their genuineness. On the other hand, this passage may be a trustworthy indication of the existence at that time of some literary work whose value would now be beyond measure. If the latter is the case, the fact that it is mentioned in a Grail story as corroborating that narrative seems to indicate that the Fécamp document dealt with this legend; and it needs no stretch of imagination to see that at the place where the legend of the Holy Blood had long been particularly located, there might be a special interest in the legend of the vessel in which the blood had been contained; and the surroundings would be favorable for the consideration and development of this latter legend.

Notes

1 Cf. *William of Malmesbury,* etc., by W.W. Newell in Publications of Modern Language Association, vol. xviii (1903).

2 Cf. *The Voyage of Bran,* by A. Nutt, London, Grimm's Library, vols. iv and vi.

3 Cf. *Melwas Roi des Morts,* article by Ferdinand Lot in *Romania,* vol.xxiv.

4 Argante-Morgana-Morgain la Fée, "the Fairy Queen of Arthurian legend;" see Miss Lucy Allen Paton's *Studies on the Fairy Mythology of Arthurian Romances,* Radcliffe College Monograph 13. Miss Paton discusses Morgain, the Lady of the Lake, and Niniane (Viviane). Morgain is the only one of the three who is found in other than Arthurian literature. The Lady of the Lake and Niniane are sometimes confused. Miss Paton holds that the three fairies do not represent the same mythical conception, but that they were originally three distinct beings.

5 Cf. *Glastonbury the Holy Grail,* article by W.A. Nitze in *Modern Philology,* Vol.1.

6 Cf. *Le Saint Graal,* article by P. Paris in *Romania,* vol.i.

7 Cf. *Essai sur l'abbaye de Fécamp,* by Le Roux de Lincy, Rouen, 1840.

PART THREE

The Continuing Search

The Continuing Search

In our own time the Story of the Grail has once again become hugely popular, with dozens of new books and studies appearing every year. With the revival of interest in mysticism and spirituality that has dominated much of the last thirty years, the Grail has become the focus for a new questing spirit, which continues to lead pilgrims in search of many possible Grails — both physical and spiritual. The selection of chapters that constitutes this final section of the book, concentrates on some of the furthest reaching and deepest of the works that have both charted and contributed to this resurgence of interest in the Grail and its secrets.

We begin with a chapter from A.E. Waite's book *The Hidden Church of the Holy Graal* (1909), which sets the tone for much of what has been written on the mystical history of the Grail in the last century. Waite is perhaps best known today for his involvement in the Hermetic Order of the Golden Dawn, an esoteric society that did more than any other to bring the subjects of magic, alchemy and other arcane aspects of the mystical discipline out of the darkness of the Middle Ages and into the light of modern scholarship. Waite's own work ranged from books on the Kabalah to Freemasonry, but he wrote two books dedicated to exploring the inner history of the Grail, in which he set out to show that a hidden, mystical Church existed within orthodox Christianity. His works influenced several generations of writers who came after, including Jessie Weston, Francis Rolt-Wheeler and Charles Williams, whose own cycles of Arthurian poems *Taliesin Through Logres* (1938) and *The Region of the Summer Stars* (1944) are among the finest works on the Grail ever written. Waite himself wrote in a heavy and sometimes difficult style — prompted partly by his desire to show the seriousness of his subject matter — but his knowledge of the sources was profound, and his perceptions often deep. Anyone wishing to seriously study the inner history of the Grail should have recourse to his books.

This is followed by three chapters that, each in their own way, explore the ritual aspect of the Grail's history. The first of these: "The Holy Grail: Qui on en Servoit?" ("Whom Does it Serve?") by D. Swinscow, actually rejects the Ritual theory in favour of a more pragmatic, psychological interpretation. Indeed, having examined the symbolic resonances of the Quest itself, the Wounded King and the mysterious Question, Swinscow refers to the words of Christ: Ask, and you shall be given — a statement that, he notes, is found nowhere else in the revealed religions of West or East. At another juncture he suggests that the pre-Christian, folk-loric sources should be dismissed, and that the legends are primarily Christian — noting, however, that the Grail has yet to be admitted to the canon of officially recognized relics. An odd fact in itself, as there was such a trade in relic hunting during the Middle Ages, with various Abbeys and Cathedrals vying with each other for possession of various pieces of the True Cross, or the bones of various saints. To be sure, Glastonbury Abbey claimed the bones of Arthur (among others) and successfully financed a rebuilding programme with the resulting rush of pilgrims, but even they did not claim the Grail — recognizing that if it existed at all, and that even if it had been kept there, it was no longer present.

Robert Crutwell, whose article follows, has no reservations about the ritual pattern present within the Grail texts. He sets forth a carefully worked out argument, based on the sources themselves, and finds a distinct and recognizable resonance within the stories of the Grail and the figure of the Maze or Labyrinth — a symbol rich in symbolic application from Classical times that continued to exert a strong fascination into the Middle Ages (as witness the great pavement maze in Chartres Cathedral). From this Crutwell admirably establishes the ritual shape of the Grail myths.

Following this we advance to the work of Jessie Weston, one of the foremost Arthurian scholars of the early twentieth century. Her work numbered many volumes, translations (of which several are featured in this collection), as well as essays on almost every aspect of the legends. Her work has had a wide and continuing influence on several generations of scholars and writers, not least T.S. Eliot who drew heavily on her writings for the Grail symbolism of his poem "The Waste Land."

In the paper reprinted here, which was first read at a meeting of the Folk Lore Society in 1906, Miss Weston examines the Grail with reference to the rites and ritual associated with the Greek God Adonis. Here she finds strong parallels between the Wounded Fisher King and the Wounded God, and shows that not only are the words "ritual" and "mystery" appropriately applied to the subject of the Grail, but that the common factor in both stories is that they are "Cults of Life," both bestowing the largess of spiritual nourishment.

D.F. de l'Hoste Ranking, in another paper originally read to the Folk-Lore society (in 1917), turns to the history of the Knights Templar for inspiration. The Templars — whose name reflects the title "Templiesen" given to the guardians of the Grail in Wolfram von Eschenbach's *Parzival* — were originally founded in 1119 to offer protection to pilgrims travelling to the Holy Land. However, during the next two hundred years they became one of the most powerful organizations in Christendom — bankers to most of the crowned heads of the West, and the official "Soldiers of Christ," the military arm of the Church of Rome. This brought its own price, and the order was brought down, under the accusations of heresy and evil practices in 1312. Rumours have persisted ever since that the Order possessed the secrets of the Grail, and that when they fell into disrepute they took the mystery with them. Much ink has been spilled in attempting to prove this, and it certainly forms an interesting link in the chain of the Grail's inner history — though it must be said that little firm evidence exists to prove the theory, which remains no more than that. Ranking's account and his conclusions are, none the less, fascinating, and he puts his case with passion and anchors it firmly within the textual sources.

There are many fine works of fiction and poetry that derive their inspiration from the story of the Grail. To have included even a reasonable selection of these would have more than doubled the length of the manuscript. I have therefore elected to include just a handful of representative texts of this kind, choosing each one both for its intrinsic merits and for its position within the ongoing canon of the Grail. Three specific works are included here: The *Quest for the Sangraal* by Robert Stephen Hawker, *Percival at Corbenic* by Rachel Anand Taylor (which forms a brief prelude to the entire collection), and *The Mass of the Sangreal* by Arthur Machen. Each of these, in its own way, has contributed to the vision of the Grail that informs this collection.

Robert Stephen Hawker (1803–75) the eccentric vicar of Morwenstow in Cornwall, published his mystical poem *The Quest of the Sangraal* in 1864. Despite drawing on Malory for its basic story it departs considerably from the original, and concentrates on just four seekers: Lancelot, Galahad, Perceval and (surprisingly) Tristan, who were each destined to seek the Grail in four quadrants of the world. Only the first of a projected quartet was published, gaining some notice after the huge success of Tennyson's *Idylls of the King,* but Hawker wrote no more that has survived. He was somewhat embittered by Tennyson's success, having discussed Arthurian matters at length with the Poet Laureate and lent him books and manuscripts relating to the Grail and the Quest. The poem itself reads surprisingly well today, thanks largely to its rough-hewn rhythms and highly mystical vision. The last part of the poem, a series of visions of the future called up for Arthur by Merlin, are apocalyptic and obscure, while his vision of the Grail is based on a considerable knowledge of the texts and commentaries of the day. Hawker's poem certainly influenced the far more important work of Charles Williams which followed some seventy years later.

Perronik the Innocent, which follows here, is one of the most unusual pieces in this collection. The origins of the story are unclear, though it has been circulating as a folk-tale in Brittany since at least the end of the eighteenth century. Several versions have appeared since then, including this one by the American writer Kenneth Sylvan Guthrie. The brief introduction to the original edition (omitted here) mentions his own search for the original site of the mystical palace of "Ker-Glas," which he found in 1914 to be located near Vannes on the Elven Road (sic) at Chateau de Porhoet. The story very clearly derives from Chrétien and others, though its hero's name has metamorphosed into the Breton-sounding Perronik. Guthrie's own version is translated from the great Breton folk-lorist Emile Souverstre, and though a late composition it may well preserve some details from a more primitive version of the Quest. Certainly the Golden Basin and the Diamond Lance possess a more Celtic resonance, and Perronik's wanderings take him into an Otherworld landscape peopled by faery folk.

Francis Rolt-Wheeler's book *Mystic Gleams from the Holy Grail* is, to my mind, one of the most interesting products of the renewed interest in the Grail among the esoteric fraternity of Europe. Rolt-Wheeler, originally from Ireland, settled in the South of France in the 1930s and there came upon materials relating to the heretical sect known as the Cathars. Outlawed and finally suppressed during the Middle Ages, there were persistent rumours (which have still failed to die out) that the Cathars possessed the secret teachings of the Grail — if not the Grail itself — and that they had hidden either documents or the priceless relic itself in the caves below their stronghold at Montségur. So persistent were these rumours that an association was founded in 1937 called *Les Amis de Montségur et du Saint Graal,* which numbered among its ranks the anthropologist Maurice Magre, the historian and Grail scholar René Nelli and a schoolmaster from Ussat-les-Bains named Antonin Gadal, who was to found his own organization, the *Lectorium Rosicrucianum,* some years later. Rolt-Wheeler became the secretary of the *Amis* and worked assiduously to promote interest in the connections between the Grail and the Cathars. His book makes little mention of them however, but concentrates instead on the more general mysticism of the story. Three extracts are reprinted here, one from each of the three sections of the book. They deal with the miraculous, the faery and the chivalric mysteries and explore the interior landscape of the Quest in a highly unorthodox fashion. The whole book is of considerable interest for those who wish to pursue the Grail search in our own time, and it is hoped that it will be reprinted in its entirety in the near future.

Isabel Wyatt's chapter "The Arthurian Pilgrimage to the Grail" continues this inner circuit of the Grail lands. Her work draws heavily on Anthroposophy and the works of Rudolf Steiner, whose own vision of the Grail is no small contribution to the literature of the subject. The chapter reprinted here comes from her interesting book *From Round Table to Grail Castle.* Her other books include work on the *Chymical Wedding of Christian Rosenkreutz* and the esoteric mysteries of Shakespeare, as well as

361

many plays, poems and stories for children. Retelling the central story of the Grail in her own words she goes on to explore the implications of this in the light of Steiner's view of the inner history of mankind, the links with both the Cathars and the Templars, and the significance of all these forces upon the development of the human spirit.

This is followed by Arthur Machen's luminous story "The Mass of the Sangraal." Machen (1863–1947) was a mystic, an actor, a journalist and a novelist whose works influenced both Charles Williams and C.S. Lewis. He wrote extensively of the Grail, which he saw as "the glorified version of early Celtic Sacramental Legends" and as an expression of the numinous teachings of the outlawed Celtic Church. He was much influenced by the works of A.E. Waite, whose mystical interpretation of the Hidden Church (see Chapter 19) he found much to his taste. The magical power of his novels *The Great Return* (1915) and *The Secret Glory* (1922) still make enjoyable reading today.

In recent years several writers have drawn attention to some all but forgotten connections between the Grail tradition and the early history of the Americas. In particular, two fascinating studies *The Holy Grail Across the Atlantic* (1988) by Michael Bradley and Deanna Theilmann-Bean, and *The Sword and the Grail* (1994) by Andrew Sinclair, have explored some unusual evidence suggesting that members of the outlawed Templar Order may have taken flight to the continent of America some ninety years before Christopher Columbus reached its shores, and that they took with them the secrets of the Grail. In the final chapter of this collection, the American scholar Ari Berk, in a newly commissioned article, takes the story of the Grail into a further dimension of this new direction in the long history of this most holy of relics, finding within the symbolism and story-telling of the Native American peoples some new and fascinating resonances.

This brings the current collection to an end. But is by no means the end of the story. The fascination with the Grail shows no sign of diminishing, and books continue to be produced which explore ever new and fascinating aspects of the story. Whether or not we shall ever discover the true origin of this theme, remains doubtful — nor is it, perhaps, ultimately needful that we should do so. The Grail remains a powerful symbol of the numinous and the mystical for seekers of our own time just as of the past. New discoveries will certainly be made, but the truths embodied in and by the Grail can only transcend time and space, as they have ever done and as they will continue to do as long as seekers after such truths continue to set forth in Quest of this holiest of relics.

CHAPTER 19

Mystic Aspects of the Graal Legend

A.E. WAITE

I. The Introductory Words

Seeing that we have not found in the Celtic Church anything which suffices to explain the chief implicits of the literature and that the watchwords call us forward, there remains another method of research, and of this I will now proceed to make trial. I suppose that there is no need to exhibit in formal words after what manner the Quest of the Holy Graal became in the later texts a religious experiment, and thus justified the titles from which it began in that story of Robert de Borron which is the earliest extant history. Any one who has proceeded so far in the present inquisition as to have reached these lines — even if he is wholly unfamiliar with the old treasury of books — will be aware that the Quest was ruled throughout by the counsels of perfection. These ruled in fact so strongly as to have reached that stage when two of them were implied only — that is, they were taken for granted: (a) Voluntary poverty, for the knights possessed nothing, and what ever came into their hands was distributed there and then; (b) entire obedience, in dedication to the proposed term, and all the ships of the world burnt with fire behind them; when change came there followed complete *avortement*, as that of Gawain in the Great Quest; (c) perpetual chastity, as the only counsel which stands declared — and in this connection it will be remembered that Bors returned to Logres. The zeal of these counsels does not appear — as I have said — to guarantee election utterly: it is rather the test of merit. And I have said also that there may be a certain success without their fulfilment in the absolute degree. In the *Longer Prose Perceval* Gawain received signal favours, yet it is admitted that he was wanting in purity, and hence he could make no response when the questionable mystery appeared once in his presence. The King also beheld the arch-natural Eucharist on the manifested side thereof: but Perceval alone possessed the plenary qualifications in this text. On the other hand, in the story of stories there was one who surpassed him, but not so utterly that they were otherwise than classed together as companions of the Quest. The distinction seems to have been that Galahad dissolved temptation, as one more than human. Perceval carried within him the latent desires of the body, and after beholding the Graal he required the purgation of a hermit's life before he entered into the true inheritance of those thrones which are above. By some of my fellowship in research it has been said most truly, though they do not understand Galahad, that the *haut prince* was just as fit for the Quest at its beginning as he was at its end. Now, that is exactly the sign of perfect vocation — of election as well as calling; the criterion of those who are meant for heaven is that they might ascend thither at any moment. Another test of Galahad was that he knew really from the beginning the whole mystery by the tradition thereof.

I am enumerating here the general implicits of the subject which should be latent in the minds of those whom I address; they do not constitute a question put forward for sifting with a view to a settlement, but of fitness and power to see — of the *verus certusque intuitus animi,* in some degree and proportion. This being passed by those who can suffer the ruling, it will be obvious that the religious experiment about which I begin to speak can depend only from two considerations: (1) the attainment of the sanctified state in the Questing Knights, and (2) the descent of a peculiar Grace upon them. I enumerate both points, though it is obvious that one of them has in another form but now passed through review, but in dealing with a very difficult subject it is necessary to look at it in more than a single light, and I wish to make it clear that the specifics of the sanctified state — by which I mean the counsels of perfection — are not things that are determined in the given case by a trend of thought and emotion at the given period, and are not therefore to be dismissed as a presentation of the ascetic life or as the definition of canons which have now passed into desuetude. The same experiment always demands the same conditions for its success, and to set aside these is really to renounce that, or in this instance it is to reject the experiment as one of the old ecstasies which never came to a term. On the contrary, the experiment of sanctity is always approximating to a term, and the measure of success is the measure of zeal in its pursuit. I propose therefore to look a little closer at one of the counsels of perfection. The essential point regarding the condition of *virgo intacta* — not in respect of the simple physical fact, which has no inherent sanctity, but in respect of its conscious acceptance at what cost soever — is that there neither was nor can be a more perfect symbol of the prepared matter of the work. It is the analogy in utter transcendence of that old adage: *Mens sana in corpore sano*, and its nearest expression is: *Anima immaculata in corpore dedicato, ex hoc nunc et usque, &c.* In other words, the banns of marriage in the higher degrees cannot be proclaimed till the contracting parties are warranted in their respective orders to have that proportion and likeness apart from which no union could be effected. The consummated grade of sanctity is an intimate state of union, and the nearest analogy thereto is found in human marriage; as the latter presupposes in the sacramental order an antecedent or nominal purity, and has for its object the consecration of intercourse which in its absence is of the animal kind, so the antecedent condition in sanctity — or the life of perfect dedication — is in correspondence with the state of *virgo intacta*. I need not say that because these things are analogical so the discourse concerning them partakes of the language of symbolism or that the state itself is a spiritual state. Entire obedience involves no earthly master; voluntary poverty is of all possibility in a palace, and the law would not deny it at the headquarters of an American Trust; as regards chastity, that is guaranteed to those who receive the sacrament of marriage worthily, and it is to be noted that this sacrament differs from baptism, which is administered once and for all, while marriage, in the effects thereof, is administered in continuity as an abiding presence and a grace abounding daily so long as its covenants are observed. On the other hand, the perpetuity of spiritual chastity in the life within does not mean of necessity that man or woman has never known flesh in the physical order. Galahad in the story had the outward signs as well as the inward grace. His Quest was an allegory throughout and sometimes the allegorical motive obtrudes into the expressed matter, which is an error of art.

The term which is proposed in the Quest, as the consideration thereof, will be best given in the words of the Quest itself:

> Now at the yeres ende and the self daye after Galahad
> had borne the croune of gold, he arose up erly and his
> felawes, and came to the palais, and sawe to fore hem the
> holy vessel, and a man knelynge on his knees in lykenes
> of a Bisshop that had aboute hym a grete felaushyp of
> Angels as it had ben Jhesu Cryst hym self, & thenne he
> arose and beganne a masse of oure lady. And whan he
> cam to the sacrament of the masse, and had done, anone
> he called Galahad and sayd to hym, come forthe the
> servaunt of Jhesu Cryst and thou shalt see that thou hast
> moche desyred to see, & thenne he began to tremble
> ryght hard, when the dedely flesshe beganne to beholde
> the spyrytuel thynges. Thenne he held vp his handes
> toward heuen and sayd, lord I thanke the, for now I see
> that that hath ben my desyre many a daye. Now blessyd
> lord wold I not lenger lyue yf it myghte please the lord,
> & there with the good man tooke our lordes body
> betwixe hys handes, and profered it to Galahad, and he
> receyued hit ryghte gladly and mekely ... And there with
> he kneled doune to fore the table, and made his prayers,
> and thenne sodenly his soule departed to Jhesu Crist and
> a grete multitude of Angels bare his soule vp to heuen ...

In this citation the most important point for our purpose at the living moment rests neither in that which it expresses nor in that which it conceals: it is assumed and realized that such a term is always hidden because it always exceeds expression, and is the closer veiled wherein it is announced the most. But here was the consummation of all, and here was that more open seeing than was granted at Corbenic wherein all the outward offices of things archnatural were set aside utterly. Herein

367

therefore was no vision of transubstantiation changes, and as evidence that this was of concert and not of chance, I have the same report to make concerning the *Longer Prose Perceval;* when the questing knight comes to his own therein no signs and wonders are connected with the Holy Graal. As regards the vision itself, we may remember the words of Nasciens when he attempted to penetrate the secrets within the new Ark of the Covenant. *"Et Nasciens dist que il l'en descouverroit tant comme nule mortieus langue em porroit descouvrir, ne deveroit. Je ai, dist-il, véut la coumenchaille dou grant hardiment, l'ocoison des grans savoirs, le fondement des grans religions, le dessevrement des grans félonnies, la démoustranche des grans mierveilles, la mervelle de totes les altrez mervelles, la fin des bontés et des gentillèces vraies."* This extract from the *Book of the Holy Graal* is thus rendered in the halting measures of Lovelich:

> "I have sein,' quod the sire Nasciens,
> Of alle manere of wykkednesse the defens;
> Of alle boldnesse I have sene the begynneng,
> Of all wittes the fowndyng.
> I have sein the begynneng of Religeown
> And of alle bowntes, bothe al & som,
> And the poyntes of alle gentrye,
> And a merveil of alle merveilles certeinlye."

Other masters have expressed the same wonder in other terms, which are the same — as, for example: *quaedam praelibatio aeternae vitae, gustus et suavitas spiritualis, mentis in Deum suspensa elevatio,* &c.

The qualifications of Galahad and Perceval in the Great Quest are not therefore things which are the fashion of a period, like some aspects of what is termed the ascetic mind, but they obtain from *Aleph* to *Tau,* through all grades of expression. Those who speak of the ethical superiority of the *Parsifal* are saying that which, in all moderation and tenderness, signifies that they are still learning the elements of true discipline.

I have now dealt with the indispensable warrants of the state, and the mode of the descent of Grace belongs to the same category; it was a manifestation to the spiritual flowers of Christian knighthood through the Eucharist — the form of symbolism made use of for this purpose being that of transubstantiation. I have already set down what I believe to be the Divine Truth on this subject, but here again we must as our research proceeds approach it from various standpoints; and, for the rest, it must be obvious that of all men I at least should have no call imposed on me to speak of the Holy Graal were it not for its connection with the Blessed Sacrament. It is the passage of the putative reliquary into the Chalice of the Eucharist, the progressive exaltation of its cultus and the consequent transfiguration of the Quest which have substituted insensibly a tale of eternity for a medieval legend of the Precious Blood; in place of the Abbey of Fécamp, we have Corbenic and Mont Salvatch shining in the high distance, and where once there abode only the suggestion of some relative and rather trivial devotion, we have the presence of that great sign behind which there lies the Beginning and the End of all things.

The romance-writers, seeking in their symbolism a reduction to the evidence of the senses, selected and exaggerated the least desirable side of Eucharistic dogma; but we have no occasion to dispute with them on that score, seeing that — for the skilled craftsman — any material will serve in the purposes of the Great Work. The only point which stands out for our consideration is that — following the sense of all doctrine and the testimony of all experience — the gate by which faith presses into realization is the gate of that Sacrament from which all others depend — of that Sacrament the institution of which was the last act of Christ and the term of His ministry; thereafter He suffered only until He rose in glory. When therefore the makers of the Graal books designed to show after what manner, and under what circumstances, those who were still in flesh could behold the spiritual things and have opened for them that door of understanding which, according to the keepers of the Old Law, was not opened for Moses, they had no choice in the matter, and it is for this reason that they represent the Bread of Life and the Chalice of the Everlasting Testament as being lifted up in the secret places of Logres, even in the *palais espiriteux*.

Hereof are the mystic aspects of the Great Quest, and it seems to follow that the secret temple of the soul was entered by those who dwelt in the world of romance as by those in the world of learning. The adepts of both schools were saying the same thing at the same period, seeing that during the twelfth and thirteenth centuries, which moved and had their being under the wonderful aegis of the scholastic mind, there began to arise over the intellectual horizon of Europe the light of another experience than that of spiritual truth realized intellectually; this was the experience of the mystic life, which opened — shall we say? — with the name of Bonaventura and closed for the period in question with that of Ruysbroeck.

II. The Position of the Literature Defined

The books of the Holy Graal are either purely of literary, antiquarian and mythological interest, or they are more. If literary, antiquarian and mythological only, they can and should be left to the antiquaries, the critics and the folk-lore societies. But if more it is not improbable antecedently, having regard to the subject, that the excess belongs to the mystics, and to those generally who recognize that the legends of the soul are met with in many places, often unexpectedly enough, and wherever found that they have issues outside that which is understood commonly and critically by the origin of religious belief. The ascetic and mystic element — to repeat the conventional description — outside the considerations which I have put forward, is for those of all importance, and it is otherwise and invariably the only thing that is really vital in legends. The impression which is left upon the mind after the conclusions of the last subsection is assuredly that the "divine event" is not especially, or not only, that "towards which creation moves," but a term, both here and now, towards which souls can approximate and wherein they can rest at the centre. Over the threshold of the Galahad Quest we pass as if out of worlds of enchantment, worlds of faerie, worlds of the mighty Morgan le Fay, into realms of allegory and dual meaning, and then — transcending allegory — into a region more deeply unrealized; so also, after having reflected on the external side of the romances and the preliminary analogies of things that are inward, we pass, as we approach the end of our research, into a world of which nothing but the veils and their emblazonments have been so far declared. No other romances of chivalry exhibit the characteristics which we discern in the perfect and rectified books of the Holy Graal, but if we do not know categorically why romance came to be the vehicle for one expression of man's highest experience, we have reasons — and more than enough — to determine that it was not automatic, not arbitrary, and yet it was not fortuitous; it came about in the nature of things by the successive exaltation of a legend which had the capacity for exaltation into transcendence. The genesis of the story of Galahad is not like the institution of the ritual belonging to the third craft grade in Masonry, which seems without antecedents that are traceable in the elements actual or symbolical — of the early building guilds. By successive steps the legend of the Graal was built till it reached that height when the hierarchies could begin to come down and the soul of Galahad could go up. It is important for my own purpose to establish this fact, because in that which remains to be said I must guard against the supposition that a conventional secret society or a sect took over the romances, edited them and interpenetrated the texts with mystic elements. That is the kind of hypothesis which occult interests might have manufactured sincerely enough in the old days, and it would have had a certain warrant because there is ample evidence that this is exactly the kind of work which in given cases was performed by the concealed orders. The Graal, as a literature, came into other hands, which worked after their own manner, and worked well.

There is another fact which is not less important because of certain tendencies recognisable in modern criticism. I will mention it only at the moment, that the reader may be put on his guard mentally; there is no single text in the literature which was or could have been put forward as a veiled *pronunciamento* against the reigning Church on the part of any historical sect, heresy, or rival orthodoxy. The pure Christianities and the incipient principles of reform took their quack processes into other quarters. The voices which spoke in the books of the Holy Graal as no voices had ever spoken in romance were not putting forward a mystery which was superior specifically to the mysteries preserved by the official Church. They trended in the same direction as the highest inquisitions move, and that invariably. The most intelligent of all the heresies is only the truth of the Church foreshadowed or travestied. The reforms of the Church are only its essential lights variously refracted. Even modern science, outside the true prerogatives of its election as our growing physical providence, is the notification of the things which do not ultimately matter in comparison with the science of the Church, which is that of the laws ruling in the search after the eternal reality. The Graal at its highest is the simulacrum or effigy of the Divine Mystery within the Church. If she, as an institution, has failed so far — and as to the failure within limits there is no question — to accomplish the transmutation of humanity, the explanation is not merely that she has been at work upon gross and refractory elements — though this is true assuredly — but that in the great mystery of her development she has still to enter into the fruition of her higher consciousness. Hereof are the wounds of the Church, and for this reason she has been in sorrow throughout the ages.

So far I have defined, but in one sense only, the position of the literature. It remains to be said that what I have termed from the beginning the major implicits, as they project vaguely and evasively upon the surface, are integral elements of the mystic aspects. But they must be taken here in connection with one feature of the quests which is in no sense implied, because this will concern us in a very important manner in the next book. I refer to the Recession of the Graal. I have no need to remind any one after so many enumerations that the final testimony of all the French Quests is that, in one or another way, the Graal was withdrawn. It is not always by a removal in space; it is not always by assumption to heaven. In the German cycle the Temple was inaccessible from the beginning and the Palladium never travelled, till — once and for all — it was carried in a great procession to the furthest East. Wolfram left it in primeval concealment; but this did not satisfy one of the later poets, who married — as we have seen — the Graal legend to that of Prester John. Now, it might be more easy to attain translation, like St Paul, than to find that sanctuary in India where, by the assumption, it must be supposed to remain. But having regard to the hidden meaning which seems to lie behind Wolfram's source he was within the measures of his symbolism when he left the Graal at Mont Salvatch, not removing to the East that which in his case did not come therefrom. Albrecht, who tells of the transit, first took the precaution to change the hallowed object. I believe that the testimony to removal was inherent to the whole conception from the beginning, concurrently with the Secret Words, and that the latter were reflected at a later period into the peculiar claim concerning sacerdotal succession. They were all Eucharistic in their nature. The testimony itself is twofold, because, in addition to the withdrawal of the Living Sign, the texts tell us of the House that is emptied of its Hallows; these are in particular the *Longer Prose Perceval* and the *Quest of Galahad*. There is also Manessier's conclusion of the *Conte del Graal,* but no very important inference is to be drawn therefrom. One of our immediate concerns will be to find the analogies of this prevailing conception elsewhere in the world; the present study of Graal mystic aspects is simply preliminary thereto, and the eduction of the significance behind the major implicits. It is at this point curiously that one element of Graal history which has been somehow ascribed to Guiot comes to our assistance, providing an intermediary between the literature of mystical romance and — as we shall learn — the obvious text-books of the secret schools. It opens, I think, strange vistas of intellectual wonder and enchantment. We have heard already that the Stone which is identified with the Graal in Wolfram was at one time a stone in the crown of Lucifer, and seeing that, according to other legends, the thrones left vacant by the fallen angels are reserved for human souls, it becomes intelligible why the Graal was brought to earth and what is signified by the mystic jewel. The Stone in the crown of Lucifer symbolizes the great estate from which the archangel fell. It was held by the fathers of the Church that, when still in the delights of Paradise, Lucifer was adorned by all manner of precious stones, under-standing mystically of him what in the text of the prophet Ezekiel is said literally of the Prince of Tyre: *In deliciis paradisi Dei fuisti; omnis lapis preciosus operimentum tuum: sardius, topazius, et jaspis, chrysolithus, et onyx, et beryllus, sapphirus, et carbunculus, et smaragdus* — nine kinds of stones, according to Gregory the Great, because of the nine choirs of angels. And Bartolocci, the Cistercian, following all authorities, understands these jewels to signify the knowledge and other ornaments of grace with which Lucifer was adorned in his original state as the *perfecta similitudo Dei* — in other words, the light and splendour of the hidden knowledge. It follows on this interpretation (1) That the Graal

Stone in no sense belongs to folk-lore; (2) that it offers in respect of its origin no connection with the idea of physical mainten-ance, except in the sense that the things which sustain the soul maintain also the body, because the *panis quotidianus* depends from the *panis supersubstantialis*; (3) that the wisdom of the Graal is an Eucharistic wisdom, because the descent of an archnatural Host takes place annually to renew the virtues thereof; (4) that the correspondence of this is, in other versions of the legend, the Host which is consecrated extra-validly by the Secret Words, and so also the correspondence of the Stone which comes from heaven is the Cup which goes thereto; but in fine (5) that the jewel in the crown of Lucifer is called also the Morning Star, and thus it is not less than certain that the Graal returns whence it came.

III. *Concerning the Great Experiment*

If there be any who at this stage should say that the term of the Holy Graal is not the end of the mysteries — which is the Vision that is He — I would not ask him to define the distinction, but the term in either case, for that which must be said of the one is said also of the other, and if he understands the other it is certain that he understands the one. The Quest of the Holy Graal is for the wonder of all sacredness, there where no sinner can be. The provisional manifestation is in the *Longer Prose Perceval* and the full disclosure — not as to what it is but as to what it is about — is in the romance of Galahad. If, after the *haut prince* had given his final message, "Remember of this unstable world," he had been asked what he had seen which led him to exercise his high prerogative and call to be dissolved, he might have answered: *Visi sunt oculi mei salutare suum*, yet he would have said in his heart: "Eye hath not seen." But it has been divined and foretasted by those who have gone before the cohorts of election in the life that is within and have spoken with tongues of fire concerning that which they have seen in the vista. One approximation has told us that it is the eternal inter-course of the Father and the Son wherein we are enveloped lovingly by the Holy Spirit in that love which is eternal. And him who said this the wondering plaudits of an after-age termed the Admirable Ruysbroeck. He knew little Latin and less Greek, and, speaking from his own root, he had not read the authorities; but he had stood upon that shore where the waves of the divine sea baptize the pilgrim, or in that undeclared sphere which is *Kether,* the Crown of Kabalism, whence those who can look further discern that there is Ain Soph Aour, the Limitless Light. The equivalent hereof is in that which was said by Jesus Christ to the men of the Quest: "My Knyghtes and my seruantes & my true children whiche ben come oute of dedely lyf in to spyrytual lyf I wyl now no longer hyde me from yow, but ye shal see now a parte of my secretes & of my hydde thynges." And in the measure of that time they knew as they were known in full, that is, by participation in, and correspondence with the Divine Knowledge. Meat indeed: it is in that sense that Christ gave to Galahad "the hyghe mete" and "then he receyved his saueour." The monk who wrote this might have exhausted all the language of the schools, but he also knew little Latin and less Greek, if any, so he said only of the communicants: "They thoughte it soo swete that hit was merveillous to telle." And of Galahad he said later: "He receyued hit ryghte gladly and mekely." But yes, and that is fuller and stronger than all the eloquence of the Master of Sentences. It is the voice of Ruysbroeck — but further simplified — saying the same thing: "And he tastes and sees, out of all bounds, after God's own manner, the riches which are in God's own self, in the unity of the living deep, wherein He has fruition of Himself, according to the mode of His uncreated essence."

This is the Great Term of the Great Experiment followed by the Mystic Schools, and here by its own words the Graal legend is expressed in the terms of this Experiment. It has been made, within their several measures, by all churches, sects and religions, for which reason I have said elsewhere that the skilled craftsman does not quarrel with his tools. All materials are possible; the ascent to eternal life can be made by any ladder, assuming that it is fixed in the height; there is no need to go in search of something that is new and strange. And those who can receive this assurance will, I think, understand why it is that the Church of a man's childhood — assuming that it is a Church and not a latitudinarian chapel of ease or a narrow and voided sect — may and perhaps should contain for him the materials of his work, and these he will be able to adapt as an efficient craftsman. There is neither compulsion nor restraint, but the changes in official religion, the too easy transition from one to another kind, taking the sanctuaries as one takes high grades in Masonry, are a note of weakness rather than a pledge of sincerity, or of the true motive which should impel the soul on its quest.

There are, of course, many helpers of that soul on that progress:

> "We, said the day and the night
> And the law of gravitation;
> And we, said the dark and the light
> And the stars in their gyration;
> But I, said Justice, moving
> To the right hand of the Throne;
> And I, said Fate, approving;
> I make thy cause mine own."

Among these there are certain of the secret orders — those, I mean, which contain the counterparts of the Catholic tradition — and it is necessary to mention them here because of what follows. They offer no royal road, seeing that such roads there are none; but they do in cases shorten some of the preliminaries, by developing the implicits of a man's own consciousness, which is the setting of the prepared postulant on the proper path. There are, of course, some who enter within them having no special call, and these see very little of that which lies behind their official workings, just as there are many who have been born within the Church, as the body of Christ, but have never entered into the life which is communicated from the soul of Christ. They remain the children of this world, participating — as we hope — according to their degree, in so much of grace and salvation as is possible at the particular time. There are others who, out of all time, have received a high election, and for them the subject is often — in its undivided entirety — found resident in that state of external religious life in which it has pleased God to call them.

The Secret Doctrine in the religions equally and the schools is that of the communication of Divine Substance. I speak of it as secret in both cases, though it is obvious that in the official church there is no instituted reservation or conscious concealment on any point of doctrine or practice; but the language of the heights is not the language of the plains, and that which is heard in the nooks, byways and corners, among brakes and thickets, is not the voice of the rushing waters and the open sea. That is true of it in the uttermost which was said long ago by Paracelsus: *Nihil tam occultum erit quod non revelabitur;* but as there are few with ears to hear, it remains a voice in the wilderness crying in the unknown tongue. We know only that, according to high theology, the Divine Substance is communicated in the Eucharist — normally in the symbolical manner, but, in cases, essentially and vitally according to the true testimonies. It is therefore as if the elements were at times consecrated normally and at times by other words, more secret and efficient archnaturally. Then the enchantments terminate which are the swoon of the sensitive life in respect of the individual, who enters into real knowledge — the soul's knowledge before that supervened which is termed mystically the fall into matter. The Great Experiment is therefore one of reintegration in the secret knowledge before the Fall, and when, or if, the Holy Graal is identified with the stone in the crown of Lucifer, that which is indicated thereby is *(a)* the perpetuation of this secret knowledge, and *(b)* that under all circumstances there is a way back whence we came. So close also those times of adventure which — among other things and manifold — are the life of external activity governed by the spirit of the world, and this is accomplished by taking the great secret into the heart of the heart, as if the Blessed Sacrament, truly and virtually, into the inmost being.

Of such is the office of the Quests, but it is understood that it is not of my concern to enumerate these particulars as present consciously in the minds of the old monastic *scriptores,* who wrote the greatest of the books; they spoke of the things which they knew; without reference or intention they said what others had said of the same mysteries, and the testimony continued through the centuries. The story of the assumption of Galahad draws into romance the hypothesis of the Catholic Church concerning the term of all sanctity manifested; in both it is attained through the Eucharist. I mean to say that this is, by the hypothesis, the normal channel of the Divine Favour, and the devotion which was shown by the saints to the Sacrament of the Altar was not like the particular, sentimental disposition in minds of piety to the Precious Blood or the Heart of Jesus. Concerning these exercises I have no call to pronounce, but among the misjudgments on spiritual life in the Roman communion has been the frittering of spiritual powers in the popular devotion. If the Great Mysteries of the Church are insufficient to command the dedication of the whole world, then the world is left best under interdict, just as no pictures at all are better than those which are bad in art, and no books than those which are poor and trivial.

There is one point more, because here we have been trending in directions which will call for more full consideration presently. I have mentioned Secret Orders, and I cannot recall too early that any Secret Tradition — either in the East or the West — has been always an open secret in respect of the root-principles concerning the Way, the Truth and the Life. We are only beginning, and that by very slow stages, to enter into our inheritance from the past; and still perhaps in respect of the larger part we are seeking far and wide for the mystic treasures of Basra. It is therefore desirable to remember that the great subjects of preoccupation are all at our very doors. One reason, of which we shall hear again in another connection, is because among the wise of the ages, in whatsoever regions of the world, I do not think that there has been ever any difference of opinion about the true object of research; the modes and form of the Quest have varied, and that widely, but to a single point have all the ways converged. Therein is no change or shadow of vicissitude. We may hear of shorter roads, and we might say at first sight that such a suggestion must be true indubitably; but in one sense it is rather a convention of language and in another it is a commonplace which tends to confuse the issues. It is a convention of language, because the Great Quests are not pursued in time or place, and it would be just as true to say that in a journey from the circumference to the centre all roads are the same length, supposing that they are straight roads. It is a commonplace, because if any one should enter the byways, or return on his path and restart, it is obvious that he must look to be delayed. Furthermore, it may be true that all paths lead ultimately to the centre, and that if we descend into hell there may be still a way back to the light: yet in any house of right reason the issues are too clear to consider such extrinsic possibilities.

On this and on any consideration, we have to lay down one irrevocable law — that he who has resolved — setting all things else aside — to enter the path of the Quest must look for his progress in proportion as he pursues holiness for its own sake. He who in the Secret Orders dreams of the adeptship which they claim, *ex hypothesi,* to impart to those who can receive, and who does not say sanctity in his heart till his lips are cleansed, and then does not say it with his lips, is not so much far from the goal as without having conceived regarding it.

Now, it is precisely this word sanctity which takes us back, a little unintentionally, to the claim of the Church, and raises the question whether we are to interpret it according to the mind of the Church or another mind. My answer is that I doubt if the Great Experiment was ever pursued to its term in Christian times on the part of any person who had once been incorporated by the mystical body but subsequently had set himself aside therefrom. When the Quest of the Holy Graal was in fine achieved, there were some who, as we know, were translated, but others became monks and hermits; they were incorporated, that is to say, by the official annals of sanctity. I am dealing here with what I regard as a question of fact, not with antecedent grounds, and the fact is that the Church has the Eucharist. It may in certain respects have hampered Christian Mysticism by the restriction of its own consciousness so especially to the literal side; it may, on the historical side, have approached too often that picture of a certain King of Castle Mortal, who sold God for money; it may in this sense have told the wrong story, though the elements placed in its hands were the right and true elements. But not only is it certain that because of these elements we have to cleave as we can to the Church, but — speaking as a *doctor dubitantium* — I know that the Church Mystic on the highest throne of its consciousness does not differ in anything otherwise than *per accidentia* — or alternatively, the prudence of expression — from formal Catholic doctrine. It can say with its heart of knowledge what the ordinary churchman says with his lips of faith; the *Symbolum* remains; it has not taken on another meaning; it has only unfolded itself, like a flower, from within.

The Christian Mystic can therefore recite his *Credo in unum Deum* by clause and by clause, including *in unam sanctam catholicam et apostolicam ecclesiam,* and there is neither heresy in the construction nor Jesuitry in the *arrière pensée.* Above all, the path of the mystic does not pass through the heresies. It has seemed worth while to make this plain, because the Holy Graal is the Catholic Quest drawn into romance.

IV. The Mystery of Initiation

The Mystic Aspects of the Graal legend having been developed up to this stage, the question arises whether they have points of correspondence with any scheme of the Instituted Mysteries, whether any element which is present in the romances can be regarded as a faint and far off reflection of something which at that time was known and done in any secret schools. The possibility has presented itself already to the mind of scholarship, which, having performed admirable work in the study of the Graal texts, is still in search of a final explanation concerning them. The shadow of the old Order of the Temple has haunted them in dreams fitfully, and they have lingered almost longingly over vague imagined reflections of the Orgies of Adonis and Tammuz. As behind the Christian symbolism of the extant literature there spreads the whole world of pagan folk-lore, so — at least antecedently — there might be implied also some old scheme of the epopts. It seems permissible therefore to offer an alternative, under proper judgments of reserve, as something which — if otherwise considerable — may be held tentatively until later circumstances of research either lead it into demonstration or furnish a fitting substitute. The Graal legends are comparable to certain distinct literatures with which the theory here put forward will connect them by a twofold consanguinity of purpose. Scholarship had scarcely troubled itself with the great books of Kabalism till it was found or conceived that they could be made to enforce the official doctrines of Christianity. Many errors of enthusiasm followed, but the books of the mystery of Israel became in this manner the public heritage of philosophy, and we are now able to say after what manner it enters into the general scheme of mystic knowledge. The literature of alchemy, in like manner, so long as it was in the hands of certain amateurs of infant science and its counterfeits, remained particular to themselves, and outside a questionable research in physics it had no office or horizon until it was discovered or inferred that many curious texts of the subject had been written in a language of subterfuge, that in place of a metallurgical interest it was concerned in its way with the keeping of spiritual mysteries. There were again errors of enthusiasm, but a corner of the veil was lifted. Now, it is indubitably the message of the Graal that there is more in the Eucharist than is indicated by the sufficing graces imparted to the ordinary communicant, and if it is possible to show that behind this undeclared excess there lies that which has been at all times sought by the Wise, that *est in sacramento quicquid quaerunt sapientes,* then the Graal literature will enter after a new manner into our heritage from the past, and another corner of the veil will be lifted on the path of knowledge. It will be seen that the literature — contrary to what it appears on the surface — is not without points of comparison in other Christian cycles — that it does not stand exactly alone, even if its consanguinities, though declared by official religion, are not entirely before the face of the world but within the sanctuaries of secret fraternities. To suggest this is not to say that these stories of old are a defined part or abstract of any mysteries of initiation; they are at most a byway winding through a secret woodland to a postern giving upon the chancel of some great and primeval abbey.

Those who have concerned themselves with the subject of hidden knowledge will know that the secret claims have been put forth under all manners of guises. This has arisen to some extent naturally enough in the course of the ages and under the special atmosphere of motives peculiar to different nations. It has also come about through the institution of multiples of convention on the part of some who have become in later times the custodians of the mysteries, such wardens having been actuated by a twofold purpose, firstly, to preserve their witness in the world, and, secondly, to see that the knowledge was, as far as might be, kept away from the world. This is equivalent to saying that the paramount law of silence has of necessity a permanent competitor in the law of the sign. We may take the readiest illustration in the rituals of Craft Masonry. They contain the whole marrow of *bourgeoisie,* but they contain also the shadow of the great mysteries revealed occasionally. The unknown person or assembly which conceived the closing of the Lodge according to one of the grades had a set of moral feelings in common with those of all the retired masters in the craft of joinery, and a language like a journeyman carpenter, but this notwithstanding the words of the adepts had passed over them and they spoke of the Hidden Token as no one had ever spoken before. That closing gives the true explanation of the secret which cannot be told and yet is imparted quite simply; of that mystery which has never been expressed and can yet be recited by the least literate occupant of the chair placed in Wisdom. Nor does it prove in communication to be anything that is strictly unfamiliar. And yet the explanation, so far from making the concealed part of the rite familiar and a thing of no moment, has built about the concealment a wall of preservation which has made its real significance more profound and in the minds of the adepts more important.

The Graal literature is open to a parallel criticism, and the result is also the same. Whatever disappointment may await, in fine, the pursuit of an inquiry like the present, partly on account of the uncouth presentation of important symbolism to the mind of the early romancist, partly by reason of the inherent defect of romance as a vehicle of symbolism, and more than either by the fatal hiatus brought about through the loss of the earliest documents, there is enough evidence to show that a very strange leaven was working in the mass of the texts. Let me add in respect of it, with all necessary reservations and in no illiberal spirit, that the quality of this leaven can be appreciated scarcely by those who are unacquainted (*a*) with the inward phases of the life of Christian sanctity during the Middle Ages, after which period the voices sound uncertain and the consciousness of experience more remote, and (*b*) with the interior working of those concealed orders of which the Masonic experiment is a part only, and elementary at that. The most important lights are therefore either in the very old books or in the catholic motive which characterizes secret rituals that, whether old or not, have never entered into the knowledge of the outside world.

The testimony is of two kinds invariably — first of all, to the existence of the Great Experiment and the success with which, under given circumstances, it can be carried to its term, and, secondly, to a great failure in respect of the external world. The one is reflected by the achieved Quest of the Holy Graal, and the other by the removal of the Graal. In respect of the one it is as if a great mystery had been communicated at one time in the external places, but as if the communication had afterwards been suspended, the secret had as if died. In respect of the other, it is as if the House of Doctrine had been voided. Did these statements exhaust the content of the alternatives, the testimony might be that of a sect, but we shall see at the proper time after what manner they conform to external doctrine, even if the keepers of that doctrine should themselves be unable to see the law of the union.

The great literatures and the great individual books may be often at this day as so many counters or heaps of letters put into the hands of the mystic, and he interprets them after his own manner, imparting to them that light which, at least intellectually, abides in himself. I make this formal statement because I realize that it is perilous for my position and because it enables me to add that though literatures may be clay in our hands, we must not suppose that they who in the first place put a shape of their own kind on the material which they had ingarnered were invariably conscious that it would bear that other seal and impression which we set upon it in our own minds as the one thing that is desirable. It is too much to suppose that behind the external sense of texts there was always designed that inward and illusory significance which in some of them we seem to trace so indubitably. The Baron de la Motte Fouqué once wrote a beautiful and knightly romance in which a correspondent discovered a subtle and complete allegory, and the author, who planned, when he wrote it, no subsurface meaning, did not less sincerely confess to the additional sense, explaining in reply that high art in literature is true upon all the planes. There are certain romances which are found to connect in this manner with the mystery of our science — that is to say, in the nonintentional way, and we must only be thankful to discern that there is the deep below the deep, without pressing interpenetration into a formal scheme. It is well to notice this position and thus go before a criticism which presents itself rather than calls to be sought out. The books of the Holy Graal are not exactly of this kind. A text which says that certain secret words were once imparted under very wonderful and exceptional circumstances is certainly obtruding a meaning behind meaning; another which affirms that a certain mythical personage was ordained secretly, owing to a similar intervention, and was made thereby the first Bishop of Christendom, manifests an ulterior motive, or there are no such motives in the world. And further, when the two great Quests of the whole literature are written partly in the form of confessed allegory, it is not unreasonable to infer that they had some such motive throughout; while, in fine, as their express, undisguised intention is to show the existence of an arch-natural Mass, the graces and the mysteries of which can be experienced and seen by some who are of perfect life, then the interpretation which illustrates this intention by the mystic side of Eucharistic doctrine in the Church offers a true construction, and its valid criticism is *vere dignum et justum est, aequum et salutare.* I will pour three cups to the health and coronation of him who shall discover the speculative proto-Perceval of primeval folk-lore, yet on the present subject let him and all other brethren in the holy places of research keep silence, unless God graces them with agreement. The unknown writers of the *Longer Prose Perceval* and the *Quest of Galahad* spoke of the Great Experiment as those who knew something of their theme and bore true witness on the term of the research.

We know in our own hearts that eternity is the sole thing which signifies ultimately and great literature should confess to no narrower horizon. It happens that they begin sometimes by proposing a lesser theme, but they are afterwards exalted; and this was the case with the Graal books, which were given the early legends of Perceval according to the office of Nature, but afterwards the legend of Galahad according to the Law of Grace.

V. *The Mystery of Faith*

We have now reached a certain definite stage in the high debate and can institute a preliminary summary of the whole subject. It is known that the mystery of faith in Christianity is above all things the Eucharist, in virtue of which the Divine Master is ever present in his Church and is always communicated to the soul;

but having regard to the interdictions of our age-long exile we receive only a substituted participation in the life of the union. The Graal mystery is the declared pageant of the Eucharist, which, in virtue of certain powers set forth under the veil of consecrating words, is in some way, not indeed a higher mystery than that of the external church, but its demonstration in the transcendent mode. We have only to remember a few passages in the *Book of the Holy Graal,* in the *Longer Prose Perceval,* and in the *Quest of Galahad* to understand the imputed distinction as: *(a)* The communication in the Eucharist of the whole knowledge of the universe from *Aleph* to *Tau; (b)* the communication of the Living Christ in the dissolution of the veils of Bread and Wine; *(c)* the communication of the secret process by which the soul passes under divine guidance from the offices of this world to heaven, the keynote being that the soul is taken when it asks into the great transcendence. This is the implied question of the Galahad legend as distinguished from the Perceval question. There are those who are called but not chosen at all, like Gawain. There are those who get near to the great mystery but have not given up all things for it, and of these is Lancelot. There is the great cohort, like the apocalyptic multitude which no man can number — called, elected and redeemed in the lesser ways, by the offices of the external Church — and of these is the great chivalry of the Round Table. There are those who go up into the Mountain of the Lord and return again, like Bors; they have received the last degrees, but their office is in this world. In fine, there are those who follow at a long distance in the steep path, and of these is the transmuted Perceval of the Galahad legend. It is in this sense that, exalted above all and more than all things rarefied into a great and high quintessence, the history of the Holy Graal becomes the soul's history, moving through a profound symbolism of inward being, wherein we follow as we can, but the vistas are prolonged for ever, and it well seems that there is neither a beginning to the story nor a descried ending.

We find also the shadows and tokens of secret memorials which have not been declared in the external, and by the strange things which are hinted, we seem to see that the temple of the Graal on Mont Salvatch is not otherwise than as the three tabernacles which it was proposed to build on Mount Tabor.

Among indications of this kind there are two only that I can mention. As in the prologue to the *Book of the Holy Graal*, we have heard that the anonymous but not unknown hermit met on a memorable occasion with one who recognized him by certain signs which he carried, giving thus the unmistakable token of some instituted mystery in which both shared: as in the *Longer Prose Perceval* we have seen that there is an account of five changes in the Graal which took place at the altar, being five transfigurations, the last of which assumed the seeming of a chalice, but at the same time, instead of a chalice, was some undeclared mystery: so the general as well as the particular elements of the legend in its highest form offer a mystery the nature of which is recognized by the mystic through certain signs which it carries on its person; yet it is declared in part only and what remains, which is the greater part, is not more than suggested. It is that, I believe, which was seen by the maimed King when he looked into the Sacred Cup and beheld the secret of all things, the beginning even and the end. In this sense the five changes of the Graal are analogous to the five natures of man, as these in their turn correspond to the four aspects of the Cosmos and that which rules all things within and from without the Cosmos. I conclude therefore that the antecedents of the Cup Legend are (1) *Calix meus quam inebrians est;* (2) the Cup which does not pass away; (3) the *vas insigne electionis*. The antecedent of the Graal question is: Ask, and ye shall receive. The antecedent of the Enchantment of Britain is the swoon of the sensitive life, and that of the adventurous times is: I bring not peace, but a sword; I come to cast fire upon the earth, and what will I but that it should be enkindled? The closing of these times is taken when the Epopt turns at the altar, saying *Pax Dei tecum*. But this is the peace which passes understanding and it supervenes upon the *Mors osculi* — the mystic Thomas Vaughan's "death of the kiss" — after which it is exclaimed truly: "Blessed are the dead which die in the Lord from henceforth and for ever." It follows therefore that the formula of the Supernatural Graal is: *Panem coelestem accipiam;* that of the Natural Graal, namely, the Feeding Dish, is: *Panem nostrum quotidianum da nobis hodie;* and the middle term: "Man doth not live by bread alone." I should add: These three there are one; but this is in virtue of great and high transmutations. So, after all the offices of scholarship — pursued with that patience which wears out worlds of obstacles — it proves that there is something left over, that this something bears upon its surface the aspects of mystic life, that hereof is our heritage, and that we can enter and take possession because other claimants there are none. The books of the Holy Graal do tell us of a sanctuary within the sanctuary of Christendom, wherein there are reserved great sacraments, high symbols, relics that are of all most holy, and would be so accounted in all the external ways; but of these things we have heard otherwise in certain secret schools. It follows therefore that we as mystics can lift up our eyes because there is a Morning Light which we go to meet with exultation, *portantes manipulos nostros.* We shall find the paths more easy because of our precursors, who have cleared the tangled ways and have set up landmarks and beacons, by which perchance we shall be led more straightly into our own, though in their clearing and surveying they did not at all know that they were working for us.

It is recognized by the Catholic Church that the Eucharist is at this time the necessity of our spiritual life, awaiting that great day when our daily bread shall itself become the Eucharist, no longer that substitute provided in our material toil and under the offices of which we die. The body is communicated to the body that the Spirit may be imparted to the soul. *Spiritus ipse Christi animae infunditur,* and this is the illustration of ecstasy. But in these days — as I have hinted — it works only through the efficacy of a symbol, and this is why we cannot say in our hearts: *A carne nostro caro Christi ineffabile modo sentitur,* meaning *Anima sponsae ad plenissimam in Christum transformationem sublimatur.* Hence, whether it is St John of the Cross speaking of the Ascent of Mount Carmel or Ruysbroeck of the Hidden Stone, the discourse is always addressed to Israel in the wilderness, not in the Land of Promise. Hence also our glass of vision remains clouded, like the sanctuary; and even the books of the mystics subsist under the law of the interdict and are expressed in the language thereof. Those of the Holy Graal are written from very far away in the terms of transubstantiation, presented thaumaturgically under all the veils of grossness, instead of the terms of the *Epiclesis* in the language of those who have been ordained with the holy oils of the Comforter. In other books the metaphysics of the Lover and the Beloved have been rendered in the tongue of the flesh, forgetting that it bears the same relation to the illusory correspondence of human unions that the Bread of the Eucharist bears to material nutriment. The true analogy is in the contradistinction between the elements of bodies and minds. The high analogy in literature is the Supper at the Second Table in the poem of Robert de Borron. That was a spiritual repast, where there was neither eating nor drinking. For this reason the symbolic fish upon the table conveyed to the Warden the title of Rich Fisher, and it is in this sense — that is to say, for the same reason — that the saints become Fishers of Men. We shall re-express the experience of the mystic life in terms that will make all things new when we understand fully what is implied by the secret words: *Co-opertus et absconditus sponsus.*

VI. The Lost Book of the Graal

We have seen, in considering the claim of the Celtic Church to recognition as a possible guiding and shaping spirit of the Graal literature, that one speculation regarding it was the existence in concealment of a particular book, a liturgy of some kind, preferably a Book of the Mass. I have no definite concern in the hypothesis, as it is in no sense necessary to the interpretation which I place upon the literature; but the existence of one or more primordial texts is declared so invariably in the romances that, on the surface at least, it seems simpler to presume its existence, and it becomes thus desirable to ascertain what evidence there is otherwise to be gleaned about it. As it has been left so far by scholarship, the question wears almost an inscrutable or at least an inextricable aspect, and its connection with the mystic aspects of the Holy Graal may be perhaps rather adventitious than accidental, but it is introduced here as a preliminary to those yet more abstruse researches which belong to the ninth book.

We must in the first place set aside from our minds the texts which depend from one another, whether the earlier examples are extant or not. The vanished *Quest* of Guiot — priceless as its discovery would be — is not the term of our research. We must detach further those obviously fabulous chronicles by the pretence of which it is supposed that the several quests and histories were perpetuated for the enlightenment of posterity. No one is wondering seriously whether the knightly adventures of the Round Table were reduced into great chronicles by the scribes of King Arthur's court, for which assurance we have the evidence of the *Huth Merlin* — among several deponents. There are other sources which may be equally putative, but it is these which raise the question, and I proceed to their enumeration as follows: (1) That which contained the greatest secret of the world, a minute volume which would lie in the hollow of a hermit's hand — in a word, the text presupposed by the prologue to the *Book of the Holy Graal;* (2) that which is ascribed to Master Blihis — the *fabulator famosus* — by the *Elucidation* prefixed to the *Conte del Graal;* (3) that which is called the Great Book by Robert de Borron, containing the Great Secret to which the term Graal is referred, a book of many histories, written by many clerks, and by him communicated apparently to his patron, Walter Montbéliard; (4) that which the Count of Flanders gave to Chrétien de Troyes with instructions to retell it, being the best story ever recited in royal court; (5) that which the Hermit Blaise codified with the help of the secret records kept by the Wardens of the Graal; (6) that which the author of the *Longer Prose Perceval* refers to the saintly man whom he calls Josephus; (7) that which the Jew Flegitanis transcribed from the time-immemorial chronicles of the starry heavens.

The palmary problem for our solution is, whether in the last understanding a mystery book or a Mass book, these cryptic texts can be regarded as "seven and yet one, like shadows in a dream — or rather, as many inventions concerning one document. If we summarize the results which were obtained from them, we can express them by their chief examples thus: (1) From the prototype of the *Book of the Holy Graal* came the super-apostolical succession, the ordination of Joseph II., the dogma of transubstantiation manifested arch-naturally, and the building of Corbenic as a Castle of Perils and Wonders girt about the Holy Graal; (2) from the prototype of the *Elucidation* we have the indicible secret of the Graal, the seven discoveries of its sanctuary, the account of the Rich Fisherman's skill in necromancy and his protean transformations by magical art; (3) from the prototype of Robert de Borron we have the Secret Words, by him or subsequently referred to Eucharistic consecration; (4) from the prototype of Chrétien we have the history of Perceval le Gallois, so far as it was taken by him; (5) from the putative chronicle of Blaise and his scribes, antecedent and concurrent, we have all that which belongs to the history of Merlin, the foundation of the Round Table and the Siege Perilous; (6) from the prototype of the *Longer Prose Perceval* we have Perceval's later history, his great and final achievements — unlike all else in the literature, more sad, more beautiful, more strange than anything told concerning him; (7) from the prototype of Guiot, we have the Graal presented as a stone, and with an ascribed antecedent history which is the antithesis of all other histories. Had I set up these varying versions in the form of seven propositions on the gates of Salerno or Salamanca and offered to maintain their identity in a thesis against all comers, I suppose that I could make out a case with the help of scholastic casuistry and the rest of the dialectical subtleties; but in the absence of all motive, and detached as regards the result, I can only say in all reason that the quests and the histories as we have them never issued from a single quest or a single history. We may believe, if we please, that the book of the Count of Flanders was really the *Quest* of Guiot, reducing the sources to six, and a certain ingenuity — with courage towards precarious positions — may help us to further eliminations, but the root-difficulty will remain — that the Quests, as we have them, exclude one another and so also do some of the histories. It follows that there were many prototypes, or alternatively that there were many inventions in respect of the sources. In respect of the Perceval legends there was the non-Graal folk-lore myth, which accounts for their root-matter but not for their particular renderings and their individual Graal elements; the nearest approximation to these myths and their nearest issue in time may have been the *Quest* of Guiot. One general source of De Borron was transparently the *Evangelium Nicodemi,* complicated by later Joseph legends, including the tradition of Fécamp, but more than all by another source, of which he had heard at a distance and of which I shall speak at the close. The *Quest of Galahad* makes no claim to a prototype, but it reflects extant manuscripts of the Greater Chronicles; for the rest, its own story was all important;

it cared nothing for antecedents, and it is only by sporadic precaution, outside its normal lines, that it registers at the close after what manner it pretended to be reduced into writing. The prototypes of this text are in the annals of sanctity, except in so far as it reflects — and it does so indubitably — some rumours which Robert de Borron had drawn into romance. As regards Galahad himself, his romance is a great invention derived from the prose Lancelot. The *Longer Prose Perceval* is an invention after another manner; there is nothing to warrant us in attaching any credit to the imputed source in Josephus, but the book drew from many places and transmuted that which it drew with a shaping spirit; it is an important text for those rumours to which I have referred darkly. It works, like the *Quest of Galahad,* in a high region of similitude, and its pretended source is connected intimately with the second Joseph of the Greater Chronicles.

We are now in a position to deal with a further ascription which is so general in the literature and was once rather widely accepted — namely, that of a Latin source. It will be noted that this is a simple debate of language and it leaves the unity or multiplicity of the prototypes an open question. It is worth mentioning, because it enters into the history of the criticism of Graal literature. There is no need to say that it is now passed over by scholarship, and the first person to reject it was Robert Southey in his preface to the edition of Sir Thomas Malory's *Morte d'Arthur* which passes under his name, though he had no hand in the editing of the text itself. "I do not believe," he says, "that any of these romances ever existed in Latin, — by whom, or for whom, could they have been written in that language?" For the romances as romances, for *Meliadus de Leonnois, Gyron le Courtois,* and so forth, the question has one answer only, the fact notwithstanding that the prologue to *Gyron* draws all the prose tales of the Round Table from what it terms the Latin *Book of the Holy Graal.* There is one answer also for any version of the Graal legend, as we now know it. Even for that period, the Comte de Tressan committed a serious absurdity when he affirmed that the whole literature of Arthurian chivalry, derived by the Bretons from the ancient and fabulous chronicles of Melkin and Tezelin, was written in Latin by Rusticien de Pise, who was simply a compiler and translator into the Italian tongue and was concerned, as such, chiefly with the Tristram cycle. At the same time it is possible to take too extreme a view. In his preface to another work, *Palmarin of England,* Southey remarks that "every reader of romance knows how commonly they were represented as translations from old manuscripts," and that such an ascription, "instead of proving that a given work was translated, affords some evidence that it is original." The inference is worded too strongly and is scarcely serious as it stands, but the fact itself is certain; and indeed the Graal romances belong to a class of literature which was prone to false explanations in respect both of authorship and language. Still, there is something to be said for the middle ground suggested, now long ago, on the authority of Paulin Paris, that while it is idle to talk of romances in the Latin language, there is nothing impossible in the suggestion that the sacramental legend of Joseph of Arimathaea and his Sacred Vessel may have existed in Latin. From his point of view it was a Gradual, and he even goes so far as to speculate *(a)* that it was preserved at Glastonbury; *(b)* that it was not used by the monks because it involved schism with Rome; and *(c)* that, like the Jew of Toledo's transcript, it was forgotten for three centuries — till it was recalled by the quarrel between Henry II and the Pope. This is, of course, fantasy, but the bare supposition of such a Latin legend would account in a natural manner for an ascription that is singularly consistent, while it would not pretend to represent the lost imaginary prototypes of the whole complex literature.

In this connection we might do worse than take warning by one lesson from the literature of alchemy. The early writers on this subject were in the habit of citing authorities who, because they could not be identified, were often regarded as mythical; but all the same they existed in manuscript; they might have been found by those who had taken the trouble; and they are now familiar to students by the edition of Berthelot. In matters of this kind we do not know what a day may bring forth, and from all standpoints the existence of a pious legend — orthodox or heretical, Roman or Breton — concerning Joseph and his Hallow would be interesting, as it must also be valuable. Unfortunately, the Quest of the Holy Graal in respect of its missing literature is after the manner of a greater enterprise, for there are many who follow it and few that come to the term of a new discovery. There are authorities now in England to whom the possibility of such a text might not be unacceptable, though criticism dwells rightly upon the fact that there is no mention of the Holy Vessel in the earliest apocryphal records of the evangelization of Britain by Joseph. We have heard already of one Latin memorial among the archives of Fécamp, but of its date we know nothing, and its conversion legend does not belong to this island.

Having thus determined, as I think, the question of a single prototype accounting for all the literature, we have to realize that everything remains in respect of the mystery of origin — now the wonder element of things unseen and heard of dimly only, sometimes expressed imperfectly in Nature poems, which have no concern therein; now what sounds like a claim on behalf of the Celtic Church; now sacramental legends incorporated by Latin Christianity into the great body of romances. But I speak here of things which are approximate and explicable in an atmosphere of legend married to a definite world of doctrine. There is nothing in these to explain (a) the report of a secret sanctuary in all the texts without any exception whatever, for even the foolish *Crown of all Adventures* allocates its house of ghosts to the loneliest of all roads; (b) the Secret Words of Consecration; (c) the arch-natural Mass celebrated in three of the texts; (d) the hidden priesthood; (e) the claim to a holy and hidden knowledge; (f) the removal of this knowledge from concealment to further concealment, because the world was not worthy. These are the rumours to which I have alluded previously, and I have attached to them this name, because there is nothing more obvious in the whole cycle of literature than the fact that those who wrote of them did not — for the most part — know what they said. Now, it is a canon of reasonable criticism that writers who make use of materials which they do not understand are not the inventors thereof. It had never entered into the heart of Robert de Borron that his Secret Words reduced the ordinary Eucharist to something approaching a semblance; to the putative Walter Map that his first Bishop of Christendom put the whole Christian apostolate into an inferior place; to any one of the romancers that his Secret Sanctuary was the claim of an orthodoxy in transcendence; to the authors in particular of the *Longer Prose Perceval* and the *Quest of Galahad* that their implied House of the Hallows came perilously near to the taking of the heart out of Christendom. So little did these things occur to them that their materials are mismanaged rather seriously in consequence. Had the first Bishop of Christendom ordained those whom he intended to succeed him, I should not bring this charge against the author of that text which presents the consecration of the second Joseph in all its sanctity and wonder. But, as a matter of fact, the custody of the Holy Graal passed into the hands of a layman, and we are offered the picture of a priest anointed by Christ who does not even baptize, a hermit on one occasion being obtained to administer this simplest of all the sacraments. And yet this first bishop of Christendom had ordained many and enthroned some at Sarras. There is a similar crux in the *Lesser Holy Graal* and its companion poem. One would have thought that the possession of the Secret Words would be reserved to those bearing the seal of the priesthood; but it is not suggested that Joseph of Arimathaea was either ordained by Christ or by any bishop of the Church; his successor, Brons, was simply a disciple saved out of rejected Jerusalem; and Perceval, the *tiers hons,* was a knight of King Arthur's court. Of two things, therefore, one: either the makers of romance who brought in these elements knew not what they said, and reflected at a far distance that which they had heard otherwise, or the claims are not that which they appear on the surface; beneath them there is a deeper concealment; there was something behind the Eucharistic aspect of the mysterious formula and something behind the ordination in transcendence; there was in fine a more secret service than that of the Mass. I accept the first alternative, but without prejudice to the second, which is true also, as we shall see later, still on the understanding that what subtended was not in the mind of romance.

If it is necessary or convenient to posit the existence of a single primordial book, then the *Sanctum Graal, Liber Gradalis, or Missa de Corpore Christi* contained these elements, and it contained nothing or little of the diverse matter in the literature. It was not a liturgy connected with the veneration of a relic or of certain relics; it did not recite the legend of Joseph or account in what manner soever for the conversion of Britain. It was a Rite of the Order of Melchisedech and it communicated the archnatural sacrament *ex hypothesi.* The prologue to the *Book of the Holy Graal* has what one would be inclined to call a rumour of this Mass, after which there supervened an ecstasy as a foretaste of the Divine Rapture. The term thereof was the Vision which is He, and the motive of the dilucid experience is evaded — consciously or not, but, I say, in truth unconsciously — by the substitute of reflections upon difficulties concerning the Trinity. No Graal writer had ever seen this book, but the rumour of it was about in the world. It was held in reserve not in a monastery at Glastonbury, but by a secret school of Christians whose position in respect of current orthodoxy was that of the apex to the base of any perfect triangle — its completion and not its destruction. There was more of the rumour abroad than might have been expected antecedently, as if a Church of St John the Divine were planted somewhere in the West, but not in the open day. There was more of the rumour, and some makers of texts had heard more than others. We know that in the prologue to the *Book of the Holy Graal* there is what might be taken as a reference to this company, the members of which were sealed, so that they could recognize one another by something which they bore upon their persons. When, in the *Quest of Galahad*, the nine strange knights came from the East and the West and the North and the South to sit down, or to kneel rather, at the Table of the Graal, they entered without challenge, they took their proper places and were saluted and welcomed, because they also bore the seal of the secret order. King Pelles went out because he was not on the Quest, because his part was done, because he had attained and seen, for which reason he departed as one who says: *Nunc dimittis Servum tuum, Domine, secundum verbum tuum in pace: quia viderunt oculi mei —* elsewhere or earlier — *salutare tuum.* The minstrels and romancers knew little enough of these mysteries, for the most part, and on the basis of the rumours of the book they superposed what they had heard otherwise — the legend of Joseph, the cultus of the Precious Blood, clouds of fables, multiples of relics, *hoc genus omne.* But it is to be noted in fine that the withdrawal into deeper concealment referred more especially to the company as a hidden school, which would be sought and not found, unless God led the quester. And perhaps those who came into contact by accident did not always ask the question: Who administers the Mysteries? Yet, if they were elected they were brought in subsequently.

It will be observed that in this speculation the existence of the rumours which were incorporated does not in a strict sense involve the existence of any book to account for their comparative prevalence.

VII. *The Declared Mystery of Quest*

There follow in this place certain exotics of the subject which are not put forward as an integral part thereof, but are offered to those only who are concerned in the rumour of the Graal literature — as expressed in this book — so far as it incorporates that literature in the annals of Christian sanctity. They will know that the sins and imperfections of this our human life are attenuated by the turning of our intellectual part towards the Blessed Zion, and that, next after leading the all-hallowed life, the making of holy books to formulate the aspirations of our best part in its best moments is counted in a man towards righteousness. It is well, indeed, for him whose life is dedicated to the Quest, but at least — in the stress and terror of these our wayward times — in the heart and the inmost heart let us keep its memory green.

1. Faith is the implicits of the mind passing into expression formally, and knowledge is the same implicits certified by experience. It is in this sense that God recompenses those who seek Him out. The Mystery of the Holy Graal is the sun of a great implicit rising in the zones of consciousness.

2. If, therefore, from one point of view we are dealing with great speculations, from another we are truly concerned with great certainties; and Galahad did not question or falter.

3. There is nothing in the world which has less to do with a process or other conventions and artifices than the ascent of a soul to light. Thus, the Quest had no formulae.

4. The mistake which man has made has been to go in search of his soul, which does not need finding but entering only, and that by a certain door which is always open within him. All the doors of Corbenic were open when Lancelot came thereto, even that sanctuary into which he could look from afar but wherein he could not enter. The chief door is inscribed: *Sapida notitia de Deo.*

5. It is understood, however, that before the door is reached there are gates which are well guarded. So on a night at midnight, when the moon shone clear, Lancelot paused at the postern, which opened toward the sea, and saw how two lions guarded the entrance.

6. It is true also that the gates are not opened easily by which the King of Glory comes in; yet we know that the King comes. The key of these gates is called *Voluntas inflammata.* This will works on the hither side, but there is another which works on the further, and this is named *Beneplacitum termino carens.* When the gates open by the concurrence of the two powers, the King of Salem comes forth carrying Bread and Wine. Of the communication which then follows it is said: *Gustari potest quod explicari nequit.* Galahad and his fellows did taste and saw that the Lord is sweet.

7. For the proselytes of the gate which is external and the postulants at the pronaos of the temple, the Crucifixion took place on Calvary. For the adepts and the epopts, the question, if it can be said to arise, is not whether this is true on the plane of history, but in what manner it signifies, seeing that the great event of all human history began at the foundation of the world, as it still takes place daily in the soul of every man for whom the one thing needful is to know when Christ shall arise within him. It is then that those on the Quest can say with Sir Bors: "But God was ever my comfort."

8. All that we forget is immaterial if that which we remember is vital, as, for example, the Lord of Quest, who said: "Therefore I wote wel whan my body is dede, my sowle shalle be in grete joye to see the blessid Trynyte every day, and the mageste of oure lord Jhesu Cryst" — in other words, *Contemplatio perfectissima et altissima Dei.*

9. The first condition of interior progress is in detachment from the lesser responsibilities which — because they have not entered into the heart of hearts are external to our proper interests and distract from those high and onerous burdens which we have to carry on our road upward, until such time as even the road itself — and the burdens thereto belonging — shall assume and transport us. From the greatest even to the least the missions of knight-errantry were followed in utter detachment, and those who went on the Quest carried no

impedimenta. So also is the great silence ordained about those who would hear the *interior Dei locutio altissimi*.

10. The generation of God is outward and so into the estate of man; but the generation of man — which is called also rebirth — is inward, and so into the Divine Union. The great clerks wrote the adventures of the Graal in great books, but there was no rehearsal of the last branch, the first rubric of which would read: *De felicissima animae cum Deo unione*.

11. Most conventions of man concern questions of procedure, and it is so with the things which are above, for we must either proceed or perish. Sir Gawain turned back, and hence he was smitten of the old wound that Lancelot gave him; but no knight who achieved the Quest died in arms, unless in Holy War.

12. In the declared knowledge which behind it has the hidden knowledge, blood is the symbol of life, and this being so it can be understood after what manner the Precious Blood profiteth and the Reliquary thereof. The other name of this Reliquary is Holy Church. But such are the offices of its mercy that *in examine mortis* even Gawain received his Saviour.

13. The root from which springs the great tree of mysticism is the old theological doctrine that God is the centre of the heart. He is by alternative the soul's centre. This is the ground of the union: *per charitatem justi uniuntur cum Deo*. Gawain entreated Lancelot to "praye some prayer more or lesse for my soule;" King Arthur as he drifted in the dark barge said to Bedivere: "And yf thou here neuer more of me praye for my soule," but Perceval and Galahad knew that their reward was with them; they asked for no offerings and no one wearied Heaven.

14. In the soul's conversion there is no office of time, and this is why the greatest changes are always out of expectation. The Graal came like angels — unawares. The *castissimus et purissimus amplexus* and the *felix osculum* are given as in the dark and suddenly. There is further nothing in the wide world so swift and so silent as the *illapsus Christi in centrum animae*. So also it is said of Galahad that "sodenely his soule departed."

15. The five changes of the Graal are analogous to the five natures of man, and these in their turn correspond to the four aspects of the cosmos and that which rules all things within and from above the cosmos.

16. The consideration of eternity arises from that of the Holy

Graal, as from all literature at its highest, and if I have set it as the term of my own researches, in this respect, it is rather because it has imposed itself than because I have sought it out.

Obiter Dicta.

And now as the sum total of these mystical aspects, the desire of the eyes in the seeking and finding of the Holy Graal may, I think, be re-expressed as follows:

Temple or Palace or Castle — Mont Salvatch or Corbenic — wherever located and whether described as a wilderness of building, crowded burg or simple hermit's hold — there is one characteristic concerning the sanctuary which, amidst all its variations in the accidents, is essentially the same; the Keeper of the great Hallows has fallen upon evil days; the means of restoration and of healing are, as one would say, all around him, yet the help must come from without; it is that of his predestined successor, whose office is to remove the vessel, so that it is henceforth never seen so openly. Taking the Quest of Galahad as that which has the highest significance spiritually, I think that we may speak of it thus: We know that in the last analysis it is the inward man who is really the Wounded Keeper. The mysteries are his; on him the woe has fallen; it is he who expects healing and redemption. His body is the Graal Castle, which is also the castle of Souls, and behind it is the Earthly Paradise as a vague and latent memory. We may not be able to translate the matter of the romance entirely into mystical symbolism, since it is only a rumour at a distance of life in the spirit and its great secrets. But, I think, we can see that it all works together for the one end of all. He who enters into the consideration of this secret and immemorial house under fitting guidance shall know why it is that the Graal is served by a pure maiden, and why that maiden is ultimately dispossessed. Helayne is the soul, and the soul is in exile because all the high unions have been declared voided — the crown has been separated from the kingdom, and experience from the higher knowledge. So long as she remained a pure virgin, she was more than a thyrsus bearer in the mysteries, but the morganatic marriage of mortal life is part of her doom. This is still a high destiny, for the soul out of earthly experience brings forth spiritual desire, which is the quest of the return journey, and this is Galahad. It is therefore within the law and the order that she has to conceive and bring him forth. Galahad represents the highest spiritual aspirations and desires passing into full consciousness, and so into attainment. But he is not reared by his mother, because Eros, which is the higher knowledge, has dedicated the true desire to the proper ends thereof. It will be seen also what must be understood by Lancelot in secret communication with Helayne, though he has taken her throughout for another. The reason is that it is impossible to marry even in hell without marrying that seed which is of heaven. As she is the psychic woman, so is he the natural man, or rather the natural intelligence which is not without its consecrations, not without its term in the highest. Helayne believes that her desire is only for Lancelot, but this is because she takes him for Eros, and it is by such a misconception that the lesser Heaven stoops to the earth; herein also there is a sacred dispensation, because so is the earth assumed. I have said that Lancelot is the natural man, but he is such merely at the highest; he is born in great sorrow, and she who has conceived him saves her soul alive amidst the offices of external religion. He is carried into the lesser land of Faerie, as into a garden of childhood. When he draws towards manhood, he comes forth from the first places of enchantment and is clothed upon by the active duties of life as by the vestures of chivalry. He enters also into the unsanctified life of sense, into an union against the consecrated life and order. But his redeeming quality is that he is faithful and true, because o which, and because of his genealogy, he is chosen to beget Galahad, of whom he is otherwise unworthy, even as we all, in our daily life, fall short of the higher aspirations of the soul. As regards the Keeper, it is certain that he must die and be replaced by another Keeper before the true man can be raised, with the holy things to him belonging, which Hallows are indeed withdrawn, but it is with and in respect of him only, for the keepers are a great multitude, though it is certain that the Graal is one. The path of quest is the path of upward progress, and it is only at the great height that Galahad knows himself as really the Wounded Keeper and that thus, in the last resource, the physician heals himself. Now this is the mystery from everlasting, which is called in the high doctrine *Schema misericordiae*. It is said: *Latet, aeternumque latebit*, until it is revealed in us; and as to this: *Te rogamus, audi nos.*

CHAPTER 20

The Holy Grail:
Qui on en servoit?

D. Swinscow

It was during the last quarter of the twelfth century and the
succeeding fifty years or so that there crystallized in the form of
Romantic poems and tales a number of legends recounting the
search for and history of the Grail, a talisman that would
nourish men's spirits and bodies indefinitely, heal their ailments,
and reveal to them the most sublime splendour that man can
experience. The original legends dealing with this subject,
judging from what is extant today, appear to have been very
few, for the large number that were written during the following
150 years in all parts of Europe are derivative and often debased
versions, and even the earliest that we have show some
evidence of having had one predecessor that provided the basic
material for them all. This source has never been traced, though
certain scholars have not hesitated to exercise ingenuity in
postulating its chief characteristics, meaning, and even authorship, in efforts to attach meaning and coherence to the Grail
legends as we know them. Others, notably the late J.D. Bruce,
have now, by their accurate researches in criticizing and cor-
relating the texts rendered this practice almost impossible. The
meaning of the legends however, if they can be said to have one
implied in their incidents and properties in the way that other
myths can, is still as elusive and as fascinating as ever, startling
the imagination only to mystify it.

The stories died a natural death within about 250 years of
their appearance. After Malory's *Morte d'Arthur* England almost

entirely neglected them until the Romantic Movement of the nineteenth century, when an edition of Malory edited by Robert Southey, was issued in 1817, and their themes and characters were reintroduced into literature, especially by Tennyson and Rossetti, though in a manner as humanitarian and pallid compared with the originals as the Pre-Raphaelite paintings. No greater attention was accorded them on the Continent. However, from the last half of the nineteenth century until today a considerable body of critical literature has been produced analysing their sources, setting, and meaning with two main purposes in view: to establish their literary antecedents and relationship to each other; and to elucidate their latent meaning, usually by means of references to mythological and religious analogues. By employing the researches principally of the former group, I propose to enter the lists with the latter, and suggest an interpretation of the symbols that has not previously been put forward.

Although the quest for some ultimate value underlies much modern literature, the need for it being felt more acutely than for centuries by people dissatisfied with mechanist interpretations of destiny, the legends of the Grail have contributed little to the theme employed to express this longing, with the notable exceptions of T.S. Eliot's "The Waste Land," based as it is on a synthesis of Grail myths, vegetation rites, and various other beliefs, (a synthesis unfortunately suggested by the theories of Jessie L. Weston, which have since been shown by several authorities to be unfounded in fact; though this does not of course deny the validity of their use in the poem); and Kafka, whose work is almost a translation into modern terms of the Grail Quest, a similarity much closer than any to be found in Bunyan, and overlooked, I believe, by all his critics. It is for such reasons, rather than for their intrinsic literary merits, that the Grail legends deserve a wider public, (they are available in rather inaccessible editions at present); for it is their underlying meaning, the main points of which this essay sets out to interpret, that is of specially topical interest.

At the epoch in our culture when the legends were produced the Church jutted with grim correctitude from its rock, assailed with a fury unknown to early Christianity, and not repeated in later times, by the rising sea of Mariolatry. The Virgin Mary captured the imagination of the people with a strength that can be measured by the violent denunciations against womankind that were poured out in ecclesiastical and monastic literature. The Trinity was and is in essence a predominantly masculine manifestation of the Deity; the Church was a strict, almost mathematically inhuman structure whose girders were the formalities of patristic theology; and it is not surprising that the living mass of people, unable to revolt against the very medium that their souls were bred in, were at least forced to water it with feminine interpolations that became more and more heretical. Christ, who had come as a mediator teaching the love of God, had become a stern Judge himself, and Mary had to be introduced as a mediator to His love. Countless legends and prayers from these times exist in which she is approached because the Divinity is too remote, to be rapidly followed by more in which she almost becomes a fourth person added to the Trinity; and worse still, there are many instances where she is prayed to with success when Christ has refused to listen, where she is able to reverse His decision to reject a sinful soul, and even to save the souls of men who have openly flouted God's laws all their lives but have regularly performed some mechanical rite in her honour, or committed their souls to her care art death. Not only could she mollify the will of Christ her son, she could even controvert the decrees of the whole Trinity. The flourishing of such beliefs among the people was firmly condemned by the Church, and so strongly masculine is its basis that it was able to oppose the dogma of her Immaculate Conception, symbolising the attainment of an almost divine state, until 1854, when it was at last proclaimed. However, it could not remain entirely deaf to the movement, and by the beginning of the thirteenth century, (just when the Grail legends were growing), a cult of the Virgin was fully systematized, with chapels being built in her honour, monastic reforms devoted to her, and so on.

It was among the people as opposed to the Church (and for the great divergence that existed between them see C.G. Coulton's *Five Centuries of Religion*) that this movement originated, just as it was among the people that the Grail legends found favour. And once we realize that it is this feminine spiritual element, which was markedly deficient in orthodox Christianity, that the Grail legends are concerned with finding, their meaning becomes clearer. They describe the questing masculine spirit searching for this missing principle, for the lack of which life eventually withers away and petrifies as the Church did. People were coming to realize that though the spirit blew upon the water, it was the water that healed.

By the female element I mean the whole aspect of life existing unconsciously in men's minds as a counterpart to the male conscious attitude, a duality symbolized in mythology as Sky and Earth, Sun and Ocean, Slayer and Dragon, Hero and Princess, and so on. In all such myths both male and female elements are depicted as a complementary spiritual duality in a manner that is not found in Christianity, where the female principle, in the form of Mary, is accorded merely reverence in contradistinction to the worship permitted solely to the Trinity, (when it is not specifically characterized as evil, a much commoner thing). It was in spite of orthodox Christianity that women came to have a spiritual as well as a purely biological value, and the tide of Mariolatry, at its height a mere handmaid of the official church, was scarcely able to elevate their cultural or social status at all (C.G. Coulton). It nevertheless manifested the cultural need for such a change; the Grail legends were omens of it.

Not only was the quest especially for the female principle, but, it being recognized that that was the means to approaching the ultimate value of life, the attainment of rebirth and immortality, this theme also was woven into the myth and made dependent on the successful conjugation of the male and female spiritual principles. Perceval becomes the guardian of the Grail, that is, assimilates this principle, and thereby attains immortality. And, in so far as it is a quest for immortality, it has a considerable resemblance to the earliest poem with that theme that we know, the Gilgamesh epic, to which reference will be made again later.

A kind of lowest common denominator of the various versions of the Grail Quest may be paraphrased from the rambling maze of incident, as follows:

The Hero is reared by his Widowed Mother in a in a secluded wood, far from the society of the outer world. His father died just before or after his birth.

When he is grown to he a young man, he is wandering

through the woods one day, and comes upon some knights jousting.

He is so attracted by their noble appearance that he leaves his mother against her will, thereby causing her death (or great unhappiness), which he later hears of.

He goes to King Arthur's court and is knighted there.

Adventures follow, and one day he meets a man fishing in a lake from a boat, and, on asking where he might find a night's shelter, is directed by him to a Castle, which, in spite of the directions, proves to be difficult to find, and its approaches perilous to traverse.

He overcomes the perils, and is well received by the host, who turns out to be the same man who directed him from the boat, in fact, the Fisher King.

The Fisher King's land is waste.

They sit down to a feast, and during the meal a procession passes through, the Grail being borne by a maiden, and a bleeding sword by a youth. The Hero fails to ask a certain Question, — what the meaning of this is; and next day wakes up to find the Castle and all its inhabitants vanished.

After many adventures, during which he is not only seeking the Grail Castle, but also his Mother, whose death he must expiate, he comes to the Castle again.

The reception is as festive as before; and this time he asks the Question. Whereupon the King is healed, the land recovers, and he becomes the new custodian of the Grail, sometimes being transported to Heaven with it. In any event, it is not to be seen again on this earth.

The diverse elements that are woven together, or superimposed one upon another, in the legend may be resolved into three strands:

The myth of a hero, whose birth is "virgin" in character, the father dying before or soon after the event; who undertakes to seek the Grail; overcomes many perilous trials, and finally attains the goal, which is (a) guardianship of the Grail, (b) immortality, (c) the cure of the King and the waste land; — and (d) suspected in an earlier version, and indicated very strongly by comparison with similar tales and from hints in the legends themselves, marriage.

The setting of Arthurian Romance.

The Christian mythology, this being greatly amplified in the Histories of the Grail's origin and transportation to Britain, the earliest of which is Robert de Borron's *"Joseph of Arimathea."*

The progressively Christian character of the legends from Chrétien de Troyes' *"Conte del Graal"* to the Galahad Quest has led a number of scholars to conclude that the original story was purely pagan in origin, and that Christian strata were progressively imposed upon it. They looked for its origin in the preexisting folk lore and religion, but found there nothing but the vaguest analogies to the principle features of the Quest, the only direct predecessor being the early English romance of Syr Percyvelle de Galles, which has nothing to do with a quest, telling a simple tale of Perceval as a hero with a birth and upbringing as it was later incorporated in the Grail legends, but with no trace of those characteristics of them, the Grail and its Question. Sources in folk lore, Mithraism, Vegetation rites, etc., have all been postulated and examined at length, but have been conclusively disposed of by J.D. Bruce *(Evolution of Arthurian Romance)* and A.E. Waite *(The Holy Grail)* among others, and the primarily Christian character of the legends demonstrated.

Nevertheless, the fact remains that orthodox Christianity never admitted the Grail legends into its precincts, and the tales themselves, particularly the histories of the Grail, seem deliberately designed to prevent this happening, or at least to manifest in quite definite yet mysterious manner a toxin inimical to the established order. As the receptacle with which Christ instituted the Eucharist, and which later received His blood from the wound pierced in His side by the sword of Longinus, the Roman centurian, the Grail might be expected to have appealed strongly to the Christian imagination as a relic at least as worthy of reverence as the chips of wood from the Cross, napkins, thorns, phials of blood, and so on, that were scattered throughout Christendom and officially approved in legends that described their origin and sanctuary. And considering the extremities of belief that the all-powerful Church was able to absorb officially or exterminate, whether by sprinkling the pagan temples with water and re-dedicating them, as Saint Gregory counselled his emissaries to England to do, or by reducing the erring to ashes in purificatory fire, its inability to do either in this case is as remarkable as the unconscious need that must have existed to flout its authority in expressing a principle so alien to it. The chief manifest barrier to acceptance was the succession of guardians who had no official place among the personages figuring in the recognized mythology of the Church. The first, Joseph of Arimathea, supplants Saint Peter as the head of the succession and transmitter of the mystery of Christ's precious blood. He is followed by his son-in law Brons, or, according to the Vulgate Chronicles, his son Josephe. Perceval, son of Alain li Gros (who is the son of Brons, and in some versions has vowed celibacy), is the final guardian. His relationship with previous guardians, and therefore his standing outside the Church's traditions, is always stressed by the legends, and is a condition of his achieving the Grail. The Vulgate Chronicles introduce a number of intermediate Keepers, presumably with a view to preserving some sort of likely chronology, but the preoccupation of men at that time with the mystery of the Trinity, culminating in 1150, just before the appearance of the legends, in the establishment by the Church of the Festival of the Most Holy Trinity, possibly determined the preference for a triple guardianship. However, nothing alters the fact that this most precious of relics was relegated by the legends to a guardianship quite outside the Church's traditions, that the Church recognized the inevitability of this, and could do nothing about it.

We must now consider what the Grail was alleged to be in fact, and actually was in symbol. In the first place it must be recognized that it is the central fact in the legends in which it appears; the story of its quest is an absolutely definite entity, though embedded in and sometimes confused with other adventures in Romance. Furthermore, there are no other quests in Romance remotely similar to it.

Except in the German legend of Parzifal, where the holy object is a kind of Stone, the Grail is usually described as the vessel used by Christ at the Last Supper. It then came into the possession of Joseph of Arimathea, who collected Christ's blood in it when he took the body down from the Cross and it sustained him during a forty years' incarceration in prison before his journey towards the west. It is the chief among four hallows: Grail, Sword, Dish, and Lance; and in connection with this, one thing that strikes the reader is that it is the vessel itself that is held to be of supreme value, rather than its content, Christ's blood, which one might have supposed to be the centre of reverence. This association of four patently male and female symbols is of considerable importance; though I believe it cannot be used to demonstrate anything more than the essentially female character of the Grail, for analogies from folk lore and the Tarot pack of cards are so remote or vague as to be value-less; and this is further supported by the fact that the Grail often appears without the other hallows, and completely overshadows them in importance. The reason for this is fundamental to its conception. What is being symbolized is the formation of a quaternity; the Trinity already received sufficient emphasis in the official faith, but the balancing fourth element had to be sought for; and hence in the quest for it, it received greater em-phasis in the imagination. From the earliest time in Egypt, where a pot was the hieroglyph for a woman, vessels have been used throughout the world as female symbols, and though one cannot assume that every vessel appearing in any situation has this significance, I think it is safe to say that this one has, when it appears in such company. Additional support is obtained for this view from the fact that the Grail is nearly always carried by a Maiden when it is manifested, and the Sword by a Youth.

Furthermore, the feminality of the vessel is evidenced by one of its most remarkable properties, for besides offering spiritual nourishment to those worthy to receive it, it did not disdain to provide them with actual food of the most delicious kind on various occasions. It sustained Joseph for forty years in the dungeon. It usually appeared during the feast in the Castle. The Bowl of Plenty has an almost world-wide distribution, and symbolizes the material fount from which the spirit soars and to which it returns for refreshment; and its appearance here, linked with a Hero who is specified as seeking both it and his mother, is quite in accord with a myth which, on the mass of evidence, is first and last a Christian one.

A description of just what is meant by a female symbol now becomes necessary, particularly as I wish to combat the views of some of my predecessors in this field who agree that the Grail is female, but assign by means of that term an essentially bio-logical significance to it. In short, by referring to it as a symbol of female reproduction, it has been associated with fertility rites connected with vegetation, Adonis, Attis, Eleusinian mysteries, etc.; and in its capacity as a Bowl of Plenty its origin has been looked for in Celtic mythology and elsewhere. But I believe that to understand the meaning of a symbol correctly it must be examined in relation to its context, and to assume that a symbol having certain associations in the framework of fertility rites will have the same associations when found in a quite different tradition is an erroneous idea. Symbols do not have the same significance for a man when he is forty as they did when he was twenty, still less when he was two; and mechanist theories that suppose the contrary are in my opinion mistaken. Consequently, in affirming that the Grail is a female symbol, I mean that it represents the female principle within the context of those times, which was a Christian context; and not a symbol with female fertility associations derived from a context flourishing a thousand years previously. Miss Weston partly saw this view-point, and tried to bridge the millennium by postulating the existence of small isolated communities still practising fertility rites, who should be the authors of the legends; but the evidence that she put forward was too flimsy to withstand later criticism. However, to assume, with J.D. Bruce and A.E. Waite, that the legends are essentially Christian, is to miss the point: that they give expression to the shadow-side of Christianity, the aspirations of Christians *manqués* who could not accept the limitations of a spiritual attitude that was incapable of assimilating the feminine into its divinity.

The presence of a secret and heretical Christian Church as a propagator of the legends is suggested by A.E. Waite, but I think it is unnecessary to suppose that any such body existed; because when a belief that does not embrace the totality of experience forms the framework in which a large number of people live, desire, and fear, and that belief is notably lacking in one particular element, it is natural for some people, especially poets, to give expression to the unconscious needs felt by themselves and many of their fellows. They return to that Bowl of Plenty whence the symbol has arisen, the unconscious; as they have depicted themselves doing, they seek, like Perceval, the source of their inspiration, and bring up with it a host of related symbols. It is for this reason that the mythology of the legends appears to be so derivative from earlier pagan beliefs; these existed in the unconscious, and whether or not the poets were historically influenced by actual pre-Christian myths is immaterial; and, in point of fact, the weight of modern scholarship inclines against it. Christians dissatisfied with their faith, searched the deepest recesses of their being to discover why, reverting, in so doing, to those pagan elements that were part of official Christianity — incorporated but not wholly transmuted — and formulated their legends with symbols drawn partly from a past age, using them to impart a novel significance to the Christian faith that they were unconsciously trying to modify. Something more impersonal and more remote from tradition was needed than the Virgin Mary to express this spiritual craving; she was too much the *noble dame* with imperial whims and tenderness, and, as the mother of Christ, exalted with more logic than feeling even by the Church. A symbol on the same plane of abstraction as the Cross, with its three members held up to the heavens by the fourth buried in mother earth, was required to liberate the fourth member from the clay, and the Grail was conceived for this purpose.

So much for the female principle involved. The heresy was aggravated, however, by the clear recognition that assimilation of this principle was a necessary step towards the greatest blessedness, and in a sense, was identical with that goal, rebirth, immortality, a subject on which the Church naturally claimed to be the sole and unchallengeable authority. But analogies of detail as well as general theme are to be found, for example, with the Gilgamesh Epic, where the hero, before starting on the Quest for immortality, the secret of which has been discovered by his ancestor Ut-Napishtim, is described as follows:

"Gilgamesh wept bitterly, and lay stretched out upon the ground.

"He cried: 'Let me not die like Ea-Bani;

"I fear death.'"

The font and the chalice of the Church could bring about the transformation of this fear into qualities of high moral value, for those who could accept the limitations of its faith; but the higher and more complete attitude sought in the legends required the Grail as a symbol for its realization.

The chief personages of the myth, like those of all myths, are dramatized aspects of a single mental complex, existing only in relation to each other, rather than independent characters such

410

as are normally found in fiction (where individuals are re-presented as subject to conflicting forces that transcend them personally, not as apotheoses of the forces themselves); and in this they differ distinctly from the fuller characters living in the Arthurian background, which exhibit a certain solidity and independence, though of course not approaching that to be found in modern novels. This difference between the two types should not be emphasised too much, for the Arthurian legends themselves are closely allied to mythology; but there is such a notable distinction between the *dramatis personae* of the Grail Quests and the Arthurian characters as to enable one to distinguish readily the Grail complex as a whole in its setting. The importance of accepting this principle lies in the necessity of realizing that the Hero and the Fisher King are two aspects of the same complex, are, in fact, identical in a way that is not the case with the Hero and King Arthur, or the latter and Lancelot and Tristram. The myth, although it does merge into the fictional history without any sharp division, exists as a self-contained unit whose parts are strictly interdependent. Psychologically, the Hero plus the rescued Maiden, or the Slayer plus the Conquered Dragon, represent single complexes, the re-birth that results from coming to a stable yet dynamic understanding of one's destiny.

In this case, the relation between Perceval and the Grail is clear enough; he becomes its final guardian, and together they exist immortally far from the Earth, usually in Heaven. The two together symbolize the reborn man, the spiritual Hero; and the heresy exists just in this fact, that the re-birth has been attained outside the orthodox tradition of Mother Church. Only one born outside this orthodoxy, like Perceval, (Par-lui-fait as he is nick-named in the *Perlesvaus)*, had the power and freedom to seek for forbidden fruit as nourishment for the existing state of affairs.

Nearly equal in importance to attaining immortality in the legend is the healing of the sick Fisher King and the Waste Land that he rules over, and we must consider next just what the meaning of the symbol is. The original bestowal of his title of Fisher occurred as the result of a most interesting ritual meal, recounted in Borron's *Joseph of Arimathea* as follows:

The Grail is being brought westwards to Britain, and, while it is still in Africa, some of the retinue accompanying it have fallen into sin. In order to discover who these are, Brons, Joseph's brother-in-law, catches a fish on the instructions of a divine voice issuing from the Grail, and sets it with the Grail as a meal before the company, in a manner similar to the Last Supper. The sinners are unable to see the Grail, or experience the spiritual delights of the meal, and so are denounced by those still in grace. Thereafter Brons is to be called the Fisher King; a title that is passed on to his descendants.

The spiritual character of the meal is stressed, as is its analogy to the Last Supper; and though such a sacrament was not sanctioned by the Church at the time when the legends were written, it was frequently performed in the first few Christian centuries, and considered to be quite permissible then. A number of paintings in the catacombs depict a sacramental meal consisting of two fishes, usually with bread, and a glass of red wine. Such a practice was abandoned when the Eucharistic meal of bread and wine became established, the only remnant being the custom of eating fish on Fridays, a rite carried over from the Jews, who probably acquired it in their Babylonian exile, where they learnt to eat the creature sacred to the deity presiding over that day, Nina (R. Eisler: *Orpheus the Fisher.*) For the fish was held to be sacred to many goddesses of love and fertility: Aphrodite (Venus; Vendredi, Friday), Cybele, Ishtar, Artemis, etc., and also to the Fisher-God Orpheus. As Eisler has shown, Christianity at its birth was more closely related to Orphism than to any other pagan religion; each incorporated texts of the other's, and the fish symbolism so prevalent in the early centuries is derived from that source, with the Jewish element mixed in.

Now for the meaning of the fish symbol: it covers a group of ideas associated with fertility: at its most general it signifies a beneficent relationship with the source of life; lying in the maternal womb, as it is depicted on Babylonian seal-cylinders, or two fish forming the circular *yoni* (=vulva) of Buddhism, the idea expressed is that of conception. It is also the phallus (in Pythagorean number symbolism, $IX\Theta Y\Sigma = 9\ 22\ 8\ 20\ 18 = 77 = 21\ 1\ 11\ 11\ 15\ 18 = \Phi A\Lambda\Lambda O\Sigma$), but it is not simply and everywhere a sign for the phallus as the mechanomorphist psychologists insist. It is a symbol of fertility in its male aspect, which at the same time, in the nature of things, presupposes relationship with a female complement, the primordially female source of life, water.

The King, therefore, has dropped his line into the water to rescue this object of value from its depths, and before reaching a conclusion as to the precise meaning of this I shall consider his other important attribute, concerning which the legend is subtly accurate psychologically: he is ailing as well as fishing.

Only those who are ill and recognize themselves to be so search for the cure. The greatest spiritual discoveries have more often than not been made by the moody, the tuberculous, the unstable, artists and saints who have submitted to their disabilities more intensely than the ordinary man, so that their pursuit of the valuable may be rendered the more urgent. *"J'ai cultivé mon hystérie,"* wrote Baudelaire; and it is a commonplace that poetry is born of suffering. Christ preferred outcasts to the respectable. And it is the realization that some spiritual factor is lacking that impels the King to undertake its salvage from the lake.

The nature of his ailment has aroused a certain amount of discussion, and is of considerable significance to the theories set out here. In the legends it is variously attributed to a wound from a spear having pierced his thighs, or senility; these having been brought about by (1) a dolorous stroke in battle, or (2) yielding to earthly passion, or (3) inability to die until his successor achieves the Grail, or (4) failure of the Hero to ask the Question (this is a late version, as J.L. Weston pointed out, and can be disregarded). The point to be considered is, whether his wound in the thighs or senility are euphemisms for castration, and whether his general condition symbolizes it. There is no doubt that the state of the land is dependent on the health of the King, though in recognizing this one need not assume that the legend is derived from fertility rites; or, for that matter, from Orphic-Christian rites, though I have given some prominence to the latter as they have not, I think, been previously noticed by critics of the legends. It is true that the same ideas occur in the various myths, but since, as stated before, the evidence is strongly in favour of this being primarily a Christian legend, even though it grew from the shadow-side of Christianity, the meaning of the ailment must be related to its context, and not sought in beliefs current a millennium previously. Consequently, to describe the

King's deficiency as loss of physiological fertility through castration or senile impotence, and to support this with the contention that he is fishing for his phallus, would be to revert to a more natural and less spiritual cultural situation in which to amplify the symbol. In the myth as we find it I think it refers quite clearly to the absence of the female spiritual principle in the Christianity of the time; that is, it symbolizes the inability to establish a relationship with the female principle, and hence, since it is only our relationship with things, not the things themselves, that we know, the deficiency of the principle itself, a loss that is felt to be a misfortune, an ailment. The fish that he is trying to hook is this relationship with the female source of life, which, once established, would enable him to include the feminine in his spiritual outlook. *(Note.* — Myths were widespread in W. Asia and elsewhere in the hundred years or so before Christ, of a fish which, when drawn up from the water and cut open, was found to contain a golden vessel whose powers of producing gold for its owner were inexhaustible. Hence the King is often called "Rich Fisher." — R. Eisler.)

In fact, the King is the counterpart of the Hero, in that he depicts the contemplative quest through meditation, brooding over the eternally feminine water, whilst the other displays the active extraverted attitude. When the Grail is achieved, and the female principle thus incorporated, the Hero's wandering ends and the King's sickness is healed. They are complementary aspects of the same complex of assimilation and the freedom resulting from it.

Finally we must take up the problem that is perhaps the most obscure in all the Grail literature, the Question, the asking of which releases the King from his bondage of sickness, raises the curse from the Waste Land, and constitutes the achievement of the Grail quest. It is one of the principle features of the legends, and although its signification has been ignored by many scholars, those who have tried to elucidate it might just have well remained in the company of their fellows who did not attempt to, for their researches have led only to one conclusion, and that a negative one; that this feature is peculiar to the Grail legends, and is not to be found in folk lore, religious mythology, fertility rites, or anywhere else.

The various stories by no means agree in their accounts; it is absent altogether from the Galahad version, for example; but the greater unanimity is shown in dealing with the first of the two occasions when it should be asked, that is, the failure to ask it. The hero comes to the Castle where the Grail reposes, a journey that becomes increasingly hazardous right up to the entrance itself, the Castle being guarded by perilous bridges, ferocious animals, and engines of destruction, (just as to approach the Kingdom of Heaven within us is the more dangerous the nearer we go); but once within he is well received by the Fisher King, and a feast is set before him. During the course of it the Grail appears to be borne in a procession by a damsel, and at this point the hero is expected, and sometimes longs, to ask what the purpose of the Grail is: *"Qui on en servoit?"* But he is restrained from doing so for reasons that differ in the various accounts: he has been warned by his Mother, or a hermit, not to be inquisitive; or he is dumbfounded by the sight; or it seems too trivial a thing to do and does not occur to him. When he wakes next day the Castle is gone, and he must start the quest anew. I might mention again that the quest is now definitely concerned with his Mother, whose suffering or death, brought about by his leaving home, must be expatiated; but since this theme is implicit in all heroic quests it affords only incidental support to the specific goal of this one, the discovery of the female principle. When he eventually arrives at the Castle again, the Question is asked, the Grail achieved, and the King healed. But unfortunately this happens in only a minority of the versions, though from passing references to it throughout the legends, and implicit in the accounts of the first failure, it is evidently intended to occur. However, the Question may be asked, and a further condition, the resoldering of a broken sword, be imposed before attainment, so that although the asking was necessary it was not the final step that it should have been; or the Question may not be asked at all, the conclusion coming in some other way. Nevertheless, the gist of the situation is defined clearly enough: a Question as to the purpose of the Grail has to be asked as the termination of the quest.

Various hypotheses have been put forward at one time or another suggesting that the Grail legends recount in a veiled form some Mystery of Initiation connected with an heretical Church or pagan fertility rites, but it seems to me that the

Question, which is not only specific to the legends but holds such an important place in them, conclusively rules out such an idea. For in the very nature of initiation one comes silent to the fount of wisdom, a supplicant at the healing source, not as a questioner of a mystery that is ailing and must be healed by the aspirant; the guardian of the treasure is the healer, and to suggest that he was sick would be not only impious, but render one's attendance at his teaching rather ridiculous.

Once again, I think, the legend is presenting us with an instance of psychological acumen; it is stating in the clearest manner that to ask the meaning of a symbol being thrust up from the unconscious is half way to assimilating it. (But not the whole way; one must already be prepared to submit to the dictates of the answer invoked. And in the legends, only he who is suited by birth, adventure, and sometimes chastity, the predestined hero, asks it.) We are not accustomed nowadays to enquire very deeply into our mental motives and attitudes; we prefer to read about them in text-books of psychology, or leave the whole problem to newspaper astrologers; but when these legends were recounted men were still capable of passionately formulating beliefs about life, and sometimes of expressing them in symbols that gripped the imagination so firmly that they wholly possessed the individual and dictated his actions and feelings, compelling him to make some attempt to understand the internal forces that guided him, and to ask himself their meaning. The disturbing symbol had to be sought and its meaning questioned. The yearning of the unsatisfied Quester and of the ailing, impotent King could only be brought to an end by the achievement of the Grail, when the old order would be regenerated with the new blood of its heir. The need to diverge from orthodoxy in order to do this by assimilating a feminine spiritual attitude became so great that it was openly expressed by an alien symbol that had inevitably forced its way up, and in order to understand and accept its value one had to ask: *"Qui on en servoit?"*

Quite in keeping with all this are the various reasons given for the failure to ask the question at the first visit. In one account his silence is attributed to parental injunctions against curiosity, instilled into him when he was a lad by his Mother, or a Hermit (taking the place of the dead Father) who taught him about the Grail. The desire for knowledge of the outer world and the continual questions concerning it are manifestations of the inexorable force that drives the adolescent from home. On his journey towards complete adulthood, in his efforts to attain that state of dynamic equilibrium symbolized by the Hero, it is as natural for the parents, if they are selfish and possessive, to try to thwart his aspirations, as it is inevitable for him, still unsure of his powers, to struggle against the bonds of his love, fear, and habit that restrain him, and, whether his parents actually do impede him or not, for him to attribute his own defaults to their malign influence; to them he is still attached, and it is for them to release him, so he thinks, not he that must struggle free. He sees them as holding him back by refusing to answer his questions, telling him not to be inquisitive, and warning him (for are they not selfish, and wanting him to return to them?) that even when he is confronted by the problems that life will present him, not to pay any attention to them. And so, although Perceval has surmounted all the perils surrounding the Castle, he quails before the heart of the mystery itself when he approaches it for the first time; and although he is conscious of a longing to ask its meaning, the little fear at the back of his mind prevents him from doing so, and the blame for the episode is dismissed as a parental responsibility. His Mother's death caused by his departure for adventure, that is, the dissolution of his relationship with her, had at first left him too isolated and weak to face the most fateful secret of his life; the first triumph of his breaking away from her had made him lose sight of the source of his being entirely, the bond is severed, she is dead; but since it is impossible for him to fulfil his destiny if he cuts himself off from the very past in which it is rooted, the death of the childish relationship with that source must be replaced by an adult one, which is what is meant by Perceval, after the first failure, having to set out on adventures again to search for his Mother as well as the Grail, and, when he learns of her death, to expiate it.

This weakness that still remains also underlies his failure in the other accounts. In one version he is dumbfounded by the symbol; the Grail fascinates his imagination beyond his control; he is swept off his insecurely planted feet by it, and it leaves him as imperiously as it came "the Spirit bloweth where it listeth." In the other version his weakness is unconsciously perceived, and the symbol is not allowed to trouble him at all; it is repressed, in fact, and seems too trivial a thing to bother about, for the very reason that it is of cardinal importance. And once again he has to set out on adventure.

But why should the Question be peculiar to these legends, and absent from the labyrinths of pagan mythology that have been examined? Beyond its remarkable appositeness in the story, it may very well hark back to the occasion when Christ specified this particular method as an aid to comprehending the promptings of the soul, in the words: "Ask and ye shall receive," which as far as I know are not to be found in any other religion as an overt doctrine. The asking is performed subjectively; there is no need to look for secret churches or rites of initiation, and to do so mistakes the nature of the Question: it is a mental method that is as valuable today as it was then, when it revealed the way to cure a certain spiritual drought that was afflicting mankind.

CHAPTER 21

The Initiation Pattern and the Grail

ROBERT W. CRUTWELL

Attention has been paid lately to the group of ideas and practices which is best designated by the word initiation used in the widest sense; and recent accounts of the relation between different elements, as they are found in the ancient world and among modern peoples of arrested culture, have disclosed a unitary pattern, in which the elements have each an appropriate place. Mr W.F.J. Knight, in his paper to the Folk-Lore Society on April 22, 1936, offered a general history of the "Initiation Pattern," with identifications of some of the elements. But he did not mention the very close parallels in medieval legends of the Holy Grail; and as the pattern is unusually explicit and complete in them, and as these legends and the other material together confirm suggestions made from either side, I now add some material concerning the Grail legends, and I also propose a formula for initiation lore, suggested by them.

The correlation of the Grail Legends with the Initiation Pattern

Miss Jessie Weston, in her *Quest of the Holy Grail*, London, 1912, writes thus:

> The Grail Quest should be viewed primarily as an
> Initiation Story ... The quest, properly speaking, begins
> only when the hero, having failed at his first

unpremeditated visit to the Grail Castle to fulfil the tests to which he has been subjected, sets out with the deliberate intention of finding the vanished Temple of the Grail, and of fulfilling the conditions which shall qualify him to obtain a full knowledge of the marvels which he has beheld ... Professor Heinzel had already seen that the peculiarities of the Grail story, the nature of the test employed, the mysterious question, all partook of the character of an initiation, and that one of its elements was the record of a failure to pass an initiation test.

Miss Weston elaborated her theory in *From Ritual to Romance* (London, 1917) in which she dealt fully with the Initiation and Mystery elements in the Grail Legends. Dr Nitze has equated the Grail Mysteries with the Eleusinian Mysteries, whereas Miss Weston connects them with the mysteries of Adonis, Tammuz and the Divine King.

So much is sufficient to prove that the initiatory character of the Grail Legends is no new or unsupported theory. Indeed it had been worked out at great length many years earlier by A.E. Waite in his *Hidden Church of the Holy Graal* (London, 1909) which equates the Grail with the Philosopher's Stone, and correlates the Grail Legends not only with Alchemy, but also with Freemasonry, Rosicrucianism and Occultism. It is, however, necessary to emphasize that neither Malory nor Tennyson gave us the genuine Grail Legend, but only popularized and sentimentalized echoes at a far distance of far earlier stories which they failed to understand. The real canon of the Grail Legend covers roughly the years 1150–1200, during which it appeared in many and varied forms in many languages. But the root ideas (completely lost in Malory and Tennyson, but restored by Wagner in his *Parsifal* opera) are invariable and persistent. They centre in a mysterious Castle or Temple, situated always by water, often on a mountain, wherein dwells an equally mysterious King Priest, who is *both Dead and Alive* and who guards certain talismans or symbols — Lance, Cup, Sword and Dish (or Stone). The object of the innumerable hero-questers is to find this Castle, to witness the manifestation of its symbols and to restore the Priest King to life and health. The country

420

round the Castle is the Waste Land: it was wasted by the King's illness and "death;" and it will be restored to fertility by his recovery or "resurrection." The difficulties in the way of finding the Grail Temple are both numerous and fearsome. There are many guides to it, not all of them reliable; but the chief guide is a woman called the Grail Messenger (Kundry in Wagner) who is sometimes a hideous old hag and sometimes a lovely young girl. She is found usually by water, and near the Castle entrance, both before and after the visits of the questers. She is also, often, the bearer of the Grail, whether a cup or stone (it may be either); and she alternately urges the hero to the quest or warns him from it. When he fails, she upbraids him for not passing the necessary tests. When he succeeds, she often becomes his bride, and changes from ugliness to beauty. The quester not only finds it almost impossible to *find* the Temple. When at last he has found it, it becomes almost impossible to *enter.* There are innumerable obstacles against entry. Sometimes there is a portcullis or a drawbridge; when the hero ventures on to the bridge, either the portcullis falls with a crash and nearly beheads him, or else the bridge itself suddenly rears in the air, so that he nearly falls off it into the waters beneath, which are a wide moat, or a lake, or the sea, or a river, which is itself perilous both from its raging waves and from the water beasts which wait to devour him. In several versions, however, the quester is met by a boatman who is fishing on the castle lake, and who (if satisfied of his credentials) rows him across to the Island Temple. When at last the hero succeeds in entering the Hall of the Grail Castle (or Temple), his troubles are far from over. In many versions he is attacked from all sides, now by ghosts, now by armed knights, now by fierce beasts, who appear from the many chambers and corridors which surround the central Hall. Then often there is a sudden storm — thunder, lightning, hail, wind, so that all the windows suddenly clap too, and shrill birds are heard screeching in the hurricane.

When at last all these obstacles are overcome (they do not, of course, *all* appear in *any* one version), the hero may be welcomed to the presence of the Priest King of the Grail, who turns out to be none other than the Boatman of the Lake who rowed him across, or else one of his other previous guides in various forms. Now comes the initiation test. The King is sorely wounded unto death and of extreme old age — in fact he is really dead — the Dead King in his Ritual Tomb. The function of the hero is twofold (a) to pass an initiatory test, to prove his own fitness, and (b) to restore the Dead King to health and life. A procession appears from the various side chambers of the Hall of Initiation, and slowly *passes to and fro and round and round* the table at which King and guest are seated. The procession consists of young girls and young men, bearing the four (or five) Grail symbols. The hero is expected to ask their meaning. If he fails to ask, the test has failed; if he asks, the King begins a long story of explanation, during which the hero falls asleep. In either case of failure, he is summarily ejected from the Temple (as Parsifal in Act I of Wagner's opera) either by main force, all the inhabitants of the building rushing at him and mishandling him as an intruder, or by simply falling asleep and waking up in a meadow by the water-side, the Castle having completely vanished. It is here that the Grail Messenger lady invariably appears, and reproaches the quester for his failure to pass the initiatory tests. Now, she says, he will have to wander long years (as in Wagner) before he can find the Castle again, and overcome many fresh obstacles both human and superhuman during his quest. As a rule, the quester does at long last succeed in reaching the Castle once again, and often he is successful this second time in passing the tests, and in healing the King and restoring the Waste Land. His reward is succession to the Grail Kingdom, and the Grail King's daughter (really the Grail Messenger) as his bride. There are also innumerable visits to *Magic* Castles, with *Magic* Kings, *Magic* Symbols, *Magic* Ladies; and in these versions the hero usually kills the Magic King or Giant, and marries his queen or his daughter. Or he beheads the giant, who thereupon is released from a spell and becomes a handsome youth.

The above summary is perhaps sufficient. Now for comments. To begin with, the root ideas of the Grail Legend are these:

(1) *A Dead King* in a Castle or Temple, who is really both alive and dead at the same time, and who needs to be rescued from this condition *from outside.*

(2) *A Water Lady* who carries the chief talisman of this Castle, and who is found sometimes inside the Castle, some times

outside. The hero usually weds her, or in some way receives her favours.

(3) *A Castle,* or *Temple,* or *Palace,* always situated by water, often on an island in a lake, or by the seaside; often on a mountain; always mysterious, hard to find, liable to be lost; only found after much difficulty.

(4) *Obstacles to entry into the Castle.* These are of every conceivable kind, and extend over the entire story, increasing however as the Castle draws nearer, and reaching their maximum at the actual moment of entry and reception.

(5) A *Quester* or *Hero,* who under innumerable names and guises is alternately urged to, and warned from, the Quest; who seeks now a *Dying King,* now a *Dead Father,* now a *Hidden Bride,* and now a *Lost Mother* (corresponding to Herzeleide of *Parsifal,* Act II).

(6) *A Grail Procession,* round and round and to and fro, in and out of Hall, Chambers and Corridors.

(7) *The Quester's Mother,* who is either lost or dead and who is sought and found by him.

I think it will be clear by this time that I equate the Dead King of the Grail with the Divine King in his tomb; the Water Lady Messenger of the Grail with (a) the Earth Mother, (b) the Hidden Bride; the Grail Castle with the Cave or Hall of Initiation, which is both the Tomb of the hero's father and the Womb of his mother, as well as the Vagina of his bride; the obstacles with the Maze or Labyrinth, both within and without the Fort, i.e. Castle; the Quester with the candidate for initiation, whose object is both personal and cosmic; the Procession with the Initiation Dance; and the Quester's Mother with the Earth Mother. The nature of the Grail itself is obscure and not always the same in the legends. I am inclined to think that the word "Grail" means "a little crater" in the sense of (a) a volcanic crater and (b) a mixing bowl. It symbolizes the internal motions (a) of lava and (b) of ingredients — hence its connection with embryo life whether of womb or tomb. In conclusion, I am haunted by the suspicion that mummification is at the root of much of the whole complex. In Egypt the Dead King, who had built his Tomb during life, was eviscerated after death, and his entrails were placed in canopic jars. My suspicion is that the bearers of these canopic jars, on their way to, and within, the Pyramid, performed evolutions symbolical of the bowels which they were carrying. The Grail Vessels would thus be connected with the canopic jars, and the Grail Weapons would be the surgical instruments for disembowelment. It is to the point that the Grail King is always wounded in the side precisely where the incision was made for evisceration. But this is too long a story.

The Maze or Trojan Game in the Grail Legends

None of the Grail Legends agree entirely, and none of them contain all the elements of the initiation pattern. There are of course very many of them; but three that are tolerably typical emphasize important elements. These three concern Sir Gawain; they are published together in *Sir Gawain at the Grail Castle*, translated by Jessie L. Weston.* Among the important elements are pavilions pitched for tournaments at the start of the story, and games of chess played in the Castle.

I am fairly certain of two points: (1) That the almost invariable custom of pitching pavilions for tournaments just before a Grail Quest is a medieval form of the Troy Game; and (2) that the frequent occurrence of *Chess* in Grail Castles and Magic Castles throughout the legends, in some of which the chessmen play the game themselves without visible handling, is really another of the innumerable disguises under which the Magic and Initiation appear. The whole story is really a sort of glorified game of chess, in which we have Kings and Queens and Knights and Bishops and Pawns under various forms and in various positions. This perhaps explains the baffling way in which guides turn into hosts and hosts into guides. The maze pattern is represented by the squares of the chess board and the moves of the pieces to and fro, from square to square. (Compare Lewis Carroll's *Alice Through the Looking Glass*, which belongs to the pattern too.)

---

* *Arthurian Romances*, No. VI, London, David Nutt, 1903. See Chapter 12 of the present collection for the second of these three texts [Ed.].

There are arguments in support of this. A chess board is a pattern, and the word almost literally means "King's Maze" (for "chess" is Sháh, Persian for "King"), and so "Initiation Pattern." A.M. Hocart (*Kingship,* Oxford, 1927) cites instances of games of chess and dice played in the ritual of divine kings:

> The great interest of the Ruanda (initiation) ceremonies is that they clearly bring together kingship and initiation. The leader is the King of the Imandura; he wins his kingdom in a manner strangely reminiscent of Tibet (see below); for he plays with his opponent a game of chess to decide who will be King ...

> The victory which the (generalized) King must win on ascending the throne turns out to be really a magical victory in a magical contest ... Thus, in Tibet, at a certain festival a monk represents the person of the Dalai Lama; a man from among the people is dressed up as King of the Demons. The latter contests (his right to the throne) ... At last the dice are used to decide who is right ...

> The garments with which the Indian King is invested ... represent the various membranes of the womb into which the king is supposed to enter in order to be born again ... After putting on the womb, the priest hands to the king *five dice,* saying 'Thou art the master; may these *five regions of thine* (i.e. the four points of the compass and the zenith) fall to thy lot.' Sovereignty is thus acquired by the decision of the dice, and this reminds us of the game of chess played for supremacy between the Dalai Lama and the King of the Demons in Tibet. (Hocart, pp.152, 24f, 79)

I make these comments. The word *chess* means *King* (Persian *Sháh*) and the word *Checkmate* means "The King is Dead" (Persian *Sháh Mát*). The object, therefore, of the game of chess was *to produce a dead king.* The victor immemorially celebrates the king's death by crying out: *"Sháh Mát,* Check Mate, The King is Dead." But an essential point of the chess game is that there is another king to succeed the dead king, namely the victorious king. "The King is Dead — Long Live the King!" In other

425

words, the game symbolizes not only the Death, but the Resurrection of the King, in the person of his successor (cf. Horus) who is really himself (cf. Osiris) reborn or risen from the dead (cf. Christ and Baptism). The Chess Board, or Chequer Board, is really the labyrinth or Maze of the five regions of the king's body (cf. dice symbolizing the five regions of the world); length, depth, height, breadth and head (the head = the zenith, or pole, terrestrial and celestial). The Divine King's Body symbolizes the Universe (which is also symbolized by the Initiation Cave). The Head, or Zenith, would be the central or nodal point of the chess board.

A Universal Initiation Formula

Day	Delivery of the Queen Mother	Sun Born	=	Earth Risen	Delivery of the Queen Mother	Day
Night	King's Tomb	Sun Dead	=	Earth conceived	King's Womb	Night
Day	Delivery of the King's Father	Sun Rise	=	Earth Born	Delivery of the King's Father	Day
Night	Queen's Womb	Sun conceived	=	Earth Dead	Queen's Tomb	Night
Day	Delivery of the Queen Mother	Sun Born	=	Earth Risen	Delivery of the Queen Mother	Day
etc.	etc.	etc.		etc.	etc.	etc.

I venture to offer above a formula which I believe to be universally applicable and in the present state of knowledge to represent as well as possible the conceptions from which the practices and myths of "initiation" have been developed.

426

Thus the Sun Hero is dead while pregnant with the embryo Earth Heroine, and *his* delivery from the Tomb Labyrinth by *her* is at once her Birth from his Womb and his Resurrection from his Tomb.

Conversely, the Sun Hero is pregnant while dead; buried alive, in fact. Hence (1) Foundation burials and (2) the practice of couvade

Thus the Earth Heroine is dead while pregnant with the embryo Sun Hero, and *her* delivery from the Tomb Labyrinth by *him* is at once his Birth from her Womb, and her Resurrection from her Tomb.

Conversely, the Earth Heroine is pregnant while dead; buried alive, in fact. Hence the practice of burying pregnant vestal virgins alive.

(Womb = Tomb)
Tomb:
Entry = Death
Exit = Resurrection
Womb:
Entry = Conception
Exit = Birth

(Womb = Tomb)
Tomb:
Entry = Death
Exit = Resurrection
Womb:
Entry = Conception
Exit = Birth

An explanation follows. All initiation is a ritual attempt at participation in the interrelationship of sun and earth, the sun being regarded as King and the earth as Queen. But their interrelationship is manifold; therefore initiatory processes are manifold. Sexual intercourse, for example, although in one sense mutual, may arise from the passionate initiation either of the male or of the female partner. Rape, or violent embrace, of the female by the male involves both ceremonial "death" to the female and ceremonial "life" to the male; the male is sexually relieved by copulation with the reluctant female. Conversely, rape, or violent embrace, of the male by the female involves both ceremonial "death" to the male and ceremonial "life" to the female; the female is sexually relieved by copulation with the reluctant male. Again, ceremonially speaking, rape of the female by the male not unnaturally results in the birth of a son who is a reincarnation of his father; and rape of the male by the female, in the birth of a daughter, who is a reincarnation of her mother. Hence the innumerable instances of ritual incest, including the

"Oedipus Complex," the custom of Egyptian pharaohs marrying their sisters, matriarchy and patriarchy. All these are explicable as follows:

Father	=	(Son × Mother)	=	Daughter
Mother	=	(Daughter × Father)	=	Son

But Son and Daughter are also Brother and Sister:

Father = Son = (Brother × Sister) = Daughter = Mother

But, further, to the next generation this Brother and this Sister will be Uncle and Aunt. Brother rapes Sister; result, Boy; Sister rapes Brother; result, Girl. This Boy will be cousin to this Girl, and nephew to her parents, his Uncle and Aunt; and, conversely, this Girl will be cousin to this Boy, and niece to his parents, her Aunt and her Uncle. And all the time they are really but the two original partners:

Sun, King, Husband, Father, Son, Brother, Uncle, Cousin;
Earth, Queen, Wife, Mother, Daughter, Sister, Aunt, Cousin.

Matriarchy results from emphasis on the female *initiation;* Patriarchy, from emphasis on the male *initiation.* Matriarchy develops worship of the Earth; Patriarchy develops worship of the Sun.

It may be remembered in this connection that the Arthurian Legends abound in confused relationships. It is never certain what precise relationship exists between any of the characters, and yet one feels instinctively that they are all members of one vast family. The Grail Questers have mysterious mothers, daughters, sisters, aunts and cousins. The Kings have mysterious nephews who are also their sons, and wives who are also their sisters. Lancelot rapes the Holy Temple Maiden Elaine in order to beget Galahad, who is really the incarnation of himself, and the chroniclers make but feeble attempts to explain his crime.

There are three Guineveres, only one of whom loves Lancelot. Gawain and Modred are both sons and nephews of Arthur. The fact is that, in these legends, all the male characters represent the

428

sun, and all the female characters represent the earth. Hence the apparently inextricable tangle of their interrelationships.

In conclusion, as we began this section with the proposed universal Initiation Formula, we may end with the following table in explanation of it:

Sunset	*Conception of Prince*	*Rape of Queen by King*
	Rape of King by Queen	*Conception of Princess*
Night	*Prince conceived*	*Queen raped by King*
	King Raped by Queen	*Princess Conceived*
Sunrise	*Birth of Prince*	*Unraping of Queen*
	Unraping of King	*Birth of Princess*
Day	*Prince Born*	*Queen Unraped*
	King Unraped	*Princess Born*

For there is only one sunset, night, sunrise and day, as there is only one wedlock between sun and earth. The sexual passion of the sun for the earth does not exceed that of the earth for the sun. But either partner gives what it has to give. The sun gives an embryo sun, the earth gives an embryo earth, in order that the morrow may not prove sunless and earthless. This was the lurking dread under all the ancient practices of initiation — that this day would be the last day, this sunset the last sunset; that there would, in fact, be no tomorrow. To prevent such a catastrophe, to ensure the continuance of sun and earth, their worshippers resorted to every kind of magical stimulation for postponing the Last Day, whether universally for the macro-cosm, or individually for the microcosm. For all initiation is ultimately based upon the dread of final annihilation whether for oneself or for one's world. Hence the innumerable varieties of sympathetic initiation, of the wedlock between the sun and the earth. To name only one or two, we may surely trace the origin of the *Couvade* to the idea of the sun as lying, alive in death, while pregnant with tomorrow's new earth; *Foundation Burials* to the same thought; while the practice of *burying pregnant "virgins"* alive may be referred to the fancy of the earth, likewise, as lying, alive in death, while pregnant with tomorrow's new sun. It is this condition of Life in Death, of Death in Life; of Tomb as Womb, of Womb as Tomb; which is symbolized in that Labyrinth or Maze which Mr Knight has proved to underlie the initiation ceremonies of the archaic culture and its derivatives. While agreeing with all his arguments, I once again suggest that the Entrail Complex is closely connected with, though not originating from, the mummification of the Dead King and the Dead Queen in Egypt. Mummification demands disembowelment; the bowels were stored in canopic jars, which formed part of the procession to the tomb; and it may be suggested that these entrails in these jars, combined with the ceremonial progress and possible dancing of their bearers, are relevant both to the theory of the maze dance and of the labyrinth as symbolizing the entrails. If, as is likely, not only the jars but the surgical instruments of disembowelment were borne in the funeral procession, they at once offer a parallel to the mysterious *vessels* and the mysterious *weapons* invariably carried in solemn procession by youths and maidens in the Grail Castle; and it may be suspected that the incision of the body of the Dead King by such instruments, and the placing of the resultant *viscera* in the canopic jars, made it easier for Christian tellers of the pre-Christian Grail Legend to equate the Dead King with Christ; the instruments of incision with the Lance which pierced His side and with the Nails of the Cross; and the canopic jars, containing the entrails of the Dead King, with the Dish and Cup of Christ's Body and Blood. It is at least suggestive that the Grail King is always wounded in the side, as if for evisceration.

The labyrinth, then, may be regarded as the Embryonic State, the entry to which is either by Conception or by Death, and the exit from which is either by Birth or by Resurrection. Into this cave of Initiation repair both King and Queen; for it is that inward universe which is but the interlocked embrace of Sun and Earth at sunset. From it they issue forth once more at sunrise, rejuvenated as Prince and Princess, each the deliverer of the other, and each the other's inseparable partner. For they are twins.

430

CHAPTER 22

The Grail and the Rites of Adonis

JESSIE L. WESTON

In offering these remarks on the subject of the Grail origins, I should wish to be understood as seeking, rather than tendering, information. The result of my researches into the *Perceval* legend has been to cause me to form certain opinions as to the sources of the Grail story, which the exigencies of space, and the character of the *Studies* as a whole, prevented me from setting forth fully in the published volume. At the same time these conclusions bore so directly on folklore researches that I was strongly impressed with the desirability of bringing them to the attention of trained folklorists, that I might have the advantage of their criticism and judgment in finally formulating my theory. Not that I can claim to be the first to give expression to such views. Long since Simrock, in his translation of the *Parzival*, and Professor Martin, in his *Zur Gralsage Untersuchungen* (1880),[1] arrived at very similar conclusions, but at that time the critical material at their disposal was scanty. We lacked the illuminating labours of Mannhardt and his disciple, Dr J.G. Frazer. We had but one *Perceval* text, and that an extremely bad one, at our disposal, and in consequence the results obtained, though interesting and stimulating, were hardly convincing.

Hitherto, in criticizing the Grail legend, we have been under the grave disadvantage of uncertainty as to the relative position of the extant versions of the story; we were not sure which of the varying forms represented most faithfully the original *données* of the tale. It is obvious that this was a serious hindrance.

You cannot safely theorize as to the original form of a story while you are still in doubt as to which of certain widely differing versions is the older. Inasmuch as, in point of MS date, the *Perceval* of Chrétien de Troyes is the oldest of our Grail romances, the tendency has been to regard the story as told by him as the most nearly approaching the original, and to argue from that; although the vague and unsatisfactory details there given left it open to conjecture whether the author were dealing with a tradition already formed, or with one in process of formation.

Now, owing to recent discoveries, the standpoint has been shifted back, and we know that the earliest attainable Grail story is that of which not Perceval but Gawain was the hero, and the authorship of which is ascribed not to Chrétien de Troyes, but to Bleheris the Welshman. The date at which Bleheris lived is uncertain, but his identity alike with the Bledhericus referred to by Giraldus Cambrensis, and the Bréri quoted as authority for the *Tristan* of Thomas, has been frankly accepted by the leading French and American scholars; so far the Germans have preserved silence on the subject.[2]

The passage in Giraldus is unfortunately very vague; he simply refers to Bledhericus as *famosus ille fabulator* and says he lived "a little before our time," words which may mean anything. Giraldus may be using the editorial "we," and may mean "a little before my time," which, as he was writing in the latter half of the twelfth century, might imply that Bledhericus lived in the earlier half. But he may also have used the pronoun quite indefinitely; as M. Ferdinand Lot, with whom I discussed the question, remarked, "it may mean anything from ten to a hundred years; we might say that Bonaparte lived 'a little before our time'." When we take into consideration the fact that only three direct references to Bleheris, or Blihis, as a source, have been preserved, while the name is more frequently found in the duplicated form of Bleo-Bleheris, Blihos-Bliheris, or Bliobliheri,[3] and generally attached to a knight of Arthur's court, it seems most probable that he lived at a period sufficiently remote to allow of the precise details concerning his life and work to become obscured, while the tradition of his close connection with Arthurian romance was retained. In any case this much is certain, and this is what principally concerns us, his version of

the Grail story is older than that of Chrétien, and we are justified in seeking for indications of origin in the story as told by
him rather than in the version of the younger poet.

This is the Bleheris Grail story, as given by Wauchier de
Denain, in his continuation of the *Perceval*.[4]

Arthur, at the conclusion of his successful expedition against
Chastel Orguellous, has given the queen *rendezvous* at certain
cross roads, marked by four pine trees. Here the court awaits
him. One evening the queen is playing chess at the entrance of
her pavilion when a stranger knight rides past, and fails to offer
any salutation. Indignant at the apparent discourtesy, the queen
sends Kay after him to command his return. Kay, as is his wont,
carries out his commission in so ungracious and insulting a
manner that he is overthrown for his pains, and returns to court
with an exaggerated account of the knight's bearing and language. Gawain is then dispatched on the same errand, and, over-
taking the stranger, courteously invites his return, but is told
that he rides on a quest that will brook no delay, and which
none but he may achieve; nevertheless, he thinks it possible that
Gawain, whose identity he has learned, might succeed. On his
return he will gladly pay his respects to the queen.

Gawain, however, by soft words, persuades him to return,
pledging his honour that he shall in no wise suffer by the delay.
They turn back, but scarcely have they reached the tents when
the knight, with a loud cry, falls forward, wounded to death by
a javelin cast by an unseen hand. With his dying breath he bids
Gawain don his armour, and mount his steed, which shall carry
him to the destined goal. Gawain, furious at the slur cast on his
honour by this breach of his safe-conduct, does as requested,
and, leaving the dead body to the care of the queen, departs at
once.

Through the night he rides, and all the next day, till he has
passed the borders of Arthur's land, and at nightfall, wearied
out, he finds himself in a waste land by the seashore. A cause-
way, bordered on either side by trees, their roots in the water,
runs out from the land, and at the further end Gawain sees a
light as of a fire. The road is so dark, and the night so stormy,
he would fain delay till morning, but the steed, taking the bit in
its teeth, dashes down the pathway, and eventually he reaches
the entrance to a lighted hall. Here he is at first received as one

long-expected, but, having unhelmed, is seen to be a stranger, and left alone. In the centre of the hall stands a bier, on which lies a body, covered with a rich pall of crimson silk, a broken sword on the breast, and four censers at the four corners of the bier. A procession of clergy enters, headed by a silver cross, and followed by many folk. Vespers for the dead are sung amid general lamentation, and Gawain is again left alone. He now sees on the daïs a Lance, fixed in a silver socket, from which a stream of blood flows continuously into a golden cup, and thence, by a channel, is carried out of the hall. Servants prepare the tables for a meal, and the King of the castle, entering, greets Gawain kindly, and seats him beside him on the daïs. The butlers pour wine into the cups, and from a doorway there issues *"the rich Grail,"* which serves them; otherwise there is *"nor serjant nor seneschal,"* and Gawain marvels much at the service of the Grail, for now 'tis here, and now there, and for fear and wonder he scarce dare eat. After supper the King leads Gawain to the bier, and, handing him the broken sword, bids him resolder it. This he fails to do, and the King, shaking his head, tells him he may not accomplish the quest on which he has come; nevertheless, he has shewn great valour in coming thither, and he may ask what he will; he shall be answered. Gawain asks of the Lance: 'tis the Lance of Longinus, with it the side of the Saviour was pierced, as he hung on the Cross, and it shall remain where it now is, and bleed, till the Day Of Doom. The King will tell who it is who lies on the bier, of the stroke by which he met his death, and the destruction brought on the land thereby; but as he speaks, weeping the while, Gawain falls asleep, and wakes to find himself upon the seashore, his steed fastened to a rock beside him, and all trace of the castle vanished. Wondering much, he mounts his steed, and rides through a land no longer waste, while all the folk he meets bless and curse him; for, by asking concerning the Lance, he has brought about the partial restoration of fruitfulness. Had he also asked of the Grail, the curse would have been entirely removed.

Now, there are certain points in this story which cannot fail to strike those familiar with the Grail legend. Who are the two dead men of the tale, the knight so mysteriously slain and the Body on the bier? We never learn. Nor do we ever hear the nature of the quest — Was it to avenge the dead knight of the castle? Was it to break the spell upon the land? Manessier, who about fifty years later brought the *Perceval* compilation to a final conclusion, gives, indeed, what purports to be a continuation of the tale. Gawain is here besought by the sister of the knight slain in his company to come to her aid against a foe, but the story is *banale* to the last degree. There are points of contact with other versions: the maiden's name is *la sore pucele*, the name Chrétien gives to the Grail King's niece; her foe is King Mangons, or Amangons, the name of the oppressor of the maidens in the *Elucidation*, to which we shall refer presently; but if there be any original connection with the Bleheris version, that connection has become completely obscured. Manessier, too, makes no attempt at solving the mystery of the Body upon the bier: certain scholars have indeed identified the slain man with Goon-Desert, or Gondefer, the brother of Manessier's Grail King, whose death by treachery Perceval avenges. But this identification is purely arbitrary; there is no bier in Manessier; it is in fact, distinctively a feature of the *Gawain* version.

The connection of the wasting of the land with the death of the knight, if knight he were, is also uncertain; indeed this is a part of the story which appears to have been designedly left in obscurity — it is at this point that Gawain falls asleep. I am tempted to believe that those who told the tale were themselves at a loss here. Then the Grail is no Christian relic, it acts simply as a food-providing talisman, coming and going without visible agency. It is called the *rich,* not the *holy,* Grail. Nor does the explanation given of the Lance agree with the description; the stream of blood, which pours continuously from the weapon, and is carried out of the hall, whither, we are not told, can have no connection with the carefully guarded relic of the *Saint Sang.* In truth, we may say without hesitation that the whole machinery of the story is definitely non-Christian, and that the explanation of its peculiarities must be sought outside the range of ecclesiastical tradition. At the same time certain of these features are repeated in a persistent fashion, even in the most definitely ecclesiasticized versions; a peculiarity which, I think, justifies the supposition that they form a part of the original Grail tradition.

Now it has seemed to me that an explanation of the most characteristic features of our story may be found in the suggestion that they are a survival, misunderstood and imperfectly remembered, of a form of Nature worship closely allied to, if not identical with, the Rites of Adonis so exhaustively studied by Dr Frazer in *The Golden Bough*. It will be remembered that the essence of these rites was the symbolic representation of the annual processes of Nature, the sequence and transition of the seasons. The god, Adonis, or Tammuz, or whatever he was called in the land where the rites were celebrated, typified the vivifying principle of vegetation; his death was mourned as the death of vegetation in winter, his restoration to life was hailed as its restoration in spring. An effigy representing the dead god was honoured with all the rites of mourning, and subsequently committed to the waves. Women especially played so large a part in these rites that an Arabic writer of the tenth century refers to the festival as El-Bugât, *"the festival of the Weeping Women."*[5]

The central *motif* of the *Gawain* Grail-story is, I submit, identical with the central idea of the Adonis rites — a death, and failure of vegetation caused by that death. Both here and in the version given by the curious German poem of *Diû Crône*, where Gawain is again the Grail hero, we are told that the wasting of the land was brought about by the *Dolorous Stroke*. Thus the central figure, the Body on the bier, whose identity is never made clear, would in this view represent the dead god; the bleeding Lance, the weapon with which he was done to death (I think it more probable that the *Dolorous Stroke* was dealt by a Lance or Spear, as in the *Balin* and *Balan* story, than by a sword).

If we accept this view we can, I think, explain the origin of that mysterious figure of the Grail legend, the Maimed King. The fact that this central figure was at the same time dead and alive must, when the real meaning of the incidents had become obscured, and the story, imperfectly remembered, was told simply as a story, have been a source of perplexity to the tellers. An easy way out of the difficulty — it was a very real difficulty — would be to represent the king, or god, as desperately wounded. That such an idea was in the minds of the romance writers appears, I think, from the peculiar version of *Diû Crône*, where, when Gawain has asked concerning the Grail, the Maimed King and his attendants vanish at daybreak; they were dead, but preserved a semblance of life till the question was put.

436

If the *Gawain* versions really represent the older, and primary, group, it is possible that this particular rendering really preceded the Maimed King version, though in the form preserved it is combined with it.

Again, in the very curious and unique *Merlin* MS., No. 337 of the French MSS of the *Bibliothèque Nationale,* I we find that Perceval is called the son of the widow lady, while his father, the Maimed King, is yet alive, and it is explained that, being desperately wounded, and only to be healed when the quest is achieved, he is as good as dead, and his wife may be reckoned a widow. These two instances will suffice to shew that the transformation of the Body on the bier into the Maimed King on the litter, is neither impossible nor unnatural. The two are really one and the same.

Students of the Grail cycle will hardly need to be reminded that the identity of the Maimed King is a hopeless puzzle. He may be the Fisher King, or the Fisher King's father, or have no connection with either, as in the Evalach-Mordrains story. He may have been wounded in battle, or accidentally, or wilfully, or by supernatural means, as the punishment of too close an approach to spiritual mysteries. A proof of the confusion which ultimately resulted from these conflicting versions is to be found in the *Merlin* MS above referred to, where not only Perceval's father but two others are Maimed Kings, and all three sit at the Table of the Grail. If such confusion existed in the mind of the writers, no wonder that we, the readers, find the path of Grail criticism a rough and intricate one! Probably the characters of the Maimed King and the Fisher King were originally distinct, the Maimed King representing, as we have suggested, the god, in whose honour the rites were performed; the Fisher King, who, whether maimed or not, invariably acts as host, representing the Priest. It would be his office to preside at the ritual feast, and at the initiation of the neophyte, offices which would well fit in with the character of Host. Here, the name of Fisher King is not given to him, but in certain texts which interpolate the history of Joseph of Arimathea he is identified with that Monarch. It will readily be understood that when the idea that the god was alive gained possession of the minds of those who told the story, there would be two lords of the castle, and they would find some difficulty in distinguishing the role of the one from that of the other. We may note that in this (i.e., the Bleheris) version, in that of Wauchier de Denain at the conclusion of his section of the *Perceval,* in the Prose *Lancelot,* and in the *Queste,* the Host is not maimed.

Again, this proposed origin would explain the wasting of the land, the mysterious Curse of Logres, which is referred to alike in earlier and later versions, and of which no explanation is ever given. As we saw above, the essence of the Rites was the symbolic representation of the processes of Nature. The festival of the death and revival of the god took place at the Spring solstice; it was an objective parable, finding its interpretation in the awakening of Nature from her winter sleep. Here the wasting of the land is in some mysterious manner connected with the death or wounding of the central figure; the successful accomplishment of the Grail quest brings about either the restoration of the land to fruitfulness, or the healing of the King (Chrétien and Wolfram, for example, have no Wasted Land). Thus the object of the Quest would appear to be one with that of the Adonis-ritual.

This wasting of the land is found in three *Gawain* Grail-stories, that by Bleheris, the version of *Chastel Merveilleus,* and *Diû Crône;* it is found in one *Perceval* text, the Gerbert continuation. Thus, briefly, the object of the Rites is the restoration of Vegetation, connected with the revival of the god; the object of the Quest is the same but connected with the restoration to health of the King.[6]

I have before noted the fact that the role played by women in these rites was of such importance that eventually it gave a name to the Festival. In the Notes to my translation of three visits paid by Gawain to the Grail Castle, I remarked on the persistent recurrence in these stories of a weeping maiden or maidens, the cause of whose grief is never made clear. In *Diû Crône,* where, as we have seen, the Maimed King and his court have but the semblance of life and are in very truth dead, the Grail-bearer and her companions are the only living beings in the castle, and their grief is, in a measure, comprehensible; they desire the breaking of the spell which binds them to this uncanny company. In what, in the *Perceval Studies,* I have designated as the *Chastel Merveilleus* version, a version midway between that of Bleheris and of Chrétien, there is but one weeping maiden, the Grail-bearer. In the curious interpolation of the Heralds' College MS., when the broken sword is restored to the Fisher King, he mentions among the results of the successful achievement of the quest, that the hero shall know why the maiden weeps. I doubt very much whether the writer of the lines himself knew the reason! In the visit paid by Bohort to castle Corbenic, it is Elaine, daughter of King Pelles, who weeps, because, being no longer a maiden, she may no longer be Grail-bearer. As she is about to become the mother of the Grail winner, and knows to what honour her son is predestined, the explanation is not convincing; but there had to be a weeping maiden in the story. The most curious instance of the persistence of this part of the original tradition is to be found in Gawain's visit to Corbenic, in the prose *Lancelot*, where he sees not one, but twelve maidens kneeling at the closed door of the Grail chamber, weeping bitterly, and praying to be delivered from their torment. But the dwellers in Castle Corbenic, so far from being in torment, have all that heart can desire, and, moreover, the honour of being guardians of the (here) sacred and most Christian relic, the Holy Grail.[7]

Now, in the light of the parallels already cited, is it not at least possible that these weeping maidens, who wail so mysteriously through the Grail story, are a survival of, and witness to, the original source of that story, that they are the mourning women of the Adonis ritual, the "Women weeping for Tammuz"?

This interpretation would also explain the constant stress laid upon the *general* mourning, even when the reason for this mourning appears inadequate, as e.g. in the *Parzival*. Here we are told that the appearance of the bleeding Lance is the signal for such lamentation that *"The folk of thirty kingdoms could scarce have bemoaned them more,"* Bk. v. l. 130. Here certainly the Lance is that with which the king has been wounded, but the *folk* of the castle are in no way affected, there is no wasting of the land.

Again, in *Peredur*, at the appearance of the Lance all fell to wailing and lamentation, but here there seems to be no connection between the Lance and the wound of the king, which latter is the work of the sorceresses of Gloucester. If the original source of the story is to be found in the Adonis ritual, and if the mourning which is so marked a feature of that ritual be associated, as Drs. Robertson Smyth and Farnell have suggested, rather with the death of the god than with the consequent failure of vegetation,[8] then we might expect to find the association of the mourning with the weapon which originally dealt the fatal blow to persist in versions which had dropped out the (originally) companion feature of the Wasted Land.

We have thus the following important points of contact between the Adonis ritual and the story of the Visit to the Grail Castle: the wasted land; the slain king (or knight); the mourning, with special insistence on the part played by women; and the restoration of fertility; while certain minor points, such as the crimson covering of the bier, the incense, and the presence, in certain versions, of doves as agents in the mysterious ceremonies also find their parallel in the same ritual.[9]

To put the matter briefly, the scene enacted in the presence of the chance visitor to the Grail Castle involved the chief incidents of the Adonis rites. I would submit that whereas the presence of an isolated feature might be due to chance, that of a complete and harmonious group, embracing at once the ceremonies and the object of the cult, can scarcely be so explained.

To go a step further. Originally I entitled this paper "The Grail and the Mysteries of Adonis" for the word *mysteries* I have now substituted *ritual*, in view of the perfectly well-grounded objection that, in classical times, the worship of Adonis was not carried on in secret. Nevertheless, I am disposed to believe that the word *mysteries* might, without impropriety, be used in connection with the celebration of these rites when in later ages Christianity had become the faith "in possession," and the votaries of an older cult performed their rites under the ban of ecclesiastical disapproval. Much, of course, depends upon the character of the cult; the Adonis worship was in its essence a "Life" cult, the life of the god ensuring the life of vegetation, and that in its turn the life of man; it is obvious that such a cult might possess an esoteric as well as an exoteric significance. To the ordinary worshipper the ritual would be an object lesson, setting forth the actual processes of Nature, to the initiate it would be the means of imparting other, and less innocent, teaching as to the sources of life.

This much is certain: the Grail is perpetually treated as something strange, mysterious, awe-inspiring; its secrets are on no account to be rashly approached or lightly spoken of; he runs great danger who does so. Such terms could hardly be applied to the Adonis rites under ordinary conditions, and yet, as we have seen, the Grail story presents such a striking identity of incident with these rites that a connection between the two seems practically certain. We have to seek for some explanation which will preserve this connection while at the same time accounting for the presence of certain "occult" features in the tale.

The explanation surely lies in the fact suggested above, that the Adonis cult was essentially a Life cult, and, as such, susceptible of strange developments. Dr Frazer has laid stress on the close connection which, in the minds of primitive worshippers, subsisted between the varying forms of life: "They commonly believed that the tie between the animal and vegetable world was even closer than it really is — to them the principle of life and fertility, whether animal or vegetable, was one and indivisible."[10] Dulaure, while assigning the same *origin* as does Dr Frazer to the ritual, definitely classes the worship of Adonis among those cults which "assumed in process of time a distinctly 'carnal' character."[11]

The Lance and Cup which form the central features of the imagery of our story are also met with as "Phallic" symbols, and I am strongly of opinion that many of the most perplexing features of the legend are capable of explanation on the theory that behind the ordinary simple "Vegetation" symbolism there lay something which justified so learned and acute a scholar as the late Professor Heinzel, whose works are a veritable mine of learning and ingenuity, in regarding our records of the Visit to the Grail Castle as records of an initiation *manquée*. Long since, in his study on the Old French Grail romances (*Die Alt-Französische Gral Romanen*, 1891) he suggested that the failure to put the question was equivalent to a refusal on the part of the neophyte to submit to the ordeal,[13] but, owing probably to the form in which he cast the results of his researches, much of their value has been obscured.

Let us note first, that whatever else changes in the story, the essential framework remains the same. Always the castle is found by chance; always the hero beholds marvels he does not comprehend; always he fails to fulfil the test which would have qualified him to receive the explanation of those marvels; always he recognizes his fault too late, when the opportunity has passed beyond recall; and only after long trial is it again granted to him; Let us clear our minds once and for all from the delusion that the Grail story is *primarily* the story of a quest; it is that *secondarily*. In its primary form it is the romance of a lost opportunity; for always, and in every instance, the first visit connotes failure; it is to redress that failure that the quest is undertaken. So essentially is this a part of the story that it survives even in the Galahad version; that immaculate and uninteresting hero does not fail, of course; but neither does he come to the Grail castle for the first time when he presides at the solemn and symbolic feast; he was brought up there, but has left it before the Quest begins; like his predecessors, Gawain and Perceval, he goes forth from the castle in order to return.

Now, let us accept for the nonce Professor Heinzel's suggestion, but for the word *refusal* substitute *failure,* and recognizing that the incidents related rest upon real objective facts, we may, perhaps, hazard a guess at the cause of this failure. In the Bleheris story we have seen that the hero was overcome by slumber at the critical moment of the King's recital, and only awoke to find himself alone upon the seashore, all trace of the castle having disappeared. This is again the cause of failure in the *Chastel Merveilleus* version. In the *Perlesvaus* three drops of blood fall from the lance on to the table, and Gawain, gazing upon them, falls into a trance, and can neither speak nor stir. In *Diû Crône* we have again the mysterious slumber, though here associated with the drinking of wine, the effect of which is to plunge Gawain's comrades, Lancelot and Calogreant, into a sleep which lasts till the question has been put, and the marvels explained. In this version also, we have the blood drops; but here, though they fall from the Lance, they are swallowed by the King, thus having no connection with the trance.

In the *Perceval* version, on the contrary, the blood drops are connected with a trance, but not with the Grail; and the hero's failure is accounted for on purely rational grounds, his too rigid adherence to the counsels of Gurnemanz.[14]

As we have seen, the *Gawain* versions certainly represent the older stage of tradition, and we may, therefore, fairly assume that, in the original form of the story, the failure to ask the necessary question was due to a mysterious slumber which overtook the hero at the crucial point of his test. But what caused this slumber? Is it too bold a suggestion that the blood drops, which are often so closely associated with the Grail, and are always found in connection with a trance, were the operating cause? that, in fact, they were employed to induce an hypnotic slumber on the part of the aspirant? We know that in Mesmerism and kindred practices, the first step is to seize and fix the attention of the subject — I believe a glittering disc, or some such object, is often employed — in any case it is through the eye that the desired effect is produced upon the brain. In the case of Gawain, and of Perceval alike, we are told that it is the startling contrast of colour — the crimson blood on the white cloth, or snow — that fetters their attention. It is of course *possible* that the slumber was merely a literary device for winding up the story, but the introduction of the feature of restored vegetation shows that the tale was moulded by some one who understood its real significance; and slumber hypnotically induced would be a very natural method of getting rid of an intruder who had stumbled upon rites not intended for general knowledge, and had failed to qualify for admission to their secrets. This much is certain, if the Grail stories have their root in the ritual of Adonis, we are dealing with a set of concrete facts, which must originally have admitted of a rational explanation. I would submit that if the slumber be really a part of the original tale, and there is every reason to believe that it is, then it must be capable of a rational explanation, and I can, in no other way, account for its constant recurrence, or for its connection with the blood drops, save on the hypothesis that one of the trials to which the neophyte was exposed, and to which apparently he frequently succumbed, was the test of hypnotic suggestion.

But how shall we explain the Grail itself? Would it not be the vessel of the common quasi-sacramental feast always connected with these rites? It is interesting that the MS which gives us the best Bleheris text also, in the same section of the work, offers us the only other instance I know of the use of the word Grail. When Gawain enters the castle of Brandelis, he finds a feast prepared, and boars' heads upon Grails of silver. The other MSS have here substituted for *Grail* the word *Tailléor*. It is thus practically certain that the writer of these tales, when he used the word *Grail,* meant a Dish, and not a Cup. The magical features, the automatic service, the feeding of the guests with all kinds of meat, were probably later additions, borrowed by the story-tellers from the numerous food-providing talismans of folklore. For we must ask ourselves how was the story told, from the inside or from the outside? That is, was it intended to be a method of preserving, and handing on, the tradition of these rites; or was it simply a story composed round this ritual as a centre? The first hypothesis would appear to involve the admission that the minstrels were the *conscious* guardians and transmitters of an occult tradition; a view which, in face of the close connection now proved to exist between the minstrel guilds and the monasteries, I do not feel able to accept. Also, we should then expect to find one clear and consistent version; and I suspect that that version would have been less susceptible of Christianization. But if the tale were told from the outside, if it were a story based upon, quite possibly, the genuine experience of one who assisted by chance at the celebration of these rites, ignorant of their nature and meaning, we can understand how it would take and keep this particular form. One admitted to the full participation in this ritual might not talk about it, where one possessed of but a partial and outside knowledge would be free to speak. And as the story passed from one to the other, is it not probable that while the initiated might venture to add or correct a feature, the uninitiated would introduce details which appeared to him suitable, but which were really foreign to the original trend of the tale? How, except on the hypothesis of some such origin, explain the persistent adherence to the framework of the story, or the hints as to the mysterious nature of the talisman, and the penalties to be incurred if its secrets are revealed? Do not let us forget that it is precisely in this, the earliest form of the tale, and in the confused version of the same offered by the *Elucidation,* that the *secret* character of the Grail is insisted upon. On any other hypothesis, what is this secret?

And now that I have had occasion to mention the *Elucidation,* I would ask, does not this theory of the Grail origins provide us, at last, with a possible solution of that most perplexing text? As is known to students of the subject, the *Elucidation* purports to be an introduction to the Grail story, and is found in three texts, the Mons MS of the *Perceval,* the Middle German translation of the continuation to that poem, and the (1530) printed edition of the work. It is extremely confused, and its connection with the other Grail texts has till recently been a complete puzzle. It starts with a warning from Master Blihis against revealing the secrets of the Grail. It then relates how at one time there were maidens dwelling in the hills, or wells, (the original word, *puys,* might be translated either way; I prefer the rendering of the German text, hills), who would offer food and drink to the passer by; but when King Amangons offered force to one, and took away her golden cup, they left the country; and, the writer goes on, "the court of the Fisher King could no longer be found." Nevertheless, Gawain found it; and we then have a summary of the Bleheris visit, given in terms often verbally identical with the text of Wauchier de Denain.

Some time ago, in the course of my *Perceval* studies, I came to the conclusion that the text at the root of the *Elucidation* was another, and apparently later, form of that used by Wauchier, and that in our English *Gawain* poems we had fragments of the same collection. Now, it appears to me, that we can suggest even a closer link. What if this text be really what it purports to be, the introduction to all the Grail stories? If it be the record of an insult[15] offered by a local chieftain to a priestess of these rites, in consequence of which they were no longer openly celebrated in that land, and, as the writer puts it, "the court of the Fisher King (the Priest of this ritual) could no longer be found?" Would not that be the logical introduction to the tale of one who found, and knew not what he found? It may be that after all the *Elucidation* is not so badly named!

So far as the Christian aspect of the story is concerned, it is now beyond doubt that a legend, similar in all respects to that of the Grail, was widely current at a date long anterior to any of our extant Grail texts. The story, with Nicodemus instead of Joseph as protagonist, is told of two of the most famous of continental relics, the *Saint Sang* of Fescamp[16] and the *Volto Santo* of Lucca. The most complete MSS of the *Perceval* refer, as authority, to a book written at Fescamp. Who was the first to utilize the pseudo-Gospels as material for the history of medieval relics we cannot say, but, given the trend of popular thought, it was practically inevitable that if the Grail were to receive the Christian pedigree which in the natural process of development in a medieval atmosphere, given to edification, it was bound to receive, it was almost inevitable that it should be fathered upon either Joseph of Arimathea or Nicodemus; as a matter of fact both are called into the service of the romancers.[17]

Given these facts, on the one hand an exceedingly popular story, having for its central point of interest a vessel round which there hovered an atmosphere of mystery and dread — none dare speak of the secrets of the Grail, — and connected in some unexplained manner with drops of blood and a bleeding lance: on the other hand, an equally popular legend connected with the Passion of Christ, and relics of that Passion; and does it not become easy to understand how on the common ground of the vessel of the ritual feast the two might meet, and eventually coalesce; the vessel of the Nature-worship being first connected with the Passion and finally identified with the chalice of the Eucharist. If I be correct in my suggestion as to the hidden meaning of this ritual, and that it was in truth a Life-cult, the Grail quest would be the quest for life; the Grail itself, under all its varying forms, the vessel in which the food necessary for life was presented to the worshippers.

I would earnestly ask all students of this fascinating subject to consider seriously whether the theory here sketched may not be found capable of providing that link between the conflicting versions which all previous hypotheses have failed to supply? On the theory of a purely Christian origin, how can we account for the obviously folklore features of our tale? How could the vessel of the Christian Eucharist have become the self-acting, food-providing talisman, known not only to Bleheris, but also to the author of the *Queste?* How could Kiot (the author of the lost French poem adapted by Wolfram von Eschenbach) have dared to turn it into a mere magical stone, a Baetylus? For if there be one thing certain, it is that the Grail had been Christianized before the day of Chrétien and Isiot. If on the other hand, the vessel were a mere food-providing Pagan talisman, how, and why, did it become so suddenly Christianized? What was there about it, more than about the countless similar talismans, that would suggest such a development? But if the Grail were from the first connected with a form of religious worship, from the first surrounded with a halo of awe and reverence, we can understand that it would lend itself with admirable readiness to the process of Christianization. Even as we can understand how Kiot, who was certainly a man of unusual learning, while he might shrink from Paganizing a fundamentally Christian relic, would have no scruple in substituting the object of one mysterious Pagan cult for that of another, and in replacing the vessel of the Adonis Rites by a Baetylus. One who knew so much may well have known what was the real character of the Grail. It seems to me that on this theory, and on this theory alone, can we account logically and harmoniously, alike for the development and the diversities of the Grail romances.

It is scarcely necessary to remind members of this Society that, in the interesting series of papers on the European Sky-God, contributed by Mr Cook to the pages of *Folk-Lore,* certain stories connected alike with Cuchullin and Gawain, are claimed as dependent on, and to be explained by, precisely the set of customs and beliefs with which I am here dealing. If the Green Knight be a survival of the Vegetation god, why not the Maimed King? I do not know how far Mr Cook's theories have met with the approval of folklore experts, but it does seem to me that when two enquirers, starting from different points, and travelling by different roads, reach precisely the same goal, there is at least an initial probability that that goal was once, very long ago, no doubt, the starting point of those diverging roads.

Postscript

I would here make certain suggestions which may meet objections raised in the discussion which followed the reading of this paper. A point advanced alike by Mr Nutt and Mr Cook was that if the hypothesis of such an origin be granted, the connection of Gawain with this particular group of beliefs and practices can hardly be accidental. My own view is that the tale, based on actual and imperfectly-understood experiences, was cast into story-form by a bard who knew what the incidents connoted, and that the connection of Gawain with the tale is due to one who knew the real character of the material with which he was dealing.

Notes

1 Cf. also *Zeitschrift für Alterthumskunde*, 1878; p.84 *sqq.*

2 Cf. M.J. Bédier's edition of the *Tristan*, and Dr Schofield's *English Literature*. For my notes on Bleheris, cf. *Romania*, xxxiii. p.333; xxxiv. p.100.

3 B.N. 1453, fo.113; "*Elucidation*;" B.M. Add. *Ib.* 614, fo.138, etc.

4 A translation of this, the *Diû Crône*, and Prose *Lancelot* versions will be found in No. vi. of *Arthurian Romances*, Nutt. [See also Chapter 12 of the present collection. Ed.]

5 Cf. *Legend of Sir Perceval*, pp.330–36; *The Golden Bough* — under heading "Adonis." *Adonis, Attis, Osiris*, Chap. viii.

6 *Legend of Sir Perceval*, p.141. In the Didot MS of the prose *Perceval* we are told that as the result of the question the "Roi Pesheor" will not only be healed but restored to youth, "*revenus en sa iuvence.*" This is also the result of the question in *Parzival*. According to Dr Frazer, it was an essential part of this Nature-cult that the god should be not merely living, but *young*.

7 Cf. Notes to vol.VI of *Arthurian Romances*.

8 Cf. Farnell, *Cults of the Greek States*, vol.II, "*Aphrodite.*"

9 Cf. Frazer, *Adonis, Attis, Osiris*, p.7. The image of Tammuz was clothed in red, and incense was burnt before it. Doves were sacrificed to Adonis; *ib.*, p.64. Doves appear both in the prose *Lancelot* Grail Visit and in *Parzival*.

10 Cf. *Adonis, Attis, Osiris*, p.5.

11 Cf. Dulaure, *Divinités Génératrices*, pp.69f.

12 E.g., the wounding of the Grail king. Cf. Dulaure, pp.78, 81. The *Parzival* alone attributes the wound to his indulgence in unlawful love, but the injury is always the same.

13 Prof. Heinzel's method was very confused, and references to the question are scattered throughout the long study.

14 In the prose *Perceval*, however, there is a hint of the earlier form, as fatigue also plays a part in the hero's failure to ask the necessary question: "e li sire le metoit en mainltes manieres de paroles por çou qu'il l'en demandast, mais il n'en fist riens, car estoit anoies des 11 nuits devant qu il avoit vellie, que por un poi qu'il ne chaoit sor la table." Modena MS., fol. 59.

15 If there be really Phallic symbolism in the tale, the wording of the affront is suggestive.

16 See Robert Jaffray, Chapter 18 in the present collection. [Ed.]

17 For summaries of these legends, cf. *Legend of Sir Perceval*, Chap. V appendix.

CHAPTER 23

The Graal Legend

D.F. DE L'HOSTE RANKING

For nigh upon eight hundred years the beauty of the Graal Legend has enchanted and its mystery has enthralled the most part of Western Europe. I say Western Europe advisedly, because, as we shall see, we find no trace of the Legend in Eastern Slavonic Europe.

On the beauty of the Legend I do not propose to speak at length; it is known to and acknowledged by all, whether in the very unsatisfying version of Tennyson, or in the peculiarly English form set forth in the pages of Malory.

It is with the mystery of the Legend that I am more concerned, and this Mystery is a double one — the mystery of its origin and diffusion and the mystery of its meaning.

The mystery of its origin has, save in one point, been solved, though even on this point new suggestions are constantly being made. Quite recently two inquirers have put forth new theories, Miss M.A. Murray in the pages of *Ancient Egypt* and Mr P.S. Barto in his work on *Tannhäuser and the Mountain of Venus.* With Miss Murray's theory I am, to a great extent, in agreement: Mr Barto's views do not commend themselves to me.

The second mystery, that of the object and meaning of the Legend, has received various interpretations, and it is on this branch of the subject that I wish to enlarge. I shall set before you various sets of theories, none of which are entirely satisfactory to myself, and I shall then suggest a theory of my own, which will possibly appear to you equally unsatisfactory.

In order to do this it will be necessary to give a brief sketch of the Legend and the various forms which it takes at different times and in different countries; also we must endeavour to analyse the complete Legend into its component parts.

The central idea of the Legend, and that which is best known, is of a cup containing the Blood of our Lord, which, after the crucifixion, had been committed to a special family as guardians, and by them had been brought to Britain, where it remained with certain other sacred emblems, occasionally manifesting itself at high festivals, when some knights were privileged to see the vessel or the damsel who bore it, and all who were present were aware of sweet odours and received not only spiritual but bodily refreshment. This vessel was ultimately withdrawn to heaven owing to what in legend are known as "The Three Dolorous Strokes," whereby the kingdom of Logris fell into great distress, whereupon certain knights undertook a quest for the recovery of the vessel.

All this Legend is interwoven with the old British Legends of King Arthur and his knights. We have, therefore, a threefold strand, the threads of which have been intertwined to make the story as we have it.

The Graal story as it appears in the twelfth century romances is clearly only a Christianized version of a much earlier pre-Christian legend of a vase or cauldron connected with the Celtic mysteries. In the Welsh Mabinogion we have the cauldron of inspiration and science from which Taliesin drew his prophetic powers, while in the tale of "Kilhwch and Olwen" we find mentioned as one of the thirteen wonders of Britain the basket of Gwyddnew Garanhir, of which it is said: "If the whole world should come together, thrice nine men at a time, the meat that each of them desired would be found within it." Taliesin's poem, "Bendigeid Vran," also mentions the bowl of Peredur which could restore the dead to life, "but those who were restored to life by it were not to speak lest they should reveal the mysteries of the vessel." This Peredur, the son of Evrawc, is a character in another of the Mabinogion, and in his adventures we find the first hint of a quest. When seeking knighthood at the hands of King Arthur he was set to fulfil various adventures. In the course of one of these, at the castle of one of his uncles, he sees a mighty spear from which poured three streams of blood; this was borne by youths, who were followed by two maidens carrying a large salver whereon was a man's head

450

swimming in blood. Here we have some of the materials which we find in the Graal Legend, but with no Christian sense attached to them. Monsieur Eugène Hucher in his introduction to the Legend of the San Graal has shown that this mystic vase may be traced back beyond the sixth century by means of representations on coins and medals to the Gauls. It is first found among Armoric Tribes on coins of the Unelles and Baiocasses; that is, in the parts of Brittany nearest to Gaul. This precious vase served from the earliest times among the Gauls, and, above all, in Brittany, for the performance of certain sacred rites, and, therefore, easily transformed into the chalice of the later Christian Legend. Here in this vase of pre-Christian origin we have a symbol common to the mysteries of every religion. This symbol was in all the mysteries invariably accompanied by something in the nature of a rod: this second talisman we find appear in the tale of Peredur in the form of the spear dropping blood: both these we find transferred into the Graal Legend, and there accompanied by two lesser talismans — a sword, said in some versions to have been that with which St John the Baptist was beheaded; and a dish or paten, which in some versions seems to take the form of a miraculous stone or altar. I believe I was the first to call attention to the fact that these four talismans correspond with the four emblems in the Tarot.

It is not strange that this portion of the Legend being of Celtic origin should have become intertwined with the legends bearing on Arthur and his Knights, legends which embodied the memories and hopes of the Celtic races in their struggle against foreign oppressors. But the form of the Celtic Legends varied very greatly as they were brought into contact with the chivalric idea through French influence. Arthur becomes a hero of romance; he is the great king and the knight errant; traversing the world to free it from giants and monsters; holding high court at Caerleon upon Usk at the great festivals of the Church, notably at Whitsuntide; surrounded by vassal kings and by all the bravest and best knights of Europe who flocked to his court in search of adventures, and to qualify for admission to the fellowship of the Round Table. In 1155 Wace, a clerk of Caen, composed a long history in octosyllabic verse, called "The Brut," in which he recounted the deeds of the kings of Briton almost from the fall of Troy to AD 680. After Wace the French Troubadours

451

of the end of the twelfth century made Arthur and the Round Table the special subject of their tale. Chrétien de Troyes wrote the "Chevalier à la Charette, an episode in the Life of Sir Lancelot," "Eric and Enid," "Tristan," and the "Chevalier au Lion."

But all these French versions differ widely from their Welsh or Breton originals. The principles of chivalry, and the refinements of courtly love have been introduced into the old tale; the strong bold outline is filled with ornament, and full play is given the imagination. But there is still one element wanting in order to complete the story as we have it, the Christian and religious feature is still absent. In order to introduce this it was necessary to incorporate the Graal Legend with the Arthurian Legend.

Towards the end of the twelfth century there came a sudden outburst of Graal literature; and in the course of a few years between 1170 and 1270 the legends were combined, perfected, and took the form under which we now know them. Authorities vary so much as to the order in which the various versions appeared, and as to the influence which each had on the other, that it must be sufficient simply to give the names of some of the authors and their works with the approximate dates at which they were written. Between 1170 and 1190, Robert de Boron wrote a series of three poems, "Joseph of Arimathea," "Merlin," and "Percival." In these it is told how our Lord Himself, gave to St Joseph of Arimathea the Cup in which the Last Supper was celebrated, and in which His Blood was caught when His Side was pierced on the Cross. St Joseph is to be its keeper, and is, after himself, to appoint a keeper to whom and to whom alone he is to reveal the "secrets" of the Graal, namely certain words spoken by our Lord to St Joseph when the latter was in prison. In this Legend the Round Table was the third of a series, the first being that of the Last Supper; the second a square table founded by St Joseph of Arimathea; the third or Round Table completed, and was the symbol of the Trinity. The Graal was in the custody of King Pelles, in the Castle of Carbonek. Here we have the beginning of the actual Graal Legend, and it is worth the attention of High Grade Masons that the Legend seems to have arisen and developed during the time that the Templars were at the height of their power; and there seems some reason to think that it may have formed the central legend of the Inner Mysteries of the Templars. The Graal is in this version simply a vessel of grace, testing men's hearts when it appeared, those only being able to see it who were in the state of grace. The connection of St Joseph of Arimathea with Britain does not apparently owe its origin simply to this poem. My learned friend, Mr Henry Jenner, late of the British Museum, furnished me with particulars of an oral tradition to the same effect. A friend of his being much interested in the making of organ pipes obtained permission to visit the largest works in London to see the process of making the metal pipes. It is essential that the insides of these pipes should be absolutely smooth, and in order to obtain the necessary smoothness the molten metal is thrown with shovels on to a linen cloth stretched on a table. This process is not unattended with danger from the molten metal, and the visitor noticed that each work-man as he threw his shovelful of metal uttered a few words in a low tone as if by way of a charm. Listening attentively he found that the words were "Joseph was in the tin trade." Much puzzled as to the meaning of this, and not understanding what Joseph was referred to, he applied for information to the foreman under whose guidance he was. After some hesitation the foreman told him that the workers in tin were a very ancient guild and had curious legends and traditions of their own; one of them being that St Joseph of Arimathea, the rich man of the Scriptures, originally made his money by trading for tin from Phoenicia to Britain, and that on one occasion when trading in a ship of his own he brought our Lord Himself with him as a boy. On making further inquiry among friends in Cornwall, Mr Jenner found that the connection of St Joseph with the tin workers was a very ancient tradition there also. Mr Jenner also pointed out to me that in the "Bollandist Acta Sanctorum in the Life of St Joseph of Arimathea" (March 17), reference is made to a tradition that St Joseph was sent to preach in Britain either by St Philip the Apostle or by St Peter himself. He is also said to have gone with St James to Compostella, in Galicia, while on his way to Britain; and this again seems to connect him with the tin trade, since Galicia is the chief source of tin outside Britain.

Between the years 1175 and 1189, Chrétien de Troyes began his "Contes del Graal." This poem was continued by Gautier de

Doulens, and after him alternative conclusions were written by Manessier, and by Gerbert. Now marvellous properties are ascribed to the Graal, it feeds those who see it with all they wish. There are also introduced a bleeding lance and a magic sword.

Between the years 1200 and 1210, Wolfram von Eschenbach must have written his "Parzival" which brings us to a new and specially Teutonic phase of the Graal Legend. It is supposed to be a translation from a poem of Guiot de Provence, who himself claims to have translated it from an Arabic manuscript of Toledo written by a Jew named Flegetanis. In this version there are three Graal kings — Titurel, Frimutel, and Amfortas. There is also a special messenger of the Graal Kundrie, who is a woman of repulsive aspect; and there is an evil magician Klingsor, who is the opponent of the Graal. According to this version the Graal is not a chalice at all but a stone somewhat of the nature of an altar which is carried on a green cushion and laid on a jacinth table over against the warden. It yields all manner of food and drink to those who are present; but it appears to be of the nature of a talisman the effect of which is exhausted by use, since it is recharged every Good Friday (some say weekly) by a Host deposited upon it by a dove which descends from heaven. About the year 1270 Albrecht von Scharfenberg wrote his poem of "Titurel." This poem differs from the rest of the German cycle in that the Graal is again represented as a chalice. The Graal is in this version carried by Parzival to Prester John whose heir Parzival was. The whole Graal company is ultimately transported to India where according to this version the Graal still remains. It is worth noting that in these versions the Graal knights are constantly called Templars. To me this reference to Prester John seems very important for reasons which I will give later. The earliest mention that we have of this mythical priest-king of the East is about the year 1156 when he is spoken of by Maimonides and by Benjamin of Tudela. Pope Alexander III is said to have sent an embassy to him; and about the year 1180 the then Emperor of Constantinople is said to have received a letter from him. Leaving for the present these various versions, we will turn to the English form of the Legend, which is said to have been originally compiled in French by Walter de Map, Archdeacon of Oxford, during the reign of Henry II.

This work is commonly known as the *Morte d'Arthur*, and may be said to consist of four parts — the "Coming of Arthur," the "Lancelot," the book of the "Quest of the San Graal," and the "Passing of Arthur" — though it also contains other books dealing with the adventures of various knights of Arthur's court. From these sources was again compiled the present English version by Sir Thomas Malory, a knight who lived in the reigns of Henry IV and Edward IV. It was completed about 1470, and printed by Caxton about fifteen years later. In this version it must be a knight of the direct line of Joseph of Arimathea who shall achieve the Graal, and this knight is Sir Galahad, son of Sir Lancelot by Elayne, daughter of King Pelles. In the romance there is more than one Elayne, but Professor Rhys has shown, both in his learned *Studies in the Arthurian Legends* and in the introduction to Dent's edition of *Morte d'Arthur,* that these various Elaynes are really one, and the same — Elayne daughter of Pelles and mother of Sir Galahad, is the same with Elayne of Astolat, which is itself identical with Shallot.

Of all the knights who set out on the quest there were only six in all who made any attempt to carry to an end: there were, first, one couple of sinful knights, Sir Gawaine and Sir Hector de Maris; then one alone, penitent, but yet coming short of the grace required — namely, Sir Lancelot; then a Trinity who achieved the quest, two without stain of sin — Sir Galahad and Sir Percival; one, once foul but penitent and shriven — Sir Bohors or Bors. Of Sir Lancelot we are told how he rode "over thwart and endlong in a wild forest, and held no part but as wild adventures led him," and how he had a vision of the San Graal but might not enter within the Chapel of the Graal. This was not the first time he had seen it; in the Castle of King Pelles it had already appeared to him, and, when wounded and out of his mind, he had been healed by it; but now that of purpose he sought it, being in sin he was not found worthy to come nigh it.

After this, Sir Lancelot follows out many adventures, in each of which it is more clearly impressed upon him that, on account of his sins, he may not achieve the quest. At length, on a mystic ship he meets, and at length recognizes, his son, Sir Galahad. For six months they bide together, and then Sir Galahad is bidden to leave his father and to continue the quest. After his departure Sir Lancelot prays earnestly that he may have a sight of the Graal, and in answer to his prayer he is bidden to enter into a castle, which is indeed Carbonek, the Castle of the Graal. Here he is privileged to see the Graal, which is described in one of the most solemn and beautiful passages in the whole of Malory. Then, knowing that he should never come nearer to achieving the quest, he returned into the realm of Logris, and took his place again in the world of action.

The quest is actually achieved by his son, Sir Galahad, who reigns as King in the spiritual city of Sarras, and there passes away before the altar of the Graal. "Sithence was there never man so hardy for to say that he had seen the San Graal."

What is the source of the new mystical element introduced by the incorporation of the Graal Legend? I have already said that there are two theories, and to these I will now refer. Mr Barto, in his book on *Tannhäuser and the Mountain of Venus* (New York: Oxford University Press), would see in it simply a myth of the world of the dead, and would regard the whole development of the Graal Legend as a survival of the Teutonic Pagan ideas as to the abode of the dead. From his conclusions I must dissent, since he would seem to have based them on the Teutonic form of the Legend, the least spiritual and most materialized version of all.

Miss M.A. Murray, in the quarterly magazine *Ancient Egypt* (1916, Parts I and II), sets forth a theory which seems to me to deserve the closest attention. I may, perhaps, be induced to attach so much importance to her solution because it in a great degree upholds the conclusion at which I had arrived independently, and which I embodied some years ago in a paper read before the Lodge of "Quattuor Coronati."

Miss Murray takes the "Joseph of Arimathea" Legend and examines it geographically and from its linguistic side. She comes to the conclusion that geographically the scene is laid in Egypt, and that the names both of places and persons can be interpreted by, and only by, Arabic or Coptic. She identifies many of the places with their modern sites, and notably the spiritual city of Sarras with Sers al-Liyaneh between old Cairo and Alexandria. "Joseph of Arimathea" she believes to be a corruption of the name "Yusuf Baramusi," Joseph of Baramus: and points out that the legend of the flowering staff is also told of St John Kolobus of Baramus.

She also points out a matter on which I had insisted in the

456

paper already mentioned, namely that the description of the Graal Chapel and the Graal ritual points to an Eastern and not to a Western rite; this rite she believes to have been the Coptic, but from this conclusion I must differ, for reasons which I will state later.

Miss Murray also mentions the lost *Book of Melkyn,* referred to by John of Glastonbury as one of the sources of the Legend, and suggests that the original title was *Kètabu'l-Milkiyyin* the *Book of the Kings,* corrupted into *Liber Melkini,* the *Book of Melkin.* Her suggestion is that the Legend was of Eastern origin, and being written in Arabic was introduced into Spain by Flegetanis, and into Britain by this *Book of Melkin.*

Having glanced at the various versions of the Legend, we may now try to discover whether any meaning underlies the tale itself, and whether there is any reason why it should have taken form at the time it did.

I will discard entirely the natural or Sun-Myth interpretation favoured by some, since such interpretations always seem to me arbitrary and useless, and will lay before you four suggested solutions: one which I may call the obvious; one the highly mystical solution of Mr Waite in his book *The Hidden Church of the Holy Graal;* a solution suggested by M. Aroux more than fifty years ago; and finally, a suggestion of my own.

IDEAL OF CHIVALRY: Taking first what I call the obvious solution we may say that the story forms a picture of what may be called the ideal of chivalry. It may be said that there were two kinds of chivalry — the court chivalry, animated by earthly love, military pride, and the love of adventure. On the other hand, there was the Christian chivalry, represented by the religious military orders, mystic and severe, having for object to make of the knight a sort of monk, armed in defence of the Faith. In the later romances this distinction is marked in two ways: First, by the separation from the ordinary knights of the world at large (who are represented as often being villain knights, destitute of knightly honour and feeling), of the fellowship of the Round Table, who were the best knights then to be found within the realm of Britain, whose mission was to ride abroad aiding those who were distressed and oppressed for the love of God, and of the blessed Mother of God; secondly, by the quest undertaken by certain of these knights of the Round Table in search of the San Graal. Written at the time when chivalry was an actual living force, furnishing the main cause of action for the only portion of society that was then reckoned of any account, we must look on it not as an actual history of what chivalry was either in Arthur's day or in the twelfth century, but as an attempt to portray what chivalry might have been, if the high purpose and solemn oaths of knighthood had been truly carried out.

MYSTICAL: Turning now to the solution of Mr Waite, it is, as I have said, of a highly mystical character: there seem to be two ideas underlying it, the first being that within the Catholic Church itself there exists an esoteric body which alone retains the true secret of Christianity; that this esoteric Church is of no particular body which claims the title of Catholic (though I infer from much of his writing that he is at least inclined to regard the Roman Catholic body as being the true official representative of the Catholic Church), but that the members may exist among all those bodies which hold Catholic doctrine, that these, though perhaps unknown to one another, yet are united by a mysterious bond, the true knowledge of the inner meaning of the rites which they celebrate; they form, in fact, the salt of the Church without which the official bodies would have lost their savour; they preserve the true knowledge of the inner meaning of the great Sacrament of the Eucharist; by them the faith is kept alive, and by them the official churches will ultimately be revivified and reunited, or rather perhaps the true church will emerge from the official bodies which now conceal though they contain it.

But Mr Waite goes further than this and leads us into a region in which it is almost impossible to follow him. I quote his own words: "Having passed through many initiations I can say with the certainty which comes of full knowledge that the Graal Legend ritually and ceremonially represented is the greatest of all which lies beyond the known borders of the instituted mysteries. But it is exalted in a place of understanding of which no one can speak in public, not only because of certain seals placed upon the sanctuary, but more especially because there are no listeners. I know, however, and can say that the Cup appears;

I know now that it is the Graal Cup, and the wonders of its manifestation in romance are not so far removed from the high things which it symbolizes, whence it follows that the same story is told everywhere." These words involve a claim so tremendous and so mysterious that it is obviously impossible to discuss them in a mixed assembly; they seem to amount to this, that those of the true Church are in possession of the secret words said to have been communicated by our Lord to St Joseph of Arimathea, and that when a priest of this Order celebrates the Eucharist he celebrates not on this plane alone but on the plane of the Graal itself; there is not merely transubstantiation but there is an actual realization of the Beatific Vision.

POLITICAL-RELIGIOUS: The interpretation of which I am now going to speak is not so widely known as it deserves to be, possibly because the works in which this theory is set out are little known and difficult of access. The two chief exponents of this theory are Gabriel Rosetti, in his work on the anti-papal spirit which preceded the Reformation, and M. Aroux in his *Mystères de Chevalerie et de l'amour platonique*, and in *L'hérésie de Dante*.

Of Rosetti's work unfortunately only two volumes were ever published, two more in manuscript having been in some way lost or destroyed. M. Aroux' works, published in 1857–58, have long been out of print and are very difficult to obtain. I might add as another authority the Comte de Canteleux in his *Sectes et Sociétés Secrètes;* but he is not so directly to the point as Rosetti and Aroux. I will try to give a *résumé* of the theory propounded by these authors. The heresy of the Gnostics did not, as is often assumed die out in the sixth century: it was adopted and consolidated by the Manichaeans and gradually spread from East to West, appearing in Western Europe under different names — Bogomils, Kathari (Cathars), Paterini, Albigenses, Pauvres de Lyons, the Family of Love, and under many other names.

All these various societies were interlocked with one another, having signs and passwords, and, in addition, a veiled and allegorical language in which they communicated with one another.

These sects professed to be in possession of the purest

doctrines of Christianity; doctrines differing in the most vital points from the doctrines of the Catholic Church; they were also Socialistic and Republican in their constitution, and their unavowed aim was the subversion of all existing forms of government whether Civil or Religious. Their organization was extraordinarily perfect, and their emissaries were found everywhere.

Provence was the stronghold of these sects, and the writers to whom I have referred assert that among the most energetic of the secret agents were the Trovatore or Troubadours, who promulgated the doctrines of the sects in their poems and tales, which were of a highly allegorical character and expressed in a veiled language only known to the initiates and known as Limossin; that is, *elemosina,* the language of the Beggars, the Gueux or Pauvres de Lyons.

In the secret language the Society was always spoken of as the beloved lady, to whom the poet poured out his soul; called by Dante, one of the leaders of the Order, "Beatrice," the Society being in fact known in Provence as La Bice. The lodges or secret meetings which arranged the plans of campaign, especially against the See of Rome, were the well known Cours d'Amour, and within these was formed, according to Aroux, the Massénie du San Graal, that is a body, seated at the Round or Perfect Table to which only the Perfect Knights could belong: the members in full communion with these Gnostic bodies being known as Parfaits, the Perfecti of the Manichaeans. On this theory the Graal represented the true Gnostic Christianity hidden in the Temple of the Katharist Church.

MY OWN INTERPRETATION: I propose now to lay before you a suggested explanation of my own, which will probably prove as little satisfactory to you as the interpretations already given have proved to myself. I shall call your attention first to the time, place, and circumstances under which the Legend sprang into prominence, and then to the meaning of the word Graal, and the internal evidence to be found in the various versions of the Legend itself. I have constantly called attention to the curious fact that there are three matters which are singularly closely related to one another as regards both period and extent — the Graal Legend, the rise and culmination of the Gothic architecture, and the rise and fall of the Templars. The Graal Legend, as we have seen, first appears in its complete form about the year 1170 and finishes in 1270 with the "Titurel" of Albrecht von Scharfenberg; Gothic architecture begins in 1130 with the building of St Denis, and ends as an absolutely distinctive style about 1250 when Salisbury was built; the Templars, founded in 1118, were suppressed in 1307.

The Graal Legend originates in Provence, spreads northward to England, and eastward to Germany, southward perhaps to Spain, though the reference of Guiot de Provence to the Jew Flegetanis of Toledo is open to doubt. I know of no Italian version, and no trace of the Legend is found in any country holding the Orthodox Faith.

Gothic architecture originates in north-eastern France, extends to Kirkwall in Orkney, and to Germany; in Italy it only appears as a foreign production, the work of German architects; Spain has a style of Gothic peculiar to itself; in Orthodox countries this form of architecture was unknown. The Templars had their headquarters in Paris, and were specially powerful in the South of France; their branches spread to Scotland, Germany, and Spain; in Italy they had little power, being looked on with great suspicion by the Roman See; in Orthodox countries they had no branches, being bitter opponents of the Orthodox emperors.

As regards the circumstances, it is worthy of notice that during the period covered by the events just mentioned there was springing up a custom in the western Church of withholding the chalice from the laity and giving them communion in one kind only, though it was only in 1261 that the monks of Citaux officially in their chapter made this a rule.

What is the meaning of the word "Graal" itself? We often find it stated that it is an ancient Armoric word meaning a cup or chalice. I am not prepared to deny this; it may be true, but I should like some evidence that such a word ever existed in the Armoric language. One would expect to find some trace of a similar word in the cognate dialects of Wales and Cornwall, but I can find none. In the Welsh and in the Breton New Testament the word used is "c'hop" or "cwpan." I hoped to find the word in the Cornish Mystery plays, but it is not used. Zeuss, who, were the word ancient, would most certainly have included it in his *Grammatica Celtica,* makes no mention of it. Where, then, is the evidence? Again, why should an Armoric word — if it be indeed Armoric — be used in a legend which is, in its complete form, of Provençal origin, and was first put forth in the dialect of Provence?

My own view is that the word is a corruption of the low Latin word *gradualis* or *graduale,* and signifies an office book containing certain prayers and ceremonies; this was confused with a Provençal word *gradalis* or *gradale* (see Skeat), signifying a dish or platter, and we find accordingly that in some forms of the Legend the chief hallow was not a chalice at all, but a dish or platter from which the knights were miraculously fed, and it is only in the latest developments that we find the term "Graal" definitely associated with a chalice. In the longer prose "Graal" (bk. xxii, c. 3) the following passage occurs:

> The Graal appeared at the Sacring of the Mass in five several manners; these none ought to tell, for the sacred things of the Sacrament ought none to tell openly but he to whom God hath given it. King Arthur beheld all the changes, the last whereof was the change into a chalice.

Now, as to the internal evidence. First, I will call your attention to the curious fact which seems to have escaped notice: it is that the Graal Chapel itself and the description of the rites celebrated therein do not indicate a Western but an Eastern ritual. It would take me too long to go into the reasons which have led me to this conclusion; I believe it has escaped notice because the commentators were not familiar with Eastern rites.

Next I would point out that Wolfram von Eschenbach and Albrecht von Scharfenberg both speak of the Graal Knights as Templars. Turn next to the "High History of the Holy Graal," otherwise the "Longer Prose Graal": the hero in this case is Percival, the son of a widow, and often referred to simply as The Son of the Widow, a title well known to the Manichaean Gnostics. The castle of the Graal is defended first by three, afterwards by nine bridges, representing different degrees of initation. None could enter the castle unless he brought with him the sword with which St John the Baptist was beheaded. Percival rides to the attack mounted on a white mule having a red cross on its forehead, and bears in his hand a certain banner.

Two hermits are met by Percival; one is adoring the cross, one is smiting it. This latter, when challenged by Percival, asserts that he reverences our Lord equally as the other, and that he smites the cross since he detests it as being the instrument of the torture of our Lord. Note that one of the charges brought against the Templars was that of insulting and trampling upon the cross, and that an identical defence was offered by them. Finally, Percival was borne away by a mystic ship having on its sail the red cross of the Templars. Who and what, then, were the Templars? We know that they were a military body connected closely with the East; that, though professing themselves staunch supporters of the papal power, they were looked on with the greatest suspicion by the Roman See, and were finally dissolved on a charge of practising rites belonging to the grossest forms of gnosticism. Further, we know that their share in the Crusades was marked by a bitter hostility towards the Orthodox Christian emperors, and a marked tendency to enter into friendly relations with certain of the Saracens, especially with the Assassins, so much so that King ("The Gnostics and their Remains") agrees with Von Hanmer (*"Mysterium Baphometis Revelatum"*) in the opinion that the various degrees of the Templars, nine in number, were not only modelled upon, but directly derived from, the similar organization of the Assassins. Who, then, were the Assassins? It is ordinarily assumed that they were Mohammedans, but this I believe to be an entirely unfounded assumption. A passage in Joinville's *History of the Crusades* leads one to believe that they were identical with the sect called by the Druses "Nusari," and counted by them as "Christians" — that is, they were a gnostic sect. The original seat of the Order was at Cairo — that is, if Miss Murray is correct — in the neighbourhood of the "Spirituality of Sarras." Here was the "House of Wisdom," the great College of instruction. William of Tyre (XIX, 17) tells how Hugo of Caesarea and Geoffroi of the Temple, being sent as envoys of the Order to Cairo, were by the then Sultan conducted through this Temple. But if a tradition of the French Order of the Temple be true, there was a still closer link between gnosticism and the Templars than this, and one which would account not merely for certain of the charges brought against the Templars, but also for the importance attached in the "Longer Prose Graal" to the sword with which St John the

463

Baptist was beheaded; for the symbol of the dish or platter, one of the alternative forms of the Graal; for the Legend that Joseph of Arimathea was consecrated to the Keepership of the Graal by Christ Himself; and in the "Parzival" and "Titurel" for the final placing of the Graal in the land of Prester John. This tradition asserts that the Patriarch Theocletes, the sixty-seventh successor of the Apostle St John, transmitted in AD 1118 his powers as Grand Pontiff of the Johannite "Christians" to Hugo de Payens, whom he also appointed his successor.

These Johannites (I will not call them Christians) were a gnostic body, otherwise known as Nabatheans, Nasoroeans (Nusari), Mandoeans, or Sabians. They regarded our Lord as a false Messiah, the true Messiah being St John the Baptist. The Druse catechism, published in French by M. de Bock ("Essai sur l'Histoire du Sabéism," Paris, 1788), contains the following passage:

Q. What ought we to think of the Gospel of the Christians?

A. There is one of them which is true, and which merits our respect: it is the Gospel of the true Messiah, who also appeared in the time of the Mohammed under the name of Selman, and who is none other than Hamzah.

We have here an obvious confusion between St John the Baptist and St John the Evangelist, the two Saints John adopted by the Templars as their patrons, though they originally derived their title from St John the Almoner, a different person altogether.

The Pontiff of the Johannites was always called the Christ. Here I submit that we find a solution to certain matters in the Graal Legend:

To the statement that Joseph of Arimathea, the appointed guardian of the Graal, was consecrated by Christ Himself.

To the appearance of the miraculous dish as one form of the Graal.

To the importance attached in the "Longer Prose Graal" to the possession of the sword with which St John the Baptist was beheaded.

It also bears on the charge always brought against the Templars of worshipping a man's head, i.e. the head of St John the Baptist. It was reported a few years ago that when the Palace of the Grand Masters at Malta was being renovated one wall of the great hall was found to be covered with a fresco representing the head of St John on a charger.

To sum up what I have already said: my suggestion is that the Graal Legend was the central legend of the Templar rite — a rite of Eastern origin, but not, as Miss Murray suggests, a Coptic rite, but that of the heretical Johannites, who, perhaps, like the Marcionites, attached a peculiar magical value to the chalice. That the Templars were the mainspring and militant portion of all the heretical Paulician bodies throughout Europe, which bodies opposed the claims of St John to those of St Peter.

That the hidden meaning of the Graal itself was the Johannite church, while the real quest was intimately connected with the "secrets" of the Graal so often spoken of; that is, with the secret doctrine embodied in the words of the ritual contained in the *graduale* or office book.

The Graal is in the final custody of "Prester John," the "Presbyter Johannes," grand patron of all the Paulician heretics; that is, in the custody and guardianship of those bodies who together formed the Hidden Church of the Graal.

CHAPTER 24

The Quest of the Sangraal

ROBERT S. HAWKER

The name Sangraal is derived from San, the breviate of Sanctus *or* Saint, Holy, *and* Graal *the Keltic word for Vessel or Vase. All that is known of the Origin and History of this mysterious Relique will be rehearsed in the Poem itself. As in the title, so in the Knightly Names, I have preferred the Keltic to other sources of spelling and sound. (R.S.H.)*

Ho! for the Sangraal! vanish'd Vase of Heaven!
That held, like Christ's own heart, an hin[1] of blood!
Ho! for the Sangraal! ...
    How the merry shout
Of reckless riders on their rushing steeds,
Smote the loose echo from the drowsy rock
Of grim Dundagel, thron'd along the sea!

"Unclean! unclean! ten cubits and a span,[2]
Keep from the wholesome touch of human-kind:
Stand at the gate, and beat the leper's bell,
But stretch not forth the hand for holy thing, —
Unclean, as Egypt at the ebb of Nile!"
Thus said the monk, a lean and gnarlèd man;
His couch was on the rock, by that wild stream
That floods, in cataract, Saint Nectan's Kieve:[3]
One of the choir, whose life is Orison.
They had their lodges in the wilderness,

466

Or built them cells beside the shadowy sea,
And there they dwelt with angels, like a dream:
So they unroll'd the volume of the Book,
And fill'd the fields of the Evangelist
With antique thoughts, that breath'd of Paradise.

Uprose they for the Quest — the bounding men
Of the siege perilous, and the granite ring —
They gathered at the rock, yon ruddy tor;[4]
The stony depth where lurked the demon-god,
Till Christ, the mighty Master, drave him forth.

There stood the knights, stately, and stern, and tall;
Tristan, and Perceval, Sir Galahad,
And he, the sad Sir Lancelot of the lay:
Ah me! that logan[5] of the rocky hills,
Pillar'd in storm, calm in the rush of war,
Shook, at the light touch of his lady's hand!

See! where they move, a battle-shouldering kind!
Massive in mould, but graceful: thorough men:
Built in the mystic measure of the Cross: —
Their lifted arms the transome: and their bulk,
The Tree, where Jesu stately stood to die —
Thence came their mastery in the field of war: —
Ha! one might drive battalions — one, alone!

See! now, they pause; for in their midst, the King,
Arthur, the Son of Uter, and the Night,
Helm'd with Pendragon, with the crested Crown,
And belted with the sheath'd Excalibur,[6]
That gnash'd his iron teeth, and yearn'd for war!
Stern was that look (high natures seldom smile)
And in those pulses beat a thousand kings.
A glance! and they were husht: a lifted hand!
And his eye ruled them like a throne of light.
Then, with a voice that rang along the moor,
Like the Archangel's trumpet for the dead,
He spake — while Tamar sounded to the sea.

"Comrades in arms! Mates of The Table Round!
Fair Sirs, my fellows in the bannered ring,
Ours is a lofty tryst! this day we meet,
Not under shield, with scarf and knightly gage,
To quench our thirst of love in ladies' eyes:
We shall not mount today that goodly throne,
The conscious steed, with thunder in his loins,
To launch along the field the arrowy spear:
Nay, but a holier theme, a mightier Quest —
'Ho! for the Sangraal, vanish'd Vase of God!'

"Ye know that in old days, that yellow Jew,
Accursèd Herod; and the earth-wide judge,
Pilate the Roman — doomster for all lands,
Or else the Judgment had not been for all, —
Bound Jesu-Master to the world's tall tree,
Slowly to die ...
          Ha! Sirs, had we been there,
They durst not have assayed their felon deed,
Excalibur had cleft them to the spine!

"Slowly He died, a world in every pang,
Until the hard centurion's cruel spear
Smote His high heart: and from that severed side,
Rush'd the red stream that quencht the wrath of Heaven!

"Then came Sir Joseph, hight of Arimathèe,
Bearing that awful Vase, the Sangraal!
The Vessel of the Pasch, Shere Thursday night,
The selfsame Cup, wherein the faithful Wine
Heard God, and was obedient unto Blood.
Therewith he knelt and gathered blessèd drops
From his dear Master's Side that sadly fell,
The ruddy dews from the great tree of life:
Sweet Lord! what treasures! like the priceless gems
Hid in the tawny casket of a king, —
A ransom for an army, one by one!

"That wealth he cherisht long: his very soul
Around his ark: bent as before a shrine!

"He dwelt in Orient Syria: God's own land:
The ladder foot of heaven — where shadowy shapes
In white appparel glided up and down.
His home was like a garner, full of corn,
And wine and oil; a granary of God!
Young men, that no one knew, went in and out,
With a far look in their eternal eyes!
All things were strange and rare: the Sangraal,
As though it clung to some ethereal chain,
Brought down high Heaven to earth at Arimathèe.

"He lived long centuries and prophesied.
A girded pilgrim ever and anon,
Cross-staff in hand, and, folded at his side,
The mystic marvel of the feast of blood!
Once, in old time, he stood in this dear land,
Enthrall'd — for lo! a sign! his grounded staff
Took root, and branch'd, and bloom'd, like Aaron's rod:
Thence came the shrine, the cell; therefore he dwelt,
The vassal of the Vase, at Avalon!

"This could not last, for evil days came on,
And evil men: the garbage of their sin
Tainted this land, and all things holy fled.
The Sangraal was not: on a summer eve,
The silence of the sky brake up in sound!
The tree of Joseph glowed with ruddy light
A harmless fire, curved like a molten vase,
Around the bush, and from the midst, a voice:
Thus hewn by Merlin on a runic stone:
Kirioth : el : Zannah : aulohee : pedah

"Then said the shuddering seer — he heard and knew
The unutterable words that glide in Heaven,
Without a breath or tongue, from soul to soul —

"'The land is lonely now: Anathema!
The link that bound it to the silent grasp
Of thrilling worlds is gathered up and gone:
The glory is departed; and the disk
So full of radiance from the touch of God!
This orb is darkened to the distant watch
Of Saturn and his reapers, when they pause,
Amid their sheaves, to count the nightly stars.

"'All gone! but not for ever: on a day
There shall rise a king from Keltic loins,
Of mystic birth and name, tender and true;
His vassals shall be noble, to a man:
Knights strong in battle till the war is won:
Then while the land is husht on Tamar side,
So that the warder upon Carradon
Shall hear at once the river and the sea —
That king shall call a Quest a kindling cry:
'Ho! for the Sangraal! vanish'd Vase of God!'

"'Yea! and it shall be won! A chosen knight,
The ninth from Joseph in the line of blood,
Clean as a maid from guile and fleshly sin —
He with the shield of Sarras;[7] and the lance,
Ruddy and moisten'd with a freshening stain,
As from a sever'd wound of yesterday —
He shall achieve the Graal: he alone!'

"Thus wrote Bard Merlin on the Runic hide
Of a slain deer: rolled in an aumry chest.

"And now, fair Sirs, your voices: who will gird
His belt for travel in the perilous ways?
This thing must be fulfilled: — in vain our land
Of noble name, high deed, and famous men;
Vain the proud homage of our thrall, the sea,
If we be shorn of God. Ah! loathsome shame!
To hurl in battle for the pride of arms:
To ride in native tournay, foreign war:
To count the stars; to ponder pictured runes,

And grasp great knowledge, as the demons do,
If we be shorn of God: — we must assay
The myth and meaning of this marvellous bowl:
It shall be sought and found —"
  Thus said the King.

Then rose a storm of voices; like the sea,
When Ocean, bounding, shouts with all his waves.
High-hearted men! the purpose and the theme,
Smote the fine chord that thrills the warrior's soul
With touch and impulse for a deed of fame.

Then spake Sir Gauvain, counsellor of the King,
A man of Pentecost for words that burn: —

"Sirs! we are soldiers of the rock and ring:
Our Table Round is earth's most honoured stone;
Thereon two worlds of life and glory blend,
The boss upon the shield of many a land,
The midway link with the light beyond the stars!
This is our fount of fame! Let us arise,
And cleave the earth like rivers; like the streams
That win from Paradise their immortal name:
To the four winds of God, casting the lot.
So shall we share the regions, and unfold
The shrouded mystery of those fields of air.

"Eastward! the source and spring of life and light!
Thence came, and thither went, the rush of worlds,
When the great cone of space[8] was sown with stars.
There rolled the gateway of the double dawn,
When the mere God shone down, a breathing man.
There, up from Bethany, the Syrian Twelve
Watched their dear Master darken into day.
Thence, too, will gleam the Cross, the arisen wood:[9]
Ah, shuddering sign, one day, of terrible doom!
Therefore the Orient is the home of God.

"The West! a Galilee: the shore of men;
The symbol and the scene of populous life

471

Full Japhet journeyed thither, Noe's son,
The prophecy of increase in his loins.
Westward[10] Lord Jesu looked His latest love,
His yearning Cross along the peopled sea,
The innumerable nations in His soul.
Thus came that type and token of our kind,
The realm and region of the set of sun,
The wide, wide West; the imaged zone of man.

"The North! the lair of demons, where they coil,
And bound, and glide, and travel to and fro:
Their gulph, the underworld, this hollow orb,
Where vaulted columns curve beneath the hills,
And shoulder us on their arches: there they throng;
The portal of their pit, the polar gate,
Their fiery dungeon mocked with northern snow:
There, doom and demon haunt a native land,
Where dreamy thunder mutters in the cloud,
Storm broods, and battle breathes, and baleful fires
Shed a fierce horror o'er the shuddering North.

"But thou! O South Wind, breathe thy fragrant sigh!
We follow on thy perfume, breath of heaven!
Myriads, in girded albs, for ever young,
Their stately semblance of embodied air,
Troop round the footstool of the Southern Cross,
That pentacle of stars: the very sign
That led the Wise Men towards the Awful Child,
Then came and stood to rule the peaceful sea.
So, too, Lord Jesu from His mighty tomb[11]
Cast the dear shadow of his red right hand,
To soothe the happy South — the angels' home.

"Then let us search the regions, one by one,
And pluck this Sangraal from its cloudy cave."

So Merlin brought the arrows: graven lots,
Shrouded from sight within a quiver'd sheath,
For choice and guidance in the perilous path,
That so the travellers might divide the lands.

They met at Lauds, in good Saint Nectan's cell,
For fast, and vigil, and their knightly vow:
Then knelt, and prayed, and all received their God.

"Now for the silvery arrows! Grasp and hold!"

Sir Lancelot drew the North: that fell domain,
Where fleshly man must brook the airy fiend —
His battle-foe, the demon — ghastly War!
Ho! stout Saint Michael shield them, knight and knave!
The South fell softly to Sir Perceval's hand:
Some shadowy angel breathed a silent sign,
That so that blameless man, that courteous knight,
Might mount and mingle with the happy host
Of God's white army in their native land.
Yea! they shall woo and soothe him, like the dove.

But hark! the greeting — "Tristan for the West!"
Among the multitudes, his watchful way,
The billowy hordes beside the seething sea;
But will the glory gleam in loathsome lands?
Will the lost pearl shine out among the swine?
Woe, father Adam, to thy loins and thee!

Sir Galahad holds the Orient arrow's name:
His chosen hand unbars the gate of day;
There glows that heart, fill'd with his mother's blood,
That rules in every pulse, the world of man;
Link of the awful Three, with many a star.
O! blessèd East! 'mid visions such as thine,
'Twere well to grasp the Sangraal, and die.

Now feast and festival in Arthur's hall:
Hark! stern Dundagel softens into song!
They meet for solemn severance, knight and king,
Where gate and bulwark darken o'er the sea.
Strong men for meat, and warriors at the wine,
They wreak the wrath of hunger on the beeves,
They rend rich morsels from the savoury deer,
And quench the flagon like Brun-guillie[12] dew!

473

Hear! how the minstrels prophesy in sound,
Shout the King's Waes-hael, and Drink-hael the Queen!
Then said Sir Kay, he of the arrowy tongue,
"Joseph and Pharaoh! how they build their bones!
Happier the boar were quick than dead today."

The Queen! the Queen! how haughty on the dais!
The sunset tangled in her golden hair
A dove amid the eagles — Gwennivar!
Aishah! what might is in that glorious eye!
See their tamed lion[13] from Brocelian's glade,
Couched on the granite like a captive king!
A word — a gesture — or a mute caress —
How fiercely fond he droops his billowy mane,
And wooes, with tawny lip, his lady's hand!

The dawn is deep; the mountains yearn for day;
The hooting cairn[14] is husht — that fiendish noise,
Yelled from the utterance of the rending rock,
When the fierce dog of Cain barks from the moon.[15]

The bird of judgment chants the doom of night,
The billows laugh a welcome to the day,
And Camlan ripples, seaward, with a smile.

Down with the eastern bridge! the warriors ride,
And thou, Sir Herald, blazon as they pass!
Foremost sad Lancelot, throned upon his steed,
His yellow banner, northward, lapping light:
The crest, a lily, with a broken stem,
The legend, **Stately once and ever fair;**
It hath a meaning, seek it not, O King!

A quaint embroidery Sir Perceval wore;
A turbaned Syrian, underneath a palm,
Wrestled for mastery with a stately foe,
Robed in a Levite's raiment, white as wool:
His touch o'erwhelmed the Hebrew, and his word,
Whoso is strong with God shall conquer man,
Coil'd in rich tracery round the knightly shield.

Did Ysolt's delicate fingers weave the web,
That gleamed in silken radiance o'er her lord?
A molten rainbow, bent, that arch in heaven,
Which leads straightway to Paradise and God;
Beneath, came up a gloved and sigilled hand,
Amid this cunning needlework of words,
When toil and tears have worn the westering day,
Behold the smile of fame! so brief: so bright.
A vast archangel floods Sir Galahad's shield:
Mid-breast, and lifted high, an Orient cruse,
Full filled, and running o'er with Numynous[16] light,
As though it held and shed the visible God;
Then shone this utterance as in graven fire,
I thirst! O Jesu! let me drink and die!

So forth they fare, King Arthur and his men,
Like stout quaternions of the Maccabee:
They halt, and form at craggy Carradon;
Fit scene for haughty hope and stern farewell.
Lo! the rude altar, and the rough-hewn rock,
The grim and ghastly semblance of the fiend,
His haunt and coil within that pillar'd home.
Hark! the wild echo! Did the demon breathe
That yell of vengeance from the conscious stone?

There the brown barrow curves its sullen breast,
Above the bones of some dead Gentile's soul:
All husht — and calm — and cold — until anon
Gleams the old dawn — the well-remembered day —
Then may you hear, beneath that hollow cairn,
The clash of arms: the muffled shout of war;
Blent with the rustle of the kindling dead!

They stand — and hush their hearts to hear the King.
Then said he, like a prince of Tamar-land —
Around his soul, Dundagel and the sea —

"Ha! Sirs — ye seek a noble crest today,
To win and wear the starry Sangraal,
The link that binds to God a lonely land.

Would that my arm went with you, like my heart!
But the true shepherd must not shun the fold:
For in this flock are crouching grievous wolves,
And chief among them all, my own false kin.
Therefore I tarry by the cruel sea,
To hear at eve the treacherous mermaid's song,
And watch the wallowing monsters of the wave, —
'Mid all things fierce, and wild, and strange, alone!

"Ay! all beside can win companionship:
The churl may clip his mate beneath the thatch,
While his brown urchins nestle at his knees:
The soldier give and grasp a mutual palm,
Knit to his flesh in sinewy bonds of war:
The knight may seek at eve his castle-gate,
Mount the old stair, and lift the accustom'd latch,
To find, for throbbing brow and weary limb,
That paradise of pillows, one true breast;
But he, the lofty ruler of the land,
Like yonder Tor, first greeted by the dawn,
And wooed the latest by the lingering day,
With happy homes and hearths beneath his breast,
Must soar and gleam in solitary snow.
The lonely one is, evermore, the King.
So now farewell, my lieges, fare ye well,
And God's sweet Mother be your benison!
Since by grey Merlin's gloss, this wondrous cup
Is, like the golden vase in Aaron's ark,
A fount of manha for a yearning world,
As full as it can hold of God and heaven,
Search the four winds until the balsam breathe,
Then grasp, and fold it in your very soul!

"I have no son, no daughter of my loins,
To breathe, 'mid future men, their father's name:
My blood will perish when these veins are dry;
Yet am I fain some deeds of mine should live —
I would not be forgotten in this land:
I yearn that men I know not, men unborn,
Should find, amid these fields, King Arthur's fame!

Here let them say, by proud Dundagel's walls —
'They brought the Sangraal back by his command,
They touched these rugged rocks with hues of God:'
So shall my name have worship, and my land.

"Ah! native Cornwall! throned upon the hills,
Thy moorland pathways worn by Angel feet,
Thy streams that march in music to the sea
'Mid Ocean's merry noise, his billowy laugh!
Ah me! a gloom falls heavy on my soul —
The birds that sung to me in youth are dead;
I think, in dreamy vigils of the night,
It may be God is angry with my land,
Too much athirst for fame, too fond of blood;
And all for earth, for shadows, and the dream
To glean an echo from the winds of song!
"But now, let hearts be high! the Archangel held
A tournay with the fiend on Abarim,
And good Saint Michael won his dragon-crest!

"Be this our cry! the battle is for God!
If bevies of foul fiends withstand your path,
Nay! if strong angels hold the watch and ward,
Plunge in their midst, and shout, 'A Sangraal!'"

He ceased; the warriors bent a knightly knee,
And touched, with kiss and sign, Excalibur;
Then turned, and mounted for their perilous way!

That night Dundagel shuddered into storm —
The deep foundations shook beneath the sea:
Yet there they stood, beneath the murky moon,
Above the bastion, Merlin and the King.
Thrice waved the sage his staff, and thrice they saw
A peopled vision throng the rocky moor.

First fell a gloom, thick as a thousand nights,
A pall that hid whole armies; and beneath
Stormed the wild tide of war; until on high
Gleamed red the dragon, and the Keltic glaive

Smote the loose battle of the roving Dane!
Then yelled a fiercer fight for brother blood
Rushed mingling, and twin dragons fought the field!
The grisly shadows of his faithful knights
Perplext their lord: and in their midst, behold!
His own stern semblance waved a phantom brand,
Drooped, and went down the war. Then cried the King,
"Ho! Arthur to the rescue!" and half drew
Excalibur; but sank, and fell entranced.

A touch aroused the monarch: and there stood
He, of the billowy beard and awful eye,
The ashes of whole ages on his brow —
Merlin the bard, son of a demon-sire!
High, like Ben Amram at the thirsty rock,
He raised his prophet staff: that runic rod,
The stem of Igdrasil[17] — the crutch of Raun —
And wrote strange words along the conscious air.
Forth gleamed the east, and yet it was not day!
A white and glowing horse outrode the dawn;
A youthful rider ruled the bounding rein,
And he, in semblance of Sir Galahad shone:
A vase he held on high; one molten gem,
Like massive ruby or the chrysolite:
Thence gushed the light in flakes; and flowing, fell
As though the pavement of the sky brake up,
And stars were shed to sojourn on the hills,
From grey Morwenna's stone to Michael's tor,
Until the rocky land was like a heaven.

Then saw they that the mighty Quest was won!
The Sangraal swoon'd along the golden air:
The sea breathed balsam, like Gennesaret:
The streams were touched with supernatural light:
And fonts of Saxon rock, stood, full of God!
Altars arose, each like a kingly throne,
Where the royal chalice, with its lineal blood,
The Glory of the Presence, ruled and reigned.
This lasted long: until the white horse fled,
The fierce fangs of the libbard in his loins:

478

Whole ages glided in that blink of time,
While Merlin and the King, looked, wondering, on.

But see! once more the wizard-wand arise,
To cleave the air with signals, and a scene.

Troops of the demon-north, in yellow garb,
The sickly hue of vile Iscariot's hair,
Mingle with men, in unseen multitudes!
Unscared, they throng the valley and the hill;
The shrines were darkened and the chalice void:
That which held God was gone: Maran-atha!
The awful shadows of the Sangraal, fled!
Yet giant-men arose, that seemed as gods,
Such might they gathered from the swarthy kind:
The myths were rendered up: and one by one,
The Fire — the Light — the Air — were tamed and bound
Like votive vassals at their chariot-wheel.
Then learnt they War: yet not that noble wrath,
That brings the generous champion face to face
With equal shield, and with a measured brand,
To peril life for life, and do or die;
But the false valour of the lurking fiend
To hurl a distant death from some deep den:
To wing with flame the metal of the mine:
And, so they rend God's image, reck not who!

"Ah! haughty England! lady of the wave!"
Thus said pale Merlin to the listening King,
"What is thy glory in the world of stars?
To scorch and slay: to win demoniac fame,
In arts and arms; and then to flash and die!
Thou art the diamond of the demon-crown,
Smitten by Michael upon Abarim,
That fell; and glared, an island of the sea.
Ah! native England! wake thine ancient cry;
Ho! for the Sangraal! vanish'd Vase of Heaven,
That held, like Christ's own heart, an hin of blood!"

He ceased; and all around was dreamy night:
There stood Dundagel, throned: and the great sea
Lay, a strong vassal at his master's gate,
And, like a drunken giant, sobb'd in sleep!

Notes

1   The hin was a Hebrew measure, used for the wine of the sacrifice.

2   The distance at which a leper was commanded to keep from every healthy person.

3   Or cauldron.

4   Routor, the red hill, so named from the heath which blossoms on the hillside.

5   Logan, or shuddering stone. A rock of augury found in all lands, a relic of the patriarchal era of belief. A child or an innocent person could move it, as Pliny records, with a stalk of asphodel; but a strong man, if guilty, could not shake it with all his force.

6   A Hebrew name, signifying "champer of the steel."

7   The city of "Sarras in the spiritual place" is the scene of many a legend of medieval times. In all likelihood it was identical with Charras or Charran of Holy Writ. There was treasured up the shield, the sure shelter of the Knight of the Quest. The lance which pierced our blessed Saviour's side was also there preserved.

8   Space is a created thing, material and defined. As time is *mensura motus*, so is space *mensura loci;* and it signifies that part of God's presence which is measured out to enfold the planetary universe. The tracery of its outline is a cone. Every path of a planet is a curve of that conic figure: and as motion is the life of matter, the whirl of space in its allotted courses is the cause of that visible movement of the sun and the solar system towards the star Alcyone as the fixed centre in the cone of space.

9   The "Sign of the Son of Man," the signal of the last day, was understood, in the early ages, to denote the actual Cross of Calvary; which was to be miraculously recalled into existence, and, angel-borne, to announce the advent of the Lord in the sky.

10 Our Lord was crucified with His back towards the east: His face therefore was turned towards the west, which is always, in sacred symbolism, the region of the people.

11 Our Lord was laid in His sepulchre with His head towards the west: His right hand therefore gave symbolic greeting to the region of the south as His left hand reproached and gave a fatal aspect to the north.

12 The golden-hill, from *brun,* "a hill" and *guillie* "golden:" so called from the yellow gorse with which it is clothed.

13 This appropriate fondling of the knights of Dundagel moves Villemarque to write, "qui me plaise et me charme quand je le trouve couché aux pieds

480

d'Ivan, le mufle allongé sur ses deux pattes croisées, les yeux à demi-ouvert et rêvant."

14 See Borlase, bk. iii, Ch. iii for "Karn-idzek:" touched by the moon at some weird hour of the night, it hooted with oracular sound.

15 Cain and his dog: Dante's version of the man in the moon was a thought of the old simplicity of primeval days.

16 When the cone of space had been traced out and defined, the next act of creation was to replenish it with that first and supernatural element which I have named "Numyne." The forefathers called it the spiritual or ethereal element *coelum;* from Genesis 1:ii. Within its texture the other and grosser elements of light and air ebb and flow, cling and glide. Therein dwell the forces, and thereof Angels and all spiritual things receive their substance and form.

17 Igdrasil, the mystic tree, the ash of the Keltic ritual. The Raun or Rowan is also the ash of the mountain, another magic wood of the northern nations.

CHAPTER 25

Perronik, the innocent

KENNETH SYLVAN GUTHRIE

I. Perronik, "the Innocent" uses his Mother-wit

Most people grow old, but there have always been some in the history of the world who, though their body grew up, ever remained young in heart. Many are the causes of this, some are physically unable to take part in labor or war; others are debarred by their sex; some, on the contrary, merely manage to preserve their youth by love of nature, the fields and forests, the sea and sky. Then again others, like David of old, remain young in heart because of the fire of religious devotion in their soul; and some remain young not only because they love nature and religion, but because of the influence of holy people, like Samuel, who associated with the reverend Elf; and the Percival of the Holy Grail legends, the companion of his sainted sister. These simple-minded people, however, are by no means fools. They have a great deal of mother-wit, as was shown by David in his fight with Goliath; when the simple-minded youth succeeded where all others failed. Then again, many of them, in times past, acted as singers, bards, or entertainers. We remember that David played before Saul, and by youthful cheeriness kept away the melancholy moods that darkened that life.

So in Brittany, the extreme north-western corner of France, that juts out into the Atlantic Ocean, there has been, since time immemorial, a class of simple-minded people called "idiots," or "innocents," who were known by the white wands they carried, and the large horn-buttons on their cloaks. They wandered around the country, in the evenings stopping off at the nearest farm-house, sure of being entertained for the night. At supper, they would tell stories, or retail the news of the country-side. In the morning they would not be driven out to work, but be allowed to help the women, or do light helpful offices that required more grace and judgement than muscular effort. When they died, they were sincerely mourned, perhaps not so much for themselves, as for their being considered messengers and helpers from heaven.

It was such an "innocent," by name Perronik, who on a fine spring day knocked at the door of a farm-house a few miles north-west of the dreamy town of Vannes. The farmer's wife responded to his request for food with a bowl of fresh milk. Perronik thanked her, and sat down to enjoy it.

"Madam," said he, "this milk is the sweetest, most delicately flavored beverage I ever tasted. I can almost see the thyme-pasture where the cow who gave it must have fed. And you must be a splendid housewife to have kept it so pure!"

"I do not deserve much credit," smilingly answered the dame; "but the milk really is good, if I do say it myself. As I see that you are a judge of such things, I will bring you some of my cheese, and I would be glad to have you tell me whether you think it is good."

So she brought out some of her new cheese, cut a generous slice, and gave it to Perronik. The latter tasted it slowly. Then, after the manner of persons who are delivering a weighty judgment, he shut one eye, cocked his head, and clacked his tongue.

"I would not have believed it possible," answered he, "to find any cheese that combines so much smoothness, bouquet and tang. It is a masterpiece, that the country-side will long remember!" and then, to convince himself still more, he accepted another hunk of it, laid it on the brown rye bread, and chewed it meditatively, still expatiating on its merits.

"Wait till I bring you some of my new sausages! They will taste all the better after the cheese!"

Soon she came out of the house with a most luscious specimen of the sausage-maker's art, and Perronik had just given it one good bite when ... Here is where our story begins.

II. Perronik Becomes A Shepherd

Around the bend of the road trotted a large heavy charger, bearing a knight in full armour, with plume and helmet, shield and lance. Resplendent in gay colours, and merrily humming a tune, he stopped in front of the farm-house door, and condescendingly shouted at the respectful peasant woman, "Ho there, woman! Which is the way to the castle of Kerglas?"

"Don't go there, my lord, it is dangerous!" tremblingly answered the buxom woman.

"Dangerous it may be!" retorted the shimmering knight, "but where else can I get the Golden Basin, and the Diamond Lance?"

"You are right," answered the woman, "nowhere else can you get those; but what good will they do you, if you do not return?"

"That is where you are mistaken," boasted he. "I expect to return, because I have just been at confession to the holy hermit of Blauvelt; and with his parting benediction, he told me the dangers I should meet; and 'forewarned is forearmed,' you know!"

"Well, if you must go," said the kindly dame regretfully, "the road leads over yonder meadow, and through the dark forest!"

"Thank you," said the knight; and he was just preparing to leave, when Perronik, who, behind the safe shelter of a wall, had been listening to all that had been going on, and who, on seeing the knight prepare to leave, concluded he had nothing to fear, felt his curiosity get the better of him. "My lord," cried he deferentially, "pray tarry a moment!"

"What for?" cried the knight disdainfully.

"Would you be willing to tell us what were the dangers of which the reverend hermit of Blauvelt warned you? It would be very interesting!" pleaded Perronik, who, with a storyteller's genuine interest scented some interesting details. "Do you feel at liberty to tell them to us?"

"Of course!" growled the noble knight. "Why should I be afraid to tell them? First, I have to find my way through the Deceptive Forest. Then I must pick the Golden Apple that grows on a tree guarded by a lion — what chance will the lion have with my shield and lance? Then I must get the Nodding Flower which grows on the rock guarded by the three-headed dragon, with the iron ball, with which he attacks his enemies. Then I will come to the Lake of the Scaly Monsters; but what can they do against my armour? Then I must ride through the Forest of the Sirens; and last, I come to the River of Death. Crossing this, I shall be at the foot of the mountain on the summit of which is the castle of Kerglas."

"Thank you, my lord!" bowed the delighted Perronik, and the scornful knight trotted out of sight, shouting his war-cry, and singing about the beautiful eyes of the lady to whom he was to bring back the Golden Basin and the Diamond Lance.

Perronik sat down, and was resuming his interrupted gourmandizing of the sausage when a distant halloo apprized the mistress of the farm-house that her own lord and master, the farmer, was approaching. She hastened to give him her dutiful greeting, and Perronik modestly stood up expectantly, to meet the man whose hospitality he sought. He had not long to wait before the appearance of the old man, with wrinkled nut-brown skin, blue cloth garments, and large beribboned black felt hat. The latter greeted the "innocent" patronizingly, and invited him to sit down, which Perronik did without further ceremony. The farmer then asked him whether he would be willing to undertake guarding the sheep in the meadow, in exchange for board and lodging. Perronik bowed low, and expressed himself as delighted with the prospect of employment. So the farmer led the way along the same path the knight had taken to the sweet-grass meadow, where browsed a flock of gentle sheep. The farmer whistled for his dog to guard them, while he himself led Perronik to the edge of the forest, where he cut down a sapling and peeled off its bark, thus transforming it into the white wand characteristic of the "innocents," but which, at the same time, was to serve as shepherd's crook.

So the wandering bard became a shepherd, and like all shepherds, ever since the time of Abel, he cut little reeds, and made flutes of them, and whiled away the time by imitating the song of the many birds that made the forest vocal from early dawn, when they sang their matin chorus, until dusk, when once more they gathered on some high bushes, and after a furious orison, retired to their secret nests, twittering away into sleep. But it was the middle of the day that Perronik especially enjoyed.

Then the sheep, exhausted by the heat, would lie down in cool patches of shade. Their bells would be at rest, except for an occasional tinkle when a lamb would start in his dreams, imagining some wasp that had dashed itself at him. The winds had died down, and the birds were resting in their nests, except for an occasional chirp. Then, released from any anxiety, and even from his attempt to call the birds to himself by imitating their song, he would go over in his mind all the wonderful stories he lately had had no opportunity to tell. But chief of all, his mind was ever haunted by the gay knight on the quest of the Golden Basin and the Diamond Lance, in the castle of Ker-glas. Perronik wondered whether the gay knight had succeeded or failed. Softly he laughed at the knight's self-confidence; for who better than a bard knew that pride comes before a fall? And if the opposite were true, perhaps even he, the simple-minded "innocent," might yet in the same quest succeed.

III. How Perronik Started on the Quest

So the peaceful days followed each other. The May flowers came out, and the forest was filled with many perfumes, as the winds blew from favourite nooks of the various flowers. One day Perronik was more than usually longing to have a chance to try those hazards that the knight had told of, when he rubbed his eyes. Was he awake? Was he in a trance? He pinched himself — yea, he was awake, even though around him played all colours of the rainbow, right in and under the shadows of the trees. Then he heard loud rustling, and in view rode a giant, on an immense charger, and over his shoulder hung the Golden Basin and lay the Diamond Lance, coruscating with all the colours of the rainbow, violet, red, blue, yellow, green, and orange. Poor little Perronik, of course, was much frightened; and he hid behind the bush, trembling, until the fearsome apparition had passed by. He was just about to return to his favourite couch in the grass, when he heard another irregular rustling. After his last experience he quickly ran back to his hiding place, but nothing very terrible came up the forest-path, only a foal, coal-black like the giant's horse, indeed, but still no more than a festive baby, nibbling here at the succulent clover, then running along, kicking his heels up in the air, and behaving generally in the irresponsible manner characteristic of puppies and kittens. Perronik almost came out, but he saw among the arches of the trees an old man, with white hair flowing over his back, while a long white beard waved gracefully down to his waist. The old man came forward, and tried to catch the foal; but the rascal would let the old man approach till almost within reach, and then would slip away, and seem to laugh at the patriarch. The latter, however, was not long at a loss. He picked up a stick, and started to draw a magic circle around the foal. The latter was carelessly nibbling at a green shoot, and looked around only when it was too late to escape. Anxiously he hopped around, but the old man relentlessly coiled the magic line around him until the foal no longer could move; when the old man jumped on his back, rubbed out the line in the leaves, and the now frightened foal shot like a bolt through the green under-bush, and disappeared so fast that almost immediately perfect silence once more reigned around him.

This was certainly an extraordinary proceeding, and Perronik long sat still thinking it over. But the afternoon breezes woke up the sheep, and they shifted towards the forbidden river, and Perronik had to run after them. Yet he did not cease to question himself about the whole course of events; and when, during his first leisure, which did not occur before next noon, he again lay on his couch or spear-grass in the shade of the bush, he thought out various solutions. But hardly had he begun to do so, when once more he noticed, playing about him, strange scintillations, such as the light-birds of a mirror in the hands of an inattentive boy at school. Barely had he time to retreat to his hiding place, before he was again almost blinded by the rainbow colours streaming from the Golden Basin and the Diamond Lance on the back of the giant on horse-back. And no sooner had he passed, than Perronik again heard the playful colt disporting himself in the forest path. Even at a distance Perronik had already noticed the grey robe of the white-haired patriarch, when suddenly his curiosity spurred him to action. He picked up a stick, himself started to draw the magic circle around the còlt, closer and closer, until the colt was in his power; and then Perronik quickly turned to bar the passage of the onward rushing old man.

"Stop!" shouted Perronik, raising his stick as if to defend the circle he had drawn. The old man halted, but pleaded with Perronik to let him have his colt.

"No indeed," exulted Perronik, "you shall not have your colt, old man, until you have told me the meaning of this strange occurrence, the passing of the giant, and your riding away on the colt!"

The old man looked much relieved, and said, "The meaning is simple enough. The giant who just passed along is my younger brother Rogear, who took the Golden Basin and Diamond Lance from me one day while I was asleep; and with their possession I lost the rule of the castle of Kerglas. Therefore when he goes abroad to visit his domain and see to the safety of the Golden Apple and the Nodding Flower, I follow after him, in the hope I may wrest my property back from him in some moment of carelessness of his."

"But why do you catch and ride the foal?" insisted the inquisitive Perronik.

"Because I myself can no longer return to the castle on foot. My brother stole the black horse away from me, and only the foal knows the short way back to the castle, or can take me safe through the Lake of the Scaly Monsters, or the River of Death, even though I be the magician Bryak! Now that I have answered your impertinent questions, youth, be faithful to your promise, and give me back my foal!"

"Very well," assented Perronik, "you may take him, now you have told me your story." For Perronik was a story-teller, and he considered a good story worth even a magic foal. So the old man rushed upon the foal, jumped on him, effaced the magic circle in one place so as to release the frightened colt, and shot off into the forest even quicker than the day before.

Perronik, too, was very happy, and retired to his grassy nook, and reviewed again and again the charming story. It was so full of wonder and human interest, that his mind flew back to the brave knight he had seen confidently ride off on this quest, which must have been unsuccessful. Then rose up within Perronik, from some mysterious recess in his soul, a thought that made him catch his breath. "What if I should now try my hand at this quest, now that the proud knight has failed, and is out of it? True, I am only an 'innocent,' but God loves the innocent; and with His help, perhaps, I might accomplish what was impossible to the knight who trusted alone in his shield and spear! After all, I can do no more than fail; and should I succeed, the glory would be so great, it would be well worth the risk. Yea, I shall try it. But I will need help. Earthly aid there is none, for I have no armour; and after all, the earthly armour of the brave knights seems to have done him but little good. No! I will seek help divine; there lies my only hope!"

IV. Perronik Conquers the Lion

So Perronik prayed all afternoon, and towards evening he drove his sheep into their cote long before sunset, in spite of the plaintive objections of the mother-sheep. Then he sallied forth and made a few preparations; put everything in a "bissac," or bag he could easily sling over his shoulder, hid it in the forest under his favourite bush, and lay down on his couch at the farm with a prayer for divine help. During the night he received assurances of success in a dream; for he saw a Hand beckoning him on to the Golden Basin and Diamond Lance. Then he rose up early, before dawn; went out to the edge of the forest where he could watch the sunrise, and prayed again, till tears dimmed his sight, and he swore to the rising sun that he would start out on the great and holy quest that very day. Then he went about his daily duties, and as soon as he had driven his sheep to the field, he lay down under the trees, and listened to every bird and insect, hoping to receive some helpful suggestion from them. The birds came very near him, for he lay quite still, and their song seemed to be telling him they would help him in his hour of need. Then weariness came over him, and he dosed off into a troubled sleep, from which he suddenly started, when he felt once more playing over him the scintillations he had seen the two days before. Hastily he jumped behind the bush, only just in time to avoid attracting the attention of the scowling giant, who, on that morning, seemed to be, if possible, more ferocious than ever. Then Perronik anxiously peered down the forest-lane for the foal. This morning the foal had strayed from the forest-path; and suddenly returned to it almost where Perronik stood. The latter indeed barely had time to seize a stick and start his magic circle around the nibbling equine baby; but he succeeded, and drew the circle closer and closer till the foal could no longer move, though he struggled bravely. Perronik had had to work fast, for already he heard the frantic shouts of the magician Bryak, commanding him to desist. But Perronik jumped on to the back of the foal, effaced a little part of the circle, and just as Bryak had caught up with him, Perronik dug his heels into the panting side of the quivering beast, and sped off into the forest so fast that all the trees seemed to fuse into one long lane; and he hardly managed to readjust himself, after having been dragged through low-hanging branches, when, to his surprise, he saw that the first stage of his journey was over, in front of him, hung, on a graceful tree, the Golden Apple of which he had been told.

So glad was Perronik that he never thought of anything else; but he was recalled to stern reality by the fearsome roaring of a giant lion, who bounded into his path, opening his ravenous maw, and crouched for a spring. Now, as all little girls and boys know, "being good is a lonely and hungry job." The bigger the lion, the bigger his appetite; and yet this faithful guardian of the Golden Apple could not hunt. He had to wait till Providence sent him some food, in the shape of people who followed the quest of the Golden Basin and Diamond Lance; and they were few and far between. So you can imagine the poor animal's hunger and we can excuse his awful excitement, when he saw some prey riding right straight into his jaws, as it were.

Perronik, at first, was struck motionless with terror. But just then he heard one of his favourite bird-friends singing in the branches above him; so he recovered himself, and did some lightning-like thinking. Off he jumped from the horse; he fell on his knees, extended his hands, in supplication, and cried out most humbly:

"Please, Mr Lion, compose yourself for a minute. Listen to me, for I cannot escape you anyway. Now if you eat me up first, the edge of your appetite will be blunted and you will not be able properly to relish the delicious larks I have brought you here in my bag. If, on the contrary, you first partake of them, as candy, you will enjoy the delicious flavor to the full. Then, after having done them full justice, you can appease the body of your appetite on me, who cannot escape you anymore, even if I tried. Will you allow me to offer them to you, kind Mr Lion?"

Even lions, you know, cannot resist courtesy and thought-fulness; and with an austere nod the huge beast sat down on its haunches, and began licking its chops in anticipation of the feast. So Perronik stood up, carefully opened the mouth of his bag, and held it up before the lion, who thrust his greedy head into it. Hardly had he done so, however, when Perronik drew the bag all the way over it: and imagine the reasonable dismay of the lion when, instead of larks, he found nothing but a mixture of glue and feathers! Of course, he pulled back his head, but with the head came the bag! Then he pawed at it, he lashed his poor inoffensive flanks with his tufted tail; he roared as loud as he could under the distressing circumstances, he danced on his hind legs; he rolled over; he bent himself double, and straightened himself out like a spring when released; he rolled himself into a ball; he dug himself into the ground; but all in vain; and the poor beast would still be struggling even till the present time, had not Perronik, after climbing up the tree and dropping straight down to the ground in his hurry, drawn off his bag, jumped on the foal, and sped away, while the poor misguided lion was still trying to get the sticky feathers out of his eyes, so he could see enough to settle accounts with Perronik; but he was too late.

V. Perronik outwits the Unsleeping Dragon

So Perronik sped through the forest till he came up flat against a rock. His late experience made him a little more thoughtful; and he remembered that the Nodding Flower, that grew here, was guarded by a hellish dragon, with four eyes and an iron ball, with which he crushed his opponents. Every six hours one of the four eyes would close in slumber, relieving the others, so the dragon was awake day and night, and there was no hope of overcoming him while off his guard. This, indeed, was a puzzling proposition, and Perronik gingerly picked his way without making a noise to the opposite side of the rock. Even this very light noise had wakened the other three eyes of the hellish dragon; and Perronik was in as great trouble as possible. So he tied the foal where it could browse in sweet clover, and Perronik threw himself down on the grass, and started to think. So

Perronik thought, and thought, and thought; but no solution came to him. In despair he gave it up, and fell to enjoying the forest scenery, and relapsed into his favourite occupation, that of listening to the birds. Now if you were listening to birds, could any boy or girl keep from imitating them? So Perronik grew tired. Then, hoping to get some suggestion, he peered over the rock at the hellish dragon, who lay coiled in his lair beside the coveted flower. Of course, Perronik expected to see the hellish dragon's first eye asleep, as it should have been. But imagine Perronik's surprise on seeing the second eye also about to close; the eyelid fluttered, and finally came to rest in a complete repose. At first Perronik could not account for this; but he remembered how the eyes of the sheep in his pasture at home behaved exactly like that when he had been whistling particularly well. At first he dismissed the thought as absurd; but, on reflection he decided that he could prove the point by making an experiment on the third eye. So he lay back and whistled the best he knew. Never had he made such runs, such trills, such cadences, such rhythms, such melodies. First you might have thought he were a lark, then a whippoorwill, then a canary, and finally a nightingale. He would listen to the birds above him, and improve on their bursts and pleadings. Then he looked over the rock again and indeed, the third eyelid of the hellish dragon was fluttering down, just like that of a sleepy pussy. A few more calls like that of the finch to his mate, and the eye was closed, watching the phantasmagoria of its dreams.

Perronik was beside himself with joy. "This is easy!" almost shouted he to himself! So he settled himself down once more, and started to whistle better than ever. Indeed, he whistled so marvellously, that he surpassed even the birds whom previously he had merely imitated. The birds, who before had listened to his efforts with friendly condescension, now became envious. They fluttered angrily about him, and tried to drown his efforts, by a chorus louder even than that they sang at dusk and dawn. But Perronik only profited by their efforts, because improving on the suggestions they thus offered, he sang so much better than they that finally their hearts wilted within their little ruffled breasts, and they grew still, hungrily drinking in the magic melodies they heard. Then for the first time Perronik reached his supreme skill in whistling. Even the insects paused on the golden flowers; the bees stopped humming, and poised themselves gracefully on the buttercups.

But Perronik never forgot he was whistling for a purpose; and once more he peeped over the rock, and to his great delight he saw the hellish monster's fourth eye-lid fluttering down just as the former eye-lids had done. So Perronik whistled more gently and drowsily, like the twittering of birds when disturbed by dreams, in their sleep; and then the fourth eye closed with a snap, and for the first time in his long life the hellish monster was entirely asleep. You may well believe that it did not take Perronik very long, noiselessly, to leap over the rock, and pick the Nodding Flower. He fastened it in his cap; picked up his bag, swung it over his shoulder, vaulted onto his impatient foal, and off they sped, showing a clean pair of heels to the wakened monster who stirred uneasily, as if feeling something was wrong, hissing hellishly, out of natural spite.

VI. Perronik escapes the Scaly Monsters

But Perronik, by this time, was far and away; and nothing stopped him till he came to the Lake of the Scaly Monsters. Now, as often happens with dangerous or forbidden things, this dangerous lake was exceedingly beautiful. The blue sky was reflected in its still waters, and the willows by the side seemed to bend down lovingly to touch their perfect reflection in the slimy depths of the treacherous pool. Perronik, however, had not much time to contemplate all these beauties, for by this time the foal was not only tired but hungry; and when Perronik sought to guide the foal around the lake, the foal impatiently jumped right in and swam, so as to get home the sooner. At first all went well; and Perronik was enjoying the unusual view when his horrified gaze fixed on a circle of still water, around which was a fringe of boiling waves. Then, out of the tranquil pool he saw rising horny scales, and then what he recognized as an opening maw. Imagine the maw of a crocodile, but as big as a whale; then you will forgive brave Perronik for going all white, and trembling. The ferocious row of teeth rose in the air; the water began to flow into the enormous black hole. A current set in, and in spite of all the efforts of the plucky foal, Perronik felt himself surely, if slowly, drawn in to the monster's maw. In his extremity he prayed. A bird darted over him, and uttered a piercing shriek, that reminded him of when he had had to protect the lambs when a hawk sailed overhead. Then he remembered something he had in his bag. He reached in, and pulled out a black bean which, for safety's sake, he had had the good parish priest bless for him, the evening before his departure. This Perronik threw right into the yawning abyss. Now this scaly monster was not a holy scaly monster; and therefore, when he felt the blessed bean tickling his soft palate he felt like vomiting, and in mighty eructations that looked like water-spouts, he tried to eject the bean, which had stuck in the hairs on his inner throat. Unfortunately, however, just as happens to a boy or girl who in eating fish swallows a bone that sticks in the throat, all the branches and sticks which had easily gone down along with the swirl of water, were now turned side-wise; they stuck in his gills, and the more the beast regurgitated, the more he choked. Finally he grew green in the face, flapped his monstrous fins, turned a somersault in the air, uttered a plaintive yowl, and careening over on his back, he gave up his wicked ghost. This, however, caused a whirlpool in the water, and Perronik who was circling around in the maelstrom, was, by the last tidal wave, driven onto the opposite shore. The brave little foal, feeling under his little hoofs firm ground, snorted and shook the slimy water out of his eyes and mane. Then he braced himself, galloped up the slope, and dashed for the shelter of the forest.

VII. *Perronik escapes Sirens*

No doubt he would have been going still, had he not, with a sudden jolt that almost made Perronik come a cropper, stood still. Especially because his hairs were wet, did they look strange as they began to stand straight in horror, as the foal gazed on in stupefaction. There lay a heap of skeletons of brave knights, whose armour was strewn around in confusion. Evidently this was the most dangerous of all the hazards of the quest; knights who had escaped all former dangers, still had here fallen before the fatal charms of the enchanted sirens that infested these sylvan retreats. Indeed, through the aisles of the forest Perronik described, approaching forms of beautiful women, golden-haired and starry-eyed, waving their arms in greeting, and chanting weird threnodies. What was the unfortunate Perronik to do? Lions, hellish dragons, and even scaly monsters could be resisted; but what proper-minded youth can resist the fair charms of a lovely woman? Alas, I fear my story will have to end here; there seems no earthly rescue for our simple-minded "innocent."

Perronik himself realized this; and so he betook himself to prayer. Then suddenly an idea popped into his mind. Just as the swish of the sirens' silken garments began to becloud his reason, just as their perfume made his head whirl, and buzz, as chloroform would have done, an inspiration came into his mind. He reached up, and, in spite of velvet hands that clung like ivy-vines, he pulled the cap on his head down just far enough to reach over his eyes. Perronik being thus blinded, the sirens were powerless over him; and digging his heels into the sore ribs of the only too willing foal, Perronik, without ever stopping, was carried through the shady groves of the sirens; and not till his foal stopped still with a jerk, and his nose apprised him of the presence of a large body of water, his ears being filled with the ominous rushing of a river, did Perronik dare to push up his cap far enough to see that he had left the sirens' grove far behind, and was standing, by the side of a bush, on the very bank of the rapidly rolling River of Death, on the further side of which loomed up before him, not so very far, the noble mountain bearing the castellated outline of Kerglas itself!

He must cross; that was sure, but how? Of course, Rivers of Death have no bridges or even fords; or of what use would they be? What indeed was our hero to do? So puzzled was he, that he would be standing there till the present moment, but for a most unusual occurrence. From behind the bush sprang a beautiful lady, dressed in black silk, but with a complexion as yellow as sulphur. Perronik would have indeed retreated before her, but she, like a wise woman, did not give him the time. She jumped up on the foal before him, and reached for the reins. Here is where Perronik's presence of mind reasserted itself. He clutched them tight and only when she saw that she had no more to gain by boldness that, like many another haughty dame, the lady became as meek as butter, and as persuasive as honey. She told him that she knew that he was on the quest of the Golden Basin and the Diamond Lance; that he could not get it alone; but that if he had the Golden Apple and the Nodding Flower, and would ferry her over the River of Death which she, unaided, could never cross, she would help him in his quest. While Perronik had his doubts about the lady, nevertheless, because he had always been trained to be polite to ladies, he agreed to take her over. She, on her part, did not lose any time, but urged the willing foal. He jumped into the icy water, and, in spite of shivering, the brave little beast swam valiantly on, never stopping until he had safely reached the opposite bank. Fearful that the foal might take cold by standing still on leaving the freezing water, Perronik urged him on, and the equine trotted up the hill as fast as he could, neighing in anticipation of the oats he knew were awaiting him in the stables, beside his mother, the giant's black charger who, on her part, must be anxious, by this time, for her offspring's safety. So the horse climbed rapidly to the gate of the frowning castle, where both Perronik and the lady dismounted, and the foal trotted off by himself, neighing and capering, to the stable.

VIII. Perronik achieves his Quest

Our two travellers entered the castle's gate, which, strange to say, they found open. They entered into the courtyard, but neither there did they discover anybody, knight or servant. So the Yellow Lady led Perronik to the main entrance, and up the steps, still deserted, into the vast dining hall of the castle. Here, seated at the festive board, sat only two individuals, the giant, Rogear, and by his side his hoary-haired brother, the magician Bryak, at a lower table.

Now, of course, golden apples and fair ladies have ever, since the beginning of time, been the pray of giants, and who can blame giants for having the good taste to consider them designed for their special benefit? Therefore Rogear the giant, with a vertiginous leap, pounced upon Perronik. Rogear reached out for the Golden Apple; but as he bit into it, he sank into a seat, because it was poisoned; and as he lay hold on the willowy

496

lady, he fell down stark dead; for, be it known, she was nothing less than the "Plague"!

You can easily imagine that Perronik did not dally near her. Swiftly pulling the Nodding Flower out of his cap, he observed in which direction the flower nodded. So he followed it through a large door, down a hall, to a stairway; down this to the lower floor; then by a winding passage into the vaults. Past an iron door he went into a cave. Following a stream, in which he waded, he came into a vast amphitheatre, glistening with salt-formations, in the light of sun-rays that filtered through some cracks. Then he followed the flower's directions into a passage so narrow he had to crawl on hands and knees; but, at last, he arrived into a chapel; and on the high altar, between ever-burning candles, lay the Golden Basin and the Diamond Lance!

Perronik pounced upon them; but he was in such a hurry that the Diamond Lance knocked on the Golden Basin, emitting a peal as clear as that of a sacring-bell. When, however, Perronik came to himself, he found himself back in the meadow, among the sheep he had so long neglected, with the Golden Basin hanging on his back, and the Diamond Lance in his hand.

IX. *Perronik becomes King of Jerusalem*

Now it is evident that no one who possessed the Golden Basin and the Diamond Lance would ever be willing to remain a shepherd. Therefore, after giving the mother-sheep a parting pat, and kissing his favourite lambs farewell, Perronik turned off on to the highway, and betook himself to the picturesque town of Vannes.

Now it chanced, as happens in all well-regulated fairy-tales, that the king of Vannes had a beautiful daughter. At the same time, however, he was being pressed very hard by his enemies who, so far, had driven back all his armies, and defeated all his generals. In desperation, the king had made a proclamation that any one who would overcome his enemies should have the beautiful daughter to wife, and become king in his stead. On entering into Vannes, Perronik read the proclamation, and asked to be led to the king's palace. Having arrived there, he asked for an audience with the king. Only with great difficulty, however, did he succeed in obtaining it. Then the king laughed at Perronik, who offered to accomplish this feat; for Perronik was still garbed as an "innocent," with white staff and horn buttons. Perronik, however, offered to give a demonstration of his powers. He touched the king of Vannes' best knight, who immediately fell down in his tracks, stone dead. Then, Perronik poured some of the water of the golden basin into the dead knight's mouth, whereupon he revived, as full of life and spirits as ever, finishing the word he had had on his lips when he fell dead. The king of Vannes was convinced, and entrusted all his armies to Perronik. The latter, of course, in the might of the Golden Basin and the Diamond Lance, was victorious over the embattled hosts of the enemy, and reduced them to abject submission. Leading their chieftains in chains to the palace of the king of Vannes, the latter gave him his blushing daughter to wife, and set Perronik upon his throne, himself retiring to meditation in a monastery.

Although Perronik was, for a short time, happy as husband of his marvellously beautiful wife and as king of the good town of Vannes; who could expect the owner of the Golden Basin and the Diamond Lance to be satisfied with being king of even Vannes, that beautiful, and famous city? So Perronik demanded the crown of France. Leading his ever-victorious armies, Perronik succeeded even in this, and finally was crowned king of France, and reigned in Paris.

But, although for a brief space of time, Perronik was happy as king of France, the owner of the Golden Basin and the Diamond Lance could not be expected to be satisfied with even that dignity. He must become emperor of Rome. And indeed, leading his ever-victorious armies, Perronik achieved this supreme dignity also.

Still, though, for a short space of time Perronik was content with the domain of the empire of Rome, it would be unreasonable to suppose that the owner of the Golden Basin and the Diamond Lance could ever grow satisfied, or cease to sigh for more worlds to conquer. So Perronik started out to conquer Palestine, liberate it from the hated rule of the Saracen. At the head of his ever-victorious armies, indeed, Perronik accomplished this task also, and was crowned king of Jerusalem.

But, strange to say, Perronik was never heard of again. His

fate ever remained a mystery; but the best-informed say that one day, while he was asleep, the old magician Bryak deprived him of the Golden Basin and the Diamond Lance, and hid them again in the mountain beneath the castle of Kerglas, where they remain hidden, until they shall once more be found by some younger Perronik who shall restore to Brittany her rightful sovereignty over the world.

CHAPTER 26

Mystic Gleams from the Holy Grail

FRANCIS ROLT-WHEELER

I. The Holy Grail, the Nature of its Divine Mystery and its Initiatory Power

The soul of man, inheritor and guardian of a Divine Spark wherein dwells an ever-shining and vital mirroring of the Divine Soul, possesses thereby an inherent receptivity to the Good. This faculty enables him to distinguish between that which is spiritually true and that which is false. Too often this inner receptivity, source of our Moral Consciousness, is neglected or obstructed by other organs of reception, or resonators, attuned either to lesser emotions or to material vibrations.

None the less, this "sensitive ear of the soul" is never completely dulled. It acts upon the egregore of a people or an era. This it is which gives "The Judgment of the Centuries," that decision which consigns a commercial Carthage to the limbo of forgetfulness, and which enshrines Athens in imperishable beauty.

The Judgment of the Centuries rules impartially and its decrees have no appeal. Among the thousand myths and legends which have cradled Humanity since the beginnings of Thought, rare indeed are those which have acquired immortality. They bear within themselves that Mystery which is known as "Initiation." As examples of these immortal myths may be named: Adam and Eve in the Earthly Paradise and the Quest of the Holy Grail.

We are yet far from a full understanding of the cosmogony, the anthropogony, and the spiritual significance of the Garden of Eden. Much remains to be deciphered (or revealed) of Adam-Kadmon as a Vesture of God; of the descent of Adam-Macroprosopus and Adam-Microprosopus; of the Fall of Adam and of the Mystery of Redemption — all concealed in the ancient traditions of the Earthly Paradise. Esoteric students know well that it is one of the most profound teachings in initiatory literature.

The Legend of the Holy Grail glows likewise with an inner light of esoterism. Few, indeed, be those who have sought to follow the silver thread of Spiritual Initiation in this strange and mysterious cycle of miracle, of faërie, of chivalry, and of a super-sacrament. Constantly, in this mystical legend, there is a glimpse of the unknown; the reader may lose his way in a thicket of visions. The texts themselves are so overburdened that any effort to set them in order produces an overlaid recital, full of sensational but secondary incidents, obscuring the higher aim.

It is customary to say that this Legend is known to everybody; it would be more just to say that it is unknown, save to the very few. Philology may guide us through a labyrinth of texts, history may show a psychological stratification, exegesis may give us a dozen possible interpretations, and the mystics — who see further and higher — may illumine the Way, showing it as thorny, or as blossoming, according to their particular enlightenment. But of "The Legend of the Holy Grail," taken as a whole, no interpreter has yet come to explain fitly.

Far be it from us to attempt the impossible! A restatement would lead nowhere. Great scholars have laboured, and great works bear witness to their labours. Yet the Legend of the Holy Grail is so rich in mystery, so revealing in vision, so subtle in its high teaching, so prophetic in its initiation that it is possible to put before the reader certain esoteric meanings he may have overlooked. It may be permitted to mirror forth some gleams of a Mystic Light too dazzling unless viewed with reflected vision.

It is therefore our intention to limit our research to such parts of the vast Legend as may permit some mystical or spiritual meaning. The incidents will not be drawn from any single text.

Little will be said of the prowess of knights in combat or in tourney; nor shall stress be laid — save in so far as may serve an allegorical purpose — on romantic or passionate attachments to the maidens of Faërie and of Chivalry. True it is that there is rhythm and beauty in the love-singing of trouvère and troubadour, but such is not our theme.

The Legend of the Holy Grail, in its origin and in its development, is essentially Christian. Yet we shall miss the spiritual uplift in the story if we fail to realize that the rites and sacraments of which it tells are not celebrated on the earthly plane, but rather in "a temple not made with hands." The "Lost Word" may not be known on this Earth, but it resounds eternally where the Celestial Hierarchies abide.

This Way will also lead us into the astral world and into the Kingdoms of Faërie, where Merlin, the Enchanter, serves as guide. Those who know how to read in the Book of Nature will find the link of Celtic Initiation in these sagas, and may even hear the tread of "The Lordly Ones."

The deeds and adventures of the Knights of the Round Table form but a thin disguise for the setting forth of a Spiritual Chivalry, such as may war with the Powers of Darkness in that conflict of the soul that leads to the Holy Grail. The Grail itself is that Cup of Immortality which contains — in addition to the Precious Blood — that draught of Living Water whose source is the fourfold river that flows from the Throne of God.

Above all, this high romance is of the Supreme Quest. It is the search for God in the soul, for spiritual contact, for the ecstatic communion received in the Sanctuary of the Grail. Even if the Holy Grail itself be hidden from description, the Luminous Chalice, symbol of its glory, is not withdrawn from our spiritual vision. The accolade of knightliness awaits him who is worthy of the Quest.

Sublime, indeed, is the Reality of the Ideal to one who has entered into this Mystery. A Joy of Possession is his, and, in the mystical words of the ancient authors: "he is nourished of the Grail." It is thus that we seem to see the high esoteric meaning and the sacred inspiration of that marvellous vision of spiritual chivalry: "The Legend of the Holy Grail."

II. The Mystical Nature of the Holy Grail, as it appears on the Several Planes

The Mystery of the Holy Grail is of so interior a nature, so apart from any concrete organization, that it may be well to show forth the inner meaning of the Legend before giving a brief summary of the story to those who may have forgotten it. Only thus can we understand its extraordinary shining athwart the ages.

Truly it may be said that the Holy Grail is the Cup of the Last Supper; it is also the Heavenly Vessel borne by an angel to the Divine Sufferer in the Garden of Gethsemane; and it is the Mystic Chalice wherein Joseph of Arimathea received the drops of the Precious Blood at the Descent from the Cross. But these three Cups are not one and the same, save in a spiritual understanding.

Likewise, the Castle of the Grail may be found at Corbenic, at Montsalvatch, at Montségur and at other places. But, like the Golden Stair of Celtic legend, it can be found only by him who is worthy. It awaits the coming of the elect, for the Castle of the Grail, like to the Grail itself, is real but as a mystical reality.

To seek a tangible vessel as the Holy Grail, whether of gold, of silver or of emerald, is but simple-wittedness. It reveals the seeker to be a sordid materialist, to whom the higher understanding is closed. More than a dozen false "Grails" exist. One may mention those at Bruges, at Mantua, at Weingarten, at Fécamp, not to speak of the famous "Sacro Catino" of Genoa — supposed to have been made from a single emerald, which is but common glass. In reducing the Cup of the Holy Grail to the level of cunning handiwork, vulgar incomprehension can no further go.

The mystical interpretation abides. The Holy Grail is definitely the supreme symbol of the Immanent Presence of Christ on Earth, inspiration of a sublime faith, enshrining a sacramental mystery whose communion is of the soul.

The Holy Grail is not only a mystical symbol; it is the Mystic Life. In reverent hesitation, yet with undoubted sincerity, the *trouvères* and the poets sought to set forth this high truth. The time for its understanding was not yet come. It is for us — to whom a key may be given — to evoke from this ancient Legend its imperishable beauty, and to invoke its indwelling power.

Let us try, briefly, to set forth the main lines of the central plot which is common to these several cycles, for the texts contain more than eight hundred thousand lines, and the incidents are complex, confused and bewildering.

Tradition tells of the events of the night of the Last Supper, of the Blessing of the Cup, of the Agony at Gethsemane, of the condemnation of Jesus by Caiaphas, Herod and Pilate, and of the Crucifixion.

When Pilate accorded to Joseph of Arimathea the privilege of the sepulture of Christ, he gave him, also, the precious Cup. During the Descent from the Cross, some drops or clots of blood were caught by Joseph in this Chalice. Thus the "sang real" became the "sang Graal," or "San Graal." (There are other derivations for this term.)

Hate-filled, the Jews threw Joseph into a windowless tower, wherein he dwelt for forty years, visited only by the Risen Christ and nourished only by the Holy Grail. Vespasian, son of the Roman emperor Titus, having been healed from leprosy by the Veil of St Veronica, liberated Joseph of Arimathea.

During his incarceration Joseph had learned much from the Risen Saviour, and had been ordered to travel to the West. Traces of his voyagings may be found in Sicily, at Marseilles, on both sides of the Pyrenees, in the Landes, in Brittany, and finally in Great Britain and Wales.

"The Times Adventurous," a period of bewitchment in the Kingdom of Logres (an esoteric term), which is said to have lasted for centuries, caused the Holy Grail to remain in hiddenness.

At this point, the Christian Legend encountered the ancient initiatory Celtic myths and hero-cycles of Ireland, of Wales and of Cornwall. After centuries of literary contact, a certain fusion occurred. Thus Merlin, the bard, becomes enchanter and initiator. The Legends of the Round Table (a grouping of the hero-cycles of Arthur, of Lancelot, of Merlin, of Percival, of Galahad, etc.) came to include the Legend of the Holy Grail, which, in time, served to inspire the whole. This fusion gives an atmosphere of faërie and chivalry to a legend purely Christian in its origin and symbolism.

504

During the Great Awakening of the twelfth century, era of the Sacramental Controversy (settled in 1214), the *trouvères* chanted to the barons, knights and ladies in feudal castles these legends and their lays. There was no standard text; each minstrel sang after the joy of his heart. Some had a vision of higher things. The Holy Grail became a sacrament, even a super-sacrament of an extra-terrestrial consecration, whereof the partakers were a Spiritual Chivalry.

It is told how the Holy Grail, veiled, passed on a shaft of light about the Great Hall of the Round Table, at Camelot, and how every knight present vowed to follow the Quest for a year and a day, that he might more clearly see the Holy Grail and understand its mystery.

Wondrous were the adventures that befell the knights-errant on the Quest, and many other hero-cycles were grafted on the Legend. In this present short study, the deeds of only four of the knights of the Quest will be followed: Gawain, who found disgrace therein; Lancelot, who, by reason of his love for Guinevere, received but a partial vision; Percival, to whom the vision of the Graal was given, but not an understanding of its mystery; and Galahad, the High Prince, glory of knighthood and hero of the Quest.

It is Galahad, the Pure and Perfect Knight, who appears in a Messianic light in several of the versions, who frees the Kingdom of Logres from its sorcery-held bondage, who heals the Maimed King and participates in the Apostolic Rite of the Holy Grail. At the last, guarding the Holy Grail and the Lance of Longinus — together with other Hallows — Galahad sets forth on the Mystical Ship of Solomon, set afloat two thousand years before, for the last voyage to the Initiate City of Sarras, of whose whereabouts no man knoweth.

After the death of Percival and Galahad, the Grail was "withdrawn" from this Earth and from terrestrial vision, nor dare any man say that he has seen it since, earthly-wise. But the high Mystery of the Holy Grail calls ever to the elect and to those who have within them the will to tread this High Way of Initiation.

XVI. *The World of Faërie and of Gramarye; the Astral Plane and Celtic Initiation*

Older and deeper-rooted, reaching to the nature-sources of Being, the traditions and initiatory strivings of the Celtic Race strike athwart the Christian content in the Legends of the Holy Grail. They do neither change nor colour it, but Initiates of "The Green Ray" will recognize a focussed simultaneity on two planes very different from the fenced thoroughfare of Mosaic monotheism. No Celtic tradition will give us a Garden of Eden with pot-herbs and fruit-trees cunningly planted; nor will God appear as an exclusive tribal possession or a totem in border war.

Such is not the Celtic Way. The Celtic peoples, so richly blessed in poesy and mystic fervour, have also their holy legends, their secret lore and their hidden initiations. High Gods are theirs. They have a story of Creation, and who shall take upon him to judge the inner truth of a Cosmogony!

He knows not the Holy Grail to whom the fairy portals have not been opened. As A.E. points out, "Poesy must always be more than it can be." It is not enough to hold the Cup; one must be free of the Fountain. Seen on the two planes, the Holy Grail becomes something quite other than a holy relic, however sacrosanct. The Celtic harp vibrates to a Cosmic touch; Merlin is as vital to the Great Epic of Saintly Chivalry as is Joseph of Arimathea.

Be it remembered historically that when the *trouvères* wrote and sang, England had been robbed of her birthright. The Celt had been driven to fastnesses and wild places by Dane, Angle and Saxon. If the Normans were less barbaric, their Latin admixture made them even less able to see "the world of Faërie." To this day — save in Brittany, which is Celt — the Latin peoples are alien to the Land of Gramarye.

This abyss of misunderstanding was one of the chief causes of "The Times Adventurous." To a monk of the Roman rite, Aengus of Eternal Youth was but a pagan deity; in no wise could Tir-na-n 'Og be made to fit into an earthly Paradise of Semitic source. There is no need that this misunderstanding should continue. It may then be permitted to lift a corner of the veil and glimpse the beauty and the heart-stir of the fairy spell in Celtic lore.

The Initiation bestowed by the gods and demi-gods of Nature was once widely spread. Unknowingly, it is so still. The Greeks held Dionysian and Orphic rites on wooded mountain and vine-clad slope; at Eleusis, Demeter was goddess of meadow and planted field. In the ruder zone of the oak forest, where Druids counselled and bards sang, the gods of the woodland gave the word of Acceptance to Aspirant and Neophyte.

Is the enchantment past and all forgotten? Not so. Let those answer who feel the Divine Presence more readily in a shadowed glade than in a parish church, and who prefer the hymning of the wood-thrush to that of the urchin chorister. Are there not still Neophytes of hill and dale? How many more souls would respond, if they did but hear!

The Holy Grail of blessed Palestine, a hallow of high sanctity, given to Joseph of Arimathea and his successors, is a symbol whereby we may pierce to the Divine Transcendence. The Holy Grail of the Celtic peoples is Nature itself; the Cup in which all Life is consecrated. The "sang real" of the Celt is God Immanent, not Transcendent; it is the Absolute in Manifestation, not in Withdrawal.

The pilgrims of the Grail who followed Joseph of Arimathea beheld before them, as a Pillar of Fire, the Mystery of the Redemption. The pilgrims and children of the Dagda Mor feel, deeply and convincingly, the Divine Presence in every leaf of tree and hear the Message in every note of a bird's song. Not all men can translate that message.

The early Christians, as yet unloosed from Hebraic bondage, saw, in the Celestial Hierarchies, nought but the messengers of Jehovah; the Celts knew well their "Lordly Ones," personifications of Great Forces in perpetual activity but real and vital to be seen of those who have the Seeing. "The Lords of the Flame" and "the lords of Form" of another cosmogony have their parallels in the Celtic theogony. God, watching over all His worlds, "slumbers not, nor sleeps;" to the Celt, the gods were never far away.

From the fairy of the field-flower to the mighty elementals who upheave mountain ranges, from the sylph to the moulder of worlds, every Nature-Being vibrates with the Divine

Immanence. Divinity homes in a tuft of moss or a cedar of Lebanon, in a drop of dew or the whirling of a hurricane. The Initiate of Nature, even as the mystic, establishes the Unitive Life with God. These be the higher regions of the World of Faërie.

The Astral or Sublunary World — to use the ancient name — is a borderland, twilight-lit, the ante-chamber of the Beyond, a land of traverse wherein no one should too long time dwell. Its frontiers run with the World of Faërie; sometimes it is hard to tell where one begins and the other ends.

It is the dwelling-place of the Great Elementals, and on a very different plane, of the Welcomers, who come to meet the newly dead. Ethereal guides await the hardy adventurer and there are always deeds of rescue awaiting him to do. There is a knight-errantry of the Astral also. But it is also the abode of lying spirits, of the tormented earthbound, of enmagicked soul-shells, of larvae and lemures. A region terribly vast, terribly real, largely uncharted, wherein sorcerers may ply their noxious trade. Yet not one of all these hosts of evil and half-evil can touch the innocent and the unknowing. This shows out clearly, where the Legends of the Round Table touch the Astral World.

Not only does the Holy Grail operate differently on all these planes, it is different in itself. In the earlier centuries of Christianity, the Grail was a material relic of precious metal, chased with gems; something that might be held and lifted with the hands. It needed a Tabernacle for its hiding-place and was often accompanied with emblems which spoke of physical suffering: such Hallows as the Lance, the Nails, the Sword, the Scourge and the Crown of Thorns. It served as a chalice at Mass. It was a Cup of Miraculous Healing for Evalach, Pellahan and other sufferers of mystical wounds, the restoration being by Faith, as in the miracles of Jesus Christ.

In the days of Chivalry, when the Legend rings the note of the Quest of the Holy Grail, all this is changed. That which was sacred becomes magical. The presence of the Grail suffices to heap up dishes of food and to fill beakers of drink, without distinction of number. This is like to the Bowl of Plenitude of Celtic origin. The Cauldron of Daga or Awen, the Caire of Alba and many other vessels of pre-Christian legend have the same character.

It is almost impossible not to bracket together the Four

Talismans of the Tuatha na Danaan and the Four Hallows of the Holy Grail. Who were the Tuatha na Danaan? Heroes all, kin to the demi-gods of Homer, kin also to the dwellers of the Lands beneath the Moon, living an enchanted life in dignity and peace. Their Talismans were (1) the Cup or Cauldron of Dagda, giving food and drink in plenty to all who came to the feast; (2) the Magic Lance or Javelin, known as the Lance of Redemption; (3) the Invincible Sword of Lugh of the Long Hand; and (4) the Lir Fail or the Stone of Destiny. In the Hallows of the Grail we find the Cup, the Lance of Longinus, the Sword of David and, in *Parzival,* the Grail itself is the Stone of Destiny.

The last phase of the Legend of the Holy Grail, which transmutes the Grail to a spiritual plane, touches sublimity. It finds the Voice of Chivalry in the Great Hall at Camelot, when the Knights of the Round Table took the vow to follow the Quest for a year and a day, that they might see it clearly and understand its mystery.

Here is no Bowl of Plenitude, nor Stone of Destiny. All material significance disappears. The Grail becomes the abiding-place of the Divine Presence. The Castle of the Grail is the Temple of the Holy Spirit. And, in the Higher Mass of the Holy Grail, the Celebrant is the Christ Himself, "a priest for ever after the Order of Melchizedek."

XLVI. The Sublime Mystery of the Holy Grail; the Spiritual Plane of the Quest

Sursum corda! Two noble texts in the cycles of the Round Table serve to lead us to planes of high spiritual beauty. These are far other than the plane of Faërie where Merlin is guide, or the plane of Chivalry, wherein moves Lancelot, the Best Knight in the World. The world of Faërie opens its gates and those of the astral world to those who are akin; earthly knighthood appears in its due place as a preparation for the Fellowship of Celestial Knighthood. On the spiritual plane, there are moments when Percival will speak to the soul, and Galahad shall be the Pillar of Light, to lead.

The *Perlesvaus* or *The Longer Prose Percival* is a very special text. It has been translated into English with exquisite care and artistry of style by Dr Sebastian Evans, and is known as *The High History of the Holy Grail*. It tells specially of the adventures of Percival (and Gawain), but begins only in the middle of their career. This is not the lay of a *trouvère*, but an esoteric rendering of a part of the Legend, revealing initiatory factors held as a Mystery.

As Waite has pointed out, in the whole field of Christian literature there is not one text that speaks so richly of a Mysterious Faith, of an Esoteric School and of a Secret Church, as does the *Perlesvaus*. If its tales of wonder be always crowned with a morning Mass, be sure that the Chapel is of a surpassing fairness, and the Mass is not according to the Ordinary. Every Sanctuary seems to be the antechamber to some higher Sanctuary, the sacrament is a super-sacrament, the order of priesthood is of celestial ordination. It is written within and without, and for those who can receive it, there is the Bread of Heaven and the Wine of the Spirit.

There are mystic emanations from the Holy Grail on many planes. There is a Mysticism that may be called "Divine" and its protagonist is Joseph of Arimathea. There is a Mysticism of Faërie and of the Celtic Initiation and the wand of Merlin points to the Lordly Ones. There is a mysticism of Chivalry on Earth which prefigures a Celestial Fellowship. So, also, earthly symbols have spiritual values, and ecclesiastical rites foreshadow heavenly mysteries.

Whoso has read deeply into mystical literature and especially into the mysticism of Symbolism will not have failed to note its specific desire to be in contact with a plane that is both immanent and transcendental in its simultaneity. Though difficult to express, Jakob Boehme has made a fusion of the in-going and the out-going will. The matter is far more difficult if it is to be expressed in rite and symbol; it is an inner problem in the Quest of the Holy Grail.

In all the Legends of the Round Table may be seen this recognition of an Outer or exoteric sense of Right and of an Inner or esoteric sense. The Knight Errant was missionary as well as judge. The Holy Grail, veiled in symbol (the External Church), is not enough, its meaning and mystery (the Inner Church) must be known. "The Word that was with God," in Manifestation, is also "the Word that was God," in non-manifestation. This is a deep force in mystical Christian feeling. It has been overlaid by a material interpretation, as in St Augustine, where Rome is the be-all and end-all of everything, but the Celtic note — so strong in the legends — is always ready to go deeper.

In the Middle Ages, The Brethren of an Interior Life, precursors of a liberal yet esoteric tradition, worked on this basis. Its most definite expressions are in *The Cloud Upon the Sanctuary* by Eckartshausen, and *The Character of the Interior Church* by Loupuhin. These two didactic works evoke a definite memory of the *Perlesvaus*.

Without overstretching the point, it may be said that a number of the specific conditions set down by Eckartshausen are foreshadowed in the Legends of the Round Table, and more especially that part of those Legends which has to do with the Holy Grail. Nine such may be mentioned:

(i) That there exists an Interior Church, founded by Christ between his Resurrection and Ascension, the teaching of which was confined to a few depositaries, among them Joseph of Arimathea and St John;

(ii) That the External Church reflects these teachings, more or less justly, according as the mystical and initiatory contacts are kept or lost;

(iii) That there is a spiritual Temple, invisible to those who cannot read the soul, but where the elect may gather, and to which, after death, they will be formally admitted (Spiritual Chivalry is of the same line of thought);

(iv) That the Inmost Sanctuary is Christ and is Eternal, knowing no change, being both pre-Incarnation and post-Incarnation;

(v) That the three stages of Regeneration are ecclesiastic, interior, and spiritual; they are not secret, but shown forth in the words of Christ;

(vi) That the Two Paths are Wisdom and Love, the mind and the heart, and that these were combined in Jesus;

(vii) That the Incarnation is a continuing process in the soul of Man;

(viii) That all Mysteries which may be accomplished on Earth are inadequate of themselves and do not give salvation;

(ix) That the Eucharist on Earth is a pre-figurement, and the priesthood a forth-shadowing; their offices are not valid unless consummated in Heaven (this is definitely the setting-forth of Galahad).

If, to the line of Mysticism already mentioned, be added the Mystery of the Interior Church, many problems in the Legends become clear. It is thus shown why Joseph of Arimathea avoided Jerusalem and Rome; why the Holy Grail was brought to the countries of the Celtic Church; why there are Mysterious Words of Consecration that must be handed on orally; why the Question of the Grail requires that he who asks it shall be conscious of its inner meaning; why the Earthly Chivalry is but a prefigurement of the Spiritual Chivalry; and why the Mass of the Grail has Christ Himself as celebrant, or, at least, one of the translated saints, made a priest after the Order of Melchizedek. The esoteric teaching of the *Perlesvaus* opens great spiritual horizons.

The second text to which reference has been made, while not more spiritual, is more devotional. It is churchly, even churchy. It suggests Rule rather than ecstasy, conformity rather than the liberty of the soul, ecclesiasticism rather than individualism, the liturgy rather than the Mystery. On its finer lines it reveals unsuspected heights and sublimates doctrine. This is *La Queste del Saint Graal*. The text is attributed to Walter Map or to a Cistercian monk. Its special character is so well analysed by Pauphilet that a few words of quotation may be permitted.

"It seems as though nearly all the apparitions of the Grail (in this text)," says Pauphilet, "are of the nature of the immaterial. In a blaze of wonder it begets astonishment and enthusiasm in the half-worldly court of King Arthur; it passes before Lancelot in the heart of a forest; it accompanies the three elect (Percival, Bohors and Galahad) on the mystical Ship of Solomon; it shines in the heart of a prison. It is ubiquitous.

"Earthly hands do not touch it; angels may do so, martyrs descended from Paradise, or even the Divine Presences. The Grail is always veiled. A terrible punishment awaits those who would profane its mysteries. At its approach, life is halted, men are struck dumb, for the arrival of the Grail is a Judgment. Herein, then, the attributes of the Grail are those of God. Immaterial, omnipresent, encircled with celestial beings, it possesses Omnipotence and Miraculous Grace. The Grail is the love-bearing Manifestation of God."

These conceptions are more spiritual than the Cup as reliquary, as the Cosmic Cup of Nature, as the Bowl of Plenty or as the Chalice of the Mass. But even the *Perlesvaus* and *La Queste* do not reveal all the Mystery behind the age-old symbols. Its allegories are far other than the introspection of St John of the Cross or the pious Biblical simplicity of the Pilgrim's Progress.

Among its other Mysteries, the Quest of the Holy Grail thus appears as an illustrative initiatory rite for Adepts of some mystical Unitive Life, and its temple is "not made with hands." The "Lost Words" are not lost to those who hear the Music of the Spheres, the Cosmic Mass knows no boundaries of church, place nor time; and the Spirit of the Grail reaches from the soul of Man to the Grace of God.

CHAPTER 27

The Arthurian Pilgrimage to the Graal

ISABEL WYATT

When, in *Perceval li Gallois,** two suns appear in the sky at King Arthur's Court, one in the East, the other in the West, and a Voice announces that Perceval has won the Graal Castle and that God wills Arthur to go on a pilgrimage thither with the best knights of his Court, Arthur chooses Lancelot and Gawain to accompany him, "with more knights, and taketh one squire to wait upon his body."

Arthur would have wished also to have had Queen Guenievre's company. But she is distraught with sorrow over the death of Lohot, her son. So he leaves her at the Court as Regent in his absence.

It is a small cavalcade of four which sets out on this momentous journey.

In individual human lives one can sometimes observe fulfilments of karma unfolding so thick and fast that one receives the strong impression that the working-out of personal karma is being accelerated in order that the hands may be free to be placed at the service of world-karma. A somewhat similar impression is received as one observes the adventures of this pilgrimage unfolding.

One adventure after another presents itself as the karma of an earlier event in Arthur's or Gawain's or Lancelot's life. It is as if our own newly dawning faculty of seeing in picture-form the

---

* That is, Perlesvaus [Ed.].

karmic counterpart of a deed just done was being, in prototype, placed into outer life and exercised in concrete reality, and as if purely "Arthurian" karma were being met and paid in order that the new stage now approaching may be embarked upon with freer hands. For the Arthurian visit to the Graal castle is itself connected with world-karma; the meeting of the Arthur stream and the Grail stream is destined to work in a concealed but powerful fashion in the spiritual background of world-history to come.

Having ridden far the first day, the four pilgrims found themselves benighted in a forest "where was neither hold nor hermitage" in which they could seek harbourage for the night. The squire climbed a tall tree, and saw the glow of a fire a long way off. Towards this they rode, and, passing over a bridge of wattles, came into a deserted hall and sat down before the fire.

The squire, entering a side-chamber in search of bait for the horses, cried out in horror that it was heaped with dead men. Lancelot went in and found it was so.

A damsel entered from the forest, "her kirtle all torn with briars, her feet all bleeding for that she was unshod. She had a face of exceeding great beauty. She carried the half of a dead man, and cast it into the chamber with the others."

When she saw Lancelot, she cried joyfully:

"Ha, God, now am I quit of my penance! Sir, I am the Damsel of the Castle of Beards, that was wont to deal with knights so foully. You did away with that toll, and had me in covenant that, so the Holy Graal should appear to you, you would come back. You returned not, for that you saw not the Graal. For the shame that I did to knights was this foul penance laid upon me until such time as you should come."

A rout of fiends in the shape of knights came rushing through the forest "as they would rend it all up by the roots." As they burst into the hall, Lancelot drew a circle round the house-place with his sword, and within this they all five stood.

The fiends snatched up great blazing firebrands and hurled them within the circle, but the pilgrims held their shields against them and "smote the firebrands so that they made the red-hot charcoal fly." When they cut the fiend-knights "limb from limb, they turned to ashes, and devils all black came forth from their bodies."

A second rout of demon knights burst in, worse even then the first. "They began to press the King and his knights hard. While they were thus in the thickest of the conflict, they heard a bell sounding, and forthwith the fiends departed at a great pace."

The damsel told the King:

"Sir, this sound have I heard every night, whereby my life hath been saved."

In the morning the damsel took leave of them, and three hermits came to bury the dead men, "that the evil haunting might be stayed, and to build up the place in holiness for the service of God. The King was right joyful thereof."

We have spoken of the Arthurian mission of fighting and conquering demonic powers. In a poem written at Tintagel, where Arthur and his knights received the Sun-powers which enabled them to carry out this task, Rudolf Steiner characterizes them as "warriors against demons." The writer of *Perceval li Gallois* therefore speaks with exactitude in his description of the fight in the charnel-house. Even that the demons encountered there are connected with the corpses of dead knights is in keeping with what Steiner tells us of the demons arising out of the corruption left when the depraved Atlantean bodies died out.

When we turn back the pages of Lancelot's life till we come to the incident of which this evil haunting was the karmic counterpart, we find it bound up with the astrality of the Damsel of the Beards' evil custom; but we also find it bound up with a still unrepented and therefore still unredeemed astrality in Lancelot himself.

Lancelot had once come to a castle whose great gate was "all covered with beards fastened thereon, and heads of knights in great plenty hung thereby." Two knights had issued from the gate and demanded Lancelot's beard, for such toll was the custom of the castle. ("Sir, now pay us yours, for a right great beard it is.") Lancelot, fighting to retain his beard, had sorely wounded them both; and the Lady of the Castle had come forth and bidden him enter. At table they had been served by knights maimed in hand or foot or eye.

The Lady of the Castle had tried her hardest to keep Lancelot with her; but he had told her:

"Lady, in no castle may I abide more than one night until I have been thither whither it behoveth me to go." For he was on his way to the Graal Castle, hoping to behold the Graal and, by asking whom it served, to heal King Fisherman of his languishment. But under pressure from the lady he had pledged his faith to return to her, should his Graal quest be achieved.

After further adventures, Lancelot had come to a hermitage at the foot of the mountain beyond which lay the Graal Castle. There he had alighted and made his confession. "He rehearseth all his sins, and saith that of all he repenteth, save only one, the fairest sin and the sweetest that ever he committed."

"I love my lady, which is the Queen, more than aught else that liveth. The affection seemeth me so good and so high that I cannot let go thereof. I am willing to do penance as great as is enjoined of this sin, but my lady the Queen will I serve so long as it is her pleasure."

The hermit had warned him:

"So much am I fain to tell you, that if you shall lie in the hostel of King Fisherman, yet never may you behold the Graal for the mortal sin that lieth at your heart."

And even thus it had come to pass.

At the Graal Castle, King Fisherman, lying "on a bed so rich and so fair apparelled as never was seen a better," had conversed with Lancelot "right nobly, as one that is a right worshipful man. But when the table was dight of rich sets of vessels of gold and silver, and they were served of rich meats of venison of hart and wild boar, the Graal appeared not at this feast. Lancelot was one of the three knights of the world of the most renown and mightiest valour, but it held aloof for his great sin as touching the Queen, whom he loved without repenting him thereof."

When, later, Lancelot had come to the hermitage of King Fisherman's brother, King Hermit, the latter had told him plainly:

"Had you had the like desire to see the Graal that you have to see the Queen, the Graal would you have seen." So, in the last resort, it was because of Lancelot's love of the Queen that the Lady of the Castle of Beards had been forced to do so long and foul a penance, and that he, with King Arthur, Gawain and the squire, had been forced to battle with the demon knights to clear the hall in the forest of its evil.

The four now "rode right busily on their journeys, and came to a little castle in a combe, and the enclosure of the castle was fallen down into an abysm." A priest tells them this is Tintagel, and King Arthur now hears the story of his own birth for the first time. "King Uther Pendragon slew King Gorlois on the morrow of the night he lay with his wife, and so forthwith espoused Queen Ygerne, and in such manner was King Arthur conceived in sin that is now the best King in the world."

So Arthur gazes back upon his own beginnings as in a kind of life-panorama such as accompanies the death of the physical body and the birth of the soul into the spiritual world, or such as accompanies the mystical death and rebirth of initiation. Can we perhaps see in it such a life-panorama reviewed in preparation for the new birth of the Arthurian Mysteries into union with the Mysteries of the Grail?

And now the day draws near when Lancelot must return to the Waste City to acquit him of a pledge.

He had come to the city on leaving the Castle of Beards, and had found it "void of folk, great palaces fallen down, and the gates ruined with age." A young knight of great comeliness had approached him, "clad in a short red jerkin with a rich girdle of gold; on his head had he a great cap of gold, and he held a great axe.

He said to Lancelot:

"Sir, needs must you cut me off my head with this axe, for of this weapon hath my death been adjudged."

Lancelot had reasoned with him; but the young knight had insisted, imposing a condition in return:

"Fair sir, hold up your hand towards the minster you see yonder, and swear to me upon the holy relics that are therein that on this day year, at the hour that you shall have slain me, you will return and place your head in the same peril."

Lancelot had so sworn, and the young knight had knelt and had received the death-blow he had demanded. Lancelot, coming to his horse, had looked behind him as he mounted. Both the body and the head of the young knight had disappeared.

And now "the King embraceth Lancelot at parting, and Messire Gawain also, and they pray God preserve his life, and that they may see him again ere long." Lancelot rides again to the Waste City, and finds it as empty as before. As he dismounts, a knight approaches, wearing a close-fitting silk jerkin and carrying the great axe. He bids Lancelot "come forward without delay and kneel down and stretch your neck, even as my brother did."

> Lancelot lieth down on the ground as it were on a cross, and crieth mercy to God. He taketh three blades of grass and eateth thereof in token of the holy communion, then signeth himself of the cross and blesseth him, riseth up, setteth himself on his knees and stretcheth forth his neck.

The first blow missed. As the knight is aiming a second, a cry rings out:

"Throw down the axe and cry the knight quit!"

Two damsels "of passing great beauty" come forward, saying to Lancelot:

"Sir, we are the two sisters that you saw so poor when you lay in our brother's house. You and Messire Gawain gave us the treasure and the hold of the robber-knights you slew. This city of our brother would never again be peopled of folk save a knight had come hither as loyal as are you. Had you failed us of your covenant, we should have lost this city and its castles without recovery."

These were the two sisters "of passing great beauty, right poorly clad," who, some months previously, had been in the act of welcoming Gawain to their brother's ruined castle, when a wounded knight brought tidings that Lancelot was sore beset nearby by four robber-knights. Gawain had departed "as fast as horse may carry him," and following the blood-track of the wounded knight, had reached Lancelot in time to turn the tide of battle.

When Gawain told Lancelot that he had "the most poverty-stricken host he had ever seen," they agreed to make him a gift of the robber-knights' ill-gotten gains rich treasure, rich ornaments, rich armour for horses, rich sets of vessels that they had thrown the one over the other into a pit that was right broad."

Their rejoicing host had confessed, when they disarmed, that he had no robe to lend them, "for none have I save my own poor jerkin." The two damsels had taken off their own kirtles, and "the two knights did on the kirtles, all to-torn and ragged and worn as they were."

So now two separate threads out of the past are twined together in the Waste City, which is no longer waste, for the mystical decapitation of the young knight, and Lancelot's willingness to suffer the same sacrifice, bring about a resuscitation of the city's dried-up life-forces.

Lancelot, leaning at the windows of the hall, now "seeth the city peopled of the fairest folk in the world, and heareth how the greatest joy in the world is being made in the forest, and clerks and priests are coming in long procession, praising God that they may now repair to their church, and giving benison to the knight through whom they are free to repair thither."

Meanwhile King Arthur and Gawain, "in sore misgiving for Lancelot," have reached an assembly of knights that is being held to win the Golden Circlet, owned formerly by Perceval when he slew the Knight of the Fiery Dragon. They tarry to take part in it.

The first day of the tourney King Arthur and Gawain are adjudged to have done best; but the second day one of the damsels of their tent reminds Gawain of a covenant he had made when journeying to visit the sick King Fisherman.

At the entrance to King Fisherman's kingdom a priest had told Gawain:

"Sir, you may not enter the castle save you bring the sword wherewith St John was beheaded. But so you conquer the sword for us, this entrance will be free to you, and then will it be well known that you are worthy to behold the Holy Graal."

On his way to Albanie, the country of King Gurgalain, where this sword was kept, Gawain promised the King of Wales to show him the sword on his return journey. He found King Gurgalain distraught with grief, for a giant had carried off his son; if Gawain could bring him back his son, he pledged his word that he should have the sword.

Gawain tracked down the giant, whom he fought and killed, but not before the giant had slain the little prince. Bearing the dead child and the giant's head, Gawain returned to King Gurgalain, who not only gave him the promised sword but also himself became a Christian.

On his return journey Gawain redeemed his promise to show the sword to the King of Wales, who, instead of giving it back to Gawain, placed it in his own treasury, only yielding it up on condition that Gawain would grant the first request made by a damsel, whatever that request might be.

When Gawain had again reached King Fisherman's kingdom, he confessed his sins to a hermit, who warned him.

"Forget not to ask that which the other knight forgot." And when, in King Fisherman's rich chamber, he gave him the sword, the King, after thanking him, also begged:

"I pray you for God's sake, hold me in remembrance tonight and forget not to speak the word."

As Gawain sat at meat that night with twelve ancient knights, each a hundred years old "and yet none of them seemed as though he were forty," two damsels entered the hall, one bearing the most holy Graal, and the other the lance.

So sweet a smell and so holy came to them therefrom
that they forgat to eat. So great a joy cometh to Gawain
that nought remembereth he in his thinking save of God
only. The knights are all daunted and sorrowful in their
hearts, and look at Messire Gawain.

A second time the damsels bring in the Graal. This time Gawain sees a child in the midst of it. The Master of the Knights beckons to him; but again he speaks no word.

A third time the damsels bring in the Graal, and above it Gawain sees:

a King crowned, nailed upon a rood, and the spear still
fast in his side. He hath great pity thereof, and of nought
doth he remember him save of the pain that this King
suffereth. The Master of the Knights summoneth him by
word of mouth, but Messire Gawain is silent, as he that
heareth not the knight speak.

And next morning Gawain leaves the Graal Castle, sorely discomfited.

And now, on this second journey to the Graal Castle, he is asked to redeem the pledge he had given to the King of Wales on that first one — that the first request made to him by a damsel should be granted, whatever that request might be.

The request is that "today you shall be he that doth worst of all the knights of the assembly, and that you bear none other arms save your own only, so that you shall be known of all them that are here present."

Gawain complies, "though sore it irked him, sith thus must he lose worship." And, indeed, "in great shame and dishonour was he held, and the knights said that never had they seen so craven a knight." Even King Arthur, who knew all the circumstances, commented:

"Never thought I that so good a knight might ever have known so well how to conterfeit such a bad one."

But on the third day Gawain acquits himself so superlatively well that he wins the Golden Circlet.

King Arthur and Gawain, continuing their journey, arrive at the Waste Manor, whose lady recognises them and holds them prisoner out of her hatred for Lancelot, who has slain her brother. They break out of their prison, and are received by the seven knights guarding the bridge "on the points of their lances."

Lancelot, coming hotfoot from the no-longer-waste Waste City in his attempt to overtake them, turns the *melée* in their favour. They have taken part of the karma of Lancelot's slaying of the lady's brother on themselves; when Lancelot has himself later to face that karma, a quite new note is sounded.

The three ride on together, and come to a second assembly of knights. The prize of the tournament is the golden crown of a Queen who has just died, which carries with it the guardianship of her kingdom.

King Arthur wins the crown. The knight who had brought it tells him:

"Sir, now you may defend the land of the best earthly Queen that is dead, and whether the King be alive or dead none knoweth."

The King asks:

"Whose was the land? And what was the name of the Queen?"

The knight tells him:

"Sir, the king's name was Arthur, and the best king in the

world was he; but in his kingdom the more part say that he is dead. And this crown was the crown of Queen Guenievre, that is dead and buried, whereof is sore sorrow. Briant of the Isles and my Lord Kay with him are burning the land; there is great war toward. The knights that may not leave Cardoil sent me to go among the assemblies of knights, that so I might hear tidings of my lord King Arthur and my lords Gawain and Lancelot, and, if so I might find them, tell them how the land hath fallen under this grievous sorrow."

Arthur mourned, holding the golden crown. Lancelot mourned, saying "between his teeth that now hath his joy come to an end. Gawain may not stint of making dole."

Lancelot offers to go back and defend the kingdom while the King completes his pilgrimage. Arthur accepts his offer. Lancelot had set out on the pilgrimage to the Grail; but it was not in his destiny to complete it.

So Lancelot again takes leave of Arthur and Gawain, and, coming in the evening to the Castle of Griffons, seeks harbourage there for the night in spite of the many heads of knights that are hanging from the gateway. The lord of this castle is a brother of the knight of the Waste Manor slain by Lancelot; a damsel in the castle recognises Lancelot, and reports to her lord that he is harbouring his deadly enemy.

The lord of the castle decides that next morning he will "smite off his enemy's head and hang it above all the other;" but his daughter sends a privy messenger to Lancelot to warn him of his danger and to tell him that there is a cavern beneath the castle which runs underground as far as the forest. It is guarded by a lion and two griffons, and she sends him a brachet (hound) with whom the griffons love to play; while they are thus playing, he can pass them unharmed. At daybreak his steed will be awaiting him at the cavern's exit in the orchard at the forest's edge.

Towards daybreak Lancelot enters the cavern; the two griffons, by the light of the fire which they themselves cast forth, "espy the brachet and make her the greatest cheer in the world. Lancelot passes beyond without gainsay." He fights and slays the lion, "cometh forth into the orchard beside the forest, and wipeth his sword on the freshness of the green grass."

The freshness of green grass, the fruiting orchard, introduce a note unheard till now. The daughter of the lord of the Castle of Griffons renounces an eye for an eye; it is with good that she repays evil.

Lancelot mounts his waiting steed, and rides all day till he reaches Avalon. Here, in the chapel, beside the coffin which holds the head of her son, Queen Guenievre lies in a rich coffin with four tall wax tapers alight at its four corners.

And beside it all night Lancelot keeps vigil.

Meanwhile King Arthur and Gawain continue their journey and reach the Graal Castle; and "Perceval, that was therewithin, made right great joy of their coming." To Perceval King Arthur presents not only the Golden Circlet which Gawain had won at the first tourney, but also Queen Guenievre's gold crown, which he himself had won at the second.

> When Perceval knew that she was dead, he lamented her
> right sweetly. The King sojourneth in the castle and is
> highly honoured, and beholdeth the richness and the
> lordship and the great abundance that is everywhere.

In King Arthur's bestowal on Perceval of Queen Guenievre's golden crown one can sense an archetypal gesture. Guenievre had been Moon to Arthur's Sun; it is silver, the metal of the moon, that connects man with the cosmos. When the Queen does not accompany the pilgrimage, the Arthurian Mysteries are already being loosened from their cosmic ties; when the Queen dies, these ties are loosened further. The Arthur stream becomes free to unite with the Grail stream.

It becomes equally free to take an alternative course. The Round Table, that reflection on earth of the Zodiac, had been a most precious wedding gift to Arthur from King Leodagrance, the father of Guenievre. At the news of her death, her kinsman, Madeglant of Oriande, sent to Arthur this ultimatum:

"I am your enemy in two manner of ways; for the Round Table which you hold by wrong, sith that the Queen is dead, and for the New Law that you hold." Arthur, says Madeglant, may continue to hold the Round Table only if he renounces his Christian belief and also weds Queen Jandree, Madeglant's infidel sister.

It is as if the Arthurian Mysteries stand at the parting of the ways. They may cling to their past, but at the cost of becoming decadent, as some other noble Mysteries had done by outliving their due time. Or they may withdraw their forces from their outward framework and, together with other esoteric streams, await in a germinal condition the time of their rebirth. In defying Madeglant, in uniting with the Grail Stream, they made the latter choice.

One day, while King Arthur still "sojourneth in the Graal Castle," he is at the castle windows and sees a great procession coming from beyond the bridge; one clad in white bears a great cross at their head, and each of those who follow bears a small cross and lighted candle. Last of all came one with a bell. They are singing with sweet voices.

King Arthur cried: "Ah, God, what folk be these?"

Perceval told him: "Sir, they are the hermits of this forest, that come to chant before the Holy Graal within yonder chapel three days in the week."

King Arthur, with Perceval and Gawain, goes to meet them; together they accompany the hermits into the chapel.

> They took the bell from the last, and smote thereon at the
> altar; and then began they the service, most holy and
> most glorious. The Graal appeard at the sacring of the
> mass, in five several manners that none ought not to tell,
> for the secret things of the sacrament ought none to tell
> openly but he to whom God hath given it. King Arthur
> beheld all the changes, the last whereof was the change
> into the chalice.

We are told that King Arthur, on his return, introduces the chalice into his own kingdom, which had known no chalice till then. This would seem to be saying, in an image, that the blood Christ shed on Golgotha had become a redemptive reality for the Arthur Mysteries, which had hitherto known and served Him as the Spirit of the Sun but had not known Him, as the Grail Mysteries had done, as the Spirit of the Earth.

In *Perceval li Gallois*, then, contrary to some other versions of the legend, but in harmony, surely, with what Rudolf Steiner tells us of the uniting of the two streams, King Arthur does himself achieve the Grail.

This is the solemn climax of the story. When tidings are brought to the Graal Castle that Aristot of Moraine has carried off Perceval's sister Dinrane from their mother's castle in the Valleys of Camelot, Perceval leaves to rescue her, and King Arthur and Gawain return to Cardoil, to share with Lancelot the burden of the war with Briant, Kay and Guenievre's kinsman, Madeglant. While the Arthurian Kingdom perishes in a long, tragic and disintegrating war, the Graal Castle falls slowly and gently away into an outer ruin pervaded by an atmosphere of such holiness that it makes saints of all who enter it. But in the spiritual worlds the essences of the Arthurian Mysteries and the Grail Mysteries await their recall together.

This, then is a thirteenth-century *trouvère*'s imaginative picture of that meeting of the Arthur stream and the Grail stream in the year 869 AD of which Rudolf Steiner tells us.

This year, 869 AD, is a momentous one. In it happenings in both sensible and supersensible worlds interreact to make it a crucial turning-point in mankind's history.

The Age of the Consciousness Soul does not dawn till the fifteenth century. But it is "signalized," Dr Steiner tells us, by the ninth, and above all by the year 869 AD. It is in this ninth century that Latin floods Europe, accelerating the withering of heart-wisdom into head-knowledge, so that the profounder significances of Christianity are no longer understood. By the middle of this century it was felt by the Roman Church Fathers that the intellect, which was increasingly "storming into evolution" and becoming increasingly incapable of spiritualized thinking, made esotericism a danger for some centuries to come.

Therefore Pope Nicholas I, who occupied the papal throne from 858 to 867 AD, decided that henceforward supersensible truths were no longer to be matters of living experience of the spiritual worlds, but of dogma, of faith alone.

So alongside this outer stream of historical Christianity, the Grail and the Arthur streams, sheltered by the wings of the Celtic Archangel, flowed as an esoteric and for the most part invisible current, though from time to time, says Rudolf Steiner, in "mysterious, repeated glimpses of the Holy Grail or its secular reflection and counterpart, the Round Table of King Arthur, men did still feel the presence of something connected with vision of worlds beyond the earth, with living experience of these worlds."

The meeting of the Arthur and the Grail streams "over Europe" in 869 AD was one of three destiny-fraught meetings which happened in that year, and whose consequences still reverberate on into our own times.

Above, in the light streaming upward from this Grail-Arthur meeting, a conference took place in the spiritual worlds as to the shaping of evolution in preparation for the new Michael Age which would begin on earth in 1879.

At this heavenly conference, Aristotle, Alexander and many knights of the Round Table strove so to shape this preparation that Christian impulses should predominate; over against them, Haroun el Raschid and his counsellor strove as strongly in the cause of Arabism. The latter prevailed, and, as a consequence, human evolution on earth in the following centuries plunged ever deeper into intellectualism.

But as a result of this decision, in the knights of the Round Table who took part in this conference their Cosmic Christianity lived yet more strongly, laid up as a seed in preparation for that time when Michael should again rule on the earth.

As the Arthur-Grail meeting over Europe had sent up its light into that conference in heaven, so the latter sent down its shadow into the third meeting, held on earth.

At the eighth Ecumenical Council, held at Constantinople in 869 AD, the Church Fathers outlawed spirit from the definition of man; it was henceforward heresy to believe him to be other than a being of body and soul with certain spiritual qualities. So was opened the way for men's achievement of ego-consciousness in complete freedom, but at the same time for the rapidly strengthening earthly intellect to gain further sway.

But from beneath the sheltering wing of the Celtic Archangel, in hidden ways the Arthur stream and the Grail stream still worked on.

In the twelfth century they hovered over the School of Chartres. "In a remarkable way," says Steiner, "this School of Chartres stands midway between the Arthur-principle and the Grail-principle, whose supersensible, invisible impulses made their way, not so much into the actual content of the teachings, as into the whole attitude and mood-of-soul of the pupils."

In the same century, also, with the founding of the Knights Templars in 1118, the forces of the Grail streamed into the new Order, with its esoteric aim of establishing the Holy Land as a centre free from Rome. These forces streamed also into certain "heretical" sects, such as the Cathars and the Albigenses, whose Christianity held esoteric reverberations. And in this same twelfth century, the esoteric Arthur stream and Grail stream emerged into exoteric romances, which troubadour and minnesinger carried from castle to castle across Europe.

The thirteenth and fourteenth centuries were a kind of spiritual Ice Age. The Transubstantiation was made dogma at the Lateral Council of 1215; the partaker was no longer permitted to perceive the pure Archetype of Man in this "Third Movement" of the fourfold Mass.

In 1244, with the taking of Mount Ségur, their last stronghold, the Cathars were wiped out by the Roman Church's Crusade against them. In 1314 the Templars were wiped out by the miser-king, Philip le Bel, but with the Pope's connivance.

The way into the spiritual world seemed firmly closed.

But the Grail stream which had flowed into the Knights Templars now flowed on further into Rosicrucianism. So, at first only among "cave-dwellers of the soul," the principle and practice of Christian Initiation were preserved without interruption.

With the dawn of our own epoch in 1413, the modern consciousness, built upon sense impressions, became paramount. Haroun el Raschid, reincarnating in the sixteenth century as that Father of Natural Science, Lord Bacon, and his former counsellor as Amos Comenius, bring back their Arabism in transmuted forms, so that here on earth materialism, sense-restricted natural science and brain-bound thinking flourish.

But meanwhile, above in the spiritual worlds, in this same sixteenth century, Michael holds a great supersensible school in preparation for his own coming leadership on earth from 1879. Not only multitudes of spiritual beings take part in this, not only multitudes of elemental beings, but also multitudes of discarnate human beings on their way down to a new incarnation.

And the substance of Michael's teaching is that esoteric Christianity which in our time is to begin to come into its own again among men upon the earth — that Cosmic Christianity which combines the Arthurian experience of Christ as a Sun-Being in the aura of the Earth with the Grail experience of Him as the whole meaning of the Earth, borne in the hearts of men.

We live today in that new Michael Age which began in 1879, and for which the great supersensible school of the sixteenth century had been a preparation — that school among whose pupils we ourselves may well have been.

Man has delved deep into the intellect. Now the time is ripe for him to rise again from intellectual to imaginative thinking, bearing with him the gifts he has wrested from the intellect — clarity and clear consciousness.

Kali Yuga, the great Dark Age, ended in 1899. With the turn of the century a new Light Age began. At the turn of the century Rudolf Steiner brought us Anthroposophy.

In Anthroposophy is one of the renewals of Cosmic Christianity, of that stream that ran through the Grail Quest and through the Round Table, through the Cathars, the Templars, the Rosicrucians — a stream which runs now underground, now above-ground, and which changes its outer form from century to century, according to human needs. The Celtic cross with its sun-circle is metamorphosed into the Rose-Cross with its circle of seven red roses; the Grail cup and bleeding lance approach us in a new manifestation in the Rosicrucian meditation on the rose with its pure sap innocent of the passions colouring our own red blood.

When we ponder the legends of King Arthur and of the Grail, we are placing before our hearts in picture-form esoteric spiritual realities which long to come to a new birth in us.

CHAPTER 28

The Mass of the Sangraal

ARTHUR MACHEN

"Ffeiriadwyr Melcisidec! Ffeiriadwyr Melcisidec!" shouted the old Calvinistic Methodist deacon with the grey beard. "Priesthood of Melchizedek! Priesthood of Melchizedek!"

And he went on:

"The Bell that is like *y glwys yr angel ym mharadwys* — the joy of the angels in Paradise — is returned; the Altar that is of a colour that no man can discern is returned, the Cup that came from Syon is returned, the ancient Offering is restored, the Three Saints have come back to the church of the *tri sant*, the Three Holy Fishermen are amongst us, and their net is full. *Gogoniant, gogoniant* — glory, glory!"

Then another Methodist began to recite a verse from Wesley's hymn:

> God still respects Thy sacrifice,
> Its savour sweet doth always please;
> The Offering smokes through earth and skies,
> Diffusing life and joy and peace;
> To these Thy lower courts it comes
> And fills them with Divine perfumes.

The whole church was full, as the old books tell, of the odour of the rarest spiceries. There were lights shining within the sanctuary, through the narrow archway.

This was the beginning of the end of what befell at Llantrisant. For it was the Sunday after that night on which Olwen

Phillips had been restored from death to life. There was not a single chapel of the Dissenters open in the town that day. The Methodists with their minister and their deacons and all the Nonconformists had returned on this Sunday morning to "the old hive." One would have said, a church of the Middle Ages, a church in Ireland today. Every seat — save those in the chancel — was full, all the aisles were full, the churchyard was full; everyone on his knees, and the old rector kneeling before the door into the holy place.

Yet they can say but little of what was done beyond the veil. There was no attempt to perform the usual service; when the bells had stopped the old deacon raised his cry, and priest and people fell down on their knees as they thought they heard a choir within singing "Alleluya, alleluya, alleluya." And as the bells in the tower ceased ringing, there sounded the thrill of the bell from Syon, and the golden veil of sunlight fell across the door into the altar, and the heavenly voices began their melodies.

A voice like a trumpet cried from within the brightness:

Agyos, Agyos, Agyos.

And the people, as if an age-old memory stirred in them, replied:

Agyos y Tâd, agyos y Mab, agyos yr Yspryd Glan.
Sant, sant, sant, Drindod sant fendigeid. Sanctus Arglwydd
Dduw Sabaoth, Dominus Deus.

There was a voice that cried and sang from with the altar; most of the people had heard some faint echo of it in the chapels; a voice rising and falling and soaring in awful modulations that rang like the trumpet of the Last Angel. The people beat upon their breasts, the tears were like rain of the mountains on their cheeks; those that were able fell down flat on their faces before the glory of the veil. They said afterwards that men of the hills, twenty miles away, heard that cry and that singing, roaring upon them on the wind, and they fell down on their faces, and cried, "The Offering is accomplished," knowing nothing of what they said.

There were a few who saw three come out of the door of the sanctuary, and stand for a moment on the pace before the door. These three were in dyed vesture, red as blood. One stood before two, looking to the west, and he rang the bell. And they say that all the birds of the wood, and all the waters of the sea, and all the leaves of the trees, and all the winds of the high rocks uttered their voices with the ringing of the bell. And the second and the third; they turned their faces one to another. The second held up the lost altar that they once called *Sapphirus,* which was like the changing of the sea and the sky, and like the immixture of gold and silver. And the third heaved up high over the altar a cup that was red with burning and the blood of the offering.

And the old rector cried aloud then before the entrance:

Bendigeid yr Offeren yn oes oesoedd — blessed be the Offering unto the ages of ages.

And then the Mass of the Sangraal was ended, and then began the passing out of that land of the holy persons and holy things that had returned to it after the long years. It seemed, indeed, to many that the thrilling sound of the bell was in their ears for days, even for weeks after that Sunday morning. But thenceforth neither bell nor altar nor cup was seen by anyone; not openly, that is, but only in dreams by day and by night. Nor did the people see Strangers again in the market of Llantrisant, nor in the lonely places where certain persons oppressed by great afflictions and sorrow had once or twice encountered them.

But that time of visitation will never be forgotten by the people. Many things happened in the nine days that have not been set down in this record — or legend. Some of them were trifling matters, though strange enough in other times. Thus a man in the town who had a fierce dog that was always kept chained up found one day that the beast had become mild and gentle.

And this is odder: Edward Davies, of Lanafon, a farmer, was roused from sleep one night by a queer yelping and barking in his yard. He looked out of the window and saw his sheep-dog playing with a big fox; they were chasing each other by turns, rolling over and over one another, "cutting such capers as I did never see the like," as the astonished farmer put it. And some of the people said that during this season of wonder the corn shot up, and the grass thickened, and the fruit was multiplied on the trees in a very marvellous manner.

More important, it seemed, was the case of Williams, the grocer; though this may have been a purely natural deliverance. Mr Williams was to marry his daughter Mary to a smart young fellow from Carmarthen, and he was in great distress over it. Not over the marriage itself, but because things had been going very badly with him for some time, and he could not see his way to giving anything like the wedding entertainment that would be expected of him. The wedding was to be on the Saturday — that was the day on which the lawyer, Lewis Prothero, and the farmer, Philip James, were reconciled — and this John Williams, without money or credit, could not think how shame would not be on him for the meagreness and poverty of the wedding feast. And then on the Tuesday came a letter from his brother, David Williams, Australia, from whom he had not heard for fifteen years. And David, it seemed, had been making a great deal of money, and was a bachelor, and here was with his letter a paper good for a thousand pounds; "You may as well enjoy it now as wait till I am dead." This was enough, indeed, one might say; but hardly an hour after the letter had come the lady from the big house drove up in all her grandeur, and went into the shop and said, "Mr Williams, your daughter Mary has always been a very good girl, and my husband and I feel that we must give her some little thing on her wedding, and we hope she'll be very happy." It was a gold watch worth fifteen pounds. And after Lady Watcyn, advances the old doctor with a dozen of port, forty years upon it, and a long sermon on how to decant it. And the rector's wife brings to the beautiful girl two yards of creamy lace, like an enchantment, for her wedding veil, and tells Mary how she wore it for her own wedding fifty years ago; and the squire, Sir Watcyn, as if his wife had not been already with a fine gift, calls from his horse, and brings out Williams and barks like a dog at him, "Goin' to have a weddin,' eh, Williams? Can't have a weddin' without champagne, y' know; wouldn't be legal, don't y' know. So look out for a couple of cases." So Williams tells the story of the gifts; and certainly there was never so famous a wedding in Llantrisant before.

All this, of course, may have been altogether in the natural order; the "glow," as they call it, seems more difficult to explain. For they say that all through the nine days, and indeed after the time had ended, there never was a man weary or sick at heart in Llantrisant, or in the country around it. For if a man felt that his work of the body or the mind was going to be too much for his strength, then there would come to him of a sudden a warm glow and a thrilling all over him, and he felt as strong as a giant, and happier than he had ever been in his life before, so that a lawyer and hedger each rejoiced in the task that was before him, as if it were sport and play.

And much more wonderful than this or any other wonders was forgiveness, with love to follow it. There were meetings of old enemies in the market-place and in the street that made the people lift up their hands and declare that it was as if one walked the miraculous streets of Syon.

But as to the "phenomena," the occurrences for which, in ordinary talk, we should reserve the word "miraculous"? Well, what do we know? The question that I have already stated comes up again, as to the possible survival of old tradition in a kind of dormant, or torpid, semi-conscious state. In other words, did the people "see" and "hear" what they expected to see and hear? This point, or one similar to it, occurred in a debate between Andrew Lang and Anatole France as to the visions of Joan of Arc. M. France stated that when Joan saw St Michael, she saw the traditional archangel of the religious art of her day, but to the best of my belief Andrew Lang proved that the visionary figure Joan described was not in the least like the fifteenth century conception of St Michael. So, in the case of Llantrisant, I have stated that there was a sort of tradition about the Holy Bell of Teilo Sant; and it is, of course, barely possible that some vague notion of the Graal Cup may have reached even Welsh country folks through Tennyson's "Idylls." But so far I see no reason to suppose that these people had ever heard of the portable altar (called Sapphirus in William of Malmesbury) or of its changing colours "that no man could discern."

And then there are the other questions of the distinction between hallucination and vision, of the average duration of one and the other, and of the possibility of collective hallucination. If a number of people all see (or think they see) the same appearances, can this be merely hallucination? I believe there is a leading case on the matter, which concerns a number of people seeing the same appearance on a church wall in Ireland; but there is, of course, this difficulty, that one may be hallucinated and communicate his impression to the others, telepathically.

But at the last, what do we know?

CHAPTER 29

The Grail in
the Uttermost West

Vessels of Power, Plenty and Tradition
in American Indian Mythology
and Literature

ARI BERK

> *...vas spirituale ... vas honorabile ... vas insigne devotionis*
>
> from the medieval *Litany of Loretto*

> In proper form they took what came
> From the Grail, meat wild and tame.
> To this one his wine, to one his mead,
> To satisfy each wont and need ...
>
> Wolfram von Eschenbach, *Parzival*

> Never tell one story. Always add a second. That way, the first one won't fall over.
>
> Inuit

In the pan-European corpus of Arthurian literature, vessels of plenty symbolizing God's divine grace are central and essential. Looking farther back, early Celtic stories (such as the Welsh *Peredur*) — many of which were the prototypes of later medieval texts — likewise have a cauldron or cup as the central object of quest or attainment. These vessels perform a variety of functions often, but not limited to, supplying inexhaustible sources of food, bestowing wisdom, healing illness, reconnecting the monarch or hero with the land, establishing lineage and supplying a vital connection between mortals, the Otherworld and God.

Though widespread in the literature and mythologies of Europe, the Near East and the Mediterranean, can the Grail be considered a truly universal symbol? Do other vessels performing similar functions exist among lands and cultures far removed from the Old World?

This paper will show that the Old World is not alone in its fascination with vessels containing and dispensing power and wisdom. Indeed, the mythology and literature of the ancient Americas is bestowed with similar themes and objects. And like the Arthurian stories, quests in American Indian myths and literature are both physical journeys to acquire objects and knowledge and spiritual movements across sacred landscapes undertaken by heroes, shaman, medicine men, First People and deities.

While not comprehensive by any means this paper will, it is hoped, inform the reader as to the prevalence and variety of these themes as they exist and are shaped by the American landscape and its indigenous cultures. The sheer number and variety of specific American Indian cultures will not permit (in this limited space) an exhaustive study of all the pertinent material. Therefore, this study will confine itself to the specific discussion of mythological Grail parallels among Inuit; California Maidu, Miwok and Achumawe; Maya; Zuni and Navajo cultures.

Before embarking on the examination of these themes, it is important to note the basic subsistence patterns exhibited by most American Indian cultures. As we shall see, depending on subsistence patterns and location of the culture examined, these vessels serve a variety of purposes, each reflecting a specific aspect of geography, need and belief. These patterns, in their most general sense, may be reduced to two types, each producing a variety of religious expressions.

For the purposes of this paper, the "grails" of Hunter-gatherer societies (these include the Inuit and California Indian cultures) generally concern food abundance (calling animals, blessing hunters) and bestowing immortality. Grails of agricultural socie-ties (including, Maya and Zuni) stress connection with ancestors, sky/weather power, water acquisition and control of natural sources by connecting the patient, priest or hero to the environ-ment and essential crops. Navajo vessels contain aspects of both Hunter-gatherer and Agricultural societies. Sacred vessels from either group may be used to heal and restore.

In our quest for the Grail of the Americas, we shall follow the land itself and the ancient migration routes as they move down from the north, along the western coasts, into the southern regions of Middle America, then back northward to the Four Corners region; the cultural crossroads of the Americas.

The quest begins in the North.

> Later in the autumn, when mush ice formed along the beaches, male umialiks visited carvers who made *qattaqs* [waterpots] for the women. Umialik [male or female skinboat owners] wives would use these pots next spring. When their husbands caught whales the women would offer fresh water to the whale's soul.
>
> The construction of the pot filled several days and nights. A special song accompanied this ritual. Next the umialik took the pot home and left it in the iglu passage. A few days later he took the pot to the *qalgi* [ceremonial house] passage. Finally, the pot was brought home and hung above the oil lamp.
>
> Finally the owner fixed two feathers to the *qattaq*. These would help lift their pots to the moon, for Alinnaq, the spirit of the moon, likes water too. The feathers were from birds in the creation story. These feathers — opposite, together — gave wings to the *qattaq*.
> (Lowestein, 108)

At Point Hope, Alaska, there is an ancient village named Tikigaq. It is the furthest north-west point in the Americas and the most ancient, continuously settled American Indian site in North America (Lowestein, xi). The people living there are whale hunters. As such, they rely on the benevolence of animal powers for survival. Used in controlling these natural forces, certain waters and the vessels carrying them hold a place of singular importance in Inuit belief and ritual. Stories of these vessels may serve as a map of the sacred elements of the landscape.

> One mile east of the village, between the inlet and the lagoon, lay a fresh water pond called Umigraagvik. Here, when the shaman-who'd-been-whales had drunk their water, the umialiks walked to cut ice blocks to make qalgi passage skylights.
> The women would keep the pond-ice for their pots. That winter, they'd splash water over the moon. Next spring they'd give their whales a drink of water.
> Umigraagvik pond was sacred to the women because a supernatural whale had been created there.
> (Lowestein, 111)

Before the whale hunts, people of the village make pilgrimages to this pond to obtain its sacred water. This water, when used by the women and poured from their qattaqs, had at once the power to bless, empower and nourish. Drinking this "whale-pond water" bound the shaman to the whale spirit, but more generally to the land. The land was considered to have been formed from the body of a whale, making these transformations and the concepts underlying them vital, related and immediate. Thus, when the women give water to their whales from these pots, it is a restorative and blessing act. And when shaman drink it, the effect is transformative; they heal the land (in the form of the whale) so that the land in turn will continue to sustain them.

The pots also connect the women to the celestial realm. By connecting themselves to the sky powers, it is hoped the success of the hunt may be assured. In a winter ceremony, the women offer their qattaqs to the moon spirit, or *Inua* ("resident spirit"):

> Then, wearing a new parka and carrying her pot of water, each woman umialik came out of her iglu and stood on the roof of the entrance passage to call up to Alinnaq, the moon soul, its inua.
> They raised their pots four times to the sky-hole,

"Alinnaq! Alinnaq!"
  raising their pots to the Moon Spirit's iglu,
"Alinnaq! Drop whales in my qattaq!
  Agvaaquktuna: I want to catch a whale!"
(Lowestein, 129)

Here, the qattaq symbolically becomes the sea and the land, ready to hold the whale. In this text we see how the water pot becomes the locus of plenitude, serving as a magical magnet to draw in and center the powers of land, sea and sky. As such, each qattaq represents both the source of abundance and the path between the worlds bringing that abundance to the people.

At the heart of the stories about this water is the idea that while it may be used by men at the source, whale-pond water may only be held and dispensed by women. This theme echoes Arthurian sources which often show women as the guardians of the Grail or as keepers of wells or other sources of sacred water associated with knowledge of the land.

The keeping of qattaqs in the iglus also informs us of their power. The very construction and form of the iglu has Otherworld associations. To the Inuit, the entrance hole, or *kattak*, is a place of reverence, power and danger. The pots are left in these entrance holes to empower them. When the qattaqs are placed in the kattak, they exist "out of time," and between the worlds. This connection with the Otherworld, no doubt, adds an important facet to the qattaq's power to contain and direct Otherworld forces.

Besides being the physical entrance to the iglu, the kattak could become a ceremonial aperture to the Otherworld; spirits could be brought into the present through it; shamans could dive into it and transform into whales moving though the dark sea:

> As the stories attest, the dark, unheated passage was an ambiguous, semi-domesticated space in which frightening supernatural events were said to happen.
> Just as the passage represented a transition between the upper village and iglu living room, so there was a second transitional area. This was the entrance-hole (*kattak,* from *katak,* "to fall") which led vertically from the passage to the iglu chamber. Local stories likewise

represent this circular hole as a locus of magical, transformative activity. (Lowestein, 33)

This association of the kattak with other world doorway is vital to Inuit ceremonial practices generally and hunt rituals specifically. In the following text, the shaman transforms into a whale by going in and out of the kattak and drinking sacred whale-pond water.

> Every time the shaman came up through the kattak, one
> of the women gave him water. The shaman drank and
> dived back, whales flukes rising and diving through the
> kattak. (Lowestein, 111)

The telling of these stories keeps the power of the qattaqs fresh and vital and the repetition of the ceremonies in connection to these retellings keeps the whales coming, and keeps the land alive.

Land, whale, story, hunter — they are bound up inexorably as one. One story which sees the whale's soul escaping to return to its own country, concludes with Raven shouting, "Come again!" and ends with the line, *"The women repeat it."* (Lowestein, 172).

The message is both ancient, circular and eternal: if the stories are retold and the ceremonies associated with the qattaqs enacted, the world continues.

In certain regions, magical vessels are multi-layered symbols of abundance that connect people with the presence of ancestors who continue to aid the living. Throughout the tribes of California, such themes are commonplace. Among these cultures, themes of abundance associated with vessels exist and as always, sustenance, either physical or spiritual, lies at the center of these stories.

The Maidu, who lived along the eastern tributaries of the Sacramento River, speak of such a vessel,

> "The Creator had a tiny basket full of delicious food,
> from which all who wished might eat; and although a
> hundred might eat from it, yet it ever remained full."
> (Gifford and Block, 62)

Connected to this idea, the Miwok of central California tell similar stories. It was a practice among the Miwok for human remains to be buried in baskets (Merriam, 218). This practice may explain the ideas of sacredness connected to buried vessels among other California Indian cultures.

As containers of ancestral remains, these baskets retain a place of reverence in tribal myth and memory. Certainly, sites associated with these baskets would be known and acknowledged by members of the tribe. Eventually, the identity of the deceased may be forgotten, but the container, common to all burials, would be remembered. Thus, with the passage of time, these baskets became the containers of ancestral memory. The connection between baskets and powerful ancestors is wonderfully told in an Achumawe/Achugawe story recently recounted by Darryl Babe Wilson.

From the Pit River country of north-eastern California, stories still are told of magical baskets existing underground. One such myth tells of two boys who, searching after a magical arrow, find a spring coming from the place where the arrow entered the ground. The boys asked their Grandmother about the strange event and were told:

> It is said by the old ones that magic waters dwell within
> the earth, that these waters are held in beautiful baskets
> made by magic grandmothers long ago. It may be that
> the arrow struck such a basket. It is said that the water
> coming from such a basket gives long life to everything
> — that some things never die when drinking or touching
> this water. (Wilson, 299)

Later, their Grandfather told them, "The water comes from the heart of a basket." (Wilson, 300). These baskets represent the heart of the land. Drinking from them translates one into the ancestral realm where long life, attained through memory, is assured.

Baskets are still made by these cultures; each a container of tradition. Indeed, all baskets represent sacred prototypes; each an icon of an unfailing ever-flowing original. And even though the names of the dead they hold or their weavers are long forgotten, the ancient, mythic baskets remain. As the heart of the land, they hold and dispense the waters of ancestral memory. Like the ancient, sacred wells of Britain and Europe they are still within the land. Silent but waiting.

Like the cup used to catch the blood of Christ, some of the New World vessels also act as containers of sacred blood. On this theme, the finest and most detailed examples exist as the baskets and bowls used by the Maya of Central America in their bloodletting rituals.

Maya city-states, like those of Europe during the time of the Grail literatures, were feudal. Power, therefore, had to be consolidated. Maintenance of royal power required faith and faith required reinforcements. This was accomplished through a combination of religious ceremony and public propaganda. Central to any act of royal authority, civic or ceremonial, was the establishment of bloodline. As Maya civilization developed, blood and lineage occupied ever more important associations to the royal line.

During the Classic period (300–900 AD) Maya society reached a remarkable degree of sophistication. Expansive city-states, elaborate religious practices, systems of writing and marking time and complex social and royal hierarchies rivaling those of Europe were the hallmarks of Maya achievements. But continuation of Maya society and cosmos required sacrifice. War captives, food, young maidens, warriors and great sportsmen (a form of ballgame was played throughout most of Mesoamerica) were all important varieties of human sacrifices. The most sacred and powerful sacrifice however, came from the rulers themselves in the form of royal blood.

Blood is a complex and multi-layered symbol in Mesoamerican mythology and a hallowed offering in Maya ceremonial practices. It is at once a blessing, sanctifying element and vehicle for the invocation of ancestral spirits and deities. Growth of crops and cities required the sacrifice of blood. So did the consolidation of royal authority through the conjuration of lineage ancestors and gods. These last two categories are central to a ceremony depicted on three lintels from the Maya city of Yaxchilàn.

Of all the material culture left by the ancient Maya, three carvings from structure 23 (illustrations 1, 2 and 3) at Yaxchilàn represent the most detailed and complete record of a bloodletting ceremony known to exist. While the details of the

Illustration 1. Lintel 24, Yaxchilàn (after Graham and Von Euw).

544

chronological relationship between these events is still debated, it is clear that their placement in the doorways of structure 23 (one each in one of the three doorways "reading" left to right) is meant to show a ritual sequence. Their placement tells a remarkable story and depicts a ceremonial order of events involved in the preparation for "holy war." And as we shall see, special vessels are central in the carving's composition and vital to the performance of the ceremony.

The ritual begins on Lintel 24.

In a darkened room, the ceremony was enacted. "Shield Jaguar," Blood-lord of the City of Yaxchilàn, stands holding a large, flaming torch. At his feet, Lady Xoc ("Shark") performs the auto-sacrifice. She is kneeling. Through her tongue, she pulls a rope strung with thorns, the blood dripping down the rope and spattering upon paper resting in a basket decorated with sacred symbols.

The hem of her clothing is adorned with a band of symbols representing the sky, thus draping her in a mantle of celestial powers and associations. The headdress she wears is of central Mexican design and bears upon it the mask of Tlaloc, the chief rain god of Teotihuacan. The Maya often "wore" their names in their headdresses. This headdress therefore, ties her to the sky god and the life giving rain powers. Her lineage and her blood are thus sacred and life-engendering.

The dotted designs around her lips and mouth are blood spots. In the center of the carving, situated between both figures, is a basket. The symbols on the basket are vital to the understanding of the ceremony. The design, known as "step-fret," has been shown by various scholars to be a symbol carrying multiple meanings. It depicts water, waves, wind, light, sun, life and is considered to be a magical protection against death (Sharp, 9). It is also associated with serpents, and therefore is connected to sky, rain and lightning powers. In the Maya cosmos, water and waves marked the transition point (a line of demarcation as it were) between the Upper and Lower worlds. Wind was the breath of life. When a person died, it was said that "the wind had left them."

Regarding the multiple interpretations of this design, it appears that all are in a degree appropriate. Like many symbols in Mesoamerica, the step-fret is a multi-layered icon and

depends largely on context for interpretation. Of this pheno-
menon, Rosemary Sharp observes,

> Most, if not all, of these meanings seem plausible. The
> fact is, they are not mutually exclusive. All pertain to the
> powers of nature — both its great beneficence and its
> destructiveness for man. More specifically, its many
> possible natural associations, and the implied potency,
> even deadliness, of this symbol also help to explain why
> certain elites of the Classic period appear to have chosen
> it as an emblem. (Sharp, 10)

All at once then, this basket is a receptacle for sacred blood and
a portal for Otherworld forces, a vessel carrying life, vitality and
sky power, and it foreshadows the arrival of the creature and
supernatural power whose invocation lies at the heart of the
ceremony.

The vessels used in the next act of the ritual change to
ceramic bowls for practical reasons. While these bowls appear
unadorned, similar vessels have been found in Maya tombs,
their insides richly decorated with images of gods and Otherworld composite creatures. The bowls are similar in shape.
One is held by Lady Xoc (containing a lancet), the other (containing a rope) rests at their feet. Each is spattered with blood
spots and contains pieces of bloody paper like those seen in
lintel 24.

Lady Xoc's head is tilted back as she beholds the vision rising
up out of the bowl in front of her. Intertwined with smoke
symbols, the conjured, two-headed War Snake, *Waxaklahun-
Ubah-Kan* (Freidel, Schele and Parker, 308) opens wide its jaws.
Out of its gaping mouth two entities emerge. The vision has
risen out of the bowl. Out of the lower jaws of the serpent, the
head of Tlaloc, the rain/war deity appears, identifiable by the
goggle-shaped eyes and distinctive Teotihuacan-style headdress.
From the serpent's larger head, *Yat Balam* ("Penis," or
"Progenitor Jaguar") the founder of the royal line of Yaxchilàn
emerges wearing a Tlaloc mask in front of his face. In his hands,
the ancestor holds a flint shield and a spear.

Conjuring both ancestor and deity (they are conflated)
through her blood contained in the bowl, Lady Xoc receives a

546

Illustration 2. Lintel 25, Yaxchilàn (after Graham and Von Euw).

Illustration 3. Lintel 26, Yaxchilàn (after Graham and Von Euw).

vision of sacred sanction and blessing for Shield Jaguar for the battle he is about to embark on. The bowl (like the kattak of the Inuit) serves as both portal and container for the summoned powers of the Otherworld.

The basket (lintel 24) and the bowls (lintel 25) each serve two purposes:

1) to catch and contain the blood of Lady Xoc, and

2) to dispense the power of that blood through the conjuration of the lineage ancestor (Yat Balam) here masked as Tlaloc the god of rain while simultaneously acting as the portal that informs the ancestor into the present.

The vision ended, the ritual's conclusion is depicted on lintel 26. Lady Xoc's clothes (still bearing the sky-band hem) now bear the step-fret design as well. Shield Jaguar also now wears the step-fret design as part of his cotton quilted armour, thus bestowing upon him all the powers associated with it. All the aspects of nature — rain, wind, lightning, the undulating earth — all these powers have been bestowed upon him. After this ceremony, and while wearing this armour, symbolically speaking, the King and the land are one.

These powers come through Lady Xoc's lineage, from the Founder (Yat Balam) of the line and comprise a sacred and royal connection between Shield Jaguar and the ancestors and the rain god Tlaloc.

In grand Wagnerian style, Lady Xoc bestows Shield Jaguar with a jaguar helmet, sacred shield and spear (which he is holding in the carving). Thus adorned with both blessed weapons, symbolic clothing and ancestral empowerment, the King is ready for war; all these attributes, carried into this world by her blood. The vessels holding that blood become the portals into the present through which the celestial, ancestral and rain powers manifest.

Here, bowl and body are sacred vessels. Here, all powers of bloodline and the natural world are bound up in the person of the king. Here, through blood, the story is remembered.

Following the migration of symbols and people northward into the arid southwest, we find the Grail transformed into a container of sacred water and, as such, the reflecting pool of living myth. Perhaps due to the general scarcity of water in much of the southwest, myths of sacred vessels among the cultures there often revolve around associations with hidden water and the ability to attain, hold and provide it.

Due in part to the region's historical locus as cultural cross-roads, myths and religions of southwest tribes are complex, often sharing elements of symbolism and ritual. While retaining aspects of their place of geographic origin (the Northwest territory in the case of the Navajo), over the ages, the myths come to reflect the landscape.

Some of the stories handed down in oral tradition have been lost, or at the very least, changed dramatically over time. In these cases, archeology, combined with fragments of information preserved by cultural descendants, may be able to shed light on people who left no known literary records. Such is the case among the Mimbres and the Anasazi, the ancestors of the modern Pueblo people.

Having no written records, the ancient people of the south-west have nonetheless left us some of the most remarkable examples of sacred pottery in existence. Certain of these pots (as evidenced both the inclusion of sacred designs in the decoration and prominent placement in burials) appear to have served more than merely utilitarian functions.

For example, the contrasting black and white colours of some of the Mimbres pots (illustration 4) produce a remarkable effect (discovered by Laurel and Paul Thornburg) when the pot is spun. When spinning, the decorations on certain pots will pro-duce what is known as the "subjective colour effect" (Thornburg). This results in the illusion of intense, varying bands of colour appearing in the bowl. While it is unknown what this affect might have meant to Mimbres, we may speculate that the remarkable variation and innovation in Mimbres pottery design may have the production of better and more startling colour effects as its goal. Certainly, this effect was considered at least remarkable if not sacred by the Mimbres and may account for the inclusion of numerous bowls as grave artifacts as well as the ritual "killing" of the bowl (by breaking out a hole in the bot-tom) at the time of burial. We do know that the interplay of opposite forces (realized symbolically on the bowls by contrast-ing dark and light designs) and "cosmic" geography are both central to Pueblo belief and may be expressed in the natural world by sacred springs, lakes, mountains and directions. As

Illustration 4. A selection of Mimbres bowl designs (after Fewkes).

Brody observes, this sacred geography is closely associated with pottery symbolism,

> There are parallel structures [to sacred mountains, springs, lakes and directions] in the non-human and mythic worlds. Thus, the structuring of Mimbres nonfigurative pottery painting may be read as simply another means of representing sacred geography. Each bowl, circumscribed by a framing line, may have been conceived as a map of, or a prayer about, and orderly, bounded world. (Brody, 99)

While there was likely a distinction between sacred and secular pottery among the Mimbres and the Anasazi, most pottery found is adorned with symbols that, according to modern Pueblo people, reflect sacred designs and carry associations with mythic elements of the landscape and cosmos. These symbols and designs reflect a notion of centredness — of the world coming to center within the bowl.

As we shall see, the Navajo (who arrived in this region from the north sometime between the thirteenth and fifteenth centuries) believe the using of sacred symbols on everyday pottery is taboo and consider this practice the chief reason for the collapse and destruction of Anasazi culture.

The modern Pueblo people (who include the Zuni and Hopi), as descendants of the Mimbres and the Anasazi, tell a different story.

For the Zuni of eastern New Mexico, sacred pottery is a continuing and vitally important part of their religion. Still in use, certain vessels (present on every Zuni altar) reflect the powerful intersection and relationship between people, water and the land. This concept of convergence is evident in a Zuni prayer recited for a priest going into retreat,

> "This day, desiring waters of our fathers, the ones who had first being, in our house, having prepared prayer meal, shells, corn pollen, hither with prayers, we have made our road come forth ...
> You of the forest, you of the brush,
> All you who in divine wisdom stand here quietly,

> Carrying your waters,
> You will go before [us]
> Thus to Itiwana
> Our roads will go." (Bunzel, 643f)

In this prayer, and common to all Zuni ceremonials, sacred water is a central theme and is an ever present object in ritual observances. This water (taken from sacred springs) binds the priest to the sky powers and reminds him of his relationship to the land. Bowls which hold this water have cloud symbolism adorning their edges. While the water is specifically revered, it is the bowl holding the water on the center of the altar which serves as the omphalos of the Zuni cosmos.

The bowl and its contents help to insure that the prayers given at the altar will bring the rains needed by the people. Though not containing food, these bowls are nonetheless vessels of agricultural abundance by their association with the rains that allow the corn and other plants to grow.

More than this, these bowls (and one in particular) are believed to stand at the center of the world. The following prayer powerfully elucidates this idea. The prayer is spoken quietly while the Great Fire Society Chief sets up his altar (Bunzel, 782). It calls directional forces to center, brings animal power into attendance and remakes the ceremonial space into the center of Zuni universe. During the ceremony, the members of the society drink from the medicine bowl. By then, the bowl is no longer merely a physical container. As the White Shell Bowl it has *become* the sacred spring in which the medicines are combined and, as such, stands at the center of all as the crossroad of the worlds. The prayer begins by summoning the direction:

> I shall sit down quietly.
> I shall set down my white shell bowl.
> Then from all sides, You, my fathers, shall come.
> Yonder from the north, the Rain Maker Priests, Bringing their waters, will make their roads come hither. Where lies my White Shell Bowl, four times they will make their road come in.
> [This is repeated for each direction]

[Now the animals of the six directions are invoked.
Each is called in turn: Mountain lion, Bear, Badger, Wolf,
Knife-wing, Gopher and is followed by the same
invocation:]

You are life-giving society chief;
Bringing your medicine,
You will make your road come hither.
Where lies my White Shell Bowl,
Four times making your road come in,
Watch over my spring.
When you sit down quietly
We shall be one person.

[Finally, the stones of the six directions are called in
turn and placed in the bowl: Ancient Yellow Stone,
Ancient Blue Stone, Ancient Red Stone, Ancient White
Stone, Ancient Many Coloured Stone and Ancient Dark
Stone. Each stone's invocation is accompanied with:]

And further more, yonder below,
On all the mossy mountains,
On the tops of the mountains,
And along their slopes,
Wherever the ravines open out,
You hold the world in your keeping;
You will make your road come hither.
Where lies my White Shell Bowl,
Four times making your road come in
You will sit down quietly.
Then with your living waters
Our young ones will nourish themselves;
Reaching to Dawn Lake
Their roads will be fulfilled. (Bunzel, 782–85)

As the center of the world and the container of both animal and
ancestral power, the bowl holds vital, hallowed medicine. Drinking this water binds the Society to their past and their land,
making them one with all living things. At this crossroad, past
(ancestors), present (the act of invocation) and future (hope for
the children) converge and are contained in the White Shell
Bowl where the power is made available.

Once again, the acts that perpetuate abundance include the

retelling of stories and the chanting of the prayers about these vessels and the sacred water they hold. Nourishment, healing and the sense of belonging to a common history and landscape are all elements contained in the bowls along with the water so necessary for the continuance of life. These thoughts are expressed in a prayer recited to the sky powers when a priest returns home from his pilgrimage,

> May you pass me on my road.
> That this may be
> I have made your days.
> When your days are at an end,
> meeting me with all your waters, may you stay with us.
> Do not cause people to speak ill of your days,
> but with waters caressing the earth,
> let your days be filled.
>   With your waters will you pass me on my road.
>   Those which all my ladder descending children
> have sown with magical rites,
> all the different kinds of corn,
> yonder all over their earth mother,
> they stand poor at the borders of our land.
> With their hands a little burnt,
> with their heads brown,
> they stand poor at the borders of our land.
> That these may be nourished with fresh water,
> thus runs the thought of my prayer.
>   When the time of my days is at an end,
> though I say, "my days are at an end,"
> No — it is not so.
> Waiting anxiously until another day comes
> we shall pass the days.
> My fathers
> Now I have fulfilled your thoughts.
>   This is all." (Bunzel, 663)

This prayer itself acts as a Grail, holding and speaking of traditions that have their origin in the sacred past. The waters and the speaker are one, each nourishing a different but related aspect of life. Both the rains and the story make it possible for the thoughts of the ancestors to be realized. As it was in ancient times, it is again. The waters and the words make it so.

Within Navajo tradition, both physical and philosophical vessels of tradition occupy places of reverence. The most common and revered of the physical vessels is the wedding basket.

Wedding baskets are an integral part of numerous ceremonies and represent balance, harmony and wholeness (House, 96). These baskets are often used to hold ceremonial bundles, sacred feathers, prayer sticks and other holy artifacts. In this regard, the power associated with the baskets is basically passive. However, it must be remembered that no sacred item is "inactive" during a ceremony since merely the presence of such items exerts potency (Reichard, 340). Symbolically, the basket's design (a broken red circle with a white line leading out through it) represents Emergence. "Just as the Navajo came through three or four previous worlds to this one, the concept of emergence is replicated on this basket." (McPherson, 80). As a result of its design, the wedding basket physically, mythically and philosophically connects the Navajo to the time of creation and serves as a portal, conveying those powers into the present.

Additionally, in the Nightway chant, evil is focused and stored underneath a basket and therefore serves as both pathway and container of supernatural forces generally. After the evil is contained, it is released out of the hogan's smoke hole (Reichard, 551).

The baskets may also symbolize jewels and, therefore, wealth. In addition, these containers (including certain bowls), when used in various rites, come to be associated with sacred vessels from the myths such as the Rock-crystal Basket and the Yellow Bowl. Both of these are connected to themes of abundance and inexhaustibility. In one myth,

> unseasoned mush in a rock-crystal basket was offered to the Twins by Dawn Girl on their first visit to the Sun. The boys were urged to eat more and more, but could not empty the basket because it turned out to be the inexhaustible food supply. (Reichard, 577)

This story (in its fuller form) contains elements of quest (the Twin's journey to the house of their father, the Sun), healing and restoration (being fed from the rock-crystal basket). All themes easily recognizable in the Arthurian Corpus. In addition, these themes are directly applied and imitated for the ceremony in which the story is told. A Navajo Medicine Man tells us, "A patient should eat lots [from the basket used in the ceremony] and no mush should be left in the basket." (Reichard, 577)

The powers of the Yellow Bowl (in some texts, it is a small yellow cup) may best be understood by an examination of the attributes associated with its colour. According to Reichard, "yellow symbolizes the motion of streams or earth waters," also, "fructification, and is closely associated with pollen." (Reichard, 193) Pollen is perhaps the element most sacred to the Navajo and is used in every religious ceremony as well as to bless, consecrate and show thanks to the Gods. The food contained in the Yellow Bowl simultaneously represents all these aspects. Its association with pollen grants the basket the additional attribute of inexhaustibility and healing. In the story of the Shooting Chant, Chipmunk restores Rainboy by feeding him from the Yellow Bowl after his battle with Burrowing Monster. In this way, the Yellow Bowl became associated with both animal and godly powers.

Certain vessels (and deities) are associated with waters in a general way. The deity known as Water Sprinkler carries a pot with him from which he can create rain and generally control the waters of the earth (Reichard, 492). It is Water Sprinkler who taught the Visionary branch of the Nightway Chant story (discussed below) and is thus connected to both the physical (i.e. the rain producing pot) and the philosophical (the Nightway Chant) "grails" of the Navajo.

While not of Navajo origin, the third and last physical vessel examined is perhaps the most intriguing of the three in its remarkable ability to simultaneously explain the landscape's history and bind the Navajo to it.

In Navajo tradition, all mountains have special bowls buried beneath their summits. Rivers, springs and rain all originate from these sources. By association, these vessels are directly responsible for the continuance of all vegetation, and animal life. The bowls, called *tò asaa* or "water bowls," are an indispensable part of the mythology and religious practices of a culture existing in an arid climate.

Ironically, though they occupy an important place in Navajo belief, the bowls themselves are not of Navajo manufacture. Tradition holds that these bowls were left behind or hidden in the regions once belonging to the ancestors of the Pueblo people, the Anasazi. Created by the Anasazi, they hold the heart and history of the land now occupied by the Navajo.

It is a combination of the weather of the region and the existence of the Anasazi ruins dotting it which explains the inclusion of these bowls in Navajo mythology. McPherson observes,

> Ceremonies to obtain rain are important. Sacred springs, water seeps, river junctions, hilltops, mountaintops, rock arches, Anasazi ruins, water basins, and cliff basins where water pours over the rim all qualify as possible sites to pray to the holy beings for rain. Anasazi ruins may have a *tò asaa,* or water bowl, planted in them to which ceremonial appeals from the Blessingway may be made. (McPherson, 43)

But the quest for these water bowls was not only the search for much needed water and rain summoning power. At its core, the Navajo reverences of these objects and their quests for them (which often required entering Anasazi ruins to get them) represent attempts to locate themselves mythically and geographically in a landscape that had been occupied by other peoples.

Certain prayers, recognizing the alien (to the Navajo) past of the region, are still used to find sacred water associated with these bowls. In Navajo tradition, the gods prophesied:

> In some days to come, Earth Surface People, when they come into being, if (they) say this: "My pueblo of old, its water I shall take out," and if one digs (after) it, at once water comes out, they said.

Therefore the Navajo believe:

> if you dig at such places [ruins] and repeat the words, "I want to dig up Cliff Dweller water," the water will be found. (Haile 1981, 174)

These vessels are still strongly associated with the ancient ruins found all over the Navajo landscape. Of course, obtaining the bowls and other ruin-related artifacts meant venturing into dangerous territory.

The required act of entering ruins was a sacred and treacherous pilgrimage and these acts had to be performed in a certain, ordained manner. Navajo taboos regarding contact with the dead — the Anasazi buried their deceased under the floors of the cliff homes — while strict, could be gotten around if certain ceremonies (Enemyway) were performed and specific procedures (as contained in the Nightway Chant) followed. Clearly, the importance of these bowls (which were frequent inclusions in Anasazi graves) becomes self-evident when we consider the elaborate and necessary rites performed in order to attain them.

References to ruins in Navajo beliefs are central. The items found in ruins — considered both holy and dangerous — are essential components of many ceremonies and the stories told of them are defining elements in Navajo myth and history. So important are the stories associated with ruins and the artifacts and gods found in them, that the stories and ceremonies, performed in conjunction, comprise the sacred Chantways of the Navajo.

The stories contained often include a quest or series of trials, the end result of which is the attainment of the story/ceremony of the Chant, which is then taken to the people to help them. Questions must be asked and the origin of the Chants lie within the Chants themselves. In a philosophical but very real sense, the Chants themselves are grails; given by Gods, as the result of great trial or quest, they hold history, tradition and grant mankind the power to heal and restore. The most complex, powerful and indeed dangerous of these is the Nightway Chant.

In the Nightway ceremony, healing is accomplished through complicated and lengthy ceremonials in which stories are recounted, sand paintings are used to define sacred space and represent holy beings and masked dancers — representing gods and animals — associate with the patient to restore him to health. These ceremonies are run by the Medicine Man or Chanter (in Navajo, a *Hataalii*) whose goal is to

... identify the patient with the supernatural being
invoked. He must become one with them by absorption,
imitation, transformation, substitution, recapitulation,
repetition, commemoration and concentration.
(Reichard, 113)

The underlying belief of this ceremony (indeed, in all Navajo
religion) is that life cannot be repaired, it may only be recreated
through the religious repetition of the action of gods and
supernaturals. By returning in time to the moment of origins,
regeneration occurs (Eliade, 83). The Nightway Chant becomes
the catalyst and pathway for bringing sacred time into the
present. In these traditions, the story becomes the Grail.

Containing both the specific mention of a sacred vessel and
acting as the container of tradition and Otherworld wisdom, the
Navajo Nightway Chant contains elements closely resembling
restorative aspects of the Arthurian cycles.

As defined by Faris, "the Nightway is a healing practice
undertaken for stricken people." (Faris, 235). It is a healing
ceremony by which people attempt to regain harmony and re-
balance their relationship with the Navajo universe. "The
Nightway is corrective (rather than creative), it is curative and
re-establishing ..." (Faris, 216).

It is interesting to note that the Nightway Chant is curative
despite the dangerous affects associated with the power of ruins.
Ironically, ruins are associated with sickness, yet, the Nightway
story centers upon them. Indeed, going to the ruins (and using
objects from them, such as water bowls) is an integral part of the
ceremonial. It is perhaps for this reason that the Supernaturals
who brought the Nightway Chant to the people obtained it from
Deities residing in White House ruins (located in Canyon de
Chelly in northeastern Arizona). In all lands, the quest is
synonymous with danger. Only through great personal sacrifice
and risk may the powers that lie at the end of the quest be
attained and realized.

The Nightway Chant story has two versions, the "Visionary"
branch and the "Stricken Twins" branch. Both contain elements
of quest with an essential component of asking assistance from
supernaturals and/or deities. In its ceremonial form, Nightway
is a nine day event with ritual activities taking place during

eight days. On the ninth day, a large ceremonial dance, called a *Yeibeichai* is performed. The Nightway is considered too dangerous to perform at most times of the year and is only told/enacted during winter in its complete form. Telling the Nightway story is central to the ceremony and is combined with almost continuous singing and a variety of ritual observances including the construction of elaborate sand paintings and fetishes, invocation of gods in the form of masked dancers and ritual washings. The goal of all aspects of the ceremony is to restore the patient by associating him with deities and super-naturals, thereby taking him back to the time of the stories' creation. It must be remembered that the story (either version) as given by gods, informs the ceremony, thus serving as its prototype.

In the Visionary branch of the Nightway Chant, White House Ruins is the home of the Navajo Gods. The myth tells how Dreamer (whose Navajo name is *Bitahatini,* meaning "his visions"), after undergoing lengthy travels, enters certain ruins (thus connecting him to the Otherworld) and safely returns to his home bringing the Nightway Chant to the Navajo. As Dreamer did in ancient times, so now the modern Navajo do symbolically, with the various parts of Dreamer's journey and entrance into the ruins being commemorated and re-enacted to bring the power of the myth into the present. When the story is told, the patient becomes Dreamer and is now the center of the myth; he enters the sacred places and eats from the crystal bowl. The Nightway restores through these vital associations.

The story begins in a place of water.

At A-Delth-La-Chee-Toh, which is a spring under a rock, it begins (Faris, 177). A boy dreams of People with blue faces (Holy People) but his family does not believe him. His brothers make fun of him calling him "Dreamer," and this becomes his name.

Dreamer had a vision that came to pass. Crow and Magpie are killed by hunters (his brothers). This was bad for the people because Crow and Magpie have powers over the game animals. After this comes to be, Dreamer follows his brothers hunting but gets lost. He meets the Sheep People (who are Gods in disguise) who ask

"Why are you chasing us? ... Why are you following us?"
The boy did not answer them. Both Sheep Men each had
a bowl and a water jug, of the four colours, white, blue,
yellow and black. Also they had an extra bowl of crystal
and a crystal water pot for the dreamer. They had roasted
cornflower with them and they put this in their bowls
and poured water into them making mush and they put
some of this in the boy's crystal bowl and all ate there
together. The dreamer thought at first that he had very
little mush in this bowl, but no matter how much he ate,
there was always more left in it. (Faris, 180)

Dreamer is transformed into a Sheep and follows the Sheep
People on their travels. He witnesses many ceremonies of the
Holy People on his journey. He meets Coyote and with him,
passes safely over four rows of dangerous (they make one go
blind) sweat houses.

Finally he reaches White House Ruins in Canyon de Chelly
where a great ceremony is taking place. He is told by the Holy
People to remember everything he sees. Dreamer learns the
Nightway Chant and teaches it to his younger brother before
returning to live with the Holy People.

The Stricken Twins branch of the Nightway addresses the
problems of ritual impropriety more directly.

This version begins with a poor family living in Canyon de
Chelly. The daughter of the family hears a voice while out
gathering food but her story is not believed by her parents. The
voice speaks to her four days in a row. On the fourth day,
Talking God suggests a secret marriage. She agrees. They remain
together for four days. After this, she never sees Talking God
again.

Soon after Talking God's departure, she realizes that she is
pregnant. The girl gives birth to twin boys and refuses to reveal
the identity of the father to her family.

When still boys, the twins wander about and the family has
trouble keeping track of them. On one occasion, they are gone
for a very long time and return injured. One is lame, the other
blind. Now a burden on the family, they are told to leave.

Guarded by their father Talking God, the twins eventually
arrive at White House Ruins, the home of the Holy People. The

twins ask the Gods for help but because they do not know the proper form of offering, they are refused again and again. Finally, after undergoing a series of trials, the Holy People realize that the twins are the son of Talking God and that kinship exists between them. After this kinship is established, the ceremony begins.

The twins are told not to speak during the ceremony, but when they realize that they are about to be cured, they cry out with joy. At once, everything vanishes and they are left, once again, blind and lame.

Departing from the failed ceremony in tears, the twins' crying turns to song and the Holy People take pity on them. Vowing to never again turn away from the needs of their children, the Holy People heal the twins and teach them the Nightway Chant to take back to the people. After passing the Nightway Chant on to their family, the twins return to live with the Holy People. (Gill, 216)

Both versions of the Nightway Chant teach the Navajo the proper method of entering into a holy place and asking for supernatural assistance. When the contemporary Navajos enter the ruins, they enter the mythic realm where sacred knowledge may be obtained. The Nightway gives instruction for entering these places safely:

> Since the only approach to the sacred house was by way
> of the canyon walls, there was a song for ascending the
> cliff, one to enter the first doorway, a song for walking
> around inside of the house, and one for the visitor
> preparing to leave. (Reichard, 295)

In his discussion of the effect entering sacred places has upon the human mind, Mircea Eliade uses the term "interrupted space" to describe the feelings of suspended time and temporal disjunction. This concept is especially applicable to the travels of Dreamer and the Stricken Twins. The ruins in the Nightway act as doorways to other times and realms where Gods reside and knowledge may be gained. In this realm, time no longer functions in a linear manner. The knowledge obtained from this realm allows one to live in harmony and also helps to explain mysterious (mythical) aspects of the environment.

The Nightway also makes strong admonishments regarding proper behaviour and the nature of supernatural power. Sacred material (artifacts, prayers, stories and even symbols) must be used in sacred, prescribed contexts. To use them otherwise brings a terrible consequence.

Navajo accounts of the ruins and the destruction of their original inhabitants are closely related to these beliefs. The Navajo believe that the use of sacred symbols on pottery led (through supernatural retribution) to the destruction of the Anasazi and the abandonment of the ruins. The use of sacred designs on everyday items was an offense to the Powers and this violation of proper conduct was dealt the severest hand. It was thought that the ancient people no longer feared their gods and that the line between the sacred and the profane had grown too thin.

For the Navajo, the Nightway Chant (with its association with ruins and proper conduct) — like their accounts of the Anasazi — contains instructions of what not to do. But there is always a choice involved. This concept is supported by the Navajo ambivalence towards power in general. Even First Man, because of his medicine powers, was feared as a possible witch. Power could be used for good or evil — it was up to the individual to decide which form it would take. The Nightway, then, serves to instruct the Navajo as to which way power should be used. The Nightway and other chants are the containers of that power and vehicles of restoration and healing; like the grail, holding and dispensing traditions vital to the continuance of the people who seek them.

Each version concludes with restoration and attainment. The Nightway is both the story of the quest and the Grail waiting at the end. In each branch, the heroes return with the Nightway Chant and gift it to the people. However, contact with the Otherworld changes Dreamer and the twins completely. After their contact with Holy People and the ruins, they cannot remain in normal reality; after teaching the Nightway to their families, they return to live with the Holy People forever.

As the Nightway stories connect heroes to the land and ruins, so do the Nightway ceremonies bind the patient to the landscape's sacred past and place them, restored, in the center

564

of the world. The prayer (from Bierhorst, 307f) offered on the third morning of the ceremony re-establishes this relationship,

> Tsegìhi!
> House made of the dawn
> House made evening light
> House made of dark cloud
> House made of male rain
> House made of dark mist
> House made of female rain
> House made of pollen
> House made of grasshoppers
> Dark cloud is at the door
> The trail is out of the dark cloud
> The zigzag lightning stands high upon it.
> Male deity!
> Your offering I make
> I have prepared a smoke for you
> Restore my feet for me
> Restore my legs for me
> Restore my body for me
> Restore my mind for me
> Restore my voice for me
> This very day take out your spell for me
> Your spell remove for me
> You have taken it away for me
> Far off it has gone
> Happily I recover
> Happily my interior becomes cool
> Happily I go forth ...
> As it used to be long ago, may I walk ...
> Being as it used to be long ago, may I walk
> May it be beautiful before me
> May it be beautiful behind me
> May it be beautiful below me
> May it be beautiful above me
> May it be beautiful all around me
> In beauty it is finished
> In beauty it is finished.

As we have seen, the Grail of the Americas may take a variety of forms. Among all the cultures we've examined, it is the remembering, and retelling of the ancient stories that reactivate and empower the Grail.

As observed by Mircea Eliade:

> For all these ... peoples, what is essential is periodically to evoke the primordial event that established the present condition of humanity. Their whole religious life is a commemoration, a remembering. The memory re-actualized by the rites plays a decisive role; what happened *in illo tempore* must never be forgotten. The true sin is forgetting. (Eliade, 101)

Clearly, the prophetic words spoken by John Boorman's Merlin in the film *Excalibur* would ring true to the ancient people of the Americas: "It is the doom of men that they forget."

In Europe as well as the Americas, the Grail's function as holder of tradition and container of stories insures its continuation. The power behind this is circular (land inspires story, story creates Grail, Grail embodies story, Grail heals and sustains the land) and eternal. Every landscape informs a different Grail:

For the Inuit the Grail is the qattaq holding the whale, embodying an ancient peninsula, dispensing transformative hunt medicine.

In California, it is a basket of ancestral memory, buried deep in the earth, from which life giving waters flow.

Among the Maya, a container of sacred blood, translating ancestral powers into the present, binding the king to the land and sky.

To the Zuni, the Grail is the White Shell Bowl, holding sacred water, serving as the crossroads of the universe.

For the Navajo, it is a Crystal Basket and a Yellow Bowl from which no one leaves hungry. And finally, the Grail becomes a story, carrying traditions from the past, connecting the stricken to the powers of creation, restoring all who hear it.

Whether a basket made from tall lake reeds; a simple cup

carved from rare Arctic wood; a deep bowl formed of clay and pigments ground from stones or a spoken word molding creation to the present, these vessels express the lands they are made from. They emanate from the landscape. Stories about them are still told. And the quest continues.

References

Brody, J.J., "Mimbres Art: Form and Imagery." In Townsend, Richard (ed.), *The Ancient Americas — Art from Sacred Landscapes,* Art Institute of Chicago, 1992.

Bunzel, Ruth L., *Zuni Ceremonialism — Three Studies,* University of New Mexico Press, Albuquerque, 1992.

Eliade, Mircea, *The Sacred and the Profane,* Harcourt and Brace, New York, 1959.

Faris, James C., *The Nightway — A History and a History of Documentation of a Navajo Ceremonial,* University of New Mexico Press, Albuquerque, 1990.

Fewkes, J. Walter, *The Mimbres — Art and Archeology,* Avanyu Publishing, Albuquerque, 1993.

Freidel, David, Schele, Linda and Parker, Joy, *Maya Cosmos — Three Thousand Years on the Shaman's Path,* William Morrow and Company Inc., New York, 1993.

Gifford, Edward W. and Block, Gwendoline Harris, *Californian Indian Nights,* University of Nebraska Press, Lincoln, 1990.

Gill, Sam and Sullivan, Irene, *Dictionary of Native American Mythology,* Oxford University Press, 1992.

Graham, Ian and Von Euw, Eric, *Corpus of Maya Hieroglyphic Inscription — Volume 3, Part 1. Yax Chilan,* Harvard University Printing Office, Cambridge, MA, 1977.

Haile, Father Bernard, *Upward Moving and Emergence Way,* University of Nebraska Press, Lincoln, 1981.

House, Conrad, "The Art of Balance," in *All Roads are Good,* National Museum of the American Indian, Smithsonian Institution Press, 1994.

Lowestein, Tom, *Ancient Land: Sacred Whale — The Inuit Hunt and Its Rituals,* Farrar, Straus and Giroux, New York, 1993.

McPherson, Robert S., *Sacred Land, Sacred View — Navajo Perceptions of the Four Corners Region,* Charles Redd Center for Western Studies, Brigham Young University, 1992.

Merriam, C. Hart, *The Dawn of the World — Myths and Tales of the Miwok Indians of California,* University of Nebraska Press, Lincoln, 1993.

Newcomb, Franc J. and Reichard, Gladys A., *Sandpaintings of the Navajo Shootingway Chant,* Dover Publications, New York, 1975.

O'Bryan, Aileen, *Navaho Indian Myths,* Dover Publications, New York, 1993.

Reichard, Gladys A., *Navaho Religion — A Study of Symbolism,* Bollingen Series XVIII, Princeton University Press, New York, 1950.

Sharp, Rosemary, *Chacs and Chiefs — The Iconology of Mosaic Stone Sculpture in Pre-conquest Yucatan, Mexico,* Dumbarton Oaks, Washington DC, 1981.

Simmons, Leo W., *Sun Chief, Autobiography of a Hopi Indian,* Yale University Press, New Haven, 1967.

Tedlock, Barbara, *The Beautiful and the Dangerous — Encounters with the Zuni Indians,* Viking, New York, 1992.

Thornburg, Laurel and Paul and Stephanie Whittlseye, "Subjective Color in Mimbres Black and White Pottery." Presented at the Mogollon Conference VIII, El Paso, Texas, 1994.

Waldman, Carl, *Encyclopedia of Native American Tribes,* Facts On File, New York, 1988.

Wilson, Darryl Babe, "Akun, Jiki Walu: Grandfather Magician." In *Earth Song, Sky Spirit,* ed. Clifford E. Trafzer, Anchor Books, New York, 1992.

Zeydel, Edwin H. and Bayard Quincy Morgan, *The Parzifal of Wolfram von Eschenbach,* University of North Carolina Press, Chapel Hill, 1951.

Sources and acknowledgments

Whilst every effort has been made to trace the copyright holders of certain texts, this has not always proved succesful. Any omissions will be corrected in future editions.

Percival at Corbenic by Rachel Anand Taylor. Originally published in: *The Occult Observer*, Vol. I, 1945–50.

1 *The Spoils of Annwn* attributed to Taliesin, translated by J. Matthews

2 *Branwen, daughter of Llyr*, translated by Charlotte Guest. Originally published in: *The Mabinogion*, J.M. Dent, London, 1906.

3 *Peredur the Son of Evrawc*, translated by Charlotte Guest. Originally published in: *The Mabinogion*, J.M. Dent, London, 1906.

4 *The Elucidation*, translated by Sebastian Evans. Originally published in: *In Quest of the Holy Graal*, J.M. Dent, London, 1898.

5 *The Origin of the Holy Grail* by Sir John Rhys. Originally published in: *Studies in the Arthurian Legend*, The Clarendon Press, Oxford, 1891.

6 *The Celtic Grail* by A.G. van Hamel. Originally published in: *Revue Celtique*, Vol. XLVII, 1930.

7 *The Irish Element in King Arthur and the Grail* by Arthur C.-L. Brown. Originally published in *Mediaeval Studies* in memory of Gertrude Schoepperle Loomis, Columbia University Press, New York, 1927.

8 *Perceval: or, The Story of the Grail* by by Chrétien de Troyes, translated by Roger Sherman Loomis and Laura Hibbard Loomis. Originally published in *Mediaeval Romances*, edited by R.S. Loomis and L.H. Loomis, Random House, New York, 1957, reprinted by permission of Random House.

9 *The History of the Holy Grail* by Robert de Borron. First part translated by Adrian Paterson from the twelfth century French of the Sire Robert de Borron. Originally published in *Studies in Comparative Religion*, Vol. 8. No.1, Winter, 1974. Second part originally published in *Mediaeval Narrative: a Book of Translations* by Margaret Schlauch. Prentice-Hall: New York, 1928.

10 *Perlesvaus: or, The High History of the Holy Graal*, translated by Sebastian Evans. Originally published by J.M. Dent & Co., 1898.

11 *Parzival: a Knightly Epic* by Wolfram von Eschenbach, translated by J.L. Weston. Originally published by Stetchert, New York, 1912.

12 *Die Krone (The Crown)* by Heinrich von dem Türlin, translated by J.L. Weston. From: *Sir Gawain at the Grail Chapel,* David Nutt, London, 1903.

13 *The Quest for the Holy Grail,* translated by W.W. Comfort. Originally published in: *The Quest for the Holy Grail,* translated from the Old French, J.M. Dent, London & Toronto, 1926.

14 *Syr Percyvelle of Galles,* translated by J.L. Weston. Originally published in: *Chief Middle English Poets* by Jessie L. Weston, Houghton Mifflin, Boston, 1914.

15 *Le Morte d'Arthur* by Sir Thomas Malory

16 *The Legend of the Grail* by M. Gaster. Originally published in: *Folk-Lore,* Vol. II, 1891.

17 *Persia and the Holy Grail* by Arthur Upham Pope. Originally published in: *The Literary Review,* Farleigh Dickinson University, Vol. I, 1957.

18 *Glastonbury and Fécamp* by Robert Jaffray. Originally published in: *King Arthur and the Holy Grail,* G.P. Putnam's Sons, New York 1928.

19 *Mystic Aspects of the Graal Legend* by A.E. Waite. From: *The Hidden Church of the Holy Graal,* originally published by Robman Ltd, London, 1909.

20 *The Holy Grail: Qui on en servoit?* by D. Swinscow. Originally published in *Folk-Lore,* Vols. LV/LVI, 1944f.

21 *The Initiation Pattern and the Grail* by Robert W. Crutwell. Originally published in: *Folk-Lore* Vol. XLVIII, 1937.

22 *The Grail and the Rites of Adonis* by Jessie L. Weston. Originally published in: *Folk-Lore,* Vol. XVIII, 1907.

23 *The Graal Legend* by D.F. de l'Hoste Ranking. Originally published in: *Transactions of the Royal Society of Literature,* Vol. XXXVI, 1918.

24 *The Quest of the Sangraal* by Robert S. Hawker. Originally published in: *The Quest of the Sangraal: Chant The First.* Printed for the Author, Exeter, 1864.

25 *Perronik, the innocent* by Kenneth Sylvan Guthrie. Originally published by Comparative Literature Press, New York, 1915.

26 *Mystic Gleams from the Holy Grail* by Francis Rolt-Wheeler. Originally published in: *Mystic Gleams from the Holy Grail* by Francis Rolt-Wheeler, Rider and Co, London, n.d. [*c.* 1944].

27 *The Arthurian Pilgrimage to the Graal* by Isabel Wyatt. Originally published in: *From Round Table to Graal,* Lanthorn Press, East Grinstead 1979, reprinted by kind permission of the Lanthorn Press.

28 *The Mass of the Sangraal* by Arthur Machen. Originally published in: *The Glorious Mystery,* Corici McGee Co., Chicago, 1924, reprinted by kind permission of Mrs Janet Machen-Pollock.

29 *The Grail in the Uttermost West* by Ari Berk.

Bibliography

Texts

Borron, Robert de, *Joseph of Arimathea — A Romance of the Grail*, trans Jean Rogers, Rudolf Steiner Press, London 1990.

Bryant, N., *The High Book of the Grail*, D.S. Brewer, Cambridge 1975.

Campbell, D.E., trans, "The Tale of Balain," from *The Post-Vulgate Cycle*, Northwestern University Press, Evanston 1972.

Chrétien de Troyes, *Perceval, or the Story of the Grail*, trans Nigel Bryant, D.S. Brewer, Cambridge 1982.

Chrétien de Troyes, *Arthurian Romances*, [Erec, Cliges, The Knight of the Cart, The Knight With the Lion. The Story of the Grail], trans W.W. Kibler and C.W. Carroll. Penguin Books, Harmondsworth 1991.

Comfort, W.W., *The Quest of the Holy Grail*, [The Vulgate Quest], J.M. Dent, London 1926.

Eschenbach, Wolfram von, *Parzival*, trans A. Hatto, Penguin, Harmondsworth 1980.

———, *Titurel*, trans C.E. Passage, Frederick Ungar, New York 1984.

Gantz, J, trans, *The Mabinogion*, [Peredur], Penguin Books, Harmondsworth 1985.

Guest, Lady C., trans.*The Mabinogion*, [Peredur], John Jones, Cardiff 1977.

James, M.R., *The Apocryphal New Testament*, [Gospel of Nicodemus and Acts of Pilate], Oxford University Press 1924.

Lacy, N.S. *et al.*, eds, *The Lancelot-Grail: The Old French Arthurian Vulgate and Post-Vulgate in Translation* (5 vols), Garland Publishing, NY, 1993–96.

Malory, Sir Thomas, *Le Morte d'Arthur*, University Books, New York 1961.

Matarasso, P. *The Quest of the Grail*, [The Vulgate Quest], Penguin, Harmondsworth 1969.

Roach, William, *The Continuations of the Old French Perceval*, (3 vols) [Gerbert de Montreuil, Wauchier de Denain, Menassier], American Philosophical Society, Philadelphia 1949–52.

Scharfenburg, Albrecht von, *Der Jüngere Titurel*, ed. W. Wolf, *(Deutsche*

571

Texte des Mittelalters, 45 and 55/61) Berlin 1955, 1968.

Skeeles, D., *The Romance of Perceval in Prose,* [Didot Perceval], University of Washington Press, Seattle 1966.

Sommer, H.O., *The Vulgate Version of the Arthurian Romances,* (8 vols) [in Old French with Commentary], The Carnegie Institute, Washington 1908–16.

Thompson, A.W., *The Elucidation,* Institute of French Studies, New York 1931.

Türlin, Heinrich von dem, *The Crown,* trans D.W. Thomas, University of Nebraska Press, Nebraska 1989.

Williams, R., *Y Seint Greal,* 1876, reprinted by Jones (Wales) Publishers 1987.

Commentaries

Adolf, H., *Visio Pacis: Holy City and Grail,* Pennsylvania State University Press 1960.

Ancona, S.G., *The Substance of Adam,* Rider & Co, London 1934.

Ashe, G., *King Arthur's Avalon,* Fontana, London 1973.

Bergmann, F.G., *The San Greal,* Edmonston & Douglas, Edinburgh 1870.

Birks, W. and Gilbert, R.A., *The Treasure of Montségur,* Crucible, London 1987.

Bogdanow, F., *The Romance of the Grail,* Manchester University Press 1966.

Bradley, M. with Theilman-Bean, D., *The Holy Grail Across the Atlantic,* The Hounslow Press, Toronto 1989.

Brown, A.C.L., *The Origin of the Grail Legend,* Harvard University Press, Cambridge, Mass. 1943.

Bryce, D., *The Mystical Way and the Arthurian Quest,* Llanerch Enterprises, Llanerch, Dyfed 1986.

Cavendish, R., *King Arthur and the Grail,* Weidenfeld & Nicholson, London 1978.

Chapman, V., *The Three Damosels,* Methuen, London 1978.

Cooper-Oakley, I., *Masonry and Medieval Mysticism,* Theosophical Publishing House, London and Chicago 1977.

Coughlan, R. *The Illustrated Encyclopedia of the Arthurian Legends,* Element, Shaftesbury, Dorset 1993.

Currer-Briggs, N., *The Shroud and the Grail,* Weidenfeld & Nicholson, London 1927.

De Sede, A., *La Rose Croix,* J'ai Lu, Paris 1978.

De Sede, G., *Les Templiers,* J'ai Lu, Paris 1969.

Evans, S., *In Quest of the Holy Grail,* J.M. Dent, London 1898.

Evola, J., *Le Mystère du Graal et l'Idée Impériale Gibeline,* Editions Traditionnelles, Paris 1984.

Fisher, L.A, *The Mystic Vision in the Grail Legend and in the Divine Comedy,* AMS Press, New York 1966.

Forward, W. and Wolpert, A., *The Quest for the Grail* (The Golden Blade 47), Floris Books, Edinburgh 1994.

Gardner, E., *Arthurian Legends in Italian Literature,* Octagon Books, New York 1971.

Gilliam, R., Greenburg, M.H. and Kramer, E.E. (eds), *Grails: Quests, Visitations and Other Occurrences,* Unnamable Press, Atlanta 1992.

Gogan, L.S., *The Ardagh Chalice,* Brown & Nolan, Dublin 1932.

Goodrich, N.L., *The Ways of Love* [includes Robert de Borron], Beacon Press, Boston 1964.

Hall, M.F., *Orders of the Quest: The Holy Grail,* Philosophical Research Society, Los Angeles 1976.

Johnson, K. and Elsbeth, M., *The Grail Castle: Male Myths and Mysteries in the Celtic Tradition,* Llewellyn, St Paul, MN. 1995.

Jung, E. and Von Franz, M.-L., *The Grail Legends,* Hodder & Stoughton, London 1971.

Knight, G., *The Secret Tradition in Arthurian Legend,* Aquarian Press, Wellingborough 1983.

Lacy, N.J. and Ashe, G., *The Arthurian Handbook,* Garland Publishing, New York 1986.

Lambert, M.D., *Medieval Heresy,* Arnold, London 1977.

Lievegoed, B.C.J., *Mystery Streams in Europe and the New Mysteries,* Anthroposophic Press, New York 1982.

Littleton, C.S. and Malcor, L.A., *From Scythia to Camelot: A Radical Reassesment of the Legends of King Arthur, the Knights of the Round Table, and the Holy Grail,* Garland Press, New York 1994.

Loomis, R.S., *Celtic Myth & Arthurian Romance,* Columbia University Press, New York 1927.

————, *Wales and the Arthurian Legend,* University of Wales Press 1956.

————, *The Grail from Celtic Myth to Christian Symbol,* University of Wales Press, Cardiff 1963.

Makale J., *Le Graal,* Retz, Paris 1982.

Matthews, C., *Mabon and the Mysteries of Britain,* Arkana, London 1987.

————, *Arthur and the Sovereignty of Britain,* Arkana, London 1989.

————, *Elements of Celtic Tradition,* Element, Shaftesbury 1989.

Matthews, J., *The Grail, Quest for Eternal Life,* Thames & Hudson, London 1981.

————, *At the Table of the Grail,* Arkana, London 1987.

————, *The Aquarian Guide to British and Irish Mythology,* (with C. Matthews) Aquarian Press, Wellingborough 1988.

————, *An Arthurian Reader,* Aquarian Press, Wellingborough 1988.

————, *Elements of Arthurian Tradition*, Element, Shaftesbury 1989.

————, *The Arthurian Book of Days* (with C. Matthews). Sidgwick & Jackson, London,/ St Martins, New York 1990.

————, *The Household of the Grail*, Aquarian Press, Wellingborough 1990.

————, *A Glastonbury Reader*, Aquarian Press, Wellingborough 1991.

————, *Ladies of the Lake* (with Caitlin Matthews) Aquarian Press, Wellingborough 1992.

————, *From the Isles of Dream*, Floris Books, Edinburgh and Lindisfarne Press, New York 1993.

————, *King Arthur and the Grail Quest*, Cassell, London 1994.

————, *Within the Hollow Hills*, Floris Books, Edinburgh and Lindisfarne Press, New York 1994.

————, and Green, M., *The Grail Seeker's Companion*, Aquarian Press, Wellingborough 1988.

————, and Matthews, C., *The Arthurian Tarot: A Hallowquest*, Aquarian Press, Wellingborough 1990.

Morduch, A., *The Sovereign Adventure*, James Clarke, Edinburgh 1970.

Morizot, P., *The Templars*, Anthroposophical Publishing Co., London 1960.

Newstead, H., *Bran the Blessed in Arthurian Romance*, Columbia University Press, New York 1939.

Nutt, A., *Studies on the Legend of the Holy Grail*, Cooper Square Publishers, New York 1965.

Oldenbourg, L., *Massacre at Montségur*, Weidenfeld, London 1961.

Olschki, L., *The Grail Castle and its Mysteries*, Manchester University Press 1966.

Pearshall, L.B., *The Art of Narration in Wolfram's Parzifal and Albrecht's Jüngere Titurel*, Cambridge University Press 1981.

Ringbom, L.I., *Graal Temple und Paradies*, Stockholm 1951.

Rohr, R., *Quest for the Grail*, Crossroad, New York 1994.

Rolt-Wheeler, F., *Mystic Gleams From the Holy Grail*, Rider, London, [c.1945].

Sansonetti, P-G., *Graal et Alchimie*, Berg International, Paris 1982.

Schlauch, M., *Medieval Narrative: A Book of Translations*, Geordian Press, New York 1969.

Sinclair, A., *The Sword and the Grail*, Crown Publishing, New York 1993.

Stein, W.J., *The Ninth Century: World History in the Light of the Holy Grail* (with an introduction by John Matthews), Temple Lodge Press, London 1991.

Steiner, R., *Christ and the Spiritual World, and The Search for the Holy Grail*, Rudolf Steiner Press, London 1963.

Sussman, L., *The Speech of The Grail*, Lindisfarne Press, New York 1995.

Topsfield, L.T., *Chrétien de Troyes: A Study of Arthurian Romance*, Cambridge University Press 1981.

Weston, J.L. *From Ritual To Romance*, Doubleday, New York 1957.
————, *The Quest of the Holy Grail*, G. Bell & Sons, London 1913.
Whitehead, J., *Guardian of the Grail*, Barnes & Noble, New York 1993.
Wieland, F., *The Journey of the Hero*, Prism Press, Bridport 1991.
Williams, C., *The Descent of the Dove*, Faber & Faber, London 1939.
————, *War in Heaven*, Faber & Faber, London 1948.
————, *Charles Williams*, [includes "Taliessin through Logres" and "The Region of the Summer Stars"] ed. D.L. Dodds *(Arthurian Poets)*, The Boydell Press, Woodbridge 1994.